WESTERN
CIVILIZATIONS

SECOND BRIEF EDITION

WORLD · POLITICAL

NATIONAL BOUNDARIES

Winkel Tripel Projection

Longitude West of Greenwich

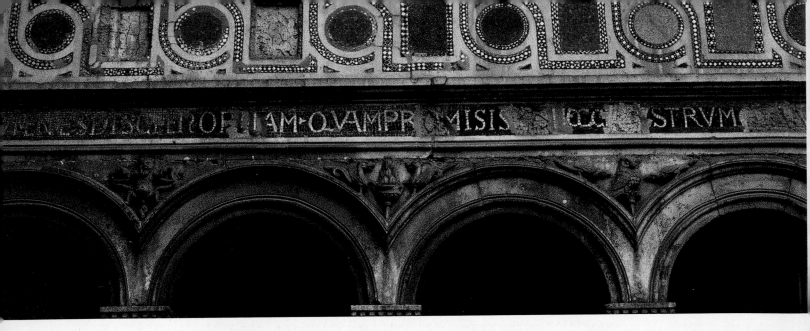

VOLUME I/SECOND BRIEF EDITION

JUDITH G. COFFIN

ROBERT C. STACEY

W · W · NORTON & COMPANY · NEW YORK · LONDON

WESTERN
CIVILIZATIONS

THEIR HISTORY
& THEIR CULTURE

W. W. Norton & Company has been independent since its founding in 1923, when William Warder Norton and Mary D. Herter Norton first published lectures delivered at the People's Institute, the adult education division of New York City's Cooper Union. The firm soon expanded its program beyond the Institute, publishing books by celebrated academics from America and abroad. By mid-century, the two major pillars of Norton's publishing program—trade books and college texts—were firmly established. In the 1950s, the Norton family transferred control of the company to its employees, and today—with a staff of four hundred and a comparable number of trade, college, and professional titles published each year—W. W. Norton & Company stands as the largest and oldest publishing house owned wholly by its employees.

Editor: Jon Durbin
Copy Editor: Candace Levy
Project Editors: Lory Frenkel and Christine D'Antonio
Managing Editor: Marian Johnson
Production Manager: Ben Reynolds
Emedia Editor: Steve Hoge
Print Ancillary Editor: Rachel Comerford
Editorial Assistant: Jason Spears
Book Design: Toni Krass
Layout Artist: Paul Lacy
Cartographer: Carto-Graphics
Manufacturing by R. R. Donnelley & Sons—Willard, Ohio

Acknowledgments and copyrights continue on page A20, which serves as a continuation of the copyright page.

The Library of Congress has cataloged the one-volume edition as follows:
Library of Congress Cataloging-in-Publication Data

Coffin, Judith G., 1952–
    Western civilizations: their history & their culture / Judith G. Coffin, Robert C. Stacey.—2nd brief ed.
        p. cm.
    "Based on Western civilizations by Edward McNall Burns, Robert E. Lerner, Standish Meacham."
    Includes bibliographical references and index.
    ISBN 978-0-393-93265-2 (pbk.)
    1. Civilization, Western—Textbooks. 2. Europe—Civilization—Textbooks. I. Stacey,
Robert C. H. Burns, Edward McNall, 1897– Western civilizations, their history and their culture.
    III. Title.

CB245.C56 2009
909'.09821—dc22   2008033268

ISBN 978-0-393-93235-5

W. W. Norton & Company, Inc., 500 Fifth Avenue, New York, N.Y. 10110
www.wwnorton.com

W. W. Norton & Company Ltd., Castle House, 75/76 Wells Street, London W1T 3QT
3 4 5 6 7 8 9 0

To our families—Robin, Will, and Anna Stacey, and Willy, Zoe, and Aaron Forbath—for their patience and support. They reminded us that books such as this are worth the work, and also that there are other things in life.

To Robert Lerner, Standish Meacham, Edward McNall Burns, and Marie Burns, our predecessors who successfully guided *Western Civilizations* for thirteen editions, spanning six decades.

ABOUT THE AUTHORS

JUDITH G. COFFIN received her Ph.D. in modern French history from Yale University. She has taught at Harvard University and the University of California, Riverside, and is currently associate professor of history at the University of Texas at Austin, where she won a 1999 University of Texas President's Associates' Award for Teaching Excellence. Her research interests focus on the social and cultural history of gender, mass culture, slavery, race relations, and colonialism. She is the author of *The Politics of Women's Work: The Paris Garment Trades, 1750-1915*.

ROBERT C. STACEY is Dean of Humanities and Arts and Professor of History and Jewish Studies at the University of Washington in Seattle. A long-time teacher of western civilization and medieval European history, he has received Distinguished Teaching Awards from both the University of Washington and Yale University, where he taught from 1984 to 1988. The author or coauthor of four books, he is a Fellow of the Royal Historical Society and has held awards from the American Council of Learned Societies and from the Guggenheim Foundation. His current research deals with the history of Jews in medieval England.

CONTENTS

PART II THE GREEK AND ROMAN WORLDS 68

PART III THE MIDDLE AGES 172

PART IV FROM MEDIEVAL TO MODERN 262

CHAPTER 13   REFORMATIONS OF RELIGION   344

CHAPTER 14   RELIGIOUS WARS AND STATE BUILDING, 1540–1660   368

PART V   EARLY MODERN EUROPE   392

CHAPTER 15   ABSOLUTISM AND EMPIRE, 1660–1789   396

CONTENTS

Maps

CHRONOLOGIES

DOCUMENTS

PREFACE

The demand for concise, affordable texts grows with each passing year. Publishers have responded by offering either bare-bones, brief editions or "value" editions of their textbooks—typically smaller format, black-and-white editions with far fewer and smaller pictures and maps. Both types of these texts are far from being highly valuable teaching tools. Fortunately, W. W. Norton, our publisher, decided to take a different approach. Welcome to *Western Civilizations*, Second Brief Edition! This new edition is full size and full color, includes innovative pedagogical tools, and is priced competitively with the most inexpensive brief books and value editions on the market. In fact, Norton has dropped the price of the book by 25 percent from the previous edition and maintained the commitment to high-quality content and production values in the text, while providing a rich and innovative support package. We hope that you will see this as the best solution for your course and students when you are considering texts.

OUR APPROACH

Western Civilizations, the title of our book, provides great insight into how we view our historical past. We mean for the plural in our title to be taken seriously, as we believe that the West cannot be understood as a single, historical culture. During much of the twentieth century however, "western" civilization meant "the civilization of western Europe," to which the history of the Ancient Near East was somewhat arbitrarily attached. Western civilization was therefore presented as beginning at Sumer, developing in Egypt, and then flowering in Greece. From Greece it spread to Rome, then made its way to France, Germany, England, Italy, and Spain, whose emigrating colonists brought it to the Americas after 1492. Rather like a train passing through stations, western civilization was thus conceived as picking up "cargo" at each of its stops, but always retaining the same engine and the same baggage cars.

This vision of western civilization was not only selective; it was often tied to a series of contentious assumptions. It cast the worldwide dominance of the European imperial powers between roughly 1800 and 1950 as the culmination of several thousand years of historical development, which it was the obligation of historians to explain. It also tended to presume that European global dominance in the nineteenth and twentieth centuries reflected and demonstrated the superiority of western

European civilization over the African, Asian, and Native American civilizations the Europeans conquered during the heyday of their imperial expansion.

Historians today are keenly aware of how much such an account leaves out. It slights the use of force and fraud in European expansion. It also ignores the sophistication, dynamism, and humanity of the many cultures it sidelines. By neglecting the crucial importance of Byzantium and Islam, it even gives a misleadingly narrow account of the development of European civilization. It also misleads us about the civilizations created in North and South America after 1492, which were hybrid cultures, not simply European cultures transplanted to other shores. This is not to argue that a study of western civilizations must give way to a study of world civilization. It is merely to insist that understanding the historical development of the West requires us to place our subject in a geographical and cultural context that is wider than western Europe alone; and that, stripped of its triumphalism, the history of these various and differing western civilizations becomes vastly more interesting.

The regular and brief editions of *Western Civilizations* have been highly successful teaching tools for more than a million students. The texts combine a vigorous narrative style with attention to the diverse ways in which ordinary people responded to changing environments, societies, and cultures. They also aim for clarity and accessibility without compromising accuracy or ignoring complexity, and by presenting politics, society, and culture as part of a single, shared world of historical experience. Add to these the innovative pedagogical program, including the new "Transformations" features (see below), and it is easy to see why these "well-balanced" texts work so well in the classroom.

We have made significant changes to the book that reflect the changing historical interests of teachers, students, and scholars. In keeping with our broadened understanding of western civilizations, we devote much more attention to the world outside western Europe. We continue to integrate new scholarly work in social and cultural history and the history of gender into our narrative, but we have also substantially increased the attention we pay to economic, religious, and military history. We also pay particular attention to the varying ways in which these different western civilizations sought to govern themselves and the territories they conquered. "Empire" has been a consistent theme in the history of the West for more than four thousand years. In revising this book, we have tried to do justice to its importance.

Western Civilizations, Second Brief Edition, is the most affordable, coherent, and full-featured brief text on the market. Most brief western civilizations text are so incoherent and depleted of the pedagogical features from their parent editions that they do not help students learn and retain key information or make connections. *Western Civilizations*, Second Brief Edition, on the other hand, provides students with a comprehensive set of in-text pedagogy and the most coherent narrative on the market—both designed to help students make connections and understand the major themes of western civilizations.

HIGHLIGHTS OF THE SECOND BRIEF EDITION

Innovative Pedagogical Program

Western Civilizations, Second Brief Edition, is designed for maximum readability. The crisp, clear, and concise narrative is also accompanied by a pedagogical program to help students study while engaging them in the subject matter. Highlights of this innovative program include:

- **Focus Question System.** To ensure that students remain alert to key concepts and questions on every page of the text, focus questions guide their reading in three ways: (1) a focus question box appears at the beginning of each chapter to preview the chapter's contents; (2) relevant questions reappear at the start of the section in which they are discussed; and (3) running heads on the righthand pages keep these questions in view throughout the chapter.

- **Map Program with Enhanced Captions.** Over seventy beautiful maps appear throughout the text, each accompanied by an enhanced caption designed to engage the reader analytically while conveying the key role that geography plays in the development of history and the societies of the world.

- **In-Text Documents.** To add depth to the more focused narrative of *Western Civilizations*, each chapter contains an average of three primary sources, two of which are paired to convey a sense of historical complexity and diversity.

- **NEW Document Questions.** Instructors requested questions for the documents in the book. We have added questions at the bottom of each box that ask students to engage the primary source or connect it to the larger issues in the chapter.

- **In-Chapter Chronologies.** Several brief chronologies built around particular events, topics, or periods appear in each chapter and are designed to provide road maps through the narrative detail.

- **End-of-Chapter Key Terms.** In response to requests from professors, each chapter includes a list of key terms to help students focus on the key ideas, events, or people in the chapter.

- **Pull Quotes.** Lifted directly from the narrative, pull quotes appear throughout each chapter to highlight key thoughts and keen insights while keeping students focused on larger concepts and ideas.

Well-Balanced, Coherent Text

Western Civilizations has always been well respected for the way it balances classic topics with contemporary research; makes connections between political, social, and cultural history; and helps students separate the forest from the trees by paying careful attention to the central narrative. The new "Transformations" features best exemplify our ongoing commitment to providing a well-balanced text.

- **New "Transformations" feature provokes students to consider the implications of major historical events.** Throughout the Second Brief Edition, we have inserted new material on important "transformations" in the history of western civilizations. Highlighted with an icon, these sections ask students to reflect on the larger political, social, or cultural consequences of major turning points in history. Frequently, they draw on cutting-edge scholarship that has transformed our understanding of these events. New "Tranformations" include:

- Chapter 1: "The Origins of Food Production in the Ancient Near East." This rewritten and expanded section focuses on the disadvantages and the advantages of agriculture.

- Chapter 6: "The Success and Impact of the German Invasions." The new material on the German-Roman relations elaborates on the economic collapse of western Rome in the fifth century, and explains how aspects of Roman life—the tax and administrative system, agricultural systems, and city life—persisted.

- Chapter 10: "The Black Death and Its Consequences." The effects of the plague rippled across Europe. It affected every aspect of life. For example, fewer people were available to work the fields, but there were also fewer people to feed. Prices of grain went up, but because there were fewer people competing for jobs, wages did, too. Consequently, ordinary people could now afford not only to buy more bread, they could also purchase dairy products, meat, fish, fruits and wine on a more regular basis. As a result, the people of Europe in the later middle ages ate a more balanced diet, and were consequently better nourished than they had been for centuries, or than some are today.

- Chapter 16: "Science and Cultural Change." This new "transformation" section deals with the cultural shifts that arose from the Scientific Revolution. Beginning in the Seventeenth century, embracing science and the scientific method was at the heart of what it meant to be "modern." This has implications for the Enlightenment, but it also became the justification for new technologies and for new empires.

- Chapter 24: "The Peace Settlement." The Treaty of Versailles marks the emergence of the United States as a world power. But it also represents the first time so many countries were involved in a peace settlement and marks the scope of the war, the growing national sentiments and aspirations, and the tightening of international communication and economic networks.

UPDATES FOR SECOND BRIEF EDITION

Throughout, we have worked to integrate the text, visual material, and pedagogy. That has meant bringing in different images as well as updating the text. These changes make the text more user-friendly while still allowing professors and students alike to tailor it to their particular course and interests.

Part I, "The Ancient Near East," was completely reorganized and rewritten for the first brief edition. However, we have made a number of changes to the text as well as to the artwork and document selections. In Chapter 1, the discussion of prehistory and the emergence of the earliest towns and villages have been updated, with particular attention to the exciting archaeological work currently underway at Çatalhöyük. We have also revised the presentation of Sumerian religion and added a discussion of Enheduanna, high priestess and daughter of Sargon I of Akkad. In Chapter 2, we have revised the discussion of Hatshepsut's role as a female pharaoh and added many new illustrations.

In Part II, readers will find a much-improved program of illustrations in all the chapters. Chapter 4 includes a revised account of Hellenistic religions, especially the so-called mystery cults. Reflecting the consensus of recent scholarly work, Mithraism is now discussed only in Chapter 5, as an example of the new religious devotions that swept through early imperial Roman society. Readers will also find in Chapter 5 a new treatment of the economy of the Roman empire. Chapter 6 offers a completely new account of the fall of the western Roman empire during the fifth century C.E., emphasizing the suddenness of Rome's collapse and the profound consequences this collapse had for the Roman economy and for standards of living within the western Roman empire. Here too, as throughout the book, we are trying to reflect the current balance of scholarly opinion.

In Part III, "The Middle Ages," Chapter 7 now includes a separate section on the Vikings. This chapter also features a revised explanation of the split between Shiite and Sunni Islam, a revised assessment of the influence of early Islamic civilization on Europe, and a new document box pairing passages from the Qur'an on Jews and Christians with the "Pact of Umar." Chapter 8 features another new document box, on the summoning of the First Crusade in 1096. Chapter 9 includes a new document box on kingship as a religious office, which we hope will make it easier for students to grasp the issues at stake in the Investiture Conflict.

Part IV, "From Medieval to Modern," begins with a completely rewritten chapter (10) on the later middle ages, which emphasizes the remarkable resilience and creativity that characterized European responses to the Black Death. The far-reaching consequences of the plague upon social, economic, and religious life are the central themes of this chapter. Interestingly, however, there is now considerable doubt among historians and epidemiologists as to whether the Black Death was in fact an outbreak of bubonic plague, or whether it may have been some other disease entirely.

In Chapter 13, "Reformations of Religion," readers will find a new section on "Reform and Discipline," and a new selection of paired documents, contrasting Lutheran and Catholic positions on marriage and celibacy.

In Part V, we have rewritten Chapter 16, "The New Science of the Seventeenth Century," to make it clearer and more accessible. It emphasizes the transformation of scientific knowledge, practice, and institutions. Here as in all our discussions of intellectual history, we foreground the context in which new ideas emerged and how those ideas came to matter for a range of people, from philosophers, rulers, and bureaucrats to explorers, artists, and artisans.

In Part VI, we have expanded discussion of Napoleon's empire and its legacy to Europe and the world. We have added to Chapter 21 an extended discussion of slavery and its abolition in the Americas which follows up on the treatment of the Haitian revolution in Chapter 18. Coming as it does before the section on the American Civil War, it places developments in the United States in a larger, comparative perspective. No course can be comprehensive, especially one dealing with a topic as hard to define as the West, but we have chosen to touch down on a few topics, like the politics of abolition, with an eye to highlighting comparisons and global connections. We have expanded the treatment of U.S. imperialism in Chapter 22 for the same reason.

Part VI continues to be organized thematically. Chapter 19, on industrial society, focuses on the relationship between social, economic, and cultural change—or on industry as a way of life. Chapters 20 and 21 break the tumultuous history of the mid-nineteenth-century revolutions into two parts, to make themes easier to follow. Chapter 20 goes from the reaction against the French Revolution of 1789 to the renewed outbreak of revolution in 1848, and includes a discussion of nineteenth-century political ideologies and cultural movements. Chapter 21 begins with the revolutions of 1848 in central and eastern Europe and then focuses on the issues those revolutions raised, nation and state building, as they played out elsewhere.

In Part VII, we have revised Chapter 24, on World War I. Readers will find more material on the long-term evolution of warfare and the emergence of total war. We have also expanded the treatment of the Paris Peace Conference, another important global moment. The new scope of war summoned global institutions to contend with the war's ramifications. Whether those international concerns could be compatible with national interests was an open question, and would become a theme of the history of the twentieth century. So would other issues central to the Peace of Paris, such as the expansion of empire, the mobilization of movements for national self determination, and the protection of minorities within new nation states.

In Part VIII, which was almost entirely rewritten for this edition, we added discussion of the history of human rights to conclude the chapter on globalization.

Why, suddenly, is the language of human rights so familiar? The change highlights the dramatic political transformation wrought by the end of the cold war; it also reflects the new horizons of a rapidly globalizing world, with all their potential and peril. Finally, a history of human rights provides the occasion to review some of the central debates of the Western political tradition.

RESOURCES FOR STUDENTS

⊚ StudySpace
wwnorton.com/studyspace

This student website provides a rich array of multimedia resources and review materials within a proven, task-oriented study plan.

Each chapter is arranged in an effective *Organize, Learn, and Connect* pedagogy:

Organize
In this section, students can work through Focus Questions, print out Chapter Outlines and summaries, or check in with Progress Reports that help them focus their studies.

Learn
This section encourages active learning with:
- **iMaps and GeoQuizzes that engage and test students' geographic knowledge** with map review worksheets and maps with zoom functions, highlighting, and labels.
- **Multiple-choice quizzes for each chapter.**
- **FlashCards** with audio pronunciations.
- **Interactive Chrono-Sequencers** that challenge students to reassemble sequences of events, reinforcing their understanding of the flow of history.
- **NEW! Document Quizzes** provide a form for students to answer the questions about the in-text documents.

Connect
In this section, students are reminded to connect to additional resources that include:
- **250 additional primary source documents**
- **Research Topics** that combine a writing prompt, documents, headnotes and sample questions.
- **NEW Interactive MapPlayer** with audio introductions, transitions, and conclusions, along with a suite of interactive functions to examine individual maps as they are presented in a progressive sequence.
- **Audio Glossary**

Study Guide
Margaret Minor and Paul Wilson, *Nicholls State University*

The *Study Guide* gives students a comprehensive means for review and self-assessment. Each chapter contains a chapter outline, identifications, multiple-choice questions, matching, and true/false questions, chronologies, and short-answer and essay questions.

RESOURCES FOR INSTRUCTORS

Norton Media Library
This newly expanded resource for multimedia lectures offers:
- PowerPoint presentations for each chapter
- High-resolution maps and graphics files from the book
- Art from the book
- Questions for Classroom Response PowerPoints (Clicker Questions)

Instructor's Manual
Steven Kreis, *American Public University*

Each chapter in the *Instructor's Manual* includes lecture outlines, key lecture topics, suggested films, and suggestions for integrating media into the classroom and using media as homework assignments.

Test Bank
Michael Prahl, *University of Northern Iowa*
Michael Halvorson, *Pacific Lutheran University*

This vastly expanded test bank includes 60 percent more questions, including true/false and essay questions. It is available in *ExamView® Assessment Suite*, WebCT, and Blackboard formats.

Blackboard and WebCT Coursepacks offer study plans that integrate review materials for each chapter, as well as ready-to-use test banks, maps, PowerPoint lecture presentations, and practice quizzes.

Map Transparencies

ACKNOWLEDGMENTS

The drafts of the manuscript have benefited from careful reading by and suggestions from a group of professors to whom we are greatly indebted. Our sincere thanks to:
- Eric Ash, Wayne State University
- Sacha Auerbach, Virginia Commonwealth University

- Ken Bartlett, University of Toronto
- Benita Blessing, Ohio University
- Chuck Boening, Shelton State Community College
- John Bohstedt, University of Tennessee– Knoxville
- Dan Brown, Moorpark College
- Kevin Caldwell, Blue Ridge Community College
- Jodi Campbell, Texas Christian University
- Annette Chamberlain, Virginia Western Community College
- Jason Coy, College of Charleston
- Benjamin Ehlers, University of Georgia
- Maryann Farkas, Dawson College
- Gloria Fitzgibbon, Wake Forest University
- Tina Gaddis, Onondaga Community College
- Alex Garman, Eastern New Mexico State University
- Norman Goda, Ohio University
- Andrew Goldman, Gonzaga University
- Robert Grasso, Monmouth University
- Sylvia Gray, Portland Community College
- Susan Grayzel, University of Mississippi
- Hazel Hahn, Seattle University
- Derek Hastings, Oakland University
- Dawn Hayes, Montclair State University
- John Houston, Fordham University
- Michael Hughes, Wake Forest University
- Bruce Hunt, University of Texas–Austin
- Ahmed Ibrahim, Southwest Missouri State University
- Kevin James, University of Guelph
- John Kearney, Cy Fair Community College
- Elizabeth Lehfeldt, Cleveland State University
- Thomas Maulucci, State University of New York–Fredonia
- Amy McCandless, College of Charleston
- Nicholas Murray, Adirondack College
- Charles Odahl, Boise State University
- Bill Olejniczak, College of Charleston
- Jeffery Plaks, University of Central Oklahoma
- Peter Pozesky, College of Wooster
- Rebecca Schloss, Texas A&M University
- Patrick Speelman, College of Charleston
- Paul Teverow, Missouri Southern State University
- James Vanstone, John Abbott College
- Kirk Willis, University of Georgia
- Ian Worthington, University of Missouri–Columbia
- Margarita Youngo, Pima Community College

We want to thank Steve Forman, Jon Durbin, and Karl Bakeman at W. W. Norton & Company for their faith in this project. We also thank Kate Feighery, Jason Spears, Ben Reynolds, and Lory Frenkel for their help with all aspects of the production process.

Robert Stacey is principally responsible for Chapters 1–15. He owes special thanks to Jason Hawke of Northern Illinois University for his extraordinary help in drafting Chapters 1–5. He would also like to acknowledge the assistance of a large number of friends and colleagues around the country who have taken the time to answer queries and offer suggestions: Jon Crump, Gerald Eck, Sandra Joshel, Mary O'Neil, Ben Schmidt, Julie Stein, Carol Thomas, Joel Walker, and Dan Waugh of the University of Washington; Michael Halvorson, University of Puget Sound; Michelle Ferry, University of California, Santa Barbara; Byron Nakamura, Southern Connecticut State University; Lawrence Duggan, University of Delaware; and Robert Stiefel, University of New Hampshire.

Judith Coffin is principally responsible for the revisions to Chapter 16–29. Many colleagues have supplied expertise and references, particularly Caroline Castiglione, David Crew, Paul Hagenloh, Tony Hopkins, Bruce Hunt, Standish Meacham, John Merriman, Gail Minault, Joan Neuberger, Paula Sanders, Daniel Sherman, James Sidbury, Robert Stephens, Michael Stoff, and Charters Wynn. Patrick Timmons, Marion Barber, Cori Crider, April Smith, and, especially, Michael Schmidt were terrific research assistants. Special thanks to Dinah Chenven and Norman Chenven who drafted Chapter 16, to James Brophy for his consistently excellent advice, to Geoffrey Clayton and Justin Glasson, who have researched, edited, and written many chapters, and to the students in Western Civ at the University of Texas, Austin.

WESTERN
CIVILIZATIONS

SECOND BRIEF EDITION

PART I

THE ANCIENT NEAR EAST

THE STORY OF Western civilizations begins in the Near East about 13,000 years ago. As the glaciers slowly receded, a new world of marshes, grasslands, and domesticable animals emerged at the eastern end of the Mediterranean Sea. In this new world, humans made a momentous transformation from small hunting-gathering bands to larger, agriculturally based communities. A second "great leap forward" occurred around 5,000 years ago when the first true cities appeared, first in Mesopotamia, in modern-day Iraq, and then throughout the Near East.

Traditions of urban independence and autonomy soon gave way to larger political configurations. In Old Kingdom Egypt, the pharaohs ruled an integrated realm that stretched for hundreds of miles along the Nile River. In Mesopotamia, Sargon of Akkad created an empire that would inspire imitators for 1,500 years. By 1500 B.C.E. (Before the Common Era, equivalent to the Christian dating system B.C., Before Christ), an "international system" of trade and diplomacy encompassed the entire eastern Mediterranean world.

Around 1200 B.C.E., however, this international system collapsed in cataclysm, taking with it most of the established empires of the era. The resulting power vacuum made space for new states to emerge, particularly in the Middle East. But the imperial hiatus proved temporary. As iron slowly replaced bronze as the essential raw material for tools and weapons, new, more powerful Near Eastern empires emerged: larger, better armed and organized, and more aggressively expansionist than the Bronze Age empires that preceded them. By 500 B.C.E., the largest of these empires, Persia, was the undisputed master of the Near Eastern world.

Equally dramatic developments were occurring in religious and cultural life. The pyramids of Egypt, the *Epic of Gilgamesh,* the works of Homer, and the religious traditions of Zoroastrianism and Judaism had all taken shape by the time the period closed around 500 B.C.E. On these foundations, all the subsequent civilizations of the Western (i.e., the Mediterranean) world have continued to rest.

B.C.E.	POLITICS	SOCIETY AND CULTURE	ECONOMY	INTERNATIONAL RELATIONS
40,000		Paleolithic Era (40,000–11,000 B.C.E.)		
		End of the Ice Age, beginning of the Neolithic Era (11,000 B.C.E.)		
10,000	The Predynastic Period in Egypt (c. 10,000–3100 B.C.E.)		Grain storage begins (9500 B.C.E.)	
		Settled agriculture in Fertile Crescent (8500 B.C.E.)		
8000		Stone walls and tower of Jericho (8000 B.C.E.)	Emergence of pottery in Jericho (8000–7000 B.C.E.)	
			Domestication of animals, raising of crops (7000 B.C.E.)	
			Copper tools appear (6000 B.C.E.)	
6000	Ubaid culture governed by priestly class (5900 B.C.E.)		Ubaid culture builds irrigation channels of stone (5900 B.C.E.)	Ubaid culture (Mesopotamia) (5900 B.C.E.)
		Agriculture established in Egypt and the Balkans (5000 B.C.E.)	Long-distance trade emerges (5000 B.C.E.)	
		Increased trade engenders social stratification (5000 B.C.E.)		
		First known settlement in Egypt (4750 B.C.E.)		
4000		Uruk Period (4300–2900 B.C.E.)		
		End of the Stone Age (4000 B.C.E.)		
		Cities form in fertile Mesopotamia (3500–3000 B.C.E.)	Building of the White Temple at Uruk (3500–3300 B.C.E.)	
			Pottery-throwing wheels (3500 B.C.E.)	
			Ubaid/Sumerians begin inscribing symbols on tablets (3300 B.C.E.)	
			Wheeled chariots (3200 B.C.E.)	
			Egyptians build fortifications, temples, settlements (3200 B.C.E.)	
	The Archaic Period in Egypt (3100–c. 2686 B.C.E.)		Appearance of cuneiform script (3100 B.C.E.)	Sumerian civilization (3100 B.C.E.)
3000		Beginning of the Bronze Age (3000 B.C.E.)	Discovery of bronze (3000 B.C.E.)	
		Egyptians develop hieroglyphs and hieratic script (3000 B.C.E.)		
	Emergence of lugal leadership in Mesopotamia (2900–2500 B.C.E.)			
	Early Dynastic Period (I and II) (2900–2500 B.C.E.)			
	The Old Kingdom in Egypt (c. 2686–2160 B.C.E.)	Great Pyramids of Giza (2640–2510 B.C.E.)		
		Royal Tombs of Ur (2550–2450 B.C.E.)		
	Early Dynastic Period (III) (2500–2350 B.C.E.)	*Epic of Gilgamesh* (2500 B.C.E.)		
	The Akkadian Period (2350–2160 B.C.E.)			Sargon of Akkad conquers Mesopotamia (2360 B.C.E.)
	Sargon organizes Mesopotamia (2350 B.C.E.)			
	First Intermediate Period (2160–2055 B.C.E.)			Gutians conquer Sumer and Akkad (2160 B.C.E.)
	Unity of Egypt dissolves (2150 B.C.E.)			
	Ur Dynasty III (2100–2000 B.C.E.)			

POLITICS	SOCIETY AND CULTURE	ECONOMY	INTERNATIONAL RELATIONS	
				B.C.E. 2000
The Middle Kingdom in Egypt (2055–c. 1650 B.C.E.) The Palace Age in Minoan culture (1900–1700 B.C.E.)	Indo-European linguistic forms appear (2000 B.C.E.)	Horses introduced to Near East (2000–1700 B.C.E.) Major expansion of trade (1900–1700 B.C.E.)	Minoan civilization flourishes in Crete (1900–1500 B.C.E.)	
Hammurabi unifies Sumero-Akkadian area (1792–1750 B.C.E.)	Code of Hammurabi (1750 B.C.E.)	Minoan trade with Egypt, Anatolia, and Cyprus (1700 B.C.E.)		
Second Intermediate Period (c. 1650–1550 B.C.E.) The New Kingdom in Egypt (1550–1075 B.C.E.)			The Hyksos overrun Egypt (1650–1550 B.C.E.) Hittites capture Babylon (1595 B.C.E.)	
	Appearance of Linear B in Mycenaean Greece (1500 B.C.E.)	Trade surges with new international-ism (1500 B.C.E.)	The Mitannians adopt cavalry and chariot technology (1500 B.C.E.)	1500
Thutmosis III and Hatshepsut take the throne (1479 B.C.E.)			Mycenaean civilization established (1500 B.C.E.) Age of internationalism begins (1500 B.C.E.) Hittite Empire (1450 B.C.E.) Mycenaeans subjugate Crete (1400 B.C.E.)	
Reign of Amenhotep III, the Magnificent (1387–1350 B.C.E.) Middle Assyrian Period (1362–859 B.C.E.) Amenhotep IV, later Akhenaten, takes the throne (1350 B.C.E.)	Rise of Amon as Egyptian national god (1350 B.C.E.)		Complex societies developed at Mycenae, Thebes, Athens, etc. (1400–1200 B.C.E.)	
			Treaty between Egypt and Hittite Empire (1286 B.C.E.) Rise of Phoenicians (Canaanites) (1200 B.C.E.) Mycenaean civilization implodes (1200 B.C.E.) Sea Peoples ravage Near East (1200–1179 B.C.E.) Ramses III defeats Sea Peoples (1179 B.C.E.)	
Saul becomes first Hebrew king (1025 B.C.E.) Reign of King David (1000–973 B.C.E.) Hebrew Kingdom splits on death of King Solomon (c. 933 B.C.E.) Neo-Assyrian Empire (883–859 B.C.E.)		Philistines introduce vine and olive tree to the Levant (1050 B.C.E.)	Philistine preeminence in the Levant (1050 B.C.E.) Egypt collapses (1000 B.C.E.)	1000
Reign of Sargon II (722–705 B.C.E.)		Assyrians master iron-smelting (700 B.C.E.)	Phoenicians establish Carthage (800 B.C.E.) Assyrian Empire expands (800–700 B.C.E.)	700
	Zoroaster, founder of Zoroastrianism (600 B.C.E.)		Hebrew captivity in Babylon begins (587 B.C.E.)	
Reign of Darius I of Persia (521–486 B.C.E.)			Athens defeats Darius I at Battle of Marathon (490 B.C.E.) Alexander the Great invades Persia (334 B.C.E.)	

THE ORIGINS
OF WESTERN
CIVILIZATIONS

THE HUMAN HISTORY of the Mediterranean world begins only about 40,000 years ago with the appearance of *Homo sapiens sapiens*, the modern human species to which we all belong. Civilization is an even more recent development. To the peoples of the ancient world, the characteristic features of civilization—government, literature, science, and art—were necessarily products of city life. Cities, however, became possible only as a result of the agricultural and technological discoveries that emerged between the end of the last Ice Age, about 13,000 years ago, and the appearance, in Mesopotamia, of the first true cities approximately 5,000 years ago. The story of Western civilizations is thus a short one. In geological time, it is merely a blip on a radar screen.

Why the world's first cities should have developed in the inhospitable region between the Tigris and the Euphrates rivers in modern-day Iraq is a question for which historians do not have a convincing answer. Once developed, however, the basic patterns of urban life quickly spread to other parts of the Near Eastern world. A steadily widening network of trading connections developed among these early cities, but so too did an intense competition for control over people and resources. Attempts during the third millennium B.C.E. to forge lasting empires out of these fiercely independent city-states did not succeed. By the middle of the second millennium B.C.E., however, it was becoming clear that the future of the ancient Near Eastern world would be determined not by the struggles of the Mesopotamian cities with one another but by the competition between the emerging imperial powers of Anatolia (modern-day Turkey) and Egypt.

More than 9,000 years ago, one of the earliest towns in human history began to develop at Çatalhöyük (*shatal-HOO-yuk*) in south-central Turkey. Over the next 2,000 years the town grew to cover an area about the size of thirty American football fields with some 8,000 inhabitants living in more than 2,000 separate houses. Yet there were hardly any streets in Çatalhöyük. Each house was built immediately next to its neighbor and generally on top of the ruins of a previous house. People

FOCUS QUESTIONS

- What were the consequences of hunting and gathering for early human societies?
- What changes allowed the transition from hunter-gatherer to sedentary societies?
- What were the principal influences behind the early emergence of urban life in Mesopotamia?

- Why did a common religion not create peace among the Sumerians?
- How did Hammurabi bind his empire together?
- In what ways did patterns of development in early Egypt differ from those in Sumer?

entered their houses by walking across their neighbors' rooftops, and then climbed down a ladder dropped through a hole in their own roof.

Despite (or perhaps because of) their beehive-like residential patterns, the people of Çatalhöyük lived in an elaborately organized and technologically sophisticated society. They wove wool cloth; made kiln-fired pottery; painted elaborate hunting scenes on the plaster-covered interior walls of their houses; and made sickles, knives, spears, arrows, and other tools from razor-sharp obsidian that they imported from the nearby mountains. They honored their ancestors with religious rites and buried their dead beneath the floors of their houses. These people were also accomplished sculptors, whose full-figured, carved female figurines may have had religious significance or could simply be evidence for Stone Age eroticism.

The people of Çatalhöyük grew grains, peas, and lentils and tended herds of domesticated sheep and goats. They also gathered fruits and nuts and hunted wild cattle, horses, and pigs. Comparisons of male and female skeletons suggest that there were few differences in occupation or diet between men and women. But despite their relatively healthy diets, life expectancy at Çatalhöyük was short, shorter in all likelihood than it was among the nomadic hunter-gatherer bands that surrounded them. At Çatalhöyük, men died, on average, at the age of thirty-four. Women died around the age of thirty.

Towns like Çatalhöyük are very recent developments in human history, but they are the foundation on which all subsequent human civilizations have rested. How, when, and why, then, did such towns emerge?

Female Figurine from Çatalhöyük. This female figurine was found in a grain storage area at Çatalhöyük. Its significance has been much debated but remains uncertain.

THE STONE AGE BACKGROUND

What were the consequences of hunting and gathering for early human societies?

"Prehistory," the era before the appearance of written records around 3000 B.C.E., is a period of much greater duration than recorded history, but it is only through archaeological discoveries that we can learn anything at all about the important developments that occurred during these years. Archaeologists generally agree that primates with some human features first appeared in Africa 4 to 5 million years ago, and that tool-making hominids (species belonging to the genus *Homo*, to which we as *Homo sapiens sapiens* also belong) evolved approximately 2 million years ago. Because early hominids made most of their tools out of stone, all human cultures down to the fourth millennium B.C.E. (the 1,000-year period ending in 3000 B.C.E.) are referred to as belonging to the Stone Age. Scholars generally divide this vast expanse of time into the Paleolithic ("Old Stone") and the Neolithic ("New Stone") Eras, with the break between them falling around 11,000 B.C.E.

Specifically human traits evolved gradually during the Old Stone Age. A burial site discovered near Burgos in Spain suggests that an early hominid species known as *Homo heidelbergenses* (sometimes called Heidelberg Man) had already developed some conception of burial as a symbolic rite some 350,000 years ago. Neanderthals, a later hominid species that lived 30,000 to 200,000 years ago, made jewelry, painted on the walls of caves, and buried their dead in oval-shaped graves with symbolic objects such as goat horns and, in one case, flowers. But could Neanderthals speak? Did they have a language? At present archaeologists cannot answer such questions.

Around 40,000 B.C.E., however, at the beginning of the Upper Paleolithic Era, the pace of human development began to accelerate dramatically. *Homo sapiens sapiens* began to produce more effective and finely crafted tools such as fishhooks, arrowheads, and sewing needles. Cave paintings became vastly more sophisticated than anything Neanderthals had produced. We also begin to get some evidence of ritual observances involving speech and perhaps even music.

But despite these important developments, virtually all human societies before 11,000 B.C.E. consisted of small bands of hunter-gatherers, probably never more

WHAT CHANGES ALLOWED THE TRANSITION FROM HUNTER-GATHERER TO SEDENTARY SOCIETIES?

THE NEOLITHIC REVOLUTION 9

than a few dozen individuals, that moved incessantly in search of food. Because early humans had no domestic animals to transport their goods, they had few possessions aside from the basic tools they could carry with them. As a result, there were few distinctions of wealth or status between the members of such bands. These bands may well have been highly organized—it is a gross error to presume that early societies were necessarily primitive—but hierarchical structures of leadership must have been uncommon and may not have existed at all.

We do not know how labor was divided among the members of these Paleolithic bands. Although scholars once assumed that men did the hunting and women the gathering, such gendered presumptions do not reflect the complex realities of modern hunter-gatherer societies, and they are probably not applicable to the Paleolithic Period either. It is more likely that all members of a Paleolithic band (except for the very young and the very old) engaged to some extent in all the basic activities of the group. Acquiring food and tools must have been the first concern of nearly everyone. Specialization—the process by which some members of the group are freed up to engage in activities other than food acquisition—was nearly impossible. Specialization requires the accumulation of storable surpluses, and this was something Paleolithic people lacked the technology to accomplish.

Neanderthal. This computer-generated model is based on a skull dating from approximately 40,000 B.C.E.

THE NEOLITHIC REVOLUTION

What changes allowed the transition from hunter-gatherer to sedentary societies?

Fundamental changes in human life began to take shape around 11,000 B.C.E., the dawn of the Neolithic Era or New Stone Age. These breakthroughs included the development of managed food production; the beginnings of semipermanent and permanent settlements; and the rapid intensification of trade, both local and long distance. For the first time, it now became possible for individuals and communities to accumulate and store wealth on a large scale. The results were far reaching. Communities became more stable, and human societies more complex. Specialization developed, along with distinctions of status and rank. This "revolution" was a necessary step before cities in the truest sense could appear toward the end of the fourth millennium B.C.E.

THE ORIGINS OF FOOD PRODUCTION IN THE ANCIENT NEAR EAST

 During the last Ice Age (c. 40,000–11,000 B.C.E.), daytime temperatures in Mediterranean Europe and Asia averaged about 60°F (16°C) in the summer and about 30°F (–1°C) in the winter. Reindeer, elk, wild boar, bison, and mountain goats roamed the hills and valleys. But as the glaciers receded northward such species retreated with them. Some humans moved north with the game, but others stayed behind to confront and create an extremely different sort of world.

Specifically, within about 3,000 to 4,000 years after the end of the Ice Age, the peoples living at the eastern end of the Mediterranean Sea accomplished one of the most momentous transformations in human history: a switch from food-gathering for subsistence to producing food for themselves. Substantial numbers of humans began to domesticate animals and raise crops. Stable settlements emerged, paving the way for the emergence of cities, the invention of writing, and the evolution of specialized social roles. A process that takes several thousand years may not seem "revolutionary," but in fact it was. In a relatively short time, people living in a small area of southwestern Asia fundamentally altered patterns of existence that were millions of years old.

The story of this momentous transformation is roughly as follows. By around 11,000 B.C.E. most of the larger game herds had left the ancient Near East. Yet people living in the territories that today comprise Turkey, Syria, Israel, and western Iran were prospering because the warmer, wetter climate created an ideal environment for wild grains to flourish. Throughout this region (known as the Fertile Crescent because of its abundant natural food supply and high agricultural productivity), humans now enjoyed plant resources plentiful enough to sustain seasonal, and sometimes even permanent, settlements. This fact made the shift to a sedentary existence possible.

The emergence of semipermanent and permanent settlements, made possible by a larger and more dependable food supply, had profound effects on human life. Women in these sedentary communities bore more children than did women who lived in hunter-gatherer groups. As a result, the human population began to increase. But this shift to sedentary, grain-dependent communities also entailed risks. Infectious diseases became more common; and as people's diets could become overly dependent on carbohydrates, they sickened and died at earlier ages than were typical of hunter-gatherer bands. But the advantages of increased fertility outweighed these disadvantages, and by about c. 8000 B.C.E. there is clear evidence that the human population was beginning to exceed the wild food supply. To support their growing numbers, humans had to increase the food-growing capacity of the land through deliberately managed agriculture.

Not only did people have to learn how to produce more food but they also had to learn how to store it. By around 9500 B.C.E., however, peoples living along the eastern coast of the Mediterranean Sea had solved this problem. Storage guaranteed that there would be food between harvests. It also allowed people to preserve seed, which they could use to produce even more grain the following year. Efficient seeding and storage also provided humans with the stable and predictable surpluses they needed to support domestic animals, which they could now afford to feed year-round.

The earliest evidence for permanent agricultural communitites comes from several areas in the Fertile Crescent between roughly 8500 and 7000 B.C.E. By 6000 B.C.E., much of the Near East had adopted sedentary agriculture as its primary mode of survival, supplemented by keeping cattle, pigs, sheep, and goats. Such animals provided a reliable supply of meat, milk, leather, wool, bone, and horn. In addition, cattle also provided power to pull carts and plows and to grind grain into flour.

THE EMERGENCE OF TOWNS AND VILLAGES

The next step in the Near East's accelerating social evolution was the emergence of towns and villages like Çatalhöyük, together with the growth of handicrafts, trade, and warfare—all signs of increasing economic specialization. Hundreds, and probably thousands, of towns and villages grew up in the Near East between 7500 and 3500/3000 B.C.E., when some towns began to evolve into cities. Most settlements were small—a typical village had around 1,000 inhabitants—but populations could vary greatly, and there was not a steady evolution from smaller to larger settlements. At first almost all able-bodied men and women probably engaged in field work, with women taking a leading role in cloth production and child rearing also. But gradually there came to be full-time specialists in handicrafts as well as a few full-time traders.

One of the earliest of these Neolithic villages was Jericho, in the disputed territories that lie between modern Israel and Jordan. Jericho emerged as a seasonal, grain-producing settlement around 9000 B.C.E., probably due to its abundant freshwater springs. Around 8000 B.C.E., however, the inhabitants of Jericho undertook a spectacular building program, constructing stone foundations for their houses and enclosing their village with a massive stone wall. At its peak, the village covered at least eight acres and had a population of around 3,000 people.

Jericho's inhabitants also produced some of the earliest known pottery. Pottery allowed them to store grain, wine, and oils more effectively than ever before. Its most important benefits, however, were in cooking. For the first time, it now became possible to produce nourishing stews, porridges, and ales. Pottery production quickly became an important industry throughout the Near East, marked by rapidly changing and easily identifiable regional styles.

Jericho and Çatalhöyük also illustrate the impact storable agricultural surpluses were beginning to have on human social relations. For the first time, significant differences began to arise in the amount of wealth individuals could acquire for themselves and their heirs. Dependence on agriculture also made it more difficult for individuals to split off from the community when

WHAT WERE THE PRINCIPAL INFLUENCES BEHIND THE EARLY EMERGENCE OF URBAN LIFE IN MESOPOTAMIA?

THE DEVELOPMENT OF URBAN CIVILIZATION IN MESOPOTAMIA   11

the consequences of social and economic differentiation became oppressive. The result was the emergence of a much more stratified human society, with more specialization of social roles than ever before.

Trade was another important development in these early Neolithic villages. By 5000 B.C.E. long-distance trade networks were operating across the Near East. Trade accelerated the exchange of commodities and ideas throughout the Fertile Crescent. But it also contributed to the increasing social stratification evident within these village communities. Because elite social status was enhanced by special access to high-prestige luxury goods, local elites often sought to monopolize long-distance trade by organizing and controlling the production of marketable goods within their own communities. Control over specialist artisans thus emerged as an important feature of elite social status in these Neolithic village communities.

What underlay all these social and economic changes was the increasing degree of specialization that agricultural surpluses made possible. In hunter-gatherer societies, every member of the community participated in the basic business of food acquisition. In a well-organized agricultural community, however, certain people could devote at least a portion of their labor to pursuits other than agriculture: making pottery or cloth, manufacturing weapons or tools, building houses and fortifications, or facilitating trade. Surpluses and specialization also led to the emergence

CHRONOLOGY	
FROM PREHISTORY TO HISTORY	
Appearance of figurative artwork	40,000 B.C.E.
End of the Ice Age	11,000 B.C.E.
Beginnings of sedentary agricultural societies	9000 B.C.E.
Emergence of villages	7500–3000 B.C.E.
Development of writing	3300–2500 B.C.E.
Emergence of cities	3100 B.C.E.

of social elites who, by organizing and exploiting the labor and production of others, were able to turn ruling itself into another specialist occupation. As villages grew larger and more sophisticated, the amount of specialization increased, until a significant fraction of the population could become full-time nonagriculturalists. This was an essential step in the development of true urban-based civilizations.

THE DEVELOPMENT OF URBAN CIVILIZATION IN MESOPOTAMIA

What were the principal influences behind the early emergence of urban life in Mesopotamia?

It is surprising that the initial shift from village to city and from prehistory to history took place in one of the most inhospitable environments imaginable—the southern desert of Mesopotamia, known to the Greeks as the "Land between the Rivers" but to modern historians as Sumer. Now part of Iraq, Sumer gets only about eight inches (20 cm) of rainfall per year, and summer temperatures there routinely exceed 110°F (44°C). The soils of the region are sandy and infertile unless irrigated. And the two rivers that supply this flat and largely featureless plain with water—the Tigris and Euphrates—are famous for their flooding and unpredictable course changes. Nevertheless, it was in this uninviting environment that the first true cities emerged.

Early Village Pottery. A shallow bowl from a western Asian village site dating from about 5000 B.C.E.

UBAID CULTURE

The founders of Ubaid culture (so called from its best-known site at al-Ubaid in modern Iraq) appear to have moved into the Sumerian desert around 5900 B.C.E. What attracted them to the unfriendly confines of the Tigris and Euphrates is unclear. But whatever it was that induced the Ubaid peoples to move into Sumer, it appears they brought their village culture with them. They were not hunter-gatherers who unluckily stumbled into difficult circumstances.

Almost as soon as we find farming settlements in Sumer, we discover evidence for fairly sophisticated sys-tems of irrigation. Ubaid farmers also constructed dikes and levies to control the seasonal flooding of the rivers and to direct the flow of water into irrigation canals. Despite the hostility of the environment, Ubaid agricul-tural communities were soon producing surpluses suffi-cient to support specialists in weaving, pottery making, metalwork, trade, and construction—the typical attrib-utes of Neolithic village life.

There is also early evidence of central structures that served religious functions. Starting out as simple and fairly humble shrines, these buildings soon evolved into impressive temples built of dried mud brick (the scarcity of stone in the region compelled Ubaid

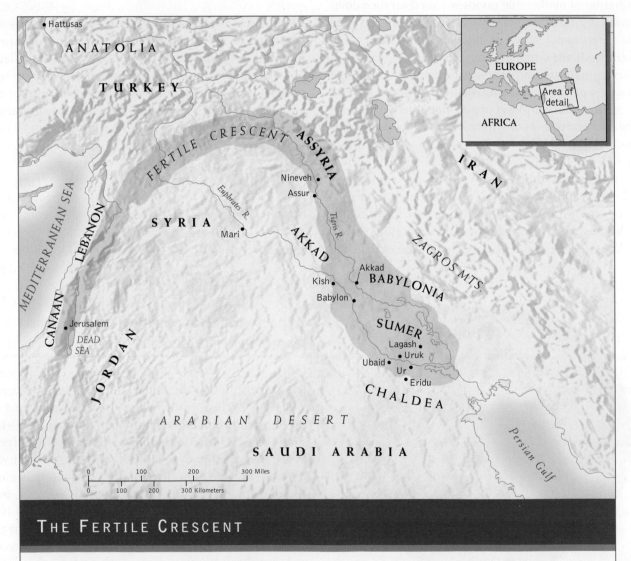

THE FERTILE CRESCENT

Notice the proximity of Sumerian cities to rivers; consider the vital role played by the Tigris and Euphrates in shaping the Mesopotamian civilizations. Also, note how close to each other the Sumerian city-states were. What challenges and opportunities did this phenomenon present? In what directions might Sumerian influence expand most quickly? Why?

WHAT WERE THE PRINCIPAL INFLUENCES BEHIND THE EARLY EMERGENCE OF URBAN LIFE IN MESOPOTAMIA?

THE DEVELOPMENT OF URBAN CIVILIZATION IN MESOPOTAMIA   13

builders to reserve that material for tools). Each larger settlement had such a building, which became progressively larger with successive rebuildings. From these temples, a priestly class acted as both the officiants of religious life and managers of the economic resources of the community, organizing the construction of ever-larger temples and maintaining the complex irrigation systems that made village life possible in the Mesopotamian desert.

URBANISM IN THE URUK PERIOD (4300–2900 B.C.E.)

From about 4300 B.C.E. on, Ubaid settlements began to develop into larger, more prosperous and more highly organized communities. This new period, named after its most impressive site at Uruk (modern Warka), witnessed the transition from the Neolithic Ubaid village to the Sumerian city-state. It marks therefore the true beginning of urban civilization in the Mediterranean world.

Among the principal developments of this period is the growing sophistication and scale of temple architecture. This trend reflects not only the centrality of religion in Sumerian culture but also the increasing wealth and control of the priestly class over economic life. The White Temple at Uruk provides a stunning example of this general trend. Sometime between 3500 and 3300 B.C.E., builders constructed a massive sloping platform that towered nearly forty feet above the surrounding flatlands. Atop the platform stood another structure, the shrine or temple proper, also dressed in brick but painted a brilliant white.

Such temples grew up across Sumer, reflecting the central role religion played in civic life. Uruk in particular seems to have owed its rapid urban growth to its importance as a religious center. By 3100 B.C.E., it sprawled across several hundred acres, enclosing a population of 40,000 people within its massive mud-brick walls. But the larger villages of Sumer were also growing rapidly, their teeming economic activity attracting immigrants just as the great cities were doing. To feed this rapidly growing population, grain and cloth production in Sumer increased tenfold during the Uruk Period. Trade routes also expanded dramatically. To manage this increasingly sophisticated and centrally directed economy, the Sumerians also began to develop a new communications technology that moved them fully into the light of history: writing.

THE DEVELOPMENT OF WRITING

Like many of the breakthroughs we have considered in this chapter, the invention of writing did not occur overnight. By 4000 B.C.E., villagers in the Near East were already using clay tokens to keep track of inventories and to facilitate the burgeoning trade of the region. Ultimately, the practice developed of placing all the tokens from a single transaction inside a hollow clay ball and inscribing, on the outside of the ball, the shapes of all the tokens it contained. By 3300 B.C.E., the priestly class (or those working for them) realized that they could dispense with the clumsy token-and-ball system altogether and replace it with flat clay tablets on which they could note the desired information by inscribing the appropriate symbols.

In its earliest phases, writing thus evolved as a means of record keeping in connection with economic pursuits. For some time, writing remained purely pictographic: each symbol marked into the clay resembled the physical object it represented. Over time, however, as the uses of writing evolved, a symbol might come to be used not only to evoke the physical object it represented but also an idea associated with that object. The symbol for a bowl of food, *ninda* (a noun), might thus be used to express a more abstract notion such as bread or sustenance—an idea not otherwise easily represented by a quick sketch into soft clay. In time, such symbols might also come to be associated with a particular phonetic sound. Thus when a Sumerian scribe needed to employ the sound *ninda*, even as part of another word or name, he would use the symbol for a bowl of food. Later, special marks were added to the script so that the reader could discern whether the writer intended the symbol to represent the object itself or the *phonogram* (the sound represented by the symbol).

By 3100 B.C.E. Sumerian scribes had largely abandoned writing with pointed sticks in favor of a more durable reed stylus. Because this stylus left an impression shaped like a wedge (the Latin word for which is *cuneus*), we refer to this script as *cuneiform* (kyoo-NEH-form). The new stylus did make it more difficult, however, to draw pictograms that accurately reflected the original shape

> By 3100 B.C.E. Sumerian scribes had largely abandoned writing with pointed sticks in favor of a more durable reed stylus. Because this stylus left an impression shaped like a wedge (the Latin word for which is *cuneus*), we refer to this script as *cuneiform*.

Cuneiform Writing. This cuneiform writing on limestone dates from about 2600 B.C.E. The inscription proclaims that a king of Ur has built a temple.

(such as a bowl of food) of the objects they were meant to represent. As a result, cuneiform symbols became more and more abstract, until they barely resembled the original pictograms at all.

Symbols ultimately were invented for every possible vowel-consonant combination in the Sumerian language. As a result, the number of symbols ran into the several hundreds. Understandably, it took many years to learn to read and write cuneiform, and only a small minority of the population ever did so. Those who did, however, became important and influential people in Sumerian society. For the entirety of the third millennium, it was largely the sons of the elite who attended the scribal schools. But despite the wide variety of symbols and the complicated nature of the script, cuneiform proved remarkably durable. For over 2,000 years it remained the principal writing system of the ancient Near East, even for societies that no longer spoke the Sumerian language.

CHRONOLOGY

ORIGINS OF MESOPOTAMIAN SOCIETY

Ubaid Period	5900–4300 B.C.E.
Uruk Period	4300–2900 B.C.E.
Early Dynastic Period	2900–2500 B.C.E.
Akkadian Period	2350–2160 B.C.E.
Ur Dynasty	2100–2000 B.C.E.

THE SUMERIANS ENTER HISTORY

Why did a common religion not create peace among the Sumerians?

After about 2500 B.C.E., the Sumerians used writing for a wide variety of economic, political, literary, and religious purposes. This makes it possible for us to know a great deal more about the Sumerians than we do about any other human society of the time. We can begin to understand their political relationships, their feelings about their gods, and the social and economic structure of their society. The Sumerians are, in this sense, the first historical—as opposed to prehistorical—society.

The great centers of Sumerian culture—such as Uruk, Ur, Lagash, Eridu, and Kish—shared a common culture, language, and religion. This common religion did not produce peace among the Sumerian cities, however. Although each Sumerian community recognized all the gods of the Sumerian pantheon (some 1,500 gods), the residents of each individual city-state viewed their city as the property of one particular god, whom they sought to glorify by exalting their city. The result was intense competition between cities, which frequently escalated into open warfare. For any city-state to surrender its independence to another city would have been an intolerable offense against the conquered city's god. The Sumerians shared a common culture and a common pantheon; but common government was impossible.

A significant proportion of the cultivable land of each city belonged outright to the temple of the patron god. During the third millennium, these great temples also began to control the production of textiles, creating protofactories that employed thousands of servile women and children. Temples also played a key role in long-distance trade, both as buyers and sellers of goods.

Each Sumerian city had a ruling aristocracy, from which the priests and important officials of the temples came; but it was the priests who stood at the top of these highly theocratic societies. In this early period of Sumerian civilization perhaps as much as half the population consisted of commoners, free persons who held a small parcel of land sufficient to sustain themselves and make required payments to the temple complex. The temples also had large numbers of legally free dependents who worked as artisans or as agricultural laborers on temple lands but who owned no land themselves.

WHY DID A COMMON RELIGION NOT CREATE PEACE AMONG THE SUMERIANS?

THE SUMERIANS ENTER HISTORY   15

There were also many slaves in Sumerian society. In Sumer, as elsewhere in the ancient world, slaves were often prisoners of war. If the slave came originally from another Sumerian city, the master's power over him or her was strictly limited, and he (or she—many slaves were women) had to be released after three years. Non-Sumerians could be held indefinitely, although slaves could sometimes buy their freedom. Despite these safeguards, slaves in Sumer were still the property of their owners. They could be beaten, punished, branded like animals, and bought and sold on their owner's whim. Ancient slavery may not have been quite so horrible as more modern examples (such as that practiced in the New World), but it was still highly undesirable to be a slave.

THE EARLY DYNASTIC PERIOD BEGINS (2900–2500 B.C.E.)

Starting around 2900 B.C.E., the intense competition between the Sumerian city-states led to the emergence of a new type of war leadership that would eventually become a kind of kingship. As the city-states grew larger (each now holding anywhere from 10,000 to 50,000 inhabitants), competition for scarce resources intensified. Warfare became a regular feature of Sumerian life, and successful war leaders, known as *lugals*, began to acquire great prestige and power.

The most striking indication of the impression this new office made on Sumerian society is the *Epic of Gilgamesh*, the first great literary work in world history, which recounts the legendary exploits of a historical king of Uruk named Gilgamesh. As he appears in the epic, Gilgamesh was a powerful lugal who became so powerful that he could ignore the constraints that bound lesser men. We hear at the start of the epic how the people complained about their king, even though they still revered him: he kept their sons away at war for too long; he showed no respect for the nobles, carousing with their wives and daughters as he pleased; he disappointed them by his sacrilegious conduct. His people prayed to the gods for relief, and ultimately the gods fashioned a wild man named Enkidu to challenge Gilgamesh.

The confrontation between Gilgamesh and Enkidu reflects the dichotomy the Sumerians perceived between city and wilderness, between what was "civilized" and what was not. We recognize in Enkidu the hunter-gatherer who was doubtless far more intimate with nature than were the Sumerians after centuries of civic life; but such "naturalness" was not a quality the Sumerians admired. Instead, the friendship that eventually formed between Gilgamesh and Enkidu illustrates the hostililty and fear Sumerians felt toward the wilderness. Given the harsh climate and unpredictable environment in which the Sumerians lived, their adversarial relationship with the natural world is understandable. As they battled uncooperative rivers, searing heat, salinization of the soil, and the raids of less civilized folk, the Sumerians' pessimistic attitude toward their natural environment is mirrored not only in their general view of life but also in their view of the gods.

SUMERIAN RELIGION

The Sumerians believed that humanity itself had been wrested from the inhospitable earth and created for one purpose, to serve the gods. The Sumerians therefore imbued every aspect of their life and culture with religiosity, reflecting their pervasive obligations to the gods. A powerful lugal might distance himself from the temple priesthood, but nonetheless, he owed his authority to the gods who had bestowed it on him.

Relations between the Sumerians and their gods were not warm. The gods wished to be exalted, and so massive temples called ziggurats evolved out of the increasingly elaborate shrines of the Uruk Period. The Sumerians also went to great pains to honor their gods with temples, festivals, and sacrifices. But the gods inspired no affection, nor did they offer any affection to human beings. Instead, they were objects of fear and suspicion: cruel, mean spirited, and capricious, with little concern for the effect their actions might have on humanity. The wide-eyed, apprehensive-looking human figures sculpted by Sumerian artists were offered to the gods by people hoping to ensure the gods' benign detachment toward humanity. To ask the gods for more positive help was a last resort in desperate circumstances and was likely to backfire, as the residents of Uruk discovered when they asked the gods to rein in the tyrant Gilgamesh.

Sumerian views of the afterlife were equally pessimistic. They expected neither eternal punishment nor eternal reward from the gods after death. Instead, the dead simply crossed a man-eating river into the "Land of No Return," a gloomy place that enjoyed no light. Relatives buried the dead with basic articles such as food and clothing and diversions such as musical instruments and games, hoping to make the glum, unhappy underworld a bit more bearable for the departed. But the improvement, if any, would have been modest. The afterlife was essentially just a continuation

THE FLOOD: TWO ACCOUNTS

The Epic of Gilgamesh *preserves a traditional account of a destructive flood sent by the gods to punish humanity. This story probably dates from the first half of the third millennium* B.C.E., *making it at least 1,500 years older than the similar account in the Hebrew Bible. The striking similarities between these two accounts is evidence of the strong cultural influence exerted by older Near Eastern civilizations on the early Hebrews.*

EPIC OF GILGAMESH

Utnapishtim spoke to Gilgamesh, saying: "I will reveal to you, Gilgamesh . . . a secret of the gods. . . . The hearts of the Great Gods moved them to inflict the Flood. Their Father Anu uttered the oath (of secrecy). . . . [But the god] Ea . . . repeated their talk [to me, saying]: 'O man of Shuruppak, son of Ubartutu: Tear down the house and build a boat! . . . Spurn possessions and keep alive living beings! Make all living beings go up into the boat. The boat which you are to build, its dimensions must measure equal to each other: its length must correspond to its width. Roof it over like the Apsu.' I understood and spoke to my lord, Ea: 'My lord, thus is the command which you have uttered. I will heed and will do it.' . . . On the fifth day I laid out her exterior. It was a field in area, its walls were each 10 times 12 cubits in height. . . . I provided it with six decks, thus dividing it into seven (levels). . . . Whatever I had I loaded on it. . . . All the living beings that I had I loaded on it. I had all my kith and kin go up into the boat, all the beasts and animals of the field and the draftsmen I had go up.

I watched the appearance of the weather—the weather was frightful to behold! I went into the boat and sealed the entry. . . . All day long the South Wind blew . . . , submerging the mountain in water, overwhelming the people like an attack. . . . Six days and seven nights came the wind and flood, the storm flattening the land. When the seventh day arrived . . .

[t]he sea calmed, fell still, the whirlwind and flood stopped up. . . . When a seventh day arrived, I sent forth a dove and released it. The dove went off, but came back to me; no perch was visible so it circled back to me. I sent forth a swallow and released it. The swallow went off, but came back to me; no perch was visible so it circled back to me. I sent forth a raven and released it. The raven went off, and saw the waters slither back. It eats, it scratches, it bobs, but does not circle back to me. Then I sent out everything in all directions and sacrificed (a sheep). I offered incense in front of the mountain-ziggurat. . . .

The gods smelled the savor . . . and collected like flies over a sacrifice. . . . Just then Enlil arrived. He saw the boat and became furious. . . . 'Where did a living being escape? No man was to survive the annihilation!' Ea spoke to Valiant Enlil, saying . . . 'How, how could you bring about a Flood without consideration? Charge the violation to the violator, charge the offense to the offender, but be compassionate lest (mankind) be cut off, be patient lest they be killed.' Enlil went up inside the boat and, grasping my hand, made me go up. He had my wife go up and kneel by my side. He touched our forehead and, standing between us, he blessed us. . . ."

Maureen Gallery Kovacs, trans. *The Epic of Gilgamesh*, Tablet XI (Stanford, Calif., 1985, 1989), pp. 97–103.

BOOK OF GENESIS

The Lord saw that the wickedness of humankind was great in the earth and . . . said "I will blot out from the earth the human beings I have created . . . for I am sorry I have made them." But Noah found favor in the sight of the Lord. . . . God saw that the earth was corrupt and . . . said to Noah, "I have determined to make an end to all flesh. . . . Make yourself an ark of cypress wood; make rooms in the ark, and cover it inside and out with pitch. . . . Make a roof for the ark, and put the door of the ark in its side. . . . For my part I am going to bring a flood on the earth, to destroy from under heaven all flesh. . . . But I will establish a covenant with you; and you shall come into the ark, you, your sons, your wife, and your sons' wives with you. And of every living thing you shall bring two of every kind into the ark, to keep them alive with you. . . . Also take with you every kind of food that is eaten." . . . All the fountains of the great deep burst forth, and the windows of the heavens were opened. . . . The waters gradually receded from the earth. . . . At the end of forty days, Noah opened a window of the ark . . . and sent out the raven, and it went to and fro until the waters were dried up from the earth. Then he sent out the dove from him, to see if the waters had subsided from the face of the ground, but the dove found no place to set its foot, and it returned. . . . He waited another seven days, and again sent out the dove [which] came back to him . . . and there in its beak was a freshly plucked olive leaf; so Noah knew the waters had subsided from the earth. Then he . . . sent out the dove, and it did not return to him anymore. . . . Noah built an altar to the Lord . . . and offered burnt offerings. And when the Lord smelled the pleasing odor, the Lord said in his heart, "I will never again curse the ground because of humankind . . . nor will I ever again destroy every living creature as I have done.". . . God blessed Noah and his sons.

Genesis 6:5–9:1, *New Revised Standard Version of the Bible* (The National Council of the Churches of Christ in the USA, 1989).

QUESTIONS FOR ANALYSIS

1. What is the significance of the *Epic of Gilgamesh*? Why was it written? What function did the *Epic of Gilgamesh* serve in ancient Mesopotamia?
2. How did the geography and climate of Mesopotamia influence this epic and Mesopotamians' attitudes toward the gods, kingship, civilization, and the afterlife?
3. How does the account of Noah in the Book of Genesis differ from that of Utnapishtim in the *Epic of Gilgamesh*? Compare both human and divine characters.

of the anxious, grim existence the Sumerians led in this world, only worse.

Even Gilgamesh, the legendary king of Uruk, could not escape the fate the gods had decreed for all mortals. When his friend Enkidu was killed by the goddess Inanna, whom they had mocked, Gilgamesh's horror at Enkidu's death propelled him on a quest for immortality. His search finally brought him to a deep pool, at the bottom of which grew a plant of eternal life. But when Gilgamesh swam down to retrieve the plant, it was stolen from him as he surfaced by a serpent, who then disappeared into the pool with the plant in his jaws. In the end, the great king of Uruk was left to ponder the futility of all human endeavor. Reflecting on the impermanence of his deeds and even of Uruk's mighty walls, Gilgamesh asked, "Why do I bother working for nothing? Who even notices what I do?"

SCIENCE, TECHNOLOGY, AND TRADE

Sumerian pessimism was deeply rooted, but it was not paralyzing. Their distrust of the gods and their adversarial relationship with their environment instead inculcated in the Sumerians a high degree of self-reliance and ingenuity. These qualities helped make them the most technologically inventive people of the ancient world.

The Sumerians became first-rate metallurgists despite the fact that their land had no natural mineral resources. By 6000 B.C.E., a number of cultures throughout the Near East and Europe had learned how to produce copper weapons and tools. Mesopotamia itself had no copper; but by the Uruk Period (4300–2900 B.C.E.), trade routes were bringing raw copper into Sumer, where the Sumerians processed it into weapons

Sumerian Ziggurat. This edifice, built in Ur c. 2100 B.C.E., is the best-preserved surviving ziggurat. As can be seen from the diagram of its original form at left, a shrine, reached by climbing four stories and passing through a massive portal, was the goal of the worshiper's ascent and the most sacred part of the temple.

and tools. Shortly before 3000 B.C.E., perhaps starting in eastern Anatolia, people discovered that copper could be alloyed with arsenic (or later, tin) to produce bronze. Bronze is almost as malleable as copper but pours more easily into molds and, when cooled, maintains its rigidity and shape better than copper. Because the Sumerians and neighboring cultures engaged in such widespread use of bronze, we refer to a Bronze Age, beginning around 3000 B.C.E.

Alongside writing, the invention of the wheel stands at the top of any list of fundamental advances in human technology. The Sumerians were using potter's wheels by the middle of the fourth millennium B.C.E., allowing them to produce high-quality clay vessels in greater quantity than ever before. By around 3200 B.C.E., the Sumerians were also using two-wheeled chariots and four-wheeled carts drawn by donkeys (horses were unknown in western Asia until they were introduced by eastern invaders sometime between 2000 and 1700 B.C.E.). Wheeled chariots were used mainly in warfare; illustrations from about 2600 B.C.E. depict them trampling the enemy. Wheeled carts were an even more important advance, however, because they dramatically increased the productivity of the Sumerian workforce. The Sumerians did not invent the wheel; they probably acquired it from nomadic peoples living on the steppes of southern Russia. But by

adapting it to so many different uses, they vastly increased its technological possibilities.

The Sumerians also pioneered the study of mathematics. To construct their elaborate systems of irrigation canals, dikes, and reservoirs, they developed sophisticated measuring and surveying techniques. Agricultural concerns probably also lay behind the lunar calendar they invented, which consisted of 12 months, 6 lasting 30 days, and 6 lasting 29 days. Since this produced a year of only 354 days, the Sumerians eventually discovered that they had to add a month to their calendars every few years to predict the recurrence of the seasons with sufficient accuracy. But the Sumerian practice of dividing time into multiples of 60 has lasted to the present day, not only in our notions of the 30-day month (which corresponds approximately with the phases of the moon) but also in our division of the hour into 60 minutes, and the minute into 60 seconds. Mathematics also contributed to Sumerian architecture, allowing the Sumerians to build domes and arches thousands of years before the Romans would adopt and spread these architectural forms throughout the Mediterranean world.

The Sumerians' ability to engage in these activities depended on the acquisition of raw materials through trade, for their homeland was almost completely devoid of natural resources. The Sumerians therefore pioneered trade routes up and down the Tigris and Euphrates and

WHY DID A COMMON RELIGION NOT CREATE PEACE AMONG THE SUMERIANS?

THE SUMERIANS ENTER HISTORY   19

Sumerian War Chariots. The earliest known representation of the wheel, dating from about 2600 B.C.E., shows how wheels were carpentered together from slabs of wood. (For a later Mesopotamian wheel with spokes, see the illustration on p. 40.)

these powerful rulers. It tells of a cycle of brutal warfare among the leading city-states, as the lugal of each sought to establish his supremacy over the others by defeating their armies in battle and then forcing the defeated cities to pay him tribute. Inevitably, however, such supremacy was fleeting: conquered cities revolted, and the cycle of warfare began again. No Sumerian lugal ever attempted to create a true and lasting empire by imposing centralized rule over the cities he conquered. As a result, Sumer remained a collection of independent city-states, compelled periodically to acknowledge the supremacy of a particular lugal but unable to forge any lasting structures of authority larger than an individual city and its patron god. This fact would prove its undoing when Sumer confronted a new style of imperial rulership in the figure of Sargon of Akkad.

into the hilly flanks of Mesopotamia, following the tributaries of these great rivers. They blazed trails across the deserts toward the west, where they interacted with and influenced the Egyptians. By sea, they traded with the peoples of the Persian Gulf and, directly or indirectly, with the civilizations of the Indus Valley. Like the Neolithic traders who conveyed goods from village to village, the Sumerians carried their ideas with them along with their merchandise, their literature, their art, their use of writing, and the whole cultural complex that arose from their urban way of life. From its Sumerian roots, the idea of civilization thus spread throughout the ancient Near Eastern world.

THE END OF THE EARLY DYNASTIC PERIOD (2500–2350 B.C.E.)

During this period, competition among the Sumerian city-states for prestige, power, and resources reached a fever pitch. Tensions between temple aristocracy and royal power were lessening, however, leading to the emergence of a more unified ruling elite, but leaving commoners with even less of a voice than they had had before.

The Royal Tombs of Ur, dating from 2550 B.C.E. to 2450 B.C.E., provide a breathtaking demonstration of the wealth of this Sumerian elite and of the divide that had now opened up between leaders and followers in Sumerian society. The rich documentary evidence from this period deals mainly with the military exploits of

THE AKKADIAN EMPIRE (2350–2160 B.C.E.)

The Akkadians were the predominant people of central Mesopotamia, to the north of Sumer. The Sumerians had greatly influenced them. But although they adopted cuneiform script along with much of Sumerian culture, the Akkadians did not adopt the Sumerian language. Instead, they preserved their own Semitic language, a member of the linguistic family that includes Assyrian, Aramaic, Hebrew, Arabic, and Ethiopic.

As an outsider to Sumerian society, Sargon, the leader of the Akkadians, was not bound by the traditional assumptions and conventions of Sumerian warfare. Instead, he launched a systematic program of conquest, designed to subject all the areas around Sumer to his authority. Only when it was too late did the Sumerians realize that Sargon now had their land by the throat. Around 2350 B.C.E., he conquered Sumer and then moved swiftly to establish direct control over all of Mesopotamia.

From his new capital at Akkad, Sargon installed Akkadian-speaking governors to rule the cities of Sumer, ordering them to pull down fortifications, collect taxes, and do his will. By so doing, Sargon transformed the independent city-states of Sumer and Akkad into a much larger political unit: a kingdom or empire. Sargon supported his empire (arguably the first true empire in human history) by managing and exploiting the network of trade routes crisscrossing the Near East. His economic influence stretched from Ethiopia to the Indus Valley in India, and his capital became the most splendid city in the world.

Sargon's imperialism also had a religious aspect. To unite the two halves of his empire, Sargon merged the Akkadian and Sumerian pantheons by identifying Akkadian divinities, such as Ishtar, with their Sumerian counterparts (in this case, the goddess Inanna). He also appointed a single Akkadian high priest or priestess (often a member of Sargon's own family) to preside simultaneously over the main temples in several different Sumerian cities. Perhaps the most successful example of this policy was Sargon's daughter Enheduanna, whom Sargon appointed as high priestess of An, the principal god of Uruk, and of Nanna, the chief god of Ur. Enheduanna herself, however, seems to have been particularly devoted to Inanna/Ishtar, her father's own patron deity. Enheduanna's hymns to Inanna are the earliest surviving literary works by a named author in world history. The precedent she established would

continue even after her father's dynasty finally fell; for several centuries thereafter, the kings of Sumer would continue to appoint their daughters to the combined high priesthoods of Ur and Uruk.

Sargon was eventually succeeded by his talented grandson Naram-Sin, who reigned, like his grandfather, for over a half century. Naram-Sin extended the Akkadian conquests and consolidated long-distance trade routes. An energetic promoter of culture and a patron of the arts, Naram-Sin encouraged literary and artistic endeavors. Through conquest and the quickened pace of commerce, he also helped stimulate the growth of cities throughout the Near East.

Although the Akkadians' emphasis on political centralization and imperial organization represented a clear break with the Sumerian past, culturally the Sumerians and Akkadians differed little from one another. By 2200 B.C.E. most people in central and southern Mesopotamia would have been able to converse in either language. Much of Akkadian literature and art was at its root Sumerian, translated and slightly transformed to appeal to Akkadian tastes. Scholars speak of a Sumero-Akkadian cultural synthesis; and indeed after the reign of Sargon

Objects from the Royal Tombs at Ur. On the right, a queen's headdress, made of gold leaf, lapis lazuli, and carnelian. Above, a helmet made of an alloy of gold and silver. Its cloth lining would have been attached through the holes visible around the edges of the helmet.

the two civilizations were virtually indistinguishable, except for their different languages. Despite its new imperial trappings, the urban civilization Sargon and Naram-Sin helped promote across the Near East was still essentially the urban model of the Sumerians.

The Dynasty of Ur (2100–2000 B.C.E.)

Court intrigue and a series of weak successors followed the long reign of Naram-Sin. Around 2100 B.C.E., however, a new dynasty from Ur, the so-called Ur Dynasty III, established itself under the rule of its first king, Ur-Nammu, and his son Shulgi. Ur-Nammu and Shulgi modeled their kingship on that of Sargon and Naram-Sin, pursuing military conquests, the centralization of Sumerian government, commercial expansion, the patronage of art and literature, and an exalted ideology of charismatic imperial rulership. Together, the Akkadian rulers and those of the Ur Dynasty III thus established a pattern of rule that would influence the region for centuries to come.

For the next two centuries, Mesopotamian history would be characterized by incessant warfare among a group of small kingdoms based on the great urban centers of the Sumero-Akkadian past. Not until the eighteenth century B.C.E. would one of these kings, the remarkable Hammurabi of Babylon, create a new imperial unity in the region.

The Old Babylonian Empire

How did Hammurabi bind his empire together?

In 1792 B.C.E. a young ruler named Hammurabi (*bah-muh-RAH-bee*) ascended the throne of Babylon, a weak kingdom in central Mesopotamia based in an insignificant city of the same name. When Hammurabi came to power, Babylon was precariously wedged among a number of other, more powerful kingdoms. Babylon's site on the Tigris and Euphrates had great potential economic and military significance; but it was also dangerous, because Babylon sat perilously amid mighty antagonists who were often tempted to "play through" the city on their way to other conquests.

Hammurabi may have been the first sovereign in world history to understand that power need not be based on brute force. He recognized that the application of intellect, political strategy, and ruthless cunning might accomplish what his army could not. Hammurabi did not try to confront his mightier neighbors directly. Rather, through letters and embassies, double-dealing diplomacy, and general deceit, he induced his stronger counterparts to embroil themselves ever deeper in armed conflict with each other. While the other kingdoms exhausted themselves in costly wars, Hammurabi fanned their hatred for one another, skillfully portraying himself as a friend to all sides. His value as a potential ally caused neighboring rulers to send him resources, in hopes that he might help them. Meanwhile, Hammurabi quietly consolidated his kingdom, augmenting his own strength, and when the time was right

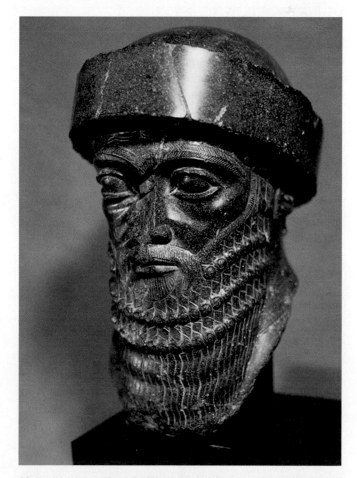

Mesopotamian Royal Head. A diorite head of a Mesopotamian king, conventionally identified as Hammurabi. Such headdresses were worn by the rulers of Mesopotamian cities between roughly 2100 and 1700 B.C.E. Hammurabi is shown wearing such a headdress on p. 22, but there is nothing else to identify this bust with Hammurabi.

fell on his depleted and weary neighbors. By such policies, he transformed his small state into what historians describe as the Old Babylonian Empire.

Mesopotamia under Hammurabi's rule achieved an unprecedented degree of political integration. His realm ultimately stretched from the Persian Gulf into Assyria. The southern half of the region, formerly known as Sumer and Akkad, would for the rest of antiquity be known as Babylonia. To help unify these territories, Hammurabi introduced an important innovation by elevating the little-known patron deity of Babylon, Marduk, to be the ruler-god of his entire empire. Although the king was also careful to pay homage to the ancient gods of Sumer and Akkad, Marduk now sat atop the official pantheon. People could continue to worship the ancient patron deities of their cities if they wished, but all now owed allegiance to Marduk.

RELIGION AND LAW

The notion that political rule rested on divine approval was nothing new, of course. Its foundations lay in the practices and beliefs of the Sumerians, and the notion was fully developed by Sargon, Narum-Sin, Ur-Nammu, and Shulgi. Hammurabi's innovation was to use Marduk's supremacy over all other gods to legitimate his own claim to rule, in Marduk's name, over all Mesopotamia because he was king of Marduk's home city of Babylon. Hammurabi thus became the first Near Eastern ruler to launch wars of aggression that he justified specifically by saying he undertook them in the name of his primary god. This precedent would become a characteristic feature of Near Eastern politics thereafter, as we will see in Chapter Two.

Hammurabi did not rely solely on religion to bind his empire together. Building on the precedents of centuries and rulers past, he also issued (and had carved in stone) a collection of laws and legal decisions in his own name, which portrayed the king as a fountain of justice and mercy for his entire empire. Preserved on an impressive eight-foot stele discovered in southwestern Iran (and now housed in the Louvre in Paris), the Code of Hammurabi was probably never intended to be a code of laws in any modern sense. Too many subjects are omitted; furthermore, the code is never cited or even mentioned in the surviving records of legal cases from Hammurabi's kingdom. Most likely, Hammurabi's code was propaganda, intended to publicize the king's devotion to justice and to urge his officials to show a similar concern in their own legal judgments.

OLD BABYLONIAN SOCIETY

Despite its propagandistic purposes, Hammurabi's code does tell us something about the structure of Old Babylonian society. Overall, the more complicated social arrangements of Sumerian civilization had given way to a simpler but more oppressive system. An upper class of nobles—palace officials, temple priests, high-ranking military officers, and rich merchants—controlled large estates and staggering wealth. Beneath this small stratum was an enormous class of legally free individuals who were nonetheless "dependents" of the palace or the temple or who leased land from the estates of the powerful. These dependents included laborers and artisans, small-scale merchants and farmers, and the minor political and religious officials of the state.

At the bottom of Babylonian society were the slaves. Far more numerous in the Old Babylonian Empire than

Code of Hammurabi. The entire code of Hammurabi survives on an eight-foot column made of basalt. The top quarter of the column depicts the Babylonian king paying homage to the seated god of justice. Directly below one can make out the cuneiform inscriptions that are the law code's text.

THE CODE OF HAMMURABI

The laws of Hammurabi, published on the authority of the king and set up throughout the Babylonian Empire, exhibit the influences both of the urban society on which they were imposed and the rough justice of Amorite tradition. Although Hammurabi built on older, urban legal traditions, he sought to extend the authority of his law into more realms of life and provide sterner punishments for its violation. This sampling of his provisions illustrates the severity of his system for criminals, while providing protections in unusual circumstances.

If a man accuses a man, and charges him with murder, but cannot convict him, the accuser shall be put to death.

If a man steals an ox or sheep, ass or pig, or boat—if it belonged to the god or palace, he shall pay thirty fold; if it belonged to a common man, he shall restore ten fold. If the thief has nothing wherewith to pay, he shall be put to death.

If a fire breaks out in a man's house and a man who goes to extinguish it . . . takes the household property of the owner of the house, that man shall be thrown into the fire.

If a man aids a male or a female slave of the palace, or a male or female slave of a common man, to escape from the city, he shall be put to death.

If a man who is a tenant has paid the full amount of money for his rent for the year to the owner of the house, and he (the owner) says to him before "his days are full," "Vacate," the owner of the house, because he made the tenant move out of the house before "his days were full" shall lose the money which the tenant paid him.

If an agent should be careless and not take a receipt for the money which he has given to the merchant, the money not receipted for shall not be placed to his account.

If the wife of a man be taken in lying with another man, they shall bind them and throw them into the water.

If a woman hates her husband and says, "Thou shalt not have me," her past shall be inquired into for any deficiency of hers; and if she has been careful and without past sin and her husband has been going out and greatly belittling her, that woman has no blame. She shall take her dowry and go to her father's house.

If a man destroys the eye of another man, they shall destroy his eye. If a man knocks out the tooth of a man of his own rank, they shall knock out his tooth . . . if the tooth of a common man, he shall pay one-third mana of silver.

Sara Robbins, ed., *Law: A Treasury of Art and Literature* (New York, 1990), pp. 20–22 (slightly revised).

QUESTIONS FOR ANALYSIS

1. Does the Code of Hammurabi sound harsh, fair, or lenient? Penalties such as exile and mutilation were less severe than death, but was harsh justice necessary in Babylonia? Based on your reading of the code, was Hammurabi an enlightened ruler?

2. In what ways does the Code of Hammurabi exhibit the influences of the urban society from which these laws were imposed? What are the general characteristics of ancient Near Eastern urban society?

they had been in the Sumerian Period, slaves were also treated much more harshly and were more readily identifiable as a separate group within society. In Babylonia, free men, whether nobles or dependents, wore long hair and beards; male slaves, however, were shaven and branded. Some Babylonian slaves were acquired through trade, another departure from Sumerian practice. Others were captured in war or were free people who had fallen into slavery through debt or as punishment for certain offenses. Slaves could accumulate property and borrow as a means of gaining their freedom, but this was probably not a frequent occurrence.

Old Babylonian society was also highly stratified by class. An offense committed against nobles carried a far more severe penalty than did the same crime committed against a dependent or slave (although nobles were also punished more severely than were commoners for crimes they committed against other nobles). Marriage arrangements and customs also reflected class differences, with bride-price and dowry depending on the status of the parties involved.

Hammurabi's code also provides evidence as to the status and treatment of women in Babylonian society. Women did enjoy certain protections under the law, including the right to divorce abusive, neglectful, or indigent husbands. If a husband divorced a wife "without cause," he was obliged to provide financial support for her and their children. Despite such protections, however, Babylonian law regarded wives as the property of their husbands. A wife who publicly defamed her husband could be drowned; she would suffer the same fate, along with her lover, if she were caught in adultery. Husbands, by contrast, had a legal right to have sexual relations not only with temple prostitutes but also with slaves and concubines.

HAMMURABI'S LEGACY

Hammurabi died around 1750 B.C.E. Although some contraction of the Old Babylonian Empire followed under his successors, Hammurabi's achievements endured. His administrative reforms, combined with his innovations in religious imperialism, created a durable and important state in Mesopotamia. For another two centuries the Old Babylonian Empire played a significant role in the Near East, until invaders from the north sacked the capital and occupied it. Babylon itself remained the region's most famous city for another thousand years.

Hammurabi's legacy extended well beyond the borders of his own kingdom. His success, and the flair and aplomb with which he achieved it, was instrumental in shaping conceptions of kingship in the ancient Near East. After Hammurabi, unifying state religions would play an increasingly important role in the policies of Near Eastern kings. Hammurabi had also demonstrated the effectiveness of writing as a political tool. Diplomacy, the keeping of extensive archives, international relations—all would characterize subsequent Near Eastern empires. So too would the claim that kings should be the protectors of the weak and the arbiters of justice within their realms. Hammurabi's law code built on the traditions of previous Mesopotamian kings, but it was his greatness that transformed law giving into an imperative for any ambitious ruler of a future Near Eastern kingdom or empire.

THE DEVELOPMENT OF CIVILIZATION IN EGYPT

In what ways did patterns of development in early Egypt differ from those in Sumer?

The other primary civilization of the Mediterranean world arose in Egypt, roughly contemporaneous with Sumer. Unlike the Sumerians, however, the Egyptians did not have to wrest their survival from a hostile and unpredictable environment. Instead, their land was renewed every year by the regular summer flooding of the Nile River. The rich black soil the river left behind made the Nile Valley the richest agricultural region in the entire Mediterranean world. Much of the distinctiveness of Egyptian civilization rests on this fundamental ecological fact.

Ancient Egypt was a narrow, elongated land, snaking along both banks of the Nile for a distance of more than 600 miles (1100 km). Outside this narrow band of territory—which ranged in breadth from a few hundred yards to no more than 14 miles (23 km)—lay an uninhabitable desert, where rain almost never falls. This contrast, between the fertile Black Land along the Nile and the dessicated Red Land beyond, deeply influenced the way the Egyptians viewed their world. Egypt itself they saw as the center of the cosmos. The lands beyond Egypt, however, they regarded as lying utterly beyond the boundaries of civilized life.

As a land, a nation, and a civilization, Egypt has enjoyed remarkable continuity. The roots of Egyptian cul-

In what ways did patterns of development in early Egypt differ from those in Sumer?

The Development of Civilization in Egypt   25

ture date back to at least 5000 B.C.E., and Egypt would continue to thrive as an independent and distinct culture until its assimilation into the Roman Empire after 30 B.C.E. From about 3000 B.C.E. on, the defining element in ancient Egyptian culture would be the pervasive influence of a powerful, centralized, bureaucratic state headed by pharaohs whom their people regarded as living gods. No other ancient civilization was ever governed so tightly for so long as was Egypt.

For convenience, historians divide ancient Egyptian history into "kingdoms" and "periods," as shown in the chronology on p. 26. As did ancient Egyptian writers,

Ancient Egypt and the Near East

Notice the peculiar geography of Egypt and the role played by the Nile. How did the lands on either side of the Nile help isolate Egyptian culture from outside influences? Consider how the Nile helped forge Egypt into a unitary state under a powerful centralized government. How was Egypt's relationship to the Nile as potentially hazardous as it was beneficial?

modern historians generally portray the Old, Middle, and New Kingdoms as times of strength, prosperity, and unity, separated by chaotic interludes when central authority broke down (the First, Second, and Third Intermediate Periods). Although we will follow these traditional divisions, we should note that they do reflect the centralizing (and perhaps therefore distorting) perspective of the ancient Egyptian state itself. As we will see, the First Intermediate Period in particular looks much less chaotic and dismal if viewed from the perspective of local society rather than from the pharaohs' court.

PREDYNASTIC EGYPT (C. 10,000–3100 B.C.E.)

Prehistoric or Predynastic Egypt is the period before the emergence of the pharaohs and their dynasties. In the Fertile Crescent, population growth forced the Mesopotamians to adopt settled agricultural life during the eighth millennium B.C.E. In Egypt, by contrast, a growing population was able to sustain itself through hunting and gathering until the fifth millennium B.C.E.

The first known permanent settlement in Egypt dates to approximately 4750 B.C.E. and was situated at the southwestern edge of the Nile Delta. Thereafter, the Egyptian economy rapidly became more sophisticated. By around 3500 B.C.E. this region already had extensive commercial contacts with the Sinai Peninsula, the Near East, and with the upper reaches of the Nile, several hundred miles to the south. Copper was a particularly important import, which allowed the residents to replace stone tools with metal ones. Many other Neolithic farming centers have also been discovered in or near the Nile Delta, where a degree of cultural unity was already developing. In later centuries, this area would be known as Lower Egypt (so called because it was downstream). Comparable developments were also occurring outside the delta. By the end of the Predynastic Period, Egyptian material culture and burial practices were more or less uniform from the southern edge of the delta all the way south to the First Cataract, a vast length of the Nile known as Upper Egypt.

Although towns in Lower Egypt were more numerous, it was in Upper Egypt that the first true Egyptian cities developed. By 3200 B.C.E., important communities such as Nekhen, Naqada, This, and Abydos had all developed high degrees of occupational and social specialization. They had encircled themselves with sophisticated fortifications and had begun to build elaborate temple and shrine complexes to honor the local gods.

This last fact may be key to explaining the growth of these towns into cities. As with Uruk in Mesopotamia, their role as regional cult centers attracted travelers and encouraged the growth of industries. But unlike in Mesopotamia, travel in Upper Egypt was relatively easy. Almost all Egyptians lived within sight of the Nile, enabling the great river to serve as a highway binding the nation together. It was due to the Nile, therefore, that the region south of the delta, despite its enormous geographical length, was able to forge a cultural, and eventually political, unity.

The Nile fed Egypt and united it. The river was a conduit for people, goods, and ideas. Centralizing rulers could project their power quickly and effectively up and down its course. By the close of the Predynastic Period the cities of Upper Egypt had banded together in a confederacy under the leadership of This. The pressure exerted by this confederacy in turn forced the towns of Lower Egypt to adopt their own form of loose political organization. By 3100 B.C.E., the rivalry between these competing regions had given rise to the two nascent kingdoms of Upper and Lower Egypt.

CHRONOLOGY

EGYPTIAN KINGDOMS AND PERIODS

Predynastic Period	c. 10,000–3100 B.C.E.
Archaic Period	3100–c. 2686 B.C.E.
Old Kingdom	c. 2686–2160 B.C.E.
First Intermediate Period	2160–2055 B.C.E.
Middle Kingdom	2055–c. 1650 B.C.E.
Second Intermediate Period	c. 1650–1550 B.C.E.
New Kingdom	1550–1075 B.C.E.

THE UNIFICATION OF EGYPT: THE ARCHAIC PERIOD (3100–C. 2686 B.C.E.)

Following the political unification of Upper and Lower Egypt, the basic features of pharaonic rule took shape along lines that would persist for the next 3,000 years. From a very early date, the pharaoh was identified closely with divinity. By the First and Second Dynasties,

IN WHAT WAYS DID PATTERNS OF DEVELOPMENT IN EARLY EGYPT DIFFER FROM THOSE IN SUMER?

THE DEVELOPMENT OF CIVILIZATION IN EGYPT   27

he was already regarded as the earthly manifestation of the falcon god Horus. These early Egyptian rulers thus laid claim to a sacred nature quite different from the early Sumerian lugal, a mortal who merely enjoyed divine favor.

How these early pharaohs established their claims to divinity is a mystery. We do know, however, that legitimating their rule over all Egypt was a difficult task. Local civic and religious loyalties remained strong, and for centuries Lower Egyptians would continue to see themselves as distinct from their cousins to the south. It seems probable that the pharaohs' claim to divinity was one approach to solving this problem of political unity. But however precisely the sacralization of Egyptian kingship occurred, it was an astonishing success. By the end of the Second Dynasty the pharaoh was not just the ruler of Egypt; in a sense he *was* Egypt, a personification of the land, the people, and their connection to the divine.

Narmer Palette, c. 3000 B.C.E. One side shows King Narmer, wearing the white crown of Upper Egypt, striking an enemy with a mace, while Horus, the falcon god, looks on approvingly. The other side shows the king, wearing the red crown of Lower Egypt, viewing the decapitated corpses of his enemies. The long-necked beasts with intertwined necks represent the two kingdoms of Upper and Lower Egypt, united under Narmer.

LANGUAGE AND WRITING

The development of hieroglyphic (*HI-roh-glif-ic*) writing in Egypt dates to around 3200 B.C.E. As in Sumer, writing quickly became an important tool for Egyptian government and administration. Unlike Sumerian cuneiform, however, Egyptian hieroglyphics never evolved very far toward a system of phonograms. Instead, the Egyptians developed a simpler, faster, cursive script for representing hieroglyphics called *hieratic*, which they employed for the everyday business of government and commerce. They also developed a shorthand version of hieratic that scribes could use for rapid note taking.

Little early hieratic writing remains, due largely to the perishable nature of the medium on which it was usually written: papyrus. Produced by hammering, drying, and processing river reeds, papyrus was lighter, easier to write on, and more transportable than the clay tablets used by the Sumerians. When sewn together into scrolls, papyrus also made it possible to record and store large quantities of information in a very small space. Production of this versatile writing material remained one of Egypt's most important industries throughout ancient times, and papyrus became a valuable export item.

THE OLD KINGDOM (C. 2686–2160 B.C.E.)

Because so few of the routine business documents of the Old Kingdom survive, writing a history of this period is a difficult venture. Funerary texts from the tombs of the elite allow us to say something about the achievements of particular individuals and to gain an impression of everyday life, but we know little about the lives of ordinary Egyptians. Further complicating our problem is the attitude of the Old Kingdom Egyptians themselves. Because of their belief in the unchanging, cyclical nature of the universe, history and historical events as we think of them were of little interest to them. It is unlikely, therefore, that we will ever be able to reconstruct their history in any detailed way.

One feature that emerges clearly, however, is the degree to which the pharaohs of the Third Dynasty (c. 2686–2613 B.C.E.) had already built a powerful, centralized administration devoted to the self-glorification of the pharaoh himself. Because the pharaoh *was* Egypt, all the resources of Egypt belonged to him. Long-distance trade was entirely controlled by the pharaoh, and systems for imposing taxation and conscripting labor were already well developed. To administer their kingdom, the pharaohs installed centrally appointed ing was difficult, but a Middle Kingdom document called "The Satire of the Trades" reminded the scribe in training how much his education would benefit him in the end, and how much better off he would be than the practitioners of other trades.

IMHOTEP AND THE STEP PYRAMID

At the dawn of the Old Kingdom, we meet one of the greatest administrative officials in the history of Egypt. Imhotep rose through the ranks of the pharaoh's administration to become the right-hand man to Djoser (*ZOH-ser*), an early pharaoh of the Third Dynasty. Earlier pharaohs had already devoted enormous resources to their burial arrangements at Abydos. It was Imhotep, however, who designed the "Step Pyramid," the first great monument in world history built entirely of dressed stone. It was not only to be the final resting place of Djoser but a symbol and expression of his transcendent power as pharaoh.

Imhotep may have intended his pyramidal design to evoke the descending rays of the life-giving sun, or perhaps the pyramid was meant as the means for the pharaoh's *ka* (his spirit after death, see below) to ascend into the sky and incorporate itself with the sun on its journey west after death. But no one could miss the pharaonic power that lay behind its construction. Imhotep had set a precedent to which pharaohs throughout the Old Kingdom would aspire. Ultimately, the competition to build ever larger and more elaborate pyramids would ruin them.

Old Kingdom Egypt reached its height in the Fourth Dynasty (2613–2494 B.C.E.), the period during which the great pyramids of Giza were built. These were true pyramids, which have become timeless symbols of Egyptian civilization. The Great Pyramid, built for the pharaoh Khufu (*KOO-foo*), was originally 481 feet high and 756 feet along each side of its base, constructed from more than 2.3 million limestone blocks and enclosing a volume of about 91 million cubic feet. With the exception of a few airways, passages, and burial chambers, the structure is completely solid. In ancient times, the entire pyramid was encased in gleaming white limestone and topped by a massive capstone gilded in gold, as were the two slightly smaller pyramids at the site built for Khufu's successors Khafre and Menkaure. During the Middle Ages, the builders and rulers of the great Muslim capital of Cairo

The Rosetta Stone. This famous stone, carved in 196 B.C.E., preserves the text of a single decree in three different forms of writing: hieroglyphs (top), demotic (middle), and classical Greek (bottom). Nineteenth-century scholars were able to use the classical Greek text (which they could read) to decipher the hieroglyphic and demotic scripts (which had previously been undecipherable).

local governors (known to the Greeks as *nomarchs*), many of whom were members of the pharaohs' own family. Old Kingdom pharaohs kept tight control over the nomarchs and their armies of lesser officials to prevent them from establishing local roots in the territories they administered.

Scribal literacy was widespread in Old Kingdom Egypt, because writing was critical to the management and exploitation of Egypt's vast wealth. And because literate bureaucrats were absolutely essential to Egyptian government at both the national and the local level, scribal administrators enjoyed power, influence, and status. Even a child just beginning his scribal education was considered worthy of great respect. Train-

> Imhotep had set a precedent to which pharaohs throughout the Old Kingdom would aspire. Ultimately, the competition to build ever larger and more elaborate pyramids would ruin them.

IN WHAT WAYS DID PATTERNS OF DEVELOPMENT IN EARLY EGYPT DIFFER FROM THOSE IN SUMER?

THE DEVELOPMENT OF CIVILIZATION IN EGYPT   29

stripped the casing stones from these pyramids and used them to construct and fortify their new city. The gold capstones had probably disappeared already. But in antiquity these pyramids, with their gleaming limestone facing, would have glistened brilliantly in the bright Egyptian sunshine, making them visible for miles in all directions.

Once thought to have been the work of slaves, the pyramids were in fact raised by tens of thousands of peasant workers, who labored most intensively on the pyramids while their fields were under water. Some workers may have been conscripts, but most probably participated willingly in the building projects, which glorifed the living god who ruled them and served as their link to the cosmic order. There can be little doubt, however, that the massive investment of labor and wealth required to build the great pyramids put grave strains on Egyptian society. Natural resources were exploited more intensively than ever before, governmental control over the lives of individual Egyptians increased, and the number of administrative officials employed by the state grew ever larger. At the same time, however, a gap was opening between the centralizing religious pretensions of the pharaoh and the continuing loyalties of Egyptians to their local gods and their local leaders. These tensions would ultimately spell the end of the Old Kingdom and usher in the important changes of the First Intermediate Period.

SOCIETY IN OLD KINGDOM EGYPT

The social pyramid of Old Kingdom Egypt was extremely steep. At its apex stood the pharaoh and his family. During the Third and Fourth

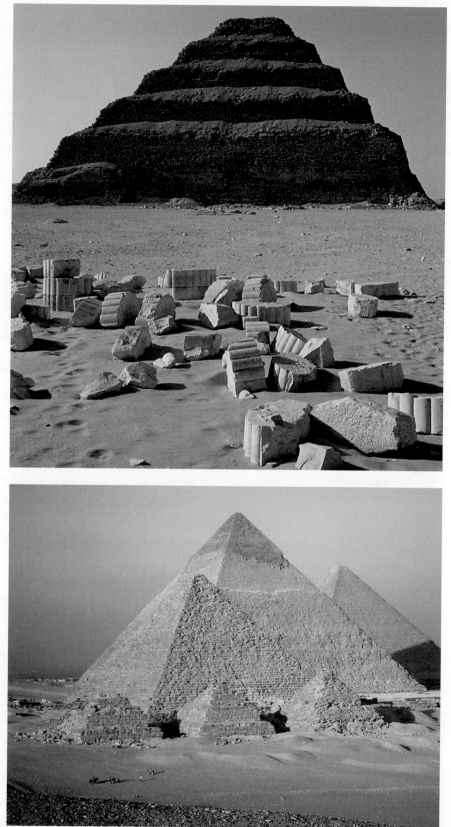

Pyramids. At top is the Step Pyramid of King Djoser, c. 2650 B.C.E. At bottom are the pyramids at Giza, with the Great Pyramid of Khufu in the center, c. 2560 B.C.E.

Dynasties their status, prestige, and power were so great as to set them entirely apart from all other Egyptians. There was a class of nobles, but until the Fifth Dynasty, their primary role was to serve as priests and officials of the pharaoh's government. Despite their subordination to the pharaoh, however, Egyptian elites lived in considerable luxury. They owned extensive estates with exotic goods and fine furniture. They kept dogs and cats and monkeys as pets and hunted and fished for sport.

Beneath the tiny minority represented by royalty and nobility was everyone else. Most Egyptians were poor, living in crowded conditions in simple mud-brick dwellings. Skilled artisans, potters, weavers, masons, bricklayers, brewers, merchants, and schoolteachers enjoyed some measure of respect and prestige, as well as a higher standard of living than most other Egyptians. The vast majority of Egyptians, however, were peasants: unskilled laborers who provided the brute force necessary for agriculture and construction. Beneath them were slaves, typically captives from foreign wars rather than native Egyptians. But despite the theocratic nature of pharaonic rule and the enormous demands the pharaohs placed on Egypt's wealth, Egyptian society does not appear to have been particularly oppressive. Even slaves had certain legal rights, including the ability to own, dispose of, and bequeath personal property.

> The Egyptians did devise effective irrigation and water-control systems, but they did not adopt such labor-saving devices as the wheel until much later than the Sumerians, perhaps because the available pool of peasant manpower seemed inexhaustible in densely populated Egypt.

WOMEN IN THE OLD KINGDOM

Egyptian women also enjoyed an unusually high degree of legal status and protection by the standards of the ancient world. They were not allowed to undergo scribal training or serve as important officials, but short personal notes between women of social standing suggest at least some degree of female literacy. In times of crisis, a woman of the royal family might assume pharaonic authority, although usually she would represent herself in rather mannish fashion. Egyptian women had standing before the courts as their own persons; they could initiate complaints (including suing for divorce), defend themselves, bear witness, and possess property on their own, without the male guardian or representative who was typically required of women in other ancient societies.

None of this should obscure the fact that Egypt was, at its heart, a rigidly patriarchal society. Aside from the role of priestess, women were barred from state office. While most Egyptians practiced monogamy, important and powerful men could and did keep harems of lesser wives, concubines, and female slaves. Furthermore, any Egyptian man could practice sexual freedom, married or not, with legal impunity; a wife who did so was subject to severe legal punishments. Gender divisions may have been less clearly defined among the peasantry than they were among the elites. Peasant women often worked in the fields during the harvest and carried out a number of menial but vital tasks. As usual in the ancient world, however, we can only glimpse the lives of Egyptian peasants through the eyes of their social superiors.

SCIENCE AND TECHNOLOGY

Their monumental architecture notwithstanding, the Egyptians lagged behind the Sumerians and Akkadians in science and mathematics, as they did in technology generally. Only in the calculation of time did the Egyptians make notable advances. The solar calendar they developed was far more accurate than the Mesopotamian lunar calendar; adopted for Rome by Julius Caesar, it is the direct ancestor of our modern Western calendar. The Egyptians did devise effective irrigation and water-control systems, but they did not adopt such labor-saving devices as the wheel until much later than the Sumerians, perhaps because the available pool of peasant manpower seemed inexhaustible in densely populated Egypt. Nor did the laws and other "civil" documents produced by the lugals of Mesopotamia have any Old Kingdom parallels. The Egyptians of the Old Kingdom apparently had no need for written law: the law was whatever their pharaoh, a living god, proclaimed it to be.

EGYPTIAN RELIGION AND WORLDVIEW

Old Kingdom Egyptians saw themselves as utterly set apart from all other civilizations. Egyptians' confidence in their own superiority stemmed from their self-conscious awareness of the uniqueness of their country, nurtured by the Nile and guarded by the brutal deserts and vast seas

IN WHAT WAYS DID PATTERNS OF DEVELOPMENT IN EARLY EGYPT DIFFER FROM THOSE IN SUMER?

THE DEVELOPMENT OF CIVILIZATION IN EGYPT   31

that surrounded it. For Egyptians, it was simply self-evident that their country was the center of the world.

Although the Egyptians constructed a variety of creation myths about the world, they did not concern themselves greatly with how humanity came to exist. Rather, what mattered to the Egyptians was the means by which life itself was created and re-created in an endless cycle of renewal. This cyclical conception gave a certain repetitive, predictable, and ultimately static cast to the way Egyptians perceived the cosmos. They viewed many phenomena as cyclical events, not surprising given the dependence of these people on the annual cycles of the Nile.

At the heart of Egyptian religion lay the myth of the gods Osiris and Isis, brother and sister, husband and wife, and two of the earliest gods in Egyptian belief. Osiris was the first to hold kingship on earth, but his brother, Seth, wanted the throne for himself. Seth betrayed and killed Osiris, sealing him in a coffin. Through great effort, Isis retrieved the corpse, but Seth seized it once again, hacked his brother into pieces, and spread his remains throughout Egypt (all Egypt could thus claim Osiris, and shrines to him were prevalent throughout the land). Still undeterred, Isis sought the help of Anubis, the god of mummification, and together they managed to reassemble Osiris. Isis then revived Osiris long enough to conceive a child by him, who became the god Horus. With the help of his mother's magic, Horus withstood the assaults of Seth and his henchmen; Horus and Seth then competed over the vacant throne of Osiris until finally Horus prevailed and avenged his father.

This mythology was extremely important to the Egyptians. The tale of Osiris is a myth about life arising out of death, but it is not a resurrection story: Osiris was revivified only temporarily. The notion the tale embodies, of new life arising from the dead, may have arisen in the earliest farming settlements of Egypt, where bodies were already being interred with extensive grave goods and special care. The promise of the continuation of life—rhythmic, cyclical, inevitable—as embodied by Osiris made him an important agricultural deity to the Egyptians.

THE EGYPTIAN DEATH CULT

Osiris was also a central deity in the death cult of the Egyptians. Unlike the Sumerians, the Egyptians did not have a bleak view of death and the underworld. Death was an unpleasant rite of passage, a necessity to be endured on the way to an afterlife that was more or less like one's earthly existence, only better. But the passage was not automatic and was full of dangers. After death, the deceased's *ka*, or otherworldly existence, would have to roam the underworld, searching for the House of Judgment. Demons and evil spirits might try to frustrate the *ka*'s quest to reach the House of Judgment, and the journey might take some time. If successful and judged worthy, however, the deceased would then enjoy immortality as an aspect of Osiris.

Because of their beliefs about death, the Egyptians developed elaborate rituals for dealing with it. It was first of all crucial that the corpse be preserved: this is why the Egyptians developed their sophisticated techniques of embalming and mummification. The body was desiccated, all its vital organs were removed (except for the heart, which played a key role in the final judgment), and then the body was treated with chemicals to preserve it. A funerary portrait mask was also placed on the mummy before burial, so that the corpse would still be recognizable in death despite being wrapped in hundreds of yards of linen. To sustain the deceased on his or

Brewing, Baking, and Butchering. This wooden model shows peasants grinding grain, baking bread, brewing beer, and slaughtering a steer. Bread and beer were the staple foods of ancient Egypt; beef was too expensive for ordinary consumption, but cattle were frequently sacrificed as a funeral offering. Such models were placed in Middle Kingdom tombs to provide food for the tomb owner in the afterlife.

Funerary Papyrus. The scene shows the heart of a princess of the Twenty-First Dynasty being weighed in a balance before the god Osiris. On the other side of the balance are the symbols for life and truth.

her journey through the underworld, food, clothing, utensils, and other items of vital importance would be placed in the grave along with the body. In the third millennium this privilege was reserved for the royal family alone, but by the Middle Kingdom participation in these death rituals had become accessible to many Egyptians.

The careful detail with which Egyptians confronted death has often led to the erroneous assumption that theirs was a "death culture," completely obsessed with the problem of death. In fact, Egyptian practices and beliefs were mostly life affirming, and the role of Osiris (also, remember, a god of returning life) and the underworld were viewed not with horror but with hope. The Egyptians' confidence in the cyclical nature of the cosmos meant that life always triumphed.

Binding together this endless cycle of life, death, and the return of life was *ma'at (MAH-aht)*. Like many words in the Egyptian language, it has no exact English equivalent. Our concepts of harmony, order, justice, and truth would all fit comfortably within *ma'at*, though none of these words captures its entire sense. Both the abstract notion and its personification as a female deity named Ma'at were what kept the universe running in its serene, repetitive, predictable fashion.

The Egyptians of the Archaic Period and the Old Kingdom were thus a supremely confident and optimistic people whose stability and peace were guaranteed by *ma'at* and their connection to it through their pharaoh.

THE END OF THE OLD KINGDOM

For reasons that are not entirely clear, the Fifth and Sixth Dynasties (2494–2181 B.C.E.) witnessed the slow erosion of pharaonic power. Although pyramid construction continued, the monuments of this period were less impressive in architecture, craftsmanship, and size, mirroring the diminishing prestige of the pharaohs who constructed them. Most tellingly, however, the nomarchs began to evolve into precisely the type of hereditary local nobility that the vigorous Third and Fourth Dynasty pharaohs had refused to permit.

Scholars are uncertain how these local officials and priests wrested power away from the pharaonic center. It may be that the extraordinarily costly building efforts of the Fourth Dynasty had overstrained the economy, leading to resentments and shortages outside the capital city of Memphis. Other evidence points to changing climatic conditions that may have disrupted

IN WHAT WAYS DID PATTERNS OF DEVELOPMENT IN EARLY EGYPT DIFFER FROM THOSE IN SUMER?

THE DEVELOPMENT OF CIVILIZATION IN EGYPT   33

the regular flooding of the Nile, leading to famine and even starvation in the countryside. To make matters worse, small states were also beginning to form in Nubia to the south, which may have restricted Egyptian access to precious-metal deposits in and around the First Cataract, further crippling the Egyptian economy.

With Egypt suffering these woes, pharaoh's claim to be a link to *ma'at* diminished accordingly. Instead, local governors and religious authorities began to emerge as the only effective guarantors of stability and order in the countryside. By 2160 B.C.E., when the First Intermediate Period begins, Egypt had effectively ceased to exist as a united country.

Beneath the political chaos, however, the First Intermediate Period witnessed some important developments in Egyptian society. Wealth became more widely and evenly distributed than had been the case during the Old Kingdom. So too did culture, and especially art. Resources that the pharaoh's court had once monopolized now remained in the localities, enabling local elites to emerge as protectors of local society and patrons for local artists. The result was a rapid diffusion of cultural forms throughout Egyptian society.

By 2160 B.C.E., when the First Intermediate Period begins, Egypt had effectively ceased to exist as a united country.

Warfare between the two competing pharaonic dynasties continued until 2055 B.C.E., when the Theban Mentuhotep II conquered the northerners and declared himself the ruler of a united Egypt. His reign marks the beginning of the Middle Kingdom of Egyptian history.

MIDDLE KINGDOM EGYPT (2055–C.1650 B.C.E.)

With the reestablishment of unified government, now centered in the south on Thebes, Egypt entered the period of the Middle Kingdom. Soon after Mentuhotep II's death, a usurper, the vizier Amenemhet (*ah-meh-NEHM-het*), established himself and his descendants as Egypt's brilliant Twelfth Dynasty. Amenemhet retained Thebes as a center of power but also built a new capital just south of Memphis. The Twelfth Dynasty remained in power for nearly 200 years, producing a succession of remarkable pharaohs.

Under this dynasty, the Egyptians began to exploit more thoroughly the potential for trade to the south. They mounted expeditions to the land of Punt (probably the coast of Somalia) and secured their border with Nubia. By the middle of the nineteenth century B.C.E., Nubia was firmly under Egypt's control, and the small states and principalities of Palestine and Syria were under heavy Egyptian influence. But despite Egypt's renewed strength, the Egyptians did not incorporate the lands to the northeast into their realm. Instead, Amenemhet I constructed the "Walls of the Prince" in Sinai to guard against incursions from Egypt's Near Eastern neighbors.

The great fortifications built along Egypt's frontiers during the Twelfth Dynasty demonstrate the power of these pharaohs, but they also betray a marked shift in the Egyptian outlook on the world. Long gone was the placid serenity epitomized by *ma'at*. Middle Kingdom Egyptians viewed the world beyond their borders with suspicion and fear. Egypt was not yet an imperial power, because Middle Kingdom pharaohs made no attempt to incorporate their conquests into their kingdom in any meaningful way. But unlike their Old Kingdom counterparts, the Egyptians of the Middle Kingdom were now taking a direct and active interest in events beyond Egypt's borders.

The pharaoh's position had also changed. None of the Middle Kingdom pharaohs portrayed himself with the serene confidence of Old Kingdom depictions. Rather, in the Middle Kingdom pharaohs represented themselves as—and were expected to be—good shepherds, tenders of their Egyptian flock. *Ma'at* could not help them in these duties; only by diligently protecting Egypt from a hostile outside world could pharaohs provide the peace, prosperity, and security desired by their subjects. Portraits of the great pharaohs of the Twelfth Dynasty poignantly reflect the concern and anxiety with which they lived.

Egyptians had lost that vision of the Old Kingdom wherein the land was a perfect and inviolable paradise. Their feelings of insecurity were justified. Egyptians recognized that they had been drawn, slowly and unwillingly, into a much wider world. But precisely because Egypt remained a highly distinct culture unto itself, this wider world beyond the frontiers appeared all the more alien, frightening, and potentially dangerous. Middle Kingdom pharaohs were greatly alarmed by the growing power and imperial ambitions of Hammurabi of Babylon. They would soon discover, however, that even greater dangers lay much closer to home.

CONCLUSION

Starting around 11,000 B.C.E., human beings in the eastern Mediterranean world began to make a slow transition from hunter-gatherer societies into settled agricultural and pastoral communities. With the ability to produce and store surpluses, larger villages began to emerge, allowing both a greater degree of functional specialization and a wider differentiation in wealth and status among individuals and families. In Sumer, where the first cities emerged during the fourth millennium B.C.E., cities were also religious centers with elaborate temple complexes and shrines to the city's gods. By around 2500 B.C.E., a sophisticated form of writing, known as cuneiform, had emerged as an important tool in trade and in the management of these temple complexes.

The third millennium B.C.E. saw the emergence of larger city-states, with more intense warfare between them. The Mesopotamian city-states were now led by kings who claimed divine sanction for their rule and whose power and wealth set them farther and farther apart from their subjects. Around 2350 B.C.E., Sumerian political life was transformed by the emergence of a new, Semitic-speaking people, the Akkadians, whose conquests resulted in the creation of the first true empire in world history. This empire would become the model future rulers of Mesopotamia would aspire to emulate.

In Egypt, the other major center of Near Eastern civilization during these centuries, political consolidation occurred around 3000 B.C.E., a process assisted by the unique importance of the Nile River system. From that time on, Egypt would be ruled by a powerful, highly centralized bureaucracy, headed by pharaohs whom their people regarded as living gods. But despite the divisions between Upper and Lower Egypt, Egypt in the Old and Middle Kingdoms was never an empire maintained through conquest. It was a highly unified but deeply parochial society, capable of mobilizing resources on a massive scale, but almost always for internal purposes.

Behind these differences in outlook lay fundamental differences in the ecology of these two civilizations. Unlike the Sumerians, the Egyptians did not have to struggle to wrest a precarious living from a forbidding environment. So long as the annual flooding of the Nile occurred, Egyptians could feed themselves easily, with a relative minimum of social tension. This fact lent an air of confidence and ease to Egyptian art that is wholly lacking in Mesopotamia.

These two civilizations have many similarities. During the third millennium, both underwent a process of political consolidation, an elaboration of religious life, and a melding of religious and political leadership. Both engaged in massive building projects; and both mobilized resources on an enormous scale for temples, monuments, and irrigation projects. At the same time, however, each of these two civilizations developed an inward focus, verging on parochialism. Although they had some trade relations with each other, there were few signficant political or cultural interactions between them. For all intents and purposes, they inhabited separate worlds. This relative isolation was about to change, however. The next millennium would see the emergence of large-scale, land-based empires in the Near Eastern world that would transform life in Mesopotamia, Egypt, and the lands that lay between them. These are the developments we examine in Chapter Two.

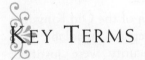

KEY TERMS

Homo sapiens	cuneiform	Hammurabi	Sumerians	Fertile Crescent
Ubaid	Gilgamesh	Sargon	Neolithic	Imhotep

SELECTED READINGS

Aldred, Cyril. *The Egyptians*. 3d ed. London, 1998. An indispensable, lively overview of Egyptian culture and history by one of the great masters of Egyptology.

Baines, J., and J. Málek. *Atlas of Ancient Egypt*. Rev. ed. New York, 2000. A reliable, well-illustrated survey, with excellent maps.

Bottéro, Jean. *Everyday Life in Ancient Mesopotamia*. Trans. Antonia Nevill. Baltimore, 2001. A wide-ranging, interdisciplinary account by an acknowledged master.

George, Andrew, trans. *The Epic of Gilgamesh: A New Translation. The Babylonian epic poem and other texts in Akkadian and Sumerian*. New York and London, 1999. The newest and most reliable translation, which carefully distinguishes the chronological "layers" of this famous text; also includes many related texts.

Hodder, Ian. *The Leopard's Tale: Revealing the Mysteries of Çatalhöyük*. London and New York, 2006. The most up-to-date account of this fascinating archaeological site, written for general readers by the director of the excavation.

Hornung, Erik. *History of Ancient Egypt: An Introduction*. Ithaca, N.Y., 1999. Concise and authoritative.

Kemp, Barry J. *Ancient Egypt: Anatomy of a Civilization*. London, 1989. An imaginative examination of Egyptian social and intellectual history.

Leick, Gwendolyn. *The Babylonians: An Introduction*. London and New York, 2002. A wide-ranging survey of Babylonian civilization across the centuries.

Lichteim, Miriam. *Ancient Egyptian Literature: A Book of Readings*. 3 vols. Berkeley, Calif., 1973–1980. A compilation used by students and scholars alike.

Mertz, Barbara. *Red Land, Black Land: Daily Life in Ancient Egypt*. Rev. ed. New York, 1990. Emphasizes the role of the Nile and the forbidding natural environment of Egypt.

Pollock, Susan. *Ancient Mesopotamia*. Cambridge, 1999. An advanced textbook that draws on theoretical anthropology to interpret Mesopotamian civilization up to 2100 B.C.E.

Redford, Donald B., ed. *The Oxford Encyclopedia of Ancient Egypt*. 3 vols. New York, 2001. An indispensible reference work, intended for specialists and beginners.

Roaf, Michael. *Cultural Atlas of Mesopotamia and the Ancient Near East*. New York, 1990. An informative, authoritative, and lavishly illustrated guide, with excellent maps.

Robins, Gay. *The Art of Ancient Egypt*. London, 1997. An excellent survey, now the standard account.

Shafer, Byron E., ed. *Religion in Ancient Egypt: Gods, Myths, and Personal Practice*. London, 1991. A scholarly examination of Egyptian belief and ritual, with contributions from leading authorities. Excellent bibliographies.

Shaw, Ian, ed. *The Oxford History of Ancient Egypt*. Oxford, 2000. An outstanding collaborative survey of Egyptian history from the Stone Age to c. 300 C.E., with excellent bibliographical essays.

Snell, Daniel C., ed. *A Companion to the Ancient Near East*. Oxford, 2005. A topical survey of recent scholarly work, particularly strong on society, economy, and culture.

CHAPTER TWO

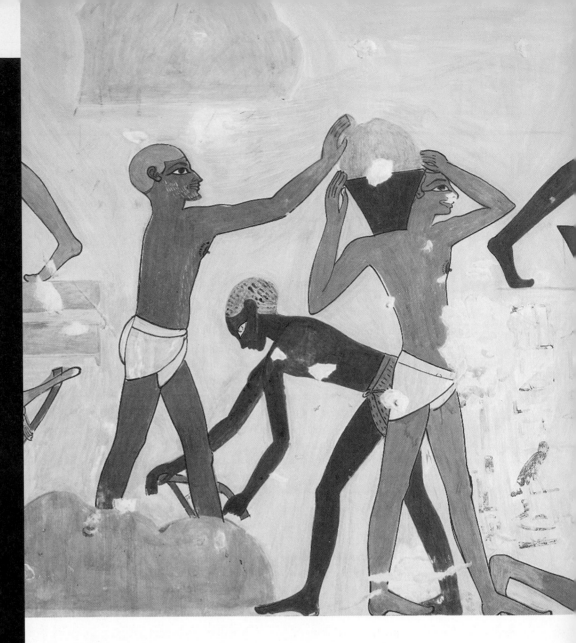

GODS AND EMPIRES
IN THE ANCIENT
NEAR EAST,
1700–500 B.C.E.

IN THE SECOND MILLENNIUM B.C.E., the ancient Near East was transformed by the arrival of new population groups and by the emergence of extensive, land-based empires built up through systematic military conquest. These migrations and conquests left a great deal of destruction and upheaval in their wake. But they also led to widespread cultural assimilation, deepening economic integration, and the emergence of an international system encompassing most of the eastern Mediterranean world.

The Late Bronze Age (1500–1200 B.C.E.) in particular was a period of intensifying diplomacy, trade, and internationalism. The two great imperial powers of this age were New Kingdom Egypt and the Hittite Empire of Anatolia (modern-day Turkey). Between these two empires a constellation of smaller states emerged along the eastern Mediterranean coast, fully engaged in the burgeoning trade and cosmopolitan culture of the age. By the thirteenth century, nations from the southern Balkans to the western fringes of Iran had been drawn into a wide-ranging web of cultural and economic relationships. By 1250 B.C.E., these early states depended in great measure on one another for their prosperity.

This international system proved more fragile than its participants had imagined. Around 1200 B.C.E., a new wave of invasions emanating from the Aegean (*ah-JEE-ahn*) Sea led to the destruction of nearly every great empire of the Late Bronze Age. Centuries-old centers of political, economic, and military power—not to mention great cultural achievement—were wiped out. As a result, we enter a new world around the turn of the first millennium B.C.E., organized along profoundly different lines from the great empires of the Near Eastern past.

In the new age that was dawning, iron would slowly replace bronze as the primary component of tools and weapons. New, larger, and more brutal empires

FOCUS QUESTIONS

• What impact did Indo-European-speaking peoples have on the patterns of Near Eastern life?

• In what ways did New Kingdom Egypt differ from the Old and Middle Kingdoms?

• What were the principal features of the Late Bronze Age international system?

• How similar was Mycenaean culture to Minoan culture?

• Why did Phoenician cities prosper during the Early Iron Age?

• What were the foundations of Assyrian imperial power?

• In what ways did the Persian Empire differ from its Near Eastern predecessors? How would you account for those differences?

• What developments marked the Hebrew transition from polytheism to monotheism?

would emerge, and new ideas about gods and their relationship to humanity would begin to displace older ones. In the Iron Age Near East, two of the Western world's most enduring religious traditions—Judaism and Zoroastrianism (*zoor-oh-AHS-tree-uh-nihz-uhm*)—were born, fundamentally altering conceptions of religion, politics, ethics, and the relationship between humanity and the natural world. The Iron Age would prove a fateful historical crossroads for Western civilizations, as elements both old and new combined to reconfigure the ancient Near Eastern world.

THE INDO-EUROPEAN MIGRATIONS

What impact did Indo-European-speaking peoples have on the patterns of Near Eastern life?

By the early nineteenth century, it was known that many of the languages of Eurasia had been derived from a common, but now extinct, linguistic source that has been labeled Indo-European, reflecting their wide distribution from India to Ireland.

Indo-European linguistic forms began to appear in the Near East and eastern Mediterranean shortly after 2000 B.C.E., when speakers of early forms of Persian and Sanskrit made their way into and across the Iranian plateau, and the Hittites arrived in their historical homeland in central Anatolia. Around this same time, another group of Indo-European-speaking peoples began to move into the Aegean basin, combining with indigenous linguistic groups to produce an early form of Greek. Other Indo-European speakers went east; some may even have reached western China.

Indo-Europeans were not the only new peoples moving into the Near East during this period. Semitic-speaking peoples were also entering the region, beginning with the Akkadians and continuing with the Amorites, the Assyrians, the Phoenicians (*feh-NEE-shuhns*), and the Canaanites. The impact of these migrations was enormous. From the second millennium onward, Western civilizations would be dominated by cultures speaking Semitic or Indo-European languages. But however rude they may have been when they first came into contact with the older civilizations of the Near East, these newcomers generally accommodated themselves quickly, spreading and developing already established patterns of urban life and organization.

HITTITES AND KASSITES

The Hittites were one of a number of Indo-European-speaking peoples who settled in Anatolia around 2000 B.C.E. Over the course of several centuries the Hittites extended their power throughout the Anatolian plateau. Combining plunder with trade, Hattusilis I transformed the Hittite Kingdom into an economic and military power. Hattusilis's grandson and successor, Mursilis I (c. 1620–1590 B.C.E.) proved even more ambitious. He sought to control the upper Euphrates and to subjugate northern Syria. In a brilliant campaign he also drove southeastward into Mesopotamia, collecting booty and tribute until he found himself before the fabled gates of Babylon. Babylon was still the center of an Amorite kingdom, now ruled by a distant descendent of Hammurabi. Mursilis I captured and sacked Babylon in 1595 B.C.E. He then withdrew and abandoned the ruined city to its fate.

A group known as the Kassites later moved into the devastated city and seized control of the Old Babylonian Kingdom. The origins and language of the Kassites are highly debatable; but like many previous invaders of Mesopotamia, the Kassites assimilated themselves speedily to the older civilization they found there. They presided over a largely peaceful and prosperous Babylonian realm for the next 500 years.

The Hittites, by contrast, brought no stability to the region. Mursilis's growing strength alarmed the warrior nobility, who were not yet ready to cede so much prestige and authority to a centralized kingship. Shortly after his arrival back in his capital Hattusas, he fell victim to a palace conspiracy. After his assassination, Hittite power ebbed for the next century or so.

THE KINGDOM OF MITANNI

Like the Hittites, the Mitannians were an Indo-European minority who first imposed themselves on the native peoples of the upper Euphrates as a ruling class, and then penetrated northern Syria around 1550 B.C.E. Assuming control of territories that Mursilis had already undermined, they knitted the upper Euphrates and northern Syria into a single kingdom, the Kingdom of Mitanni.

The Mitannians introduced a number of innovations into Near Eastern warfare, including a lighter, horse-drawn chariot with spoked wheels, which they used to carry archers around the field and strike terror into

WHAT IMPACT DID INDO-EUROPEAN-SPEAKING PEOPLES HAVE ON THE PATTERNS OF NEAR EASTERN LIFE?

THE INDO-EUROPEAN MIGRATIONS   39

their enemies. They were also masters of horse training and cavalry tactics. For a time, these innovations allowed them to keep the Hittites in check to their west, while to their east they reduced the powerful Assyrians to the status of a vassal kingdom. But when the opponents of the Mitannians began employing chariots themselves and using scale armor to protect both infantry and cavalry, the military balance of power quickly turned against Mittani.

Weakened by a dynastic dispute in the mid-fourteenth century, Mitanni finally collapsed in the face of renewed Hittite aggression. The Hittites allowed a rump kingdom of Mitanni to survive as a buffer state between themselves and Assyria. But the destruction of the Mitannian kingdom in northern Syria meant that the Egyptians and Hittites now embroiled themselves directly in military conflict with each other, with enormous consequences for both empires. To understand this conflict, however, and the emergence of New Kingdom Egypt as an imperial power, we need to return to Egypt at the end of the Middle Kingdom.

THE NEAR EAST, C. 1400 B.C.E.

How has the spread of the urban model forced us to widen our geographical focus? Notice the proliferation of cities along the eastern shores of the Mediterranean; what does this tell us about the importance of trade in this region of the Near East? Consider the centrality of this region in relation to the major empires of the time as well as the emerging civilization of the Aegean basin. Why is trade becoming so crucial to the world of the Late Bronze Age?

EGYPT IN THE SECOND MILLENNIUM B.C.E.

In what ways did New Kingdom Egypt differ from the Old and Middle Kingdoms?

Egypt too was transformed by the dynamic changes occurring in the early second millennium B.C.E. During the First Intermediate Period, foreigners from western Asia and Nubia penetrated the "center of the cosmos" in large numbers. Some came as immigrants; others were brought to Egypt as mercenaries. This strategy preserved Egypt from large-scale armed invasion. But when the pharaohs of the Middle Kingdom restored central government from Thebes soon after 2000 B.C.E., the confidence Old Kingdom Egyptians had once placed in *ma'at* had been irreparably shattered. Middle Kingdom Egypt was an anxious, uncertain place, uncomfortably aware that it could no longer safely ignore events beyond its borders but not yet committed to being an actively interventionist imperial power in Nubia, Sinai, and the Middle East. Commercial contacts with all these regions were growing, as was Egyptian influence within them. But none of this made Middle Kingdom Egyptians feel secure behind their walls.

Their concerns only deepened after 1700 B.C.E., when Egypt was conquered by a foreign army called the Hyksos (*HIHK-sohs*). These invaders—whose exact origins are unknown but who may have been Semitic speakers from the Middle East—carved out a kingdom in the eastern delta and projected their authority over most of Lower Egypt. Hyksos domination lasted about a century, from 1650 to 1550 B.C.E., and came to be regarded as the great shame of Egyptian national history, despite the fact that the Hyksos established Egypt as the most significant power in the Near East. In the south, however, the Hyksos conquest did allow the Nubians to break free and found an independent kingdom called Kush. This Nubian kingdom was a much greater threat to the native dynasty at Thebes than to the Hyksos in the north; it therefore provided additional incentive to the southern pharaohs to play on nationalist sentiment by launching "wars of liberation" against the Hyksos in the north. Ultimately, this strategy succeeded. By the end of the sixteenth century B.C.E., the southern pharaoh Ahmose had driven out the invaders, establishing the Eighteenth Dynasty and a new era in Egyptian history.

THE NEW KINGDOM (1550–1075 B.C.E.)

During the New Kingdom, Egyptian civilization reached the height of its magnificence and power. Although established forms of religious, economic, cultural, and political life continued, the New Kingdom also marked a radical departure in Egyptian history and culture. The

A Near Eastern War Chariot. Here the chariot is used for lion hunting by the Assyrian king Assurnasirpal II (883–859 B.C.E.).

In what ways did New Kingdom Egypt differ from the Old and Middle Kingdoms?

Egypt in the Second Millennium b.c.e. 41

dynamism of the New Kingdom—particularly its focus on imperialism and militarism—changed the very fabric of Egyptian life.

Pharaonic Rule in the Eighteenth Dynasty

The Eighteenth Dynasty ruled Egypt for more than two and a half centuries. Striking developments took place during this period. Most important, we witness the rise of a new type of nobility in Egyptian society, an aristocracy of military commanders and leaders whose wealth was acquired through war: not just plunder but also crown lands (and the slaves to work them) received from the pharaoh as rewards for their service.

The Eighteenth Dynasty was forged in battle. Ahmose (*AH-mose*) himself won fame as the man who expelled the Hyksos and reunited Egypt. Soon thereafter, Ahmose and his heirs turned their attention south, toward Nubia. By this time, gold had become the standard for Near Eastern commerce and finance. If Egypt was to prosper in this world, it needed to control the rich Nubian gold mines. Under Thutmose I (c. 1504–1492 b.c.e.), the Egyptians also penetrated deep into Palestine and Syria. No previous pharaoh had ever held sway over so much territory.

New Kingdom pharaohs pursued an ambitious strategy of defense through offense. The embarrassment of Hyksos domination translated itself into a steely determination to prevent such an episode from occurring ever again, not by preparing for the day when more invaders might arrive but by actively projecting Egyptian strength into regions from which danger might come. The Egyptians also learned something about battle tactics from the Hyksos, employing the horse-drawn battle chariots the Hyksos had used against them to devastating effect against their new enemies.

Queen Hatshepsut and Thutmose III

Military activity peaked during the fifteenth century b.c.e., in the wake of what could have been a crisis for the Eighteenth Dynasty. In 1479 b.c.e., Thutmose II died young, leaving a youth as his heir, the future Thutmose III. In the past, such incidents often led to instability and even changes of dynasty. On this occasion, however, family politics and a remarkable personality served as a force for cohesion and continuity. It was customary in the New Kingdom for the pharaoh—himself a manifestation of a god—to marry as his official "queen," his own sister. Such brother-sister unions do not appear to have been the routine way to produce

heirs: pharaohs also had a vast harem of subsidiary wives and concubines with whom to procreate. Such was the case with Thutmose II, whose queen was his sister Hatshepsut (*baht-SHEHP-soot*) but whose son and heir had been borne to him by another wife.

On the death of Thutmose II, Hatshepsut became regent for her stepson/nephew Thutmose III, who was still a small child when his father died. It was common practice during the New Kingdom for a widowed queen to act as regent in such cases, a reflection of the relatively high status that Egyptian women generally enjoyed compared with women in other ancient Near Eastern cultures. What is remarkable in Hatshepsut's case, however, is that within a few years of becoming regent, she declared herself to be a pharaoh in her own right and began to portray herself in pictures and statuary with the masculine figure and false beard characteristic of male pharaohs. She did not pretend to be a man—inscriptions on her statues and portraits almost always indicate her true sex—nor did she usurp the throne from Thutmose III, who continued to be described as her co-ruler. But during the twenty

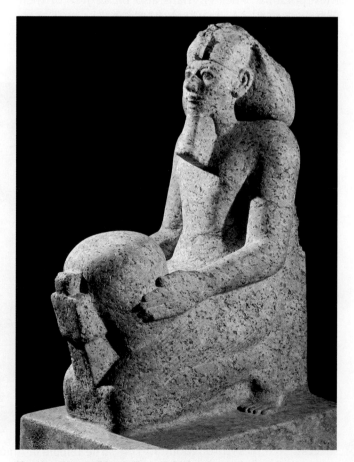

Hatshepsut as Pharaoh, c. 1460 b.c.e. Notice her masculine figure and ceremonial beard.

years that she and Thutmose III reigned together, she was clearly the ruling force within the government. Several successful military campaigns were recorded under her name, and the arts flourished, setting standards that Egyptian craftsmen would emulate for a thousand years.

Thutmose III remained in Hatshepsut's shadow until her death in 1458 B.C.E. Thereafter, he ruled alone until his own death some thirty years later. In the final decade of his rule, he began to deface Hatshepsut's monuments and to remove her name from inscriptions, to create the impression that he had always ruled alone.

Thutmose III launched a total of seventeen military campaigns that were intended not only to augment Egyptian strength but also to undermine the economic and military might of the Kingdom of Mitanni. In this they were entirely successful, but to ironic effect. Mitanni was now so weakened that the Hittites were able to reassert themselves in Syria and Mesopotamia. The Assyrians also broke free of their vassalage to Mitanni and would ultimately prove a far more aggressive foe to Egypt than Mitanni had ever been. At the time, however, the long-term consequences of Mitanni's demise were not apparent, and the Eighteenth Dynasty basked in the glow of its military accomplishments.

> By 1550 B.C.E., the Amon-Ra godhead had become something like an Egyptian national god, around whom the Thebes-based Eighteenth Dynasty rallied Egypt against the Hyksos.

as the temples became wealthy and powerful, so too did their priests. But no temple complex made out quite so well as that dedicated to Amon in Thebes.

THE TEMPLE OF AMON

Thebes was the capital of the Eighteenth Dynasty; as the city's patron deity, Amon therefore played an important role in the dynasty's own self-image. But Amon was more than just a local god. He had grown in stature and popularity throughout Middle Kingdom Egypt. Increasingly he was identified or incorporated with the sun god Ra (thus the common New Kingdom formulation Amon-Ra). By 1550 B.C.E., the Amon-Ra godhead had become something like an Egyptian national god, around whom the Thebes-based Eighteenth Dynasty rallied Egypt against the Hyksos. The dynasty thus had much reason for gratitude to Amon, whose support had been crucial in their efforts to reunite Egypt.

The favor shown to the priesthood of Amon at Thebes, coupled with the tremendous wealth deposited there, made the priests of Amon a formidable political and economic force. Indeed, by the end of

RELIGIOUS CHANGE AND RELIGIOUS CHALLENGE

The great conquests of the Eighteenth Dynasty brought mind-boggling amounts of spoil to Egypt. Much of this wealth went to the personal glorification of the pharaoh through grand temples, tombs, and other monuments. Another significant portion of the booty went to the military aristocracy that made such conquests possible. But vast quantities of wealth still remained, which went to propitiate the gods with offerings of thanks for Egypt's bountiful success. Temples throughout Egypt enjoyed the profits of conquest, and

The Temple of Amon at Karnak. This massive temple, just outside Thebes, testifies to the Eighteenth Dynasty's support for the god Amon and his priests.

In what ways did New Kingdom Egypt differ from the Old and Middle Kingdoms?

Egypt in the Second Millennium B.C.E.   43

Amenhotep III's reign (c. 1390–1352 B.C.E.), the priesthood of Amon enjoyed political clout surpassing even that of the officer class, and the priests themselves had become influential persons at the pharaoh's court. The dynasty's prestige was completely intertwined with that of Amon; but it was starting to be unclear whose was the controlling voice in this relationship.

THE REIGN OF AKHENATEN (1352–1336 B.C.E.)

All these factors came to a fateful intersection in one of history's most intriguing figures. On the death of Amenhotep III, his son succeeded him as Amenhotep IV. Amenhotep IV showed an early inclination toward sun-god worship, as distinct from worship of Amon. But soon the new pharaoh went much farther. He changed his name from Amenhotep ("Amon is pleased") to Akhenaten (*AH-keh-NAH-ton;* "He Who Is Profitable to the Aten"). As Akhenaten, he built a new capital halfway between Memphis in the north and Thebes in the south, calling it Akhetaten ("The Horizon of the Aten"), the modern site of el-Amarna. The short-lived but quite distinctive culture of Akhenaten's reign is therefore known as the Amarna Period.

Akhenaten introduced a variety of innovations into Egyptian religion and culture. Aten worship was more stringently monotheistic than the evolving view of Amon had been. Whereas Theban Amon theology recognized other gods as aspects of Amon, Akhenaten recognized only the life-giving power of light, embodied by the Aten. Unlike the ancient Egyptian deities, Aten could not be captured or represented in art. The image of the Aten, a dominant feature of Amarna-period art, is therefore an elaboration of the Egyptian hieroglyph for "light."

Great controversy still surrounds Akhenaten's motives for this religious and cultural revolution. Some see him as the world's first revolutionary intellectual, who applied imaginative force and exceptional insight to break the bonds of tradition. Others see him as a reactionary, troubled by the absorption of Ra into Amon and attempting to reassert the traditional worship of the sun. Others see him as a cagey politician, who sought to undermine the influence of Amon's priests by instituting a new religious regime.

These various explanations are not mutually exclusive. Politics and religion were inextricably intertwined in the ancient Near East, as they would be in Greece and Rome also. His own dynasty's particular identification with Amon guaranteed, however, that Akhenaten's religious revolution would also be politically revolutionary, be-cause it would require that the legitimacy of his dynasty be reestablished on new foundations.

But despite the tremendous energy Akhenaten expended in trying to achieve this revolution, most Egyptians did not follow him. Traditional Egyptian religion may seem bewilderingly complex to us, but Egyptians apparently preferred it to the remote, benevolent but impersonal god their pharaoh was offering them. The powerful priesthood of Amon also put up strenuous resistance to Akhenaten's religious innovations. To make matters worse, Akhenaten seems also to have been largely uninterested in military affairs. His exertions on behalf of his new god may even have encouraged him to neglect Egypt's interests abroad. The revolts that followed cost him the support of his military nobility. Akhenaten's revolution failed.

His failure was the harbinger of the Eighteenth Dynasty's decline. He was ultimately succeeded by Tutankhaten, who changed his name to Tutankhamon (the famous "King Tut") to reflect his rejection of Akhenaten's heresies and the restoration of the god Amon and his priesthood. The new capital city of Akhetaten was abandoned and its memory cursed; its neglect thereafter is largely responsible for its high state of preservation today. Akhenaten, meanwhile, was remembered only as "Akhetaten's heretic." His monuments were destroyed throughout the land. But the damage had been done. Egypt's position in the wider world had eroded at an astonishing rate since the outset of Akhenaten's reign. Ramses I, the founder of the Nineteenth Dynasty, would restore Egypt to glory in the Near East.

Akhenaten, His Wife Nefertiti, and Their Children. The Aten is depicted here as a sun disk, raining down power on the royal family.

AKHENATEN, THE HEBREWS, AND MONOTHEISM

One of the great literary monuments of Akhenaten's religious revolution was his "Hymn to the Aten," extolling the life-affirming virtues of the god he sought to place atop the Egyptian religious system. Although Akhenaten's experiment failed in Egypt, it may have played a significant role in shaping the religious traditions of other societies throughout the Levant, including the ancient Hebrews.

HYMN TO THE ATEN

You appear beautifully on the horizon of the heavens, living Aten, the beginning of life! When you arise on the eastern horizon, you have filled every land with your beauty. You are gracious, great, glistening, and high over every land; your rays encompass the lands to the limit of all that you have made.... When you set in the western horizon, the land is in darkness, in the manner of death. They sleep in a room, with heads wrapped up, nor sees one eye the other. All their goods which are under their heads might be stolen, but they would not perceive it....

Creator of seed in women, you who makes fluid into man, who maintains the son in the womb of his mother, who soothes him with that which stills his weeping, you nurse even in the womb, who gives breath to sustain all that he has made! ... How manifold it is, that which you have made! They are hidden from the face of man. O sole god, like whom there is no other! You created the world according to your desire, while you were alone: all men, cattle, and wild beasts, whatever is on earth, going upon its feet, and what is on high, flying with its wings....

The world came into being by your hand, according to how you have made them. When you have risen they live, when you set they die. You are lifetime itself, for one lives only through you.

Based on James B. Pritchard, ed., *Ancient Near Eastern Texts Relating to the Bible*, 3d rev. ed. with supplement (Princeton, N.J., 1969), pp. 370–371.

PSALM 104

Bless the Lord, O my soul.... You are clothed with honor and majesty, wrapped in light as with a garment. You stretch out the heavens like a tent.... You set the earth on its foundations, so that it shall never be shaken. You cover it with the deep as with a garment; the waters stood above the mountains. At your rebuke they flee.... You cause the grass to grow for the cattle, and plants for people to use, to bring forth food from the earth, and wine to gladden the human heart. You make darkness, and it is night, when all the animals of the forest come creeping out. The young lions roar for their prey, seeking their food from God.

O Lord, how manifold are your works! In wisdom you have made them all; the earth is full of your creatures.... These all look to you to give them food in due season; when you give them to them, they gather it up; when you open your hand, they are filled with good things. When you hide your face, they are dismayed; when you take away your breath they die.

New Revised Standard Version of the Bible (The National Council of the Churches of Christ in the USA, 1989).

QUESTIONS FOR ANALYSIS

1. How does the "Hymn to Aten" express monotheism? Why would a pharaoh, already acknowledged as divine, attempt a religious revolution? Why did he fail?

2. The praise of the greatness of God in Psalm 104 suggests an order in Creation. How does this idea of order differ from the *ma'at* of the Egyptians? How does the monotheism of the Hebrews differ from that of Akhenaten? Why did polytheism emerge before monotheism?

WHAT WERE THE PRINCIPAL FEATURES OF THE LATE BRONZE AGE INTERNATIONAL SYSTEM?

THE INTERNATIONAL SYSTEM OF THE LATE BRONZE AGE   45

THE INTERNATIONAL SYSTEM OF THE LATE BRONZE AGE

What were the principal features of the Late Bronze Age international system?

The fates of many nations after 1500 B.C.E., including Egypt, are intelligible only within the wider context of international relations. For the next 300 years, the destinies of the various Near Eastern kingdoms became increasingly interwoven as an international system developed throughout the eastern and central Mediterranean.

The Late Bronze Age was an age of superpowers. As we have seen, the great pharaohs of the Eighteenth Dynasty had transformed Egypt into a conquering state, feared and respected throughout the Near East. But the pressure they applied to the Kingdom of Mitanni allowed the emergence of a revived Hittite Empire after 1450 B.C.E. The Assyrians also revived, and the Kassite kingdom of Babylonia remained a significant force in the economic and military relationships of the age. Between these imperial powers numerous smaller but important states emerged, concentrated along the coasts and river valleys of Syria but extending westward to Cyprus and the Aegean Sea.

INTERNATIONAL DIPLOMACY

Though warfare remained a characteristic feature of international relations, the most powerful states of the Late Bronze Age evolved a balance of power that helped stabilize trade and diplomacy as the period progressed. Internationalism had existed to some degree since the age of Hammurabi. In the fourteenth century, however, many nations and their leaders came to understand that security and stability helped trade flourish, whereas war could prove disruptive and—in the long run—unprofitable for all concerned.

The archives discovered by modern archaeologists at Akhenaten's abandoned capital of el-Amarna provide us with a clear picture of this international diplomatic standard. Flurries of correspondence took place between the leaders of nations, sometimes over great matters, but often simply to "stay in touch" with one another. A language of diplomatic rank developed, in which the most powerful rulers would address one another as "brother," while the princes of lesser states showed their deference and respect to the pharaoh, the Hittite king, and other powerful sovereigns by calling them "father." Rulers also exchanged lavish gifts and entered into marriage alliances with each other. Professional envoys journeyed back and forth between the centers of Near Eastern power, conveying valuable gifts and handling politically sensitive missions. In Egypt, such emissaries were often merchants, sent not only to handle matters of diplomacy but also to explore trade opportunities for the pharaoh.

INTERNATIONAL TRADE

Trade became an increasingly important aspect of international relations during the Late Bronze Age. The great coastal cities of the eastern Mediterranean became wealthy entrepôts for the exchange of a bewildering variety of goods. A single merchant vessel's cargo might contain scores of distinct items originating anywhere from the interior of Africa to the Baltic Sea. At the same time, the great states of the region continued to exploit their control of overland trade routes, relying more than ever on moving goods to an international market. Trade was rapidly becoming the lifeline of all these Late Bronze Age empires.

Busy and lucrative trade routes also served as a conduit for artistic motifs, literary and religious ideas, architectural forms, and ideas in tool making and weapon smithing. Whereas in the past such influences spread slowly and unevenly, the societies of the Late Bronze Age were now developing a very self-conscious cosmopolitanism. Egyptians delighted in Canaanite glass; Bronze Age Greeks prized Egyptian amulets; and the merchants of Ugarit admired and desired Greek pottery and wool.

This cosmopolitanism was particularly marked in large merchants towns. At Ugarit, the swirl of commerce and the multiplicity of languages may have been what impelled its citizens to develop a simpler form of writing than the cuneiform system still current throughout most of the Near East. An Ugaritic alphabet appears at the end of the Bronze Age, consisting of about thirty symbols representing consonants. Vowels had to be inferred, potentially sacrificing some clarity between reader and audience; but the alphabetic system was more easily mastered and more flexible than cuneiform for recording the heady pace of trade in the city's harbors.

The search for markets, resources, and trade routes heightened economic competition but also promoted greater understanding among cultures. After a fierce battle between Egypt and the Hittites near Kadesh (c. 1275 B.C.E.), the powerful Nineteenth Dynasty pharaoh Ramses II realized that more was to be gained through peaceful relations with his northern neighbors than through endless warfare. The treaty he established with the Hittites served as a pillar of geopolitical stability in the region and allowed further economic integration to develop during the thirteenth century B.C.E. But greater integration also meant greater mutual dependence. If one economy suffered in this international system, the effects of that decline were sure to be felt elsewhere.

EXPANSION AND FRAGILITY

Over the course of several centuries, this integrated system of trade and diplomacy grew to encompass the entire eastern Mediterranean world. The farther this system spread, however, the more fragile it became. This fragility was heightened by the fact that many of these new markets involved societies whose own degree of "civilization" was modest at best. Their rough, warlike spirit made them unreliable partners but even more dangerous adversaries within this integrated, Late Bronze Age world. We turn now to their story.

AEGEAN CIVILIZATION: MINOANS AND MYCENAEANS

How similar was Mycenaean culture to Minoan culture?

The ancient Greeks treasured many legends about their heroic past, when great men mingled with the gods and powerful kingdoms—larger and stronger than any known to the later world of classical Greece—contended for power and glory. For a long time, however, scholars dismissed any suggestion that there might be a "prehistoric" component of Greek experience. Tales of the Trojan War, Theseus and the Minotaur, and the great adventures of Odysseus were regarded as myths—products of Greek imagination that reflected no historical truth whatsoever.

In the late nineteenth century, an amateur archaeologist named Heinrich Schliemann became convinced that these myths were in fact historical accounts. Using the epic poems of Homer as his guide, he found the site of the great city of Troy near the coast of northwest Anatolia. He also discovered a number of once-powerful citadels on the Greek mainland, including the home of the legendary king Agamemnon at Mycenae (MY-seh-nee). Soon thereafter, Sir Arthur Evans found a large palace at Knossos on the island of Crete that predated any of the major citadel centers on the Greek mainland. Evans dubbed this wealthy and magnificent culture "Minoan," after King Minos, the powerful ruler who later Greeks believed had once dominated the Aegean Sea from Crete.

Although many of their initial conclusions were erroneous, the discoveries by Schliemann and Evans forced a reevaluation of Greek civilization and its roots. It is now clear that Bronze Age Greece (or, as it is more often termed, Mycenaean Greece, after the mighty kingdom of Greek myth based at Mycenae) was an important and well-integrated part of the Mediterranean world during the second millennium B.C.E. and that the foundations of classical Greek culture were established during this period. Much about these cultures remains mysterious. But their importance can no longer be denied.

THE MINOAN THALASSOCRACY

In the fifth century B.C.E. the Athenian historian Thucydides wrote that King Minos had ruled a "thalassocracy"—that is, a sea empire. Until Evans's discoveries at Knossos, Thucydides' claim seemed fanciful. It now appears that he was substantially correct.

Minoan civilization flourished from about 1900 to 1500 B.C.E., making it contemporary with Middle Kingdom Egypt and the Hittite Old Kingdom. Minoan success depended on overseas trade. They exchanged a range of exotic goods with Egypt, southwest Anatolia, and Cyprus. Through Cyprus, the Minoans also had contacts with the Levantine coast of modern-day Lebanon and Syria. Artistic influences also traveled along these trade routes; among much else, Minoan-style paintings appear regularly from this period in the Nile Delta and in the Levant.

One focus of Minoan commercial activity was clearly the mainland of Greece. The presence of a wide variety of Minoan objects there, including pottery, metalwork, and textiles, suggests the export of Minoan technologies, and perhaps even Minoan craftworkers, from Crete to the mainland. But the exact nature of the relationship between Minoan Crete and Mycenaean Greece remains controversial. The myth of Theseus and the Labyrinth claims that the hero went to Crete as a hostage, intending to free Athens from the heavy tribute laid on the city by King Minos. Might this story preserve a memory of a time when Crete did so dominate the Greeks of the mainland?

Close contacts between the Minoans and the mainland led to a variety of developments in Mycenaean Greece. The quality of material culture increased, and the mainland was drawn more tightly into the network of international commercial and diplomatic relationships that characterized the Near East during these centuries. The inhabitants of the mainland learned how to build great fortified palaces, hybrids of the Minoan palaces and the imposing strongholds the Hittites favored. The Greeks also learned to write from the Minoans, taking the Minoan script and modifying it to suit their own language better. The resulting script is the one Sir Arthur Evans called Linear B—the earliest written form of Greek.

The Mycenaeans

When Linear B was finally deciphered in the 1950s, it turned the world of Greek scholarship decisively toward a reckoning with the Bronze Age past. Until then, scholars could continue to wonder whether the impressive sites unearthed by Schliemann, Evans, and others had anything at all to do with the story of classical Greek civilization. That Linear B represented an ancient but unmistakably Greek dialect proved conclusively that Greek history stretched well back into the Bronze Age. But what role did the Mycenaean Greeks play in that story?

Greek-speaking Indo-Europeans entered Greece in several waves. But there was never a single, decisive moment at which Greece became "Greek." As the eminent Mycenaean scholar John Chadwick has suggested, during the Middle and Late Bronze Age the Greeks were always in the process of "becoming Greek."

An Artist's Reconstruction of the Great Hall at Pylos. This great Mycenaean hall, with its central hearth, was the focus of life within the palace complex, which would also have included private apartments, storerooms, and meeting rooms.

CHRONOLOGY

CIVILIZATIONS OF THE LATE BRONZE AGE

Minoan civilization	1900–1500 B.C.E.
Mycenaean civilization	1600–1200 B.C.E.
Near Eastern international	
system	1550–1200 B.C.E.
New Kingdom Egypt	1550–1075 B.C.E.

Mycenaean civilization represents the culmination of this process. By 1500 B.C.E., powerful citadels dotted the Greek landscape, ruled by warriors who touted their martial prowess on their gravestones and were buried with their war gear. These early rulers based their authority on their ability to lead men successfully into battle and to reward their followers with plunder. The most successful of them managed to gain control of strategic sites from which they could exploit the major trade routes through Greece, while never straying too far from the sea, where they engaged in both trade and piracy. By the thirteenth century B.C.E., some rulers had carved out territorial kingdoms with as many as 100,000 inhabitants, dwarfing the typical Greek city-state of the Classical Period.

These palace centers were an adaptation of a Near Eastern model; but their massive size was not ideally suited to the Greek landscape. In war also, Mycenaean imitation of Near Eastern examples had its limits. Although Mycenaean kings cherished the war chariots used by their Near Eastern contemporaries, such chariots were highly impractical on Greece's rocky terrain.

Despite these and other differences from their neighbors, the Mycenaean Greeks played an important role in the closing stages of the Near Eastern Bronze Age. By about 1400 B.C.E., they had subjugated the island of Crete, taking over Knossos and using it as a Mycenaean center. In western Anatolia, at least one Mycenaean king exercised enough influence for a Hittite king to address him as "my brother." The Mycenaeans also enjoyed great prestige in the Near East as warriors and mercenaries. It was their combined activities as traders and raiders that made it possible for the Mycenaeans to support the huge populations of their citadels; by itself, the surrounding hinterland could not begin to sustain such numbers.

The political and commercial foundations of the Mycenaean world—a powerful palace, headed by a king who was also a war leader; a warrior aristocracy; a bureaucracy of local officials; state-regulated land holdings; a re-distributive economy; large territorial kingdoms—were more typical of the contemporary Near Eastern world than they were of the Greek Classical Age. Nevertheless, we can trace important features of later Greek civilization back to the Mycenaeans, including of course the Greek language. Perhaps most important, however, the Classical Greeks themselves believed that they were descended from these legendary Mycenaean forebears, whom they credited with superhuman achievements. In fact, later Greeks knew little about their Mycenaean ancestors; but the impact on the Greek imagination of what they thought they knew about them was considerable.

The Mycenaean world seems to have collapsed under its own weight around the end of the thirteenth century B.C.E. What triggered this collapse is impossible to say: natural disasters, drought, famine, disease, and social unrest have all been posited as causes. But because it was such an integrated part of this international network of commercial, political, and military relationships, the reverberations from the Mycenaean world's collapse were felt across the entire Near East.

THE SEA PEOPLES AND THE END OF THE BRONZE AGE

As the Mycenaean world collapsed, a wave of destruction swept from north to south across the Near East. The nature of this devastation is obscure because it was the handiwork of a people so thorough that they obliterated everything in their path until they reached Egypt. Were it not for the narrow victory of Ramses III in about 1176 B.C.E., we might know nothing at all of the invaders who so suddenly unraveled the international system of the Late Bronze Age.

Ramses III referred to the invaders as the "Sea Peoples." Several of the groups he named as part of this coalition were familiar to the Egyptians as mercenaries; from Ramses' depiction of their battle gear and dress, it is also clear that many of the Sea Peoples were Aegean. Most notable of these were the Peleset, who, after their defeat by Egypt, withdrew to populate the coast of the region named after them, Palestine.

The arc of annihilation started in the north and may have helped trigger the final collapse of Mycenaean Greece. Disruption of the northern trade networks must have had a profound effect on the Mycenaean kingdoms, which suddenly faced an apocalyptic combination of overpopulation, drastic food shortages, and incessant warfare. The undermining of commerce in the north also devastated the economy of the Hittites, whose kingdom collapsed with astonishing rapidity.

MYCENAEAN GREECE

Note the mountainous landscape of Greece and how the peculiar shape of the region creates thousands of miles of coastline; consider that Greece is almost devoid of major rivers but that few places are far from the sight of the open sea. Notice that a map of "Greece" in antiquity always includes the western coast of Asia Minor as well as the islands of the Aegean. How would this dry, mountainous country surrounded by the sea potentially affect the nature of Greek civilization and its economic interests? Would the Near Eastern model be a good fit for Greece?

We catch only a few glimpses in our sources of a desperate Hittite king fighting to save Hattusas against myriad enemies.

Along the Mediterranean coast we find other clues. The king of Ugarit wrote a letter to his "brother" the king of Alashiya on Cyprus, begging his counterpart for immediate help. Poignantly, however, we have his letter only because the clay tablet on which it was written was baked hard in the fire that destroyed his palace. The letter was never sent. Ugarit was destroyed, and the Sea Peoples moved on.

The eruption of the Sea Peoples destroyed much of civilization as the Mediterranean world had known it. The destruction was not total. Cities did not all disappear, and trade did not vanish. But the Hittite Empire was gone, replaced by a bewildering variety of weak, short-lived principalities. The great cosmopolitan cities of the eastern Mediterranean coast lay in ruins, and new groups—sometimes contingents of the Sea Peoples—populated the seaboard. The citadels of Mycenaean Greece also collapsed. Depopulated by as much as 90 percent over the next century, Greece entered into a dark age of cultural and economic isolation that would last for the next 250 years. The Greeks would have to reinvent urbanism, in forms better suited to their unique environment.

Egypt survived the invasions, but with its major trading partners destroyed, it too went into a long decline. Assyria likewise suffered from the effects of the invasions. The next few centuries would see the Assyrians fighting for their very survival, while to the south, the peaceful and prosperous rule of the Kassites also collapsed, along with Babylon's economy.

The centuries immediately after the Sea Peoples' invasion saw no great empires arise in the Near East. The international system of the Late Bronze Age, carefully elaborated over half a millennium, had disappeared. In the wake of its destruction, however, new traditions and new cultural experiments began to emerge. New political and religious configurations took shape, and a new metallurgical technology—based on iron—began to supplant the use of bronze. Out of the ashes of the Late Bronze Age, a more enduring, more vibrant cultural world arose, the culture of the Iron Age Near East.

> Depopulated by as much as 90 percent over the next century, Greece entered into a dark age of cultural and economic isolation that would last for the next 250 years. The Greeks would have to reinvent urbanism, in forms better suited to their unique environment.

THE SMALL-SCALE STATES OF THE EARLY IRON AGE

Why did Phoenician cities prosper during the Early Iron Age?

With the destruction of the superpower balance of the Late Bronze Age, the geopolitical map of the Near East changed significantly. In Anatolia, a patchwork of small, largely Indo-European realms emerged from the collapse of the Hittite Empire. Similar developments took place in the Levant, the eastern Mediterranean coastal area that today comprises Israel, Lebanon, and parts of Syria. For centuries, this area had been controlled by either the Egyptians or the Hittites. With the collapse of both these empires, the resulting power vacuum in the region allowed new states to emerge. As political and military powers, the small-scale states of the Early Iron Age were at best second rate. However, they had a profound impact on the intellectual and religious development of Western civilizations.

THE PHOENICIANS

The Phoenicians were Canaanites who spoke a Semitic language closely related to Ugaritic, Hebrew, Amorite, and other West Semitic dialects. Their cultural and political roots lay firmly in the ancient Near East. Phoenician cities were all independent of one another; as in Sumer, a Phoenician's first loyalty was to his or her city, not to any abstract notion of being a Phoenician.

During the Late Bronze Age, most Phoenician cities had been controlled by Egypt. The erosion of Egyptian imperial power after 1200 B.C.E. gave them the opportunity to capitalize on commercial advantages they had already established. One Phoenician city, Gubla, had been a teeming center of trade under Egyptian rule, particularly as an entrepôt for papyrus, the highly prized Egyptian writing material. This connection with the papyrus trade continued during the Iron Age, so much so that the Greek name for the city, Byblos, became the basis for the Greek word *biblion*, meaning "book." The seabeds off the Phoenician coast yielded a valuable purple reddish dye from the murex snail—hence the Greek term *Phoenician*, which essentially means "purple people." Phoenician textiles commanded a high price everywhere their merchants went. So too did timber (especially cedar) and the famous Canaanite glass. The Phoenicians also became expert metalworkers, ivory carvers, and shipbuilders.

PHOENICIAN CITIES

Tucked along a mountainous coast riven by deep valleys, Phoenician cities oriented themselves toward the sea. Phoenicians became famous as merchants and seafarers. They were also aggressive colonists, planting trading colonies across the Mediterranean. At the end of the ninth century B.C.E., colonists from Tyre established

WHY DID PHOENICIAN CITIES PROSPER DURING THE EARLY IRON AGE?

THE SMALL-SCALE STATES OF THE EARLY IRON AGE   51

Carthage in modern-day Tunisia. Carthage would ultimately become the preeminent power in the western Mediterranean, bringing it into conflict with Rome centuries later.

CULTURAL INFLUENCE

The widespread colonial and mercantile efforts of the Phoenicians meant that they influenced cultures across the Mediterranean. Among their early overseas trading partners were the Greeks. Here the Phoenicians may have played an important role in reintroducing urban life into the Greek world after the collapse of the Mycenaean citadels. They also brought with them a number of Near Eastern artistic and literary influences.

Without question, however, the most important contribution the Phoenicians made to Greek life was their alphabet.

As we have seen, a thirty-character alphabet had evolved at Ugarit by the end of the Bronze Age. Around 1100 B.C.E., the Phoenicians refined this writing system to twenty-two characters. This simpler, more flexible writing system probably helped facilitate trade and accounting. Why they chose to share their invention with the Greeks is less certain; but whatever the explanation, the Greeks remained very aware of their debt to the Phoenicians. Later Greek legends ascribed the invention of their alphabet to Cadmus, a Phoenician who had settled in Greece. The debt is also clear from the close relationship

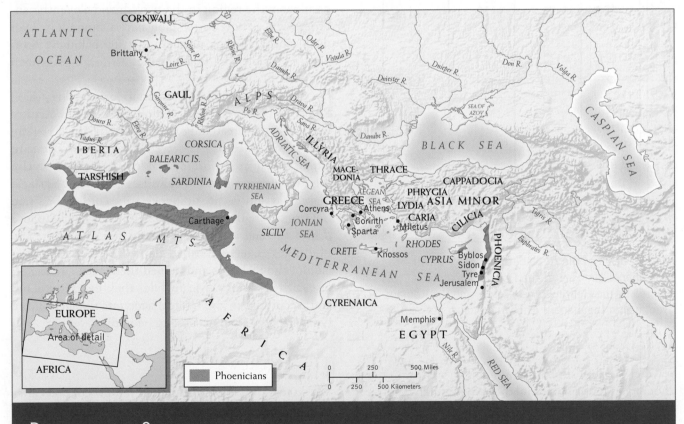

PHOENICIAN COLONIZATION

Examine the map and compare the more detailed one of Palestine on p. 53. Why would overseas colonization be of such crucial importance to Phoenician city-states? Consider in what ways the Phoenicians may have been partly driven by necessity. Notice that Phoenician colonization is concentrated in the western Mediterranean; then consider that the Phoenicians were the most active merchants of the eastern Mediterranean as well. What does their westward colonization imply about the Phoenicians' aims and the level of civilization in the West as compared with the East?

Phoenician	Hebrew	Classical Greek	Modern Alphabetic
𐤀	א	A	A
𐤁	ב	B	B
𐤂	ג	Γ	G
𐤃	ד	Δ	D
𐤄	ה	E	E
𐤅	ו	Y	V
𐤆	ז	Z	Z
𐤇	ח	H	H
𐤈	ט	Θ	T
𐤉	י	I	Y
𐤊	כ	K	K
𐤋	ל	Λ	L
𐤌	מ	M	M
𐤍	נ	N	N
𐤎	ס	Ξ	S
𐤏	ע	O	O
𐤐	פ	Π	P
𐤑	צ		TZ
𐤒	ק		Q
𐤓	ר	P	R
𐤔	ש	Σ	S
𐤕	ת	T	T

The Evolution of the Alphabet. This table illustrates how letter shapes changed as the Phoenician alphabet was adapted by the Hebrews, the Greeks, and the Romans (from whom the modern English alphabet derives).

between Greek (alpha, beta, gamma, delta . . .) and Phoenician letter names (aleph, bayt, gimel, dalet . . .) and from the obvious similarities in letter shapes evident in the table above.

THE PHILISTINES

South along the Levantine coast from Phoenicia lay the land of the Philistines. Few cultures have enjoyed historical reputations as bad as theirs. The Philistines were among the great villains of the Hebrew scriptural tradition. *Philistine* continues today as a word to describe a boorish, uncultured, and ignorant person. Their infamy

stems from their unique position in the Levant at the beginning of the Iron Age, where as descendants of the Peleset—one of the Sea Peoples defeated by Ramses III—they settled, urbanized, and quickly gained the upper hand over their neighbors in the region. Among those peoples were the Hebrews, for whom the Philistines were the great national enemy.

The Philistines retained a separate identity from the other peoples of the region for several generations; each new archaeological discovery roots this identity more firmly in their Aegean past. We know little about the Philistine language—few written materials survive, and they gradually adopted a Canaanite dialect—but their material culture, behavior, and organization all exhibit close affinities with the Mycenaean world. The Philistines introduced grapevines and olive trees to the Levant from the Aegean basin. With the profits from these industries, they created powerful armies that dominated the region in the twelfth and eleventh centuries B.C.E. They also established a monopoly over metalsmithing in the southern Levant, making it virtually impossible for their enemies to forge their own weapons.

The Hebrews had good reason to fear the Philistines. Philistine pressure on the central Hebrew hill country was constant, threatening the holy sanctuary at Shiloh, the resting place of the sacred Ark of the Covenant, which contained the original tablets of the law given by the Hebrew god Yahweh to Moses on Mount Sinai. In Hebrew tradition, the desperate tribes of Israel carried the Ark before them against the Philistines, only to lose it in battle and witness the destruction of Shiloh. The Philistines then established garrisons throughout the land of the Hebrews and denied them access to metallurgical technology. Meanwhile, they exacted tribute and, according to the biblical account, engaged in the typical abuses of an occupying people.

THE HEBREWS

We discuss the central feature of Hebrew cultural experience, the development of their monotheistic conception of divinity, at the end of this chapter. In this section, we focus our attention on the political development of Hebrew society within the Iron Age Levant. In any discussion of Hebrew society, however, religious conceptions and practices can never be far from the surface. Like all ancient cultures, the Hebrews initially made little distinction between politics and religion. What set them apart, however, was their unusual theology and the impact it had on their development as a people. Were it not for the resilience of their religious

WHY DID PHOENICIAN CITIES PROSPER DURING THE EARLY IRON AGE?

THE SMALL-SCALE STATES OF THE EARLY IRON AGE   53

tradition and the fundamental influence it has had on the subsequent development of Western civilizations, we would have little reason to discuss the early Hebrews at length. As it is, however, the Hebrews were one of the most important cultures in world history.

ORIGINS

We are blessed as historians with one of the unique achievements of the Hebrews: the Hebrew Bible, known to Christians as the Old Testament. The Bible is an unparalleled historical resource, full of extraordinary detail about cultural practices and historical events, as well as being a guide to the intellectual unfolding of one of the most important religious traditions of the Western world. It is not, however, a history as modern people would conceive of it. Although it contains some ostensibly historical accounts, the Bible is essentially a story about the relationship between a transcendent creator god and the Hebrews, whom he chose to be his special people; of the covenant that was forged between them; and of the trials by which that relationship was repeatedly tested and reaffirmed.

The historical accounts contained in the first five books of the Bible are particularly problematic. Aside from the chronological difficulties posed by a series of impossibly long-lived patriarchs (Methusaleh, for example, is said to have lived for more than 900 years), much of this material appears to have been borrowed from other Near Eastern cultures. The creation and flood stories have Sumerian parallels; the laws and practices of the patriarchs have clear Hurrian antecedents; and the tale of Moses' infancy is virtually a replica of Sargon's legend. Even the story of the exodus from Egypt is fraught with problems from a historical standpoint. Although the Book of Joshua claims that the Hebrews who returned from Egypt conquered and expelled the native Canaanites, archaeological and linguistic evidence suggests that the Hebrews were themselves essentially inland Canaanites, who may have merged with scattered Hebrew refugees from Egypt in the aftermath of the Sea Peoples' invasions but who for the most part had been continuously resident in Canaan for centuries. Important religious and cultural developments clearly occurred among the Hebrews of the second millennium B.C.E., but the first five books of the Bible have the look and feel of retrospective extrapolation and justification, not secure historical record.

Once we move into the so-called historical books of the Bible, the information becomes more credible; but it remains extremely difficult to confirm any of it from archaeological sources. In the Book of Judges, for example, the Hebrews appear as wandering pastoralists who were just beginning to establish permanent settlements. The Hebrews were organized into twelve tribes—extended clan units in which families owed mutual aid and protection to one another in times of war, cattle raiding, and judicial dispute. Each tribe was ruled over by a judge, who exercised the typical functions of authority in a clan-based society: war leadership, high priesthood, and dispute settlement. By the middle of the twelfth century B.C.E.,

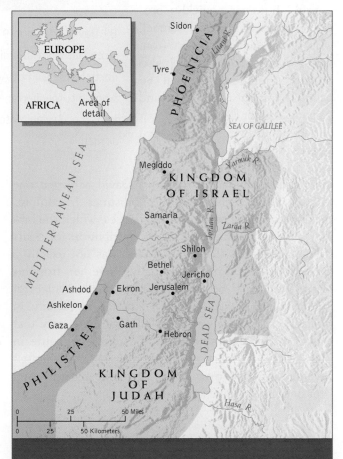

THE HEBREW KINGDOM, c. 900 B.C.E.

Notice the scale of the map and consider the comparatively small size of this world. Why did the Philistines and Phoenicians present such a perceived cultural challenge to the Hebrews? What advantages did the Philistines and Phoenicians possess, geographically and otherwise? What political and religious consequences might have resulted from the division of the Kingdom of Israel after the death of King Solomon, especially given the position of Jerusalem and the Temple in the south?

these tribes had established some kind of rough territorial turf, those in the south calling themselves Judah, and those in the north Israel.

In practice, however, the Hebrew tribes had few effective mechanisms for concerted action, a fact made plain when the Philistines conquered the Levantine coastal region around 1050 B.C.E. To meet the Philistine threat, a tighter, "national" form of government was needed. Accordingly, around 1025 B.C.E., Samuel, a tribal judge and holy man, selected a king named Saul to lead Hebrew resistance against the Philistines.

Saul, however, quickly provoked the resentment of Samuel, who withdrew his support from the embattled king. Saul also proved an indifferent general. So Samuel threw his support behind a young warrior, David, a member of Saul's court who now schemed actively to draw popular support away from Saul. Waging his own independent military campaigns, David achieved one triumph after another over the Philistines. In contrast, the armies of Saul met frequent reverses, which the biblical authors portrayed as divine retribution for Saul's own inadequacies. David, however, was not exactly a national patriot. When Saul finally drove him from his court, David first became an outlaw on the fringes of Hebrew and Philistine society, then a mercenary in Philistine service. It was as a Philistine mercenary that David fought against Saul in the climactic battle in which Saul was killed. Soon thereafter, David himself became king, first over Judah, his home territory, and later over Saul's home kingdom of Israel also.

> By David's death in 973 B.C.E., his kingdom stretched from the middle Euphrates in the north to the Gulf of Aqaba in the south, and from the Mediterranean coast in the west into the Syrian deserts beyond the river Jordan.

CONSOLIDATION OF THE HEBREW KINGDOM

With David's ascension to the throne around 1000 B.C.E., the most glorious period in the political history of the ancient Hebrew kingdom began. Through cunning, opportunism, and inspired leadership, David reduced the Philistines to an inconsequential strip of coastal land in the south and extended his control east of the river Jordan and Dead Sea. By David's death in 973 B.C.E., his kingdom stretched from the middle Euphrates in the north to the Gulf of Aqaba in the south, and from the Mediterranean coast in the west into the Syrian deserts beyond the river Jordan. Israel was now a serious force in the politics of the Near East, its status increased by the temporary weakness of its imperial neighbors Egypt and Assyria.

As David's power and prestige grew, he was able to impose on his subjects a highly unpopular system of taxation and forced labor. His goal was to build a glorious political and religious capital at Jerusalem, a Canaanite settlement that he transformed into the central city of his kingdom. It was a shrewd choice. As a newly conquered city, Jerusalem had no previous affiliation with any of Israel's twelve tribes and so stood outside the ancient rivalries among them. Geographically too, Jerusalem lay between the southern tribes of Judah (of which David was a member) and the northern tribes of Israel (from which Saul had come). David also took steps to exalt the city as a religious center by making Jerusalem the resting place of the sacred Ark of the Covenant and reorganizing the priesthood of Yahweh. By these measures, he sought to forge a new national identity, focused on the House of David and its connections to Yahweh, that would transcend the old divisions between Israel and Judah.

THE REIGN OF KING SOLOMON (973–937 B.C.E.)

Continuing his father's policies but on a much grander scale, David's son King Solomon built a great temple complex at Jerusalem to house the sacred Ark of the Covenant. Such visible support of the Yahweh cult played particularly well with the writers of the Hebrew scripture, who portrayed Solomon's reign as a golden age for the Hebrews.

Despite his proverbial wisdom, however, Solomon was a ruthless and often brutal ruler whose promotion of the Yahweh cult coincided with a program of

CHRONOLOGY

THE TRANSFORMATION OF HEBREW SOCIETY

Early efforts to form national government	1025 B.C.E.
David crowned king of Israel	1000 B.C.E.
Split between Israel and Judah	924 B.C.E.
Fall of Judah and start of Babylonian Captivity	586 B.C.E.

despotic rule and royal self-aggrandizement. His palace complex—of which the temple was a part—allowed him to rule in the grand style of ancient Near Eastern potentates. To finance his expensive tastes and programs, Solomon instituted a variety of oppressive taxation and administrative schemes. He imposed customs duties on the lucrative caravan trade that passed through his country. With the help of Hiram, the Phoenician king of Tyre, Solomon also constructed a commercial fleet based at the head of the Gulf of Aqaba. These ships plied the waters of the Red Sea and beyond, trading among other commodities the gold and copper mined by Solomon's slaves in the southern Negev. Wealth poured into Israel as never before.

But it was not enough. To undertake his ambitious building program, Solomon required many of his subjects, particularly from the agricultural north, to perform forced labor four months out of every year. This level of oppression was too much for many Israelites. The north seethed with rebellion against the royal capital, and after Solomon's death, his son and successor was faced with revolt. Before long the united monarchy had split in two, the House of David ruling the southern Kingdom of Judah with its capital at Jerusalem, the ten northern tribes banding together into the Kingdom of Israel with its capital at Shechem.

Although the two Hebrew kingdoms would maintain their independence for several centuries—the north until 722 B.C.E., the south until 586 B.C.E.—the changing political situation of the Near East made their divided state increasingly vulnerable. The united Hebrew monarchy created by David and Solomon arose at a time when the traditional imperial powers in the region were temporarily in eclipse. Within a few generations of Solomon's death, however, the Hebrews and the other small states of the Near and Middle East would find themselves menaced by the revived Mesopotamia-based empire of the Assyrians.

THE ASSYRIAN EMPIRE

What were the foundations of Assyrian imperial power?

The Assyrians were a Semitic-speaking people whose homeland lay in northern Mesopotamia. As we saw in Chapter One, by 1900 B.C.E. the Assyrians were already taking advantage of their geographical position to establish trade routes between Mesopotamia and Anatolia.

They also played an important role in spreading urban society and organization across the Anatolian Plateau. Thereafter, however, they struggled to protect themselves against a series of aggressive neighbors: first the Old Babylonian Empire of Hammurabi, then the Egyptians, the Mittanians, the Hittites, and finally the Sea Peoples.

This centuries-long fight for existence had a profound effect on the Assyrian worldview. Starting in the ninth century B.C.E., the Assyrians became the aggressors, extending their power and influence through brutal, systematic victimization of their neighbors. Its terrors notwithstanding, their aggression helped shape the religious and political traditions of their neighbors, extending Near Eastern culture to the Aegean basin, synthesizing a new type of imperial organization, and imparting important lessons about what did and did not make for successful governance of a far-flung, international empire.

THE MIDDLE ASSYRIAN PERIOD (1362–859 B.C.E.)

The decline of the Kingdom of Mitanni in the fourteenth century B.C.E. gave the Assyrians their first opportunity to establish themselves as a great realm. As Hittite pressure wore down Mitanni from the west, local Assyrian potentates extended their control in the east. Finally one such ruler, the governor of the city of Assur (sometimes spelled Ashur), adopted the name of his city's patron deity and declared himself king of Assyria. Assur-uballit I (1362–1327 B.C.E.) and his successors extended their power over northern Mesopotamia. But otherwise, they did little to upset the delicate balance of power in the region.

With the succession of Tukulti-Ninurta I in 1244 B.C.E., however, the restraint was dropped. Tukulti-Ninurta sacked Babylon, carrying its Kassite king and its patron deity, Marduk, into captivity and claimed the prestigious kingship of Babylon for himself. To maintain his tenuous grip over Babylonia, however, Tukulti-Ninurta had to engage in constant campaigning. This, plus his sacrilegious treatment of the Babylonian god, alienated his own subjects, who murdered him in about 1208 B.C.E.

A century of Assyrian decline followed as its neighbors sought both vengeance and control over the vital trade routes that crisscrossed Assyrian territory. This struggle for survival continued until the close of the Middle Assyrian Period, when a brutal but brilliant ruler, Assurnasirpal II (*ab-sur-NAH-sur-PAHL*; 883–859 B.C.E.)

revived Assyrian strength and founded the neo-Assyrian Empire. Under his ruthless leadership, the Assyrians conducted aggressive military campaigns on an annual basis. The targets of Assyrian might had to pay tribute or face the full onslaught of the Assyrian war machine, which under Assurnasirpal acquired a deserved reputation for savagery and viciousness.

THE NEO-ASSYRIAN EMPIRE (859–627 B.C.E.)

The conquests of Assurnasirpal and his son Shalmeneser (*SHAHL-meh-NEE-zehr*) III, inspired stiff resistance to Assyrian expansion. The northern Kingdom of Israel, along with several other states in the region of Syria-Palestine, formed an alliance to stop the Assyrians. Ultimately this coalition fought to a standstill, forcing the Assyrian ruler to settle for smaller victories, until a great revolt within Assyria ended his reign. But the respite proved brief. A usurper who took the name

<table>
<tr><td colspan="2">CHRONOLOGY</td></tr>
<tr><td colspan="2">EVOLUTION OF ASSYRIA IN THE IRON AGE</td></tr>
<tr><td>Assyria begins to reestablish
its influence</td><td>1362–883 B.C.E.</td></tr>
<tr><td>Assurnasirpal II founds
neo-Assyrian Empire</td><td>883–859 B.C.E.</td></tr>
<tr><td>Birth of the Sargonid dynasty</td><td>722 B.C.E.</td></tr>
<tr><td>Destruction of the Assyrian state</td><td>612–605 B.C.E.</td></tr>
</table>

Tiglath-Pileser III seized the Assyrian throne in 744 B.C.E. and immediately prepared a great western campaign. In his first year he demanded tribute from various western kingdoms that had not paid up for generations. Those who refused fell victim to an immediate Assyrian onslaught.

When Tiglath-Pileser III died in 727 B.C.E., many of the recently conquered states rebelled, perhaps hoping that a familiar pattern of Assyrian dynastic instability would reassert itself on the death of the usurping monarch. But Tiglath-Pileser's son energetically crushed the rebellions. When he died in battle, he was quickly replaced by one of his military commanders, who took the name Sargon II (722–705 B.C.E.). With typical Assyrian historical consciousness, Sargon II regarded Sargon of Akkad as the "first" Sargon; he was thus claiming to be the direct successor to a Near Eastern empire nearly 1,500 years in the past. The dynasty that Sargon II founded is called the Sargonid; its century of rule proved the most magnificent in all of Assyrian history.

The Sargonids extended the frontiers of the Assyrian Empire from western Iran to the shores of the Mediterranean. Briefly, they even subjugated parts of Egypt. Sargon himself put an end to the Kingdom of Israel and scared the southern Kingdom of Judah into remaining a loyal and quiet vassal. By the seventh century B.C.E. Assyria was the unrivaled power of the ancient Near East.

Assyrian Winged Human-Headed Bull. This relief was found in the palace of King Sargon II (722–705 B.C.E.). It measures sixteen feet wide by sixteen feet high and weighs approximately forty tons.

THE ASSYRIAN MILITARY-RELIGIOUS ETHOS

Assyrian religious, political, and military ideas took shape in the centuries during which Assyria fought for its survival. As the Assyrians gained the upper hand, however, this ethos became the foundation for their empire's relentless conquests.

The two fundamental characteristics of this Assyrian military-religious ethos were holy war and the exaction of tribute through terror. The Assyrians were convinced that their god Assur demanded that his worship be extended through military conquest. Even more than to the king, therefore, the Assyrian army belonged to Assur; and all who did not accept Assur's supremacy were, by that fact alone, enemies of Assur's people, the Assyrians. Ritual humiliation of a defeated city's gods was therefore a regular feature of Assyrian conquests. Frequently the conquered gods would be carried off to the Assyrian capital, where they would "live" as hostages at the "court" of Assur. Meanwhile, an image of Assur himself (usually represented as a sun disk with the head and shoulders of an archer) would be installed in the defeated city, where the conquered people would be required to worship him. Worship of Assur did not necessarily mean that conquered peoples abandoned their previous gods altogether. But in Assyrian eyes, there was no question that Assur should be the supreme deity for all the peoples of their empire.

Rather than defeat their foes once and impose tribute thereafter, the Assyrians raided even their vanquished foes each year, extracting tribute by force. This strategy succeeded in terrifying Assyria's subjects and keeping

THE ASSYRIAN EMPIRE, C. 700 B.C.E.

What do you find striking about the geography of the Assyrian Empire? Why would the Assyrians concentrate their efforts in the river valleys and along the coast, leaving the Syrian interior largely alone? Notice the location of the Assyrian capitals of Nineveh and Assur; how was their situation in Mesopotamia likely to affect the Assyrians' sense of their own historical identity? Consider the position of Egypt. Why did the Assyrians find it difficult to subjugate Egypt permanently, despite the violence of their conquests?

THE SENJIRLI STELE OF KING ESARHADDON

Set up in northern Syria by the Assyrian king Esarhaddon (681–669 B.C.E.), this inscribed stone monument is one of the most important records of his reign. Accompanying the text (which proclaims his victories over Egypt and the Phoenician coast of Syria) was a depiction of Esarhaddon holding a cup in his right hand and a mace in his left. His left hand also grasped reins fastened to shackles holding a captured prince of Egypt and a Syrian ruler, both begging for mercy. The inscription demonstrates Assyrian kingship's bombastic propaganda, its conscious connection to the Sumero-Akkadian past, and the cruelty that characterized Assyrian conquests. (Assur, Anu, Ba'al, Ea, and Ishtar were all gods or goddesses.)

To Assur, father of the gods, lover of my priesthood, Anu mighty and pre-eminent, who called me by name, Ba'al, the exalted lord, establisher of my dynasty, Ea, the wise, all-knowing . . . Ishtar, lady of battle and combat, who goes at my side . . . all of them who determine my destiny, who grant to the king, their favorite, power and might . . . the king, the offering of whose sacrifices the great gods love . . . their unsparing weapons they have presented him as a royal gift . . . [he] who has brought all the lands in submission at his feet, who has imposed tribute and tax upon them; conqueror of his foes, destroyer of his enemies, the king, who as to his walk is a storm, and as to his deeds, a raging wolf; . . . the onset of his battle is powerful, he is a consuming flame, a fire that does not sink: son of Sennacherib, king of the universe, king of Assyria, grandson of Sargon, king of the universe, king of Assyria, viceroy of Babylon, king of Sumer and Akkad. . . . I am powerful, I am all powerful, I am a hero, I am gigantic, I am colossal, I am honored, I am magnified, I am without an equal among all kings, the chosen one of Assur . . . the great lord [who] in order to show to the peoples the immensity of my mighty deeds, made powerful my kingship over the four regions of the world and made my name great. . . . Of Tirhakah, king of Egypt and Kush, the accursed . . . without cessation I slew multitudes of his men, and him I smote five times with

the point of my javelin, with wounds, no recovery. Memphis, his royal city, in half a day . . . I besieged, I captured, I destroyed, I devastated, I burned with fire. . . . The root of Kush I tore up out of Egypt and not one therein escaped to submit to me.

Daniel David Luckenbill, ed., *Ancient Records of Assyria and Babylonia*, vol. 2 (Chicago, 1926–1927), pp. 224–227.

QUESTIONS FOR ANALYSIS

1. Ancient inscriptions and chronicles often exaggerate when describing royal accomplishments. Can we separate Esarhaddon's actual accomplishments from his boastful propaganda? What function did this inscription serve?

2. The Assyrians have a reputation for arrogance and cruelty toward defeated enemies. What features of this text suggest that reputation may be well deserved?

3. "I slew multitudes of his men," Esarhaddon boasted. Recall that "Saul slew his thousands, and David his ten thousands" (1 Samuel 29:5). Would it surprise you if the harsh Hebrew justice of "an eye for an eye, a tooth for a tooth" (Exodus 21:24; Leviticus 24:20; Deuteronomy 19:21) echoed Assyrian laws? What lasting influence did the Assyrians have on other cultures of the ancient Near East?

the Assyrian military machine primed for battle. But perpetual reconquests did little to inspire loyalty among subject peoples, who eventually reached a point of desperation at which they had little to lose through rebellion.

Assyrian warfare was also notoriously savage. Ancient warfare was always brutal: mutilations of prisoners, decapitations, rape, and the mass deportations and/or enslavement of civilian populations were commonplace. The Assyrians, however, relished and celebrated such barbarities as did no other ancient empire. Their artwork and inscriptions revel in the butchering and torture of their enemies. Smiling Assyrian archers are shown shooting fleeing enemies in the back, while remorseless soldiers fling the citizens of a captured Judean town from the walls, impaling them on stakes below.

The army itself had developed by the ninth century into a devastating force. Like many ancient societies,

Assyrian Atrocities. These Judean captives are being impaled on stakes after their city has fallen to the Assyrian king Sennacherib (704–681 B.C.E.). This carving comes from the walls of Sennacherib's palace at Nineveh.

the Assyrians had originally employed a seasonal peasant army of part-time soldiers. But from the reign of Assurnasirpal II onward, the Assyrians recruited a massive standing army of more than 100,000 soldiers. The Assyrians also mastered large-scale iron-smelting techniques, and by the ninth century could equip their fighting men with high-quality steel weapons that overwhelmed opponents still reliant on bronze.

THE END OF ASSYRIA AND ITS LEGACY

The successors of Sargon II continued Assyrian military policies while devoting great energy to what we might broadly consider "culture." Sargon's immediate successor Sennacherib (704–681 B.C.E.) rebuilt the ancient Assyrian city of Nineveh, fortifying it with a double wall with a circuit of nine miles. He constructed an enormous palace there, raised on a giant platform decorated with marble, ivory, and exotic woods and ordered the construction of a massive irrigation system, including an aqueduct that carried fresh water to the city from thirty miles away. His son rebuilt the conquered city of Babylon and was a famous patron of the arts and sciences.

Assurbanipal (669–627 B.C.E.) was perhaps the greatest of all the Assyrian kings. He maintained a strong military presence throughout the empire and for a time ruled the entire delta region of Egypt. After the Assyrian adventure in Egypt ultimately ended in failure, he turned his attention to a series of internal reforms, seeking ways to govern his empire other than through the traditional weapons of military terror and religious imperialism. Assurbanipal was an "enlightened" Assyrian king, who hoped to transform the empire into something more enduring than an armed camp in a perpetual state of warfare with its subjects and neighbors.

When Assurbanipal died in 627 B.C.E., the Assyrian Empire appeared to be at its zenith. Its borders were secure, the realm was largely at peace with its neighbors, and its kings had adorned their capitals with magnificent artwork and hanging gardens. The end of Assyria is therefore all the more dramatic for its suddenness. Within fifteen years of the mighty Assurbanipal's reign, Nineveh lay in ruins; a few years later, the Assyrian state was no more, obliterated from the face of the earth with the same speed and violence by which it had established itself.

After the death of Assurbanipal, a coalition formed between the Indo-European-speaking Medes of Iran and the Chaldeans, a Semitic-speaking people who once controlled the southern half of Babylonia. The Chaldeans succeeded to Assyria's position as the predominant imperial power in Mesopotamia and the Levant. They proved little better than the hated Assyrians, exercising the same cruelty that had made the Assyrians infamous, including the mass deportation of conquered foes from their homelands. The most famous example of this policy came in 587/586 B.C.E., when the ruthless Chaldean king Nebuchadnezzar (*neb-byoo-kuhd-NEHZ-ehr*) captured Jerusalem. He destroyed the temple and removed tens of thousands of Hebrews to Babylon, an exile known in Jewish history as the Babylonian Captivity.

THE PERSIANS

In what ways did the Persian Empire differ from its Near Eastern predecessors? How would you account for those differences?

Built as it was on plunder and fear, the Chaldean Empire (612–539 B.C.E.) had a very short life. It was the Persians who would emerge to topple the Chaldeans and reunite the ancient Near East.

THE ORIGINS OF THE PERSIAN EMPIRE

The Persians emerged from obscurity suddenly, under an extraordinary prince named Cyrus, who succeeded to the rule of a single Persian tribe in 559 B.C.E. Shortly thereafter Cyrus made himself ruler of all the Persians. Around 549 B.C.E. he threw off the lordship of the Medes, claiming dominion over lands stretching from the Persian Gulf well into Asia Minor. Cyrus thus became a neighbor of the kingdom of Lydia. In 546 B.C.E., Cyrus defeated the wealthy Lydians obtaining their gold and silver.

He invaded Mesopotamia in 539 B.C.E., striking so quickly that he took Babylon without a fight. Once he was in Babylon, the entire Chaldean Empire was his. Cyrus allowed the Hebrews captive in Babylon since the time of Nebuchadnezzar to return to Israel and set up a semi-independent vassal state. Cyrus allowed other conquered peoples considerable self-determination as well, especially in religion, making Persian rule a welcome change from that of the Assyrians and Chaldeans. When Cyrus fell in battle in 530 B.C.E., he left behind the largest empire the world had yet seen. Persian

expansion continued, however, even after his death. In 525 B.C.E., his son would conquer Egypt.

THE CONSOLIDATION OF THE PERSIAN EMPIRE

Cyrus's son died young and without a son, leaving open the question of succession. After a short period of civil war, Darius I ruled Persia from 521 to 486 B.C.E. He concentrated on consolidating his predecessors' military gains by improving the administration of the Persian state. Darius divided the empire into provinces called satrapies, each administered by a satrap. The satraps enjoyed extensive powers and considerable political latitude, but they owed fixed tributes and absolute loyalty to the central government, as did vassal states such as the technically autonomous Hebrew Kingdom.

Adhering to the tolerant policy of Cyrus, Darius allowed the various peoples of the Persian Empire to retain most of their local institutions while enforcing a standardized currency and system of weights and measures. Throughout their empire the Persians required modest tribute payments; but otherwise, they were little interested in imposing onerous taxes, martial law, or their own religious practices on subject peoples. After centuries of Assyrian and Chaldean tyranny, the light hand of Persian rule was welcomed throughout the Near East.

Darius was also a great builder. He erected a new royal residence and ceremonial capital, which the Greeks called Persepolis ("Persia City"). Darius also expanded the Assyrian road system to enhance trade and communications in his far-flung realms. The most famous was the "Royal Road," stretching 1,600 miles from Susa near the Persian Gulf to Sardis (the old Lydian capital) near the Aegean. Government couriers along this road were the first postal system, carrying messages and goods in relay stages from one post to another. An extensive imperial spy network also used this postal system to inform the crown of developments throughout the massive empire. The "intelligence service" founded by Darius was famed throughout Persian history as "the eyes and ears of the king."

Darius was an extraordinarily gifted administrator. As a military strategist, however, he made an enormous mistake when he attempted to extend Persian hegemony into Greece. Cyrus's conquest of Lydia had made Persia the ruler of the Greek-speaking cities on the western coast of Asia Minor, but these cities disdained

In what ways did the Persian Empire differ from its Near Eastern predecessors?

THE PERSIANS   61

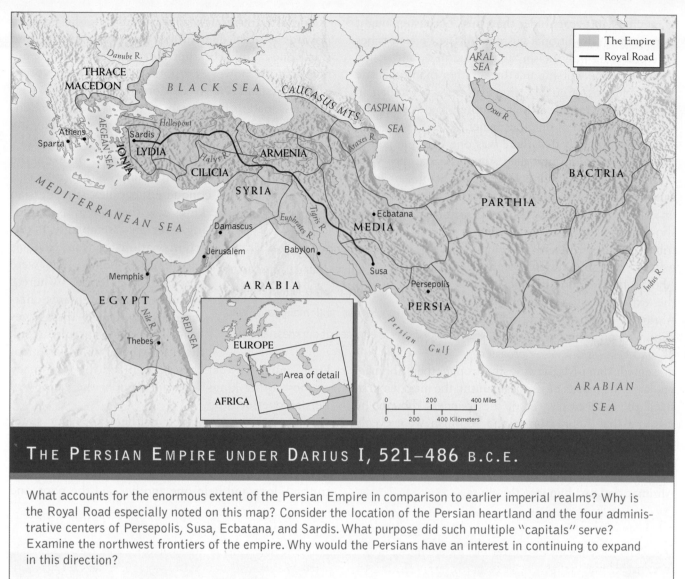

THE PERSIAN EMPIRE UNDER DARIUS I, 521–486 B.C.E.

What accounts for the enormous extent of the Persian Empire in comparison to earlier imperial realms? Why is the Royal Road especially noted on this map? Consider the location of the Persian heartland and the four administrative centers of Persepolis, Susa, Ecbatana, and Sardis. What purpose did such multiple "capitals" serve? Examine the northwest frontiers of the empire. Why would the Persians have an interest in continuing to expand in this direction?

Persian rule and yearned for the idealized freedom of other Greek city-states. Consequently, between 499 and 494 B.C.E. the Greeks on the Asian mainland waged a war for independence and briefly gained the support of troops from Athens, who joined the Asian Greeks in burning the important Persian regional administrative center at Sardis. After quelling the uprising in Asia, Darius sent a force across the Aegean to punish Athens and serve notice of his dominion to all European Greeks. At the battle of Marathon in 490, the Athenians dealt Darius the only major setback of his reign. In 480 his son and successor, Xerxes (ZERK-zees), attempted to avenge this humiliation by crushing Greece with a tremendous army, but heroic resistance by Athens and Sparta forced him to retreat and abandon his plans a year later. At that point the Persians realized that they had reached the limits of their expansionism. Thereafter, they concentrated on their Asian possessions and used money and diplomacy to keep the Greeks in check.

ZOROASTRIANISM

Even more enduring than Persia's political legacy was its religious one, embodied in Zoroastrianism. This important world religion, along with Buddhism and Judaism, was one of the three major universalizing religions known to the world before Christianity and Islam. The religion's founder was Zoroaster (the Greek form of the Persian name Zarathustra). Zoroaster was a Persian who probably lived shortly before 600 B.C.E., although some of the writings attributed to him may be as much as 400 years older than this. Zoroaster sought to reform the traditional customs of the Persian tribes by eradicating polytheism, animal sacrifice, and magic and to redefine worship in ethical rather than ritualistic terms. He was, arguably, the first true theologian in world history, insofar as he attempted to devise a fully developed system of religious belief.

Zoroaster taught that there was one supreme god in the universe, whom he called Ahura-Mazda, the "Wise Lord." Ahura-Mazda embodied the principles of light, truth, and righteousness; there was nothing wrathful or evil about him, and his light shone everywhere, not just on one tribe. Because evil and suffering were inexplicable by reference to Ahura-Mazda, Zoroaster posited the existence of a counterdeity, Ahriman, treacherous and malignant, who presided over the forces of darkness and evil. Zoroaster presented Ahura-Mazda as vastly stronger than Ahriman; but later, the priests of Zoroastrianism, the magi, emphasized the dualistic aspect of the founder's thought by insisting that Ahura-Mazda and Ahriman were evenly matched, engaged in a desperate struggle for supremacy. Only on the last day would "light" decisively triumph over "darkness," when Ahura-Mazda would overpower Ahriman and cast him into the abyss.

> Because evil and suffering were inexplicable by reference to Ahura-Mazda, Zoroaster posited the existence of a counterdeity, Ahriman, treacherous and malignant, who presided over the forces of darkness and evil.

Zoroastrianism was a personal religion, making private, spiritual demands as opposed to public and ritual ones. Unlike earlier Near Eastern cults, it did not exalt the power of a godlike king. The devotion of the Persian Dynasty to Zoroaster's teachings nevertheless made Zoroastrianism important to the conduct of Persian government and helps explain the general eclecticism and tolerance of Persian rule. Unlike the Assyrians, the Chaldeans, or even the Egyptians, all of whom tried to impose their own cultural practices on conquered peoples, the Persian kings saw themselves as presiding over an assemblage of different nations whose customs and religious beliefs they were prepared to tolerate. Whereas Mesopotamian potentates characteristically called themselves "true king," Persian rulers took the title "king of kings" or "great king," implying that they recognized the legitimacy of those other kings who ruled under the canopy of Persian overlordship.

Ahura-Mazda patronized neither tribes nor states but only individuals who served his cause of truth and justice. Humans possessed free will and could choose to sin or not to sin. Zoroastrianism urged people to be truthful, love and help one another, aid the poor, and

A Cylindrical Seal of King Darius the Great of Persia, 522–486 B.C.E. The seal shows the king in a chariot, hunting lions with a bow, with the winged representation of the god Ahura-Mazda rising above the scene behind him.

WHAT DEVELOPMENTS MARKED THE HEBREW TRANSITION FROM POLYTHEISM TO MONOTHEISM?

THE DEVELOPMENT OF HEBREW MONOTHEISM   63

practice generous hospitality. Those who did so would be rewarded in an afterlife, for the religion posited the resurrection of the dead on judgment day and their consignment to a realm either of bliss or flames. In the scriptures of the Zoroastrian faith, known as the Avesta, the rewards for righteousness are explicit.

Zoroastrianism has numerous similarities to Judaism and Christianity. Its ethical universalizing resembles the teachings of the Hebrew prophets; its heaven and hell resemble Christian ideas about the afterlife; and its concern with the day of judgment is paralleled in both these other traditions. We should not, however, think of these similarities as simple borrowings from one faith by another. The religious and intellectual traditions of the ancient Near East took shape in a world characterized by pervasive cross-cultural influences. Rarely if ever is it possible to trace an idea or a religious belief to a single, original source. Zoroastrianism, Judaism, and Christianity all emerged out of the rich cultural soup of the Iron Age Near Eastern world, as of course did the very idea of a universal religion itself.

> Although Moses is often credited with beginning the ascendancy of the cult of Yahweh, the promotion of the Yahweh cult probably took place later, under the auspices of the Levites, a tribe whose unique claims to priestly authority made them a religious elite within Hebrew society.

THE DEVELOPMENT OF HEBREW MONOTHEISM

What developments marked the Hebrew transition from polytheism to monotheism?

Of all the cultural developments that took place in the Iron Age Near East, none was of greater significance to the civilizations of the West than monotheism—the belief, that is, in but a single god, the creator and ruler of all things. This development is traditionally, and rightly, associated with the Hebrews. But even the Hebrews were not always monotheists. Those who argued for the exclusive worship of Yahweh—a group whom we shall refer to as the Yahwists—were often a minority within Hebrew society, albeit a vocal and assertive one. That the Hebrews came ultimately to regard Yahweh as the only divine being in the universe, and to root their identity as a people in such an exclusive religious outlook, is a development that can be explained only against the backdrop of the tumul-

tuous and confusing world in which Hebrew society itself arose.

FROM MONOLATRY TO MONOTHEISM

Hebrew monotheism emerged in a world conditioned by polytheism. For those who later advocated the exclusive worship of Yahweh, the early history of the Hebrews was full of embarrassments. At every turn, the Hebrews of the twelfth through tenth centuries B.C.E. can be found worshiping gods other than Yahweh. Later Hebrew kings also continued to tolerate non-Yahwist cult practices, regardless of the protests of religious purists advocating the exclusive worship of Yahweh.

Despite lingering polytheism, however, by the beginning of the first millennium Hebrew religion had clearly moved into a new stage of national *monolatry*—the exclusive worship of one god, without denying utterly the existence of others. Although Moses is often credited with beginning the ascendancy of the cult of Yahweh, the promotion of the Yahweh cult probably took place later, under the auspices of the Levites, a tribe whose unique claims to priestly authority made them a religious elite within Hebrew society. The Levites sought to enhance their own power and prestige by exalting Yahweh above the other gods traditionally revered in Hebrew and Canaanite society.

The Levites also enjoyed a higher degree of literacy than most of their fellow Hebrews. In an age of constant threats to Hebrew religious and political sovereignty, the literacy of the Levites helped preserve and promote Yahweh worship. So too did the House of David, which by promoting the Yahweh cult and centralizing it in Jerusalem helped link the political and the religious identity of the Hebrews to the worship of Yahweh as the supreme (if not yet the only) god of the universe. Nevertheless, the worship of other gods persisted. Religious figures as late as Jeremiah (c. 637–587 B.C.E.) continued to rail against "foreign" cults, and to warn of the disastrous consequences that would arise if Yahweh's people did not remain faithful to Yahweh alone.

Despite these polytheistic holdovers, some of the Hebrews' most important contributions to subsequent Western religious thought had emerged by the middle of the eighth century B.C.E. One was their unique *transcendent theology*. In the eyes of his priests and prophets, Yahweh was not part of nature but entirely outside of it.

He could therefore be understood in purely intellectual or abstract terms, entirely apart from the operations of the natural world he had created. Complementing this principle of divine transcendence was the belief that Yahweh had appointed humans to be the rulers of nature by divine mandate. The famous line from Genesis in which Yahweh orders Adam and Eve to "be fruitful and multiply, and replenish the earth and subdue it, and have dominion over . . . every living thing," stands in striking contrast with Babylonian creation accounts, in which humans are created merely to serve the gods, "so that the gods might be at ease." Finally, while not fully developed, universalizing ethical considerations are also present in Hebrew religious thought during this period.

The Hebrews honored Yahweh during the period of monolatry by subscribing to moral precepts, rituals, and taboos. The exact form of the Ten Commandments may not have existed before the Babylonian Captivity. But the Hebrews certainly observed some commandments, including injunctions against murder, adultery, bearing false witness, and "coveting anything that is thy neighbor's." In addition they observed ritualistic demands,

Seal of Abdi, Servant of Hosea. An eighth-century B.C.E. Hebrew seal whose owner, Abdi, was a royal official for Hosea (732–722 B.C.E.), the last ruler of the Northern Kingdom of Israel. The winged sun disk on which the figure stands and the figure's strongly Egyptian appearance hint at the religious diversity of the Northern Kingdom in its final centuries.

such as refraining from labor on the seventh day and not boiling a kid in its mother's milk. But the moral standards enjoined by Yahweh on the Hebrew community were not necessarily binding when the Hebrews dealt with outsiders. Lending at interest, for example, was not acceptable between Hebrews, but was quite acceptable between a Hebrew and a non-Hebrew. Such distinctions applied also to more serious issues, such as the killing of civilians in battle. When the Hebrews conquered territories in Canaan, they took "all the spoil of the cities, and every man they smote with the sword . . . until they had destroyed them, neither left they any to breathe." Rather than having any doubts about such a brutal policy, the Yahwists believed it had been ordered by their Lord himself—indeed, that Yahweh had inspired the Canaanites to resist so that there would be reason to slaughter them: "For it was of the Lord to harden their hearts, that they should come against Israel in battle, that He might destroy them utterly" (Joshua 11:20).

The fragmentation of the united Hebrew Kingdom after Solomon's death was accelerated by the Assyrians, who under Sargon II absorbed the northern kingdom as a province and deported nearly 28,000 Hebrews—the famous Ten Lost Tribes of Israel—to the interior of the Assyrian Empire. The southern Kingdom of Judah survived but found it expedient to become an Assyrian vassal state. As we have seen, however, political collaboration with the Assyrians also meant acceptance of the Assyrian god Assur.

This Assyrian threat was the whetstone on which the Yahwist prophets sharpened their demands for an exclusive monotheism. Prophets were political as much as religious figures, and most understood that military resistance to the Assyrians was futile. If the Hebrews were to survive as a people, then they had to exalt the one thing that separated them from everyone else in the region: the worship of Yahweh. The prophets' insistence, during the eighth and seventh centuries B.C.E., that Yahweh alone should be worshiped and that no other gods even existed, was thus an aggressive reaction to the equally aggressive promotion of Assur by the Assyrians. Nor could there be any room for compromise in the Yahwists' demand for a thoroughgoing and exclusive monotheism. Only by worshiping Yahweh alone could the Hebrews combat the insinuating effects of Assyrian religious imperialism.

Despite some differences in emphasis, the Hebrew prophets' messages were sufficiently similar to each other to warrant treating them as if they formed a single coherent body of religious thought. Three doc-

WHAT DEVELOPMENTS MARKED THE HEBREW TRANSITION FROM POLYTHEISM TO MONOTHEISM?

THE DEVELOPMENT OF HEBREW MONOTHEISM   65

trines made up the core of the prophets' teachings: (1) Absolute monotheism: Yahweh is the ruler of the universe, he even makes use of nations other than the Hebrews to accomplish his purposes, and the gods of others are false gods. (2) Yahweh is exclusively a god of righteousness: he wills only the good, and evil in the world comes from humanity, not from him. (3) Because Yahweh is righteous, he demands ethical behavior above all else and he cares less for ritual and sacrifice than that his followers should "seek justice, relieve the oppressed, protect the fatherless, and plead for the widow."

JUDAISM TAKES SHAPE

Through their revolutionary insistence that Yahwist monotheism was the cornerstone of the Hebrews' identity as a people, the Yahwists made it possible for the Hebrews to survive under Assyrian domination. As the Assyrian threat receded in the late seventh century B.C.E., the Yahwists triumphed religiously and politically. The new king of Judah, Josiah (621–609 B.C.E.) was a committed monotheist who employed prominent prophets at his court, including Jeremiah.

To the dismay of the Yahwists, however, Josiah died in battle against the Egyptians. With his death, the monotheists fell hard from power. The great prophet Jeremiah was placed under house arrest, denied the right to speak in public, and finally carried off into Egypt where he was murdered. All the while, he continued to denounce the corruption of the Hebrews, suggesting that they would fall before the Chaldeans just as they had before the Assyrians, in punishment for their disobedience to Yahweh.

Within a generation of King Josiah's death, Jeremiah's predictions were fulfilled. The Chaldeans under Nebuchadnezzar conquered Jerusalem, destroyed the Temple, and carried thousands of Hebrews off to Babylon. The Babylonian Captivity brought many challenges for the Hebrews living there, paramount among them being the maintenance of their religious and ethnic identity. The leading voices in defining that identity continued to be the patriotic Yahwists, the same people who would later spearhead the return to Palestine after Cyrus's capture of Babylon. Among the Yahwists, the prophetic tradition thus continued, even in a foreign land. The prophet Ezekiel stressed that salvation could be found only through religious purity,

The Babylonian Captivity brought many challenges for the Hebrews living there, paramount among them being the maintenance of their religious and ethnic identity.

which meant ignoring all foreign gods and acknowledging only Yahweh. States and empires and thrones did not matter in the long run, Ezekiel said. What mattered for the Hebrews living in exile was the creature God had made in his image—man—and the relationship between that creator god, his chosen people, and his creation.

The disassociation of political identity from religious practice that triumphed during the Babylonian Captivity was decisive for the emergence of Judaism as a universalizing religion. In Babylon, Judaism became something more than simply the national cult of the Hebrews. No longer was Yahweh's worship tied to any particular political entity or dynasty, for after 586 B.C.E., neither a Hebrew state nor a Hebrew ruling dynasty existed. Nor was his worship tied to any specific place. In Babylon and in the Holy Land, Judaism survived the destruction of the Temple and the exile of the Hebrew people from their land. In the ancient world, this was an unparalleled achievement. No other ancient people is known to have survived so long an exile from its central holy place.

After 538 B.C.E., when Cyrus permitted the Hebrews of Babylon to return to the Holy Land and rebuild the Temple, Jerusalem became once again the central holy place of Hebrew religious life. But the new developments that had arisen within Judaism during the captivity would prove lasting. Increasingly, Jewish religious teachings would be presented in ethical terms, as obligations owed by all human beings toward their creator, independent of place or political identity. Ritual requirements and religious taboos, by contrast, would remain the exclusive obligation of Jews, for whom they symbolized the special covenant that bound Yahweh to his people.

The notion of a creator god who existed outside time, nature, place, and kingship became ever more powerful in Second Temple Judaism, and would be taken up later by Christianity and Islam. So too would the Hebrew claim that Yahweh was a jealous god who would not permit his followers to worship any other divinity in any form. In the context of the ancient world, both remained peculiar ideas that would not be fully absorbed for a millennium. But despite their peculiarity, the transcendental monotheism developed by the Hebrews would ultimately become a fundamental feature of the religious outlook of all Western civilizations.

CONCLUSION

The centuries from 1700 to 500 B.C.E. were an age of empires. The two great powers of the second millennium B.C.E. were New Kingdom Egypt and the Hittite Empire of Anatolia. But a host of lesser empires also emerged during this period, including Minoan Crete, Mycenaean Greece, the Kingdom of Mitanni, and Middle Kingdom Assyria. All these empires were sustained by a sophisticated network of international trade and diplomacy; we can speak even of an international system binding them together by the Late Bronze Age. At the heart of all these Bronze Age empires, however, lay a very old model of social organization: the Mesopotamian city-state as it had developed in Sumer. With the arguable exception of New Kingdom Egypt, none of these empires came close to being an integrated, territorial state. Instead, they were collections of cities, ruled by kings who claimed some sort of divine sanction for their rule.

Between 1200 and 1000 B.C.E., the devastation wrought by the Sea Peoples cleared the way for a number of new, small states to emerge in the Near and Middle East, including the Phoenicians, the Philistines, the Hebrews, and the Lydians. Many of the crucial cultural and economic developments of the early Iron Age began in these small states, including alphabetic writing, coinage, exclusive monotheism, and mercantile colonization. But the dominant states of the early Iron Age Mediterranean world continued to be the great land empires centered in western Asia: first the Assyrians, then the Chaldeans, and finally the Persians.

On the surface, it may therefore appear as if nothing very dramatic had changed since the middle of the second millennium B.C.E. But such geographical continuities can be deceiving. The empires of the early Iron Age were quite different from the collections of quasi-independent city-states that had dominated the Near East a thousand years before. These new empires were much more highly unified than earlier empires had been. They had capital cities, centrally managed systems of communication, sophisticated administrative structures, and ideologies that justified their aggressive imperialism as a religious obligation imposed on them by a single, all-powerful god. They commanded armies of unprecedented size, and they demanded from their subjects a degree of obedience impossible for any Bronze Age empire to imagine.

At the same time that these great land empires were declaring themselves to be the chosen instruments of their god's divine will, we also mark the emergence of more personalized monotheistic traditions in the early Iron Age. Zoroastrianism in particular proved fully compatible with an imperialist ideology and became the driving spiritual force behind the Persian Empire. Judaism, by contrast, was forged in the struggle to resist the religious imperialism of Assyria and Chaldean Babylonia. But both Zoroastrianism and Judaism added an important new emphasis on personal ethical conduct as a fundamental element in religious life, and both pioneered the development of authoritative, written scriptures as a foundation for their religious teachings. These developments would exercise an enormous influence on Western religious life, and would provide the models on which Christianity and Islam would ultimately erect their own imperial traditions.

KEY TERMS

Indo-European

Hittites

Assyrians

Mycenaeans

Akhenaten

Minoans

Phoenicians

Cyrus

Zoroastrians

David

SELECTED READINGS

On New Kingdom Egypt, see also the readings listed in Chapter One.

Aubet, Maria Eugenia. *Phoenicia and the West: Politics, Colonies, and Trade*. Trans. Mary Turton. Cambridge, 1993. An intelligent and thought-provoking examination of Phoenician civilization and its influence.

Boardman, John. *Assyrian and Babylonian Empires and Other States of the Near East from the Eighth to the Sixth Centuries B.C.* New York, 1991. Scholarly and authoritative.

Boardman, John. *Persia and the West*. London, 2000. A great book by a distinguished classical scholar, with a particular focus on art and architecture as projections of Persian imperial ideologies.

Boyce, Mary. *Textual Sources for the Study of Zoroastrianism*. Totowa, N.J., 1984. An invaluable collection.

Bryce, Trevor. *The Kingdom of the Hittites*. Oxford, 1998. And *Life and Society in the Hittite World*. Oxford, 2002. An extraordinary new synthesis, now the standard account of Hittite political, military, and daily life.

Curtis, John. *Ancient Persia*. Cambridge, Mass., 1990. Concise, solid, reliable.

Dever, William. *Who Were the Early Israelites and Where Did They Come From?* Grand Rapids, Mich., 2003. A balanced, fair-minded account with excellent bibliographical guidance to recent work.

Dickinson, O. T. P. K. *The Aegean Bronze Age*. Cambridge, 1994. An excellent summary of archaeological evidence and scholarly argument concerning Minoan, Mycenaean, and other cultures of the Bronze Age Aegean basin.

Dothan, Trude, and Moshe Dothan. *Peoples of the Sea: The Search for the Philistines*. New York, 1992. The essential starting point for Philistine culture and its links to the Aegean basin.

Drews, Robert. *The End of the Bronze Age: Changes in Warfare and the Catastrophe ca. 1200 B.C.* Princeton, N.J., 1993. A stimulating analysis and survey, with excellent bibliographies.

Finkelstein, Israel, and Nadav Na'aman, eds. *From Nomadism to Monarchy: Archaeological and Historical Aspects of Early Israel*. Jerusalem, 1994. Scholarly articles on the Hebrews' transformation from pastoralists to a sedentary society focused on Yahweh worship.

Fitton, J. Lesley. *Minoans: Peoples of the Past* (British Museum Publications). London, 2002. A careful, reliable debunking of myths about the Minoans, written for nonspecialists.

Kamm, Antony. *The Israelites: An Introduction*. New York, 1999. A short, accessible history of the land and people of Israel up to 135 C.E., aimed at students and general readers.

Kuhrt, Amélie. *The Ancient Near East, c. 3000–330 B.C.* 2 vols. London and New York, 1995. An outstanding survey, written for students, that includes Egypt and Israel as well as Mesopotamia, Babylonia, Assyria, and Persia. Excellent bibliographies.

Luckenbill, Daniel David, ed. and trans. *Ancient Records of Assyria and Babylonia*. 2 vols. Chicago, 1926–1927. Still one of the best and most readily accessible collections of primary sources on Assyrian attitudes and policies in war, religion, and politics.

Metzger, Bruce M., and Michael D. Coogan, eds. *The Oxford Companion to the Bible*. New York, 1993. An outstanding reference work, with contributions by leading authorities.

Niditch, Susan. *Ancient Israelite Religion*. New York, 1997. A short, suggestive introduction designed for students, emphasizing the diversity of Hebrew religious practice.

Redford, Donald B. *Egypt, Canaan, and Israel in Ancient Times*. Princeton, N.J., 1992. An up-to-date overview of the interactions between these peoples from about 1200 B.C.E. to the beginning of the Common Era.

Renfrew, Colin. *Archaeology and Language: The Puzzle of Indo-European Origins*. Cambridge, 1987. A masterful but controversial work by one of the most creative archaeologists of the twentieth century.

Saggs, H. W. F. *The Might That Was Assyria*. London, 1984. A lively narrative history of the Assyrian Empire, with analysis of the institutions that underlay its strength.

Sandars, Nancy K. *The Sea Peoples: Warriors of the Ancient Mediterranean*. Rev. ed. London, 1985. An introductory account aimed at students and scholars.

Tubb, Jonathan N., and Rupert L. Chapman. *Archaeology and the Bible*. London, 1990. A good starting point for students that illustrates clearly the difficulties in linking archaeological evidence to biblical accounts of early Hebrew history and society.

Wood, Michael. *In Search of the Trojan War*. New York, 1985. Aimed at a general audience, this carefully researched and engagingly written book is an excellent introduction to the late Bronze Age context of the Trojan War.

PART II
THE GREEK AND ROMAN WORLDS

THE CLASSICAL CIVILIZATIONS of Greece and Rome dominated the Mediterranean world from the sixth century B.C.E. until the sixth century C.E. Both drew heavily on the traditions and achievements of the ancient Near East, but each represented a distinct departure from this earlier world. Together, however, Greece and Rome constituted the seedbed out of which all subsequent Western civilizations would develop.

Beginning in the eighth century B.C.E., Greek civilization took shape in the warring, particularistic, and fiercely independent city-states that grew up around the Aegean and the Adriatic seas. But it was not until the end of the fourth century B.C.E., when the conquests of Alexander the Great created an empire that stretched from Greece through Persia to India and Egypt, that Greek civilization became the common cultural currency of the Mediterranean and Near Eastern worlds.

In central Italy, the city of Rome was slowly extending its dominion over the Italian peninsula. In the last two centuries B.C.E., Rome expanded its rule throughout the entire Mediterranean world and into western Europe. By the end of the first century C.E., Rome had built an empire larger even than Alexander's. In an extraordinary triumph of organization, discipline, and cultural adaptability, the Romans maintained that empire, substantially intact, for the next 400 years.

	POLITICS	SOCIETY AND CULTURE	ECONOMY	INTERNATIONAL RELATIONS
B.C.E. 1150		The Dark Age of Greece (1150–800 B.C.E.)	Greek trade increases in Aegean Sea (1000–800 B.C.E.)	
		Introduction of Phoenician alphabet into Greece (900 B.C.E.)		
	Birth of the Greek polis (800 B.C.E.)	Archaic Greece (800–480 B.C.E.)		Carthage founded (800 B.C.E.)
		Homer's *Iliad* and *Odyssey* are written down (800 B.C.E.)		
		First Greek colonies appear (800–600 B.C.E.)		Rome founded (753 B.C.E.)
		First Olympic games (776 B.C.E.)		
	Spartans enslave Messenians (700–680 B.C.E.)			
	Kylon sent into exile for tyranny (632 B.C.E.)			
600	Hoplite tactics become military standard (600 B.C.E.)		Solon encourages cash-crop farming and urban industries (600–550 B.C.E.)	Miletus becomes colonial power (600–400 B.C.E.)
	Tarquin the Proud gains kingship over Rome (543 B.C.E.)			
500	Roman Republic (527–500 B.C.E.)		Athens becomes principal exporter of olive oil, wine, and pottery (500 B.C.E.)	
	Xerxes succeeds Darius the Great (486 B.C.E.)	Sophocles, author of *Oedipus*, (496–406 B.C.E.)		The Ionian Revolution (499–494 B.C.E.)
	Plebian rebellion leads to Law of the Twelve Tables (480 B.C.E.)	Emergence of Greek sculpture (490–480 B.C.E.)		Persians sack Eritrea (490 B.C.E.)
		Golden age of Greek civilization (480–323 B.C.E.)		Hellenic League formed (480 B.C.E.)
		Socrates (469–399 B.C.E.)		Persian army defeated at battle of Salamis (480 B.C.E.)
	Pericles elected strategos of Athens (462–461 B.C.E.)	Thucydides (460–400 B.C.E.)		
		Sophists emerge (450 B.C.E.)		Athens gains control of Delian League (450s B.C.E.)
		Parthenon built in Athens (447–438 B.C.E.)		Peloponnesian War (431–404 B.C.E.)
		Plato, author of the *Republic* (429–349 B.C.E.)		
		Aristotle, author of *Nicomachean Ethics* (384–322 B.C.E.)		Corinthian War (394–387 B.C.E.)
	Reign of Philip II (359–336 B.C.E.)	Greek migrations into western Asia (325–225 B.C.E.)	Alexander's conquests open commercial routes between Greece and Asia (323 B.C.E.)	Philip II defeats Greek alliance and forms League of Corinth (338 B.C.E.)
	Reign of Alexander III, the Great (336–323 B.C.E.)	Euclid, *Elements of Geometry* (300 B.C.E.)		Reign of Alexander the Great (336–323 B.C.E.)
300				Ptolemy establishes dynasty in Egypt (332 B.C.E.)
				Alexander defeats the Persian army (331 B.C.E.)
				Seleucus establishes dynasty in Persia (281 B.C.E.)
			First standard coinage in Rome (269 B.C.E.)	Punic Wars (264–146 B.C.E.)
	Roman slave revolts (146–130 B.C.E.)			Carthage razed (146 B.C.E.)
100		Cicero (106–43 B.C.E.)	Roman commerce relies on 1 million slaves (100 B.C.E.)	
	Spartacus' revolt (73–71 B.C.E.)	Virgil, author of the *Aeneid* (70–19 B.C.E.)		
		Horace (65–8 B.C.E.)		
	Caesar defeats Pompey (48 B.C.E.)	Livy, author of *History of Rome* (59 B.C.E.–17 C.E.)		
	Octavian becomes emperor (27 B.C.E.)	Ovid, author of *Metamorphoses* (43 B.C.E.–17 C.E.)		
	The Principate of early Roman Empire (27 B.C.E.–180 C.E.)			

POLITICS	SOCIETY AND CULTURE	ECONOMY	INTERNATIONAL RELATIONS	
				C.E. 10
	Jesus (c. 4 B.C.E.–c. 30 C.E.)			
	Saul of Tarsus, or Paul the Apostle (10–67 C.E.)			
	Christians begin arriving in Rome (40 C.E.)		Claudius enters Britain (48 C.E.)	
Pax Romana (96–180 C.E.)	Gospel of Mark is written (70 C.E.)	Romans excel in engineering aqueducts and roads and develop new tax system under Trajan (98–117 C.E.)	Romans destroy the Temple of Jerusalem (70 C.E.)	
			Romans destroy the city of Jerusalem (135 C.E.)	100
The Third-Century Crisis in Roman Empire (180–284 C.E.)				
	Neoplatonism (200–300 C.E.)	Roman Empire loses one third of population due to disease, low birthrate, and war (180–294 C.E.)		
	Growth of monasticism (300s C.E.)		Goths defeat Romans and cross the Danube (251 C.E.)	
The Dominate or later Roman Empire (284–610 C.E.)		Currency is stabilized and new coinage introduced under Diocletian (284–305 C.E.)		
Diocletian, soldier-emperor (284–305 C.E.)				
	The Great Persecution of Christians (303–313 C.E.)			300
Reign of Constantine over Western Roman Empire (312–324 C.E.)	Conversion of Constantine to Christianity (312 C.E.)			
Reign of Constantine over Roman Empire from Constantinople (324–337 C.E.)	Saint Jerome (c. 340–420)		Council of Nicea condemns Arianism (325 C.E.)	
	Saint Ambrose (c. 340–397)		Visigoths defeat Romans (378 C.E.)	
	Saint Augustine, author of *Confessions* and *On the City of God* (354–430)			
	Christianity becomes official Roman religion (c. 392)		Visigoths sack Rome (410 C.E.)	400
	Saint Benedict (480–547)			
			Vandals sack Rome from the sea (455 C.E.)	500
Justinian rules as emperor in East (527–565 C.E.)			Justinian recaptures Italy from Ostrogoths (536 C.E.)	
Corpus Juris Civilus (534 C.E.)			The Lombards seize northern parts of Italy (568 C.E.)	
Tenure of Pope Gregory I (Saint Gregory the Great) (590–604 C.E.)	Papacy of Saint Gregory the Great (590–604)			

CHAPTER THREE

THE GREEK
EXPERIMENT

THE IMAGE that comes most often to mind when Americans or Europeans think of the ancient world is the Acropolis of Athens, its gleaming temples and shrines still impressive despite their age and ruined condition. The rationality, harmony, and repose of this symbol of Greek culture seem to many to bespeak something quintessentially "Western": the triumph of reason and freedom over the "superstition" and "despotism" of "Eastern" cultures such as Assyria or Persia.

Such easy and self-congratulatory contrasts tell us more about ourselves than they do about the ancient Greeks. In fact, Greek civilization has been deeply influenced by its Near East neighbors from the Mycenaean Period until the present day. The achievements of classical Greek civilization would have been impossible without the debt Greece owed to Phoenician, Assyrian, and Egyptian examples.

The flowering of Greek civilization during the first millennium B.C.E. is nonetheless a watershed in the development of Western civilizations. Building on their historical experiences after the Bronze Age collapse, the Greeks of the Iron Age came to cherish assumptions and values that differed greatly from those of their Near Eastern neighbors. Human dignity, individual liberty, participatory government, artistic innovation, scientific investigation, constitutional experimentation, confidence in the creative powers of the human mind—the Greeks espoused all of these values, although, as ever in human affairs, practice often fell short of their ideals.

What we mean by such terms as *democracy, equality, justice,* and *freedom* differs from what the Greeks meant by them. Nonetheless, the modern West can find an intelligibility in the institutions and beliefs of this tenacious, quarrelsome, and energetic people, whose small-scale societies started a cultural revolution and created a civilization distinctly different from any before it. The democracies of the modern Western world are not the only heirs of this Greek experiment, but they are unimaginable without it.

FOCUS QUESTIONS

• What cultural changes marked the end of the Dark Age of Greece?

• How did the emergence of hoplite tactics affect Greek political norms?

• How and why did the Athenian, Spartan, and Milesian poleis differ from each other?

• How were the Greek armies able to defeat the much larger Persian forces?

• To what extent was the culture of Athens in the golden age the product of Athenian democracy?

• How did the Peloponnesian War influence Greek philosophy?

THE DARK AGE OF GREECE (1150–800 B.C.E.)

What cultural changes marked the end of the Dark Age of Greece?

By the end of the twelfth century, the last remnants of Mycenaean civilization had vanished, and Greece entered an undocumented Dark Age. Mainland Greece witnessed depopulation of up to 90 percent in the century or so following 1200 B.C.E. Except at Athens, the great citadels were destroyed in the conflagrations at the end of the Bronze Age; and even at Athens, the population steadily declined.

Depopulation had severe effects on the social organization, economy, and material culture in Greece. Settlements shrank in size and moved inland, away from vulnerable locations near the sea. Pottery and burial remains suggest a world that remained static and backward, cut off from the centers of Near Eastern civilization. Even nearby Greek communities had little economic contact with each other. Some villages may have had chiefs, but a chief's home and material possessions differed little from those of his neighbors. This Dark Age background, with its presumptions of the political and economic equality of self-sufficient households, had a profound effect on the later political assumptions of the classical Greeks.

HOMER AND THE HEROIC TRADITION

By the year 1000 B.C.E., the complete isolation of Greece was ending, and Greek society was becoming gradually more complex. Pottery also became more sophisticated, reflecting an upswing in the material culture and prosperity of the Greek mainland, and providing Greek traders with a valuable commodity to exchange for luxury goods from abroad.

As trade became an increasingly important feature of the Dark Age Greek economy, wealth increased and social stratification became more pronounced. A small group of aristocrats began to emerge, who justified their preeminence as a reflection of their own superior qualities as the "best men." Wealth alone was not sufficient to establish aristocratic standing. A great man had also to be a singer of songs, a doer of deeds, a winner of battles, and above all favored by the gods. In short, he had to be a hero.

Most of what we know about the heroic ideal of late Dark Age Greece derives from the *Iliad* and the *Odyssey*, epic poems ascribed to the authorship of Homer, but not written down until after 800 B.C.E. Homer depicts a world in which competition and status are of paramount concern to the warrior elite. Competition among aristocratic households frequently led to violence, as it did during the Trojan War. But it could also take religious form in the creation of hero cults. The heroic ideal thus became a deeply ingrained feature of Greek society, which Homer's epics would preserve and propagate throughout the classical period and beyond.

FOREIGN CONTACTS AND THE RISE OF THE POLIS

The ninth century B.C.E. saw dramatic changes throughout the Aegean basin. Contacts between Greeks and Phoenicians intensified. Most crucial, the Greeks adopted the Phoenician alphabet, improving it by converting unneeded consonantal symbols to represent vowels. The rolling melody and power of Homeric epic could now not only be heard but also recorded and read. The Phoenicians also introduced many artistic and literary traditions of the Near East into Greece, which the Greeks incorporated and reshaped to their own purposes.

The Phoenicians also pointed the way to a new activity among the Greeks—seafaring. Until the tenth century B.C.E., most Greek traders waited at home for the Phoenicians to come to them. By the end of the Dark Age, however, Greeks had copied Phoenician designs for merchant vessels, allowing them to set out on trading ventures of their own and also to engage in piracy. As commercial activity increased, significant numbers of Greeks began to move among the homeland, the islands, and Anatolia, foreshadowing the colonial explosion that would issue from the Aegean in the eighth and seventh centuries B.C.E.

These economic and cultural developments were accompanied by dramatic growth in the Greek population. Around Athens, the population may have quadrupled during the ninth and early eighth centuries. Such rapid population growth placed heavy demands on the resources of Greece, a mountainous country with limited agricultural land. As smaller villages grew into towns, the inhabitants of these rival communities came into more frequent contact with each other. Some degree of economic, political, and social cooperation

How did the emergence of hoplite tactics affect Greek political norms?

Archaic Greece (800–480 b.c.e.) 75

The Parthenon. The largest and most famous of Athenian temples, the Parthenon is considered the classic example of Doric architecture. Its columns were made more graceful by tapering them in a slight curve toward the top. Its friezes and pediments were decorated with lifelike sculptures of prancing horses, fighting giants, and confident deities.

among the inhabitants of these towns soon became necessary. But the heroic values of Dark Age Greek society did not make such cooperation easy. Each local community treasured its traditional autonomy and independence, celebrated its own religious cults, and honored its own aristocratic luminaries. On what basis, then, could such communities unite?

The Greek solution to this challenge was the *polis*. The Greek polis was a unique blend of institutional and informal structures of organization. Although poleis (the plural of polis) differed widely in size and organization, most were structured around a political and social center known as the *asty*, where markets and important meetings were held and where the basic business of the polis was conducted in the open air. Surrounding the urbanized asty was the *khora*, the "land." The khora of a larger polis might support several other towns besides the asty, as well as numerous villages; for example, all the residents of the entire territory of Attica were considered to be citizens of Athens. The vast majority of Athenian citizens were thus farmers, who might come to the asty to participate in the affairs of their polis but who did not reside in the urban center.

Synoikismos (the "bringing together of dwellings") was how Greeks described the process of early polis formation. Some poleis took shape around defensible hilltops such as the Acropolis in Athens. Greeks may also have borrowed a Near Eastern (and particularly Phoenician) practice of orienting an urban center around a temple precinct. In Greece, however, the central temple site of a polis was not always located within the city's walls; at Argos, for example, the massive temple to Hera was located several miles away from any sizable settlement. As was typical of Greek life generally, there was probably no standard pattern by which the early Greek poleis took shape.

Archaic Greece (800–480 b.c.e.)

How did the emergence of hoplite tactics affect Greek political norms?

With the emergence of the polis and the return of writing and literacy, the Archaic Age begins. After languishing in obscurity for nearly four centuries during the Dark Age, Greek civilization now burst forth with breathtaking dynamism and energy. Archaic Greece is remarkable not only for its achievements but also for its willingness to explore new avenues in religion, society, and politics. Aptly, this period has also been called the "Age of Experiment."

COLONIZATION AND PANHELLENISM

In the eighth and seventh centuries B.C.E., smaller-scale Greek trading ventures and migrations throughout the Aegean developed into a full-fledged colonization effort. Each colony was an independent foundation, with emotional and sentimental ties to its mother city, but no political obligations. By the end of the sixth century B.C.E., Greeks had founded several hundred new colonies from the Black Sea to the western Mediterranean, permanently altering the cultural geography of the Mediterranean world. The western shores of Anatolia would remain a stronghold of Greek culture until the end of the Middle Ages; so many Greeks settled in southern Italy and Sicily that the Romans called the region Magna Graecia, "Greater Greece." By the fourth century B.C.E., more Greeks lived in Magna Graecia than in Greece itself. Greek colonies could also be found farther westward, along the southern coasts of France and Spain.

Colonial expansion intensified Greek contacts with other cultures, especially Egypt and Phoenicia. At the same time, however, intensified contact with other cultures sharpened Greeks' awareness of their own common identity and peculiarity as "Hellenes" (the Greeks' name for themselves). Such self-conscious "Hellenism" did not necessarily lead to greater political cooperation among the fiercely independent poleis. Like the Sumerians, the Greeks were particularists who had little use for permanent political associations larger than the individual polis. But it did encourage the growth of Panhellenic ("all-Greeks") cult sites such as the Oracle of Delphi, and of Panhellenic festivals such as the Olympic Games. Predictably, such competitions did little to stop contentiousness and rivalry among the poleis; but they did strengthen the Greeks' sense that they shared a common culture, despite their political and linguistic differences.

HOPLITE WARFARE

During the Dark Age, the military power of a Greek community rested with the elite, who had the time, resources, and training to become "Homeric" warrior heroes. Common foot soldiers played a secondary role as followers and supporters of the aristocratic warriors who dueled in single combat. This aristocratic monopoly on military prowess gave the aristocracy tremendous political and social leverage within the nascent poleis. As a result, aristocrats dominated political offices and priesthoods as well as economic life.

The introduction of hoplite tactics during the Archaic Period brought aristocratic military dominance to an end. Hoplites were foot soldiers, armed with spears

Hoplite Infantry Advancing into Combat. This Corinthian vase, dating to around 620 B.C.E., is the earliest known depiction of hoplites fighting in a phalanx formation.

How did the emergence of hoplite tactics affect Greek political norms?

Archaic Greece (800–480 b.c.e.) 77

or short swords, and protected by a large round shield (a *hoplon*), a breastplate, a helmet, and sometimes wrist and leg guards. In battle, hoplites stood shoulder to shoulder in a close formation called a phalanx, several rows across and several lines deep, with each hoplite carrying his shield on the left arm to protect the un-shielded right side of the man standing next to him. In his right hand each hoplite carried a thrusting weapon such as a spear or short sword, so that an approaching phalanx presented a nearly impenetrable wall of armor and weaponry to its opponents. If a man in the front rank fell, the one behind him stepped up to take his place; indeed, the weight of the entire phalanx was liter-ally behind the front line, each soldier aiding the assault by leaning with his shield into the man in front of him. The tight formation and heavy armor (as much as sev-enty pounds including the shield) required but one skill: the ability to stay together. As long as the phalanx remained intact, it was a nearly unbeatable formation. By the end of the seventh century b.c.e., hoplite tactics were a standard element in Greek warfare.

The result was a social and political revolution. Because every polis needed a hoplite force to protect its independence, farmers who could afford the requisite armor soon became a political and social force within the archaic polis—a "hoplite class." But the sacrifices demanded by hoplite warfare were great, and the men who had now become indispensable to the polis's survival quickly grew restless without a share in its decision making. Scholars once believed their disquiet was sufficient by itself to force concessions from the aristocrats, including access to political decision mak-ing and the writing down of laws to guarantee "equal" justice. But the real impetus toward political change may in fact have come from disgruntled aristocrats.

ARISTOCRATIC CULTURE AND THE RISE OF TYRANNY

The aristocrats of the Archaic Age pursued not only wealth, power, and glory but also a distinct culture and defining lifestyle. Holding office and participating in politics was part of this lifestyle; but so too was the symposium, an intimate gathering at which elite men would enjoy wine (sometimes in prodigious quantities), poetry (ranging from epics to bawdy drinking songs), dancing competitions, and female courtesans who pro-vided both musical and sexual services. Respectable women were excluded from such meetings, as they were from all other aspects of social and political life. So too were nonaristocratic men. The symposium was

thus far more than a social occasion. It was an essential feature of aristocratic male life within the polis.

Homosexuality was another important aspect of aristocratic culture in the Archaic Period. Appropriate aristocratic homosexual behavior was regulated by social custom. Typically, a man in his late twenties to late thir-ties and on the rise in political life would take as his lover and protégé an aristocratic youth in his early to mid-teens. The two would form a close and intimate bond of friendship, in which sexual intercourse played an im-portant role. This intimate bond between man and boy was believed to benefit the younger partner, as he learned the workings of government and society, and through his older lover made important political and so-cial connections that would benefit him later in life.

A whole complex of values, ideas, practices, and assumptions thus informed aristocratic identity in the Archaic Period. As a result, it was impossible for those outside this elite world to participate fully in the public life of the polis. By the middle of the Archaic Age, however, the circle of the aristocratic elite was narrow-ing even further. As a result, many aristocrats were left on the outside of their own culture, looking in.

As the circles of political power narrowed during the seventh century b.c.e., violence between aristocratic groups increased, ultimately giving rise to the emer-gence of tyranny as an alternative form of government. The word *tyrannos* was not originally Greek but bor-rowed from Lydia, signifying someone who seized

A Bearded Greek Male and His Young Lover. This illus-tration is from a red-figure cup, c. 480 b.c.e.

THRASYBOULOS ON HOW TO BE A TYRANT

The fifth-century historian Herodotus relates how Periander, tyrant of Corinth from 627 to 587 B.C.E., sought advice from his older contemporary Thrasyboulos of Miletus on how best to secure tyrannical power. The excerpt here describes Thrasyboulos's response to Periander's emissary and the Corinthian's response to his strange reply. Although Herodotus's negative attitude toward tyranny is typical of later classical thought, Periander and his father before him had in fact been instrumental in breaking a narrow aristocratic regime and increasing Corinth's commercial prosperity.

At the beginning Periander was gentler than his father [Cypselus] had been. But afterwards, when he had dealt with Thrasyboulos, prince of Miletus, he became yet bloodier than Cypselus. . . . Thrasyboulos had led out Periander's messenger, outside the city, and with him entered a sown field; then he walked through the corn, questioning, and again questioning the herald, about his coming from Corinth. And ever and again as he saw one of the ears growing above the rest he would strike it down, and what he struck down he threw away, until by this means he had destroyed all the fairest and strongest of the corn. So he passed through the whole place and, having added no suggestions, sent the herald away. When the herald came back to Corinth, Periander was anxious to know what suggestion Thrasyboulos had made. But the man said that Thrasyboulos had made no suggestion at all, and indeed he wondered what sort of man this was he had been sent to, a madman and a destroyer of his own property. . . . But Periander understood the act of Thrasyboulos and grasped in his mind that what he was telling him was that he should murder the most eminent of the citizens. And so from this time forth he displayed every form of wickedness toward his fellow countrymen. Whatever Cypselus had spared of death and banishment, Periander completed.

Herodotus, v. 92. Trans. David Grene (Chicago and London, 1987), pp. 397–398 (somewhat revised).

QUESTION FOR ANALYSIS

1. Tyrants in Greece sometimes ruled by terror and other times by popular consent. Can you suggest positive aspects of tyrant rule in the Greek states? Was Thrasyboulos simply a bad example, an unheroic character lacking in aristocratic virtue?

power and ruled outside the traditional constitutional framework. A tyrant in Archaic Greece was thus not necessarily an abusive ruler. Often, he was an aristocrat who had tired of his exclusion from the elite or had become frustrated with the petty rows of aristocratic factions within the polis. To strengthen themselves, tyrants appealed instead to the hoplite class, whose armed might could propel them to a position of sole power. In return, tyrants would then extend rights of political participation to the hoplites, while striving to retain the reins of power in their own hands. This was an inherently unstable state of affairs, because after the original tyrant had fulfilled the wishes of the hoplites, the continuance of tyranny became an obstacle to even

How and why did the Athenian, Spartan, and Milesian poleis differ from each other?

THE ARCHAIC POLIS IN ACTION   79

greater power for the people, the *demos*. For this reason, tyrannies rarely lasted for more than two generations. Tyranny more often served as a way station on the road from aristocracy to more broadly participatory forms of government, such as democracy.

THE ARCHAIC POLIS IN ACTION

How and why did the Athenian, Spartan, and Milesian poleis differ from each other?

The Archaic poleis developed in very different ways. To illustrate this diversity, we examine three particularly well documented examples: Athens, Sparta, and Miletus. None, however, is "typical" of the historical development of the Greek poleis as a whole. There were approximately 1,000 such poleis in Greece. About most of them we know almost nothing. It seems unlikely, however, that amid such diversity we will ever be able to describe a "typical" polis.

ATHENS

Athens emerged from the Dark Age with a distinctly agricultural economy. The city's orientation toward the Aegean, together with the excellent harbors along the Attic coast, would eventually make Athens famous as a mercantile and seafaring polis. But until the sixth century B.C.E., the aristocracy of Athens remained firmly entrenched on the land.

Aristocratic dominance over Athens rested on the elected magistracies, which they monopolized, and the council of state, which was composed of former magistrates. By the early seventh century B.C.E., aristocratic officials called archons wielded executive power in Athens; ultimately nine archons in all presided over the civil, military, judicial, and religious functions of the polis. The archons served a term of one year, after which they became lifetime members of the Areopagus (*ahr-ee-OP-ah-guhs*) Council. The council was where the real power in Athens resided. The Areopagus elected the archons, thus controlling its own future membership. It also served as a kind of "high court," with tremendous influence over the judicial procedures of Athens.

Deep economic and social divisions developed in Athenian society during the seventh century B.C.E., as a significant proportion of the population fell into debt slavery (the practice of securing a loan with one's person as collateral and, when unable to pay up, becoming indentured to the creditor). Rivalries between aristocratic political factions also destabilized the polis. In 621 B.C.E., an aristocrat named Drakon was charged with "setting the laws"; in particular, he sought to control homicide through harsh ("draconian") punishments. His attempt at stabilizing Athens failed, however, and the city soon found itself on the brink of civil war. Hoping to avoid this, in 594 B.C.E. aristocrats and hoplites alike agreed to make Solon the sole archon for one year and to give him sweeping powers to reorganize Athenian government. Solon was an aristocrat who had made his name and fortune as a merchant; this led everyone in Athenian society to trust Solon because he was not beholden to any single interest.

Solon's reforms laid the foundations for the later development of Athenian democracy. He forbade the practice of debt slavery and set up a fund to buy back Athenian debt slaves sold abroad. He encouraged the Athenians to cultivate olives and grapes, thus spurring cash-crop farming and the urban industries (such as pottery, oil production, and shipbuilding) necessary to make Athens a commercial power. He also broadened rights of political participation. Solon set up courts in which a broader range of citizens served as jurors and to which any Athenian might appeal if he disliked a decision of the Areopagus. He based eligibility for political office on property qualifications,

Ostracism. The system took its name from the pot shards (in Greek, *ostraka*) on which the names of unpopular citizens were scratched. Many of the "ballots" have survived.

thus making it possible for someone not born an aristocrat to gain access to power through the accumulation of wealth. He also gave the Athenian citizen assembly (known as the *ekklesia*) the right to elect the archons. This was a significant step because all free-born Athenian men over the age of eighteen could participate in the assembly.

Solon's reforms did not succeed. The aristocracy thought them too radical, the demos (common people), not nearly radical enough. In the resulting turmoil, an aristocrat named Peisistratos (*pi-SIS-trah-tohs*) finally succeeded in establishing himself as tyrant in 546 B.C.E. By enforcing Solon's reforms, Peisistratos strengthened the demos and encouraged the taste for self-government. He remained a popular ruler until his death. His sons, however, were quickly overthrown. Two generations of increasing access to power left the Athenian demos with no interest in returning to an elite oligarchy. For the first time in history, the populace at large spontaneously rose up and overthrew the government. They rallied behind Cleisthenes (*CLIS-the-nees*), an aristocrat who had served the Peisistratid government ably and championed the cause of the demos. Once voted in as archon in 508–507 B.C.E., Cleisthenes quickly took steps to limit aristocratic power. He also introduced the practice of ostracism, whereby the Athenians could decide each year whether they wanted to banish someone for ten years and, if so, whom. Cleisthenes believed that with this power, the demos could prevent the return of a tyrant and quell factional strife if civil war seemed imminent.

By 500 B.C.E., Athens had become the principal exporter of olive oils, wines, and pottery in the Greek world. The political struggles of the sixth century had also given it a far more democratic temper than any other Greek polis possessed. Athens was poised to assume the role it would claim for itself during the fifth century B.C.E., as the exemplar of Greek culture and the proponent of its own style of participatory democracy.

SPARTA

Located in the southern part of the Peloponnesus (*pel-oh-poh-NEE-subs*)—the large peninsula that forms southern Greece—the Spartans represented everything that Athens was not. Athens was cultured, sophisticated, cosmopolitan; Sparta was basic, earthy, and traditional. Depending on one's point of view, either set of adjectives might serve as admiration or criticism.

Sparta took shape when four villages (and ultimately a fifth) combined to form the polis of Sparta. Perhaps as a relic of the unification process, Sparta retained a dual monarchy throughout its history, with two royal families and two lines of succession. Although seniority or capacity usually determined which of the two ruling kings had more influence, neither was technically superior to the other, a situation that led to political intrigue within Sparta.

The Spartan system depended on its conquest of Messenia, an agriculturally wealthy region west of Sparta. Around 720 B.C.E., the Spartans subjugated the region and enslaved the population. These *helots* (as the enslaved Messenians were now called) remained to work the land, which was now parceled out among the Spartiates. Around 650 B.C.E., however, the helots revolted, gaining support from several neighboring cities and briefly threatening Sparta with annihilation. Eventually, Sparta triumphed; but the shock of this rebellion brought about a permanent transformation in Spartan society.

Determined to prevent another uprising, Sparta became the most militarized polis in Greece. By 600 B.C.E., everything in Sparta was oriented to the maintenance of its hoplite army, a force so superior that the Spartans confidently left their city unfortified. The Spartan system made every full citizen, called a Spartiate, a professional soldier of the phalanx. At a time when Athenian society was becoming more democratic, in Sparta the citizenry was "aristocratized," making every citizen-soldier into a warrior-champion of the hoplite phalanx.

Sparta became a society organized for war. At birth, every child was examined by Spartan officials, who determined whether the child was healthy enough to raise (if not, the infant was abandoned in

CHRONOLOGY

THE CHANGING LANDSCAPE OF ARCHAIC GREECE

Panhellenic colonial expansion by Greek poleis	900–800 B.C.E.
Hoplite tactics become standard in Greek warfare	725–650 B.C.E.
Emergence of tyrannical governments	700–600 B.C.E.
Militarization of Sparta	650–600 B.C.E.
Solon's reforms	594 B.C.E.
Cleisthenes' reforms	508 B.C.E.

HOW AND WHY DID THE ATHENIAN, SPARTAN, AND MILESIAN POLEIS DIFFER FROM EACH OTHER?

THE ARCHAIC POLIS IN ACTION   81

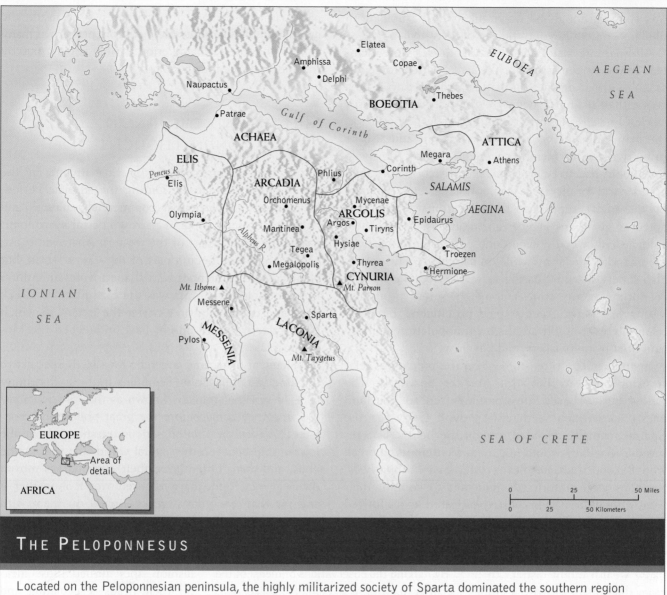

THE PELOPONNESUS

Located on the Peloponnesian peninsula, the highly militarized society of Sparta dominated the southern region known as Laconia. How might Sparta's geographical position have influenced its outlook on foreign affairs? Did geography make conflict between Athens and Sparta inevitable?

the mountains). If deemed worthy of upbringing, a child was placed at age seven in the state-run Spartan educational system. Boys and girls trained together until age twelve, participating in exercise, gymnastics, and other physical drills and competitions. Boys then went to live in the barracks, where their military training would commence in earnest. Girls continued an education in letters until they married, usually around the age of eighteen.

Barracks training was rigorous, designed to accustom the young Spartan male to physical hardships. At age eighteen, the young man would try to gain member-

ship in a *syssition*, a communal mess tent as well as a kind of fighting brotherhood. Failure meant that the young man could not become a full Spartiate and would lose his rights as a citizen. If accepted into a syssition, however, men remained in the barracks until they were thirty years of age. Although they were required to marry between the ages of twenty and thirty, men living in the barracks were permitted to meet their wives only secretly—a fact that may account in part for the notably low birthrate among Spartiate couples. After age thirty, a Spartiate male could live with his family. He remained on active military duty, however, until he was sixty, although he was unlikely to participate in phalanx combat beyond the age of forty-five.

All Spartiate males aged thirty and over were members of the citizen assembly, the *apella*, which voted yes or no, without debate, on matters proposed to it by a council consisting of twenty-eight elders (the *gerousia; gher-OO-see-ah*) plus the two kings. The gerousia was the main policymaking body of the polis and also its primary court. Its members were elected by the apella for life but had to be over the age of sixty before they could stand for election. Five ephors, elected annually by the apella, supervised the educational system and acted as guardians of Spartan traditions. In the latter role, an ephor could even depose an errant king from command of the army while on campaign. The ephors also supervised the Spartan secret service, the *krypteia*, recruiting agents from among the most promising young Spartiates. Agents spied on citizens, but their main job was to infiltrate the helot population, identify potential troublemakers, and kill them.

Spartan policy often hinged on the precarious relationship between the helots and the Spartiates. The helots outnumbered the Spartiates ten to one, and Messenia routinely seethed with revolt. Every year the Spartans ritually declared war on the helots, as a reminder that they would not tolerate attempts to break free. But the Spartiates never rested easy in their beds; Spartans were notoriously reluctant to commit their army abroad, in part because they feared its prolonged absence might encourage a helot uprising at home.

Spartiates were forbidden to engage in trades or commerce, because wealth might distract them from the pursuit of martial virtue. Nor did Spartiates farm their own lands. Economic activity in the Spartan state fell either to the helots or to the free residents of the other Peloponnesian cities (known as the *perioikoi*, "those dwelling round about"). The perioikoi enjoyed certain rights and protections within Spartan society, and some grew wealthy handling its business concerns. They exercised no political rights within the Spartan state, however, and Sparta conducted their foreign policy for them. Spartiates who lost their rights as citizens also became perioikoi.

The fatal flaw in the Spartan system was demographic. There were many ways to fall from the status of Spartiate, including criminal behavior and cowardice. The only way to become a Spartiate, however, was by birth—and the Spartan birthrate simply could not keep pace with the demand for Spartiates. As a result, the number of full Spartiates declined from perhaps as many as 10,000 in the Archaic Period to only about 1,000 by the middle of the fourth century B.C.E.

MILETUS AND THE IONIAN REVOLUTION IN THOUGHT

Across the Aegean from the Greek mainland lay the Greek cities of Anatolia. During the Archaic Period, Miletus was the foremost commercial, cultural, and military power of Ionia, a narrow coastal strip dominating the central part of the western Anatolian coast. Miletus had long been a part of the Greek world, but Near Eastern influences also shaped Milesian culture in important ways. Ionia was the birthplace of Greek epic, and debate continues over the extent to which Near Eastern models might have influenced the Homeric epics.

Miletus also became a center for Greek speculative thinking and philosophy. Beginning in the sixth century B.C.E., a series of thinkers known as the "pre-Socratics" (because they came before the great philosopher Socrates; *SAH-kruh-tees*) raised serious questions about the relationship between the natural world (the *kosmos*), the gods, and men. Oftentimes, their explanations moved divine agency to the margins or removed it altogether—and for that, everyday Greeks looked on them with suspicion. All built on older traditions of Near Eastern learning, such as Babylonian astronomy; but in typically Greek fashion, they turned those ideas on their heads. Calculating and observing the movements of the heavens, the thinkers of the Milesian School sought physical explanations for what they saw, refusing to presume that the heavenly bodies were gods. By making the observations of men, not the will of the gods, the starting point for their thinking, the Milesian School began to formulate rational theories to explain the physical universe they observed.

> By making the observations of men, not the will of the gods, the starting point for their thinking, the Milesian School began to formulate rational theories to explain the physical universe they observed.

Stimulated by the cosmopolitanism of their city, Milesian philosophers also began to rethink their place in the human world, inaugurating what has sometimes been called "the Ionian revolution in thought." Xenophanes (*zee-NAHF-un-nees*) of Colophon concluded that human beings made gods in their own image, not the other way around. If oxen could speak and make ob-

How were the Greek armies able to defeat the much larger Persian forces?

THE PERSIAN WARS   83

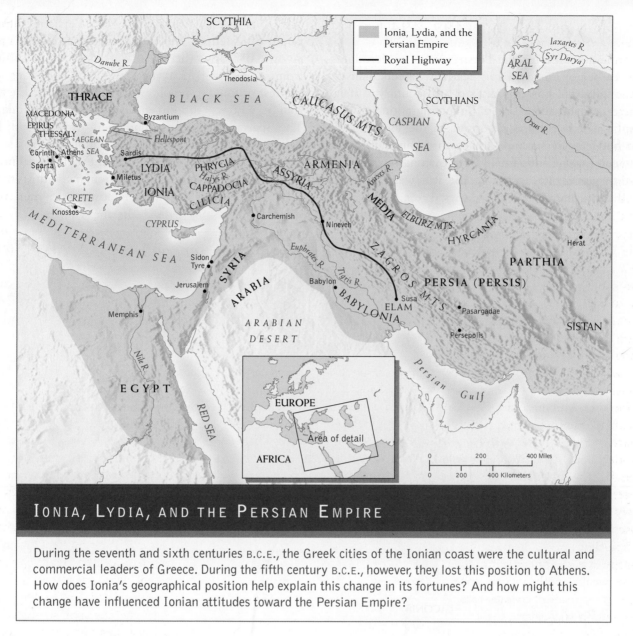

IONIA, LYDIA, AND THE PERSIAN EMPIRE

During the seventh and sixth centuries B.C.E., the Greek cities of the Ionian coast were the cultural and commercial leaders of Greece. During the fifth century B.C.E., however, they lost this position to Athens. How does Ionia's geographical position help explain this change in its fortunes? And how might this change have influenced Ionian attitudes toward the Persian Empire?

jects, Xenophanes declared, they would pray and fashion idols to gods who looked like oxen. Such relativism was new, but it would become a distinctive strand in later Greek philosophy.

This widening fissure between religious belief and philosophical speculation was a crucial development in the history of Western thought. It was less complete, however, than is often imagined. Philosophy was a game for a few, not for the average Greek; and as philosophers turned their attention to humanity's relationship to the gods, citizens in even the most progressive poleis were unnerved. The gods were too central a part of daily life for the average Greek not to feel threatened by such impious philosophizing.

THE PERSIAN WARS

How were the Greek armies able to defeat the much larger Persian forces?

The Archaic Period of Greek history closed with dramatic struggles against Persia. For two decades the threat of Persian conquest loomed on the Greek horizon. When finally the threat to Greek freedom receded, the experience of war had changed the Greek world immeasurably.

THE IONIAN REVOLT (499–494 B.C.E.)

Our main source for the Persian Wars is Herodotus, the "Father of History." His account reflects many of the intellectual currents of mid-fifth-century Athens, where he lived and worked. Reflecting a kind of geographical and cultural determinism, he ascribed the war between Persia and Greece to an ancient hatred between Europe and Asia. But his own narrative shows that the immediate cause of the war was a political conflict in Miletus.

By 501 B.C.E., Aristagoras—the Persians' puppet tyrant of Miletus—grew concerned that his days as a favorite of Darius the Great were numbered. Turning from puppet to patriot, he roused the Milesians and the rest of Ionia to revolt against Persian rule. He also sought military support from the Greek mainland. The Spartans refused to send their army abroad, but Athens and the city of Eretria on Euboea sent a small force that captured and burned the Persian administrative center of Sardis. The Athenians and Eretrians then sailed home, leaving the Ionians to their own

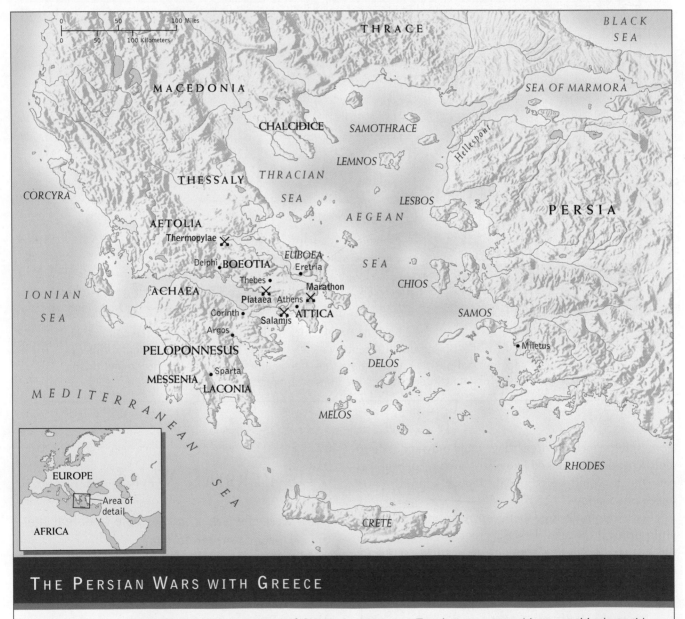

THE PERSIAN WARS WITH GREECE

Imagine you are Xerxes, planning the conquest of Greece in 480 B.C.E. To what extent would geographical considerations dictate your military strategy? Xerxes' attempt at conquest failed. What would you have done differently? Could any Persian expedition have succeeded in conquering Greece?

How were the Greek armies able to defeat the much larger Persian forces?

The Persian Wars   85

devices. After five years of brave struggle, the rebels were finally overwhelmed by the vastly superior might of Persia in 494 B.C.E.

Darius realized, however, that so long as his Greek subjects in Asia Minor could cast a hopeful eye to their cousins across the Aegean, they would long for freedom. Darius therefore set out on a punitive expedition to teach Athens and Eretria a lesson. Landing on Euboea in the summer of 490, Persian forces sacked and burned Eretria and sent its population into captivity in Persia. They then crossed the narrow strait to Attica, landing in the plain of Marathon.

Marathon and Its Aftermath

Recognizing the danger they now faced, the Athenians sought help from the Spartans, who responded that they were unable to assist due to an ongoing religious festival. Only the small, nearby polis of Plataea offered the Athenians aid. The Athenian phalanx would have to engage the mighty Persians on its own.

Heavily outnumbered, the Athenian phalanx took a position between two hills blocking the main road to the asty. After a standoff of several days, the Athenian general Miltiades received word that the Persians were watering their horses and that the Persian infantry (numerically superior but poorly equipped compared to the 10,000 Athenian hoplites) was vulnerable. Miltiades led a charge that smashed the Persian force and resulted in catastrophic losses for the Persians. Herodotus records that 6,400 Persians fell, compared with only 192 Athenians. The Persians withdrew.

The Athenians had defeated the world's greatest empire, and they had done it without Spartan help. It was a tremendous boost to Athenian confidence, and many exulted in their victory, a victory of the demos. The Athenian politician Themistocles (*the-MIS-tah-klees*) believed, however, that Greece had not seen the last of the Persians, who would inevitably return in much greater force. In 483 B.C.E., the Athenians discovered a rich silver vein in the Attic countryside. Themistocles persuaded them not to divide the windfall among themselves (the customary practice) but to use it to build a fleet of 200 triremes, state-of-the-art warships. Athens thereby transformed itself into the preeminent naval power of the Greek world just in time to confront a new Persian onslaught.

The defense at Thermopylae failed, but their sacrifice allowed the fleet, under Themistocles' guidance, to inflict heavy losses on the Persians and then withdraw safely to the south.

Xerxes' Invasion

Darius died in 486 B.C.E. and was succeeded by his son Xerxes, who began preparing a massive overland invasion of Greece designed to conquer the entire country. Supported by a fleet of 600 ships, Xerxes' grand army (which numbered at least 150,000 men and may have been as large as 300,000) set out from Sardis in 480 B.C.E., crossing the narrow strait separating Europe from Asia on pontoon bridges. Unlike his father, who had dispatched talented generals against Athens, Xerxes led this campaign himself.

Many Greek cities capitulated immediately. Athens, Sparta, Corinth, and some thirty others refused to bow, however, and formed the Hellenic League to defeat the Persian menace. Under the military leadership of Sparta, the outnumbered Greek allies confronted Xerxes at the pass of Thermopylae (*ther-MO-pih-lee*) in August of 480. For three days the Greeks held off the Persian multitude, while the Greek fleet engaged a Persian flotilla at nearby Artemisium. The defense at Thermopylae failed, but their sacrifice allowed the fleet, under Themistocles' guidance, to inflict heavy losses on the Persians and then withdraw safely to the south.

Realizing he could no longer defend the city, Themistocles abandoned Athens for the island of Salamis off the coast of Attica. In early September, the Athenians watched the Persians put Athens to the torch.

CHRONOLOGY

The Persian Wars

Croesus, king of Lydia, conquers Greek cities of Anatolia	c. 560 B.C.E.
Cyrus, king of Persia, conquers Lydia and controls Greek cities	546 B.C.E.
Ionian Revolt	499–494 B.C.E.
Battle of Marathon	490 B.C.E.
Xerxes invades Greece	480 B.C.E.
Battles of Thermopylae and Salamis	480 B.C.E.
Battle of Plataea	479 B.C.E.
Formation of the Delian League, led by Athens	478–477 B.C.E.

Time, however, was on Themistocles' side. Xerxes' massive army depended on his fleet for supplies. Bad weather made sailing the Aegean in autumn a risky business; the Persians were now desperate to force a decisive battle before the season turned against them.

In late September, the numerically superior Persian fleet, believing the Greeks were about to flee Salamis, sailed into the Bay of Eleusis, only to find that Themistocles had the Greek fleet ready for combat. The Greeks smashed the Persian fleet while Xerxes watched the disaster from a throne above the bay. The following year, a Greek army prevailed on land at the battle of Plataea, driving the Persians completely from mainland Greece. Against all odds, the small, fractious, outnumbered Greek poleis had defeated the mightiest empire of the Mediterranean world. It was a turning point in the history of Greece, ushering in the Classical (or golden) Age.

THE GOLDEN AGE OF CLASSICAL GREECE

To what extent was the culture of Athens in the golden age the product of Athenian democracy?

In the half century after the battle of Salamis, Athens enjoyed a meteoric rise in power and prestige, becoming the premier naval power of the eastern Mediterranean and a military rival even of Sparta. Athens also emerged as the leader of the Delian League, a group of poleis pledged to continue the war against Persia. As the leader of the league, Athens controlled its funds and resources. This fact allowed the Athenians to make their polis—in the words of their brilliant political leader Pericles (PEHR-eh-klees)—the "school of Hellas." The

Bust of Pericles. A Roman copy, in marble, of a Greek original made during Pericles' lifetime. Like the tyrant Peisistratos, Pericles is said to have had a deformed head. Pericles wore a helmet to conceal this potentially provocative resemblance.

fifth century B.C.E. witnessed the greatest achievements of Greek culture and the flowering of Athenian democracy. Both were fueled, however, by the increasingly awkward relationship Athens enjoyed with its allies, who by the 430s had begun to look more like Athenian subjects than free poleis.

PERICLEAN ATHENS

The reforms of Cleisthenes encouraged further experiments in Greek democracy, including the selection of major officeholders by lot. Only one key position was now filled by traditional voting: the office of *strategos*, or general. Because a man could be elected strategos year after year, this office became the focus for Athens' most talented and ambitious public figures. Themistocles had been strategos, as was Cimon (*KI-mahn*), who led the Delian League to stunning victories over Persia in the 470s and 460s. But Cimon also turned the league against members who tried to opt out, suppressing their "revolts" by force of arms, and turning the league more and more into an instrument of Athenian policy.

Cimon's military successes made him the most powerful politician in Athens. By the 460s, however, the political mood in Athens was changing. New voices were demanding a greater role in government, especially the *thetes*, the lowest of the four classes established by Solon. As rowers, these men were the backbone of the all-important Athenian fleet; as citizens, however, they played little role in the government of their polis.

Pericles was elected strategos for 462–461 after he used a platform of greater enfranchisement of the thetes and an anti-Spartan foreign policy to defeat Cimon. He then pushed through reforms to make Athens more fully democratic. He gave every Athenian citizen the right to propose and amend legislation, not just to vote yes or no in the citizen assembly. He also made it easier for poorer citizens to participate in the assembly and the great appeals courts of Athens by paying an average day's wage for attendance. Through these and other measures, the thetes became a dominant force in politics, loyal to the man who had made that dominance possible.

To what extent was the culture of Athens the product of Athenian democracy?

The Golden Age of Classical Greece 87

Pericles glorified Athens' democracy with an ambitious scheme of public building and lavish festivals to the gods, especially Athena. He was also a generous patron of the arts, sciences, and literature, attracting the greatest minds of the day to Athens. His populist political stance, combined with his ability to inspire a sense of Athenian superiority, ensured his reelection as strategos for the next three decades. During these years, Athenian culture flourished as never before. Pericles would prove to be a disastrous political leader; but Periclean Athens represents a dramatic and brilliant moment in the history of Western civilizations.

LITERATURE AND DRAMA

Periclean Athens was not the only city to produce great works of literature during the golden age, but our knowledge of classical Greek literature is dominated by the poetry and drama (both tragic and comedic) produced there. Epic and lyric poetry were already well-established Greek literary forms when the fifth century began. Drama, however, appears to have been an innovation that developed in Athens out of the poetic odes chanted by choruses to the god Dionysius at the great spring festival devoted to him. Credit for transforming the Dionysian odes into a genuine drama with characters and a chorus belongs to the great tragedian Aeschylus (*AH-skihl-uhs*; 525–456 B.C.E.), who by introducing a second (and later a third) character into the performance, made it possible to present conversation, and hence human conflict, on the stage for the first time. Staging remained very simple, but the emotional impact of tragic drama could be overwhelming.

The themes of Greek tragedy—justice, law, and the conflicting demands of piety and obligation that drove a heroic man or woman to destruction—were derived from Homer. But tragedy could also have a decidedly contemporary aspect. Sophocles' (496–406 B.C.E.) great masterpiece, *Oedipus (ED-ih-pus) at Colonus*, was presented in the midst of Athens' disastrous war with Sparta. Euripides' (485–406 B.C.E.) *Trojan Women* was presented in 415, the year of the expedition to Syracuse and the turning point in the Athenians' march toward defeat in the Peloponnesian War (discussed later in this chapter). Tragedy dealt in absolutes, most memorably perhaps in Sophocles' *Antigone*, the story of a clash between justice and law and the competing obligations of familial piety and civic necessity; but its context was inevitably the history of Athens in the period of its own greatest achievements and failures.

Comedy was even more directly a genre of direct political commentary. Comedy was crude, parodic, and outspoken, full of slapstick, absurdity, and vulgarity. Its themes were (in the scholar Peter Levi's words) "sex, life on the farm, the good old days, the nightmare of politics, the oddities of religion, the strange manners of the town." Aristophanes (*EHR-ih-STAHF-ah-nees*; c. 448–382 B.C.E.), the greatest of the Athenian comedic playwrights, ridiculed everything that offended or amused

Greek Theater in Epidauros. Greek dramas were invariably presented in the open air. The construction of this theater, which takes advantage of the slope of the hill, and the arrangement of the stage are of particular interest.

him: the philosophy of Socrates, the tragedies of Euripides, and especially the imperialistic warmongering of contemporary politicians such as Cleon. But above all else, Aristophanes was a social critic, who routinely savaged the powerful political figures whom he believed (with justice) were leading Athens to its doom. He was repeatedly dragged into court to defend himself against the politicians whom he had attacked. But despite their anger, the politicians never dared to shut down the comedic theater for long. It was too much a part of the spirit of democratic Athens.

Periclean Athens was also fertile ground for the development of Greek prose. During the sixth century, Greeks typically expressed ideas through poetry. In the fifth century, however, prose emerged as a distinct literary form. Herodotus found a ready market for his "inquiries" (*historiai*) in Athens. His younger contemporary

Thucydides (*thu-SID-ih-dees;* c. 460–c. 400 B.C.E.) wrote a masterful history of the great war between Athens and Sparta. Between them, these two historians developed a new approach to history, emphasizing the reliability of their sources and looking for human explanations for historical events. The development of prose would make possible in the fourth century even further literary achievements, such as the great philosophical treatises of Plato and Aristotle and the stirring political and legal speeches of the great Attic orators we will meet in the next chapter.

ART AND ARCHITECTURE

The Greeks of the golden age revealed the same range of genius in the visual arts as they did in their drama. Their comic gift—exuberance, cheerful sensuality, and

Apollo of Tenea, Apollo of Piombino, and the "Critian Boy." These three statues, dating from about 560, 500, and 480 B.C.E. respectively, display the progressive "unfreezing" of Greek statuary art. The first stiff and symmetrical statue is imitative of Egyptian sculpture. Roughly half a century later it is succeeded by a figure that begins to display motion. The last figure introduces genuine naturalism in its delicate twists and depiction of the subject's weight resting on one leg.

TO WHAT EXTENT WAS THE CULTURE OF ATHENS THE PRODUCT OF ATHENIAN DEMOCRACY?

THE GOLDEN AGE OF CLASSICAL GREECE 89

coarse wit—can be seen especially in their "black figure" vases and jugs, whose characters often look like glinting rascals up to some sort of mischief, usually sexual. More dignified were the marble statues and sculptured reliefs the Greeks made for temples and public places. Athenian sculptors in particular took human greatness as their theme, depicting the beauty of the human form in statuary that was simultaneously naturalistic and idealizing.

The Athenians also made exceptional contributions to architecture. All Greek temples sought to create an impression of harmony and repose, but the Parthenon of Athens, built between 447 and 438 B.C.E., is generally considered the finest example of its genre. Construction of this stunning, expensive, and difficult building was urged on the Athenians by Pericles, who saw it as a symbol of devotion to their patron goddess, Athena, and a triumphant celebration of their own power and confidence.

> Athenian sculptors in particular took human greatness as their theme, depicting the beauty of the human form in statuary that was simultaneously naturalistic and idealizing.

WOMEN AND MEN IN THE DAILY LIFE OF ATHENS

Toward the end of his famous Funeral Oration, Pericles urged the married women of Athens to do three things: rear more children for the sake of Athens; show no more weakness than was "natural to their sex"; and avoid gossip. His remarks reveal widely held male attitudes toward women in classical Greece, but especially in Athens.

Rather than leading to greater equality among the sexes, the growth of democracy had the opposite result. In the Dark Age, aristocratic women were sometimes portrayed as possessing extraordinary traits of beauty, wisdom, or courage. These women gave shrewd advice on political and military matters and played an active role in the world around them. But as aristocratic ideals gave way to more democratic ones, life in the shadows increasingly became women's lot. Public spaces were restricted to male activities such as athletics and political gatherings, while domestic, private spaces were reserved for female activities such as child rearing and weaving. By the fifth century B.C.E., "respectable" women lived in seclusion, rarely if ever venturing forth from their houses.

In Athens, girls could be married at age fourteen—as soon as they were biologically capable of childbearing—to husbands more than twice their age. A girl's father arranged her marriage and provided a dowry that her husband could use for her support. Shortly after a wife entered her new home, a regular schedule of childbearing would usually begin. Typically the interval between births was between two and four years, meaning that the average young wife would bear between four and six children before she died, usually around the age of thirty-five.

Women seldom went out of doors, as it was thought immodest for them to be seen by other men. Slaves did whatever shopping or marketing the household required. Even at home, women were expected to withdraw into private rooms if visitors arrived. Because the

Women and Weaving. Wool-working and weaving were highly gendered activities in ancient Greece, in which women of all social ranks were expected to participate. On this red-figure vase, dating from 460–450 B.C.E., we see the woman on the left carding wool and the two women on the right spinning it into wool threads, which could then be woven into cloth.

ideology of democratic Athens opposed excessive displays of wealth or leisure, women were not supposed to sit around idly; their main occupation was probably cloth weaving. But because "women's work" was basically menial, men looked down on women for engaging in it. Available evidence suggests that husbands customarily had little emotional attachment to their wives, regarding them as natural inferiors. In a revealing passage Herodotus says of a certain Lydian king, "[T]his Candaules fell in love with his own wife, a fancy that had strange consequences." An Athenian orator remarked, "[P]rostitutes we have for pleasure, concubines for daily physical attendance, wives to bear us legitimate children and be our faithful housekeepers."

Athenian society was as dependent on its slaves as the Spartans were on the helots. Without slavery, none of the extraordinary Athenian accomplishments in politics, thought, or art would have been possible. The Athenian ideal of dividing and rotating governmental duties among all free men depended on slaves who worked in fields, businesses, and homes while free men engaged in politics. Freedom and slavery were inescapably linked.

LEAGUE BUILDING AND THE PELOPONNESIAN WAR

How did the Peloponnesian War influence Greek philosophy?

Athenians saw themselves as the freest of men, but their freedom rested on the servitude of others. Slaves performed much of the labor at home, while Athens' allies in the Delian League provided the resources that underlay Athenian greatness. Without the surplus wealth flowing into Athens from the league, none of the projects Pericles undertook—pay for political participation, massive building projects (also, incidentally, an employment program for poorer citizens), the patronage of Athenian drama—would have been possible. These projects kept Athens powerful, its democracy vibrant, and Pericles popular and in power. But Athens' democratic achievements rested on its control over an alliance it had transformed into an empire.

Since the 470s, Athens had faced attempts by its allies to break away, and it had crushed those efforts ruthlessly. Through the 450s, such revolts were rare.

But in the early 440s, Pericles determined on a more aggressive policy toward Sparta, by then Athens' only real rival for supremacy in the Greek world. To give himself a freer hand, he concluded a formal peace with Persia. After this peace, the purpose of the Delian League evaporated, and Athens had no justification for compelling its allies to remain within it. Many remained loyal nonetheless, paying their contributions and enjoying the economic benefits of warm relations with Athens. Others, however, did not, and Athens found itself increasingly forcing its allies back into line, often installing Athenian garrisons and planting Athenian colonists—who retained their Athenian citizenship—to ensure future loyalty.

In the context of Greek culture, such behavior was disturbing. The Delian League had been established to preserve Greek independence against the Persians. Now many Greeks accused Athens of having become a tyrannical empire itself. Foremost among the accusers were the Corinthians, whose own economic standing was seriously threatened by Athenian dominance of the Aegean. The Corinthians were close allies of the Spartans, the dominant power in what historians call the "Peloponnesian League." (The Greeks called it simply "the Spartans and their allies.") When war finally erupted between Athens and Sparta, the great historian Thucydides ascribed it to the growing power of Athens and the fear and envy this inspired in Sparta. No modern historian has improved on Thucydides' formulation. For the Athenian democracy and its leader, there could be no question of relinquishing the empire, the cornerstone of Athens' cultural and political ascendancy. By the 430s, however, Athens could not preserve that empire without threatening the interests of Sparta and its allies.

THE PELOPONNESIAN WAR ERUPTS

After a series of provocations, the Athenians and Spartans found themselves at war with one another in 431 B.C.E. Athens could not defeat Sparta on land; but neither Sparta nor its allies had a fleet capable of facing the Athenians on the seas. Pericles therefore developed a bold strategy: he would pull the entire population of Attica within the walls of Athens and its harbor, abandoning the countryside to Sparta, while the superior Athenian fleet supplied Athens from the sea and ravaged the Spartan coastline. As in many of history's pivotal contests, both sides believed a conclusion would come quickly.

Time appeared to be on Athens' side, but in 429 B.C.E. the crowded conditions of the besieged city

THE PELOPONNESIAN WAR

Consider the balance of power between Athens and Sparta at the outbreak of the Peloponnesian War. Which side had the geographical advantage? Which neutral powers might have been able to tip the balance by entering the war on one side or the other? What strategic and military choices did geography impose on the two combatants and their allies?

gave rise to an epidemic that killed over a third of the Athenian population, including Pericles. Pericles' death showed that he was the only man capable of managing the democratic political forces he had unleashed. His successors were mostly demagogues, ambitious men who played to the worst instincts of the demos to gain power for themselves.

A short-lived truce ultimately ensued. But the Athenian demos was in no mood for a long peace, and

hostilities reopened in 415 B.C.E. with an ill-advised attack on the distant city of Syracuse in Sicily. The expedition failed, with thousands of Athenians killed or enslaved in Sicily.

News of the Syracusan disaster shattered the Athenian demos. Recriminations began immediately. Many political leaders were driven from the polis, and in 411 B.C.E. the demos suffered a momentary but monumental lack of self-confidence. While the rowers in the

A Modern Replica of an Athenian Trireme. These versatile warships were powered by both oars and sail.

fleet were away from the city, the Athenians essentially voted the democracy out of existence, replacing it with an oligarchy of 400 citizens. The oligarchy proved to be brief, and democracy was restored to Athens by 409. But the fact that the war could force such desperation did not bode well for the future.

THE END OF THE WAR

The Spartans too despaired of bringing the war to an end. Despite Athens' problems, its fleet was still invincible. Finally, Sparta turned to the Persians, who agreed to supply the gold and the naval expertise necessary to create an effective Spartan fleet. By 407, a talented and ambitious Spartan commander, Lysander, was successfully harrying the Athenians throughout the Aegean Sea.

Lysander destroyed the poorly led Athenian fleet in 404 B.C.E. Without their fleet the Athenians could neither feed themselves nor defend their city. Lysander sailed around the Aegean unopposed, installing pro-Spartan oligarchies among the former allies of Athens. Finally, he besieged Athens itself. Facing the inevitable, the Athenians surrendered. Corinth and Thebes called for Athens' destruction. The Spartans refused to allow this but imposed harsh terms: the dismantling of Athens' walls, the scrapping of its fleet, and the acceptance of an oligarchic government of thirty Athenians.

For the Greeks, the Peloponnesian War was a disaster. From the long perspective of historical distance, we may view it as demonstrating the limitations of the polis system. The competitive ethos that characterized the Greek poleis proved to be their tragic flaw. To the Greeks themselves, however, the war offered no such clear lessons. Instead, it brought demoralization and a questioning of all the old certainties. Democracies had collapsed and empires had crumbled. Sparta too proved incapable of rising to the challenges it now confronted. Even the gods seemed to be in disarray. These were the circumstances in which the great Athenian philosopher Socrates (469–399 B.C.E.) attempted to refound ethical and political life on new and more certain principles. To understand his accomplishments, however, we must trace briefly the history of philosophical speculation in the half century before his birth.

THE LIFE AND THOUGHT OF SOCRATES

Before Socrates, philosophy in Athens was dominated by a new group of professional teachers known as *Sophists*, a term simply meaning "those who are wise." The Sophists were not a coherent philosophical school. Their work did display some common threads, however, that are best exemplified by Protagoras, who was active in Athens from about 445 to 420 B.C.E. His famous dictum, "man is the measure of all things," meant that goodness, truth, and justice are relative to the needs and interests of human beings. In religious matters Protagoras was agnostic, declaring that he did not know whether the gods existed or what they did. Because he knew nothing of the gods, he concluded that there could be no absolute truths or eternal standards of right and wrong. If sense perception was the only source of knowledge, there could be only particular truths valid for the individual knower.

Such teachings struck many Athenians as dangerous. By encouraging people to examine each new situation on its own terms and merits, Sophists for the first time made everyday life a subject for philosophical discussion. But the relativism of such Sophists as Protagoras could easily degenerate into the doctrine that the wise man is the one who knows best how to manipulate others and gratify his own desires. To some critics, such ideas were antidemocratic; to others, they smacked of atheism and anarchy. If there was no final truth, and if goodness and justice were merely relative to the whims of the individual, then religion, morality, the state, and society itself could not be maintained.

In response, a new philosophical movement emerged, grounded on the theory that truth is real and absolute standards do exist. The initiator of this new trend was Socrates. Socrates was an ardent patriot who believed Athens was being corrupted by the shameful doctrines of the Sophists. But he was not an uncritical patriot. Rather, he wished to submit every presumed truth to rigorous examination to reconstruct Athenian life on a firm foundation of ethical certainty. It is bitterly ironic that such a dedicated idealist should have been put to death by his own countrymen. Shortly after the end of the Peloponnesian War, in 399 B.C.E., when Athens was

Socrates. According to Plato, Socrates looked like a goatman but spoke like a god.

reeling from the shock of defeat and violent internal upheavals, a political faction decided that Socrates was a threat to the state. A democratic court agreed, condemning him to death for impiety and "corrupting the youth." Although his friends made arrangements for him to flee, Socrates decided to accept the popular judgment and abide by the laws of his polis. He died by calmly drinking a cup of poison.

Because Socrates wrote nothing himself, it is difficult to determine exactly what he taught. Contemporary reports, however, especially by his student Plato, make a few points clear. First, Socrates subjected all inherited assumptions to rigorous criticism. He continually engaged his contemporaries in "Socratic" questioning, seeking to show them that all their supposed certainties were merely unexamined prejudices resting on false assumptions. According to Plato, an oracle once said that Socrates was the wisest person in the world and Socrates agreed: everyone else thought he knew something, but he was wiser because he knew he knew nothing. Second, he sought to base his philosophical

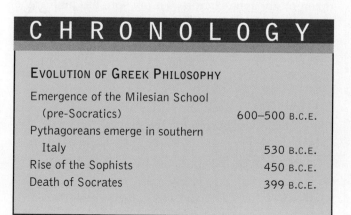

CHRONOLOGY

Evolution of Greek Philosophy

Emergence of the Milesian School (pre-Socratics)	600–500 B.C.E.
Pythagoreans emerge in southern Italy	530 B.C.E.
Rise of the Sophists	450 B.C.E.
Death of Socrates	399 B.C.E.

TWO VIEWS OF SOPHISM

SOCRATES AS A SOPHIST

The image of Socrates held by most people is of the sage thinker who challenged the prevailing prejudices of his day and opposed the Sophists. During his own time, however, he was not so universally admired. In his comedy The Clouds, *Aristophanes' protagonist Strepsiades—ruined by the wastefulness of his son—goes to Socrates and his "Thought Shop" so that Socrates can make him and his son Pheidippides orators capable of winning lawsuits and thus enriching himself. Aristophanes implies throughout that Socrates is essentially just another Sophist, a man who teaches word games and logic tricks for hire. The first excerpt is from Aristophanes' play.*

During the truce authored by the Athenian statesman Nicias in 421 B.C.E., *both Athens and Sparta continued to pursue a "dirty war," living by the letter of their agreement but not its spirit, while preparing for the inevitable reopening of the conflict. The Aegean island of Melos—originally a Spartan colony—had so far maintained a policy of neutrality between Athens and Sparta. In* 416, *however, the Athenians insisted on their submission, and the Athenian envoys justified their position with a chillingly logical argument that "might makes right," reprinted in part in the second selection.*

STREPSIADES: See that he [Pheidippides] learns your two Arguments, whatever you call them—oh yes, Right and Wrong—the one that takes a bad case and defeats Right with it. If he can't manage both, then at least Wrong—that will do—but that he must have.

SOCRATES: Well, I'll go and send the Arguments here in person, and they'll teach him themselves.

STREPSIADES: Don't forget, he's got to be able to argue against any kind of justified claim at all.

RIGHT: This way, Let the audience see you. . . .

WRONG: Sure, go wherever you like. The more of an audience we have, the more soundly I'll trounce you.

RIGHT: What sort of trick will you use?

WRONG: Oh, just a few new ideas.

RIGHT: Yes, they're in fashion now, aren't they, [to the audience] thanks to you idiots. . . . [to Pheiddipides] You don't want to be the sort of chap who's always in the agora telling stories about other people's sex lives, or in the courts arguing about some petty, filthy, little dispute. . . .

WRONG: People here at the Thought Shop call me Wrong, because I was the one who invented ways of proving anything wrong, laws, prosecutors, anything. Isn't that worth millions—to have a really bad case and yet win? . . . Suppose you fall in love with a married woman—have a bit of fun—and get caught in the act. As you are now, without a tongue in your head, you're done for. But if you come and learn from me, then you can do whatever you like and get away with it . . . and supposing you do get caught with someone's wife, you can say to him. . . . "What have I done wrong? Look at Zeus; wasn't he always a slave of his sexual passions? And do you expect a mere mortal like me to do any better than a god?" . . .

STREPSIADES [to Socrates]: I wonder if you'd accept a token of my appreciation? But my son, has he learned that Argument we were listening to a moment ago?

SOCRATES: Yes, he has.

STREPSIADES: Holy Fraud, how wonderful!

SOCRATES: Yes, you'll now be able to win any case at all.

STREPSIADES: Even if the witnesses were actually there when I was borrowing the money?

SOCRATES: Even if there were a thousand of them.

Aristophanes, *The Clouds*. Trans. Alan H. Sommerstein (New York, 1973), pp. 148–150, 154, 159–160 (slightly revised).

Sophistry in Action: The Melian Dialogue

ATHENIANS: For ourselves, we will not trouble you with specious pretenses—either of how we have a right to our empire because we overthrew the Mede, or are now attacking you because of wrong that you have done us—and make a long speech which would not be believed; and in return we hope that you, instead of thinking to influence us by saying that you did not join the Spartans, although their colonists, or that you have done us no wrong, will aim at what is feasible, holding in view the real sentiments of us both; since you know as well as we do that right, as the world goes, is only in question between equals in power, while the strong do what they can and the weak suffer what they must. . . . We would desire to exercise empire over you without trouble, and see you preserved for the good of us both.

MELIANS: And how, pray, could it turn out as good for us to serve as for you to rule?

ATHENIANS: Because you would have the advantage of submitting before suffering the worst, and we should gain by not destroying you.

MELIANS: So you would not consent to our being neutral, friends instead of enemies, but allies of neither side?

ATHENIANS: No; for your hostility cannot so much hurt us as your friendship will be an argument to our subjects of our weakness, and your enmity of our power.

MELIANS: Is that your subjects' idea of equity, to put those who have nothing to do with you in the same category with peoples that are most of them your own colonists, and some conquered rebels?

ATHENIANS: As far as right goes they think one has as much of it as the other, and that if they maintain their independence it is because they are strong, and that if we do not molest them it is because we are afraid; so that besides extending our empire we should gain in security by your subjection. . . .

MELIANS: What is this but to make greater the enemies that you have already, and to force others to become so who would otherwise have never thought of it? . . . we know that the fortune of war is sometimes more impartial than the disproportion of numbers might lead one to suppose; to submit is to give ourselves over to despair, while action still preserves for us a hope that we may stand. . . .

ATHENIANS: Hope . . . may be indulged in by those who have abundant resources, if not without loss, at all events without ruin; but its nature is to be extravagant, and those who go so far as to stake their all upon the venture see it in its true colors only when they are ruined. . . . Let not this be the case with you, who are weak and hang on a single turn of the scale; nor be like the vulgar, who, when abandoning such security as human means may still afford, when visible hopes fail them in extremity, turn to the invisible, to prophecies and oracles, and other such inventions that delude men with hopes to their destruction. . . . When we come to your notion about the Spartans, which leads you to believe that shame will make them help you, here we bless your simplicity but do not envy your folly. . . . You do not adopt the view that expediency goes with security, while justice and honor cannot be followed without danger; and danger the Spartans generally court as little as possible. . . . Is it likely that while we are masters of the sea they will cross over to an island?

MELIANS: Should the Spartans miscarry in this, they would fall upon your land, and upon those left of your allies . . . and instead of places which are not yours, you will have to fight for your own country and your own confederacy.

ATHENIANS: Some diversion of the kind you speak of you may one day experience, only to learn, as others have done, that the Athenians never once yet withdrew from a siege for fear of any. . . . Think over the matter, therefore, and reflect once and again that it is for your country that you are consulting, and that upon this one deliberation depends its prosperity or ruin.

Thucydides, *The Landmark Thucydides*, Book 5, ed. Robert Strassler (New York, 1995), pp. 352–356.

QUESTIONS FOR ANALYSIS

1. Socrates reportedly denied being a sophist and refused to teach the art of "making the weaker argument defeat the stronger"—a mark of sophism. In *The Clouds*, Aristophanes shows him teaching Right and Wrong how "to win any case at all." From your reading of the text, was Socrates really a sophist? What is the true meaning of *sophisticated*?

2. Rhetoric and the philosophy of persuasion became more important in classical Greece than in earlier cultures. How was this related to politics and government in the polis?

speculations on precise definitions of words. Third, he focused his attention on ethics rather than on studying the physical world. He shunned the traditional discussions of Milesian philosophers about why things exist, why they grow, and why they perish. Instead, Socrates urged people to reflect on principles of proper conduct, both for their own sake and for that of society. One should consider the meaning of one's life and actions at all times, for according to one of his most memorable sayings, "the unexamined life is not worth living."

All this might make Socrates sound rather like a Sophist; indeed, he felt compelled at his trial to insist that he was not. Like the Sophists, he was a "philosopher of the marketplace" who held tradition and cliché up to doubt to help people improve their lives. But the overwhelming difference between Socrates and the Sophists lay in his belief in certainties—even if he avoided saying what they were—and in the standard of absolute good rather than expediency he applied to all aspects of life. Socrates' death made clear, however, that to reestablish the polis, it would be necessary to go farther than Socrates himself had, by constructing a system that revealed a positive framework of truth and reality. This was the task Socrates' most brilliant student, Plato, would undertake in the wake of the disasters of the Peloponnesian War. In so doing, he would lay the groundwork for all subsequent Western philosophical thinking up to the present day.

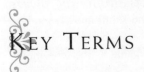

CONCLUSION

Ever since the Renaissance, Europeans have liked to think of themselves as the heirs of the classical Greeks, and to imagine the Greeks as mirror images of themselves. Such uncritical admiration is misleading. Despite the religious skepticism of a few intellectuals, the Greeks were neither secularists nor rationalists. Although they invented the concept of democracy, only a small percentage of the population was ever permitted to play a role in political affairs. Greek

statecraft was characterized by imperialism and aggressive war. The Greeks made no great advances in economic enterprise, and they scorned commerce. Finally, not even the Athenians could be described as tolerant. Socrates was not the only man put to death merely for expressing his opinions.

And yet the profound significance of the Greek experiment for the history of Western civilizations is undeniable. The typical political regime of the ancient Near Eastern world was that of an absolute monarch supported by a powerful priesthood. Culture was mainly an instrument to enhance the prestige of rulers and priests, and economic life tended to be controlled by palaces and temples. In contrast, the civilization of Greece, notably in its Athenian form, was founded on ideals of freedom, competition, individual achievement, and human glory. As Herodotus has a Greek (in this case a Spartan) say to a Persian, "You understand how to be a slave, but you know nothing of freedom. . . . If you had but tasted it you would counsel us to fight for it not only with spears but with axes."

Another way of appreciating the enduring importance of Greek civilization to the Western world is to recall some of the words that come to us from this civilization: politics, democracy, philosophy, metaphysics, history, tragedy. These are all ways of thinking and acting that have enriched human life immeasurably, but that had hardly been known before the Greeks invented them. To a startling degree the Western concept of "humanity" itself—the exalted role within nature of the human race in general and the individual human being in particular—comes to us from the Greeks. For the Greeks, the aim of existence was the fullest development of one's human potential; the work of becoming a person, called in Greek *paideia*, meant that every free man was supposed to be the sculptor of his own statue. When the Romans took up this ideal from the Greeks, they called it *humanitas*, from which we derive the English word *humanity*. The Romans admitted their indebtedness when they remarked that "Greece was where humanity was invented." It is hard to doubt that they were right.

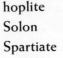

KEY TERMS

hero cults	hoplite	pre-Socratics	Sophists
polis	Solon	Pericles	Socrates
Oracle at Delphi	Spartiate	Peloponnesian War	

SELECTED READINGS

Penguin Classics and the Loeb Classical Library both offer reliable translations of Greek literary, philosophical, and historical texts.

Boardman, John, Jaspar Griffin, and Oswyn Murray, eds. *Greece and the Hellenistic World*. Oxford, 1988. A reprint of the Greek and Hellenistic chapters from *The Oxford History of the Classical World*, originally published in 1986. Excellent, stimulating surveys, accessible to a general audience but provocative to specialists.

Brunschwig, Jacques, and Geoffrey E. R. Lloyd. *Greek Thought: A Guide to Classical Knowledge*. Trans. Catherine Porter. Cambridge, Mass., 2000. An outstanding, up-to-date work of reference.

Buckley, Terry, ed. *Aspects of Greek History, 750–323 B.C.: A Source-Based Approach*. London, 1999. An outstanding new collection of source materials.

Cartledge, Paul A. *The Spartans: An Epic History*. New York, 2003. A lively and authoritative history of Sparta from its origins to the Roman conquest.

Dover, Kenneth J. *Greek Homosexuality*. Cambridge, Mass., 1978. The standard account of an important subject.

Fantham, Elaine, Helene Foley, Natalie Kampen, Sarah B. Pomeroy, and H. A. Shapiro. *Women in the Classical World: Image and Text*. Oxford, 1994. Wide-ranging analysis drawing on both visual and written sources, covering both the Greek and the Roman periods.

Fornara, Charles W., and Loren J. Samons II. *Athens from Cleisthenes to Pericles*. Berkeley, Calif., 1991. An excellent narrative history of Athenian politics during the first half of the fifth century B.C.E.

Freeman, Charles. *The Greek Achievement: The Foundation of the Western World*. New York, 1999. An admiring survey written for a general audience.

Garlan, Yvon. *Slavery in Ancient Greece*. Ithaca, N.Y., 1988. Now the standard account.

Hanson, Victor Davis. *The Other Greeks: The Family Farm and the Agrarian Roots of Western Civilization*. New York, 1995. Occasionally polemical and idiosyncratic but convincing in its emphasis on small-holding farmers as the backbone of Greek urban society.

Jones, Nicholas F. *Ancient Greece: State and Society*. Upper Saddle River, N.J., 1997. A concise survey from the Minoans up to the end of the Classical Period that emphasizes the connections between the social order and politics.

Lefkowitz, Mary, and Maureen Fant. *Women's Life in Greece and Rome: A Source Book in Translation*. 3d ed. Baltimore, Md., 2005. A remarkably wide-ranging collection, topically arranged, and invaluable to scholars and students.

Levi, Peter. *Atlas of the Greek World*. New York, 1984. Excellent maps and illustrations supplement an outstanding text.

Morris, Ian, and Barry Powell, eds. *A New Companion to Homer*. Leiden, 1997. A collection of thirty specialist but accessible scholarly articles, encompassing the most recent research on Homer and Dark Age Greece.

Pomeroy, Sarah B., Stanley M. Burstein, Walter Donlan, and Jennifer Tolbert Roberts. *Ancient Greece: A Political, Social, and Cultural History*. New York, 1999. An outstanding new textbook: clear, lively, and up-to-date, with good bibliographies.

Price, Simon. *Religions of the Ancient Greeks*. Cambridge, 1999. Concise and authoritative, this survey extends from the Archaic Period up to the fifth century C.E.

Strassler, Robert B., ed. *The Landmark Thucydides*. New York, 1996. Reprints the classic Richard Crawley translation with maps, commentary, notes, and appendices by leading scholars.

Thomas, Carol G., and Craig Conant. *Citadel to City-State: The Transformation of Greece, 1200–700 B.C.E.* Bloomington, Ind., 1999. A lucid and accessible study that examines developments at a number of different Dark Age sites.

CHAPTER FOUR

THE EXPANSION
OF GREECE

THE SUPREME TRAGEDY OF THE GREEKS was their failure to solve the problem of internecine political conflict. The fifth century B.C.E. in Greece had ended with a debilitating and destructive war of attrition between Athens and Sparta. The fourth century continued along much the same path, as the major poleis—Sparta, then Thebes, then Athens again—jockeyed for dominance within the Greek world. But the independent temper of Greek political life could not suffer such dominance for long; and so as each great polis appeared on the brink of realizing its goals, a coalition of age-old enemies would form to defeat it. Despite mounting calls for the Greeks to set aside their local differences and unite in a common cause, they could not escape their heritage of particularism.

Social and economic difficulties were also mounting, stemming from ideologically driven civil wars within the poleis as well as from the endemic warfare among them. Faith in the old ideals of equality decayed as a vast gulf opened up between the rich and the poor. Increasingly, the wealthy withdrew from politics altogether; meanwhile, the number of free citizens declined as poverty-stricken freemen and freewomen descended into slavery. The result was despair and cynicism.

The age did not lack for creative energy. Philosophy, science, and literature blossomed in the fourth century B.C.E., as men of talent shunned public life, turning their attention instead to the life of the mind. As the polis system decayed, thinkers debated what the polis was, how and why it functioned, and how it might be improved. But even the greatest of these thinkers remained enclosed within the parochial world of the polis.

The unhappy equilibrium of the Greek world was shattered in the last half of the fourth century by the sudden emergence of the kingdom of Macedonia. The extraordinary conquests of Philip of Macedon unified Greece. Those of his son

FOCUS QUESTIONS

• What conditions led to the growing number of mercenaries in the fourth century B.C.E.?

• Why did Plato's ideal polis differ from Aristotle's?

• What accounts for the remarkable success of the Macedonian conquests?

• What characteristics defined and distinguished the three major Hellenistic kingdoms?

• Why was prosperity so unevenly distributed in the Hellenistic economy?

• What was the relationship between Epicureanism and Stoicism?

• What were the principal themes of Hellenistic architecture and sculpture?

• Why did science and medicine flourish in this period?

• What changes occurred during the Hellenistic period to the polis-based culture of classical Greece?

Alexander the Great extended Greek culture by force of arms from Egypt to Persia to the frontiers of India. Alexander's empire did not last. But the cosmopolitan, Greek-like (hence *Hellenistic*, as opposed to *Hellenic*) culture to which it gave rise became the most powerful and pervasive cultural influence the Near Eastern world would know until the rise of Islam almost 1,000 years later.

FAILURES OF THE FOURTH-CENTURY POLIS

What conditions led to the growing number of mercenaries in the fourth century B.C.E.?

The Peloponnesian War had left Sparta as the pre-eminent power in the Greek world, but the Spartans showed little talent for the position their unexpected victory had thrust on them. In 395, a significant portion of Greece—including such traditional enemies as Athens, Argos, Corinth, and Thebes—aligned itself against Sparta in the Corinthian War (395–387 B.C.E.). The Spartans, for their part, could bring matters to a resolution only by forcing a peace on their fellow Greeks brokered from the outside—essentially composed and guaranteed by the Persians. This pattern was repeated time and again over the next fifty years, during which the advantage shifted steadily toward Persia.

SOCIAL AND ECONOMIC CRISES

Incessant warfare, combined with internal political struggles, profoundly affected society and economy throughout the Greek world. Even wealthy cities such as Athens and Sparta exhausted their resources through war. Personal fortunes were lost, and many ordinary people were driven from their homes or reduced to slavery. Country towns were ravaged, some repeatedly, as were farmlands throughout Greece. The destruction of orchards and vineyards was particularly devastating, because of the long time it takes to nourish olive trees and grapevines to a productive state; but even arable land was now less productive than it had been earlier. As a result, standards of living declined significantly during the fourth century B.C.E.

Unemployment was widespread, especially among the growing population of the cities. During wartime, men might find employment as rowers or soldiers in the service of their city. When their city was at peace, many turned instead to mercenary service. The Greek states of Sicily and Italy hired mercenaries from the mainland, as did Sparta to supplement its own campaigns in Asia Minor. But when mercenaries could not find work abroad, they were likely to terrorize the local Greek countryside. Such depredations only added to the disastrous cycle of destruction, inflation, and overpopulation caused by land failure.

THE CULTURAL AND INTELLECTUAL RESPONSE

Why did Plato's ideal polis differ from Aristotle's?

The breakdown of polis society during the fourth century B.C.E. had a profound impact on philosophy, the arts, and political thought. Scholars have sometimes presented fourth-century culture as if it represented a decline from the great artistic and intellectual achievements of the fifth century B.C.E. But such a sweeping verdict on fourth-century B.C.E. culture is unjustified. It underestimates not only the continuities between fifth- and fourth-century Greek culture but also the originality and creativity of these new developments.

ART AND LITERATURE

Sculptors were already attempting to achieve a heightened sense of realism, especially in portraiture, when the fourth century B.C.E. began. Realism had been a hallmark of classical art as well; but in the fourth century artists tried increasingly to render objects as they actually looked, rather than portraying them in an idealized, dignified form. Fourth-century artists also paid more attention to life and movement, a trend that would culminate in the breathtaking works of the Hellenistic period.

Drama, by contrast, changed profoundly. No fourth-century authors emerged to match the great tragedians of the Athenian golden age. Nor did the comic genius of Aristophanes have any true fourth-century successors. Even in his own lifetime, however, Aristophanes' biting, satirical style was beginning to give way to a milder, less provocative drama that bears some resemblance to modern television comedies. It was this new style that laid the groundwork for the "New Comedy" of the fourth and third centuries B.C.E.

Perhaps the most striking development in fourth-century drama is the flight from social and political commentary. Fourth-century audiences looked to drama for diversion and escape; they no longer cared for the scathing indictments of society and of prominent individuals that Aristophanes had pioneered. Comedic humor was now based on mistaken identities, tangled familial relationships, comic misunderstandings, and breaches of etiquette. Similar trends are apparent in novels, a new literary genre that emerged during the fourth century. Here, too, lovers face extraordinary obstacles, but their affairs almost always end happily, with the lovers reunited after perilous adventures and a long separation.

PHILOSOPHY AND POLITICAL THOUGHT IN THE AGE OF PLATO AND ARISTOTLE

The intellectual shift begun by Socrates was carried on brilliantly by his most talented student, Plato. Born in Athens to an aristocratic family around 429 B.C.E., Plato joined Socrates' circle as a young man and soon saw his mentor condemned to death. This experience made such an indelible impression on Plato that from then until his own death around 349 B.C.E. he shunned direct political involvement, seeking instead to vindicate Socrates by constructing a philosophical system based on Socratic precepts. Plato taught this system in Athens in an informal school (no buildings, tuition, or set curriculum) called the Academy, and also by writing a series of *dialogues* (treatises expressed in dramatic form) in which Socrates was the main speaker. The Platonic dialogues, including the *Phaedo*, the *Symposium*, and the *Republic*, are enduring works of literature as well as the earliest surviving complete works of philosophy.

Plato was influenced by the two worlds in which he lived. As a young man, he had watched his teacher engage the relativism of the Sophists; as an adult, he lived in a rapidly changing world that had lost confidence in absolute truths. Plato understood that to combat skepticism and refute the Sophists he needed to provide a secure foundation for ethics. This he did by means of his doctrine of Ideas. He conceded that relativity and change are characteristics of the world we perceive with our senses, but he denied that this world of appearances was an appropriate foundation for philosophy. A higher, spiritual realm exists, composed of eternal forms or Ideas that only the mind can grasp. These unchanging Ideas are not mere abstractions but have a real existence. The things we perceive through our senses are merely imper-

fect copies of the supreme realities, the Ideas, and relate to them as shadows relate to material objects. By understanding and contemplating the Idea of the Good, one might achieve the ultimate goal of fulfillment through virtue.

Plato addressed himself to politics in his most famous dialogue, the *Republic*, the first systematic treatment of political philosophy ever written. Because Plato sought social harmony and order rather than liberty or equality, he argued for an elitist state in which most of the people—the farmers, artisans, and traders—would be governed by an intellectually superior group of "guardians." Guardians would be chosen for their naturally superior attributes of intelligence and character. These enlightened rulers would see to it that every aspect of life was subordinated to the Idea of the Good, and would in turn choose only the wisest to succeed them. Later commentators have often found this ideal of rule by the wisest to be seductive, but they ask of Plato, "Who will guard the guardians?" Plato's system presumed that properly educated rulers would never be corrupted by power or wealth—a proposition that has yet to be sustained in practice.

Plato.

ARISTOTELIAN THOUGHT

Such practical considerations were more typical of the thought of Plato's own greatest student, Aristotle (384–322 B.C.E.). Aristotle was the son of a physician, who learned from his father the importance of carefully observing natural phenomena. He accepted Plato's assumption that there are some things only the mind can grasp, but his own philosophical system was based on his confidence that the human mind could understand the universe through the rational ordering of sense experience. In contrast to Plato, who taught that everything we see and touch is but an untrustworthy reflection of some intangible truth, Aristotle believed in the objective reality of material objects and taught that systematic investigation of tangible things, combined with rational inquiry into how they function, could yield full comprehension of the natural order and of human beings' place within it.

Aristotle surveyed a wide variety of subjects in separate but interrelated treatises on logic, metaphysics, ethics, poetics, and politics. Aristotle's central belief was that all things in the universe consist of the imprint of form on matter. This was a compromise between Platonism, which tended to ignore matter, and materialism, which saw no underlying patterns in the universe at all. For Aristotle, forms are the purposeful forces that shape the world of matter, thus the presence of the form of humanity molds and directs the human embryo until it ultimately becomes a human being. Because everything has a purposeful form, the universe for Aristotle is teleological—that is, every item and every class of items is inherently aiming toward its own particular end. Aristotle's universe is therefore in a constant state of motion, as everything within it moves toward its ultimate perfected form (known in Greek as its *telos*).

Aristotle's moral philosophy was expressed most fully in his *Nicomachean (NEE-ko-MAH-kee-an) Ethics*, although important aspects of his ideas are also contained in his *Politics*. Aristotle taught that the highest good consists in the harmonious functioning of the individual human mind and body. Humans differ from the animals by virtue of their rational capacities, and so they find happiness by exercising these appropriately. For most peo-

ple this will mean exercising reason in practical affairs. Good conduct is virtuous conduct, and virtue resides in aiming for the golden mean: courage rather than rashness or cowardice, temperance rather than excessive indulgence or ascetic denial. Better than the practical life, however, is the contemplative life, for such a life allows those few men equipped for it by nature to exercise their rational capacities to the utmost. Aristotle believed therefore that philosophers were the happiest of men, but he understood that even they could not engage in contemplation without interruption. As a practical person, moreover, he deemed it necessary for them to intersperse their speculative activities with practical life in the real world.

Whereas Plato conceived of politics as a means to an end, the orderly pursuit of the supernatural Good, Aristotle thought of politics as an end in itself, the collective exercise of the good life. But Aristotle also took it for granted that some people—"barbarians"—were not fully human and so were meant by nature to be slaves. He also excluded women from the life of the polis and so from a full measure of humanity. All male citizens, however, were meant to share in it, for, as Aristotle proposed, "man is by nature a political animal" (or, to be more faithful to the Greek, "a creature of the polis"). This did not mean that the best form of government was democracy; like Plato, Aristotle saw that as a "debased" form of government. What he preferred was the polity, in which monarchical, aristocratic, and democratic elements were combined by means of checks and balances. Such a government would allow free men to realize their rational potential, above the animals and right below the gods.

> Whereas Plato conceived of politics as a means to an end, the orderly pursuit of the supernatural Good, Aristotle thought of politics as an end in itself, the collective exercise of the good life.

For all of their brilliance and originality, Plato and Aristotle offered few prescriptions for reforming their own societies. Both imagined the perfect society as one made up of a few thousand households, largely engaged in agriculture and living in a face-to-face, participatory society. Although Greek civilization had begun in such a world, the realities of fourth-century political life were very different. The fact that Plato and Aristotle considered the problem at all is testament to their recognition that something was wrong with the polis; but for both men, the answer was a reorganization of the existing polity, not something new in its place.

WHAT ACCOUNTS FOR THE REMARKABLE SUCCESS OF THE MACEDONIAN CONQUESTS?

THE RISE OF MACEDON AND THE CONQUESTS OF ALEXANDER   103

THE RISE OF MACEDON AND THE CONQUESTS OF ALEXANDER

What accounts for the remarkable success of the Macedonian conquests?

By the middle of the fourth century B.C.E., the Greeks had become so embroiled in turmoil that they at first barely noticed the growing power of Macedon, a kingdom on the northern fringes of the Greek world. They had little reason to do so; until the fourth century, Macedon had been a weak kingdom, ruled by a royal house barely strong enough to control its own nobility and beset by intrigue and murderous ambition from within. Most Greeks viewed the Macedonians as barbarians, despite the efforts of a few Macedonian kings to add a bit of Hellenic culture to their court. When a young and energetic Macedonian king named Philip II consolidated the southern Balkans under his rule, many Greek patriots therefore saw it as a development no less troubling than the approach of the Persian "barbarians" in the fifth century B.C.E.

THE REIGN OF PHILIP II
(359–336 B.C.E.)

Philip came to the throne of Macedon after his older brother died fighting a barbarian invasion, leaving as his heir a small boy. Philip had himself made regent for the boy, but soon dispensed with that fiction and took the throne himself. By 356, he certainly considered himself king. That same year a son was born to him; Philip named the child Alexander and marked him out as his successor.

Philip's first problem was to stabilize his northern borders. Through a combination of warfare and diplomacy, he subdued the tribes of the southern Balkans and incorporated their territory into Macedonia. Philip's success had much to do with his reorganization of the Macedonian army. Philip turned the Macedonian phalanx from an ill-organized peasant army into a highly drilled, well-armed fighting machine. The mineral resources Philip captured early in his reign made him wealthy enough to establish what was in essence a professional army—just one of his gold mines produced as much in one year as the Delian League collected annually at its height. Philip also organized an elite cavalry squad—the Companions—who fought with and beside the king. Philip recruited future Companions (and gained valuable hostages) by bringing the most promising sons of the nobility to his capital at Pella, where they trained as pages with the crown prince Alexander. Through a series of dynastic marriages, Philip also managed to gain the good will and alliance of many neighboring kingdoms.

The growing power of Macedon alarmed some in the Greek world, most notably an Athenian orator named Demosthenes. Whereas some Greeks, like Isocrates, saw in Philip a potential answer to Greece's woes, Demosthenes and others believed that Philip's ultimate aim was to subject Greece to his rule.

There is no doubt of the threat that Philip now posed; but Demosthenes misunderstood Philip's true goals. Philip's expansion in the north was not aimed at Athens; instead, it was designed to secure his frontiers and the resources necessary to support an invasion of Persia. From 348 on, he was keen to conciliate the major Greek poleis, especially Athens. At one point, he even asked for

Macedonian Phalanx. Philip of Macedon's infantry—and Alexander the Great's thereafter—was armed with two-handed pikes and massed in squares sixteen rows deep and wide. Members of the phalanx were trained to wheel in step in any direction or to double their front by filing off in rows of eight.

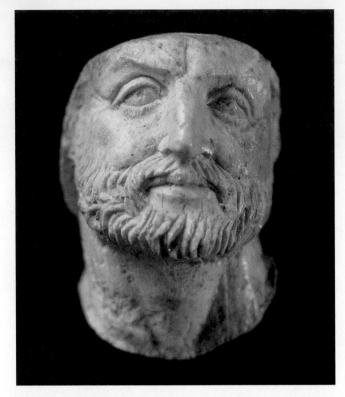

Philip II of Macedon. This tiny ivory head was discovered in the tomb of Philip of Macedon. The damaged right eye strongly suggests that it is a portrait of Philip himself, whose eye was damaged by a catapult bolt.

gruntled lover charged into the arena and assassinated him. The kingship now fell to the twenty-year-old young man who had led his father's cavalry at Chaeronea, Alexander III. To the Greeks he would be known as Alexander Poliorcetes, the "Sacker of Cities." To the Romans, far more impressed by conquerors than were the Greeks, he was Alexander the Great.

THE CONQUESTS AND REIGN OF ALEXANDER (336–323 B.C.E.)

Alexander is a difficult figure for historians to understand, not least because in his own lifetime romantic legend had already built up around him and his achievements. Scholars have seen in Alexander a visionary, a genius, and a butcher; what he did was nothing less than transform the world, translating Greek culture from its parochial, small-scale homeland into a world culture, spreading it as far as the modern states of Afghanistan and Pakistan.

an alliance whereby the Athenians would provide the war fleet for his proposed invasion of the Persian Empire; in return he would support their claim to hegemony over Greece. The Athenians took Demosthenes' advice and refused to cooperate with Philip. This miscalculation would prove disastrous for Athens.

Philip's inability to reach any understanding with Athens, despite his strenuous diplomatic efforts, ultimately led to war between the Macedonians on one side and Athens, Thebes, and a number of smaller poleis on the other (Sparta remained aloof). At the battle of Chaeronea in 338 B.C.E., the Macedonians won a narrow victory over the Athenians and their allies. In the aftermath, Philip called delegates from around mainland Greece to Corinth, where he established a new league. By and large, he left the independence of the major Greek poleis unaffected. The main purpose of the "League of Corinth" was to provide forces for the invasion of Persia by electing Philip as their military commander. But the league also played some role in maintaining peace among the rival Greek poleis.

Philip never realized his dream of invading Persian territory. At a festival in Macedon in 336 B.C.E., a dis-

Marble Head of Alexander. Alexander the Great was reputed to have been very handsome, but all surviving representations doubtless make him more handsome still. This one dates from about 180 B.C.E. and is typical in showing Alexander with "lion's-mane hair."

WHAT ACCOUNTS FOR THE REMARKABLE SUCCESS OF THE MACEDONIAN CONQUESTS?

THE RISE OF MACEDON AND THE CONQUESTS OF ALEXANDER   105

Alexander's military victories are well known. After first quelling revolts in Greece that erupted immediately on his father's death, by 334 he was ready to invade the Persian Empire, then under the rule of Darius III. The Macedonian king won a series of startling victories. Within three years, Alexander had subdued Anatolia and the Syria-Palestine coast and had detached Egypt from the Persian Empire. In 331 B.C.E., Darius mustered the remaining strength of his empire to face Alexander's Greco-Macedonian army in what is today northern Iraq. At the battle of Gaugamela, Alexander destroyed the Persian army. Darius himself fled to the hills, where he was captured and slain by a chieftain hoping to ingratiate himself to Alexander. The next spring, Alexander destroyed the Persian capital of Persepolis, lest it serve as a rallying point for Persian resistance.

Over the next few years, Alexander campaigned in the mountains of Bactria (modern Afghanistan), the hardest fighting of the campaign. He ultimately succeeded in conquering much of the region, but his grasp there was tenuous. Among the Bactrians he found the woman he would take as his queen, Roxane. From there he moved down the Indus Valley, meeting stiff resistance. At the mouth of the Indus, his soldiers mutinied and refused to press on. Alexander reluctantly led them back toward Babylon, arriving there by the end of 324 B.C.E.

What Alexander planned to do with his new empire is difficult to say. Some scholars see him merely as a pirate, bent on conquest and plunder in a self-serving quest for glory worthy of the Homeric heroes from whom he claimed descent. Others counter by pointing to his

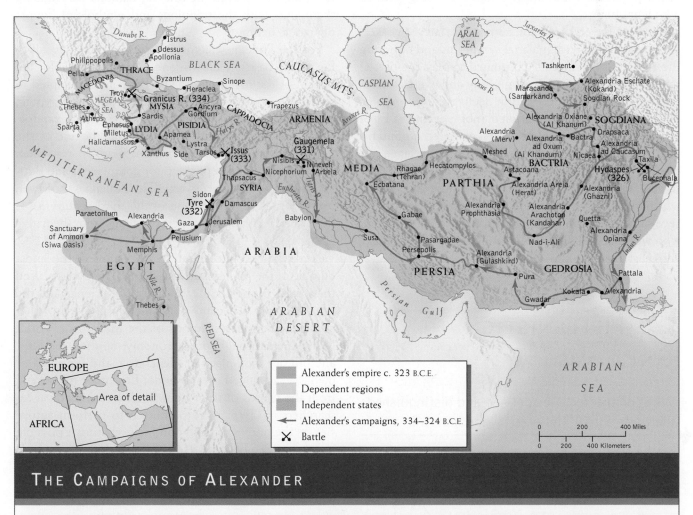

THE CAMPAIGNS OF ALEXANDER

The conquests of Alexander the Great brought Greek culture to the vast area of the former Persian Empire as far east as the Indus River. Notice the number of cities named after Alexander. Why did Alexander and his followers establish so many new cities, particularly in regions that were already highly urbanized?

systematic foundation of Greek-style cities along his campaign route. These new cities served not only as garrisons to control the local population but also as foci of Greek culture. There is also the bizarre mass marriage he forced on his officers, compelling them to put aside their wives and take Persian noblewomen as brides. Once seen as a reflection of Alexander's supposed visionary desire to eliminate ethnic distinctions within his empire, this act is now viewed as an attempt to breed a new nobility, loyal not to Macedonian or Persian concerns but to him and his successors alone. Alexander took no realistic steps to create an administration for his new realm, although he did move various officers and groups of veterans about in an attempt to reshuffle certain responsibilities. Our sources hint at plans for further conquests, perhaps Arabia, perhaps toward Italy and Sicily in the west. Given what we know about Alexander, it is hard to imagine him ever being satisfied with what he had.

We will never know for certain. In late May 323, Alexander fell ill with malarial symptoms and, ignoring the advice of his doctors, continued to play the part of the Homeric king, drinking mightily and exerting himself incautiously. His condition declined, until on June 10, 323 B.C.E., Alexander died, not yet thirty-three years old. His friends and officers, gathered around his deathbed, asked to whom he wished to leave his empire. One source states that, just as he went unconscious, a wry smile adorned Alexander's face as he whispered "To the strongest." This might mean any of several talented and ambitious generals around him, who were second only to Alexander himself in prestige and martial skill.

The Hellenistic Kingdoms

What characteristics defined and distinguished the three major Hellenistic kingdoms?

The wars and intrigues that took place in the two generations after Alexander's death are too involved to describe in detail. By 275 B.C.E., however, three separate axes of military and political power had emerged, each with a distinctive outlook despite their common background and their Greco-Macedonian ruling class.

Ptolemaic Egypt

Following Alexander's death in Babylon, his inner circle met to decide the fate of his empire. The rest of Alexander's generals seem to have been glad to let Ptolemy (*TAHL-uh-mee*) have the hot, sweltering land of Egypt, but Ptolemy himself recognized the country's vast potential and its virtual invulnerability to attack. As soon as he arrived, Ptolemy set about making Egypt an independent kingdom under his rule. The dynasty he established would rule Egypt for the next 300 years. The male heirs of the line all took the name Ptolemy, hence Ptolemaic Egypt.

Ruling from Alexandria, the great coastal city founded by Alexander, the Ptolemies acted as Macedonian kings toward their Greek and Macedonian subjects living in the thriving capital. Outside of Alexandria, however, they played the role of pharaohs, surrounding themselves with the trappings and symbols of Egypt's pharaonic heritage.

For the Ptolemies as for the ancient pharaohs, all of Egypt was basically crown land, to be exploited for the benefit of the royal house. The Ptolemies attempted to squeeze every last drop of wealth from the Egyptian countryside. Most of this wealth ended up in Alexandria. There was little interest in improving the lot of the Egyptian peasantry; in the ancient world it was often assumed that what kept the poor complacent and dutiful was their desperate poverty. The Ptolemies, however, overdid it, and from the end of the third century B.C.E. they faced regular and dangerous revolts from the native peasantry.

Nevertheless, Ptolemaic Egypt proved the most durable of the Hellenistic kingdoms. The dynasty used the wealth of the country to patronize science and the arts. Alexandria became a center of scholarship that attracted the greatest minds of the Hellenistic world. Many breakthroughs in astronomy, applied sciences, and physics took place in Alexandria, and the study of medicine advanced greatly under Ptolemaic rule. Freed from the taboos of their homeland, Greek medical researchers in Egypt were permitted to perform autopsies on the bodies of dead criminals, making it possible for anatomy to become a scientific discipline in its own right. The Ptolemies were not selfless patrons. They were largely interested in the glory and prestige their patronage brought them, rather than the practical benefits that might arise from the research they sponsored. But whatever its motives, Alexandrine scholarship left a permanent mark on the Mediterranean world.

SELEUCID ASIA

The vast Asian possessions of Alexander the Great eventually fell to another Macedonian, Seleucus (*seh-LOO-kuhs*), by 281 B.C.E. Unlike the Ptolemies, however, the Seleucid Dynasty struggled with the problem of secession throughout its history. Their hold on the easternmost provinces was especially tenuous—even during Alexander's lifetime that had been the case—as Seleucus recognized. He therefore ceded much of the Indus Valley to the great Indian warrior-king Chandragupta in exchange for peace and a squad of war elephants. By the middle of the third century, the Seleucids had also lost control of Bactria, where a series of Indo-Greek states were emerging with a unique cultural complex of their own. By the 260s, they had also lost control of the western half of Asia Minor. The Seleucid heartland now became Syria–Palestine, Mesopotamia, and the western half of Persia: still a great, wealthy kingdom, but far less than what Alexander had left.

Like the Ptolemies, the Seleucids offered two faces to their subjects, one rooted in ancient Near Eastern tradition for their Persian and Mesopotamian subjects, another decidedly more Greek for the heavily Hellenized populations of the coast. Seleucus' son, Antiochus I, proclaimed in terms reminiscent of Sargon or a Esarhaddon: "I am Antiochus, the Great King, the legitimate king . . . king of Babylon, king of all countries." Throughout their empire, shrines and temples were built for the cult of the living ruler.

Seleucid rulers continued the tradition of Alexander, planting new cities throughout their empire, cities that were fundamentally Greek in their assumptions but that grew to be thriving commercial and industrial centers. Although their bureaucracy was less organized than that of the Ptolemies, in an empire of as many as 30 million

Legend:
- Antigonid Kingdom (and dependencies 240 B.C.E.)
- Independent Greek states
- Ptolemaic Egypt and dependencies
- Seleucid Kingdom
- Hellenized non-Greek kingdoms

ALEXANDER THE GREAT AND THE HELLENISTIC WORLD

Note the position of the three successor kingdoms to Alexander's empire; notice how each was based on one of the three major axes of civilization we have studied so far: Egyptian, ancient Near Eastern, and Aegean. What might the division of Alexander's empire along such "traditional" lines suggest about the durability of his empire even if he had lived to rule it?

inhabitants even haphazard tax collection could reap huge sums. Like their Persian predecessors, however, the Seleucids did not reinvest their gains into what we would call capital improvements. Instead, they hoarded their wealth in great state treasuries. All the same, they had more than enough cash to provide for the smooth operation of their government and to defend their borders against the Ptolemies. It was not until the second century, when Antiochus III lost a costly war with the Romans, that he had to plunder temples and private wealth to pay off his war indemnity.

ANTIGONID MACEDON AND GREECE

The Macedonian homeland remained highly unstable from the time of Alexander's death until 276 B.C.E., when a general named Antigonus was finally able to establish his rule over the area. Macedon drew its strength from natural resources and Aegean trade, as well as its de facto overlordship of the Greek homeland. Furthermore, the Macedonians could still field the finest army of any of the successor states, and the Antigonid kings of Macedon held what many of the monarchs of the Hellenistic world desired, the kingship of the land once held by Philip and Alexander.

The Greeks, however, were restive under the Antigonids, and two emergent forces within the Greek world served as rallying points for cries of freedom and war against the "barbarian." These two forces, the Aetolian League and the Achaean League, were a departure in Greek political organization. Unlike the defensive alliances of the classical period, these two leagues represented a real political unification. So impressive was the degree of cooperation and unification that James Madison, John Jay, and Alexander Hamilton employed the Achaean League as one of their models in advocating federalism in the United States.

THE GROWTH OF TRADE AND URBANIZATION

Why was prosperity so unevenly distributed in the Hellenistic economy?

The Hellenistic world was generally prosperous, owing to the growth of long-distance trade, finance, and cities. Alexander's conquests opened up a vast trading area stretching from Egypt to the Persian Gulf, dominated by Greek-speaking rulers and merchant communities. These conquests also stimulated the economy by putting into circulation hoards of gold and silver coins, jewelry, and utensils acquired through plunder. Industries also benefited, because manufacturing was encouraged by autocratic rulers as a means of increasing their revenues through trade.

New trading ventures were particularly vigorous and lucrative in Ptolemaic Egypt and Seleucid Syria. Every facility was provided by the Ptolemies and the Seleucids for the encouragement of trade. Harbors were improved, warships were sent out to police the seas, and roads and canals were built. The Ptolemies even employed geographers to discover new routes to distant lands and thereby open up valuable markets. As a result of such methods Egypt developed a flourishing commerce in the widest variety of products. Into the port of Alexandria came spices from Arabia, gold from Ethiopia and India, tin from Britain, elephants and ivory from Nubia, silver from Spain, fine carpets from Asia Minor, and even silk from China. Profits for the government and for some of the merchants were often as high as 20 or 30 percent.

Cities grew enormously during the Hellenistic Age. Alexander the Great himself had founded some 70 cities as outposts of Greek domination, and in the next two centuries his successors founded about 200 more. But urbanization also increased because of the expansion of commerce and industry and the proliferation of governmental bureaus. At Antioch in Syria, the population quadrupled during a single century. Seleucia on the Tigris grew from nothing to a metropolis of several hundred thousand in less than two centuries. Alexandria in Egypt, the largest and most famous of all the Hellenistic cities, had 0.5 million inhabitants. Before imperial Rome, no other city in ancient times surpassed it in size or in magnificence. Its streets were well paved and laid out in regular order. It had splendid public buildings and parks, a museum, and a library of half a million scrolls.

Despite the overall growth of the Hellenistic economy, by no means did everyone enjoy prosperity. Agriculture remained the major occupation and primary source of wealth in the Hellenistic world, and small farmers in particular suffered severely from the exploitative tax policies of Hellenistic monarchs. Although industrial production increased, industry continued to be based on manual labor by individual artisans, most of whom lived in poverty. Among the teeming populations of Hellenistic cities, unemployment was a constant concern. Those who could not find work were forced to beg, steal, or prostitute themselves to survive.

Even those who prospered in the new economy were often subject to drastic fluctuations in their fortunes. Merchants were particularly exposed to the "boom-and-bust" syndrome. A merchant, thinking he would make a fortune during an upward price spiral, might go into debt to take advantage of the upward trend, only to find that supply in the commodity he traded suddenly exceeded demand, leaving him nothing with which to pay back his creditors.

All told, therefore, it seems clear that the economic landscape of the Hellenistic world was one of contrasting extremes, an image worth remembering as we move to a consideration of Hellenistic thought and culture.

Hellenistic Culture: Philosophy and Religion

What was the relationship between Epicureanism and Stoicism?

Hellenistic philosophy exhibited two trends that ran almost parallel throughout the civilization. The major trend, exemplified by Epicureanism and Stoicism, saw reason as the key to resolving the anxieties of human life. The minor trend, exemplified by the Skeptics and various cults, tended to reject reason, to deny the possibility of attaining truth, and in some cases to turn toward mysticism. But despite the differences in their teachings, the philosophers and religious enthusiasts of the Hellenistic Age generally agreed on one thing: the necessity of finding some release from the trials of human existence, for with the decline of free civic life as a means for the expression of human idealism, alternatives needed to be found to make life seem meaningful, or at least endurable.

EPICUREANISM AND STOICISM

Epicureanism and Stoicism both originated about 300 B.C.E. The founders were, respectively, Epicurus (c. 342–270 B.C.E.) and Zeno (fl. after 300 B.C.E.), both residents of Athens. The two philosophies had several features in common. Both were individualistic, concerned not with the welfare of society but with the good of the individual. Both were materialistic, denying the existence of any spiritual substances; even divine beings and the soul were declared to be formed of matter. Stoicism and Epicureanism also contained elements of universalism. Both taught that people are the same the world over and recognized no distinctions between Greeks and non-Greeks.

But in most ways the two systems were quite different. The Stoics believed that the cosmos is an ordered whole in which all contradictions are resolved for ultimate good. Evil is, therefore, relative; the particular misfortunes that befall human beings are but necessary incidents to the final perfection of the universe. Everything that happens is rigidly determined in accordance with rational purpose. No individual is master of his or her fate; people are free only in the sense that they can accept their fate or rebel against it. But whether they accept or rebel, they cannot overcome it. Their supreme duty is to submit to the order of the universe in the knowledge that this order is good. Through such an act of resignation the highest happiness will be attained, which consists of tranquillity of mind. Those who are most truly happy are thus the ones who by the assertion of their rational natures have accomplished a perfect adjustment of their lives to the cosmic purpose and purged their souls of all bitterness and protest against evil turns of fortune.

The Stoics' ethical and social theory grew from their general philosophy. Believing that the highest good is serenity of mind, they emphasized duty, self-discipline, tolerance, and forgiveness as cardinal virtues. They urged participation in public affairs and condemned slavery and war, although they took no real actions against these evils because they believed that the results that might arise from violent measures of social change would be worse than the diseases they were meant to cure.

The Epicureans based their philosophy on the materialistic "atomism" of an earlier Greek thinker named Democritus, who lived in the latter part of the fifth century B.C.E. According to this theory, the ultimate constituents of the universe are atoms, infinite in number, indestructible, and indivisible. Every individual object or organism in the universe is the product of a fortuitous combination of atoms. Epicurus and his followers concluded, therefore, that because there is no ultimate purpose in the universe, the highest good is pleasure—the moderate satisfaction of bodily appetites, the mental pleasure of contemplating excellence, and above all, serenity of soul in the face of death. An individual who understands that the soul is material and therefore cannot survive the body, that the universe operates of itself, and that no gods intervene in human affairs, will not fear death or the supernatural. The Epicureans thus came by a different route to the same general conclusion as the Stoics—nothing is better than tranquillity of mind.

The practical moral teachings and the politics of the Epicureans rested on utilitarianism. In contrast to the Stoics, they did not insist on virtue as an end in itself but taught that the only reason why one should be good is to increase one's own happiness. In like manner, they denied that there is any such thing as absolute justice: laws and institutions are just only insofar as they contribute to the welfare of the individual. Certain rules have been found necessary in every society for the maintenance of order. These rules should be obeyed solely because it is to each individual's advantage to do so. Epicurus considered the state as a mere convenience and taught that the wise man should take no active part in politics. Because the evils in the world cannot be eradicated by human effort, the wise individual will withdraw from it to study philosophy and enjoy the fellowship of a few congenial friends.

> The Epicureans thus came by a different route to the same general conclusion as the Stoics—nothing is better than tranquillity of mind.

SKEPTICISM

A more radically defeatist philosophy was propounded by the Skeptics. Skepticism reached the zenith of its popularity about 200 B.C.E. under the influence of Carneades. The chief source of its inspiration was the teaching that all knowledge is derived from sense perception and, therefore, must be limited and relative. From this the Skeptics deduced that people cannot prove anything. Because the impressions of our senses deceive us, no truth can be certain. All we can say is that things appear to be such and such; we do not know what they really are. We have no definite knowledge of the supernatural, of the meaning of life, or even of right and wrong. It follows that the sensible course to pursue is suspension of judgment; this alone can lead to happiness. If we will abandon the fruitless quest for absolute truth and cease worrying about good and evil, we will attain peace of mind, which is the highest satisfaction that life affords. The Skeptics were even less concerned than the Epicureans with political and social problems. Their ideal was one of escape from a world neither reformable nor understandable.

RELIGION

Religious developments in the Hellenistic period also encouraged escape from collective political commitments. Greek religion in the age of the city-states had emphasized the worship of the gods who protected the polis. This sense of connection between a locality and its gods continued during the Hellenistic period. For many people, however, such civic-oriented worship was losing its vitality in the rootless, cosmopolitan world of the second and third centuries B.C.E. In its place, elite members of society gravitated toward Stoicism, Epicureanism, and Skepticism, while ordinary people began to embrace emotional personal religions that offered elaborate ritual in this world and salvation in the next.

In Greek-speaking communities especially, cults that stressed ascetic atonement for sin, ecstatic mystical union with divinity, and otherworldly salvation attracted many followers. Among these mystery cults, so called because their membership was secret and their rites held in private, one of the most popular was based on the death and resurrection of the god Dionysius. The Egyptian cult of Isis sounded these same themes of death and rebirth; so too did Zoroastrianism, which became increasingly dualistic, insisting that everything material was evil and demanding that believers practice austerities to prepare their souls for the afterlife.

Like the peoples of the Hellenistic world, the gods migrated to new lands. Temples to Greek gods and goddesses were dedicated throughout the Near East and Egypt, and temples to Near Eastern divinities were constructed in the Greek homeland. Greek and non-Greek cults thus combined to create a dizzying variety of religious possibilities.

Even where such assimilationist impulses met with resistance, as they did among the Jews of Palestine, Hellenistic culture was deeply influential. Outside Palestine, where by the end of the second century B.C.E. the majority of Jews lived, Hellenistic influence on Judaism was pervasive. To meet the religious needs of these Greek-speaking Jewish communities, a Greek translation of the Hebrew Bible was produced, probably in Alexandria. Legend had it that seventy scribes, each working independently, produced exactly the same translation from Hebrew into Greek. This proved that the "Septuagint" (so called from the Greek word for *seventy*) was the product of divine inspiration, and it

THE GREEK INFLUENCE ON ISRAEL

Greek culture was a powerfully intoxicating force throughout the Hellenistic world, even in a comparative cultural backwater like Israel. In the second century B.C.E., *the Hellenized ways of the Jewish upper classes in Jerusalem finally occasioned a revolt by a native Hebrew dynasty known as the Maccabees, who decried the "debaucheries" Greek culture had introduced into Jewish life. In the passage that follows, note that even the high priest of the Temple bears the Greek name Jason.*

In those days [the reign of Antiochus IV Epiphanes, 175–164 B.C.E.] certain renegades came out from Israel and misled many, saying, "Let us go and make a covenant with the Gentiles [Greeks] around us, for since we separated from them many disasters have come upon us." . . . Some of the people went to the king, who authorized them to observe the ordinances of the Gentiles. So they built a gymnasium in Jerusalem, according to Gentile custom, and removed the marks of circumcision, and abandoned the holy covenant. They joined with the Gentiles and sold themselves to do evil. . . . When Antiochus succeeded to the kingdom, Jason the brother of Onias obtained the high priesthood by corruption. . . . He at once shifted his compatriots over to the Greek way of life. . . . Despising the sanctuary and neglecting the sacrifices, they hurried to take part in the unlawful proceedings in the wrestling arena after the signal for the discus-throwing, disdaining the honors prized by their ancestors and putting the highest value upon Greek forms of prestige. . . . When the quadrennial games were being held at Tyre and the king was present, Jason sent envoys . . . to carry three hundred silver drachmas for the sacrifice to Heracles. . . . Harsh and utterly grievous was the onslaught of evil.

For the Temple was filled with debauchery and reveling by the Gentiles, who dallied with prostitutes and had intercourse with women within the sacred precincts. . . . The altar was covered with abominable offerings that were forbidden by the laws.

1 Maccabees 2 and 2 Maccabees 4–6, *New Revised Standard Version of the Bible* (The National Council of the Churches of Christ in the USA, 1989).

QUESTIONS FOR ANALYSIS

1. The Jews had disobeyed their religious leaders many times before they encountered Hellenistic culture. Why did Hebrew priests and prophets think the Greeks were so dangerous? What did they personally have to fear from corruption?

2. Why was the building of a gymnasium, or "Greek secondary school," in Jerusalem particularly symbolic and offensive to Jews? Could anyone have stopped the project? By their insistence on maintaining separatism, were the Jews resisting or demanding special privileges from the rulers of the Hellenistic successor kingdoms?

soon came to be accepted as authoritative even in Palestine, lending a distinctly Greek coloring to Jewish understandings of the Hebrew Bible.

HELLENISTIC CULTURE: LITERATURE AND ART

What were the principal themes of Hellenistic architecture and sculpture?

Both the literature and the art of the Hellenistic Age were characterized by a tendency to take aspects of earlier Greek accomplishments to extremes, as writers and artists sought to demonstrate their formal skills to please their autocratic patrons. The greater uncertainties of existence in Hellenistic times may also have led consumers of art to seek gratification from more dramatic and less subtle forms of artistic expression. Whatever the explanation, rather than being an integral expression of civic life, art during this period became more of a commodity. Artistic works became more numerous and more widely available: we know the names of at least 1,100 Hellenistic authors. Many of these works are mediocre but some are enduring masterpieces of art and literature.

PASTORAL LITERATURE

The most prominent Hellenistic verse form was the pastoral, a new genre depicting a make-believe world of shepherds and wood nymphs. The inventor of the genre was a Greek named Theocritus, who wrote around 270 B.C.E. in the big-city environment of Alexandria. Theocritus was a merchant of escapism. In the midst of urban bustle, faced with despotic rulers, and within sight of overcrowded, slumlike conditions, he celebrated the charms of hazy country values and idealized the "simple pleasures" of rustic folk. One of his pastorals might start like this: "Begin my country song, sweet muses, begin, I am Thrysis from Etna, this is Thrysis's lovely voice." To many the falseness of such verse is alienating; how could shepherds talk this way? But other readers enjoy its poetic lushness.

PROSE

Hellenistic prose literature was dominated by historians and biographers. By far the most profound of the writers of history was the mainland Greek Polybius, who lived during the second century B.C.E. From the standpoint of historical method, Polybius deserves to be ranked second only to Thucydides among all the historians of ancient times, and he even surpassed Thucydides in his grasp of the importance of social and economic forces. Although most biographies of the time were light and gossipy, their popularity bears eloquent testimony to the literary tastes of the Hellenistic period.

ARCHITECTURE

Consonant with the despotic style of rule, the main traits of Hellenistic architecture were grandeur and ornamentation. In place of the balance and restraint that had characterized Greek architecture of the fifth and early fourth centuries B.C.E., Hellenistic public building drew on Greek elements but moved toward standards set by Persian monarchs and Egyptian pharaohs. Two examples (neither of which survives) are the great lighthouse of Alexandria, which rose to a height of nearly 400 feet, and the citadel of Alexandria, built of stone covered with blue-tinted plaster and said by a contemporary to have "risen into mid-air." In Pergamon in Asia Minor an enormous altar to Zeus (transported in modern times to Berlin) and a huge open-air theater looked out over a high hill. In Ephesus, not far away, the streets were paved with marble. The "signature" of Hellenistic architecture of whatever dimension was the Corinthian column, a form of column more ornate than the simple and dignified Doric and Ionic alternatives that had predominated in earlier Greek building.

The Corinthian Order of Architecture. This characteristically Hellenistic style for constructing columns was much more ornate than its classical predecessors.

The Winged Victory of Samothrace. In this figure, done around 200 B.C.E., a Hellenistic sculptor preserved some of the calmness and devotion to grace and proportion characteristic of Hellenic art in the golden age.

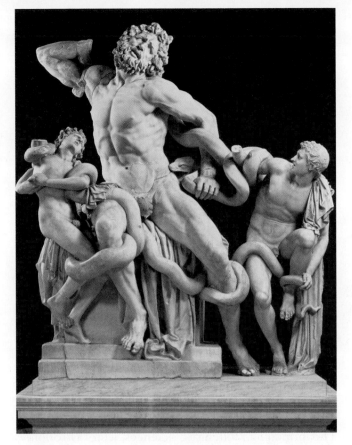

Laocoön. In sharp contrast to the serenity of the *Winged Victory* is this famous sculpture group from the first century B.C.E., depicting the death of Laocoön. According to legend, Laocoön warned the Trojans not to touch the wooden horse sent by the Greeks and was punished by Poseidon, who sent two serpents to kill him and his sons. The intense emotionalism of this work had a great influence on western European art from Michelangelo onward.

SCULPTURE

Whereas earlier Greek sculpture had sought to idealize humanity and to express Greek ideals of modesty by understated restraint, Hellenistic sculpture emphasized extreme naturalism and unashamed extravagance. Sculptors went to great lengths to re-create facial furrows, muscular distensions, and complex folds of drapery. Awkward human postures were considered to offer the greatest challenges to the artist in stone, to the degree that sculptors might prefer to show people stretching themselves or balancing themselves on one leg in ways that hardly ever occur in real life. Because most Hellenistic sculpture was executed for wealthy private patrons, it is clear that the goal was to create something unique in its conception and craftsmanship that a collector could show off as the only one of its type. It is not surprising, therefore, that complexity came to be admired for its own sake, and extreme naturalism sometimes teetered on the brink of distorted stylization. Yet when moderns see such works they frequently experience a shock of recognition, for the bizarre and exaggerated postures of Hellenistic sculp-

tures exerted an enormous influence on Michelangelo and his followers, and later inspired some of the most "modern" sculptors of the nineteenth and twentieth centuries.

SCIENCE AND MEDICINE

Why did science and medicine flourish in this period?

The Hellenistic period was the most brilliant age in the history of science before the seventeenth century C.E. There are two major reasons for this. One was the enormous stimulus given to intellectual inquiry by the fusion of Mesopotamian and Egyptian science with the learning and the curiosity of the Greeks. The other was that many Hellenistic rulers were generous patrons of scientific research, supporting scientists just as they did sculptors.

Practical aims motivated the patronage of science in some areas, above all in medicine and anything that might relate to military technology. But the rulers who financed scientific endeavors did so primarily for motives of prestige: rulers could show off a scientific gadget to visitors just as they would show off their sculptures. Even purely theoretical achievements were so much admired among the Greek-speaking leisure classes that a Hellenistic prince who subsidized such a breakthrough would share the prestige for it in the way the mayor of an American city might bask in prestige today if his or her city's football team were to win the Super Bowl.

ASTRONOMY, MATHEMATICS, AND GEOGRAPHY

The principal Hellenistic sciences were astronomy, mathematics, geography, medicine, and physics. The most renowned of the earlier Hellenistic astronomers was Aristarchus of Samos (310–230 B.C.E.), sometimes called the "Hellenistic Copernicus." His primary accomplishment was his deduction that the earth and the other planets revolve around the sun. This view was not accepted by his successors because it conflicted with the teachings of Aristotle and with the conviction of the Greeks that humanity, and therefore the earth, must be at the center of the universe. Later the fame of Aristarchus was overshadowed by that of Ptolemy of Alexandria (second century C.E.). Although Ptolemy made few original discoveries, he systematized the work of others. His principal writing, the *Almagest*, based on the view that all heavenly bodies revolve around the earth, was handed down to medieval Europe as the classic summary of ancient astronomy.

Closely allied with astronomy were mathematics and geography. The most influential Hellenistic mathematician was Euclid, the master of geometry. Until the middle of the nineteenth century his *Elements of Geometry* (written around 300 B.C.E. as a synthesis of the work of others) remained the accepted basis for the study of that branch of mathematics.

Hellenistic geography owed most of its development to Eratosthenes (c. 276–c. 196 B.C.E.), an astronomer and librarian of Alexandria. By means of sundials placed some hundreds of miles apart, he calculated the circumference of the earth with an error of less than 200 miles. Eratosthenes was also the first to suggest the possibility of reaching eastern Asia by sailing west. One of his successors divided the earth into the five climatic zones that are still recognized and explained the ebb and flow of the tides as due to the influence of the moon.

MEDICINE

Other Hellenistic advances in science were in the field of medicine. Especially significant was the work of the Alexandrian scholar Herophilus of Chalcedon (c. 335–c. 280 B.C.E.). Herophilus was the greatest anatomist of antiquity and probably the first to practice human dissection. Among his achievements were a detailed description of the brain, with an insistence (against Aristotle) that the brain is the seat of human intelligence; the discovery of the significance of the pulse and its use in diagnosing illness; and the discovery that the arteries contain blood alone (not a mixture of blood and air as Aristotle had taught) and that their function is to carry blood from the heart to all parts of the body. About the middle of the third century B.C.E., Erasistratus of Alexandria discovered the valves of the heart and distinguished between motor and sensory nerves. In addition, he rejected Hippocrates' theory that the body consists of four "humors" and consequently criticized bloodletting as a method of cure. Unfortunately the humoral theory and bloodletting were revived by Galen, the great encyclopedist of medicine who lived in the Roman

CHRONOLOGY

SCIENTIFIC LUMINARIES OF THE HELLENISTIC WORLD

Herophilus of Chalcedon	c. 335–c. 280 B.C.E.
Euclid	330?–270? B.C.E.
Aristarchus of Samos	310–230 B.C.E.
Archimedes of Syracuse	c. 287–212 B.C.E.
Eratosthenes	c. 276–c. 196 B.C.E.

Empire in the second century C.E. Galen's baleful influence lasted until the eighteenth century C.E.

PHYSICS

Before the third century B.C.E., physics had been a branch of philosophy. It was made a separate, experimental science by Archimedes of Syracuse (c. 287–212 B.C.E.), who discovered the law of floating bodies, or specific gravity, and formulated with scientific exactness the principles of the lever, the pulley, and the screw. Among his memorable inventions were the compound pulley and the screw propeller for ships. Although he has been considered the greatest technical genius of antiquity, he preferred to devote his time to pure scientific research. Tradition relates that he discovered "Archimedes' principle" (specific gravity) while pondering possible theories in his bath: when he reached his stunning insight he dashed out naked into the street crying "Eureka" ("I have found it").

THE TRANSFORMATION OF THE POLIS

What changes occurred during the Hellenistic period to the polis-based culture of classical Greece?

 The Hellenistic period saw the creation of great kingdoms in Egypt and Asia Minor and the rise of new forms of political organization in the Greek world such as the Achaean League. What, however, became of the polis, the foundation of classical Greek culture?

The apparent eclipse of the poleis is to some extent misleading. Some poleis continued to thrive as centers of trade. It is also important to remember that the great Hellenistic kingdoms remained, in many respects, collections of cities and that, for the most part, their Greco-Macedonian rulers continued to carry with them the cultural and political baggage of the polis world.

Nevertheless, the Hellenistic polis—even when it had not become a sprawling megalopolis such as Alexandria or Antioch—was in many ways a fundamentally different place from its classical precursor. As we have seen, changes in the fourth century were already disrupting the traditional bonds of Greek social and political life. Alexander's conquests had created a cosmopolitan world full of economic opportunity for a Greek-speaker. By 300 B.C.E., a common Greek-based culture encompassed the eastern Mediterranean and western Asia, and a sense of "Greekness" had emerged that transcended political and geographical boundaries. Into this vast, exciting world, Greeks poured en masse, reducing the population of the Greek mainland by as much as one half between 325 and 225 B.C.E. Hundreds of thousands of Greeks left Greece to seek their fortunes in a Mediterranean world of massive empires and cosmopolitan cities whose scale dwarfed anything imaginable even in Periclean Athens.

Such a transformation had serious effects on Greek culture and the polis. The small-scale Dark Age communities and archaic poleis from which classical Greek culture grew were societies in which everybody knew virtually everyone else; innumerable social and political ties bound the citizens. Greek traditions of participation in government had led to a greater share in the franchise than any other culture had achieved in antiquity. Every citizen of the Greek world, to a lesser or greater extent, had some share, some stake in his society, its institutions, its gods, its army, and its cultural life.

If we transport this ingrained outlook into the swirling cosmopolitanism of the Hellenistic city, we can perhaps appreciate the magnitude of the change. All of those things that defined one's life as a person and a citizen were by and large gone. The intimate connection with the political life of the state had vanished. In place of the nexus of social and familial relationships prevalent in the Greek mainland, an average Greek in one of the Hellenistic kingdoms might have only his immediate family to rely on, if even that. What resulted was a traumatic separation between the traditional values and assumptions of Greek life and the social and political realities of the day.

CONCLUSION

Judged from the vantage point of classical Greece, Hellenistic civilization may at first seem no more than a degenerate phase of Greek civilization. The autocratic governments of the Hellenistic Age appear repugnant by comparison to Athenian democracy, and the Hellenistic penchant for extravagance may appear debased in contrast to earlier Greek ideals. Even the best Hellenistic literary works lack the inspired majesty of the great Greek tragedies, and none of the Hellenistic philosophers matched the profundity of Plato and Aristotle. Yet Hellenistic civilization had its own achievements that the classical age could not match. Most Hellenistic cities offered a greater range of public facilities, such as museums and libraries, than earlier Greek cities did, and Hellenistic thinkers, writers, and artists left to posterity important new ideas, impressive new genres, and imaginative new styles. Scientific advances also demonstrate the intellectual creativity that marked the Hellenistic world.

Probably the most important contribution of the Hellenistic era to subsequent historical development was the role it played as intermediary between Greece and Rome. In some cases the Hellenistic contribution was simply that of preservation. Most of what the ancient Romans would know of classical Greek thought came to them through copies of Greek philosophical and literary texts preserved in Hellenistic libraries. In other areas, however, transfer involved transmutation. Hellenistic art, for example, evolved from earlier Greek art into something related but quite different, and it was this "Greek-like" art that exerted the greatest influence on the tastes and artistic accomplishments of the Romans. A similar case might be made for drama.

Two aspects of Hellenistic culture deserve special comment—Hellenistic cosmopolitanism and Hellenistic "modernity." The word *cosmopolitan* itself comes from a Greek word meaning "universal city," and it was the Greeks of the Hellenistic period who came closest to turning this ideal of cosmopolitanism into reality. Around 250 B.C.E. a leisure-class Greek could have traveled from Sicily to the borders of India, always meeting people who "spoke his language," both literally and in terms of shared ideals. Nor would this same Greek have been a nationalist in the sense of professing any exclusive loyalty to a city-state or kingdom. He would more likely have considered himself a "citizen of the world."

Hellenistic cosmopolitanism was partly a product of the cosmopolitanism of Persia and helped, in turn, create the cosmopolitanism of Rome; but in contrast to both it was not imperialistic even though it was achieved by exploiting subject peoples. Other aspects of Hellenistic civilization will seem even more familiar to observers today. Authoritarian governments, ruler cults, economic instability, extreme skepticism side by side with intense religiosity, rational science side by side with irrational superstition, flamboyant art and ostentatious art collecting: all these aspects of the Hellenistic Age might make the thoughtful student of history regard it as one of the most relevant in the entire human record for comparison with our own.

KEY TERMS

Plato's *Republic*	Ptolemy	Stoicism
Nicomachean Ethics	Seleucus	Euclid
Philip II	Antigonus	
Alexander	Epicureanism	

SELECTED READINGS

Penguin Classics and the Loeb Classical Library both offer reliable translations of scores of literary and historical texts from this period. Particularly important are historical works by Arrian (*Anabasis of Alexander*) and Plutarch (*Lives*).

Adcock, F. E. *The Greek and Macedonian Art of War*. Berkeley, Calif., 1957. Still a valuable introduction to the guiding principles and assumptions of Greek and Macedonian warfare.

Austin, M. M. *The Hellenistic World from Alexander to the Roman Conquest: A Selection of Ancient Sources in Translation.* Cambridge, 1981.

Bagnall, R. S., and P. Derow. *Greek Historical Documents: The Hellenistic Period.* Chico, Calif., 1981.

Bosworth, A. B. *Conquest and Empire: The Reign of Alexander the Great.* Cambridge, 1988. A political and military analysis of Alexander's career that successfully strips away the romance, maintaining a clear vision of the ruthlessness and human cost of his conquests.

Bosworth, A. B. *The Legacy of Alexander: Politics, Warfare, and Propaganda under the Successors.* Oxford, 2002. Surveys Egypt, Persia, and Macedon during the half century following Alexander's death.

Borza, Eugene N. *In the Shadow of Olympus: The Emergence of Macedon.* Princeton, N.J., 1990. The standard account of the rise of Macedon up to the accession of Philip II.

Burstein, Stanley M., ed. and trans. *The Hellenistic Age from the Battle of Ipsos to the Death of Kleopatria VII.* Cambridge, 1985. An excellent collection, with sources not found elsewhere.

Cartledge, Paul A. *Agesilaus and the Crisis of Sparta.* Baltimore, Md., 1987. A thorough but readable analysis of the social and political challenges besetting Sparta in the fourth century B.C.E.

Green, Peter. *Alexander of Macedon, 356–323 B.C.* Berkeley, Calif., 1991. Revised edition of the author's 1972 biography; entertainingly written, and rich in detail and insight.

Green, Peter. *Alexander to Actium: The Historical Evolution of the Hellenistic Age.* Berkeley, Calif., 1990. An outstanding, comprehensive, and wide-ranging history of the period; balanced and sensible.

Hammond, Nicholas G. L. *The Genius of Alexander the Great.* Chapel Hill, N.C., 1998. A clear, authoritative, admiring account, distilling a lifetime of research on the subject.

Hansen, Mogens H. *The Athenian Democracy in the Age of Demosthenes.* Oxford, 1991. An intelligent examination of the political institutions of Athens in the fourth century B.C.E.

Lloyd, Geoffrey, and Nathan Sivin. *The Way and the Word: Science and Medicine in Early China and Greece.* New Haven, Conn., 2002. An extraordinary comparative study of scientific thinking between 400 B.C.E. and 200 C.E. in the Hellenistic world and in China.

Pollitt, Jerome J. *Art in the Hellenistic Age.* New York, 1986. The standard account, written from the perspective of cultural history as well as art history.

Sherwin-White, Susan, and Amélie Kuhrt. *From Samarkhand to Sardis: A New Approach to the Seleucid Empire.* London, 1993. A stimulating examination of the relationship between rulers and ruled in the vast expanses of the Seleucid empire.

Shipley, Graham. *The Greek World after Alexander, 323–30 B.C.* New York and London, 2000. Emphasizes social and cultural developments, with extensive bibliography.

Tritle, Lawrence A. ed. *The Greek World in the Fourth Century: From the Fall of the Athenian Empire to the Successors of Alexander.* New York, 1997. A wide-ranging collection of scholarly essays.

Worthington, Ian. *Alexander the Great: A Reader.* London and New York, 2002. A collection of influential interpretations of Alexander by modern historians.

Worthington, Ian. *Alexander the Great: Man and God.* London, 2004. Nicely illustrated biography aimed at scholars and general readers.

CHAPTER FIVE

ROMAN
CIVILIZATION

WHILE THE GREEKS STRUGGLED against the Persians and then each other, a new civilization was emerging on the banks of the Tiber River in central Italy. By the end of the fourth century B.C.E., Rome was already the dominant power on the Italian peninsula. For five centuries thereafter Rome's power steadily increased. By the first century C.E., it ruled most of the Hellenistic world as well as most of western Europe. Rome's conquests united the Mediterranean world for the first time and made the Mediterranean itself a "Roman lake." Rome's empire brought Greek institutions and ideas not only to the western half of the Mediterranean world but also to Britain, France, Spain, and Romania. Rome was thus the builder of a great historical bridge that connected Europe to the cultural and political heritage of the ancient Near East. Without Rome, European civilization as we know it would not exist.

Rome was deeply influenced by Greek culture, but it was also a distinctive civilization in its own right. The Romans were much more mindful of tradition than the Greeks. Rome revered its old agricultural traditions, its household gods, and its stern military values. But as their empire grew, Romans also came to see themselves as having a divinely ordained mission to civilize the world by teaching it the arts of law and government that were Rome's own peculiar genius. Virgil (70–19 B.C.E.), the great epic poet of Rome, expressed this self-conscious sense of Rome's historical mission in the *Aeneid*, which tells one of the several competing legends Romans treasured about the founding of their city. Here, Anchises of Troy speaks prophetically to his son Aeneas, who (in Virgil's account) would go on to become one of the founders of the city of Rome. Speaking about the Romans, Anchises tells his son of his people's future:

FOCUS QUESTIONS

• How did the Etruscans and Greeks influence early Roman society?

• How democratic was the early Roman Republic?

• What were the consequences of Roman territorial expansion during the third and second centuries B.C.E.?

• What impact did Rome's expanding empire have on Roman society and culture?

• What issues caused the social struggles of the late republic?

• Why did the Augustan system succeed?

• Why did so many critics of Roman life during the Principate focus their criticisms on the behavior of women?

• What factors brought the Roman Empire to the brink of ruin?

• Did Roman civilization come to an end in the third century C.E.?

"Others will cast more tenderly in bronze
Their breathing figures, I can well believe,
And bring more lifelike portraits out of marble;
Argue more eloquently, use the pointer
To trace the paths of heaven accurately
And accurately foretell the rising stars.
Roman, remember by your strength to rule
Earth's peoples—for your arts are to be these:
To pacify, to impose the rule of law,
To spare the conquered, battle down the proud."

Virgil, *Aeneid*, Book VI, lines 848–857, trans. Robert Fitzgerald (New York, 1982), p. 190.

Not all the peoples whom Rome conquered welcomed the experience. But all were transformed by it.

EARLY ITALY AND THE ROMAN MONARCHY

How did the Etruscans and Greeks influence early Roman society?

Ancient Italy had sizable forests and much fertile land. But it had few mineral resources, aside from excellent supplies of marble. Its extensive coastline had only a few good harbors. Nor did it have any secure natural defenses. In short, Italy was rich enough to be attractive but difficult to defend. The Romans were a sternly military society almost from the moment they settled on Italian soil, because they were continually forced to defend their own conquests against other invaders.

THE ETRUSCANS

The dominant early settlers on the Italian peninsula were a non-Indo-European-speaking people known as the Etruscans. By the sixth century B.C.E., the Etruscans had established a confederation of independent city-states in north-central Italy. They were skilled metal-workers, artists, and architects, from whom the later Romans took their knowledge of the arch and the vault, among much else. The Roman practice of centering urban life around massive stone temples with their attendant cults probably also derived from Etruscan example. Even the two most famous myths the Romans told about the founding of Rome itself they probably drew from the Etruscans: that involving Aeneas of Troy

(noted earlier in connection with Virgil's *Aeneid*) and that involving the infant twins Romulus and Remus, who were raised by a female wolf after being abandoned by their parents.

The Romans also borrowed heavily from the Greek settlers of Italy. Colonists from mainland Greece began to arrive in southern Italy and Sicily in large numbers during the eighth century B.C.E. Such famous Greeks as Pythagoras, Archimedes, and even Plato for a time lived in Greek Italy, which became a key battleground in the Peloponnesian War between Athens and Sparta. From the Greeks, the Romans derived their alphabet, many of their religious concepts, and much of their art and mythology. The high culture of Rome thus became thoroughly and pervasively Greek in inspiration and imitation.

THE RISE OF ROME

The Romans were descended from a cluster of Indo-European-speaking peoples who crossed the Alps into Italy during the second millennium B.C.E. Rome's strategic location along the Tiber brought it many advantages. Trading ships—but not large war fleets—could navigate the Tiber as far as Rome, but no farther; the city could thus serve as a port without being threatened by attack from the sea. Rome's famous hills increased the defensibility of the site. Rome also sat astride the first good ford across the Tiber River, making it a major land and river crossroads. Its location on the frontier between Latium (the territory of the "Latins"—that is, the Romans) and Etruria (the Etruscan homeland) also contributed to its commercial and strategic importance.

At an early date, Rome established with the other Latin communities a series of common "rights," including intermarriage and legal migration between cities. These privileges, known as the "Latin Right," stand in sharp contrast to the rigid particularism and jealous suspicion that divided the cities of Sumer or Greece. Roman willingness to extend the Latin Right even beyond Latium was a key factor in the success of their later expansion within Italy.

Roman government was initially a monarchy advised by a senate, or council of elders (*senex* is Latin for "old man"). The monarchy, however, did not last. Legend has it that in 534 B.C.E. an Etruscan tyrant, Tarquin the Proud, gained control of the kingship in Rome. Tarquin used Rome's strategic location to dominate Latium and the agriculturally wealthy district of Campania to the south, but he ruled the Romans with extreme cruelty. The final indignity came in 510 B.C.E.,

Romulus and Remus. A sixth-century B.C.E. Etruscan bronze statue known as the *Capitoline Wolf*. Although the statues of the twins were added during the fifteenth century C.E., there were probably comparable figures of Romulus and Remus in the same basic posture in the original statue.

when Tarquin's son raped a virtuous Roman wife, Lucretia. When Lucretia committed suicide rather than living on "in dishonor," the Romans rose up in revolt, overthrowing not only the Etruscan tyranny but the entire form of monarchical government itself.

The story of Lucretia is probably patriotic myth, but there was a change in government in Rome around 500 B.C.E. (whether gradual or sudden is unknown) that ended the kingship and replaced it with a republic. Thereafter, the Romans would hold kingship in the same fear and contempt with which Greeks ultimately held the name "tyrant." Whatever the truth of Lucretia's story, it does tell us something important about early Roman attitudes toward government and the family.

THE EARLY REPUBLIC

How democratic was the early Roman Republic?

The early Roman Republic was marked by almost constant warfare. The Romans were initially on the defensive; but as time went on they steadily gained ground, conquering first the other Latin territories, then Etruria and the Greek cities of southern Italy. The Romans did not usually impose heavy burdens on the cities they conquered. More often, they demanded that their defeated foes contribute soldiers to the Roman army. Rome also extended the Latin Right to many of the cities it conquered, giving them a further stake in Rome's continued political and military success.

This long series of conflicts confirmed among the Romans a steely military ideal. Many of the most familiar Roman legends of martial heroism date from the early republican period, including the story of Horatius, who held a key bridge against an entire army, and the retired soldier and statesman Cincinnatus (with whom George Washington would be frequently compared) who left his farm at a moment's notice to fight for Rome on the battlefield.

THE GOVERNMENT OF THE EARLY REPUBLIC

Meanwhile, Rome underwent a very gradual political evolution. Even the replacement of the monarchy was highly conservative: its chief effects were to substitute for the king two elected officials called *consuls* and to exalt the position of the Senate by granting it control over the public funds. The consuls, who each served a one-year term, were inevitably senators who acted as the agents of aristocratic interests. Each consul exercised the full executive and judicial authority that the king had previously wielded, limited by the right each possessed to veto the action of the other. If a conflict arose between them, the Senate might be called on to decide; or in time of grave emergency, a dictator might be appointed for a term not greater than six months.

After the establishment of the republic, the political dominance of the aristocracy, known as the *patricians*, began to be challenged by the *plebeians*, who made up nearly 98 percent of the citizen population but who initially had no access to political power. The 200-year struggle between them is sometimes known as the "Struggle of the Orders." The plebeians were a diverse group. Some had grown wealthy through trade or agriculture, but most were small-holding farmers, merchants, or the urban poor. The grievances of the plebeians were numerous. Forced to serve in the army in time of war, they were nevertheless excluded from holding office. They frequently felt themselves the victims of discriminatory decisions in judicial trials. They did not even know what legal rights they were supposed to enjoy, for the laws were unwritten, and the patricians alone had the power to interpret them. Worst was the oppression that could stem from debt because a debtor could be sold into slavery outside Rome by his creditor.

These grievances prompted a plebeian rebellion in the early fifth century B.C.E. that forced the patricians to agree to the election of new officers known as *tribunes* who could protect the plebeians by vetoing unlawful patrician acts. This victory was followed by a successful demand for codification of the laws. Roughly a generation later the plebeians won eligibility to positions as lesser magistrates, and about 367 B.C.E. the first plebeian consul was elected. Gradually, plebeians also gained access to the Senate. The final plebeian victory came in 287 B.C.E. with the passage of a law stipulating that measures enacted by the *concilium plebis* (an assembly composed only of plebeians) would be binding on the Roman government whether the Senate approved them or not. It is from the decisions of this citizen assembly that English derives its modern word *plebiscite*.

These reforms had several important consequences. Because successful plebeians could now work their way into the upper reaches of Roman society and government, the Roman aristocracy gradually shifted (at least to some degree) from one of birth to one of wealth. In an attempt to prevent wealth from becoming too much of a factor in Roman political life, laws were passed barring senators from engaging directly in commerce. But this restriction only fueled the rise of the "equestrian" order: men who had the wealth and influence of senators, but who chose a life of business rather than one in politics. Meanwhile, those few families who managed to win election generation after generation became increasingly prestigious and disproportionately influential. As a result, by the first century B.C.E. even powerful and aristocratic Romans were coming to feel excluded from real political influence within their city, tempting some to pursue their private political agendas by styling themselves the champions of a downtrodden public interest.

CULTURE, RELIGION, AND MORALITY

Political changes in early republican Rome moved glacially. So too did intellectual and cultural ones. Although writing had been adopted as early as the sixth century B.C.E., the Romans made little use of it except for laws, treaties, and funerary inscriptions. Education was largely limited to instruction imparted by fathers to sons in manly sports, practical arts, and military virtues; as a result, literary culture long remained a minor part of Roman life, even among the aristocracy. War and agriculture continued to be the chief occupations for the bulk of the population. A few artisans could be found in the cities, and a minor development of trade had occurred. But the fact that the republic had no standard system of coinage until 289 B.C.E. reflects the comparative insignificance of Roman commerce at this time.

During the early republic, religion assumed the character it retained through the greater part of Roman history. In many ways Roman religion resembled that of the Greeks. But there were also significant differences between the two religions. One was that Romans literally revered their ancestors; their "household gods" included deceased members of a lineage who were worshiped to ensure a family's contin-

> In an attempt to prevent wealth from becoming too much of a factor in Roman political life, laws were passed barring senators from engaging directly in commerce.

CHRONOLOGY

THE RISE OF ROME, 753–THIRD CENTURY B.C.E.

Legendary founding of the city of Rome	753 B.C.E.
Establishment of the Latin Right	493 B.C.E.
Roman Republic established	c. 500 B.C.E.
Struggle of the Orders	c. 450–287 B.C.E.
Concilium plebis gains power	287 B.C.E.
Equestrian order established	third century B.C.E.

ROMAN EXPANSION TO 265 B.C.E.

- Controlled by Rome in 485 B.C.E.
- To 387 B.C.E.
- To 334 B.C.E.
- To 300 B.C.E.
- To 290 B.C.E.
- To 265 B.C.E.

ROMAN EXPANSION IN ITALY, 485–265 B.C.E.

This map illustrates the pattern of early Roman expansion in central and southern Italy. What does this pattern of expansion suggest about the threats Rome faced? Why did the Romans wait so long to conquer Etruria, even though it was so close to Rome? By transforming itself into the dominant power on the Italian peninsula, whose interests would Rome threaten after 265 B.C.E.?

ued prosperity. Another difference was the extent to which Roman religion was tied up with political life. Religion and politics were always closely integrated in

the ancient world. But the Roman state appointed committees of priests virtually as branches of government to tend to the worship of the city's gods, preside over public rites, and serve as guardians of sacred traditions. These priests were not full-time professionals but rather prominent aristocrats who rotated in and out of priestly offices while also serving as leaders of the Roman state. Their dual role as priests and politicians made Roman religion an even more integral part of the fabric of public and political life than it had been in Greece.

Roman morality emphasized patriotism, duty, masculine self-control, and respect for authority and tradition. Its chief virtues were bravery, honor, self-discipline, and loyalty to country and family. A Roman's primary duty was to honor his ancestors by his conduct, but the greatest honor attached to those who sacrificed themselves for Rome. For the good of the republic, therefore, citizens had to be ready to sacrifice not only their own lives but, if necessary, those of their family and friends. The cold-bloodedness of certain consuls who put their own sons to death for breaches of military discipline was to the Romans a matter of deep admiration bordering on awe.

THE FATEFUL WARS WITH CARTHAGE

What were the consequences of Roman territorial expansion during the third and second centuries B.C.E.?

By 265 B.C.E. the Romans controlled most of the Italian peninsula, freeing them to engage in overseas ventures. Scholars disagree as to whether the Romans continually extended their rule as a matter of deliberate policy, or whether their conquests grew more accidentally, by a series of reactions to changes that seemed to threaten Rome's security. Probably the truth lies between these extremes. Whatever the case, beginning in 264 B.C.E., a year after its final victory over the Etruscans, Rome became embroiled in a series of wars with overseas nations that decidedly altered the course of its history.

THE PUNIC WARS

By far the most crucial was the struggle with Carthage, a great maritime empire that stretched along the northern coast of Africa from modern-day Tunisia to the Strait of Gibraltar and included parts of Spain, Sicily, Sardinia,

A Roman Noble of the First Century B.C.E. The man shown here is holding the busts of two of his ancestors. Honoring one's ancestors was an important part of Roman social and religious life, especially among the aristocracy.

WHAT WERE THE CONSEQUENCES OF ROMAN TERRITORIAL EXPANSION DURING THE THIRD AND SECOND CENTURIES B.C.E.?

THE FATEFUL WARS WITH CARTHAGE   125

and Corsica. Carthage had been founded about 800 B.C.E. as a Phoenician colony, but it developed into a rich and powerful independent state. In naval might, commercial prowess, and material resources, Carthage in the third century B.C.E. was far superior to Rome.

The protracted struggles between Rome and Carthage are known collectively as the Punic Wars because the Romans called the Carthaginians Poeni, that is, "Phoenicians." The First Punic War began in 264 B.C.E., apparently because of Rome's genuine fear that the Carthaginians might gain control of Messina, a Sicilian port directly across from the Italian mainland. Twenty-three years of bitter fighting ensued. Finally, by a peace agreement in 241, Carthage was forced to cede all of Sicily to Rome and to pay a large indemnity. Sicily thus became Rome's first overseas province.

Because the Romans had fought so hard to defeat Carthage, they were determined not to let their enemy extend its control to other Mediterranean areas. Accordingly, in 218 the Romans interpreted Carthage's attempt to expand its rule in Spain as a threat to Roman interests and responded with a declaration of war. The renewed struggle, known as the Second Punic War, raged for sixteen years. At first Rome was thrown off guard by the brilliant exploits of the famous Carthaginian commander Hannibal, who brought a Spanish army, including war elephants, through southern France and then over the Alps into Italy. With Carthaginian troops on Italian soil, Rome escaped defeat by the narrowest of margins.

Deep reserves of Roman manpower and the discipline of Rome and its closest allies ultimately overcame Hannibal's military genius. From 212 B.C.E. on, the Romans increasingly put the Carthaginians on the defensive in Italy, Sicily, and even Spain. The architect of the Spanish offensive, Publius Cornelius Scipio, then invaded North Africa and defeated Hannibal at Zama, near Carthage, in 201 B.C.E. His victory ended the

CHRONOLOGY

THE WARS WITH CARTHAGE

First Punic War	264–241 B.C.E.
Second Punic War	218–201 B.C.E.
Third Punic War	149–146 B.C.E.
City of Carthage destroyed	146 B.C.E.

Second Punic War, and Scipio was honored with the additional name "Africanus," the conqueror of Africa.

Carthage was now compelled to abandon all its possessions, except the city of Carthage itself and its surrounding territory in Africa, and to pay an indemnity three times greater than that paid at the end of the First Punic War. Yet Roman suspicion of Carthage remained obsessive. By the mid-second century B.C.E. Carthage had recovered some of its former prosperity—and this was enough to provoke the displeasure of the Romans. Nothing short of the total demolition of the Carthaginian state would now satisfy influential Roman senators such as Cato the Censor, who ended every speech he made in the Senate with the same words: "Carthage must be destroyed." The Senate agreed, and in 149 B.C.E. seized on a minor pretext to demand that the Carthaginians abandon their city and settle at least ten miles from the coast. Because this demand amounted to a death sentence for a nation dependent on commerce, it was refused—as the Romans probably realized it would be. The result was the Third Punic War, fought between 149 and 146 B.C.E. When the Romans finally breached the walls of Carthage, frightful butchery took place. The 55,000 Carthaginians who survived the massacre were sold into slavery, and their once magnificent city was razed to the ground.

A Hannibal Coin. This coin was issued by Hannibal's family in Spain around 230 B.C.E. Its front shows the Carthaginian god Melqart in the guise of Hercules (notice the club over his shoulder). The other side of the coin shows a war elephant with a mounted rider, like the ones that would be used by Hannibal against Rome a generation later.

TERRITORIAL EXPANSION

The wars with Carthage brought an enormous increase in Roman territory, leading to the creation of new overseas provinces in Sicily, North Africa, and Spain. This was the beginning of a policy of westward expansion that proved to be one of the great formative influences on the history of Europe.

Rome's expanding overseas commitments also brought it into conflict with eastern Mediterranean powers, paving the way for further conquests. During the Second Punic War, Philip V of Macedon entered into an alliance with Carthage; soon afterward, he moved aggressively into Greece and was rumored to have designs on Egypt. Rome sent an army to eject Philip from Greece; a decade or so later, another Roman army thwarted similar plans by the Seleucid monarch Antiochus III. In neither campaign did Rome set out to conquer Greece militarily; by 146 B.C.E., however, both Greece and Macedon had become Roman provinces, Seleucid Asia had been deprived of most of its territories, and Ptolemaic Egypt was largely a pawn of Roman commercial and naval interests.

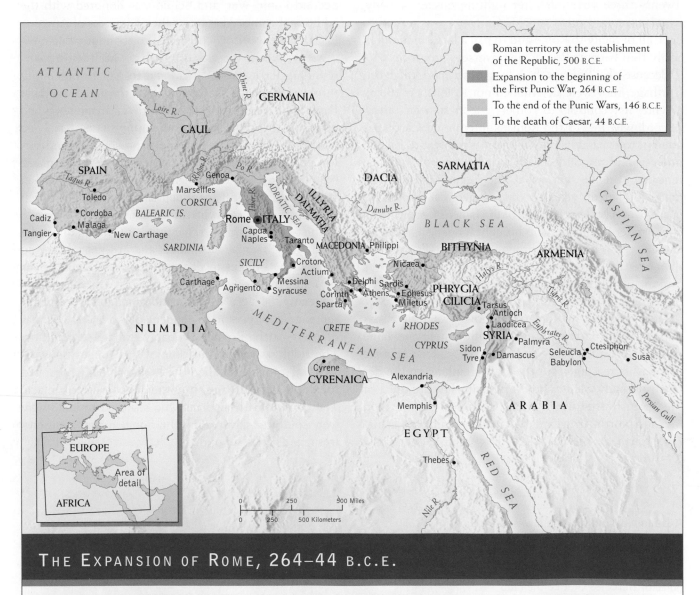

THE EXPANSION OF ROME, 264–44 B.C.E.

By the death of Julius Caesar in 44 B.C.E., the Roman world had become an empire that united the eastern and the western Mediterranean regions. How did these two parts of the empire differ from one another? How were these differences likely to have affected the way Rome ruled its empire? What particular problems did Julius Caesar create by extending Roman rule into Gaul, well away from Rome's Mediterranean roots?

WHAT IMPACT DID ROME'S EXPANDING EMPIRE HAVE ON ROMAN SOCIETY AND CULTURE?

SOCIETY AND CULTURE IN THE LATE REPUBLIC   127

SOCIETY AND CULTURE IN THE LATE REPUBLIC

What impact did Rome's expanding empire have on Roman society and culture?

Rome's "inadvertent" conquest of Greece and Asia Minor transformed the later republic. Vast new wealth poured into Rome, increasing the social and economic inequalities within Roman society and undermining traditional Roman values of austerity and self-sacrifice. Small farmers left the land for the cities, unable to compete with the huge agricultural estates (known as *latifundia*) owned by aristocrats and worked by gangs of slaves. Slaves also played an increasing role in Roman society as artisans, merchants, and household servants. Roman rule over the Hellenistic East also had a pervasive impact on the cultural life of the late republic; so much so, indeed, that by the end of the republican period, Romans were wondering openly whether they had conquered Greece, or whether it was Greece that had conquered Rome.

ECONOMIC AND SOCIAL CHANGE

Like nearly all the peoples of the ancient world, Romans took slavery for granted. Nothing in Rome's earlier experience prepared it, however, for the huge increase in slave numbers that resulted from its western and eastern conquests. By the end of the second century B.C.E., there were 1 million slaves in Italy alone, making Roman Italy one of the most slave-based economies known to history.

The majority of these slaves worked as agricultural laborers on the vast (and growing) estates of the Roman aristocracy. Some of these estates were the result of earlier Roman conquests within Italy itself. But others were constructed by aristocrats buying up the land holdings of thousands of small farmers who found themselves unable to compete with the great *latifundia* in producing grain for the market. Soldiers in particular —who might now be required to serve for years at a time on campaigns in Spain or the Greek East—often found it impossible to maintain their family farms. Instead, they moved to the city, selling their farms (often at a very good price) to aristocrats eager to invest in land the huge profits they had made from war and empire. In the cities, however, there was often little work to be had. Rome never made a transition to industrialism. With slaves to do all the hard work, a great disincentive existed for the technological initiative that might have led to industrialism; but without large-scale manufacturing, the urban population remained underemployed and politically volatile. By the first century B.C.E., almost a third of Rome's 1 million inhabitants were receiving free grain from the state, partly to keep them alive and partly to keep them quiet.

As we have seen, the Roman economy remained fundamentally agrarian and noncommercialized until the mid-third century B.C.E. During the following century, however, Rome's eastern conquests brought it fully into the sophisticated commercial economy of the Hellenistic world. The principal beneficiaries of this economic transformation were the equestrians, the second of the four orders into which the society of republican Rome was divided (senatorial aristocrats, commoners, and slaves being the other three). As overseas merchants, the equestrians profited handsomely from Rome's voracious appetite for foreign luxury goods. As representatives of the Roman government in the provinces, they operated mines, built roads, and collected taxes, always with an eye toward their own profit. They were also the principal moneylenders to the Roman state and to distressed individuals. Interest rates were high, and when the state could not pay its bills, it would often allow the moneylenders to repay themselves by exploiting the defenseless population of the provinces.

Commoners who lost their lands certainly suffered from these economic changes; but the principal victims of Rome's transformation were its slaves. Roman slaves were scarcely considered people at all but instruments of production like cattle. Notwithstanding the fact that some were cultivated foreigners taken as prisoners of war, the standard policy of their owners was to get as much work out of them as possible until they died of exhaustion or were released in old age to fend for themselves. The ready availability and cheapness of slaves, a consequence of Rome's conquests, made slavery a far more impersonal and brutal institution in Rome than it had been in other ancient civilizations. Although domestic slaves were sometimes treated decently, and some slave artisans in the city of Rome were permitted to run their own businesses, the general lot of the slave was horrendous.

This extreme reliance on slave labor, combined with the relative cheapness of slaves, encouraged a mind-set wherein the Romans had little use for labor-saving inventions. Water mills and a crude steam engine, among many potential industrial innovations, were known to the Romans during the course of their history, but they showed little interest in them. They had little need for such devices when cheap human labor seemed inexhaustible.

FAMILY LIFE AND THE STATUS OF WOMEN

Another change that accompanied the acquisition of new territories was a change in the nature of family life and the status of women. In earlier times, the Roman family was based on the husband's nearly absolute powers over his household. During the second century B.C.E., however, changes in the laws governing divorce and property holding gave wives greater legal independence. The slave system also gave wealthy women greater practical independence, for slaves could now take over women's traditional tasks of child rearing and household maintenance. Upper-class Roman women now spent more time away from the home and began to engage in a range of social, intellectual, and artistic activities.

The conquest of the Hellenistic East also brought the wide-scale adoption of Greek ideas and customs into upper-class Roman life. In earlier centuries, Romans had taken pride in the simplicity of their cultural lives. Now, however, upper-class Romans began to see Greek culture as a mark of refinement that they had the wealth to pursue. The creature comforts that Hellenistic Greeks enjoyed in Syria and Egypt were also quickly adopted by the Roman conquerors of the Mediterranean world. Some Romans viewed such changes with repugnance. For them the "good old Roman ways" of paternal authority and stern military discipline were giving way to the debilitating allure of soft living. Their protests struck a chord, but they did little to stem the tide of change. Rome was being irreversibly transformed from a republic of farmers into a complex society with vast gaps between rich and poor and new habits of personal autonomy for both men and women.

EPICUREANISM AND STOICISM

The late republic was also deeply influenced by Greek philosophical ideas. The most renowned of the Roman exponents of Epicureanism was Lucretius (98–55 B.C.E.), the author of a book-length philosophical poem, *On the Nature of Things*. In writing this work Lucretius wished to explain the universe in such a way as to remove fear of the supernatural, which he regarded as the chief obstacle to peace of mind. Though he admitted the existence of the gods, he conceived of them as living in eternal peace, neither creating nor governing the universe. Everything that exists on earth, including the human mind, is the result of a fortuitous combination of atoms. Since mind is indissolubly linked with matter, death means utter extinction; consequently, no part of the human personality can survive to be rewarded or punished in an afterlife. Lucretius's conception of the good life was simple: "peace and a pure heart."

Stoicism was introduced into Rome about 140 B.C.E. and soon numbered among its converts many influential leaders of public life. The greatest of these was Cicero (106–43 B.C.E.), the "father of Roman eloquence." Cicero's ethical philosophy was based on the Stoic premises that virtue is sufficient for happiness and tranquillity of mind is the highest good. He conceived of the ideal human being as one who has been guided by reason to an indifference toward sorrow and pain. But Cicero diverged from the Greek Stoics in his greater approval of the active, political life. To this degree he still spoke for the older Roman tradition of service to the state.

Cicero never claimed to be an original philosopher; his goal was to bring the best of Greek philosophy to the West. In this he was remarkably successful, for he wrote in a rich and elegant Latin prose style that immediately became a standard for Latin composition and has remained so until the present century. Thus even though not a truly great thinker, Cicero was the most influential Latin transmitter of ancient thought to medieval and modern Europe.

RELIGION

The religious beliefs of the Romans also altered in various ways in the last two centuries of the republic—again mainly because of Rome's interaction with the Hellenistic world. Most pronounced was the spread of Eastern mystery cults, including the Persian cult of Mithraism, which offered awe-inspiring underground rites and a doctrine of the afterlife of the soul. But despite the attractions of these new cults, most Romans

> Cicero's ethical philosophy was based on the Stoic premises that virtue is sufficient for happiness and tranquillity of mind is the highest good.

THE INFLUENCE OF GREEK LUXURY

Lucius Licinius Lucullus (106?–57 B.C.E.) was a partisan of the dictator Sulla and a member of Rome's highest aristocracy. He commanded Roman forces admirably in the East, but his demands for discipline from the army and his intolerance of corruption among the equestrians and senatorial governors made him powerful enemies. His conquests made him quite wealthy and, once he tired of trying to preserve his political career against his foes, he retired from public life. This passage from Plutarch's biography of him demonstrates the effects Eastern luxury could have on the Roman elite, the staggering wealth they could acquire, and their enjoyment of it especially once they abandoned the public career for one of private pleasure.

And indeed, Lucullus' life, like the Old Comedy, presents us at the commencement with acts of policy and of war, at the end offering nothing but good eating and drinking, feastings, and revelings, and mere play. For I give no higher name to his sumptuous buildings, porticos, and baths, still less to his paintings and sculptures, and all his industry about these curiosities, which he collected with vast expense, lavishly bestowing all the wealth and treasure he got in the war upon them, insomuch that even now, with all the advance of luxury, the Lucullean gardens are counted the noblest the emperor has. Tubero the Stoic, when he saw his buildings at Naples, where he suspended the hills upon vast tunnels, brought in the sea for moats and fish-ponds round his house, and built pleasure-houses in the waters, called him Xerxes in a toga. He had also fine seats in Tusculum, belvederes, and large open balconies for men's apartments, and porticos to walk in, where Pompey, coming to see him, blamed him for making a house which would be pleasant in summer, but uninhabitable in winter; whom Lucullus answered with a smile, "You think me, then, less provident than cranes and storks, not to change my home with the season." . . . Lucullus's daily entertainments were ostentatiously extravagant, not only with purple coverlets, and plate adorned with precious stones, and dancings,

and interludes, but with the greatest diversity of dishes and the most elaborate cookery, for the vulgar to admire and envy. . . . Cato [the Younger] was his friend and connection, but, nevertheless, so hated his life and habits that when a young man made a long and tedious speech in praise of frugality and temperance, Cato got up and said, "How long do you mean to go on making money like Crassus, living like Lucullus, and talking like Cato?"

Plutarch, *Life of Lucullus*, based on John Dryden, trans., *Plutarch's Lives* (New York, 1992), pp. 621–622.

QUESTIONS FOR ANALYSIS

1. Why does Plutarch recount the life of Lucius Licinius Lucullus, who went from high commands in the army and offices in the state to a buffoon-like private life? What can we learn from this gossipy account?

2. Despite having left office, Lucullus had powerful friends, such as Sulla, Pompey, and Cato, which implied that he was still politically influential. How might his wealth and entertainments corrupt Roman politics just as much as military intervention did?

Roman Mystery Rites. The "Villa of the Mysteries" in Pompeii preserves an astonishing cycle of wall paintings done around 50 B.C.E. The exact meaning is debatable, but the most persuasive interpretation is that it shows a succession of cult rites. Here a young woman is being whipped, probably an initiation ceremony, while a cult member performs a solemn dance in the nude.

continued to honor the traditional gods of their household and their city. Roman polytheism was not an exclusive system. So long as the traditional gods were paid the reverence due them, newer gods could be added and honored also.

THE SOCIAL STRUGGLES OF THE LATE REPUBLIC

What issues caused the social struggles of the late republic?

The period from the end of the Third Punic War in 146 to about 30 B.C.E. was one of enormous turbulence. Social conflicts, assassinations, struggles between rival dictators, wars, and insurrections were common occurrences. Slave uprisings were also part of the general disorder. Some 70,000 slaves defeated a Roman army in Sicily in 134 B.C.E. before this revolt was put down by Roman reinforcements. Slaves ravaged Sicily again in 104 B.C.E. But the most threatening slave revolt of all was led by a slave named Spartacus. Spartacus, who was being trained to become a gladiator (which meant certain death in the arena), escaped with a band of fugitives to Mount Vesuvius near Naples, there attracting a huge host of other fugitive slaves. From 73 to 71 B.C.E. the escapees under his leadership held off Roman armies and overran much of southern Italy until they were finally defeated and Spartacus was slain in battle. Almost 6,000 of those captured were left crucified along the length of a road from Capua to Rome (about 150 miles) to provide a terrible warning.

THE GRACCHI

Meanwhile, an extended conflict among elements of the Roman governing class began in 133 B.C.E. with the attempts at social and economic reform instituted by the two Gracchus brothers. Though of aristocratic lineage himself, Tiberius Gracchus proposed to alleviate social and economic distress by granting government lands to the landless. Conservative aristocrats bitterly opposed this proposal and engineered its veto by Octavius, Tiberius's fellow tribune. Tiberius then removed Octavius from office, a highly irregular action, and when his own term expired attempted to stand for reelection. These moves seemed to threaten a dictatorship and offered the conservative senators an excuse for resistance. Armed with clubs, they went on a rampage during the elections and murdered Tiberius and many of his followers.

Nine years later, Tiberius's younger brother Gaius renewed the struggle. Though Tiberius's land law had finally been enacted by the Senate, Gaius believed that the campaign had to go further. Elected tribune in 123 B.C.E., and reelected in 122, he enacted several laws for the benefit of the less privileged. One stabilized the price of grain in Rome by building public granaries along the Tiber. Another imposed controls on governors suspected of exploiting the provinces

WHAT ISSUES CAUSED THE SOCIAL STRUGGLES OF THE LATE REPUBLIC?

THE SOCIAL STRUGGLES OF THE LATE REPUBLIC   131

for their own advantage. Gaius also proposed to extend full Roman citizenship to vast numbers of Italian allies. These measures provoked so much anger among the vested interests that they resolved to eliminate their enemy. The Roman Senate proclaimed Gaius Gracchus an outlaw and authorized the consuls to take all necessary steps for the defense of the republic. In the ensuing conflict Gaius was killed, and about 3,000 of his followers lost their lives in vengeful purges.

ARISTOCRATIC REACTION

After the downfall of the Gracchi, two military leaders who had won fame in foreign wars successively made themselves rulers of the state. The first was Marius, who was elevated to the consulship by the plebeian party in 107 B.C.E. and reelected six times. Marius, however, accomplished little beyond demonstrating how easily a general with an army behind him could override opposition. Partly for political motives and partly to meet the shortfall in manpower, Marius scrapped the property qualification for the army altogether. Thereafter, Rome's soldiers would come increasingly from the ranks of the urban poor and the landless country dwellers. The result was that gradually Roman armies became more loyal to the individual interests of their commanders than they were to the republic itself, because the political success of their generals could best guarantee rewards for the impoverished soldiers of the army.

Following Marius's death in 86 B.C.E., conservatives took a turn at governing through the army. Their champion was Sulla, another victorious commander. Appointed dictator in 82 B.C.E. for an unlimited term, Sulla ruthlessly exterminated his opponents. He extended the powers of the Senate (whose ranks, depleted by civil war, he packed with men loyal to himself) and curtailed the authority of the tribunes. After three years of rule Sulla decided his job was done and retired to a life of luxury on his country estate.

POMPEY AND JULIUS CAESAR

The effect of Sulla's decrees was to give control to a selfish aristocracy. Soon, however, new leaders emerged to espouse the cause of the people. The most prominent were Pompey (Gnaeus Pompeius Magnus, 106–48 B.C.E.) and Julius Caesar (100–44 B.C.E.). For a time they cooperated in a plot to gain control of the government, but later they became rivals and sought to outdo each other in bidding for popular support. Both were men who, despite their successes, failed to gain complete acceptance from the established elite. Pompey won fame as the conqueror of Syria and Palestine, and Caesar devoted his energies to a series of campaigns against the Gauls. These added to the Roman state the territory of modern Belgium, Germany west of the Rhine, and France, greatly increasing Caesar's reputation and cementing the loyalty of his army. They came at a high price to the Gauls, however: perhaps 1 million Gauls were killed in these campaigns, and another million were enslaved.

In 52 B.C.E., after protracted mob disorders in Rome, the Senate turned to Pompey and engineered his election as sole consul. Caesar, stationed in Gaul, was branded an enemy of the state, and Pompey conspired with the Senate to deprive him of political power. The result was a deadly war between the two men. In 49 B.C.E. Caesar marched on Rome. Pompey fled to the East in the hope of gathering an army large enough to regain control of Italy. In 48 B.C.E. the forces of the rivals met at Pharsalus in Greece. Pompey was defeated and soon afterward murdered by supporters of Caesar.

Caesar then intervened in Egyptian politics at the court of Cleopatra (whom he left pregnant). Then he conducted another military campaign in Asia Minor in which victory was so swift that he could report,

CHRONOLOGY

STRUGGLES OF THE LATE REPUBLIC, 146–27 B.C.E.

Third Punic War	149–146 B.C.E.
Slave revolts in Sicily	134–104 B.C.E.
Gracchian reforms	133–122 B.C.E.
Rule of Marius	107–100, 86 B.C.E.
Sulla becomes dictator	82 B.C.E.
Spartacus leads slave revolt	73–71 B.C.E.
Pompey becomes sole consul	52 B.C.E.
Caesar becomes sole consul	48 B.C.E.
Caesar becomes dictator	46 B.C.E.
Caesar assassinated	44 B.C.E.
Rule of Octavian, Mark Antony, and Lepidus	42–31 B.C.E.
Octavian becomes sole consul	31 B.C.E.
Octavian becomes emperor	27 B.C.E.

"I came, I saw, I conquered" (*Veni, vidi, vici*). After that Caesar returned to Rome. No one now dared challenge his power. With the aid of his veterans he cowed the Senate into granting his every desire. In 46 B.C.E. he was named dictator for ten years, and two years later for life. In addition, he assumed nearly every other title that could augment his power. He obtained from the Senate full authority to make war and peace and to control the revenues of the state. For all practical purposes he was above the law, and rumors spread that he intended to make himself king. Such fears led to his assassination on the Ides of March (the 15th) in 44 B.C.E. by a group of conspirators under the leadership of Brutus and Cassius, who hoped to return Rome to republican government.

Although Caesar was once revered by historians as a superhuman hero, he is now often dismissed as insignificant. Both extremes of interpretation should be avoided. Certainly he did not "save Rome," nor was he the greatest statesman of all time. He treated the republic with contempt and made the problem of governing more difficult for those who came after him. Yet some of the measures he took as dictator did have lasting effects. With the aid of a Greek astronomer he revised the calendar so as to make a 365-day year (with an extra day added every fourth year). This "Julian" calendar—adjusted by Pope Gregory XIII in 1582—is still with us. Appropriately, the seventh month is named after Julius as "July." By conferring citizenship on thousands of Spaniards and Gauls, Caesar took an important step toward eliminating the distinction between Italians and provincials. He also helped relieve economic inequities by settling many of his veterans and some of the urban poor on unused lands. Vastly more important than these reforms, however, was Caesar's farsighted resolve, made before he seized power, to invest his efforts in the West. Whereas Pompey, and before him Alexander, went to the East to gain fame and fortune, Caesar was the first Roman leader to recognize the potential significance of northwestern Europe. By incorporating Gaul into the Roman world he brought Rome great agricultural wealth and helped bring urban life and culture to what was then the wild West. Western European civilization, later to be anchored in just those regions that Caesar conquered, might not have been the same without him.

THE PRINCIPATE OR EARLY EMPIRE (27 B.C.E.–180 C.E.)

Why did the Augustan system succeed?

In his will, Julius Caesar had adopted as his heir his grandnephew Octavian (63 B.C.E.–14 C.E.), then a young man of eighteen. On learning of Caesar's death, Octavian hastened to Rome to try to claim his inheritance. He soon found that he had to join forces with two of Caesar's powerful friends, Mark Antony and Lepidus. The following year the three formed an alliance to crush the political faction responsible for Caesar's murder. The methods employed were not to the new leaders' credit. Prominent members of the opposition were hunted down and slain and their property confiscated. The most notable of the victims was Cicero, brutally slain by Mark Antony's thugs; though he had taken no part in the conspiracy against Caesar's life, Cicero had actively sought to undermine Antony during his term as consul and have him branded a pub-

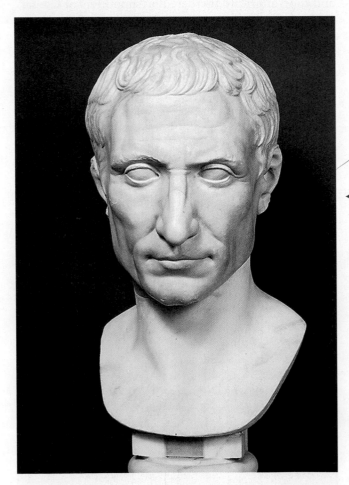

Julius Caesar.

lic enemy. Caesar's real murderers, Brutus and Cassius, escaped and organized an army, but they were defeated by Antony and Octavian near Philippi in 42 B.C.E.

With the "republican" opposition effectively crushed, tensions mounted between the members of the alliance, inspired primarily by Antony's jealousy of Octavian. The subsequent struggle became a contest between East and West. Antony went to the East and made an alliance with Cleopatra, hoping to use the resources of the Egyptian kingdom in the power struggle with Octavian. Octavian, as the junior partner, established himself in Italy and the West. It was a risky move. Octavian had to deal with the problems of resettling veterans while maintaining his position in the roiling political environment in Rome. But Italy provided him with manpower and the opportunity to style himself as the protector of Rome and its heritage against Antony, whom he skillfully portrayed as being in the clutches of a foreign, female potentate who intended to become queen over Rome. As in the earlier contest between Caesar and Pompey, the victory went to the West. In the naval battle of Actium (31 B.C.E.) Octavian's forces defeated those of Antony and Cleopatra, both of whom soon afterward committed suicide. Egypt's independent existence came to an end, and Rome reigned supreme throughout the Mediterranean world.

THE AUGUSTAN SYSTEM OF GOVERNMENT

The victory at Actium ushered in a new period in Roman history, the most glorious and the most prosperous that Rome ever experienced. When Octavian returned to Rome he announced the restoration of complete peace. This was a great relief to the people of Italy, who had suffered grievously from a decade of civil war. For four years he ruled as consul, until he accepted from the Senate the honorific titles of *imperator* (emperor) and *augustus*, a step that historians count as the beginning of the Roman Empire. At the time, *imperator* meant only "victorious general"; *augustus* signified "venerable" or "worthy of honor." But gradually, after his successors took the title of emperor as well, it became the primary designation for the ruler of the Roman state. The title Octavian himself preferred was the more modest *princeps*, or "first citizen." For this reason the period of his rule and that of his successors is called the Principate (or, alternatively, the early empire), to distinguish it from the periods of the republic (c. 500–27 B.C.E.), the "Third-Century Crisis"

(180 C.E.–284 C.E.), and the later empire or "Dominate" (284–610 C.E.).

Octavian, or Augustus as he was now called, was determined not to appear to be a dictator. He therefore left most republican institutions in place even though they now exercised little independent power. In theory the Senate and the citizens remained the supreme authorities; but in practice, Augustus himself controlled the army and determined governmental policy. Fortunately, he was an able ruler. He instituted a new coinage system throughout the empire; he introduced a range of public services in the city of Rome; he reorganized the army; and he allowed cities and provinces more substantial rights of self-government than they had enjoyed before.

Augustus presented himself as a stern defender of traditional Roman morality. He rebuilt temples and prohibited Romans from worshiping foreign gods. In

Octavian. When Octavian gained sole rule he became known as Augustus. Many statues of him survive, all of them idealized.

an attempt to increase the Roman birthrate, he penalized citizens who failed to marry and required widows to remarry within two years of their husbands' deaths. He also introduced laws punishing adultery and making divorces more difficult to obtain. To hammer the message home, Augustan propaganda portrayed the imperial family as a model of domestic virtue and sexual propriety. These portrayals were only moderately successful. The emperor's own extramarital affairs were well known; and the sexual promiscuity of his daughter Julia finally led Augustus to exile her to a distant island.

From the time of Augustus until that of Trajan (98–117 C.E.), the Roman Empire continued to expand. Augustus gained more land for Rome than did any other Roman ruler. His generals advanced into central Europe, conquering the modern-day territories of Switzerland, Austria, and Bulgaria. Only in what is today central Germany did Roman troops meet defeat, a setback that convinced Augustus to hold the Roman borders at the Rhine and Danube. Subsequently, in 43 C.E., the emperor Claudius began the conquest of Britain, and at the beginning of the next century Trajan pushed beyond the Danube to add Dacia (now Romania) to the empire's realms. Trajan also conquered territories in Mesopotamia, but in so doing he aroused the enmity of the Parthian rulers of Persia. His successor, Hadrian, halted the conquests and embarked on a defensive policy epitomized by the construction of Hadrian's Wall in northern Britain. The Roman Empire had now reached its territorial limits; in the third century these limits would begin to recede.

When Augustus died in 14 C.E. after four decades of rule, his remarkable experiments in statesmanship might have died with him. His system was so ingenious, however, that Rome enjoyed nearly two centuries of peace, prosperity, and stability as a result of his reforms. Aside from one brief period of civil war in 68 C.E., the transition of power between emperors was generally peaceful, and the growing imperial bureaucracy managed affairs competently even when individual emperors proved to be vicious. Nevertheless, the fact that Rome had become an autocratic empire became harder and harder to conceal. Several talented men succeeded Augustus, but few of them had his panache for disguising the true power of the princeps.

Aside from one brief period of civil war in 68 C.E., the transition of power between emperors was generally peaceful, and the growing imperial bureaucracy managed affairs competently even when individual emperors proved to be vicious.

The height of the Augustan system came between 96 and 180 C.E., under the so-called Five Good Emperors: Nerva (96–98 C.E.), Trajan (98–117 C.E.), Hadrian (117–138 C.E.), Antoninus Pius (138–161 C.E.), and Marcus Aurelius (161–180 C.E.). All were capable administrators, and all proved worthy successors of Augustus, respecting the Senate and preserving republican forms while running an essentially autocratic government. Until 180, none had a son who survived him, and so each adopted a man worthy to succeed him. They thus avoided the difficulties of dynastic politics, one of the great horrors of first-century imperial life.

Rome's successful governance of such a vast empire from the time of Augustus to that of Marcus Aurelius was certainly one of its greatest accomplishments. During these two centuries, Rome had few external enemies. The Mediterranean was now under the control of a single military power; on land, Roman officials ruled from the borders of Scotland to those of Persia. A contemporary orator justly boasted that "the whole civilized world lays down the arms which were its ancient burden, as if on holiday . . . [A]ll places are full of gymnasia, fountains, monumental approaches, temples, workshops, schools; one can say that the civilized world, which had been sick from the beginning . . . has been brought by right knowledge to a state of health."

ROMANIZATION AND ASSIMILATION

This Roman Peace (*Pax Romana*) was not universal. In Britain, the Roman army massacred tens of thousands of Britons in the aftermath of Queen Boudicca's revolt. In Judea, perhaps the most restive of all the Roman provinces, a Roman army destroyed the Temple at Jerusalem in 70 C.E. in the wake of one rebellion, and in 135 C.E. destroyed the entire city of Jerusalem in the wake of another, massacring its inhabitants and scattering the survivors throughout the empire. Upwards of 0.5 million people may have been killed in Judea during these years, and an equal number enslaved. Jerusalem, meanwhile, was refounded by the emperor Hadrian as a pagan capital named Aelia Capitolina. For the next 500 years, Jews would be forbidden to live there.

Such rebellions were not the norm, however, even in Judea. Although the Roman Empire rested on the

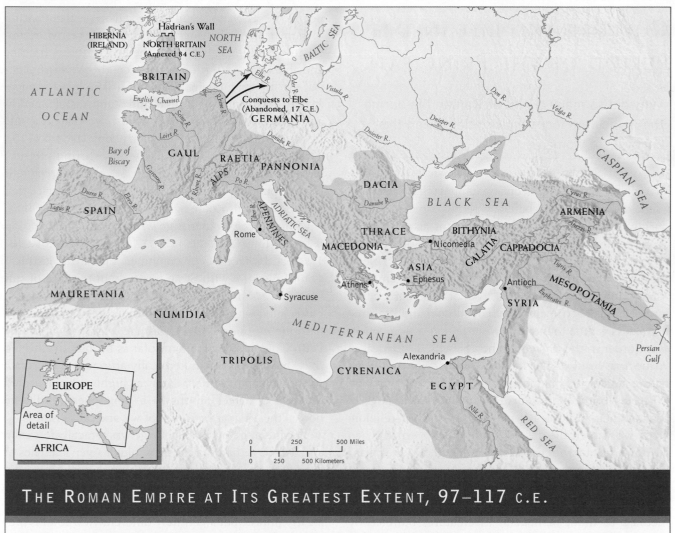

THE ROMAN EMPIRE AT ITS GREATEST EXTENT, 97–117 C.E.

By the second century C.E., Roman expansion had pushed well beyond the Mediterranean basin and into northern and central Europe. This expansion largely followed the courses of the major European river systems. Why do you suppose this was so?

backs of its armies, the empire was not really a military occupation. Rome controlled its far-flung territories by assimilating their residents into the common cultural and political life of Rome itself. Local gods became Roman gods and were adopted into the Roman pantheon of divinities. Cities were constructed, and the amenities of urban life introduced: baths, temples, amphitheaters, aqueducts, and paved roads. Rights of citizenship were extended, and able provincials could rise far in Roman service. Some, like Trajan and Hadrian, even rose to become emperors.

Even the frontier areas of the empire need to be understood in this light. Although for convenience's sake historians speak of the empire's "borders," in fact these borders were highly fluid and permeable. We ought, more properly, to speak not of "borders" but of "frontiers," and to see these frontiers as zones of particularly intensive cultural interaction between provincial Romans and the non-Roman peoples who lived beyond them. Roman influence thus reached far beyond the frontier areas, across the Rhine and the Danube into the heartland of Germany and the Gothic lands to the east. When, in the third century, frontier garrisons were withdrawn to take part in civil wars within the empire itself, many of these Romanized Germans and Goths moved into the empire, sometimes as plunderers but often as settlers and aspiring Romans.

CULTURE AND LIFE IN THE PERIOD OF THE PRINCIPATE

Why did so many critics of Roman life during the Principate focus their criticisms on the behavior of women?

The cultural and intellectual changes that began in Rome during the late republican period came to fruition during the Principate. Three eminent exponents of Stoicism lived in Rome during this period: Seneca (4 B.C.E.–65 C.E.), a wealthy adviser for a time to Nero; the slave Epictetus (60?–120 C.E.); and the emperor Marcus Aurelius (121–180 C.E.). All of them agreed that inner serenity is the ultimate human goal and that true happiness can be found only in surrender to the benevolent order of the universe. They preached the ideal of virtue for virtue's sake, deplored the evils of human nature, and urged obedience to conscience. Seneca and Epictetus both expressed deep mystical yearnings as part of their philosophy, making it almost a religion. They worshiped the cosmos as divine, governed by an all-powerful Providence that ordained all that happened for ultimate good. Marcus Aurelius was more fatalistic and less hopeful. Although he did not reject the concept of an ordered and rational universe, he was inclined to think of humans as creatures buffeted by evil fortune for which no distant perfection of the whole could fully compensate. He urged, nevertheless, that people should continue to live nobly, that they should not abandon themselves to gross indulgence or angry protest, but should derive what contentment they could from dignified resignation to suffering and tranquil submission to death.

LITERATURE OF THE GOLDEN AND SILVER AGES

Roman literature of the Principate is conventionally divided into two periods: works of the Golden Age, written during the reign of Augustus, and works of the Silver Age, written during the first and early second centuries C.E. Most of the literature of the Golden Age was vigorous, affirmative, and uplifting, and—it should be noted—much of it served the propagandistic purposes of Augustus's government. The poetry of Virgil (70–19 B.C.E.), was prototypic. In a set of pastoral poems, the *Eclogues*, Virgil expressed an idealized vision of human life led in harmony with nature, while implicitly extolling Augustus as the bringer of such peace and abundance. Virgil's masterpiece, the *Aeneid (ih-NEE-ihd)*, is an epic poem about a Trojan hero, Aeneas (whom the family of Caesar and Augustus claimed as an ancestor), who was reputed to have played a role in the formation of the Roman people (see p. 119). Written in elevated, yet sinewy and stirring metrical verse ("Arms and the man, I sing. . . ."), the *Aeneid* tells of the founding of a great state through warfare and toil and foretells Rome's glorious future.

Other major Golden Age writers were Horace (65–8 B.C.E.), Livy (59 B.C.E.–17 C.E.), and Ovid (43 B.C.E.–17 C.E.). Horace's *Odes* combined Epicurean justification of pleasure with Stoic fortitude in the face of suffering. Livy's *History of Rome* is often factually unreliable but is filled with dramatic stories designed to appeal to patriotic emotions. Ovid was the least typical of the Latin Golden Age writers insofar as his outlook tended to be more satiric than heroically affirmative. His main poetic accomplishment was a highly sophisticated retelling of Greek myths in a long poem of fifteen books, the *Metamorphoses*, full of wit and eroticism.

The literature of the Silver Age was typically less calm and balanced than that of the Golden Age. The tales of Petronius and Apuleius describe the sometimes sordid aspects of Roman life. The aim of these authors is less to instruct or uplift than to tell an entertaining story or turn a witty phrase. But an entirely different viewpoint is presented by two other important writers of this age. The satirist Juvenal (60?–140 C.E.) wrote with savage indignation about the moral degeneracy he saw in his contemporaries. A similar attitude toward Roman society characterized the writings of Tacitus (55?–117? C.E.). His *Annals* offer a subtle but devastating portrait of the political system constructed by Augustus and ruled by his heirs; his *Germania* contrasts the manly virtues of the German barbarians with the effeminate vices of the decadent Romans. Like Juvenal, Tacitus was a master of ironic wit and brilliant aphorism. Referring to Roman conquests, he makes a barbarian chieftain say, "They create a wilderness and call it peace."

ART AND ARCHITECTURE

Roman art first assumed its distinctive character during the Principate. Before this time what passed for an art of Rome was really an importation from the Hellenistic East. Conquering armies brought back to Italy wagonloads of statues, reliefs, and marble columns as part of

WHY DID SO MANY CRITICS FOCUS THEIR CRITICISMS ON THE BEHAVIOR OF WOMEN?

CULTURE AND LIFE IN THE PERIOD OF THE PRINCIPATE   137

the plunder from Greece and Asia Minor. These became the property of the wealthy and were used to embellish their sumptuous mansions. As demand for such works increased, hundreds of copies were made by Roman artisans. None, however, represents a truly indigenous Roman artistic style.

Encouraged by the patronage of Augustus himself, the Principate witnessed the development of a more distinctively Roman art. This art was more varied than is often assumed, running from the most magnificent public architecture to the most intimate wall paintings. Roman architecture was often grandiose, its massive proportions made possible by the expertise Roman engineers had developed in working with concrete. Among the largest such public buildings were the Pantheon, with its 142-foot-diameter dome, and the Colosseum, which could accommodate 50,000 spectators at gladiatorial combats. Except on public monuments, Roman sculpture was less bombastic. Relief sculpture was particularly notable during this period for its delicacy and naturalism. Even on their coins, emperors were portrayed very much as they looked in real life; and since the images on coins were recut annually,

we can trace on successive issues a ruler's receding hairline or his advancing double chin. Painting, however, was the Romans' most original and most intimate art. Romans loved intense colors; those who could afford to do so surrounded themselves with brilliant wall paintings and mosaics (pictures produced by fitting together small pieces of colored glass or stone). These created a gamut of effects from fantastic seascapes to dreamy landscapes to introspective portraiture.

Closely related to their achievements in architecture were Roman triumphs in engineering. The imperial Romans built marvelous roads and bridges, many of which still survive. Under Trajan, eleven aqueducts brought water into Rome from the nearby hills and provided the city with 300 million gallons daily for drinking and bathing and for flushing a well-designed sewage system. Water was cleverly funneled into the homes of the rich for their private gardens, fountains, and pools. The emperor Nero built a famous "Golden House" in the center of Rome with pipes fitted for sprinkling his guests with perfume, baths supplied with medicinal waters, and an artificial lake. In addition, a spherical ceiling in the banquet hall revolved day and

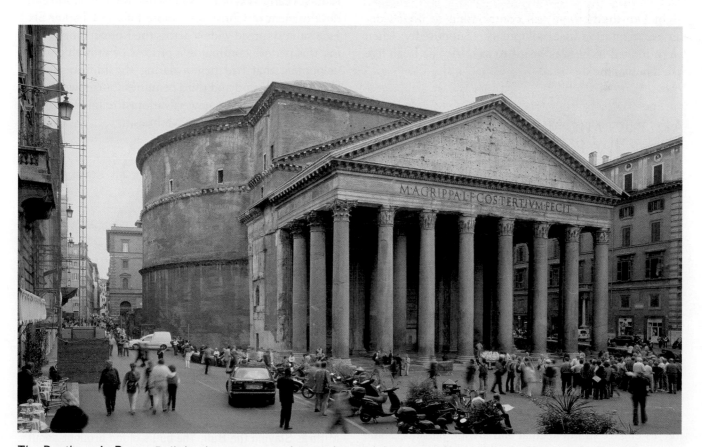

The Pantheon in Rome. Built by the emperor Hadrian, it boasted the largest dome without interior supports of the ancient world. The dome forms a perfect sphere, exactly as high as it is wide.

A Roman Floor Mosaic. This fine mosaic from Roman London shows Bacchus, the god of wine, mounted on a tiger, a reference to the myth that the god had visited India.

night like the heavens, all contributing to Nero's deserved reputation as a voluptuary. (Supposedly, when Nero moved in he was heard to say, "At last I can live like a human being.")

ARISTOCRATIC WOMEN UNDER THE PRINCIPATE

One of the most striking aspects of Roman society under the Principate was the important role played by upper-class women. As we have seen, the wealthy women of late-republican Rome were much less confined to domesticity than were their counterparts in Classical Athens. This trait became even more pronounced during the Principate. Despite laws that kept them formally under the legal supervision of a male guardian, in practice wealthy women could own property, invest in commercial ventures, and make public benefactions. They could not hold political office, but they could act as priestesses and civic patrons. Both roles gave them considerable influence in public affairs. With numerous slaves to take care of their households and wealth of their own on which to draw, upper-class Roman women were free to engage in intellectual and artistic pursuits. Some wrote poetry, others studied philosophy, and others presided over literary salons. They also exercised a degree of sexual freedom unknown elsewhere in the an-

cient world and profoundly shocking to conservative male critics. Aristocratic Roman women often had their portraits painted or chiseled in stone. Several emperors' wives or daughters even appeared on Roman coinage.

The lives of lower-class women are far less well known. Most were probably married at some point in their lives, and the wives of shopkeepers in particular played an important role in the businesses that sustained their families. Married women who survived the dangers of childbirth could probably expect to give birth to three or four children, not all of whom would live to adulthood. But death rates were high, especially for women. In Rome, the median recorded age at death for women was thirty-four; for men, between forty and forty-six. If enslaved women were more fully represented in these figures, they would likely be even lower.

NEW RELIGIONS

The age of the Principate was characterized by an even greater interest in salvationist religions than had prevailed during the late Republic. One of these religions was Christianity, which began to attract adherents in Rome as early as 40 C.E. (We discuss the origins and early development of Christianity more fully in Chapter Six.) Judaism too spread widely across the Roman Empire during this period, continuing a process of growth and development that had begun during the Hellenistic era. During the second and third centuries C.E., however, the most popular of these new salvationist religions was not Christianity or Judaism, but Mithraism.

Mithras Slaying the Bull. The bull's blood brought about the rebirth of light at midwinter and so the revival of life. Mithras's Phrygian cap and leggings emphasize his eastern origins.

A SCATHING CRITIQUE OF ROMAN SOCIETY

Roman society, even at its height under the Five Good Emperors, was not without its critics. Among the most famous and resonant indictments were those of Juvenal, whose Satires *attacked everything from the general erosion of public morality to the effete tastes of the elite. His language is often bitter, and he did not shy away from lacing his elegant verses with a vulgarity still shocking across the centuries. Like those of Aristophanes, many of his references are highly topical, and their exact meaning is lost to us. No doubt his audience understood the allusions, making his public excoriations all the more personal and pointed. Contrast this portrayal of contemporary women with the model of the virtuous Lucretia.*

What conscience has Venus drunk? Our inebriated beauties can't tell head from tail at those midnight oyster suppers when the best wine's laced with perfume, and tossed down neat from a foaming conch-shell, while the dizzy ceiling spins round, and the tables dance, and each light shows double. Why, you may ask yourself, does the notorious Maura sniff at the air in that knowing, derisive way as she and her dear friend Tullia pass by the ancient altar of Chastity? And what is Tullia whispering to her? Here, at night, they stagger out of their litters and relieve themselves, pissing in long hard bursts all over the goddess's statue. Then, while the Moon looks down on their motions, they take turns to ride each other, and finally go home. So you, next morning, on your way to some great house, will splash through your wife's piddle. Notorious, too, are the ritual mysteries of the Good Goddess, when flute-music stirs the loins, and frenzied women, devotees of Priapus, sweep along in procession, howling, tossing their hair, wine-flown, horn-crazy, burning with the desire to get themselves laid. . . . So the ladies, with a display of talent to match their birth, win all the prizes. No make-believe here, no pretense, each act is performed in earnest, and guaranteed to warm the age-chilled balls of a Nestor or a Priam.

Juvenal, *Sixth Satire* 301–326, based on Peter Green, trans., *Juvenal: The Sixteen Satires* (New York, 1974), pp. 138–139.

QUESTIONS FOR ANALYSIS

1. Why did Juvenal focus his outrage so specifically on the misbehavior of women?
2. What sort of an audience would a satire like this one appeal to? Who would have been its intended audience?
3. Do you think Juvenal was describing actual people and events? Why or why not?

Mithraism took its name from a minor Zoroastrian deity named Mithras. The cult's origins, however, are much more securely Roman than Persian. As was true of other mystery cults, the beliefs and practices of Mithraism were closely guarded secrets, revealed only to the cult's initiates and never written down. As a result, we know relatively little about them. We do know, however, that Mithraism was a cult limited to men, that its adherents worshiped in caves or cellars, and that its central visual symbol portrayed Mithras as a young man killing a bull. During the second century, Mithras came to be identified with the unconquered god of the sun, *Sol invictus,* and in this form became one of the favored gods of the Roman army. Initiates to Mithraism shared a common meal of bread and wine, honored Sunday as the most sacred day of the week, and regarded December twenty-fifth as the most sacred day of the year because, as the approximate date of the winter solstice, it was the "birthday" of the sun, when its life-giving powers began to increase again for the benefit of humanity. Early Christians were well aware of the similarities between their own religious practices and those of Mithraism but saw them as examples of the devil's tricks, designed to woo Christians away from their faith.

Perhaps the most startling religious development during the Principate, however, was the emergence and popularity of emperor worship. Although most emperors of the first and second centuries avoided claiming to be divine during their lifetimes, they were routinely recognized as gods after their deaths. The form such worship took varied from place to place within the empire. It is clear, however, that the imperial cult was not imposed on unwilling subjects by an all-powerful Roman state. Rather, the widespread popularity of emperor worship reflected a deeply held and widely shared vision of the essential connections between rulers and the divine order of the world.

ROMAN LAW

One of the most important legacies the Romans left to succeeding cultures was their system of law. This too was largely a product of the Principate. Augustus and his successors appointed a small number of eminent jurists to deliver opinions on the legal issues raised by cases under trial in the courts. Their legal opinions came to embody a systematic philosophy of law unlike anything that had gone before and became the foundation for all subsequent Roman jurisprudence.

Roman law as it was developed by the jurists comprised three branches or divisions: civil law, the law of peoples, and natural law. Civil law was the law of Rome and its citizens. It included the statutes of the Senate, the decrees of the emperor, the edicts of magistrates, and certain ancient customs operating with the force of law. The law of peoples was held to be common to all people regardless of nationality. This law authorized slavery and private ownership of prop-

> One of the most important legacies the Romans left to succeeding cultures was their system of law.

erty and defined the principles of purchase and sale, partnership, and contract. It was not superior to the civil law but supplemented it, especially with respect to the alien inhabitants of the empire.

The most interesting and in many ways the most important branch of Roman law was the natural law, a product not of judicial practice but of philosophy. The Stoics had developed the idea of a rational order of nature that is the embodiment of justice and right. They had affirmed that all men are by nature equal and that they are entitled to certain basic rights that governments have no authority to transgress. The father of the law of nature as a legal principle, however, was Cicero. "True law," he declared, "is right reason consonant with nature, diffused among all men, constant, eternal. To make enactments infringing this law, religion forbids, neither may it be repealed even in part, nor have we power through Senate or people to free ourselves from it." This law was prior to the state itself, and any ruler who defied it automatically became a tyrant.

The practical law applied in local Roman courts often bore little resemblance to the laws of nature. Nonetheless, the development of a concept of abstract justice as a legal principle was one of the noblest achievements of Roman civilization.

THE ECONOMY OF ITALY DURING THE PRINCIPATE

The establishment of stable government by Augustus ushered in a period of prosperity for Italy that lasted more than two centuries. Trade routes led from Rome throughout the Mediterranean world and on to Arabia, India, and China. Manufacturing increased, and the mass production of pottery, textiles, metal, and glasswork throughout the empire brought even the poor a level of material abundance and domestic comfort unmatched by any previous Mediterranean society.

But there were also signs of strain in this sophisticated, complex, but fragile economic world. The upper classes lived in spectacular luxury in their city and country houses. In the countryside, however, the diminishing number of slaves captured in war was beginning to result in labor shortages on the great aristocratic *latifundia*. The economic and social position of small farmers also continued to decline, with many winding up as semiservile agricultural workers tied to these great aristocratic estates.

The western empire in general, and Italy in particular, also had a serious trade imbalance with the eastern parts of the empire. Western bulk goods—wine, grain, oil, and pottery—traveled eastward in massive quantities, but this trade was still not enough to balance the cost of luxury goods imported from the east. So long as imperial revenues continued to flow from east to west to support the army and the government, the economic system of the later Principate was relatively stable. Should that flow of cash dry up, however, or should the trade routes between east and west be disrupted, the economy of Italy and the western empire risked being thrown quickly into crisis.

THE CRISIS OF THE THIRD CENTURY (180–284 C.E.)

What factors brought the Roman Empire to the brink of ruin?

With the death of Marcus Aurelius in 180 C.E. the period of beneficent imperial rule came to an end. One reason for the success of the Five Good Emperors was that the first four designated particularly promising young men, rather than sons or close relatives, for the succession. But Marcus Aurelius broke this pattern with unfortunate results. Although he was one of the most thoughtful rulers who ever reigned, he was not wise enough to recognize that his son, Commodus, was a self-indulgent adolescent who lacked the discipline or the capacity to rule effectively. His erratic and frequently violent behavior resulted in a conspiracy originating inside his own palace: his wrestling coach finally strangled him in 192 C.E. Matters thereafter became worse. With no obvious successor to Commodus, the armies of the provinces raised their own candidates and civil war ensued. A provincial general, Septimius Severus (193–211 C.E.), emerged victorious, making it clear that provincial armies could now interfere in imperial politics at will.

THE SEVERAN DYNASTY

Severus and his successors aggravated the problem by eliminating even the theoretical rights of the Senate and ruling as military dictators. On his deathbed, Severus advised his two sons, "Enrich the soldiers, boys, and ignore the rest." His son Caracalla was little more than a thug who murdered his brother and co-emperor Geta. So desperate was Caracalla to raise revenues and pay bonuses to his increasingly covetous armies (especially to appease them after he assassinated his more popular brother), that he made everyone in the empire a Roman citizen. This was hardly an act of enlightenment but rather was aimed at increasing the tax base of the Roman state. In the process, he cheapened Roman citizenship, once the prized glue that held the vast empire together. His successors in the Severan Dynasty proved no better. The growing prominence of the army over time made it increasingly uncontrollable. Once the role of brute force was openly revealed, any aspiring general could try his luck at seizing power. In 235 C.E. the army overthrew the last of the Severan Dynasty rulers. Fifty years of endemic civil war followed. From 235 to 284 C.E. there were no fewer than twenty-six "barracks emperors," of whom only one managed to escape a violent death.

Commodus. The self-deluded ruler encouraged artists to portray him as the equal of the superhuman Hercules.

THE HEIGHT OF THE THIRD-CENTURY CRISIS

In the half century between 235 and 284 C.E. political chaos combined with other factors to bring the empire to the brink of ruin. Civil wars undermined the economy, not only by interfering with agriculture and trade but also by encouraging aspiring emperors to enrich their soldiers by debasing the coinage and imposing exorbitant taxation on civilians. The result was runaway inflation. The poorest suffered the most. Many were driven to abject destitution. In the wake of war and hunger, disease also ran rampant. In the reign of Marcus Aurelius a terrible plague had swept through the empire, decimating the army and the population at large. In the middle of the third century the pestilence returned.

The resulting decline in population came at a time when Rome could least afford it, for still another threat to the empire in the middle of the third century was the advance of Rome's external enemies. With Roman ranks thinned by disease and Roman armies fighting each other, Germans in the west and Persians in the east broke through the old Roman defense lines. In 251 C.E. the Goths defeated and slew the emperor Decius, crossed the Danube, and marauded at will in the Balkans. An even more humiliating disaster came in 260 C.E. when the emperor Valerian was captured in battle by the Persians and made to kneel as a footstool for their ruler. When he died his body was stuffed and hung on exhibition. For a time, the western provinces broke free as an independent empire in their own right, despairing of Rome's ability to defend them. Clearly the days of Augustus were far in the past.

ROMAN RULE IN THE WEST: A BALANCE SHEET

Did Roman civilization come to an end in the third century C.E.?

As Rome was not built in a day, so it was not lost in one. As we will see in the next chapter, strong rule returned in 284 C.E. Thereafter the Roman Empire endured in the west for 200 years more and in the east for a millennium. But the restored Roman state differed greatly from the old one—so much so that it is proper to end the story of characteristically Roman civilization here and to review the reasons for Rome's transformation into a distinctly different type of society, one that we will examine in detail in the next chapter.

EXPLAINING THE "DECLINE AND FALL" OF ROME

More has been written on the decline and fall of Rome than on the death of any other civilization. The theories offered to account for the decline have been many and varied. Perhaps the strangest recent one is that Rome fell from the effects of lead ingested from cooking utensils, but if this were true we would have to ask why Rome did so well for so long. Moralists have found the explanation for Rome's decline in the descriptions of lechery and gluttony presented by such authors as Juvenal and Petronius. But such an approach overlooks the facts that much of this evidence is patently overdrawn and that nearly all of it comes from the period of the early Principate. In later centuries, when the empire was more obviously collapsing, morality became more austere. One of the simplest explanations is that Rome fell because of the severity of German attacks. But German "barbarians" had always stood ready to attack Rome: German invasions succeeded only when Rome was already weakened internally. Indeed, from the fourth century C.E. onward, increasing numbers of Germanic tribes were less interested in destroying Rome than in becoming a part of it. Many of the Germanic tribes who would overrun the western empire during the fifth century C.E. were in fact Roman allies, provoked to invade the empire by Roman bigotry, maladministration, and abuse.

POLITICAL FAILURES

It is best then to concentrate on Rome's most serious internal problems. Some of these were political. The most obvious failing of the Roman constitution under the Principate was the lack of a clear law of succession. Especially when a ruler died suddenly, there was no certainty about who was to follow him. For all of Augustus's achievements, this was his system's greatest failure. Indeed, because the reality of autocratic rule was disguised behind republican forms, there was little any emperor could do to provide for an orderly succession to an imperial position that did not officially exist. So long as respect for the institutions of republican Rome remained, transitions might be effected more or

DID ROMAN CIVILIZATION COME TO AN END IN THE THIRD CENTURY C.E.?

ROMAN RULE IN THE WEST: A BALANCE SHEET   143

less smoothly. But from 235 to 284 C.E. warfare and instability fed on each other. Civil war was also nurtured by the lack of constitutional means for reform. If regimes became unpopular, as most did after 180 C.E., the only means to alter them was to overthrow them. But resorting to violence always bred more violence, especially as the soldiery became the arbiter of the success or failure of an imperial regime.

ECONOMIC CRISIS

The Roman Empire also had its share of economic problems. Rome's worst economic problems derived from its slave system and from labor shortages. Roman civilization was based on cities, and Roman cities existed largely by virtue of an agricultural surplus produced by slaves. Slaves were worked so hard that they did not normally reproduce to fill their own ranks. Until the time of Trajan (98–117 C.E.), Roman conquests provided fresh supplies of slaves to keep the system going, but thereafter the economy began to run out of human fuel. Landlords could no longer be so profligate with human life, barracks slavery came to an end, and the countryside produced less of a surplus to feed the towns.

Labor shortages also aggravated Rome's economic problems, especially in the west. With the end of foreign conquests and the decline of slavery there was a pressing need for people to stay on the farm, but barbarian pressures meant that there was also a steady need for men to serve in the army. The plagues of the second and third centuries sharply reduced the population just at the worst time. It has been estimated that between the reign of Marcus Aurelius and the restoration of strong rule in 284 C.E., disease, warfare, and a declining birthrate combined to reduce the population of the Roman Empire by one third. The result was that there were neither sufficient farmers to work the land nor enough soldiers to fight Rome's enemies.

Despite all of this, it is important to remember that Rome was scarcely poverty stricken. Wealth still poured into Roman society from the east, but in the western provinces especially it tended to be concentrated in the hands of a very few families. These families gradually accrued to themselves such extensive privileges that they rarely contributed anything to the coffers of the Roman state. The upkeep of cities thus fell increasingly on a local elite that could not shoulder it. As these men were reduced to poverty or fled the cities altogether, the urban basis of classical Roman civilization and its civic ideals were further undermined. Regional differences were also growing more pronounced, leading to a series of secessionist movements among the western provinces. Enormous dedication and exertion on the part of its citizenry might just possibly have saved the empire, but too few citizens were now willing to work hard for the public good. Ultimately, the decline of Rome was marked by a lack of interest among its citizens in preserving it. As a result, the Roman world came to an end not so much with a bang as with a whimper.

ROMAN ACHIEVEMENTS

Attention to the dynamics of Rome's decline in the west should not cause us to overlook the many ways in which Roman society was a towering success. No state has ever encompassed so much territory, with so many people under its dominion, for so long a span of time. Roman rule maintained its vitality in the west from the first century B.C.E. until the fifth century C.E. In the east, the Roman Empire survived until 1453. Part of that success resulted from the Roman government's ability to create and maintain systems of communication, trade, and travel as no other state had done before and as none would do again until modern times. Underlying these successes was the fundamental strength of the Roman economy. Until the third century crisis, the Romans had maintained a relatively stable currency and a prosperous international trade for four centuries without any of the mechanisms or safeguards of a modern market economy. This too remains an unparalleled achievement.

Most fundamental, however, the Roman Empire's survival was a political achievement. The Roman political system was inclusive to a degree no modern empire has ever matched. Through their willingness to extend the franchise to non-Romans, to allow even provincials to become senators and ultimately emperors, Rome gave a share of power to its population that no Near Eastern or Greek empire ever imagined. Although the Persians were tolerant of foreign cultic practice, and the Athenians generous with political rights among their own citizenry, extending real political power to "outsiders" was out of the question. For

> The upkeep of cities thus fell increasingly on a local elite that could not shoulder it. As these men were reduced to poverty or fled the cities altogether, the urban basis of classical Roman civilization and its civic ideals were further underminded.

the Romans, extension of the franchise was key to their success, from the Latin Right in early Italy to the granting of citizenship to all the inhabitants of the empire under Caracalla. As a prominent historian of Rome once remarked, if the British Empire had been as willing to extend its franchise as the Romans were to extend theirs, the American Revolution might never have occurred.

CONCLUSION

Resemblances between Roman history and the history of Great Britain or the United States in the nineteenth and twentieth centuries have often been noted. Like America's, the Roman economy evolved from a simple agrarianism to a complex urban system with problems of unemployment, gross disparities of wealth, and financial crises. Like the British Empire, the Roman Empire was founded on conquest. And like both the British and the American empires, the Roman Empire justified itself by celebrating the peace its conquests allegedly brought to the world.

Ultimately, however, such parallels are superficial. Rome was an ancient, not a modern, society that differed profoundly from any of the societies of the modern Western world. The Romans disdained industrial activities. Neither did they have any idea of the modern national state. The Romans never developed an adequate representative government, and they never solved the problem of succession to imperial power. Nor were Roman social relations in any way comparable with those of more recent centuries. The Roman economy rested on slavery to a degree unmatched in any modern society. Technology was primitive, social stratification was extreme, and gender relations were profoundly unequal. Roman religion rested on the assumption that religious practice and political life were inseparable from one another, and Roman emperors were worshiped as living gods.

Nevertheless, the civilization of Rome exerted a great influence on later cultures. Roman architectural forms survive to this day in the design of many of our government buildings, and Roman styles of dress continue to be worn by the clergy of the various Christian churches. Roman law was handed down to the Middle Ages and on into modern times. Roman sculpture provided the model on which virtually all modern sculpture rests, and Roman authors set the standards for prose composition in Europe and America until the twentieth century. Even the organization of the Catholic Church was adapted from the structure of the Roman state; today the pope bears the title of supreme pontiff (*pontifex maximus*), once borne by the emperor in his role as head of the Roman civic religion.

But perhaps the most important of all Rome's contributions to the future was its role in transmitting Greek civilization throughout the length and breadth of its empire. When, finally, the united Roman Empire did collapse, three different successor civilizations would emerge to occupy Rome's former territories: Byzantium, Islam, and western Europe. Each of these civilizations would be characterized by a distinctive religious tradition, and each would adopt and adapt different aspects of its Roman inheritance. What these three Western civilizations shared, however, was a common cultural inheritance derived from Greece by way of Rome—an inheritance of urbanism, cosmopolitanism, imperialism, and learning that would forever mark the West as a unique experiment in human history.

This cultural inheritance would be Rome's epitaph; and in the mid-third century C.E., it must have seemed that an epitaph was the only thing needed to bring the Roman Empire to an end. But in fact, the Roman Empire did not collapse. It went on to enjoy another several centuries of life. Rome did not fall in the third century, or the fourth century, or even the fifth. But it was transformed; and in this transformed state the Roman inheritance would pass to the Western civilizations of the Middle Ages. It is to those transformations that we now turn.

KEY TERMS

Etruscans	plebeians	Cicero	Augustus	aqueducts
patricians	Carthage	Julius Caesar	Virgil	Gaul

SELECTED READINGS

Translations of Roman authors are available in the Penguin Classics series and in the Loeb Classical Library.

Barker, Graeme, and Tom Rasmussen. *The Etruscans.* Oxford and Malden, Mass., 1998. A fine survey, from the Blackwell *Peoples of Europe* series.

Beard, Mary, John North, and Simon Price. *Religions of Rome,* vol. 1: *A History.* Cambridge, 1998. An authoritative account, full of new ideas.

Beard, Mary, John North, and Simon Price. *Religions of Rome,* vol. 2: *A Sourcebook.* Cambridge, 1998. A definitive source collection that supplements vol. 1.

Boardman, John, Jasper Griffin, and Oswyn Murray. *The Oxford History of the Roman World.* Oxford, 1990. Reprint of relevant portions of the excellent *Oxford History of the Classical World* (1986). Stimulating, accessible topical chapters by British specialists.

Cornell, T. J. *The Beginnings of Rome: Italy and Rome from the Bronze Age to the Punic Wars (c. 1000–264 B.C.).* London, 1995. An expert, ambitious survey of the archaeological and historical evidence for early Rome.

Crawford, Michael. *The Roman Republic.* 2d ed. Cambridge, Mass., 1993. A lively, fast-paced survey of republican Rome. An excellent place to start.

Fantham, Elaine, Helene Peet Foley, Natalie Boymel Kampen, Sarah B. Pomeroy, and H. Alan Shapiro. *Women in the Classical World.* Oxford, 1994. A lively, expert survey of both Greece and Rome.

Garnsey, Peter, and Richard Saller. *The Roman Empire: Economy, Society, and Culture.* Berkeley, Calif.,1987. A straightforward short survey.

Gruen, Erich S. *The Hellenistic World and the Coming of Rome.* 2 vols. Berkeley, Calif.,1984. A massive survey, focused on the unpredictable rise of Rome to a position of dominance within the Mediterranean world.

Harris, William V. *War and Imperialism in Republican Rome, 327–70 B.C.* Oxford, 1979. A challenging study arguing that Rome's need for military conquest and imperial expansion was deeply embedded in the political and social fabric of Roman life.

Lancel, Serge. *Carthage: A History.* Trans. Antonia Nevill. Oxford, 1995. An up-to-date account of Rome's great rival for control of the Mediterranean world.

Lewis, Naphtali, and M. Reinhold. *Roman Civilization: Selected Readings.* 2 vols. New York, 1951–1955. The standard collection, especially for political and economic subjects. Vol. 1 covers the republic; vol. 2, the empire.

Millar, Fergus G. B. *The Crowd in Rome in the Late Republic.* Ann Arbor, Mich., 1999. A revisionist account that emphasizes the reality of Roman democracy in the late republic, against those who would see the period's politics as entirely under the control of aristocratic families.

Millar, Fergus G. B. *The Emperor in the Roman World, 31 B.C.–A.D. 337.* London, 1977. A classic work that showed (among much else) the importance of emperor worship to the religious outlook of the Roman Empire.

Ward, Allen M., Fritz Heichelheim, and Cedric A. Yeo. *A History of the Roman People.* 3d ed. Upper Saddle River, N.J., 1999. An informative, well-organized textbook covering Roman history from its beginnings to the end of the sixth century C.E.

Wells, Colin. *The Roman Empire.* 2d ed. Cambridge, Mass., 1992. An easily readable survey from the reign of Augustus to the mid-third century C.E., particularly useful for its treatment of the relationship between the Roman central government and its Italian provinces.

Chapter Six

Christianity and the Transformation of the Roman World

THE ROMAN EMPIRE declined after 180 C.E., but it did not collapse. In 284 C.E. the soldier-emperor Diocletian began a reorganization of the empire that gave it a new lease on life. Throughout the fourth century the Roman state continued to encompass the entire Mediterranean world. During the fifth century the western half of the empire fell under the political control of German-speaking invaders; but many Roman institutions continued to function in these new Germanic kingdoms, and in the sixth century the emperor Justinian reconquered much of the western Mediterranean shoreline. Only in the seventh century did it become clear that the divisions between the eastern and western halves of the Roman Empire would be permanent, and that the two regions would thereafter develop in fundamentally different ways. With this transition, the world of classical antiquity came to an end.

Historians used to begin their discussions of medieval history in the third, fourth, or fifth century C.E. But it is now more customary to conceive of ancient history as continuing after 284 C.E. and lasting until the Roman Empire lost control over the Mediterranean in the seventh century. The period from 284 to about 610 C.E., although transitional (as, of course, all ages are), has certain themes of its own and is best described as neither Roman nor medieval but as the age of late antiquity.

Three major cultural trends characterized the world of late antiquity. The first was the spread and triumph of Christianity throughout the Roman world. At first Christianity was just one of many otherworldly religions that appealed to increasing numbers of people during the later empire. But in the fourth century it was adopted as the Roman state religion and thereafter became one of the greatest shaping forces in the development of Western civilizations.

The gradual extension of Christianity, first from city to city, and then from city to countryside, was one element in a larger process of cultural assimilation that characterized the entire late-antique world. New cultural developments were more widely

FOCUS QUESTIONS

• What were the principles by which Diocletian reformed the Roman Empire?

• How did Christianity become the majority religion within the Roman Empire?

• What major changes did Christianity undergo during the fourth century?

• Why did the Germanic invasions succeed?

• What distinctive themes of Western Christian thought were emerging during the fourth and fifth centuries?

• How was classical culture Christianized?

• Why did Justinian's plan to reunite the Roman Empire fail?

diffused than ever before, and a wider range of people participated in them. As Roman culture became more uniform and more widespread, however, it also became less sophisticated and distinctive. The result was a watering down of the high culture of the classical era—a process we shall call "vulgarization."

Cultural influences from outside the Mediterranean world were also having an increasing impact, especially on the western parts of the empire. The Romans called this process "barbarization," from the Greek word *barbaros*, meaning "foreigner." Barbarian culture was not necessarily primitive, but it was nonurban and non-Greek—and in the eyes of Mediterranean elites, these facts alone were enough to stigmatize it. But barbarian influence grew steadily nonetheless, first within the army and then throughout society. None of these processes was cataclysmic; but by the end of the sixth century C.E., Christianization, vulgarization, and barbarization had combined to bring the ancient Mediterranean world to an end.

For the barracks emperors of the earlier third century, too much familiarity with their soldiers and courtiers had bred contempt.

THE REORGANIZED EMPIRE

What were the principles by which Diocletian reformed the Roman Empire?

The chaos of the mid-third century C.E. might well have destroyed the Roman Empire. That it did not is largely due to the efforts of a remarkable soldier named Diocletian, who ruled as emperor from 284 to 305 C.E. Diocletian imposed a number of fundamental political and economic reforms on the empire. Most important, however, he restored the majesty and prestige of the emperorship itself. By so doing, Diocletian laid the foundations on which all subsequent Roman and Byzantine emperors would base their authority.

THE REIGN OF DIOCLETIAN

Like Augustus, Diocletian was acutely aware of the dignity of his imperial office and of the importance of political symbolism in maintaining it. But unlike Augustus, who tried to cloak the reality of his power in the trappings of republicanism, Diocletian presented himself to his subjects as an undisguised autocrat. His title was not

princeps ("first citizen"), but *dominus* ("lord"). Diocletian himself remained apart from the ordinary business of his court, physically removed behind a maze of doorways, rooms, and curtains. Those lucky enough to gain an audience with him had to prostrate themselves before him; a privileged few would be allowed to kiss his robe. For the barracks emperors of the earlier third century, too much familiarity with their soldiers and courtiers had bred contempt. As a soldier-emperor himself, Diocletian was determined to avoid their mistake.

In another breach with Augustan tradition, Diocletian also took steps to define formal rules of imperial succession. Realizing that the empire had now become too large for a single ruler to control it effectively, Diocletian divided the empire in half, entrusting the western part to a reliable junior colleague named Maximian while retaining the wealthier, eastern half for himself. The two "augusti" (as Diocletian and Maximian called themselves) then each chose a lieutenant, called a caesar, to govern a subsection of their respective territories. When the two augusti retired, the caesars would step into their place, and appoint new caesars in turn to assist them. This system (known as the tetrarchy, the "rule of four") was intended to provide more effective governance over the empire by permitting a degree of decentralization. But it was also designed to end the succession disputes that had proven to be the fatal weakness of the Augustan political system and that had brought the third-century empire to its knees.

Diocletian was also an energetic administrative reformer. Although he retained close personal control over the army, he took steps to separate military from civilian chains of command. Never again would Roman armies make and unmake emperors as they had done in the third century. To control the devastatingly high rates of inflation that were undermining the economy of the empire, Diocletian stabilized the currency and attempted (without much success) to fix prices and wages by legislative fiat. He reformed the tax system, adjusting tax assessments and appointing a small army of new (and immensely unpopular) tax collectors. He also moved the administrative capital of the empire itself from Italy to Nicomedia in modern-day Turkey. Rome remained the spiritual and symbolic capital of the empire, not least because the Senate continued to meet there. But Diocletian had little need for the Senate's advice, and the growing disparities of wealth between the eastern and western regions made Nicomedia a

What were the principles by which Diocletian reformed the Roman Empire?

The Reorganized Empire   149

Legend:
- District of Constantius as caesar
- District of Maximian as augustus
- District of Galerius as caesar
- District of Diocletian as augustus
- Diocese boundary
- District capitals

DIOCLETIAN'S DIVISION OF THE EMPIRE, C. 304 C.E.

In a desperate bid to save the Roman Empire from collapse, Diocletian divided it in half. He would control the eastern portion, and Maximian would have the west. Each emperor then chose a lieutenant, thus creating what was called the tetrarchy (the "rule of four"). To what extent do the divisions shown on this map mirror those that would characterize the later history of the Mediterranean and European worlds?

more appropriate capital than Rome for an empire that now rested on the backs of its bureaucrats.

THE REIGN OF CONSTANTINE

In 305 C.E. Diocletian built a palace for himself at Split (Croatia) and retired there to raise cabbages—an unprecedented move for a late Roman ruler. At the same time he obliged his colleague Maximian to retire also, and their two caesars moved peacefully up the ladder of succession. But the concord did not last. Civil war broke out among Diocletian's successors and continued until Constantine, the son of one of the original caesars, emerged victorious. From 312 until 324 Constantine

ruled as augustus over the western empire, while a junior augustus ruled in the east. In 324 Constantine did away with this arrangement and ruled the reunited empire single-handedly until his death in 337.

In keeping with Constantine's grandiose conception of himself, he built a new capital starting in 324 C.E. and named it Constantinople. Founded on the site of the ancient city of Byzantium, this new capital epitomized the continuing shift in the "weight" of Roman civilization toward the east. Situated at the mouth of the Black Sea on the border between Europe and Asia, Constantinople had commanding advantages as a center for communications, trade, and defense. Surrounded on three sides by water and protected on land by walls, it would remain the political and economic center of the Roman Empire until 1453, when the city was finally conquered by the Ottoman Turks.

In one crucial respect, however, Constantine abandoned the precedents established by Diocletian. By making succession to the imperial throne hereditary within his own family, Constantine brought Rome back to the principle of dynastic monarchy it had thrown off 800 years before. To make matters worse, Constantine divided the empire among his three sons on his death. Civil war was the predictable result, made worse by differences in the type of Christianity each son espoused.

Dynastic conflicts among Constantine's descendants would continue for most of the fourth century. But these conflicts were never so serious as the civil wars of the third century, and from time to time a contestant would still be able to reunite the empire. The last to do so was Theodosius I (379–395 C.E.). Before Theodosius died, however, he too divided the empire between his two sons: this time with disastrous results, as we shall see in a moment.

Behind these quarrels over the imperial throne we can also discern some larger developments in the history of the fourth-century empire. Most fundamental, divisions between the eastern and the western halves of the empire were becoming steadily more pronounced. As the Greek-speaking east grew more populous, more prosperous, and more central to imperial policy, the Latin-speaking west was becoming poorer and more peripheral to the political, economic, and cultural life of the empire. Many western cities now relied on transfers of funds from the east to keep them going; when these funds dried up, or military units were transferred away, these cities declined. Even Rome was becoming something of a backwater in its own empire. When emperors did reside in the west, they found it more convenient to live at Milan, or Ravenna, or on the Rhine frontier at Trier. After the early fourth century, no emperors lived in Rome, and only twice thereafter did an emperor even visit the city. Beneath the surface of imperial autocracy, the fourth-century empire was slowly dissolving into its constituent parts.

Colossal Head of Constantine. This enormous statue of the seated emperor was located just outside the Forum in Rome. It stood forty feet high; the head alone weighed nine tons. The enlarged eyes emphasize the emperor's spiritual vision.

THE EMERGENCE AND TRIUMPH OF CHRISTIANITY

How did Christianity become the majority religion within the Roman Empire?

Between the first and fifth centuries C.E., Christianity grew from obscure beginnings in Judea to become the official state religion of the Roman world. Thereafter, it became a dominant force in shaping the civilizations of the Western world. For Christians, their religion's extraordinary growth and impact is testimony to its truth. For historians, however, it poses an enormous interpretive problem: how can we explain the appeal of early Christianity without making its eventual success seem predictable or inevitable?

In attempting to do this, it may be useful to recognize at the outset that Christianity appealed to differing groups of people at different stages in its early history, and that each of these groups understood its appeal in rather different ways. Christianity began with the teachings of Jesus, delivered to the Jews of Judea and Galilee around the year 30 C.E. It took firm root, however, largely among the Greek-speaking town dwellers of the eastern Mediterranean during

HOW DID CHRISTIANITY BECOME THE MAJORITY RELIGION WITHIN THE ROMAN EMPIRE?

THE EMERGENCE AND TRIUMPH OF CHRISTIANITY   151

the second and third centuries C.E. Then, starting with Constantine, it became the favored religion of the imperial family and ultimately the official religion of the Roman Empire. We will examine these stages in order, starting with the career of Jesus himself.

THE CAREER OF JESUS

There is no doubt that Jesus was a historical figure, but it is difficult to know very much about him. No strictly contemporary sources mention him, although we do have references to some of his opponents, including the Roman governor Pontius Pilate and the high priest Caiphas. The earliest written sources that mention Jesus are the letters of one of his followers, the apostle Paul, written during the 50s and 60s C.E., and the four "gospel" accounts of Jesus' life plus the Acts of the Apostles, all written between c. 70 and 100 C.E. All these works, together with a number of later sources, are contained in the New Testament, a collection of Christian writings added to the text of the Hebrew Bible during the first three centuries C.E. Other sources also circulated during those years, including a now-lost compilation of Jesus' sayings from which the gospel writers drew some material. It is possible, therefore, that even fairly late, nonbiblical sources such as the second-century Gospel of Thomas may preserve some authentic record of Jesus' teachings. Most historians, however, prefer to rely on the first-century sources in trying to interpret his career.

Jesus was born to a Galilean Jewish family sometime shortly before the beginning of the Common (or Christian) Era. He was not born precisely in the "year one"—we owe this mistake in our dating system to a sixth-century monk. When Jesus was around thirty years old, he was acclaimed by a preacher of moral reform, John the Baptist, as one "mightier than I, whose shoes I am not worthy to untie." Thereafter, Jesus' career was a continuous course of preaching, healing, and teaching, mostly in the rural areas of Galilee and Judea. Around the year 30 C.E., however, he staged an openly messianic entry into Jerusalem during Passover, a religious holiday that brought large and excitable crowds of Jews into the city. The city's

Jesus. This depiction of Jesus with long hair and a beard from a third-century C.E. stone inlay is strikingly different from the Roman style.

religious leaders quickly arrested him and turned him over to Pontius Pilate, the Roman governor, for sentencing. Pilate chose to make an example of Jesus by condemning him to death by crucifixion, a standard Roman criminal penalty for those judged guilty of sedition against Rome.

This might have been the end of the story. But soon after Jesus' execution, rumors began to spread that Jesus was alive and had been seen by some of his followers. He had risen from the dead, his followers now proclaimed, and after forty days had ascended into heaven, promising to return again at the end of time. In life Jesus had been a religious teacher and healer; in death, however, he had been revealed as something more. His entire career now had to be rethought and reinterpreted by his followers. The evidence of this reinterpretation has come down to us in the letters of Paul and in the gospel narratives of Matthew, Mark, Luke, and John.

JESUS AND SECOND TEMPLE JUDAISM

In 1947, a Bedouin boy discovered an extraordinary cache of Jewish religious texts that had been hidden in a cave near Qumran at some point during the first century C.E. Only recently, however, has the bulk of this material, known collectively as the Dead Sea Scrolls, been made widely available to scholars. These scrolls have revolutionized our understanding of Jewish religious practice and belief around the time of Jesus. Most of all they emphasize its extraordinary diversity.

When Jesus was born, the Roman conquest of Judea was less than a generation old. Banditry, sometimes tinged with nationalism, was commonplace in the countryside; in the cities and villages, there was talk of rebellion and hope for a messiah who would restore Jewish rule over the holy land of Israel. Most extreme of those who sought hope in politics were the Zealots, who sought to expel the Romans by force of arms. Their activities eventually led to two disastrous revolts. The first, between 66 and 70 C.E., brought about the destruction of the Jewish Temple at Jerusalem by the avenging Romans. The second, in 132–135 C.E., caused the destruction of the city of Jerusalem and the expulsion of its entire Jewish population.

This political context is important to understanding Pilate's decision to execute Jesus; but it tells us little about what Jesus actually taught or how his teachings might have been understood by his fellow Jews. To this purpose, the religious divisions within contemporary Judaism are much more important.

In the centuries after the Jews' return from Babylon and the rebuilding of the Temple, Judaism became an uncompromisingly monotheistic religion, built on the covenantal relationship between Yahweh and his chosen people. By the first century B.C.E., however, important differences had emerged in how Jews understood what that covenant required of them. Jesus' teachings need to be seen in the context of these debates.

The guardians of the written traditions enshrined in the Torah (the first five books of the Hebrew Bible) were the hereditary Temple priesthood and their aristocratic allies, a group known as the Sadducees.

Their main rivals for the religious allegiance of the people were the Pharisees. In contrast to the Sadducees, who considered most of the requirements of religious law to pertain only to the priesthood, the Pharisees insisted that all 613 of Yahweh's commandments were binding on all Jews. The Pharisees urged rigorous devotion to religious law, but they were also quite flexible in applying it to daily life. They also believed in a life after death characterized by individual rewards and punishments. They actively sought out converts through preaching and looked forward to

the imminent arrival of the messiah whom God had promised to his people. In all these respects they differed from the more traditional Sadducees.

Jesus' emphasis on the ethical requirements of the law (love of God and neighbor; the obligation to do good even to those who harm you and to forgive those who wrong you), his apparent belief in life after death and in the imminent coming of "the kingdom of God," and his exhortations to obey the spirit rather than the letter of religious law all fitted well within a Pharisaic framework. Nevertheless, he seems to have carried these principles considerably further than did most Pharisees. When, for example, his followers broke the laws of the Sabbath by gathering grain to eat, Jesus justified them by declaring, "The Sabbath was made for man, not man for the Sabbath." By extending Pharisaic reasoning to such a degree, Jesus' teachings threatened to undermine completely the obligatory nature of Jewish law as the Pharisees understood it.

> In the centuries after the Jews' return from Babylon and the rebuilding of the Temple, Judaism became an uncompromisingly monotheistic religion, built on the covenantal relationship between Yahweh and his chosen people.

None of these groups was monolithic, and the vast majority of Jews would not have identified themselves with any of these groups. Even the Sadducees are best regarded as a sect within the larger Temple priesthood. For most Jews at the time of Jesus, Judaism consisted of going up to the Temple at Jerusalem a few times a year on holy days, paying the annual Temple tax, reciting the morning and evening prayers, and observing certain fundamental religious laws such as circumcision (for men) and ritual purity.

While Jesus may have stretched such observances, there is no evidence he sought to end them. Rather, what made him controversial within the larger Jewish community was his followers' claim that he was the messiah promised by God to deliver Israel from its enemies. After his death and alleged resurrection, such claims grew louder and more assertive; but they never persuaded more than a small minority of Jesus' fellow Jews. As his followers began to preach to non-Jewish audiences, however, they began to reinterpret Jesus' role as messiah in terms that drew on Greek theological ideas. Jesus, his followers now proclaimed, was not merely a messiah for the Jews. He was the "Christ" (from the Greek for "anointed one"), the divine Son of God sent to earth to suffer and die for the sins of all humanity, who had risen from the dead and ascended into heaven and who would return to judge all the world's inhabitants at the end of time.

How did Christianity become the majority religion within the Roman Empire?

The emergence and Triumph of Christianity   153

The Growth of Christianity in the Hellenistic World

The key figure in developing this new theological understanding of Jesus' messiahship was Saul of Tarsus (c. 10 – c. 67 C.E.). Saul was a Jew born in southeast Asia Minor. A staunch Pharisee, Saul was initially a persecutor of Jesus' followers; but after a blinding conversion experience, he joined the "Jesus movement," changed his name to Paul, and devoted his limitless energy to interpreting and preaching the new faith to the Greek-speaking, mainly non-Jewish communities of Greece and Asia Minor. Declaring himself to be the apostle to the Gentiles (non-Jews), Paul rejected the binding nature of Jewish religious law, declaring it to be irrelevant to salvation for Jesus' followers. This stance initially caused offense among the Jewish Christians of Jerusalem, a group led by Jesus' brother, James; but after a wrenching debate, Paul's position triumphed. Some Christians would continue to obey Jewish religious law, but the movement's future now lay clearly with the non-Jewish converts it was making outside Judea and Galilee.

It is not entirely clear who the majority of these new converts were. By the first century C.E., sizable Jewish communities existed in most major cities of the eastern Mediterranean world, including Rome itself. These communities had already begun to reinterpret Jewish religious ideas within a Greek intellectual and cultural

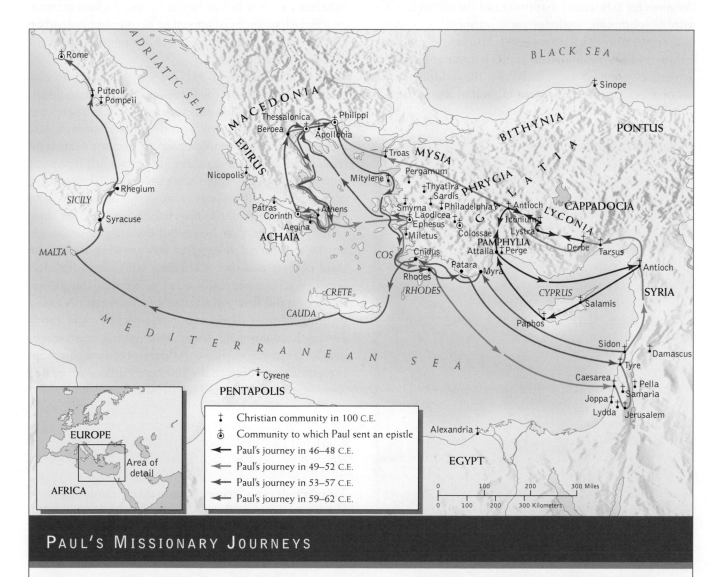

PAUL'S MISSIONARY JOURNEYS

Why did the message of Paul and the Jesus movement appeal to the non-Jews of the Mediterranean world? What was the main issue that divided Paul and the Christian Jews of Jerusalem? What were the consequences of Paul's travels throughout the Greek world?

context. As Paul's own example suggests, to some of these Hellenized Jews the new Christian teachings must have been attractive. Even more so, however, Christianity probably appealed to the groups of non-Jews (known as "God-fearers") who tended to gather around these Greek-speaking Jewish communities. God-fearers did not follow all the precepts of Jewish law, but they admired Jews for their monotheism and for their uncompromising moral and ethical standards, and modeled their own lives after Jewish example. But Christianity must also have made inroads among ordinary Greeks, many of whom would already have been familiar with other, superficially similar cults (such as Mithraism) that also stressed elaborate initiation ceremonies (for Christians, baptism) and the importance of special religious knowledge for salvation.

Certain differences between Christianity and these other mystery religions do stand out. Organizational structures evolved very early; by the middle of the second century, the Christian church at Rome already had a bishop who presided over a small army of lesser officeholders, including priests, deacons, confessors, and exorcists. Women were also notably prominent in these early Christian communities, not only as patrons and benefactors (a role upper-class Roman women had often played in new religious cults) but also as officeholders (although we know of no female bishops or priests, female deacons are well attested). This relatively high status of women was quite unusual and distinguished Christianity markedly from Mithraism, which excluded women even from membership in the cult, much less from holding any office within it. Christians were also well known for supporting their poorer members through charity. Christianity drew its adherents from a broad range of social classes, but it may have had a special appeal to people (such as urban artisans) whose livelihoods could disappear with a shift of the economic winds.

All these factors help explain the appeal of the new religion, especially to the Greek-speaking urban dwellers who made up the vast majority of Christian converts during the second and third centuries C.E. Nevertheless, why people chose to become Christians remains an impossible question for historians to answer with certainty. It is often suggested that Christianity's promise of salvation was a powerful inducement to conversion, especially in the chaotic world of the third century C.E. This may be so; but the claim rests simply on the facts that Christianity was growing during the third century and that Christians believed in life after death. We have no real way to prove that the second fact led to the first. All we can say for certain is that a growing number of people in the second- and third-century Mediterranean world believed Christian teachings to be true and that they were prepared to accept these teachings despite the disapproval they generated within Greco-Roman and Jewish society.

Saint Paul. This early Christian mosaic depicts the self-declared apostle to the Gentiles, formerly known as Saul of Tarsus, who was a key figure in developing the theological understanding of Jesus' messiahship.

CHRISTIANITY AND THE ROMAN EMPIRE

Throughout the second and third centuries C.E., Judaism remained a legally recognized religion within the Roman Empire. Whatever their attitudes toward Jewish belief and practice, Romans respected the fact that Jews were at least maintaining the religious customs of their ancestors. Christianity, however, was an innovation; and in the eyes of traditional Romans, novelty in religion was not a good thing. Nevertheless, the official attitude of the Roman state toward Christianity

PROSECUTING CHRISTIANS

Until the third century, the Roman imperial government rarely initiated the persecution of Christians. Local administrators, such as the younger Pliny, were anxious to follow proper legal procedures in dealing with the new sect, which they regarded as absurd but not particularly dangerous. But neither Pliny nor the emperor Trajan (98–117 C.E.) wanted to see the Roman state actively seek out Christians for punishment.

THE LETTERS OF PLINY THE YOUNGER AND THE EMPEROR TRAJAN

LETTER 97: PLINY TO TRAJAN

It is a rule, Sir, which I inviolably observe, to refer myself to you in all my doubts; for who is more capable of removing my scruples, or informing my ignorance? Having never been present at any trials concerning those who profess Christianity, I am unacquainted not only with the nature of their crimes, or the measure of their punishment, but how far it is proper to enter into an examination concerning them. . . .

The method I have observed towards those who have been brought before me as Christians, is this: I interrogated them whether they were Christians; if they confessed I repeated the question twice again, adding threats at the same time; when, if they still persevered, I ordered them to be immediately punished: for I was persuaded, whatever the nature of their opinions might be, a contumacious and inflexible obstinacy certainly deserved correction. . . .

But this crime spreading (as is usually the case) while it was actually under prosecution, several instances of the same nature occurred. An information was presented to me without any name subscribed, containing a charge against several persons, who upon examination denied they were Christians, or had ever been so.

They repeated after me an invocation to the gods, and offered religious rites with wine and frankincense before your statue (which for the purpose I had ordered to be brought together with those of the gods); and even reviled the name of Christ: whereas there is no forcing, it is said, those who are really Christians, into a compliance with any of these articles: I thought proper therefore to discharge them. . . .

I judged it . . . necessary to endeavor to extort the real truth [about Christian rites and beliefs] by putting two female slaves to the torture, who were said to administer in their religious functions: but I could discover nothing more than an absurd and excessive superstition. I thought proper therefore to adjourn all further proceedings in this affair, in order to consult with you. . . . For this contagious superstition is not confined to the cities only, but has spread its infection among the country villages. Nevertheless, it still seems possible to remedy this evil and restrain its progress. The temples, at least, which were once almost deserted, begin now to be frequented; and the sacred solemnities, after a long intermission, are again revived. . . . From hence it is easy to imagine, what numbers might be reclaimed from this error, if a pardon were granted to those who shall repent.

LETTER 98: TRAJAN TO PLINY

The method you have pursued, my dear Pliny, in the proceedings against those Christians which were brought before you, is extremely proper; as it is not possible to lay down any fixed plan by which to act in all cases of this nature. But I would not have you officiously enter into any enquiries concerning them. If indeed they should be brought before you, and the crime is proved, they must be punished; with the restriction, however, that where the party denies himself to be a Christian, and shall make it evident that he is not, by invoking our gods, let him (notwithstanding any former suspicion) be pardoned upon his repentence. Information without the accuser's name subscribed ought not to be received in prosecutions of any sort, as it is introducing a very dangerous precedent, and by no means agreeable to the equity of my government.

W. Melmoth, trans., *The Letters of Pliny the Consul*, vol. 2 (London, 1770), pp. 671–677. Reprinted in *Western Societies: A Documentary History*, vol. 1, ed. Brian Tierney and Joan Scott (New York, 1984), pp. 166–168.

QUESTIONS FOR ANALYSIS

1. Pliny and Trajan were friends, but Pliny was careful to get the emperor's approval of his legal procedures. He was unsure whether simply being a Christian was a crime, but he knew that lying about church membership constituted perjury and refusal to perform ritual honors to the emperor was equal to rebellion and treason, all crimes that should be punished. What does this say about official Roman ideas of honor, propriety, and justice?

2. During judicial examinations, subjects were routinely tortured to extort more information from them. Yet when Pliny tortured two deaconesses, he found only "absurd and excessive superstition." What did he conclude from this? What seemed the best way to fight this superstition?

was usually one of indifference. During the first and second centuries C.E., Christians were tolerated by Roman authorities except when local magistrates chose to prosecute them for refusing to worship the official state gods. During the third century there were some concerted, centrally organized persecutions; the last of these took place toward the end of Diocletian's reign and the beginning of the reign of his successor Galerius. But these were too intermittent and short lived to do irreparable damage; and by the early fourth century, the religion had gained too many adherents to be wiped out by persecution, a fact Galerius finally recognized by issuing an edict of toleration just before his death in 311 C.E.

Still, however, the number of Christians was not large. No reliable statistics exist, but most scholars now believe that in the year 300 only 1 to 5 percent of the total population of the empire was Christian. Even in the relatively more Christianized eastern parts of the empire, no more than 10 percent of the population was Christian, and this estimate is probably generous. Christian numbers were growing, and

might have continued to grow. But it seems unlikely Christianity would ever have become the majority religion in the empire without the help of the emperor Constantine.

Constantine's decision to become a Christian continues to puzzle historians. He must have had some contact with Christianity as a young man; he may even have been a nominal Christian at the time he launched his bid for the imperial throne. His real commitment to the faith came later, however, after he saw a Christian symbol in the sky while preparing for battle at the Milvian Bridge (312 C.E.) and heard a heavenly voice declaring, "In this sign, conquer." Constantine ordered his soldiers to paint the symbol on their shields; the victory they won that day propelled him to the imperial throne.

As emperor, Constantine showered favors on the Christian clergy and patronized the construction of churches throughout the empire. But Constantine did not make Christianity the official religion of the empire, nor did he prohibit pagan worship. He did, however, make Christianity the favored religion of the imperial family, transforming Christianity, almost over-

> As emperor, Constantine showered favors on the Christian clergy and patronized the construction of churches throughout the empire. But Constantine did not make Christianity the official religion of the empire, nor did he prohibit pagan worship.

WHAT MAJOR CHANGES DID CHRISTIANITY UNDERGO DURING THE FOURTH CENTURY?

THE NEW CONTOURS OF FOURTH-CENTURY CHRISTIANITY   157

night, into a prestigious religion for the ruling classes of the empire to adopt. Gradually, the rest of the citizens of the empire followed suit. By the end of the fourth century C.E., a clear majority of the empire was Christian, and bishops had emerged as dominating influences in the political life of their cities.

Constantine himself retained both pagan and Christian officials around his court and was careful in his public pronouncements to speak in terms that would be acceptable to a non-Christian audience. His successors, however, became more and more uncompromisingly Christian in their orientation and less and less inclined to tolerate competing faiths. A brief exception was the reign of Julian "the Apostate" (360–363 C.E.), who abandoned Christianity and attempted to revive traditional Roman paganism. But Julian was killed in battle with the Persians, his pro-pagan edicts were revoked, and the Christian officials around the imperial court became more insistent that imperial power be used to suppress competing cults. Theodosius the Great (379–395 C.E.) finally suppressed competing cults, prohibiting pagan worship of any sort within the empire and removing the altar of the goddess Victory from the Senate house in Rome. Fifteen years later, Rome fell to the Goths. Pagan spokesmen noted the connection.

THE NEW CONTOURS OF FOURTH-CENTURY CHRISTIANITY

What major changes did Christianity undergo during the fourth century?

As Christianity became politically influential and socially prestigious, it underwent major changes in doctrine, organization, and outlook. As a result, Christianity at the end of the fourth century was in many respects a quite different religion from the one persecuted by Diocletian and Galerius only a century before.

DOCTRINAL QUARRELS

One consequence of Christianity's new prominence was the flaring up of bitter doctrinal disputes. Christians had of course disagreed about doctrinal matters before; but as long as Christianity remained the religion of an unimportant minority, these disagreements were of little political or social consequence. With Constantine's accession to the imperial throne, however, such disagreements now had the potential to ignite political quarrels (even rioting) among bishops and their opponents and to undermine imperial support for the church itself. It was imperative, therefore, that such doctrinal disputes be resolved, if necessary through the active intervention of the Christian emperor himself.

The most fundamental doctrinal dispute to erupt was between the Arians and Athanasians over the nature of the Trinity. The Arians—not to be confused with Aryans (a racial term)—were followers of a priest named Arius who rejected the idea that Jesus, as the Christ, could be equal with God. Instead Arians maintained that Jesus as the Son of God was created by the Father in time and therefore was not co-eternal with him or formed of the same substance. The followers of Saint Athanasius argued the opposite: even though Christ was the Son he was also fully God; and so Father, Son, and Holy Ghost (the Trinity) were all absolutely equal and composed of an identical substance. After protracted struggles, the Athanasian doctrine became the orthodox Christian position, and Arianism was declared a heresy. But Arianism continued to attract followers for the next 200 years.

Resolving such doctrinal disputes was intensely difficult. Often they involved not only doctrinal differences but regional and political differences as well. As a result, the Roman state became increasingly enmeshed in the governance of the church, especially in the eastern half of the empire. Constantine himself began this process in 325 C.E., when he presided over the Council of Nicea which condemned Arianism. His successors carried it much further. Gradually, these Christian emperors began to claim that in presiding over such councils, they were assuming a role as Christ's representative on earth, which entitled them to decide what Christian doctrine was and should be. Some even dispatched troops to suppress Christian groups who refused to accept the emperor's decisions on orthodoxy. Those who rejected such decisions were labeled heretics and could suffer both legal and ecclesiastical penalties.

GROWTH OF ECCLESIASTICAL ORGANIZATION

During the fourth century, the church became a much more clearly defined hierarchical organization, as urban-centered bishops (often from powerful local families) began to assert closer control over the priests and deacons of their surrounding areas. Distinctions of rank among the bishops themselves also began to emerge. Bishops who ruled from the larger cities came to be called metropolitans (today known in the West as archbishops), with authority over the clergy of an entire province. In the fourth century the still higher rank of patriarch was established to designate bishops who ruled over the oldest and largest Christian communities, such as Rome, Jerusalem, Constantinople, Antioch, and Alexandria. By 400 C.E., the Christian clergy thus was made up of a definite hierarchy of patriarchs, metropolitans, bishops, priests, and deacons—from which women were now firmly excluded.

The climax of this development was the primacy of the bishop of Rome, or the rise of the papacy. The bishop of Rome's claim to preeminence over the other patriarchs of the church rested on several foundations. Rome itself was venerated by the faithful as the place where the apostles Peter and Paul had been martyred. Peter was widely regarded as having been the first bishop of Rome; and the New Testament said (Matthew 16:18–19) that Jesus himself had commissioned Peter as his representative on earth, with the power to admit or deny the entrance of any Christian to the kingdom of heaven. As Peter's successors, subsequent bishops of Rome claimed to exercise the same powers Jesus had given to Peter.

The bishops of Rome also enjoyed some more prosaic advantages over the other bishops within the church.

Unlike the eastern bishops, the Roman bishop after 330 C.E. rarely had an emperor on his doorstep. As a result, he could act with more independence than could the patriarch of Constantinople. At the same time, however, it was often convenient for eastern emperors to support papal claims to authority over the western bishops as a way of maintaining some semblance of imperial control over the western empire. This was probably what lay behind the decree in 445 C.E. by the eastern emperor Valentinian III commanding all western bishops to submit to the jurisdiction of the pope. Centuries later, this decree would be cited to justify the dominance the papacy had by then achieved over the western church. At the time, however, it was ignored by everyone except the pope himself. Most eastern bishops regarded the pope's claims to primacy over the entire church as brazen effrontery, and even many western bishops paid no attention to him. The prestige of the bishops of Rome was nonetheless growing during the fourth and fifth centuries; and although the popes were not yet the monarchical rulers they would eventually become, the roots of their primacy lie here.

The increasing effectiveness of ecclesiastical organization and administration during the fourth century helped the church conquer the Roman world and minister to the needs of the faithful. As the western Roman Empire collapsed during the fifth century, western bishops took over many of the functions of urban government and preserved the vestiges of Roman rule. As a result, when barbarian armies arrived it was usually with the local bishop whom they negotiated.

THE SPREAD OF MONASTICISM

To most Christians, the increasing administrative responsibilities of the church seemed natural: religion and politics had always been closely connected throughout the history of the Roman Empire. To some Christians, however, the new world seemed a far cry indeed from the simple faith of Jesus and his apostles. Monasticism was one outgrowth of such disillusionment. Today we tend to think of monks as groups of priests who live communally and dedicate themselves to contemplation and prayer. In their origins, however, monks were not priests but laymen, who almost always lived alone and who sought extremes of self-denial rather than ordered lives of corporate prayer and service.

Monasticism began to emerge in the third century, but it became a dominant movement within Christianity only in the fourth century. There were two main reasons for monasticism's appeal. As persecution of Christians

CHRONOLOGY

THE GROWTH OF CHRISTIANITY, FIRST–FOURTH CENTURIES C.E.

Life of Jesus	c. 4 B.C.E.–c. 30 C.E.
Paul's missionary journeys	46–62 C.E.
Destruction of the Temple at Jerusalem	69–70 C.E.
Expulsion of the Jews from Jerusalem	132–135 C.E.
Constantine becomes the first Christian emperor	312 C.E.
Council of Nicea	325 C.E.
Christianity becomes official religion of the Roman Empire	c. 392 C.E.
Era of doctrinal quarrels	fourth–fifth centuries C.E.

ended, extreme asceticism sometimes functioned as a substitute for martyrdom. More obviously, however, the growth of monasticism was a response to the increasing worldliness of the fourth-century church. Christians seeking to avoid earthly temptations fled to the deserts and woods to practice an ascetic lifestyle altogether different from the lives led by the well-to-do men and women who were now flocking to join the religion of their emperor. In a church filled with such "social Christians," monasticism seemed to some purists the only certain road to salvation.

Monasticism did not initially spread so quickly in the west as it did in the east. Only in the sixth century, when Saint Benedict of Nursia (c. 480–c. 547) drafted his famous Rule, did monasticism begin to grow rapidly in western Europe. Benedict copied much of his Rule from an earlier and much harsher Latin text known as the "Rule of the Master." Benedict, however, produced a very different document: a "simple rule for beginners" as he called it, notable for its brevity, flexibility, and moderation. The Rule established a carefully defined cycle of daily prayers, lessons and communal worship. It laid down guidelines for how monks ought to live together; what they should eat; and how the work of the monastery should be performed. Physical labor was encouraged—idleness, Benedict declared, was "an enemy of the soul"—but he also reserved time for private study and contemplation. In all such matters, however, Benedict left much to the discretion of the abbot, the leader of the monastery, whom all the monks were expected to obey without hesitation.

THE GERMANIC INVASIONS AND THE FALL OF THE WESTERN ROMAN EMPIRE

Why did the Germanic invasions succeed?

The western Roman Empire had already suffered a devastating series of attacks by Germanic tribes during the mid-third century C.E. Throughout the fourth century, however, relations between Romans and Germans were largely peaceful. But starting in the early fifth century, a series of German-led invasions overwhelmed the western half of the empire. Out of this collapse a group of new Germanic kingdoms emerged in western Europe

that would permanently alter the region's history and culture.

GERMAN-ROMAN RELATIONS

The Germans were barbarians in Roman eyes because they did not live in cities and were illiterate; but in no sense were the Germans savages. They were settled agriculturalists and sophisticated metalworkers who had enjoyed trading relationships with the Roman world for centuries. In some frontier areas, entire tribes of Germans had been settled inside Roman borders as *foederati*, to reinforce depleted or withdrawn Roman garrisons. By the end of the fourth century, many German tribes had also adopted Christianity, albeit of the heretical, Arian variety. All these interactions made the barbarians very familiar with Roman civilization and substantially favorable to it.

It was actually Roman mistreatment rather than German aggression that began the sequence of events that led to the collapse of the western empire. During the 370s, a large group of Goths had been invited to settle on Roman lands along the Danube to guard that frontier against incursions by other barbarians. In 378, however, the Goths revolted when the Romans failed to supply the food and agricultural land they had been promised. A Roman army sent to suppress them was defeated at the battle of Adrianople, and the emperor Valens (who led the expedition) was killed. The new emperor, Theodosius the Great (379–395), quickly restored peace by accommodating the Goths' demands and enrolling them in the Roman army under their own military leaders.

Before Theodosius died, however, he divided the empire between his two young sons, whose advisers quickly set about trying to undermine each other. In these promising circumstances, the Goths increased their demands on the empire. The eastern emperor bought them off, encouraging them instead to attack his imperial rival in the west. Under the brilliant military leadership of Alaric, the Goths did precisely that. After several years of wandering through the western empire in search of booty, food, and land, in 410 they arrived at the gates of Rome. Rome, however, had little to offer in the way of food or land. After sacking the city, the Goths moved on, eventually settling in southern Gaul and Spain where they established a Visigothic ("West Gothic") kingdom.

Meanwhile, on New Year's Eve 406–407, a group of allied Germanic tribes led by the Vandals crossed the frozen Rhine. Capitalizing on the western emperor's preoccupation with the Goths, they streamed into Gaul and Spain. Ultimately the Vandals crossed the straits of Gibraltar and settled in the rich agricultural regions of Roman North Africa from which, in 455, they launched a seaborne attack on Rome. Further Germanic tribes, including the Alans, the Franks, the Burgundians, and the Alemans, soon followed them across the Rhine into Gaul, where they too set about erecting kingdoms.

In 476, the last Roman emperor in the west, an ineffectual usurper derisively known as Romulus Augustulus ("little Augustus"), was toppled by a mixed army of Germans, Huns, and disgruntled Romans. This event conventionally marks the ending date of the western Roman Empire. In the east, however, a Roman emperor continued to rule and continued to claim authority over the western half of the empire.

THE BARBARIAN INVASIONS OF THE ROMAN EMPIRE

What do the invasion routes followed by these different barbarian-led armies suggest about the invaders' identity and motives? Why did so many different armies attack the city of Rome, even though the city was no longer the capital even of the western Roman Empire?

ROMANIZED BARBARIANS AND BARBARIANIZED ROMANS

These two letters from Sidonius Apollinaris (c. 430–c. 480) illustrate the ways in which cultural assimilation in the late-fifth-century western empire was rapidly blurring the boundaries between Roman and barbarian. Sidonius himself was the descendant of an illustrious Roman provincial family in Gaul. He was one of the admired Latin stylists of his day, in both poetry and prose. Although he eventually became a bishop and was regarded locally as a saint after his death, his letter collection (from which these extracts are taken) tells us much more about the late Roman literary culture of Visi-gothic southern Gaul than it does about his Christianity. Arbogastes was the Frankish governor of Treves; Syagrius was from an ancient Gaulish Roman family.

LETTER 4:17: SIDONIUS TO HIS FRIEND ARBOGASTES

My honored Lord, your friend Eminentius has handed me a letter written by your own hand, a really literary letter, replete with the grace of a three-fold charm. The first of its merits is certainly the affection which prompted such condescension to my lowly condition, for if not a stranger I am in these days a man who courts obscurity; the second virtue is your modesty. . . . In the third place comes your urbanity which leads you to make a most amusing profession of clumsiness when as a matter of fact you have drunk deep from the spring of Roman eloquence and, dwelling by the Moselle, you speak the true Latin of the Tiber: you are intimate with the barbarians but are innocent of barbarisms, and are equal in tongue, as also in strength of arm, to the leaders of old, I mean those who were wont to handle the pen no less than the sword.

Thus the splendor of the Roman speech, if it still exists anywhere, has survived in you, though it has long been wiped out from the Belgian and Rhenic lands: with you and your eloquence surviving, even though Roman law has ceased at our border, the Roman speech does not falter. For this reason . . . I rejoice greatly that at any rate in your illustrious breast there have remained traces of our vanishing culture. If you extend these by constant reading you will discover for yourself as each day passes that the educated are no less superior to the unlettered than men are to beasts.

LETTER 5:5 SIDONIUS TO HIS FRIEND SYAGRIUS

You are the great-grandson of a consul, and in the male line too—although that has little to do with the case before us; I say, then, you are descended from a poet, to whom his literary glory would have brought statues had not his magisterial glories done so . . . and the culture of his successors has not declined one whit from his standard, particularly in this respect. I am therefore inexpressibly amazed that you have quickly acquired a knowledge of the German tongue with such ease.

And yet I remember that your boyhood had a good schooling in liberal studies and I know for certain that you often declaimed with spirit and eloquence before your professor of oratory. This being so, I should like you to tell me how you managed to absorb so swiftly into your inner being the exact sounds of an alien race, so that now after reading Virgil under the schoolmaster's cane and toiling and working the rich fluency of [Cicero] . . . you burst forth before my eyes like a young falcon from an old nest.

You have no idea what amusement it gives me, and others too, when I hear that in your presence the barbarian is afraid to perpetrate a barbarism in his own language. The bent elders of the Germans are astounded at you when you translate letters, and they adopt you as umpire and aribitrator in their mutual dealings. . . . And although these people are stiff and uncouth in body and mind alike, they welcome in you, and learn from you, their native speech combined with Roman wisdom.

Only one thing remains, most clever of men: continue with undiminished zeal, even in your hours of ease, to devote some attention to reading; and, like the man of refinement that you are, observe a just balance between the two languages: retain your grasp of Latin, lest you be laughed at, and practice the other, in order to have the laugh of them. Farewell.

W. B. Anderson, ed., *Sidonius, Poems and Letters*, vol. 2 (Cambridge, Mass., 1980), pp. 127–129, 181–183.

QUESTIONS FOR ANALYSIS

1. What is the topic of the letter from Sidonius Apollinaris to Arbogastes?
2. In his letter to Syagrius, Sidonius says that he is amazed that Syagrius has "quickly acquired a knowledge of the German tongue." He remembers that Syagrius had "a good schooling in liberal studies." How does that help Syagrius in his official duties? Why is it amusing to Sidonius that barbarians fear to make mistakes in their own language when they appear before Syagrius? Why does Sidonius advise him to continue reading and to maintain his knowledge of both Latin and German?

THE SUCCESS AND IMPACT OF THE GERMANIC INVASIONS

 The collapse of the fifth-century western empire is in many ways surprising. The armies that invaded the empire were small, and their leadership was divided among competing warlords. Nor was the western Roman Empire already in a state of collapse when the invasions began. Recent archaeological work has shown that in the year 400 the population of the western empire was stable, the rural economy was buoyant, and local and long-distance trading networks were still active. By the year 500, however, the western Roman Empire had ceased to exist as an economic and political entity. How can we explain this sudden and sweeping collapse?

First and foremost, the western empire's collapse was a military failure. Many army units along the western frontiers had been withdrawn to protect the eastern half of the empire before the invasions began. Those that remained were undermanned and underfunded. Nor could resources to support the army be easily increased. Tax levels were already high; any attempt to raise them further risked sparking a revolt by disgruntled taxpayers.

Civilian morale was also low. Even among aristocrats, the bureaucratic regime of the fourth-century emperors inspired little loyalty. In the early fifth century, rivalries between the eastern and western imperial courts undermined what little loyalty remained. The Germans, meanwhile, were seldom regarded with horror, having become a familiar element in western Roman society over several centuries. As a result, few pitched battles were fought between "Romans" and "Germans" during the fifth-century invasions. Often, the invading armies triumphed by default, because local residents did not care enough to defend themselves. When battles were fought, they were usually between mixed armies of Romans, Germans, and Huns on both sides, with each army fighting on behalf of its own warlord.

The western empire lacked the resources necessary to defend itself even when the invasions began. Once begun, however, the invasions quickly tipped the western empire into a spiral of collapse. Every territory plundered or captured by the invaders further reduced the tax revenues available to the western empire with which to pay its soldiers. And as the invaders began to establish their own kingdoms, taxes from these areas ceased to be paid to the Roman government at all. After 439, when the Vandals captured North Africa,

What themes emerged in Christian thought during the fourth and fifth centuries?

The Shaping of Western Christian Thought   163

the richest of all Rome's western provinces, the western empire drew its revenues only from the parts of Italy that it still controlled. Everything else was now in the hands of the new barbarian rulers.

The economic consequences of this collapse were profound. In the year 400, the economy of the western Roman Empire was still built on the mass production of low-cost, high-quality consumer goods that were transported in huge quantities throughout the empire. By the year 500, this world was gone. Although regional and local trade continued, only luxury goods now traveled long distances. As a result, factories in the western empire shut down and standards of craftsmanship declined. Living standards also dropped dramatically, as did the number of people living in the western empire. In the richer, more densely populated eastern empire, traditional patterns of Roman life continued throughout the fifth and sixth centuries. In the west, however, standards of living and overall population would not return to their fourth-century levels for 1,000 years.

Other aspects of Roman life in the western empire changed more gradually. Roman tax systems often survived, even though their proceeds now went into the purses of the new barbarian rulers. So too did Roman legal and administrative customs. On the land, Roman agricultural patterns continued in most areas, often under the same landlords. Roman aristocrats continued to dominate civic life, and Roman cities continued to dominate their surrounding regions, especially in southern Gaul and Spain. Nor did the invasions bring an end to Roman culture or to the influence of Roman example on the new immigrants. As Theodoric, the Ostrogothic conqueror of Italy, was fond of remarking: "An able Goth wishes to be like a Roman; but only a poor Roman would want to be like a Goth."

The Shaping of Western Christian Thought

What distinctive themes of Western Christian thought were emerging during the fourth and fifth centuries?

As the western Roman Empire declined during the fourth and fifth centuries, a small group of Western Christian thinkers formulated a theological outlook on the world that would guide Western thought for the next 800 years. This concurrence of political decline and theological advance was not coincidental. As the western empire collapsed, it seemed clearer than ever to thinking Christians that the classical inheritance was passing away and that God had not intended the world to be anything more than a transitory testing place. How, then, should Christians live? What did God require of them?

Answers to these questions were worked out by the four great "fathers" of the Western church: Saint Jerome (c. 340–420), Saint Ambrose (c. 340–397), Saint Augustine (354–430), and Pope Saint Gregory the Great (540–604). Jerome, Ambrose, and Augustine were contemporaries who knew and influenced one another. We will deal with their work here. Pope Gregory's contributions will be discussed in Chapter Seven.

Saint Jerome and Saint Ambrose

Jerome's greatest contribution was his translation of the Bible from Hebrew and Greek into Latin. His translation, known as the Vulgate (or "common" version), was not the first Latin Bible, but it quickly became the standard one, and would remain so until the sixteenth century. Jerome's translation was vigorous, colloquial, and clear; its powerful prose and poetry would influence all subsequent Latin authors for 1,000 years. Jerome was also important for arguing that classical learning could and should be studied by Christians, so long as it was thoroughly subordinated to Christian aims. Jerome himself was not certain, however, that he had succeeded in subordinating his love for the classics to his love for God. When, in a dream, he imagined himself arriving at the gates of heaven, God reproved him for being more of a follower of Cicero than of Christ.

Jerome was primarily a scholar. Saint Ambrose, in contrast, was principally a man of the world. As archbishop of Milan, the aristocratic Ambrose fearlessly rebuked even the Christian emperor Theodosius the Great for massacring innocent civilians at Thessalonica. Theodosius of course remained emperor; but until he did penance as a Christian for his sin, Ambrose refused to admit him into the church, declaring that on matters of faith, "The emperor is within the church, not above the church."

Like Jerome, Ambrose was an admirer of Cicero. Unlike Cicero, however, Ambrose argued that the beginning and end of human conduct should be reverence for God rather than social or political advancement. Ambrose also argued that although God assists all Christians by sharing with them the power of divine grace, God nonetheless gives more grace to some Christians than to others. Ambrose's emphasis on the necessity and mystery of grace (Why does God give more grace to some than to others?) would be refined and greatly amplified by his disciple, Saint Augustine of Hippo.

THE LIFE AND THOUGHT OF SAINT AUGUSTINE

Augustine was the greatest of all the Latin fathers; indeed he was one of the most powerful Christian thinkers of all time. Augustine's influence on medieval thought was incalculable, but his theology also had a profound influence on the development of Protestantism. Even in the twentieth century many leading Christian thinkers would describe themselves as neo-Augustinians.

Augustine's Christianity may have been so searching because he began his career by searching for it. Although his mother was a Christian, he hesitated until the age of thirty-three to be baptized, passing from one philosophical system to another without finding intellectual or spiritual satisfaction in any. Only his increasing doubts about all other alternatives, the appeals of Saint Ambrose's teachings on grace, and a mystical experience movingly described in his autobiographical *Confessions* led Augustine to embrace the faith wholeheartedly in 387. Thereafter he advanced rapidly in ecclesiastical positions, becoming bishop of the North African city of Hippo in 395. Although he led an extremely active life as bishop (he died in 430 while defending Hippo against the Vandals), he still found time to write more than 100 profound, complex, and powerful treatises analyzing the most fundamental problems of Christian belief.

Augustine's theology revolved around a single, fundamental question: How could humanity be so profoundly sinful, if human beings were created by an all-powerful God whose nature is entirely good? Augustine's answer to the question of evil went back to the Garden of Eden, where God had given Adam and Eve, the first human couple, the freedom either to follow his will or to follow their own. By eating the one fruit that God had forbidden them to eat, Adam and Eve chose to follow their own wills rather than God's will. Thereafter, says Augustine, God simply left Adam and Eve's descendants to their own devices, by withdrawing from human beings the divine power (grace) by which they might overcome their own wills to follow his. All the evils that plague the world are thus ultimately the result of the innate human propensity to place our own desires ahead of God's.

God would be justified if he condemned all human beings to hell; but because he is also merciful he chose instead to save some human beings through the sacrifice of his son, Jesus. No one, however, has by nature the grace necessary to become a Christian, much less to deserve salvation. God alone makes this choice; by granting grace to some and not to others, he predestines a portion of the human race to salvation and sentences the rest to be damned. If this seems unfair, Augustine's answer is, first, that strict "fairness" would condemn everyone to hell and, second, that the basis for God's choice is a mystery far beyond the realm of human comprehension.

To respond to those who blamed Christianity for the fall of Rome in 410, Augustine wrote one of his most famous works, *On the City of God*. In this work, he developed his ideas about predestination into an interpretation of all human history. Augustine argued that the entire human race from the creation until the last judgment was and will be composed of two opposing societies, those who "live according to man" and love themselves, and those who "live according to God." The former belong to the "City of Man"; their rewards are the riches, fame, and power they may garner on earth. The City of Man is not useless; earthly rulers bring peace and order and therefore deserve the obedience of Christians. But only those predestined to salvation, and who are thus members of the "City of God," will on Judgment Day put on the garment of immortality. Christians should therefore behave on earth as if they were travelers or "pilgrims," never forgetting that their true home lies in heaven.

Augustine was convinced that the Bible contained all the wisdom worth knowing. But he also believed that a certain amount of education was needed to understand it thoroughly. Augustine therefore approved of some Christians' acquiring an education in the liberal arts (as he himself had done), so long as they directed their education toward its proper end: the study of the Bible. Along with Jerome, Augustine thus laid the groundwork for Western Christians to preserve the literary and educational traditions of the

> To respond to those who blamed Christianity for the fall of Rome in 410, Augustine wrote one of his most famous works, *On the City of God*.

CHRONOLOGY

SHAPING OF WESTERN CHRISTIAN THOUGHT, FOURTH–SIXTH CENTURIES

Saint Jerome	
Translates Bible from Hebrew	
and Greek into Latin	c. 340–420
Saint Ambrose	
Furthers the church's autonomy	
on religious matters	c. 340–397
Saint Augustine	
Writes *Confessions,*	
On the City of God	354–430
Cassiodorus	
Justifies monks' studying and	
copying classical literature	c. 490–c. 583

classical past. But Augustine intended liberal education only for an elite; most Christians simply needed to be taught the faith. He also thought it was far worse to study classical thought for its own sake than for someone to know nothing at all about Latin and Greek learning. The true wisdom of mortals, he insisted, was piety.

THE CHRISTIANIZATION OF CLASSICAL CULTURE IN THE WEST

How was classical culture Christianized?

The Christian intellectuals of late antiquity were not prepared to throw out altogether the classical traditions of learning they had inherited. For all of them, however, this tradition posed severe challenges. It was, in the first place, thoroughly pagan, and paganism remained a significant threat to Christianity even after the empire became formally Christian. Classical learning was also associated with syncretism—that is, with the easy acceptance of both Christian and pagan beliefs simultaneously, which had been so marked a feature of aristocratic culture during the fourth century. Christian intellectuals

—indeed, the Christian clergy generally—wanted desperately to replace the doctrines of pagan philosophy with the doctrine of Christ. To do this, however, they needed a way of Christianizing the classical inheritance and conveying it to the Christian masses in an intellectually satisfying way. It was, therefore, to the preservation and reinterpretation of classical Latin culture for a mixed audience of vulgar Romans and aspiring barbarians that the Christian intellectuals of the fourth, fifth, and sixth centuries devoted themselves.

Their challenge was to arrive at an understanding of the purposes of classical culture for a Christian audience. Tertullian had raised this question around 200 C.E. by asking, "What has Athens [the symbol of classical learning] to do with Jerusalem [the symbol of Christian salvation]?" Tertullian's answer had been "Nothing"; but this answer did not suit the changed circumstances of the Christian church from the fourth century on. Jerome and Augustine were more hopeful about Christianizing the classical tradition; but on the whole, the early monastic movement sided with Tertullian. Despite the role Benedictine monasteries would later play in copying and preserving Latin literary texts, Saint Benedict himself was no admirer of classical culture. Quite to the contrary, he wanted his monks to serve only Christ—not literature or philosophy. But unlike some of his monastic contemporaries, he did believe that monks should be able to read well enough to study the Bible. To guarantee this, some schooling within the monastery would be necessary, especially for boys given over from birth to the monastic profession. For Benedict, however, preserving classical learning was no part of a monastery's proper duties.

CASSIODORUS AND THE BENEDICTINE TRADITION OF LEARNING

The impetus behind the development of Benedictine monasticism's tradition of learning came not from Benedict himself, but from Cassiodorus (c. 490–c. 583), an official at Theodoric's court. Early in his career, Cassiodorus wrote *History of the Goths* for his barbarian overlord. He also composed (and eventually published) several volumes of his official correspondence, reflecting his training in the classical rhetorical tradition. During the last forty years of his life, however, Cassiodorus turned his attention toward religion, composing commentaries on the Psalms and founding an important monastery at Vivarium in southern Italy.

Cassiodorus. This frontispiece from a Bible, drawn in an English Benedictine monastery around 700 C.E., depicts Cassiodorus as a copyist and preserver of books. Because books were expensive and rare until the invention of printing in the fifteenth century, they customarily were stored in cupboards, lying flat, as we see them here.

It was for his monks that Cassiodorus composed his most influential work, the *Institutes*. Inspired by Saint Augustine, Cassiodorus believed that study of classical literature was the essential preliminary to a proper understanding of the Bible and the church fathers. His *Institutes* were basically a reading list, making up first the essential works of classical, pagan literature a monk should know before he moved on to the more difficult and demanding study of theology and the Bible. Through the *Institutes*, Cassiodorus thus defined a classical literary canon that would influence Christian educational practice until the end of the Middle Ages.

Cassiodorus also encouraged his monks to copy manuscripts, arguing that such copying was in itself "manual labor" of the sort that Saint Benedict had demanded, and that it might even be more appropriate work for monks than laboring in the fields. As

Benedictines began to subscribe to these ideas, Benedictine monasteries emerged as the most important centers for the preservation and study of classical literature in the Latin-speaking West. Hardly any works of classical Latin literature would survive today had they not been copied and preserved during the early Middle Ages by Benedictine monks following the example of Cassiodorus.

EASTERN ROME AND THE WESTERN EMPIRE

Why did Justinian's plan to reunite the Roman Empire fail?

The reconquest of Italy was part of a larger plan to revive the Roman Empire conceived and directed by the eastern emperor Justinian (527–565). The eastern empire, with its capital at Constantinople, had faced many external and internal pressures since the time of Theodosius (d. 395). But by the early sixth century it had recovered much of its strength. Although the eastern empire—which then encompassed the modern-day territories of Greece, Turkey, most of the Middle East, and Egypt—was largely Greek and Syriac speaking, Justinian himself came from a western province (modern-day Serbia) and spoke Latin. A student of history, he saw himself as the heir of imperial Rome, whose ancient power and western territories he aspired to restore. Although his efforts ultimately failed, they had a lasting impact on the entire Mediterranean world.

THE CODIFICATION OF ROMAN LAW

One of Justinian's most lasting accomplishments was his codification of Roman law. To carry out this work he appointed a commission of lawyers under the supervision of his minister Tribonian. Within two years the commission published the first result of its labors. This was the Code, a systematic compilation of all the imperial statutes that had been issued from the reign of Hadrian to Justinian's own. The Code was later supplemented by the Novels, which contained the legislation of Justinian and his immediate successors. By 532 the commission had also completed the Digest, a summary of the writings of the great jurists. The commission's final product was the Institutes, a textbook of the legal

Justinian and Theodora. Sixth-century mosaics from the Church of San Vitale, Ravenna. The emperor and empress are presented here as holy figures (notice the halos around their heads) who exercise priestly responsibilities. As they advance toward the altar, they carry the communion dish and the chalice, symbols of the body and blood of Christ. On the hem of Theodora's gown, the "three wise kings from the East" who visited the infant Jesus are represented. Just as these three magi once had supernatural knowledge of Christ, so now do their counterparts, Justinian and Theodora.

principles reflected in the Digest and the Code. All four volumes together constitute the *Corpus Juris Civilis,* or the "body of civil law."

Justinian's *Corpus* was a brilliant achievement: the Digest alone has been justly called "the most remarkable and important lawbook that the world has ever seen." In the East, the *Corpus* immediately became the foundation on which all subsequent legal developments would rest. In the West, by contrast, the *Corpus* was initially little known; most early medieval law codes drew instead on the fifth-century compilation of the emperor Theodosius II (408–450). From the twelfth century on, however, Justinian's *Corpus* would be intensively studied in the West as well, influencing both the conduct of government and the developing legal systems of late medieval and early modern Europe.

JUSTINIAN'S MILITARY CONQUESTS

Justinian's initial attempts to reconquer the western Roman Empire succeeded easily. In 533 his brilliant general Belisarius conquered the Vandal Kingdom in northwest Africa; by 536 Belisarius appeared to have conquered Italy, where he was welcomed by the Catholic subjects of the Ostrogoths. But the early victories of the Italian campaign were illusory; the war would drag on for decades until the exhausted imperial forces finally reduced the last Gothic outposts in 563.

THE MEDITERRANEAN WORLD UNDER JUSTINIAN, 527–565 C.E.

Compare this map with the one on p. 160. Which areas of the former Roman Empire did Justinian not attempt to reconquer? Was there any strategic logic to Justinian's reconquests? What would have been necessary to hold this newly reconstituted Roman Empire together after Justinian's death?

Because Justinian had already recaptured northwest Africa and the coastal parts of Spain, the Mediterranean was once again a "Roman" lake when he died in 565. But the costs of this endeavor had been enormous and would soon call into question the very existence of the eastern Roman Empire.

Justinian's western campaigns were ill-advised for two reasons. One was their enormous cost. Belisarius seldom had enough troops to do his job properly: he began his Italian campaign with only 8,000 men. To provide the troops his generals needed, Justinian imposed oppressive taxation which undermined support for the empire in such vitally important regions as Egypt and Syria. Even the Catholic Christians of Italy and North Africa resented the costs their liberation imposed on them. Justinian's western campaigns also distracted attention from dangers closer to home: in particular, the developing strength of Persia. To respond to the Persian threat, Justinian's successors were forced to withdraw their troops from Italy and North Africa; this left both regions dangerously exposed to further barbarian invasions, and was still not sufficient to guarantee the safety of the eastern empire. Only a heroic reorganization of the eastern empire after 610 saved Constantinople from falling to the Persians; but this reorganization also marked the final end to Justinian's dream of reuniting the eastern and the western Mediterranean worlds.

CHRONOLOGY

THE ROMAN REVIVAL OF JUSTINIAN, 527–568 C.E.

Reign of Justinian	527–565
Publication of the *Corpus Juris Civilis*	529–534
Justinian conquers the Vandal Kingdom of northwest Africa	533
Justinian reconquers Italian peninsula	536
Justinian defeats last Gothic outposts	563
Justinian rules over Mediterranean world	563–565
Death of Justinian	565
Germanic Lombards conquer Italian peninsula	568

CONCLUSION

From its earliest days, Rome had been characterized by its remarkable capacity to assimilate the disparate cultures of the lands Rome conquered. In this process, both Rome and its empire were steadily transformed. The pace of these transformations accelerated markedly, however, from the mid-third century on—so much so that historians now commonly refer to the period from the mid-third century to the early seventh century as "late antiquity" to distinguish it from the classical Roman world that preceded it. During these centuries, larger numbers of immigrants entered the Roman Empire than ever before, drawn by a combination of land hunger, opportunity, and the desire to participate in the material and cultural benefits of Roman life. In the western empire especially, the number of these new immigrants became so large during the late fourth and fifth centuries that the frontier areas of the empire ceased to be distinguishable from the more "Romanized" areas of the interior.

At the same time, two internal cultural processes were transforming what it meant to be Roman. The learned culture of the Greek and Roman world was being steadily extended to larger numbers of people; but in the process, learned culture itself was increasingly vulgarized. And finally, the empire itself became Christian, first by persuasion, as Constantine and his successors made it attractive for individuals to convert to the new religion, and later by coercion, as Christianity became the official religion of the entire Roman Empire. As a result, a new fusion of Christian culture and late Roman governance began to evolve, not only around the imperial court at Constantinople but also in the provinces.

What did not change, however, was the Mediterranean focus of this evolving late-antique world. Despite the emergence of new political units in the western Roman Empire, Roman civilization in the fifth and sixth centuries remained firmly centered on the Mediterranean Sea. That too, however, was soon to change. The seventh century would witness the final fracturing of this unified Mediterranean world and the emergence in its place of three quite different Western civilizations: Byzantium, western Europe, and Islam. This development marks the end of the classical world and the beginning of the Middle Ages. It is to this development that we now turn.

KEY TERMS

tetrarchy	Pharisees	Arians	Saint Benedict of Nursia	Cassiodorus
Constantinople	Paul	papal	Saint Augustine	Justinian

SELECTED READINGS

Saint Augustine. *The City of God.* Trans. Henry Bettenson. Baltimore, Md., 1972.

Saint Augustine. *Confessions.* Trans. Henry M. Chadwick. Oxford, 1991.

Saint Augustine. *The Enchiridion on Faith, Hope and Love.* Trans. H. Paolucci. Chicago, 1961.

Saint Augustine. *On Christian Doctrine.* Trans. D. W. Robertson Jr. New York, 1958.

Boethius. *The Consolation of Philosophy.* Trans. R. Green. Indianapolis, Ind., 1962.

Bowersock, G. W., Peter Brown, and Oleg Grabar. *Late Antiquity: A Guide to the Postclassical World.* Cambridge, Mass., 1999. An authoritative compilation. The first half is devoted to essays on the cultural features of the period; the second half is organized as an encyclopedia.

Brown, Peter. *Augustine of Hippo.* Berkeley, Calif., 1967. A great biography, by the greatest living scholar of late antiquity.

Brown, Peter. *The Body and Society: Men, Women and Sexual Renunciation in Early Christianity.* New York, 1988. A revealing study of one of the fundamental transformations Christianity brought to the late-antique world.

Brown, Peter. *Power and Persuasion in Late Antiquity: Toward a Christian Empire.* Madison, Wisc., 1992. An important revisionist account of the impact of Christianization on the political culture of the later Roman Empire.

Brown, Peter. *The Rise of Western Christendom: Triumph and Diversity, 200–1000.* 2d ed. Oxford, 2002. Evocatively written picture of the diverse forms Christianity took as it spread east and north from the Mediterranean world.

Brown, Peter. *The World of Late Antiquity.* New York, 1971. Still the best short survey of the period, with excellent illustrations.

Cameron, Averil. *The Later Roman Empire, A.D. 284–430.* London, 1993. Now the standard account of its period, with an emphasis on imperial politics.

Cameron, Averil. *The Mediterranean World in Late Antiquity, A.D. 395–600.* London, 1993. Masterful, with excellent, succinct bibliographical essays.

Cassiodorus. *An Introduction to Divine and Human Readings.* Trans. L. W. Jones. New York, 1946.

Chadwick, Henry M. *Augustine.* Oxford, 1986. The best short introduction to Augustine's thought.

Chadwick, Henry M. *Boethius.* Oxford, 1981. The best intellectual biography of this important thinker.

Clark, Gillian. *Christianity and Roman Society.* Cambridge, 2004. A short, stimulating survey that places early Christianity firmly in its Roman social context.

Clark, Gillian. *Women in Late Antiquity.* Oxford, 1993. A clear, compact account of an important subject.

Coogan, Michael, ed. *The Oxford History of the Biblical World.* Oxford, 1998. A reliable, but rather traditional account of the historical events recounted in the Hebrew Bible and the New Testament.

Eusebius. *Eusebius' Life of Constantine.* Trans. Averil Cameron and Stuart Hall. Oxford, 1999. An admiring life that reflects Constantine's own vision of his religious authority.

Eusebius. *The History of the Church.* Trans. G. A. Williamson. Baltimore, Md., 1965. An indispensable narrative account of Constantine's reign, written by one of his courtier-bishops.

Jones, A. H. M. *The Later Roman Empire, 284–602: A Social, Economic, and Administrative Survey.* 2 vols. London, 1964. An immense, detailed analysis, difficult to read but packed with information.

Lane Fox, Robin. *Pagans and Christians.* New York, 1987. A subtle, perceptive, lengthy, but highly readable exploration of the pagan world within which Christianity grew up.

Lawrence, Clifford Hugh. *Medieval Monasticism.* 3d ed. London, 2000. Concise, intelligent, perceptive survey of monasticism from its beginnings to the end of the Middle Ages.

Markus, R. A. *The End of Ancient Christianity.* New York, 1990. An expert synthetic study of Christianity in the western Roman Empire between 350 and 600 C.E.

Moorhead, John. *Justinian.* New York, 1994. An up-to-date survey of the emperor and his times.

Pelikan, Jaroslav. *The Christian Tradition, Volume I: The Emergence of the Catholic Tradition.* Chicago, 1971. A history of Christian doctrine that is one of the tours de force of twentieth-century scholarship. Synthetic, clear, and objective.

Potter, David. *The Roman Empire at Bay, A.D. 180–395*. London and New York, 2004. The most recent and readable account of Rome during the third and fourth centuries.

Procopius. *The Secret History*. Trans. G. A. Williamson. Baltimore, Md., 1966. All the gossip from Justinian's court, much of it salacious.

Sanders, E. P. *The Historical Figure of Jesus*. London and New York, 1993. The best of the recent studies of Jesus in his first-century Jewish context.

Shanks, Hershel, ed. *Christianity and Rabbinic Judaism: A Parallel History of Their Origins and Early Development*. Washington, D.C., 1992. Accessible chapters written by top authorities, describing both Jewish and Christian developments from the first to the sixth centuries C.E.

Wallace-Hadrill, John Michael. *The Barbarian West*. 3d ed. London, 1966. Still the most interesting and suggestive analysis of the Romano-Germanic world created by the invasions of the fifth century C.E.

Whittaker, C. R. *Frontiers of the Roman Empire: A Social and Economic Study*. Baltimore, Md., 1994. A convincing picture of the frontiers of the Roman Empire as zones of intensive cultural interaction.

Williams, Stephen. *Diocletian and the Roman Recovery*. New York, 1997. A recent account that modifies, but does not replace, A. H. M. Jones.

Wolfram, Herwig. *The Roman Empire and Its Germanic Peoples*. Berkeley, Calif., 1997. The best recent survey of its subject.

PART III
THE MIDDLE AGES

THE TERM *MIDDLE AGES* was coined by Europeans in the seventeenth century to express their view that a long and dismal period of interruption extended between the glorious accomplishments of Greece and Rome and their own "modern age." Because the term became so widespread, it is now an ineradicable part of our historical vocabulary; but no serious scholar today uses it with the sense of contempt it once invoked. To the contrary, most scholars would now argue that it was during the Middle Ages—roughly the years between 600 and 1500—that the cultural, political, and religious foundations of all three Western civilizations were established. Whether we speak of Byzantium, the Islamic world, or Europe, the Middle Ages were a formative and creative period in the history of Western civilizations.

Only with respect to Europe, however, do the years between 600 and 1500 constitute a true middle age. For the Islamic world, these centuries witnessed the birth, expansion, and maturation of a new civilization that drew heavily on its classical past but fused that past with a sweeping new religious vision. For Byzantium, the so-called Middle Ages ended in 1453 with the conquest of the Byzantine Empire by the Ottoman Turks. Even for Europe, the metaphor of a middle age is to some extent misleading. Like Islamic civilization, European civilization began to take shape from the seventh century on, but it was not until the twelfth century that a truly distinctive European tradition with respect to politics, religion, and art emerged.

	POLITICS	SOCIETY AND CULTURE	ECONOMY	INTERNATIONAL RELATIONS
570	Muhammad, founder of Islam, born (570) Pope Gregory I (Saint Gregory the Great) (590–604) Ascension of Byzantine emperor Heraclius (610) Shiite–Sunni schism (661) Umayyad family governs Islamic world (661–750)	Growth of monasteries (600–700) The Hijrah (622)	Economic unity of Mediterranean world ends (650)	Arabs, under Abu-Bakr, rout Byzantine army in Syria (636) Arabs take Antioch, Damascus, and Jerusalem (636) Attempts by Muslims to take Constantinople (677, 717)
700	The Carolingians share power with the Merovingian kings (717–751) Abbasid family governs Islamic world (750–1258) Pepin becomes king of the Franks (751)	Iconoclast Controversy begins (717)	Agricultural revolution (700–1300)	Arabs take Visigothic Spain (717)
800	Charlemagne crowned Holy Roman emperor (800) Charlemagne dies (814)			Rus sack Constantinople (860)
900	Capetian dynasty (987–1328)	Cluniac reform of monasteries (900–1050) Islamic civilization's "middle period" (900–1250) Rise of Romanesque architecture (900–1150) Avicenna, author of *Canon of Medicine* (980–1037) European population triples (1000–1300)	Invention of iron horseshoe (900) Rus establish principality near Kiev (900s)	Otto I defeats Hungarians at Lechfeld (955)
1000	Split between Roman and Byzantine churches (1054) Saxon civil war begins (1073) Investiture Conflict (1075–1122)	*Song of Roland* (1050) Number of monks increases tenfold (1066–1200) Peter Abelard (1079–1142) Cisterian order flourishes (1090–1153) Hildegard of Bingen (1098–1179)	Invention of tandem harness for plowing (1050) Water mill becomes widely used in Europe (1050)	Battle of Hastings, England falls to the Normans (1066) Norman Conquest (1066) Seljuk Turks overrun eastern Byzantine provinces (1071) Battle of Manzikert, Turks take Anatolia (1071) First Crusade (1095–1099)
1100	Concordat of Worms distinguishes temporal power of kings from spiritual power of clergy (1122) Reign of Frederick I, Barbarossa, as Holy Roman emperor (1152–1190)	Rise of Gothic architecture (1100–1300) Umar Hayyam, author of the Rubiyat (d. 1123) Averroës, Spanish philosopher, theologian, and physician (1126–1198) Catharism in southern France (1150–1300) Rise of chivalry (1150) Troubadour poets travel Europe (1150–1300) Chretien de Troyes, author of Arthurian legends (1165–1190) Saint Dominic (1170–1221) Rome decrees all cathedrals must support one schoolteacher (1179) Saint Francis of Assisi (1182–1226)	Manorial lords begin trading serfs' freedom for cash (1100s) Proliferation of windmills (1170s)	Muslim leader, Saladin, recaptures Jerusalem (1187)

POLITICS	SOCIETY AND CULTURE	ECONOMY	INTERNATIONAL RELATIONS
	Theater appears outside of church (1200)		Crusaders sack Constantinople (1204)
			England ousted from Normandy, Anjou, and Brittany (1204)
			Mongols conquer eastern Slavic region (1200s)
Magna Carta (1215)	The Cid and Norse sagas are written down (1200s)		Mongols take Kiev (1240)
Fourth Lateran Council (1215)	Saint Thomas Aquinas, author of Summa Theologica (1225–1274)		Mongols dispose of Abbasid caliphate (1258)
	Dante Alighieri, author of The Divine Comedy (1265–1321)		
Emergence of English Parliament (1272–1307)	Giotto of Florence, painter (1267–1337)		
Formation of French Estates General (1285–1314)	William of Ockham, founder of nominalism (1285–1349)		Jews expelled from southern Italy, England, and France (1288–1306)
French King Philip IV (1285–1314)			

CHAPTER SEVEN

CHAPTER CONTENTS

ROME'S THREE HEIRS: THE BYZANTINE, ISLAMIC, AND EARLY MEDIEVAL WORLDS

A NEW PERIOD in the history of Western civilizations began in the seventh century. In the year 600, it was still possible for the rulers of the Roman Empire living in Constantinople to imagine their empire as uniting the entire Mediterranean world. By the end of the seventh century, however, three different successor civilizations to the Greco-Roman world of antiquity had emerged: the Byzantine, the Islamic, and the western European, each with its own language and distinctive ways of life. The history of Western civilizations from the seventh to the eleventh centuries is largely a story of the rivalries and interactions among these three emerging worlds, each of which preserved and extended different aspects of the late-antique inheritance they shared.

Like the provinces of the eastern Roman Empire over which it ruled, Byzantine civilization after 610 was Greek-speaking. It combined the bureaucratic and imperial traditions of late Roman governance with an intense pursuit of the Christian faith. This fusion had been pioneered in the fourth century by Constantine and his successors and was continuously elaborated in the eastern Roman Empire thereafter. Islamic civilization, in contrast, was Arabic-speaking. It was the most cosmopolitan and wide ranging (both geographically and culturally) of the three successor civilizations. The Islamic world was the heir both to the Roman vision of an expansive empire and to Roman ideals of cultural and religious assimilation as essential attributes of imperial rule. By combining the philosophical and scientific interests of the Hellenistic world with the literary and artistic culture of Persia, Islam created the most dynamic cultural amalgam of the early Middle Ages.

Western Christian civilization in the early Middle Ages was rooted in Latin, but with important cultural influences from Germanic, Celtic, and Latin-derived vernacular languages. In contrast to Byzantium and Islam, it owed relatively little to Roman ideals of empire, except briefly under the Carolingians. It was, however, profoundly influenced by Roman ideals of law and local government, which carried with them a continuing influence from the republican traditions of ancient Rome. For western Europe in the early Middle Ages, law and Latin Christianity were

FOCUS QUESTIONS

- How did the Byzantine state survive for nearly a millennium?

- How was Islam able to spread so rapidly?

- What forces combined to undermine the political unity of the Islamic world?

- What caused economic and social change in seventh-century western Europe?

- How did Charlemagne redefine the relationship between Christianity and kingship?

the pinnacles of Roman cultural achievement. They were, indeed, the very essence of what it meant to be Roman; and to be Roman remained an almost universal aspiration in early medieval Europe. If we measure civilizations by their highest philosophical and literary accomplishments, western Europe in the early Middle Ages was a laggard in comparison with Byzantium and the Islamic world. It was also the least economically advanced of these three successor states and faced the greatest organizational weaknesses in both government and religion. By the twelfth century, however, Latin Christian civilization was no longer on the defensive against its rivals in military, economic, or religious terms. Rather, it stood at the beginning of an extraordinary period of expansion and conquest that would bring it ultimately to a dominant position in world affairs during the early modern and modern eras.

THE BYZANTINE EMPIRE AND ITS CULTURE

How did the Byzantine state survive for nearly a millennium?

It is impossible to date the beginning of Byzantine history with precision because the Byzantine Empire was the uninterrupted successor of the Roman state. Justinian's reign was clearly an important turning point in the direction of Byzantine civilization because it saw the crystallization of new forms of thought and art that can be considered more "Byzantine" than "Roman." But only after 610 did a new dynasty emerge that came from the east, spoke Greek, and maintained a fully Eastern or "Byzantine" orientation. Hence, although good arguments can be made for beginning Byzantine history with Diocletian, Constantine, or Justinian, we will begin here with the accession in 610 of the emperor Heraclius.

It is also convenient to begin in 610 because from then until 1071 the main lines of Byzantine military and political history were determined by resistance against successive waves of invasion from the east. When Heraclius came to the throne the very existence of the Byzantine Empire was being challenged by the Persians, who had conquered almost all of the empire's Asian territories. By enormous effort Heraclius rallied Byzantine strength and turned the tide, routing the

Persians and recapturing Jerusalem. But soon thereafter new armies began to invade Byzantine territory, swarming out of hitherto placid Arabia. Inspired by the new religion of Islam and profiting from Byzantine exhaustion after the struggle with Persia, the Arabs made astonishingly rapid gains. By 650 they had taken most of the Byzantine territories that the Persians had occupied in the early seventh century, including Jerusalem, which became a holy site for Muslims no less than for Christians and Jews. Arab armies also conquered Persia itself, and rapidly made their way westward across North Africa, where Byzantine control had long been resented. Having become a Mediterranean power, the Arabs also took to the sea. In 677 they tried to conquer Constantinople with a fleet. They attempted to take the city again in 717 by means of a concerted land and sea operation.

The Arab threat to Constantinople in 717 marked a new low in Byzantine fortunes, but the threat was countered by the emperor Leo the Isaurian (717–741) with the same resolution Heraclius had shown against the Persians a century before. Leo's defense of Constantinople in 717 was one of the most significant battles in European history. Had the Islamic armies taken Constantinople there would have been little to stop them from sweeping through the rest of Europe. Over the next few decades, however, the Byzantines reconquered most of Asia Minor, which became the heartland of their empire for the next 300 years. In the eleventh century, however, a new Islamic power, the Seljuk (sehl-JOOK) Turks, reversed the Byzantine gains. In 1071 the Seljuks annihilated a Byzantine army at Manzikert in Asia Minor, a stunning victory that allowed them to overrun Byzantium's eastern provinces. Constantinople was now thrown back on itself more or less as it had been in the days of Heraclius and Leo. By and large, it would remain on the defensive for the next 400 years. The last remnants of the Byzantine Empire fell to the Ottoman Turks in 1453. Turks continue to rule in Constantinople—which they renamed Istanbul—to the present day.

SOURCES OF STABILITY

Because Byzantine power was so completely focused on the imperial court at Constantinople and because rulers followed their late Roman predecessors in claiming the powers of divinely appointed absolute monarchs, there was no way of opposing them other than by intrigue and violence. Hence Byzantine history was marked by repeated palace revolts involving mutilations, murders,

How did the Byzantine state survive for nearly a millennium?

The Byzantine Empire and Its Culture   179

Byzantine Soldiers Clashing with Arab Soldiers. This illustration from the Scylitzes chronicle dates back to the eleventh century, when the Seljuk Turks started to reverse the Byzantine gains in Asia in an offensive that would ultimately end the Byzantine Empire in the fifteenth century.

Historians emphasize Byzantine trade and industry because these provided most of the surplus wealth that supported the state. But agriculture lay at the heart of the Byzantine economy. Byzantine agricultural history was marked by the struggles of independent peasant farmers to stay free from control by wealthy aristocrats and monasteries. Until the eleventh century the free peasantry managed to maintain its position with the help of state legislation. After 1025, however, the aristocracy gained power in the government and began to transform the peasants into impoverished tenants. This had many unfortunate results, not least that peasants became less interested in resisting the enemy. The defeat at Manzikert in 1071 was in part the result of the government's short-sighted acquiescence to aristocratic ambitions.

and blindings. Fortunately for the empire, some very able rulers did emerge from time to time to wield their unrestrained powers effectively. Even more fortunately, an efficient bureaucracy continued to function even during times of palace upheaval.

Efficient bureaucratic government was one of the major reasons for Byzantine success and longevity. Literate Byzantine bureaucrats supervised education and religion and presided over all forms of economic endeavor. Even chariot racing fell under strict governmental supervision, with the populace of Constantinople being assigned by governmental command to root for particular teams. Bureaucratic methods also regulated the army and navy, the courts, and the diplomatic service, endowing these agencies with organizational strengths incomparable for their time.

Another explanation for Byzantine endurance was the comparatively sound economic base of the state, at least until the eleventh century. Commerce and cities continued to flourish in the Byzantine East, as they had done in the late-antique period. Constantinople in the ninth and tenth centuries was a vital trade emporium for Far Eastern luxury goods and Western raw materials. The empire also nurtured and protected its own industries, most notably silk making, and it was renowned until the eleventh century for its stable gold and silver coinage.

BYZANTINE RELIGION

So far we have spoken about military campaigns, government, and economics as if they were the keys to Byzantine survival. Seen from hindsight they were, but what the Byzantines themselves cared about most was the religious orthodoxy of their empire. Byzantines fought and died over statements of religious doctrine. This intense preoccupation with questions of doctrine could cause great harm during periods of religious dissension, but it also endowed the Byzantine state with a powerful sense of confidence and mission.

Byzantine doctrinal disputes were complicated by the fact that the emperors took an active role in them. Emperors exercised great power in the life of the church. Nonetheless, rulers could never force all their subjects to believe the same doctrines they themselves did. Even Byzantine governmental authority did not stretch that far. Only after the loss of many eastern provinces and the refinement of doctrinal formulae did religious peace seem near in the eighth century. But then it was shattered for still another century by what is known as the Iconoclastic Controversy.

The Iconoclastic movement was initiated by Emperor Leo the Isaurian, and subsequently directed with even greater energy by his son Constantine V (740–775). The Iconoclasts wished to prohibit the veneration of icons—that is, images of Christ and the saints. Honoring such images seemed to the Iconoclasts to smack of idolatry and paganism. Traditionalists responded that it was not the images themselves that worshipers honored, but the heavenly reality that lay beyond them. Like Byzantine art generally, icons were intended to act as windows through which a glimpse of heaven might be granted to human beings on earth.

The Iconoclastic Controversy was resolved in the ninth century by a return to the status quo—namely the veneration of images, but the century of turmoil over the issue had lasting results. One was the destruction by imperial order of a large amount of religious art. Pre-eighth-century Byzantine religious art that survives today comes mostly from places such as Italy and Palestine, which were beyond the reach of the Iconoclastic emperors. A second consequence of the controversy was the opening of a serious religious breach between the Greek East and the Latin West. The pope, who until the eighth century had usually been a close ally of the Byzantine emperors, strongly opposed Iconoclasm, not least because Iconoclasm tended to question the cult of saints, and the claims of papal primacy were based on the pope's role as Saint Peter's successor. Papal hostility to Iconoclasm during the eighth century led to worsening relations between East and West that culminated with the crowning of the Frankish leader Charlemagne as the new Roman emperor in the West on Christmas Day 800.

The ultimate defeat of Iconoclasm also led to a renewed emphasis on the traditional, Orthodox faith of the empire as the key to its political unity and military success. Religious tradition became the touchstone of doctrinal correctness and political legitimacy. This helped the religion gain new adherents in the ninth and tenth centuries. But it also reinforced the hegemony of Constantinople's own religious traditions within the empire, thus marginalizing even further the rival religious traditions of Syrian and Armenian Christianity. Fear of heresy also tended to inhibit free speculation, not just in religion but also in related intellectual matters. Although the Byzantine emperors founded and supported a university in Constantinople, they never permitted it to exercise any significant degree of intellectual freedom, in marked contrast with the freewheeling intellectual atmosphere of the growing universities of twelfth- and thirteenth-century western Europe.

> The Iconoclasts wished to prohibit the veneration of icons—that is, images of Christ and the saints. Honoring such images seemed to the Iconoclasts to smack of idolatry and paganism.

BYZANTINE CULTURE

Religion dominated Byzantine life; but commitment to Christianity by no means inhibited the Byzantines from preserving and revering their ancient Greek heritage. Byzantine schools based their instruction on classical Greek literature, and especially Homer, to an astonishing degree. Educated people around the Byzantine court could quote but a single line of Homer and expect that their audience would know immediately the entire passage from which it came. Byzantine scholars also studied intensively the philosophy of Plato and the historical prose of Thucydides. Aristotle's works were regarded with less interest. By and large, the Greek scientific and mathematical tradition was neglected by the Byzantines, and even philosophy was considerably restricted. Justinian, for example, shut down the Athenian philosophical academies that had existed since Plato's day, declaring that everything worth knowing was already known. Preservation rather than innovation was the hallmark of Byzantine classicism. Nevertheless, such dedicated classicism enriched Byzantine intellectual and literary life and helped preserve the Greek classics for later ages. The bulk of classical Greek literature that we have today survives only because it was copied by Byzantine scribes.

CHRONOLOGY

THE BYZANTINE EMPIRE, 610–1100

Ascension of the emperor Heraclius	610
Arabs seize most of Byzantine territory	c. 650
Constantinople nearly falls to the Arabs	717
Byzantines reconquer most of Asia Minor	717–750
Stalemate between Arabs and Byzantines	750–950
Byzantines reconquer most of Syria	c. 950–1000
Seljuk Turks overrun eastern Byzantine provinces	1071
First Crusade	1095–1099

How did the Byzantine state survive for nearly a millennium?

The Byzantine Empire and Its Culture   181

Byzantine classicism was a product of an educational system for the laity that extended to women as well as to men. In the Byzantine world of the ninth through eleventh centuries, learned women were praised for being able to discourse like Plato or Pythagoras. There were also female physicians in the Byzantine Empire, a fact of note given their scarcity in western European society until recent times.

Byzantine achievements in architecture and art are more familiar. The finest example of Byzantine architecture was the church of Santa Sophia (Holy Wisdom) in Constantinople, constructed at enormous cost by the emperor Justinian in the sixth century. Its purpose was not to express pride in human accomplishment but

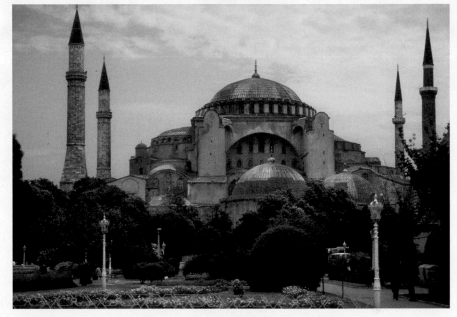

Santa Sophia. The greatest monument of Byzantine architecture. The four minarets were added when the Turks turned the church into a mosque.

rather to symbolize the inward and spiritual character of the Christian religion. For this reason the architects gave little attention to the external appearance of the building. Nothing but plain brick covered with plaster was used for the exterior walls; there were no marble facings, graceful columns, or sculptured friezes. The interior, however, was decorated with richly colored mosaics, gold leaf, colored marble columns, and bits of tinted glass set on edge to refract the rays of sunlight like sparkling gems. To emphasize a sense of the miraculous, the building was constructed in such a way that light appeared not to come from the outside at all, but to be generated within. So many windows were placed around its rim that the dome appears to be suspended in midair.

Byzantium and the Western Christian World

After the Iconoclastic period relations between Eastern and Western Christians remained tense, partly because Constantinople resented Western claims (initiated by Charlemagne in 800) to rule a rival Roman Empire, but most of all because religious differences between the two continued to grow. In 1054, papal claims to primacy over the Eastern church provoked a religious schism that has never healed. Soon thereafter the Crusades drove home the dividing wedge.

After the sack of Constantinople in 1204 by crusaders, Byzantine hatred of Westerners became intense.

"Between us and them," one Byzantine wrote, "there is now a deep chasm: we do not have a single thought in common." Westerners called Easterners "the dregs of the dregs . . . unworthy of the sun's light." Easterners called Westerners the children of darkness, alluding to the fact that the sun sets in the west. The beneficiaries of this hatred were the Turks, who conquered Constantinople in 1453 and soon thereafter conquered most of southeastern Europe.

In view of this long history of hostility (which we will discuss more fully in the next chapter), it is best to end our treatment of Byzantine civilization here by recalling how much the western European world owes to it. The Byzantine Empire acted as a bulwark against Islam from the seventh to the eleventh centuries, thus helping preserve an independent and Christian West. Western Europeans also owe an enormous cultural debt to Byzantine scholars, who preserved much of the classical Greek literary tradition during centuries when these texts were entirely unknown in western Europe. Byzantine art has also exerted a profound influence on the art of western Europe. Saint Mark's Basilica in Venice reflects this influence; so too does the art of such great Western painters as Giotto and El Greco. Modern travelers who view Byzantine mosaics in such cities as Ravenna and Palermo are awestruck; those who make their way to Istanbul still find Santa Sophia breathtaking. In such jeweled beauty, the light from the Byzantine Empire continues to glow.

BYZANTINE CLASSICISM

This poem, by an eleventh-century Byzantine scholar, illustrates the sense of continuity learned Byzantines felt between their own Christian world and the world of the ancient Greek philosophers and authors.

May Christ Save Plato and Plutarch from Eternal Damnation

If perchance you wish to exempt certain pagans from punishment, my Christ,
May you spare for my sake Plato and Plutarch,
For both were very close to your laws in both teaching and way of life.
Even if they were unaware that you as God reign over all,
In this matter only your charity is needed,
Through which you are willing to save all men while asking nothing in return.

Deno John Geanokoplos, ed. and trans., *Byzantium: Church, Society, and Civilization Seen through Contemporary Eyes* (Chicago, 1984), p. 395.

QUESTIONS FOR ANALYSIS

1. The poetic prayer by an eleventh-century Byzantine scholar expresses a pious hope not only for Plato and Plutarch but also for the author, who wanted to hold on to both pagan classics and Christianity. From a Christian point of view, what problems arise from this position?

2. What would have to be changed in Plato's works (such as the *Republic*) to make them acceptable to orthodox Christians? Do the Platonic dialogues assist Christianity in any way? Would Christianity be something very different without Plato?

THE GROWTH OF ISLAM

How was Islam able to spread so rapidly?

Believers in Islam, known as Muslims, currently make up about one seventh of the global population: in their greatest concentrations they extend from Africa through the Middle East and the states of the former Soviet Union to South Asia and Indonesia. Islam has always demanded from its followers not just adherence to common forms of worship but also adherence to certain social and cultural norms. Indeed, more than Judaism or Christianity, Islam has been a great experiment in trying to build a worldwide society based on the fullest harmony between religious requirements and precepts for everyday existence. In this section we trace the early history of Islam, with primary emphasis on its westward expansion. Nonetheless we must remember that Islam expanded in many directions and that it ultimately had as much influence on the history of Africa and South Asia as it did on that of Europe or western Asia.

THE RISE OF ISLAM

Islam was born in Arabia, a desert land so backward before the founding of Islam that the two dominant neighboring empires, the Roman and the Persian, had not even bothered to conquer it. In the second half of the sixth century the protracted wars between Byzantium and Persia made Arabia a safer transit route than other alternatives for caravans passing between Africa and Asia. Towns grew up to direct and take advantage of this trade. The most prominent of these was Mecca, which not only lay on the junction of major trade routes but also had long been a local religious center. In Mecca was located the Kabah, a pilgrimage shrine that served as a central place of worship for many different Arabian clans and tribes. The men who controlled this shrine belonged to the tribe of Quraish (*kur-RAYSH*), an aristocracy of traders and entrepreneurs who provided the area with what little government it knew.

Muhammad, the founder of Islam, was born in Mecca to a Quraish family in about 570. Orphaned early in life, he entered the service of a rich widow whom he later married, thereby attaining financial security. Until middle age he lived as a prosperous trader little different from his fellow townsmen, but around 610 he underwent a religious experience that changed the course of his life and ultimately that of a good part of the world. Although most Arabs until then had been polytheists who recognized at most the vague superiority of a more powerful god they called Allah, Muhammad in 610 heard a voice from heaven tell him that there was no god but Allah alone. Thereafter he received further messages that commanded him to accept the calling of "Prophet" to proclaim the new monotheistic faith to the Quraish. At first he was not very successful in gaining converts beyond a limited circle, perhaps because the leading Quraish tribesmen believed that a new religion would deprive the Kabah, and therewith Mecca, of its central place in local worship with its attendant economic benefits. The town of Yathrib to the north, however, had no such concerns, and its representatives invited Muhammad to emigrate there to serve as a neutral arbiter of local rivalries. In 622 Muhammad and his followers accepted the invitation. Because their migration—called in Arabic the Hijrah (*HIJ-ruh;* or Hegira)—saw the beginning of an advance in Muhammad's fortunes, Muslims regard it as marking the beginning of their era: as Christians begin their era with the birth of Christ, so Muslims begin their dating system with the Hijrah of 622.

Muhammad changed the name of Yathrib to Medina ("city of the Prophet") and quickly established himself as ruler of the town. He also began to organize his converts into a political as well as a religious community. But he still needed to find some means of support for his original Meccan followers, and he also wanted vengeance on the Quraish for not heeding his calls to convert. Accord-

ingly, he started leading his followers in raids on Quraish caravans traveling beyond Mecca. In 630, after several desert battles, Muhammad entered Mecca in triumph. The Quraish thereupon submitted to the new faith, and the Kabah was not only preserved but made the main shrine of Islam, as it remains today. After the capture of Mecca, other tribes throughout Arabia in turn accepted the new faith. Thus, although Muhammad died in 632, he lived long enough to see the religion he had founded become a success.

THE RELIGIOUS TEACHINGS OF ISLAM

The word *islam* means "submission," and the faith of Islam calls for absolute submission to Allah, the Creator, God Almighty—the same omnipotent deity worshiped by Christians and Jews. Instead of saying, then, that Muslims believe "there is no god but Allah," it is more correct to say Muslims believe that "there is no divinity but God." In keeping with this strict monotheism, Muslims believe that Muhammad himself was God's last and greatest prophet, but not that he was God himself.

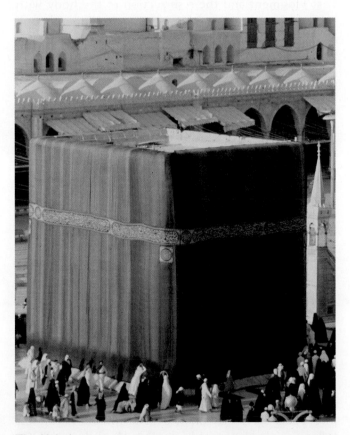

The Kabah. It contains the black stone that was supposed to have been miraculously sent down from heaven and rests in the courtyard of the great mosque in Mecca.

Men and women must surrender themselves entirely to God because divine judgment is imminent. Mortals must choose to begin a new life of divine service: if they do, God will guide them to blessedness, but if they do not, God will turn away from them and they will become irredeemably wicked. The practical steps the believer can take are outlined in the Qur'an (kuh-RAHN), which contains the revelations sent by God to Muhammad. These steps include moral rectitude, compassion, and fidelity to set religious observances— a regimen of prayers and fasts, pilgrimage to Mecca, and frequent recitation of parts of the Qur'an.

Islam resembles Judaism and Christianity in its strict monotheism; its emphasis on personal morality and compassion; and its reliance on written, revealed scripture. Although for Muslims the Qur'an is the ultimate source of religious authority, Islam accepts both the Hebrew Bible and the Christian New Testament as divinely inspired. From Christianity Muhammad may also have derived his doctrines of the Last Judgment and the resurrection of the body with subsequent rewards and punishments. But although Muhammad regarded Jesus as one of the greatest of a long line of prophets, he did not regard Jesus as divine. Nor did Muhammad claim to have performed any miracles himself, beyond his role in transmitting the Qur'an from heaven to earth.

Islam is a religion without sacraments or priests. Instead of priests there are only religious scholars who comment on problems of Islamic faith and law and who act as judges in disputes. Muslims are expected to pray together in mosques, but there is no such thing as a Muslim liturgy. The absence of clergy makes Islam more like Judaism, a similarity that is enhanced by Islamic stress on the inextricable connection between the religious, social, and political aspects of communal life. Unlike Judaism, however, Islam has historically aspired to unite the world into a single community of believers under the rule of Allah.

The Islamic Conquests

Because the Arabs had no clear concept of political succession, it was unclear whether Muhammad's community would survive at all after his death. But his closest followers—led by his father-in-law, Abu-Bakr (ah-BOO-BAK-uhr), and a zealous early convert named Umar— quickly took the initiative by naming Abu-Bakr caliph, meaning "deputy of the Prophet," and so the supreme

Although for Muslims the Qur'an is the ultimate source of religious authority, Islam accepts both the Hebrew Bible and the Christian New Testament as divinely inspired.

religious and political leader of all Muslims. Immediately after becoming caliph Abu-Bakr began a military campaign to subdue various Arab tribes that had followed Muhammad but were not willing to accept his successor's authority. In the course of this successful military action Abu-Bakr's forces began to spill northward beyond the borders of Arabia, where they met only minimal resistance from Byzantine and Persian forces.

Abu-Bakr was succeeded as caliph by Umar, who continued to direct his armies against Byzantium and Persia. In the following years Arab triumphs were virtually uninterrupted. In 636 the Arabs routed a Byzantine army in Syria and occupied Antioch, Damascus, and Jerusalem. In 637 they destroyed the main Persian army and marched into the Persian capital of Ctesiphon. By 651 the Arabian conquest of the entire Persian realm was complete. The Islamic forces now turned west toward North Africa, capturing Byzantine Egypt and extending their control throughout the rest of North Africa. Attempts in 677 and 717 to capture Constantinople failed; but in 711 the Arabs crossed from North Africa into Visigothic Spain and quickly took almost all of that area too. Thus within less than a century the forces of Islam had conquered all of ancient Persia and much of the late Roman world.

The Shiite-Sunni Schism

Despite the success of the Arab conquests, succession disputes soon began to divide Muslims against one another. In 644, when the caliph Umar died, he was replaced by Uthman, a weak ruler who belonged to the Umayyad (oo-MY-yad) family, a wealthy clan from Mecca whose members had initially resisted Muhammad's call. Uthman's opponents rallied around the Prophet's cousin and son-in-law Ali, whose warrior spirit and family ties to Muhammad made him seem a more appropriate choice to be caliph. When Uthman was murdered in 656 by mutineers, some declared Ali to be the new caliph. But Uthman's powerful family refused to accept Ali. Soon thereafter, Ali was murdered, and Uthman's party emerged triumphant. In 661 another member of the Umayyad family took over as caliph, and that house ruled the Islamic world from its capital at Damascus until 750.

Ali's followers, however, did not accept defeat. As time went on they hardened into a minority religious party known as Shiites (shi'a is Arabic for "party" or

The Expansion of Islam to 750

This map shows the steady advance of Islam from the time of Muhammad to the middle of the eighth century. Note the rapid expansion in the generation after Muhammad's death. Which aspects of Islam's organization and fervor helped contribute to the spread of Muslim armies? What does the rapid advance suggest about the preparedness of their initial foes, such as Byzantium and Persia? Why were these foes not better able to resist? Why was the capture of Constantinople so crucial to successive Muslim rulers even after Islam had spread well beyond the eastern Mediterranean?

"faction"). The Shiites insisted that only descendants of Ali and his wife, Fatimah (the daughter of the Prophet), could legitimately rule the Muslim community (the *umma*). Nor did the Shiites accept as binding the customary religious practices (*sunna*) that had developed under the first two caliphs, Abu-Bakr and Umar. The Shiites' opponents did regard these customs as binding and thus were called Sunnis. This division between Shiites and Sunnis, which crystallized during the tenth century, has lasted until the present day. Often persecuted by the Sunni majority as heretics, Shiites developed a powerful commitment to martyrdom and a deep sense of themselves as being the only true exponents of Islam. During the Middle Ages, Shiites sometimes held political power

in Egypt and North Africa, but the largest number of Shiites lived farther east. Today, Shiites rule Iran and are the largest single Muslim group in Iraq, but they make up only about one tenth of the worldwide population of Islam.

Umayyads and Abbasids

The triumph of the Umayyads in 661 began a more settled period in the history of the caliphate that would last until the tenth century. During these centuries there were two major governing orientations: the westward-looking one represented by the Umayyads, and the eastward-looking orientation of their successors, the Abbasids. The Umayyad capital was

MUSLIMS, JEWS, AND CHRISTIANS UNDER ISLAMIC RULE

THE "PACT OF UMAR"

When the caliph Umar (d. 644) conquered the city of Jerusalem, he issued a charter of protection to the people of the city, defining the relationship that should exist in the future between the Muslim conquerors and their Christian subjects. In its surviving form, the "Pact of Umar" contains provisions that were probably not in Umar's original document. Nonetheless, the Pact, as seen from the first excerpt here, does describe accurately the rules that governed Christians and Jews living under Muslin rule during the early Middle Ages.

This letter is addressed to Allah's servant Umar, the Commander of the Faithful, by the Christians of such-and-such city. When you advanced against us, we asked you for a guarantee of protection for our persons, our offspring, our property, and the people of our sect, and we have taken upon ourselves the following obligations toward you, namely:

We shall not build in our cities or in the vicinity any new monasteries, churches, hermitages, or monks' cells. We shall not restore . . . any of them that have fallen into ruin or which are located in the Muslims' quarters.

We shall keep our gates wide open for passersby and travelers. We shall provide three days' food and lodging to any Muslims who pass our way. . . .

We shall not teach our children the Koran.

We shall not hold public religious ceremonies. We shall not seek to proselytize anyone. We shall not prevent any of our kin from embracing Islam if they so desire.

We shall show deference to the Muslims and shall rise from our seats when they wish to sit down.

We shall not attempt to resemble the Muslims in any way. . . .

We shall not ride on saddles.

We shall not wear swords or bear weapons of any kind, or ever carry them with us. . . .

We shall not display our crosses or our books anywhere in the Muslims' thoroughfares or in their marketplaces. We shall only beat our clappers in our churches very quietly. We shall not raise our voices when reciting the service in our churches, nor when in the presence of Muslims. Neither shall we raise our voices in our funeral processions. . . .

We shall not build our homes higher than theirs. . . .

Norman A. Stillman, ed. and trans., *The Jews of Arab Lands: A History and Source Book* (Philadelphia, 1979), pp. 157–158.

PASSAGES FROM THE QUR'AN ON JEWS AND CHRISTIANS

Like the Hebrew and Christian Bibles, the Qur'an is a complex compilation of materials of varying dates and differing perspectives. The second excerpt contains selections that reflect the range of views to be found in the Qur'an on the way Muslims should deal with Jews and Christians.

Wretchedness and baseness were stamped upon [the Jews], and they were visited with wrath from Allah. That was because they disbelieved in Allah's revelations and slew the prophets wrongfully. That was for their disobedience and transgression (Sura 2:61).

There is to be no compulsion in religion. Rectitude has been clearly distinguished from error. So whoever disbelieves in idols and believes in Allah has taken hold of the firmest handle. It cannot split. Allah is All-hearing and All-knowing (Sura 2:256).

Have you not seen those who have received a portion of the Scripture? They purchase error, and they want you to go astray from the path. But Allah knows best who your enemies are, and it is sufficient to have Allah as a friend. It is sufficient to have Allah as a helper. Some of the Jews pervert words from their meanings . . . twisting with their tongues and slandering religion. . . . But Allah has cursed them for their disbelief, so they believe not, except for a few (Sura 4:44–46).

Indeed, you will find that the most vehement of men in enmity to those who believe are the Jews and the polytheists. But you will also surely find that the closest of them in love to those who believe are those who say, "We are Christians." That is because there are among them priests and monks, and because they are not arrogant (Sura 5:82).

The Jews say, "Ezra is the son of Allah," and the Christians say, "The Messiah is the son of Allah." Those are the words of their mouths, conforming to the words of the unbelievers before them. Allah attack them! How perverse they are! They have taken their rabbis and their monks as lords besides Allah, and so too the Messiah son of Mary, though they were commanded to serve but one God. There is no God but He. Allah is exalted above that which they deify beside Him (Sura 9:30–31).

Norman A. Stillman, ed. and trans., *The Jews of Arab Lands: A History and Source Book* (Philadelphia, 1979), pp. 150–151.

QUESTIONS FOR ANALYSIS

1. Why did the Muslims tolerate other religions? If they believed all other religions were false, why didn't they stamp them out? Was early Christianity a religion of tolerance?
2. According to the Qur'an, how should Muslims deal with Jews and Christians?

Damascus in the old Byzantine territory of Syria, and in many ways the Umayyad caliphate functioned as a Byzantine successor state, continuing even to employ formerly Byzantine bureaucrats. The Umayyads concentrated their energies on dominating the Mediterranean and conquering Constantinople. When their massive attack on the Byzantine capital failed in 717, Umayyad strength was seriously weakened.

A new perspective came with the takeover of the caliphate by a new family, the Abbasids, in 750. Their rule stressed Persian more than Byzantine elements. The Abbasid caliph built his new capital at Baghdad in Iraq, near the ruins of the old Persian city. The Abbasids also modeled their administration and their absolutist style of rule on Persian example, imposing heavy taxation to support a large professional army and presiding over an extravagantly luxurious and elaborate court. This is the world described in the *Arabian Nights*, a collection of stories of dazzling splendor set in Baghdad under the Abbasids. The dominating presence in these stories, Harun al-Rashid, ruled as caliph from 786 to 809. His lavish but brutal reign marked the height of Abbasid power.

After 750, the Umayyad dynasty continued to rule only in Spain. Relations between the Spanish Umayyads and the Persian Abbasids were cold, with each dynasty claiming to be the only legitimate successor of the Prophet. But because their capitals were so far apart, the hostility between them rarely erupted in war. Instead, the two courts competed for preeminence through

Exterior and Interior of the Great Umayyad Mosque at Damascus. This mosque was built by Caliph al-Walid between 705 and 715 on the former site of a pagan Roman temple; it incorporates a shrine to St. John the Baptist. Byzantine influence is apparent in its arched colonnades, its mosaics (the ones over the main door indicate that the worshiper is entering paradise), and its series of domes. Its horseshoe arches and interior striping influenced much subsequent Islamic architecture.

literary and cultural patronage. Philosophers, artists, and especially poets flocked to both courts, which became important cultural and intellectual centers. The *Arabian Nights* was but one product of this rivalry. At Cordoba, the caliph Al-Hakem II (961–976) amassed a library of more than 400,000 volumes at a time when, in western Europe, a monastery with 100 books qualified as a center of learning. Nothing remotely comparable had been seen in the western Mediterranean world since the heady days of imperial Rome.

For the Christians of Byzantium and western Europe, the Abbasid caliphate was significant not only for its cultural achievements but also because its eastern orientation took a certain amount of military pressure off the Mediterranean West. The Byzantine state, accordingly, was able to recover somewhat after a century of military pressure from the Umayyads. Farther west, the Franks of Gaul also benefited from the advent of the Abbasids. The great Frankish ruler Charlemagne (*SHAR-leh-mayn*; r. 768–814) maintained diplomatic and trade relations with the Abbasid caliphate of Harun al-Rashid against their common Umayyad enemy. The most famous symbol of this connection was the elephant that Harun al-Rashid sent to Charlemagne. More important, however, was the flow of silver that found its way from the Abbasid Empire north through Russia and the Baltic and into the Rhineland in exchange for

Frankish furs, slaves, wax, honey, and leather. Jewels, silks, spices, and other luxury goods from India and the Far East also flowed north and west into the Frankish world through the Abbasid Empire. These trading links with the Abbasid world helped fund the extraordinary cultural achievements of the Carolingian Renaissance, which we describe in the next section of this chapter.

THE CHANGING ISLAMIC WORLD

What forces combined to undermine the political unity of the Islamic world?

During the ninth and tenth centuries the power of the Abbasid dynasty rapidly declined. An extended period of decentralization followed that was mirrored during the eleventh century in Umayyad Spain. A major cause of the Abbasid collapse was the gradual impoverishment of their economic base—the agricultural wealth of the Tigris-Euphrates basin—resulting from ecological crises and a devastating revolt by the enslaved African workforce that farmed the southern Iraqi

WHAT FORCES COMBINED TO UNDERMINE THE POLITICAL UNITY OF THE ISLAMIC WORLD?

THE CHANGING ISLAMIC WORLD   189

marshlands. Tax revenues from the Abbasid Empire were also declining, as provincial rulers in North Africa, Egypt, and Syria retained larger and larger portions of those revenues for themselves. As their revenues declined, the Abbasids found themselves unable to support either their large civil service or the new-style mercenary army they had built up. Massively expensive building projects, including the refoundation of the Abbasid capital of Baghdad, further exacerbated the fiscal, military, and political crisis.

Behind the Abbasid crisis lay two fundamental developments of great significance for the future of the Islamic world: the growth of regionalism and the sharpening religious divisions between Sunnis and Shiites and among the Shiites themselves. In 909 a local Shiite dynasty known as the Fatimids seized control of the Abbasid province of North Africa. In 969, the Fatimids succeeded in conquering Egypt also. Meanwhile, another Shiite group, rivals of both the Fatimids and the Abbasids, attacked Baghdad in 927 and Mecca in 930, seizing the Kabah. Thereafter, the effective power of the Abbasids over their empire collapsed entirely. In its place a new order began to emerge in the eastern Muslim world centered around an independent Egyptian kingdom and a new Muslim state based in Persia.

In Spain, Umayyad weakness was more directly a consequence of political failures and succession disputes than of economic collapse. Muslim Spain in the ninth and tenth centuries was an enormously wealthy agricultural and commercial region. But from the mid-ninth century on, renewed military pressure from the reviving Christian kingdoms of northern and eastern Spain increased the internal political difficulties of the Umayyad caliphate. In the opening years of the eleventh century, the united Umayyad caliphate in Spain finally dissolved, to be replaced by a host of small-scale kingdoms, some of which were now paying tribute to the Christian rulers of the north. One by one, these local kingdoms gradually fell victim to the advancing forces of the Christian kings of Spain. Although the last Muslim kingdom, the principality of Granada, would not fall to the Christians until 1492, the Christian reconquest of Spain was essentially complete by the middle of the thirteenth century.

Extravagance and incompetence by the Abbasid and Umayyad caliphs certainly played a role in their collapse. But there were larger factors at work in breaking up the unity of the Islamic world that transcended the failures of particular caliphs. Although Islamic society was religiously tolerant, at least with respect to Jews and Christians, ethnic tensions within the Islamic world were rampant and grew more divisive as the early idealism of the initial conquests faded with time. These ethnic tensions among Arabs, Turks, Berbers, sub-Saharan Africans, and Persians also complicated the deep regional divisions that had characterized this area of the world for centuries before the Islamic conquests began. Adding further to the political instability of the Muslim world was the uncompromising monotheism and religious egalitarianism of Islam itself. Muslim rulers (such as some of the Abbasids) who took on Persian styles of semidivine rulership were frequently murdered as blasphemers. Tensions between the universality of Islamic belief and the realities of regional particularism, ethnic hostility, and religious conflict between Sunnis and Shiites thus combined to undermine the political unity of the Islamic world.

> Tensions between the universality of Islamic belief and the realities of regional particularism, ethnic hostility, and religious conflict between Sunnis and Shiites thus combined to undermine the political unity of the Islamic world.

MUSLIM SOCIETY AND CULTURE, 900–1250

The political decentralization of the Muslim world did not automatically bring cultural decay, however. In fact, Islam's most creative cultural period was only beginning as the ninth century came to an end.

Islamic culture and society were extraordinarily cosmopolitan and dynamic. Islam inherited the sophistication of Byzantium and Persia and remained centered at the crossroads of long-distance trade between the Far East and West. Urban life in most Muslim territories grew enormously, resulting in striking geographical and social mobility. Since literacy was remarkably widespread—a rough estimate for around the year 1000 is that 20 percent of all Muslim males could read the Arabic of the Qur'an—many could rise through education. Offices were seldom regarded as hereditary, and "new men" could arrive at the top by enterprise and skill.

There was one major exception to Muslim egalitarianism: the treatment of women. The Qur'an allowed a man to marry four wives, so women were at a premium, and married women were segregated from other men. A wealthy man would also have a number of female servants and concubines, whom he kept in a part of his residence called the harem, where they were guarded by eunuchs—that is, castrated men. Although large harems could be kept only by the wealthy, the system was imitated as far as possible by all classes. Based on the principle that women were chattel property, these practices did much to emphasize attitudes of domination in sexual life. Although male homosexual relations were tolerated in upper-class society, these relationships too were based on patterns of domination, usually of a powerful adult over an adolescent boy, much as they had been in the ancient Greek world.

Two major avenues were open to men wishing to devote themselves to Islamic religious life. One was that of the *ulama,* learned men whose job was to study and offer advice on all aspects of religion and religious law. Complementary to them were the *Sufis,* religious mystics who stressed contemplation and ecstasy as the ulama stressed religious law. Sufis were usually organized into "brotherhoods" that did much to convert outlying areas such as Africa and India. Throughout the Islamic world Sufism provided a channel for the most intense religious impulses. The ability of the ulama and the Sufis to coexist is testimony to the cultural pluralism of the Islamic world. But the absence of any avenues for religious women comparable with the convents of the Christian world is a reminder of the limits imposed by gender on that pluralism.

CHRONOLOGY

THE SPREAD OF ISLAM, 622–750

Expulsion of Muhammad from Mecca (Hijrah)	622
Muhammad returns to Mecca	630
Muhammad dies	632
Abu-Bakr becomes caliph	632
Umar becomes caliph	634
Arabs occupy Antioch, Damascus, Jerusalem	636
Arabs occupy Persian capital	637
Arabs invade Egypt	646
Arabs conquer Persian Empire	651
Shiite-Sunni schism	661
Arabs conquer North Africa	646–711
Umayyad dynasty	661–750
Arabs invade Spain	711
Beginning of Abbasid dynasty	750

MUSLIM PHILOSOPHY, SCIENCE, AND MEDICINE

The two greatest influences on medieval Islamic philosophy were Aristotelianism and Neoplatonism. Muslim philosophers strove to reconcile these two quite different philosophical traditions with each other and with the tenets of Islamic theology. Reconciling Aristotelianism and Neoplatonism was in some ways the easier task. Reconciling Greek philosophy with Islamic theology was more difficult. Like Judaism and Christianity, Islam holds firmly to the view that a single omnipotent God created the world in time as an act of pure will, and that the world will continue to exist only for so long as God wills it to do so. Islamic theology also believes in the immortality of the individual human soul, another doctrine flatly in conflict with Aristotelian and Neoplatonic thought. There were also conflicts over predestination and free will. Although medieval Muslim theologians strongly emphasized the individual responsibility of believers to choose between good and evil, virtually all Muslims agreed that nothing good could occur unless God actively willed it. At times, such convictions could rise to a kind of fatalism wholly at odds with Greek philosophical presumptions.

The most famous Islamic philosopher was the Spaniard Averroës (*ah-VER-oh-eez*; Ibn Rušd, 1126–1198). A consummate rationalist and the greatest Aristotelian scholar of his day, Averroës wrote a series of commentaries on the works of Aristotle that sought to purge them of all Neoplatonic influences. Translated from Arabic into Latin, these commentaries influenced the way all thirteenth-century Christian scholars, including Aquinas and Dante, read and understood Aristotle. Averroës was also an expert in Muslim law and theology and a physician, but he thoroughly subordinated theology to philosophy. Averroës considered both theology and philosophy to be true, but in different ways. Philosophical assertions were true in their literal meaning; theological statements, however, were often true only when interpreted allegorically or symbolically—and only philosophers were capable of determining which theological statements were literally true because philosophers alone were the experts on literal meaning.

Such views did not sit well with the Islamic rulers of Spain. After burning several of Averroës' works, they exiled him to Morocco, where he died in 1198. His death marks a turning point in Islamic philosophy. Thereafter, philosophy tended either to blend into Sufistic mysticism or became too constrained by the

WHAT FORCES COMBINED TO UNDERMINE THE POLITICAL UNITY OF THE ISLAMIC WORLD?

THE CHANGING ISLAMIC WORLD   191

demands of Islamic orthodoxy to lead an independent existence. But in its heyday between 900 and 1200, Islamic philosophy was far more advanced and sophisticated than anything found in Byzantium or western Europe.

Islamic philosophers were often distinguished physicians and scientists also. Muslim observations of the heavens were so accurate, indeed, that some astronomers concluded that the earth must rotate on its axis and revolve around the sun, rather than remaining stationary with the sun and planets revolving around it. Islamic accomplishments in medicine were equally remarkable. Avicenna (Ibn Sinā, 980–1037) discovered the contagious nature of tuberculosis, described pleurisy and several varieties of nervous ailments, and noted that diseases could spread through contaminated water and soil. His *Canon of Medicine* would remain an authoritative textbook in the Islamic world and in western Europe until the seventeenth century. Islamic scientists also made important advances in optics, chemistry, and mathematics. Islamic physicists studied the theory of magnifying lenses and the velocity, transmission, and refraction of light. Islamic mathematicians united the geometry of the Greeks with the number science of the Hindus. Using what Westerners know as "Arabic numerals" (but which are in fact Hindu in origin), Muslim mathematicians developed a decimal arithmetic based on place values (the zero was critical to this). They also made fundamental advances in algebra and algorithms (both Arabic words) and in spherical trigonometry. Muslim mathematicians thus brought together and pushed forward all the areas of mathematical knowledge that would be adopted and developed in western Europe from the sixteenth century on.

TRADE AND INDUSTRY

Although the economy of seventh-century Arabia was relatively primitive, many of the territories conquered by Muhammad's followers were wealthy and highly urbanized. Syria, Egypt, and Persia in particular lay at the crossroads of the Mediterranean world, linking the major trade routes among Africa, Europe, India, and China. Conversion to Islam did not diminish their economic importance; if anything, it increased it, as their

Aristotle Teaching Arab Astronomers, Thirteenth-Century Manuscript. Greek philosophers, particularly Aristotle, greatly influenced Islamic philosophy and science.

trading contacts grew in tandem with the growth of the Islamic world. By the tenth century, Muslim merchants had penetrated into southern Russia and equatorial Africa and had become masters of the caravan routes that led eastward to India and China. Ships from the Muslim world established new trade routes across the Indian Ocean, the Persian Gulf, and the Caspian Sea and for a time dominated the Mediterranean world also. During the tenth and eleventh centuries, however, Western Christian merchants gradually took control over the Mediterranean sea routes; in the sixteenth century, they would extend that control into the Indian Ocean. Both these developments were serious blows to the economy of the Muslim world.

The growth of Muslim commerce in the early Middle Ages reflects the development of a number of important industries. One product that deserves special mention, however, is paper. Muslims learned papermaking from the Chinese and quickly became masters of the art. Paper was cheaper to produce, easier to store, and far easier to write on than papyrus or parchment. As a result, by the early eleventh century, paper had replaced papyrus even in Egypt, the heartland of papyrus production for almost 4,000 years.

The ready availability of paper brought about a revolution in the Islamic world. Many of the characteristic features of Islamic civilization—bureaucratic record keeping, high levels of literacy and book production (especially copies of the Qur'an), even the standard form of cursive Arabic script known as Kufic—would have been impossible without the widespread availability of paper. Only in the thirteenth century would western Europeans master papermaking; when they did, however, they quickly began to undercut the market for Islamic paper. By the end of the fifteenth century, the Muslim world was importing almost all of its paper from western Europe, despite the fact that the watermarks on European papers often contained Christian symbols offensive to Islam.

THE EFFECT OF EARLY ISLAMIC CIVILIZATION ON EUROPE

Until the twelfth century, the cultural, economic, intellectual, and political achievements of Islamic civilization completely overshadowed those of Latin Christian Europe. And when Latin Europe did move forward, it relied heavily on what it had learned from the Islamic world. Europeans adopted a good deal of Muslim technology, including irrigation systems, papermaking, and the distillation of alcohol (an Arabic word). Similarly, the commercial influence of the Muslim world on Europe is reflected in the large number of common English words of Arabic and Persian origin: traffic, tariff, magazine, muslin, damask, orange, lemon, alfalfa, saffron, sugar, syrup, and musk, to name just a few.

Latin Europe was equally indebted to the Muslim world in intellectual and scientific life. Islamic civilization preserved and extended Greek philosophical and scientific knowledge throughout the early Middle Ages at a time when such knowledge was almost entirely forgotten in the Latin-speaking world. Most of the important Greek scientific works surviving today were translated into Arabic, and from the twelfth century on were translated from Arabic into Latin through the combined efforts of Muslim, Jewish, and Latin Christian scholars. Above all, the preservation and interpretation of the works of Aristotle was one of Islam's most enduring contributions to western European culture. Arabic numerals, adopted from India by Muslim mathematicians, are another crucially important intellectual legacy from the Islamic world, as anyone will discover after trying to balance a checkbook using Roman numerals.

WESTERN CHRISTIAN CIVILIZATION IN THE EARLY MIDDLE AGES

What caused economic and social change in seventh-century western Europe?

In western Europe also, the seventh century marked the transition between the late antique and the early medieval worlds. At the end of the sixth century, the Frankish chronicler Gregory of Tours still saw himself as living in a discernibly Roman world of cities, trade, taxation, and local administration. Gregory was proud of his family's status as Roman senators and took it for granted that he and his male relatives should be bishops who ruled, by right of birth and status, over their episcopal cities and the surrounding countryside. Like others of his class, Gregory still spoke and wrote Latin—a quite different Latin from the polished prose of Cicero 600 years before, but a Latin that was nonetheless the same language and that had certainly changed less since Cicero's day than English has changed since the time of Chaucer. Gregory was of course aware that the western Roman Empire was now in the hands of Frankish, Visigothic, and Lombard kings. But he saw those kings as Romans nonetheless because they ruled in accordance with Roman models and, in the case of the Franks, because they ruled with the approval of the Roman emperor in Constantinople. It was also a source of satisfaction to Gregory that in recent years, all these barbarian kings had converted to Catholic Christianity. This too, for Gregory, reinforced their *romanitas* ("Romanness"), and thus lent legitimacy, both earthly and heavenly, to their rule.

However, 200 years later, when Charlemagne, the greatest of all the Frankish rulers, was crowned as the new Roman emperor in the West, the sense of direct continuity that Gregory of Tours had had with the Roman world was gone. When Charlemagne set out to reform the cultural, religious, and political life of his empire, his goal was to revive a Roman Empire from which he and his contemporaries now saw themselves as estranged. Charlemagne sought a *renovatio Romanorum imperii*—a renewal of the empire of the Romans—

> Charlemagne sought a *renovatio Romanorum imperii*—a renewal of the empire of the Romans—thus conceding in his very motto that he sought to revive an empire that had fallen.

WHAT CAUSED ECONOMIC AND SOCIAL CHANGE IN SEVENTH-CENTURY WESTERN EUROPE?

WESTERN CHRISTIAN CIVILIZATION IN THE EARLY MIDDLE AGES   193

thus conceding in his very motto that he sought to revive an empire that had fallen. This awareness of a break with the Roman past developed during the seventh century. It marks the beginning of a new era in the history of western European civilization.

ECONOMIC DISINTEGRATION AND POLITICAL INSTABILITY

The Mediterranean world remained a reasonably well-integrated economic unit until the late sixth century. By 650, however, the economic unity of the Mediterranean world had broken down. This breakdown resulted partly from the destructiveness of Justinian's efforts to reconquer the western empire. Partly it was a consequence of ruinous Byzantine taxation of agricultural land. Piracy by Muslim raiders also played a role in undermining the economy of the seventh-century Mediterranean world—although Muslims quickly became important maritime traders, and in the long run Muslim conquests did more to reconstruct than to destroy the patterns of Mediterranean commerce.

For western Europe, however, the most important causes of these seventh-century economic changes were internal. The cities of Italy, Gaul, and Spain continued to decline. Agricultural land was passing out of cultivation, and the late Roman system of land taxes was also collapsing. The coinage systems of western Europe were also breaking down. From the 660s on, western European rulers shifted from a gold to a silver coinage. Europe would remain a silver-based economy for the next 1,000 years.

During the seventh century, western Europe thus became a basically two-tier economy. Gold, silver, and luxury goods circulated among the wealthy, but the peasantry relied mainly on barter and various currency substitutes to facilitate their transactions. Lords collected rents from their peasants in foodstuffs but found it difficult to convert these payments of grain, wine, and meat into the weapons, jewelry, and silks that brought prestige in seventh-century aristocratic society. In a world in which the power of lords depended on their ability to give such high-prestige gifts to their military followers, the inability to convert peasant rents into cash was a serious handicap.

Another factor contributing to the instability of power in this world was the difficulty all the royal dynasties of the early Middle Ages experienced in trying to regulate the succession to their thrones. The kings who established themselves during the invasion period

of the fifth and sixth centuries did not come from the traditional royal families of their peoples. Moreover, the barbarian armies who took over the western Roman Empire during these years were rarely if ever composed of a single people anyway. They were usually made up of many different peoples, including a sizable number of disaffected Romans. Such unity as they possessed was largely the creation of the charismatic warrior-kings who led them, and this charisma was not easily passed on by inheritance.

Of all the barbarian groups that set up kingdoms in the western empire during the fifth and sixth centuries, only the Franks succeeded in establishing a single royal dynasty from which the future kings of the Franks would be drawn for the next 250 years. This dynasty was established by Clovis (d. 511), the great warrior-king of the Franks, who by converting to orthodox Catholic Christianity also established an alliance between his dynasty and the powerful Roman bishops of Gaul. But the dynasty itself came to be known as the Merovingians, after Clovis's legendary grandfather Merovech, who was a sea dragon. We need not take this claim seriously; but it does suggest that no one was sure who Clovis's grandfather actually was.

Even in Gaul, however, the Merovingians were not the only noble family with a plausible claim to be kings; and in Visigothic Spain, Anglo-Saxon England, and Lombard Italy, the numbers of such rival royal families were even greater. In Visigothic Spain, the bloody succession disputes that resulted when a reigning king died so horrified the resident Roman population that they spoke of this inability to regulate the succession as a kind of a sickness: the *morbus Gothorum*, the "sickness of the Goths." In Gaul, the Franks were more successful in restricting claims to kingship to descendants of the Merovingian dynasty; but the Merovingians' custom of dividing the kingdom up into its constituent, regional parts, and installing a different king over each part, guaranteed plenty of civil strife in Merovingian Gaul also.

MEROVINGIAN GAUL

The brutal conflicts between these rival Merovingian kings can easily obscure the real strength and sophistication of Merovingian governance. Many elements of late Roman local administration survived throughout the Merovingian period. Literacy remained an important element in Merovingian administration, providing a foundation on which the Carolingians would build. Even the cultural renaissance associated with the reign of Charlemagne really began in the late seventh century, with the production of deluxe biblical and other manuscripts at Merovingian monasteries.

Monasteries grew remarkably under the Merovingians, especially during the seventh century, reflecting the great wealth of the country. The Frankish bishoprics also prospered under the Merovingians, amassing three quarters of their total landed possessions by the end of the seventh century. This massive redistribution of wealth reflected a fundamental shift in the economic gravity of the Frankish kingdom. In the year 600, the wealth of Gaul was still concentrated in the south, where it had been throughout the late Roman period. By the year 750, however, the economic center of the kingdom lay north of the Loire, in the territories that extended from the Rhineland westward to the North Sea. It was here that most of the new monastic foundations of seventh-century Gaul were established.

MONASTICISM AND CONVERSION

Throughout Christian Europe, the seventh century witnessed a rapid increase in the number of monastic houses. Monasteries had existed in Gaul, Italy, and Spain since the fourth century, but most were located in the highly Romanized cities of southern Spain, Gaul, and northern Italy. Most of the new monastic foundations of the seventh century were deliberately located in rural areas, however, where they played an important role in the continuing struggle to Christianize the countryside. The most famous example of such monastic missionary activity is the conversion of Anglo-Saxon England. In northern England, the work of Christianization began in the late sixth century, led by missionary monks from Ireland. The decisive moment came in 597, however, when a group of forty Benedictine monks, sent by Pope Gregory I (590–604), brought the traditions of Roman Christianity to southeastern England. Despite some initial setbacks, by the end of the seventh century all of England had been brought firmly within the boundaries of the Roman, Christian world, and English monks had begun their own missionary campaigns in Frisia and Saxony. Frankish missionaries were also active in these areas. But it was the particular loyalty the English monks felt toward the papacy that was to have the most momentous consequences, not only for the papacy, but also for Gaul.

THE REIGN OF POPE GREGORY I

The architect of this new alliance between the Roman papacy and Benedictine monasticism was Pope Gregory I, known as Saint Gregory the Great. Until his time the Roman popes were generally subordinate to the emperors in Constantinople. Byzantine power in Italy was declining, however, and although Gregory worked hard to prevent a breach with Constantinople, he also sought to create a more autonomous, Western-oriented Latin church. As a theologian—the fourth great "Latin Father" of the church—he built on the work of Saint Jerome, Saint Ambrose, and especially Saint Augustine of Hippo, in articulating a theology with distinctively Western elements. Among these were an emphasis on the necessity of penance for the forgiveness of sins and the concept of purgatory as a place where the soul was purified before it was admitted into heaven. (Western belief in purgatory was thereafter to become one of the major differences in the teachings of the Eastern and Western churches.) Gregory emphasized the importance of pastoral care by bishops toward the laity, and popularized a powerful liturgical chant with unaccompanied vocal music that has become known as "Gregorian chant." All these innovations helped make the Christian West religiously and culturally more independent of the Greek-speaking East than it had ever been before.

Pope Gregory the Great. In this tenth-century German ivory panel the pope is receiving inspiration from the Holy Spirit in the form of a dove.

HOW DID CHARLEMAGNE REDEFINE THE RELATIONSHIP BETWEEN CHRISTIANITY AND KINGSHIP?

THE RISE OF THE CAROLINGIANS   195

Gregory was also a statesman and ruler in the model of his Roman forebears. Within Italy he ensured the survival of the papacy against the barbarian Lombards by clever diplomacy and expert management of the papacy's estates and revenues. He maintained good relations with Byzantium while asserting his authority as pope over the other bishops of the Western church. Above all, he supported Benedictine monks. Gregory's patronage helped the Rule of Saint Benedict become the predominant monastic rule in the West; through his encouragement, Benedictine monks emerged as the most important missionary group of the early Middle Ages. Their missionary work in Frisia and Germany brought both regions into the Western Catholic Church and laid the groundwork for an alliance between the papacy and the Frankish monarchy that would transform early medieval Europe.

THE RISE OF THE CAROLINGIANS

How did Charlemagne redefine the relationship between Christianity and kingship?

In Gaul, the weaknesses of the Merovingian dynasty were becoming steadily more apparent as the seventh century drew to a close. Tensions between noble families in the Merovingian heartland of Neustria and those in the border region of Austrasia were increasing. But not until 717, when Pepin of Heristal's illegitimate son Charles Martel ("the Hammer") finally triumphed over his Neutrian opponents was Pepin's family secure in its control over the Merovingian court. Thereafter, however, the Merovingian kings were largely figureheads in a kingdom ruled by Charles Martel and his sons.

Charles Martel is sometimes considered the second founder (after Clovis) of the Frankish state. His claim to this title is twofold. First, in 733 or 734 (the traditional date of 732 is erroneous), he turned back a Muslim force from Spain at the battle of Tours (not Poitiers), some 150 miles from the Merovingian capital of Paris. Although the Muslim contingent was a raiding party rather than a full-scale army, the incursion was nonetheless the high-water mark of Umayyad progress toward northwestern Europe, and Martel's victory won him great prestige. Equally important, Martel began to develop an alliance with the English Benedictine missionaries who were attempting to convert Frisia and

central Germany to Christianity. Martel's family had long been active in the drive to conquer and settle these areas, and he understood clearly how missionary work and Frankish expansion could go hand in hand. Martel assisted Saint Boniface and his followers in their conversion efforts. In return, the English Benedictines brought Martel and his descendants into contact with the papacy and assisted him in his efforts to reform (and so control) the Frankish church.

Martel died in 741. Although he never sought to become king himself, during the last years of his life he was so clearly the effective ruler of Gaul that he did not even bother to arrange for a new king to be selected when, in 737, the reigning Merovingian king died. In 743, however, Martel's sons, Carloman and Pepin, bowed to the forces of legitimism, and a new Merovingian king took the throne. By 750, however, Pepin had decided to seize the throne for himself. To effect such a change in dynasties, Pepin sought papal approval. Through his family's support for Saint Boniface, Pepin was already well regarded in Rome. And the papacy, locked in a bitter fight with the Byzantine emperors over Iconoclasm and with the Lombard kings for control over central Italy, proved only too happy to cooperate in Pepin's elevation, hoping that a powerful new Frankish ruler would take over from the Byzantines the responsibility for protecting papal interests in Italy against the Lombards.

In 751 Saint Boniface, acting as papal emissary, anointed Pepin as king of the Franks. The last Merovingian king was deposed and sent to a monastery, and a new king, who had not a drop of Merovingian blood, was raised to the Frankish throne for the first time in almost three centuries. Pepin's coronation symbolized the integration of the new Frankish monarchy into the papal-Benedictine orbit. For the moment, however, Pepin had his hands full simply trying to control his new kingdom.

THE REIGN OF CHARLEMAGNE

The real consolidation of this new pattern of papal-Frankish-Benedictine relations took place during the reign of Pepin's son, Charlemagne, from whom the new dynasty takes its name of Carolingian (from "Carolus," the Latin form of "Charles"). When Charlemagne came to the throne in 768, it seemed possible that the Frankish kingdom would break up into its hostile regional parts of Austrasia, Neustria, and Aquitaine. But in an astonishing series of military campaigns, Charlemagne united the Franks by leading them on a series of conquests that annexed the Lombard kingdom of Italy, the greater part of Germany including Saxony, portions of central Europe, and Catalunya. These conquests set a seal of divine approval on the new Carolingian dynasty. They also provided the plunder, booty, and new lands that enabled Charlemagne to promote his Frankish followers to dizzying heights of wealth and grandeur.

To rule the vast empire he had conquered, Charlemagne appointed Frankish aristocrats called counts to supervise local administration within their territories. Among the counts' many duties were the administration of justice and the raising of armies. Charlemagne also established a network of local administrators to supervise courts, collect tolls, administer crown lands, and extract taxation. Charlemagne also created a new coinage system, based on a division of the silver pound into 240 pennies, which would last in France until the French Revolution and in Great Britain until the 1970s, when it was finally replaced by a decimal-based currency.

Like Carolingian administration generally, this new monetary system depended on the regular use of written records and instructions. But Charlemagne did not rely on the written word alone to make his will felt. Periodically he sent special representatives from his court through the countryside to relay his instructions personally and check up on local administrators. Charlemagne's governmental system was far from perfect. Local officials abused their positions; nobles sought to turn free peasants into unfree serfs; justice in local courts was often denied. But Charlemagne's system produced the best government Europe had seen

since the Romans, and it became the model on which Western rulers would base their own administrations for the next 300 years.

CHRISTIANITY AND KINGSHIP

Charlemagne took seriously his responsibilities as a Christian king. As his empire expanded, however, he came to see himself not only as the ruler of the Franks but as the leader of a unified Christian society, Christendom, which he was obliged to defend both militarily and spiritually against its enemies. The Carolingian world did not make the distinctions between the religious and the political realms that would characterize European life from the twelfth century on, any more than did Byzantium or Islam. Especially among churchmen, kingship in early medieval Europe was regarded as a sacred office created by God to protect the church, defend the Christian people, and promote their salva-

Pepin and Charlemagne Giving Edicts to a Clerk.
Cementing the papal–Frankish–Benedictine commitment, Charlemagne's reign outshone that of his father, Pepin.

CHRONOLOGY

THE RISE OF THE CAROLINGIAN EMPIRE, 717–814

Charles Martel becomes mayor of the palace	717
The Carolingians (Charles, Pepin, and Carloman) share power with the Merovingian kings	717–751
Pepin becomes king of the Franks	751
Charlemagne succeeds Pepin	768
Charlemagne is crowned Holy Roman emperor	800
Louis the Pious becomes emperor	813
Charlemagne dies	814

How did Charlemagne redefine the relationship between Christianity and kingship?

The Rise of the Carolingians   197

tion. Religious reforms were therefore no less central to proper kingship than were justice and defense. In some ways, a king's responsibilities for his kingdom's religious life were even more important than his other responsibilities: for surely no kingdom could prosper if the lives of its subjects were displeasing to God.

These ideas about the spiritual responsibilities of kingship were not new in the late eighth century, but they took on a new importance as a result of the extraordinary power Charlemagne wielded over his empire. Like other early medieval kings, Charlemagne appointed and deposed bishops and abbots, just as he did his counts and other officials. But he also changed the liturgy of the Frankish church, reformed rules of worship in Frankish monasteries, declared changes in basic statements of Christian belief, prohibited pagan observances, and imposed Christian observances, including baptism, on the conquered peoples of Saxony. To Charlemagne, such measures were clearly required if God's new Israel, the Franks, were to avoid the fate that befell biblical Israel whenever its people turned away from their obedience to God.

THE CAROLINGIAN RENAISSANCE

Similar ideals lay behind the Carolingian Renaissance, a cultural and intellectual flowering that took place around the Carolingian royal court. Like their biblical

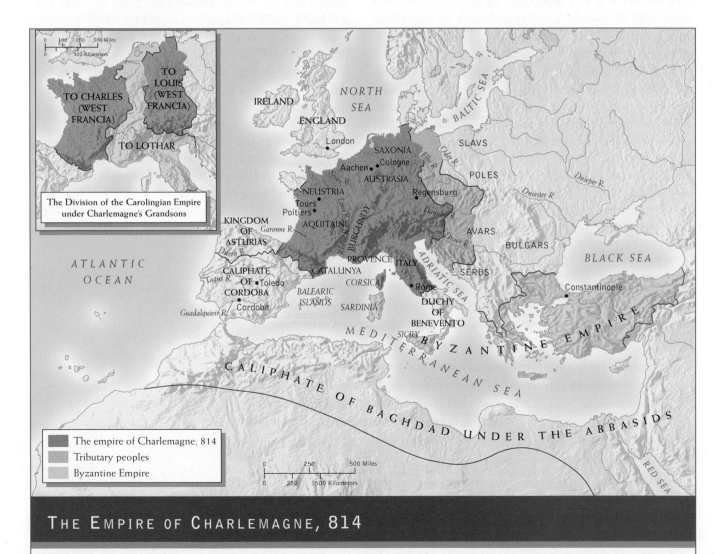

The Division of the Carolingian Empire under Charlemagne's Grandsons

■ The empire of Charlemagne, 814
■ Tributary peoples
■ Byzantine Empire

THE EMPIRE OF CHARLEMAGNE, 814

By 814, Charlemagne had created an empire that embraced most of the territory of the former western Roman Empire. Could he legitimately claim to be renewing the Roman Empire? How did his possession of Rome strengthen such a claim? How might it complicate his family's traditional alliance with the papacy? Note the inset in the upper left. What forces led to the division of Charlemagne's empire along these particular borders?

exemplars, the Hebrew kings David and Solomon, Charlemagne and his son, Louis the Pious, took seriously their role as patrons of poetry and learning. In so doing, they created an ideal of the court as an intellectual and cultural center that would profoundly influence western European cultural life until the nineteenth century. What lay behind the Carolingians' support for scholarship, however, was their conviction that classical learning was the foundation on which Christian wisdom rested and that such wisdom was essential to the salvation of God's people. Supporting scholarship was therefore a paramount obligation for a Christian king.

To promote classical learning and Christian wisdom, Charlemagne recruited scholars from throughout Europe to his court. Carolingian scholars produced a good deal of original Latin poetry and an impressive number of theological and pastoral tracts. However, their primary efforts were devoted to collating, correcting, and recopying classical Latin texts, including the text of the Latin Bible, which had become corrupted by generations of copyists' mistakes. They also developed a new style of handwriting, with simplified letter forms and spaces inserted between words, that further reduced the likelihood that subsequent copyists would misread the corrected texts. This new style of handwriting, known as Carolingian minuscule, is the foundation for the typefaces in which almost all European books, including this one, are still printed.

CHARLEMAGNE AND THE REVIVAL OF THE WESTERN ROMAN EMPIRE

The climax of Charlemagne's career came in Rome on Christmas Day 800, when he was crowned as the new Roman emperor in the West by Pope Leo III. Centuries later, popes would cite their role in this event as precedent for the political superiority they claimed over the Holy Roman emperor (a title that became common only in the twelfth century but that can be used for convenience to designate the Western emperors from Charlemagne on). In the year 800, however, Pope Leo was entirely under Charlemagne's thumb. Although Charlemagne said later that he would never have gone to church that day had he known Leo's plans to crown him, it is highly unlikely Pope Leo would have mounted such a ceremony without Charlemagne's consent, not least because it was certain to anger the Byzantines, with whom Charlemagne already had strained relations. Nor did the imperial title add much to Charlemagne's position as king of the Franks. Why, then, did he accept it, and in 813 transfer it to his son, Louis the Pious?

Historians do not know. What is clear, however, is the symbolic significance of the action. Until 800 only the Roman emperor who ruled in Constantinople could lay claim to being the direct heir of Caesar Augustus. Although the Byzantines had lost most of their influence in the West, they continued to regard it vaguely as

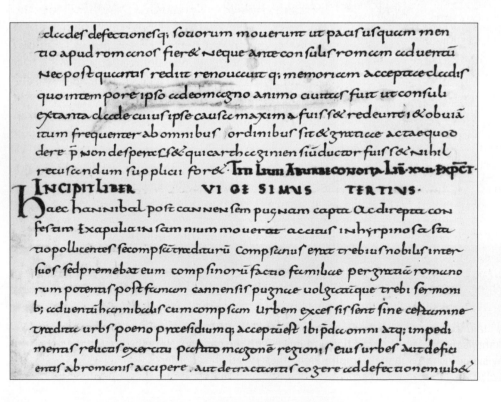

Carolingian Handwriting. Even the untrained reader has little difficulty in reading this excerpt from a Carolingian manuscript. For example, the first two words in the heading read "Incipit Liber," and the two words below them "Haec Hannibal."

How did Charlemagne redefine the relationship between Christianity and kingship?

The Rise of the Carolingians   199

an outlying province of their empire. Charlemagne's assumption of the imperial title was a clear slap in the face to the Byzantines. In the West, however, it was a declaration of self-confidence and independence that was never forgotten. Whatever his specific motives may have been, Charlemagne's revival of the western Roman Empire thus proved to be a major step in the developing self-consciousness of western European civilization.

THE COLLAPSE OF THE CAROLINGIAN EMPIRE

When Charlemagne died in 814, his empire descended intact to his only surviving son, Louis the Pious. Under Louis, however, the empire rapidly began to disintegrate. When Louis died in 843, the empire was divided between his three sons. Western Francia, which became France, went to Charles the Bald; Eastern Francia, which became Germany, went to Louis the German; and the so-called Middle Kingdom, stretching from the Rhineland to Rome, went to Lothair, along with the imperial title. When Lothair's line died out in 856, a civil war erupted between the East Franks and the West Franks for control over Lothair's former territories and the imperial mantle. These territories, known as Lotharingia (or, in French, Alsace-Lorraine), would remain a flashpoint for hostilities between France and Germany until the end of World War II.

Louis was not an incompetent ruler, but he faced an almost impossible task in trying to hold together the empire his father had created. Charlemagne's empire had been built on successful conquest. By 814, however, Charlemagne had pushed the borders of his empire as far as they could reasonably go. The pressures that had driven the Frankish conquests, however—the need for booty, land, and plunder with which to reward and promote one's followers—had become even more pronounced as a result of Charlemagne's successes. Under Charlemagne, the number of counts in the Frankish empire had tripled, from approximately 100 to 300. Louis the Pious could not possibly turn 300 counts into 900. The resources to do so simply did not exist.

Frustrated by their emperor's inability to reward them, Frankish nobles turned on each other. Civil wars erupted among Louis's quarrelsome and difficult sons; regional hostilities among Austrasians, Neustrians, and Aquitanians flared up again. As central imperial authority broke down, free peasants, a critical group in the eighth-century Carolingian world, found themselves increasingly under the thumb of powerful local nobles who treated them as if they were unfree serfs, bound to the soil and forbidden to leave it. At the same time, internal troubles in the Abbasid Empire caused a breakdown in the foreign trade routes through which Viking traders brought Abbasid silver into Carolingian domains. The Vikings then turned to destructive raiding along the coasts and up the river systems. Under these combined pressures the Carolingian Empire fell apart completely, and a new political map of Europe began to emerge.

THE VIKINGS

Scandinavian traders were already familiar figures in the North Sea and Baltic ports of Europe when the Carolingian era began. Starting in the 790s, however, Scandinavian raiders (known to their enemies as Vikings, a word meaning "robbers") began to attack the coastal ports of northern Europe. Initially, these raids were driven by the desire for profit through plunder, ransom, tribute collection, and slaving. By the mid-ninth century, however, some Viking attacks involved organized armies with thousands of men, whose aim was to conquer and settle independent principalities in England, Scotland, Ireland, and northern France.

By the early eleventh century Vikings had also established settlements in Iceland, Greenland, and Newfoundland; Viking leaders ruled principalities in Scotland, Ireland, Normandy ("the land of the Northmen"—that is, the Vikings), and Russia; and a Viking army had just placed King Cnut of Denmark on the throne of England. Thereafter, however, the threat of Viking attacks lessened. In Scandinavia, conversion to Christianity proceeded rapidly from the late tenth century on; in France, Scotland, Ireland, and England, Viking rulers and settlers were rapidly assimilated into the cultural and political world of northwestern Europe. In 1066, an army of Norman Vikings conquered England at the Battle of Hastings; but to the conquered English (many of whom were themselves the descendants of Viking invaders), their Norman conquerors in 1066 were perceived as Frenchmen rather than Vikings.

The impact of the Vikings on Europe continues to be controversial. Although the destructiveness of Viking raids is undeniable, the Vikings were not the only source of disorder in the ninth and tenth centuries. Civil wars in Carolingian France, Muslim attacks in southern Italy and Provence, Hungarian attacks in southeastern Germany, and local political rivalries nearly everywhere contributed to the chaos of the post-Carolingian world. Nor were the Vikings solely a source of disorder. In Ireland and eastern England, Vikings founded a series of new towns where they mass-produced high-quality pottery for the first time since the Roman period. As long-distance traders, Vikings transported large quantities of silver into western Europe from the Abbasid Empire, fueling the European economy. And as we shall see in a moment, in those areas of Europe where rulers did succeed in fending off Viking attacks, the prestige resulting from their victories enabled them to construct much more powerful kingdoms and principalities than had existed before. By focusing so many of their raids on monasteries, the Vikings destroyed much of the intellectual and cultural work of the Carolingian renaissance. Nonetheless, the wide geographical range of their influence, combined with their conversion to Latin Christianity, helped tighten the cultural and political links that bound the European world together.

THE LEGACY OF THE CAROLINGIANS

The Carolingians' vision of a united, Christian Europe collapsed in the chaos of the ninth and tenth centuries. In its place, however, new political divisions within Europe began to emerge that would have decisive consequences for the future. England, which had never been part of Charlemagne's empire and which hitherto had been divided into at least half a dozen small kingdoms at war with each other, emerged as a unified kingdom for the first time under King Alfred the Great (871–899) and his successors. Alfred and his heirs reorganized the army, reformed local government, founded new towns, and codified English laws. In addition, Alfred established a court school and fostered an interest in Anglo-Saxon writing and other elements of a national culture. In all these respects, Alfred modeled himself closely on Carolingian example. The increasing prosperity of the country, largely a product of the wool trade, also brought increasing power to the monarchy. By the year 1000, Anglo-Saxon England had become the most administratively sophisticated state in western Christian Europe.

On the Continent, the most powerful monarchs of the tenth century were the dukes of Saxony, who became kings of Germany (East Francia) in 917 after the Carolingian line of kings expired. Like the West Saxon kings of England, the Saxon kings of Germany modeled their kingship closely on Carolingian example. In Germany, however, royal power in the tenth century rested more on the profits of successful conquest than it did on trade and administration. In the eighth century, the Carolingians had built their power on successful conquests in Saxony. In the tenth century, the Ottonian kings of Germany, based in Saxony, built their authority on successful conquests into the Slavic lands that lay on their "soft" eastern frontier.

They were also careful to nurture their image as Christian kings on the Carolingian model. In 955, Otto I defeated the pagan Hungarians in a decisive battle while carrying a sacred lance that had once belonged to Charlemagne. This victory established Otto as the dominant power in central Europe and as a man worthy to inherit Charlemagne's imperial throne. In 962 Otto went to Rome to be crowned western emperor by the pope, a thoroughly dissolute young man named John XII, who hoped to use Otto in his own factional squabbles in Rome. Otto, however, refused to go home when Pope John had no further use for him. Scandalized by John's behavior as pope, Otto instead deposed John and selected a new pope to replace him.

By becoming emperor, Otto hoped to strengthen his control over the church in Germany and to claim a variety of potentially lucrative imperial rights in northern Italy and Burgundy, parts of the Middle Kingdom once held by the emperor Lothair. Protecting the papacy was, of course, Otto's responsibility as a Carolingian-style emperor, but Otto also needed papal support to achieve these other, more concrete objectives. In Italy, however, Otto quickly discovered that unless he was prepared to remain in Rome full time, he could not even control the papacy, much less the rapidly growing and highly independent towns of northern Italy. If he remained in Italy too long, however, his authority in Saxony would break down, as local lords began to lead and profit from the continuing conquests in the Slavic east. Balancing their local concerns in Saxony with their imperial concerns in Italy presented a dilemma neither Otto I nor his son (Otto II, 973–983) nor his grandson (Otto III, 983–1002) was able to solve. The result was a gradually increasing alienation of the Saxon

> The increasing prosperity of the country, largely a product of the wool trade, also brought increasing power to the monarchy. By the year 1000, Anglo-Saxon England had become the most administratively sophisticated state in western Christian Europe.

How did Charlemagne redefine the relationship between Christianity and kingship?

The Rise of the Carolingians   201

nobility from their emperor. This alienation accelerated dramatically after 1024, when the German throne passed to a new dynasty, the Salians, centered not in Saxony but in Franconia. It was not until the 1070s that the Salian king Henry IV attempted to reassert his control over the formerly royal lands in Saxony and the Slavic east. When he did so, he touched off a civil war between himself and the Saxon nobility that was to have momentous repercussions not only for Germany but for the entirety of western Europe. The consequences of this great Saxon war are discussed more fully in Chapter Nine.

EUROPE IN THE ELEVENTH CENTURY

This map shows the alignment of geopolitical power that had emerged by 1050. Based on the map, which political entities would you expect to dominate the twelfth-century European world? Why? Consider the geographical position of Kievan Russia. What influences pulled it toward the West? In what respects was it isolated from the West?

The tenth century also witnessed a remarkable growth of towns and cities in western Europe, particularly in areas where rulers patterned themselves on Carolingian example. In Anglo-Saxon England, the West Saxon kings established new towns and encouraged existing ones. By 1066, when England fell to the invading Normans, at least 10 percent of the English population lived in towns, making it the most highly urbanized country in eleventh-century Europe. Cities also grew rapidly in the Low Countries and the Rhineland, fueled by long-distance trade (especially in wool and wool cloth) and by the discovery of silver deposits in the mountains of Saxony. In Catalunya, the growth of Barcelona was beginning to transform the political and social life of the country; while in Aquitaine, both Poitiers and Toulouse prospered from their location along the overland trade route that connected the Mediterranean with Atlantic Europe.

In tenth- and eleventh-century Italy, however, urban growth occurred in the absence of an effective Carolingian-style ruler. Instead, the prosperity of tenth-century Italian cities depended on the success of the Byzantine emperors in suppressing Muslim piracy in the eastern Mediterranean. The most prosperous cities in tenth-century Italy lay in the Byzantine-controlled areas of the peninsula: Venice in the north, Amalfi, Naples, and Palermo in the south. Their prosperity rested on their role in the trade that brought silks, spices, and other luxury goods from the Byzantine and Muslim worlds into western Europe. In the eleventh century, however, Norman invasions of southern Italy disrupted this trade, as Turkish invasions of Asia Minor turned Byzantine attentions eastward. By the end of the eleventh century, it would be the north Italian cities whose navies controlled the eastern Mediterranean and that would profit from their role as middlemen in the lucrative traffic among Byzantium, the Muslim world, and western Europe.

On the Carolingian heartland, however, these developments had little influence. Here, Carolingian-style kingship disintegrated during the tenth century under the combined weight of Viking raids, economic collapse, and the growing power of local lords. In some areas, a few Carolingian institutions, such as public courts and a centrally minted coinage, survived in the hands of counts and dukes who used them in building up new, essentially autonomous territorial principalities such as Anjou, Normandy, Flanders, and Aquitaine. Elsewhere in France, even this modicum of continuity with the Carolingian world disappeared. France still had a king who continued to be recognized as the ruler of the western part of Charlemagne's former territories. After 987, however, the kings of France were no longer Carolingians. Instead, a new dynasty, the Capetians, had taken the throne, after having established their reputation as counts of Paris by defending that city against the Vikings. But it would be another century before the Capetian kings of France could reverse the trends that had destroyed their predecessors and begin to rebuild monarchical power in France on new foundations.

Conclusion

This spectacle of Carolingian collapse may suggest that little had changed in western Europe between 750 and 1000. Any such impression would, however, be seriously misleading. It is certainly true that compared with Byzantium or the Muslim world, western Europe remained an intellectual and cultural backwater, more so perhaps by the year 1000 than it had been two centuries before. Politically, no western European ruler in the year 1000 could approach the power of the Byzantine emperor or the Umayyad caliph of Córdoba. Economically also, western Europe was a dependency of Byzantium and Islam, importing finished and luxury goods, and exporting furs, leather, and slaves. Beneath the surface, however, western European society was becoming steadily more formidable. Urbanization was proceeding rapidly on the margins of the collapsing Carolingian world. Long-distance trade was growing and Europe's borders were expanding. By the year 1000, its boundaries extended from the Baltic to the Mediterranean Sea, and from the Pyrenees to Poland. Within this vast territory, moreover, every ruler was, or would soon be, Christian. The Latin Christian church was as yet highly localized, but the emergence of new confederations of reformed Benedictine monasteries (discussed in more detail in Chapter Nine) was beginning to point the way toward a more unified and centralized church. Political omens were less promising. But out of the chaos of tenth-century western Europe, effective territorial principalities and kingdoms were beginning to emerge. During the early Middle Ages, Europe had become a society mobilized for war to a degree unmatched in either Byzantium or the Islamic world. This was, to be sure, a mixed blessing. In the centuries to come, however, the militarization of western European society was to prove a decisive factor in the steadily shifting balance of power among Europe, Byzantium, and the Muslim world.

KEY TERMS

Santa Sophia	Mecca	caliphs	Shiites	Pope Gregory I
caravans	Qur'an	harem	Sunnism	Charlemagne
Muhammad	mosque	Shiism	Sufism	

SELECTED READINGS

Bede. *A History of the English Church and People.* Trans. Leo Sherley-Price. Baltimore, Md., 1955. A fascinating account by the greatest historian of eighth-century Europe.

Saint Boniface. *Letters of Saint Boniface.* Trans. Ephraim Emerton. New York, 1972.

Campbell, James, ed. *The Anglo-Saxons.* Oxford, 1982. The best and most interesting treatment of its subject, splendidly illustrated.

Collins, Roger. *Early Medieval Europe, 300–1000.* 2d ed. New York, 1999. Dry and detailed, but a useful textbook nonetheless.

Einhard and Notker the Stammerer. *Two Lives of Charlemagne.* Trans. Lewis Thorpe. Baltimore, Md., 1969. Lively and entertaining.

Geanakoplos, Deno John, ed. *Byzantium: Church, Society and Civilization Seen through Contemporary Eyes.* Chicago, 1984. An outstanding source book, with a great deal of fresh material.

Geary, Patrick J. *Before France and Germany: The Origins and Transformation of the Merovingian World.* New York, 1988. Accessible introduction to recent scholarship, much of it otherwise unavailable in English.

Gregory of Tours. *History of the Franks.* Trans. Lewis Thorpe. Baltimore, Md., 1974. Difficult to follow, but by far the most revealing single source on Merovingian kingship.

Gregory, Timothy E. *A History of Byzantium.* Oxford and Malden, Mass., 2005. The most accessible of the recent textbooks on Byzantium. An excellent place to start.

Herrin, Judith. *The Formation of Christendom.* Princeton, N.J., 1987. A synthetic history of the Christian civilizations of Byzantium and western Europe from 500 to 800, written by a prominent Byzantinist.

Hodges, Richard, and David Whitehouse. *Mohammed, Charlemagne and the Origins of Europe.* London, 1983. An analysis and recasting of the "Pirenne thesis," which claimed (wrongly, as this book shows) that the advent of Islam disrupted the economic unity of the Mediterranean world.

Hourani, Albert. *A History of the Arab Peoples.* New York, 1992. A sympathetic, clear, and intelligent survey written for non-specialists.

Kazhdan, Alexander P., ed. *The Oxford Dictionary of Byzantium.* 3 vols. Oxford, 1991. An authoritative reference work.

Kennedy, Hugh. *The Early Abbasid Caliphate: A Political History.* Totowa, N.J., 1981. A standard account.

Kennedy, Hugh. *The Prophet and the Age of the Caliphates.* London, 1986. A lucid introduction to the political history of Islam from the sixth through the eleventh centuries.

McKitterick, Rosamond. *The Frankish Kingdoms under the Carolingians, 751–987.* New York, 1983. An authoritative account of politics and intellectual developments.

McKitterick, Rosamond, ed. *The Uses of Literacy in Early Medieval Europe.* New York, 1990. A superb collection of essays representing some of the freshest recent thinking on this subject.

Reuter, Timothy. *Germany in the Early Middle Ages, 800–1056.* New York, 1991. The best survey in English.

Sawyer, Peter, ed. *The Oxford Illustrated History of the Vikings.* Oxford, 1997. The best one-volume account, lavishly illustrated.

Stillman, Norman A. *The Jews of Arab Lands: A History and Source Book.* Philadelphia, 1979. An essential resource.

Wallace-Hadrill, John Michael. *The Frankish Church.* Oxford, 1983. A masterful account that links together the Merovingian and the Carolingian churches.

Watt, W. Montgomery. *Islamic Philosophy and Theology.* 2d ed. Edinburgh, 1985. The standard English account.

Whittow, Mark. *The Making of Orthodox Byzantium, 600–1025.* London, 1996. Emphasizes the centrality of orthodoxy in shaping Byzantine history. Particularly good on Byzantine relations with the peoples outside the empire.

Wood, Ian. *The Merovingian Kingdoms, 450–751.* New York, 1994. Full of the latest thinking, but detailed and difficult for beginners.

CHAPTER EIGHT

THE EXPANSION OF EUROPE: ECONOMY, SOCIETY, AND POLITICS IN THE HIGH MIDDLE AGES, 1000–1300

BETWEEN 1000 AND 1300, the balance of power among western Europe, Byzantium, and the Islamic world shifted profoundly. In the year 1000, Europe remained politically fractured and militarily threatened by Viking, Hungarian, and Muslim attacks. Although towns in western Europe were beginning to grow, none could compare in size or sophistication with the cities of Byzantium and the Islamic world. Economically, western Europe continued to depend on Byzantine and Islamic traders for its cotton, silk, spices, and gold. With respect to literature and learning, the imbalances were even greater. Europeans had access to only a small portion of the cultural and intellectual riches Byzantium and Islam had inherited from the classical world. Outside Sicily, Venice, and the Muslim-controlled areas of Spain, western Europeans knew no Arabic and virtually no Greek. Even Latin, the language of Western learning for more than 1,000 years, was increasingly a foreign tongue.

By the year 1300, however, Europe was the dominant military, economic, and political power among the three Western successor civilizations to Greece and Rome. Hungary, Poland, Scandinavia, and Bohemia were now thoroughly integrated parts of a Catholic, European world. Combining conquest with conversion, European Christians had forcefully pushed their borders eastward into Prussia, Lithuania, Livonia, and the Balkans. They had conquered Spain from the Muslims and Constantinople from the Byzantines. They had also established (and in 1300, just lost) a Latin kingdom in the Middle East, with its capital at Jerusalem. European navies controlled the Mediterranean Sea and had outposts on the Black Sea and the Caspian Sea, allowing European traders to dominate the long-distance trade routes that brought Eastern luxury goods into western Europe. European missionaries and traders were beginning to follow these trade routes back through Central Asia, opening up connections with Mongolia and China. To the west, Italian merchants had initiated a seaborne trade route through the Strait of Gibraltar, thus connecting the Mediterranean and the north Atlantic world.

FOCUS QUESTIONS

- What impact did the medieval agricultural revolution have on the lives of Europeans?

- What were the major causes of urban growth during the High Middle Ages?

- How did the First Crusade alter the balance of power between Europe and Byzantium?

- What was the relationship between chivalry and the cult of courtly love?

- How did government and politics change during the High Middle Ages?

- What was the relationship between feudalism and the rise of national monarchies?

This expansion of European commerce, both local and long distance, was accompanied by significant urbanization. By 1300, Europe could claim at least a dozen cities with populations between 50,000 and 100,000 people, with hundreds of smaller towns and cities scattered across the landscape. The growth of cities mirrored the general growth in the European population which, on a rough estimate, tripled between 1000 and 1300. The economy grew even more rapidly, however, leading to increased per capita wealth and a rising standard of living. By no means, however, were these economic gains distributed equally among the entire population. Governments grew more powerful, and social stratification increased. New wealth increased the demand for luxury goods among social elites and freed up huge sums of money for investment in agriculture, commerce, and construction. It also fueled remarkable new religious, cultural, and intellectual developments, which will be discussed in the next chapter.

THE MEDIEVAL AGRICULTURAL REVOLUTION

What impact did the medieval agricultural revolution have on the lives of Europeans?

Like all premodern economies, the western European economy in the Middle Ages rested on agriculture. Between 700 and 1300, however, revolutionary changes occurred in European farming techniques. Technological innovations combined with a warming climate and a new crop-rotation system; and increased investments in tools, livestock, and mills brought dramatic improvements in agricultural productivity. As productivity increased, so too did the marketing of agricultural surpluses, leading to increasingly specialized and efficient agriculture. Without these changes, western Europe could never have supported the tripling of its overall population or the massive investments in buildings, ships, books, armies, and art that shaped the high medieval world.

TECHNOLOGICAL ADVANCES

The basic technological advances that made possible the increasing productivity of high medieval agriculture were developed in the early Middle Ages. The heavy-wheeled plow, fitted with an iron-tipped coulter and dragged by a team of oxen or horses, could cut and turn the rich, wet soil of northern Europe to a depth impossible for the Mediterranean scratch plow to reach, thus aerating the soil and providing excellent drainage for water-logged territories. The new plow also saved labor, allowing more frequent plowing and better control of weeds.

Despite the advent of the heavy-wheeled plow, most of the work of raising crops continued to be done by individual peasant farmers using hand tools. As iron became more common during the High Middle Ages, the efficiency of hand tools steadily improved. Wheelbarrows were another homely but important technological innovation. Technology also had an impact on cooking techniques. Iron pots allowed food to be boiled rather than just warmed, reducing the chances of contamination; cooking food in communal ovens preserved more nutrients than did boiling.

Mills represented another major technological innovation in food processing. The Romans had known about water mills but relied mainly on human- and animal-powered wheels to grind grain into flour. Starting around 1050, however, there was a veritable craze in northern Europe for building water mills of steadily increasing efficiency. Once Europeans had mastered the complex technology of building water mills, they turned their attention to windmills, which proliferated rapidly from the 1170s on, especially in flat lands such as Holland that had no swiftly flowing streams. Although the major use of mills was to grind grain, they could be adapted to drive saws, process cloth, press oil, provide power for iron forges, and crush pulp for manufacturing paper. The importance of such mills cannot be overstated. They would remain the world's only source of mechanical power for manufacturing until the eighteenth-century invention of the steam engine.

With the exception of the windmill, most of the technological innovations that lay behind the medieval agricultural revolution were already known to the Carolingians. Only from the mid-eleventh century, however, did these innovations become sufficiently widespread as to have a decisive effect on European agricultural production. Various explanations for this delay have been offered, but the fundamental change lay in the growing confidence of entrepreneurial peasants and lords that if they invested labor and money in agricultural improvements, they would profit from the resulting surpluses.

More than anything else, it was the expanding demand for agricultural produce that encouraged peas-

WHAT IMPACT DID THE MEDIEVAL AGRICULTURAL REVOLUTION HAVE ON THE LIVES OF EUROPEANS?

THE MEDIEVAL AGRICULTURAL REVOLUTION   207

The Heavy Plow. The major innovation of the heavy plow (often wheeled) was the long moldboard, which turned over the ground after the plowshare cut into it. The picture shows a second crucial medieval invention as well—the padded horse collar, which allowed horses to throw their full weight into pulling.

ants and landlords to make productive investments in the land. Behind the growing demand for foodstuffs lay the two fundamental economic factors that drove the high medieval economy forward: a rapidly increasing European population and an increasingly efficient market for goods.

MANORIALISM, SERFDOM, AND AGRICULTURAL PRODUCTIVITY

In England, northern France, and western Germany, increasing use of the heavy-wheeled plow between 800 and 1050 coincided with an important change in patterns of peasant settlement. During the early Middle Ages, most free peasant farmers lived on individual plots of land that they farmed with their own resources and for which they paid their landlord some kind of customary rent. Starting in the ninth century, however, many of these individual peasant holdings began to be consolidated into large, common fields that were farmed communally by peasants living in villages. The resulting complex of rents, renders, dues, fines, and fields is sometimes called a "manor."

> Behind the growing demand for foodstuffs lay the two fundamental economic factors that drove the high medieval economy forward: a rapidly increasing European population and an increasingly efficient market for goods.

In some areas, the impetus for these changes in settlement patterns probably came from the peasants themselves. Large common fields and pastures allowed villagers to experiment with new crops, to plow more efficiently, and to support larger numbers of animals. Peasants living together in a village might be able to support communal institutions such as a parish church, a communal oven, a blacksmith, and a tavern. In a difficult natural environment, help from neighbors could be an enormous advantage.

Elsewhere, however, manorialism was imposed by lords, who found it easier to control peasants living in villages than peasants living on scattered individual farms. Manorialism also allowed lords to claim a larger share of their peasants' agricultural production. On many manors, the common fields were divided into narrow strips assigned to individual peasants, for which each peasant landholder paid rent to the lord, but from which each peasant took the profits. In addition to their rents, however, most lords also claimed a third to a half of the total acreage in the common fields as their own land, from which they took all the produce for their own use. To farm this land, manorial lords imposed or increased labor services on peasant farmers, reducing many formerly free peasants to the status of serfs.

Serfs had existed in Europe for centuries, even in areas where the manorial system never took hold. There is no doubt, however, that the number of serfs increased in manorialized areas. Unlike free peasants, serfs could not leave their land or their lord without his permission. Serfs worked for their lords regularly without pay; paid humiliating fines to their lord when they fornicated illicitly, married, or died; and were subject to the jurisdiction of their lord's manorial court. Like slaves, their servile status was heritable; but unlike slaves, their obligations to their lord were fixed by custom, and they were not supposed to be sold apart from the lands they held.

NEW CROP-ROTATION SYSTEMS

From the standpoint of agrarian productivity, the greatest advantage of the manorial system was the fact that it made possible the adoption of new, more efficient crop-rotation systems. For centuries, farmers had known that if they sowed the same crop on the same land year after year, they would eventually exhaust the soil. The traditional solution to this difficulty was to divide one's land, planting half in the fall to harvest in the spring, and leaving the other half to lie fallow. In the Mediterranean, this remained the most common cropping pattern throughout the Middle Ages. In the wet, fertile soils of northern Europe, however, farmers slowly discovered that a three-field crop-rotation system could produce a sustainable increase in overall agricultural production. Under this system, one third

of the land would lie fallow, often being used for pasturage, so that the animals' droppings would fertilize the soil; one third would be planted with winter wheat or rye, which was sown in the fall and harvested in the early summer; and one third would be planted with another crop (usually oats, legumes, or barley) that could be sown in the spring and harvested in the fall. The fields were then rotated over a three-year cycle.

This system immediately increased the amount of land under cultivation in any given year. It also produced higher yields per acre of wheat and rye. With two separate growing seasons, the system provided some insurance against loss from natural disasters. It also produced new types of food. Oats could be consumed by both humans and horses, while legumes provided a source of protein to balance the major intake of cereal carbohydrates from bread and beer, the two main staples of the peasant diet in northern and central Europe. The new crop-rotation system also helped spread labor more evenly over the course of the year, allowing more careful attention to weed control, liming, and fertilizing of the common fields.

SERFDOM AND THE LIMITS OF MANORIALISM

It is important to remember that, by and large, the manorial system was limited to England, northern France, and western Germany. Even in these areas, moreover, it was beginning to break down by the end of the twelfth century, as lords began to commute labor services into cash payments, to free their serfs (again in return for cash payments), and to live from rents rather than from the actual agricultural produce of their estates.

The reasons for the decline of serfdom during the thirteenth century are complex and did not affect all areas of Europe equally. As the European economy became increasingly monetarized, many lords simply found it more convenient to collect their revenues directly from their peasants in cash, rather than taking the risks associated with marketing agricultural produce directly. In England and Catalunya, however, which had two of the most thor-

Peasants Harvesting Grain. This illustration, drawn around 1340, shows two women harvesting grain with sickles, while a third woman stretches out her back and a man bundles up the sheaves.

WHAT WERE THE MAJOR CAUSES OF URBAN GROWTH DURING THE HIGH MIDDLE AGES?

THE GROWTH OF TOWNS AND COMMERCE   209

oughly commercialized agricultural economies in medieval Europe, serfdom lasted longer than almost anywhere else in western Europe. In Austria and Poland, which were far less monetized, serfdom also increased during the thirteenth century, as it did in northern Spain. There is thus no simple correlation between commercialization and the decline of serfdom. In most of Europe, however, the generalization holds: serfs and free peasants became increasingly indistinguishable during the thirteenth century as lords freed serfs in return for cash. Even in France, however, some servile obligations would continue to exist as nagging indignities right down to the French Revolution in 1789. And in central and eastern Europe and Russia, serfdom underwent a resurgence during the later Middle Ages that would carry it into the eighteenth and nineteenth centuries.

THE GROWTH OF TOWNS AND COMMERCE

What were the major causes of urban growth during the High Middle Ages?

This agricultural revolution was the foundation on which the commercial revolution of the High Middle Ages rested. Here too, the groundwork for new developments had been laid in the ninth and tenth centuries, especially around the North Sea, where a lively trade among England, Flanders, and the Rhineland was fueled by silver production from the Harz Mountains in Saxony. During the eleventh and twelfth centuries, however, the greatest developments in long-distance commerce took place in the burgeoning cities of northern Italy. The growing prosperity of western European nobles and churchmen created an expanding market for Eastern luxury goods, while the improved domestic security of high medieval Europe made it possible for merchants to provide such goods with at least a modicum of security and safety. In the twelfth century, an organized system of fairs emerged in the central French region of Champagne, where Flemish merchants sold cloth to Italians, and Italian merchants sold Muslim spices and Byzantine silks to Flemish, French, and German merchants. By 1300, however, these fairs were declining, as Italian merchants succeeded in opening up a direct route by sea between Italy and Atlantic ports of northern Europe.

COMMERCE

Long-distance trade was a risky enterprise. Piracy was commonplace, and the Mediterranean Sea was notoriously dangerous to sailors and their ships. To facilitate investment in such a risky business, Italian merchants developed new forms of commercial partnership contracts, new methods of accounting, and new credit mechanisms, some of which they borrowed from Byzantine and Muslim examples. Some of these new credit arrangements ran afoul of the Western Christian church, which condemned almost all forms of money-lending as usury. But the demand for capital to fuel the new commercial economy was irresistible, and slowly attitudes began to change. From the thirteenth century on, leading churchmen also began to speak more favorably of merchants. Saint Bonaventura, a thirteenth-century Italian Franciscan, argued, for example, that in Old Testament times, God had shown special favor to shepherds such as King David; in New Testament times, he had favored fishermen such as Saint Peter; but in modern times, God's favor now went out to merchants such as Saint Francis of Assisi.

It would be misleading, however, to think of the commercial revolution or the urban revolution of the High Middle Ages as principally the result of long-distance trade. Some towns did receive great stimulus from such trade, and the growth of such major cities as Venice (about 100,000 people in 1300) and Genoa (80,000) would have been impossible without it. But the prosperity of most towns, including such enormous cities as Paris, Florence, Milan, and London, depended primarily on the wealth of their surrounding hinterlands, from which they drew their food supplies, their raw materials, and the bulk of their population. The quickening of economic life in general was the major cause of urban growth during the High Middle Ages. Long-distance trade was but one aspect of this larger economic and commercial transformation of European life.

> To facilitate investment in such a risky business, Italian merchants developed new forms of commercial partnership contracts, new methods of accounting, and new credit mechanisms, some of which they borrowed from Byzantine and Muslim examples.

TOWNS

Towns, both large and small, depended on the countryside around them. Towns provided markets and manufactured goods, lived off the rural food surplus, and expanded through the immigration of free peasants and escaped serfs in search of a better life. Once towns started to flourish, many of them began to specialize in certain enterprises. Paris and Bologna became the homes of leading universities; Venice, Genoa, Cologne, and London became centers of long-distance trade; Milan, Florence, Ghent, and Bruges specialized

MEDIEVAL TRADE ROUTES

This map details the routes by which long-distance trade moved in and around Europe during the eleventh century. What was the relationship between trade routes and rivers, and why? Why was the agricultural revolution and the revival of trade crucial to the extension of major trade routes in the West? What factors led to the intense proliferation of trade routes among England, Bruges, and the Rhine Valley? What trade patterns emerged as different regions began specializing in certain goods?

WHAT WERE THE MAJOR CAUSES OF URBAN GROWTH DURING THE HIGH MIDDLE AGES?

THE GROWTH OF TOWNS AND COMMERCE   211

View of Paris. The city looked this way at the end of the Middle Ages, around 1480. Note the prominence of the Cathedral of Notre Dame in the center and the large number of other church spires; note, too, how closely all the buildings are packed behind the walls.

in manufactures. The most important urban industries were those devoted to the making and finishing of wool (and in Venice, cotton) cloth. Most urban manufacturing was done by individual artisans in small, privately owned workshops whose production was regulated by professional associations known as guilds.

Usually only master artisans, who were experts at their trade and ran their own shops, were allowed to be full voting members of a craft guild. As a result, guilds generally promoted the interests of their richest and most successful members by trying to preserve monopolies and limit competition. If an apprentice or a journeyman (someone who had completed his apprenticeship but still worked for a master craftsman) wished to become a master, he had to produce a "masterpiece" for judging by the masters of the guild. Craft guilds controlled prices and wages, prohibited afterhours work, and formulated detailed regulations governing methods of production and the quality of materials to be used by their members. They also served important social functions as religious associations, benevolent societies, and drinking clubs, looking

after their members in times of trouble and supporting the dependents of a master craftsman who died.

Merchants also established guilds, which in some towns became so powerful that membership in a merchant guild became a prerequisite for service in town government. Merchant guilds sought to maintain a monopoly of the local market for their members by restricting competition and enforcing uniform pricing. Often they also controlled admissions to citizenship in the city. By their nature, guilds were exclusionary organizations. Because they were explicitly Christian, they were almost invariably closed to Jews and Muslims. They also significantly restricted the economic opportunities available to ordinary wage earners, and especially to women. Women were not automatically excluded from most guilds, and a few craft guilds were specifically female. But, despite the important role women played as urban wage earners, the male-dominated guilds ensured that women would have no influence over the terms and conditions under which they worked or the wages they would be paid for their labor.

> But, despite the important role women played as urban wage earners, the male-dominated guilds ensured that women would have no influence over the terms and conditions under which they worked or the wages they would be paid for their labor.

To modern eyes, most medieval towns and cities would still have seemed half rural even in 1300. Streets were often unpaved, houses had gardens for raising vegetables, and farm animals were everywhere. Sanitary conditions were poor and the air reeked of excrement, both animal and human. Disease ran rampant, especially in the overcrowded neighborhoods where the poorest urban dwellers lived. At every level of urban society, however, fertility rates were low and infant mortality high. Most cities sustained their population only through continuing immigration from the countryside. Fire was a constant danger, and economic tensions and family rivalries could lead to bloody riots. Yet for all this, urban folk took great pride in their new cities and ways of life.

BYZANTIUM, ISLAM, AND THE CRUSADES

How did the First Crusade alter the balance of power between Europe and Byzantium?

As the power of the Abbasid caliphate declined during the ninth and tenth centuries, the Byzantine Empire expanded. By 1025, Byzantium's position had been transformed. After several centuries of missionary inactivity, ninth-century Byzantine missionaries, most famously Saints Cyril and Methodius, converted the Balkan Slavs to Orthodox Christianity, devising for them a written language known as Old Church Slavonic and creating the Cyrillic alphabet, which is still used today in Bulgaria, Serbia, and Russia. Military conquest quickly followed. By 1025, the Byzantines had firmly annexed Greece, Bulgaria, and modern-day Serbia to their empire. They had also established a military and commercial alliance with the western Rus kingdom centered around Kiev, decisively reorienting the Rus toward Constantinople and away from Islam.

THE BYZANTINE REVIVAL

Between the 930s and the 970s, the Byzantines also launched a series of successful campaigns against the Abbasids, reconquering territories that had not been in Byzantine hands since the seventh century. Although most of the peoples of the reconquered territories had remained Christian through three centuries of Islamic rule, the Armenians and the Syrians in particular had their own distinctive Christian traditions that were at odds, both doctrinally and linguistically, with the Greek-speaking church at Constantinople. For an empire that had defined itself for centuries on the basis of its orthodoxy (the word itself means "correct belief"), incorporating such "heretics" threatened the foundations on which the unity of the empire rested.

These eastern conquests also increased the power of the local noble families who led them, creating for the first time a center of power within the empire that lay outside the imperial capital at Constantinople. Tensions and rivalries between these Eastern noble families and the imperial officials at the capital disturbed Byzantine politics for most of the tenth century. After an attempted coup by the head of one such family, the emperor Basil II (976–1025) savagely suppressed the leading Eastern magnate families. But this check on the Eastern magnates' ambitions proved only temporary. After Basil's death, the imperial throne passed to a series of aged and incompetent relations. In the resulting power vacuum, noble military families came more and more to dominate the countryside; while at court, tax revenues decreased as imperial expenditures rose. To pay the bills, the emperors debased the Byzantine gold coinage, undermining Byzantine commerce precisely when Venice, Genoa, and Pisa were consolidating their control over the eastern Mediterranean trade routes. By 1081, when the Eastern magnate families triumphed by placing Alexius Comnenus on the imperial throne, the Byzantine Empire had been crippled as a Mediterranean power.

THE INVASION OF THE TURKS

By the late eleventh century, Byzantium faced new threats from several quarters. Venice, Genoa, and Pisa had emerged as the dominant naval powers in the east-

CHRONOLOGY

BYZANTINE EMPIRE, 900–1204

Successful campaigns against the Abbasid rulers	930–970
Russia converts to orthodoxy	911–989
Annexation of Greece, Bulgaria, and Serbia	1025
Turkish invasions (defeat of Manzikert)	1071
Reign of Alexius Comnenus	1081–1118
First Crusade	1095–1099
Fourth Crusade, capture of Constantinople	1204

HOW DID THE FIRST CRUSADE ALTER THE BALANCE OF POWER BETWEEN EUROPE AND BYZANTIUM?

BYZANTIUM, ISLAM, AND THE CRUSADES   213

ern Mediterranean and had to a considerable extent taken over the lucrative trade between Islamic North Africa and the West. The growing power of Fatimid Egypt was beginning to roll back Byzantine gains along the empire's southeastern frontier with Syria. But most disastrous of all, a new Sunni Muslim power, the Seljuk Turks, had emerged in Central Asia and had begun to move into Asia Minor, the very heartland

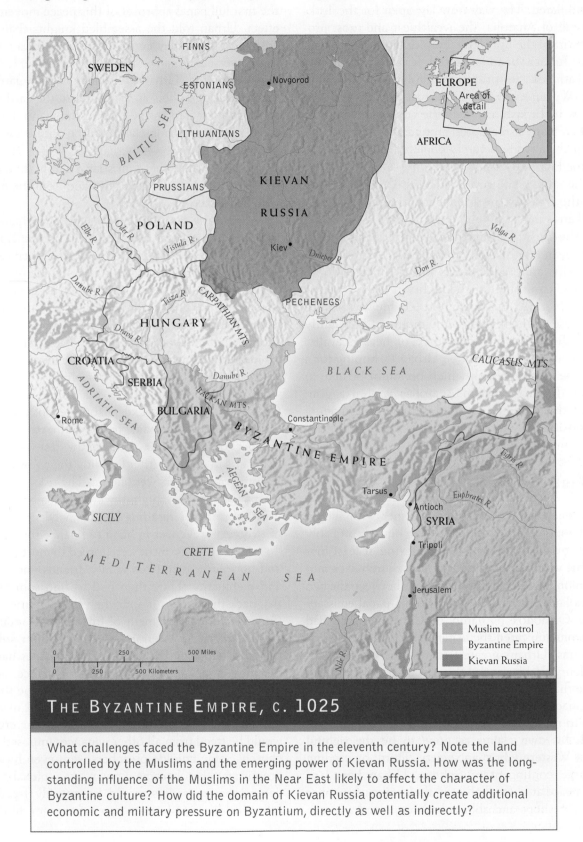

THE BYZANTINE EMPIRE, C. 1025

What challenges faced the Byzantine Empire in the eleventh century? Note the land controlled by the Muslims and the emerging power of Kievan Russia. How was the long-standing influence of the Muslims in the Near East likely to affect the character of Byzantine culture? How did the domain of Kievan Russia potentially create additional economic and military pressure on Byzantium, directly as well as indirectly?

of the Byzantine Empire. When the Turks captured Armenia, the emperor tried to eject them; but the Eastern noble families refused their support, and in the decisive battle of Manzikert (1071), the imperial army was annihilated. The way now lay open for the Turks to seize all of Anatolia, the wealthiest and most productive part of the Byzantine Empire. In the same year, another Turkish band captured Jerusalem from the Shiite Fatimids, restoring the Holy City to Sunni control. Within five years, almost all of Syria and Asia Minor lay in Turkish hands. In the west, a rebellion by the Balkan Slavs also erupted around this time, further reducing the already severely depleted treasury of the Byzantine Empire.

By the 1090s, however, Alexius Comnenus had rebuilt the treasury, restored Byzantine control over the Balkans, and was beginning to plan a campaign against the Turks. During the eleventh century, western European knights had emerged as the most effective heavily armored cavalry troops in the world. Alexius had confronted such knights in 1085, when he repelled a Norman invasion of Greece. He was anxious to make use of them against the mounted but lightly armored Turks. To recruit a force of heavy cavalry, Alexius sent a request to Pope Urban II, hoping for a few thousand troops with which he might be able to roll back Turkish gains in Anatolia. Within a year, however, the pope had set in motion a vast crusading army of 100,000 Westerners to retake the Holy City of Jerusalem for Christendom.

THE FIRST CRUSADE

The reasons that Urban's summons met with such a massive response are complex. Urban himself probably saw the crusade as a means for achieving at least four ends. One was to bring the Orthodox church back into communion with the papacy. Relations between the two churches had ruptured in 1054, when a papal emissary and the Orthodox patriarch of Constantinople had each excommunicated the other. A second motive was to embarrass Urban's greatest enemy, the German emperor Henry IV. Henry and the papacy had been at war for more than twenty years over their respective claims to supremacy within Christendom. By calling a mighty crusade to retake Jerusalem, Urban probably hoped to establish his own claims as pope to be the rightful leader of Western Christian society. Third, by sending off a large contingent of fighters, Urban hoped to achieve peace at home. Earlier in the century, a number of French bishops and abbots had supported a "peace movement" that prohibited attacks on noncombatants and prohibited fighting on certain holy days. At the 1095 ecclesiastical council at Clermont where he announced the First Crusade, Urban also promulgated the first full papal approval of this peace movement. In effect, Urban told the assembled knights that if they wished to fight, they could do so justly for a Christian cause overseas. Finally, the goal of Jerusalem itself genuinely inspired Urban. Jerusalem was regarded by medieval geographers as the center of the earth as well as the most sacred shrine of the Christian religion because it was Jesus' homeland. To the untutored knights of Western Europe, as perhaps to Urban himself, it seemed only right that Christian knights should assist their Lord Christ to recover his land from the Muslims who had seized it.

As with any large enterprise, the participants' motives for joining the crusade varied. Some hoped to win lands or establish principalities for themselves in the East. Others were drawn simply by the prospect of adventure. Many were dependents of greater men, accompanying their lords because it was their duty to do so. Some may have been motivated by obscure prophecies and apocalyptic fervor. Most probably had no idea how long a journey would be involved or even what direction they would be traveling.

But the dominant motive for going on the First Crusade was religious. Except for a few of the greatest lords—mostly Normans from southern Italy—the prospect of winning new lands in the East was both unlikely and undesired. After fulfilling their vows, the vast majority of crusaders went home. The risks of dying on such a journey were high; the costs of embarking on it were enormous. Crusading knights needed a minimum of two years' revenues in hand to finance their journey. To raise such sums, most were forced to mortgage lands and borrow heavily from family, friends, monasteries, and merchants. They then had to find some way to pay back these loans if and when they returned home. On any rational judgment of financial advantage, the crusade was a fool's errand. But it did offer solace to the Christian soul. For centuries pilgrimages had been the most popular type of Christian penance, and the pilgrimage to Jerusalem was considered to be the most sacred and efficacious one of all. Urban II made this point explicit at Clermont, promising that crusaders would be freed from all other penances imposed by the church. Some crusade preachers went even further by promising what became known as a plenary indulgence: that crusaders would be entirely freed from otherworldly punishments in purgatory for all the sins

CALLS TO CRUSADE, 1074–1100

These documents illustrate how appeals to Europeans to embark on a military expedition to the east developed between 1074 and c. 1100. The first selection is a letter from Pope Gregory VII in 1074 to all Christians. The second document is an account by Fulcher of Chartres of Pope Urban II's call at the Council of Clermont in 1095. Fulcher is thought to have attended the council.

POPE GREGORY VII'S CALL TO ASSIST THE GREEKS, MARCH 1074

Gregory, bishop, servant of the servants of God, to all who are willing to defend the Christian faith, greeting and apostolic benediction.

We hereby inform you that the bearer of this letter, on his recent return from across the sea came to Rome to visit us. He repeated what we had heard from many others, that a pagan race had overcome the Christians and, with horrible cruelty, had devastated everything almost to the walls of Constantinople, and were now governing the conquered lands with tyrannical violence, and that they had slain many thousands of Christians as if they were but sheep. If we love God and wish to be recognized as Christians, we should be filled with grief at the misfortune of this great empire and the murder of so many Christians. But simply to grieve is not our whole duty. The example of our Redeemer and the bond of fraternal love demand that we should lay down our lives to liberate them. . . . Know, therefore, that we are trusting in the mercy of God and in the power of his might and that we are striving in all possible ways and making preparations to render aid to the Christian empire as quickly as possible. Therefore, we beseech you by the faith in which you are united through Christ . . . and by the authority of Saint Peter, prince of the apostles, we admonish you that you be moved to proper compassion by the wounds and blood of your brethren and the danger of the aforesaid empire and that, for the sake of Christ, you undertake the difficult task of bearing aid to your brethren [that is, the Byzantines].

Send messengers to us at once to inform us what God may inspire you to do in this matter.

O. J. Thatcher and E. H. McNeal, eds., *A Sourcebook for Medieval History, Selected Documents Illustrating the History of Europe in the Middle Ages* (New York, 1905), pp. 512–513.

POPE URBAN II'S CALL AT CLERMONT, NOVEMBER 1095

Most beloved brethren: Urged by necessity, I, Urban, by the permission of God chief bishop and prelate over the whole world, have come into these parts as an ambassador with a divine admonition to you, the servants of God. . . .

Although, O sons of God, you have promised more firmly than ever to keep the peace among yourselves and to preserve the rights of the church, there remains still an important work for you to do. Freshly quickened by the divine correction, you must apply the strength of your righteousness to another matter which concerns you as well as God. For your brethren who live in the east are in urgent need of your help, and you must hasten to give them the aid which has often been promised them. For, as most of you have heard, the Turks and Arabs have attacked them and have conquered the territory of Romania [the Byzantine Empire] as far west as the shore of the

Mediterranean and the Hellespont, which is called the Arm of Saint George. They have occupied more and more of the lands of those Christians, and have overcome them in seven battles. They have killed and captured many, and have destroyed the churches and devastated the empire.

If you permit them to continue thus for a while with impunity, the faithful of God will be much more widely attacked by them. On this account I, or rather the Lord, beseech you as Christ's heralds to publish this everywhere and to persuade all people of whatever rank, footsoldiers and knights, poor and rich, to carry aid promptly to those Christians and to destroy that vile race from the lands of our friends. I say this to those who are present, but it is meant also for those who are absent. Moreover, Christ commands it.

All who die by the way, whether by land or by sea, or in battle against the pagans, shall have immediate remission of sins. This I grant them through the power of God with which I am invested. O what a disgrace, if such a despised and base race, which worships demons, should conquer a people which has the faith of omnipotent God and is made glorious with the name of Christ! With what reproaches will the Lord overwhelm us if you do not aid those who, with us, profess the Christian religion!

Let those who have been accustomed to wage unjust private warfare against the faithful now go against the infidels and end with victory this war which should have been begun long ago. Let those who for a long time have been robbers now become knights. Let those who have been fighting against their brothers and relatives now fight in a proper way against the barbarians. Let those who have been serving as mercenaries for small pay now obtain the eternal reward. Let those who have been wearing themselves out in both body and soul now work for a double honor. Behold! On this side will be the sorrowful and poor, on that, the rich; on this side, the enemies of the Lord, on that, his friends. Let those who go not put off the journey, but rent their lands and collect money for their expenses; and as soon as winter is over and spring comes, let them eagerly set out on the way with God as their guide.

S. J. Allen and Emilie Amt, eds., *The Crusades: A Reader* (Peterborough, Ont., Canada, 2003), pp. 39–40.

QUESTIONS FOR ANALYSIS

1. Do these letters help explain why Urban's call received so much more of a response than did Gregory's?
2. Consider the message implicit in Pope Gregory's and Urban's calls to the crusades. Why would king and commoner alike join a holy crusade to unknown and hostile lands?
3. Why do the authors of these letters present the oppression of Greek Christians primarily as a religious, rather than ethnic, problem?

they had committed up to that point in their lives, and that the souls of those who died on crusade would go straight to heaven.

Crusade preaching emphasized the vengeance that Christ's soldiers should exact on his enemies in the East. But to some crusaders, it seemed absurd to wait until they arrived in Jerusalem to undertake this aspect of their mission. Muslims might hold Jesus' property at Jerusalem, but Christian theology held Jews responsible for the death of Jesus himself. During the course of the eleventh century, Jewish communities had grown up in most of the larger cities of the Rhineland and in many of the smaller towns and cities of northern France. Assaults by bands of crusaders against Jewish communities began in northern France in the spring of 1096 and quickly spread to the Rhineland as the crusaders moved east. Hundreds of Jews were killed throughout western Europe, and hundreds more were forcibly baptized as the price for escaping death at the hands of crusading knights. Despite the efforts of church authorities to prevent them, attacks on Jews would remain a regular and predictable feature of Christian crusading thereafter.

> Despite the efforts of church authorities to prevent them, attacks on Jews would remain a regular and predictable feature of Christian crusading thereafter.

Surprised by the nature and scale of the Western response to his appeal, Alexius Comnenus did his best to move the crusaders quickly through Constantinople and into Asia Minor. Differences in outlook between the Western crusaders and the Byzantine emperor quickly became apparent, however. From Alexius's standpoint, the crusader army

How did the First Crusade alter the balance of power between Europe and Byzantium?

Byzantium, Islam, and the Crusades   217

was a threat, not least because it contained within it several of the Norman leaders who had attempted to conquer his empire only ten years earlier. The crusaders, however, saw themselves as on a mission from God. They did not understand the Byzantine emperor's willingness to make alliances with some Muslim rulers against other Muslim rulers, and they speedily concluded that the Byzantines were in fact working to undermine the crusading effort. Such suspicions were unfounded, but they contributed to a growing Western conviction that the Byzantine Empire itself was an obstacle to the successful recovery of Jerusalem for Christendom.

Against great odds the First Crusade succeeded. In 1098 the crusaders captured Antioch and with it most of the Syrian coast. At the end of 1099, they took Jerusalem, mercilessly slaughtering its inhabitants. Their success stemmed mainly from the fact that the crusaders' Muslim opponents were at that moment internally divided. The Fatimids had recaptured Jerusalem from the Turks just months before the crusaders arrived, and the Turks themselves were at war with each other. But Western military tactics, in particular the dominance in the open field of the heavily armored knights, also played an important role in the crusaders' success.

Equally critical was the naval support the First Crusade received from Genoa and Pisa, which hoped that a successful crusade would allow them to control the Indian spice trade that passed through the Red Sea and on to Alexandria in Egypt. In this respect, the First Crusade contributed to the further decline of Byzantine commerce, which was already suffering both from Italian competition in the Mediterranean and from the disruptive impact of the Turkish invasions on the trade routes that connected Constantinople with Baghdad and the silk route to China. All these trends were under way before the First Crusade began, but the establishment of the Latin kingdom accelerated them. To that extent, the First Crusade contributed significantly to the changing balance of power between Byzantium and western Europe.

The Later Crusades

The First Crusade had much less of an impact on the balance of power between the Islamic world and Europe. The crusader kingdom was never more than an underpopulated, narrow strip of colonies along the coastline of Syria and Palestine. So long as the crusaders did not control the Red Sea, the main routes of Islamic commerce with India and the Far East were unaffected by the change in Jerusalem's religious allegiance. Nor, for that matter, did the crusaders in any way wish to interfere with the overland caravan routes that led through their new territories. For the Muslims, the loss of Jerusalem was a religious affront much more than an economic one, and it was for religious reasons that they began to plan its recovery. By 1144, most of the crusader principalities in Syria had been recaptured. When Christian warriors led by the king of France and the emperor of Germany came east in the Second Crusade to recoup the losses, they suffered crushing defeats. Not long afterward, Syria and Egypt were united by the great Muslim leader Saladin, who finally recaptured Jerusalem in 1187. In response, the Third Crusade was launched, led by the German emperor Frederick Barbarossa, the French king Philip Augustus, and the English king Richard the Lionheart. This campaign also failed. Barbarossa drowned in Asia Minor on the way to Jerusalem, and Philip Augustus soon went home. Richard the Lionheart's heroic efforts enabled the Latin kingdom to survive for another century, but even he could not recapture Jerusalem.

The dream, however, did not die. When Innocent III became pope in 1198, his main ambition was to win back Jerusalem. He summoned the Fourth Crusade to that end, but it proved a disaster. Civil war in Germany, combined with war between England and France, severely reduced the number of knights willing to participate; and when the Venetians, who had contracted to transport the crusader army to the Holy Land, discovered that only half the predicted crusaders would arrive and that they would therefore not be properly paid, they diverted the crusade toward a successful attack on Constantinople itself in 1204. The result was an enormous commercial windfall for Venice, but the effective destruction of the Byzantine Empire, which for the next sixty years was divided into Latin-ruled and Greek-ruled provinces. In 1261 the Venetians' rivals, the Genoese, helped a new imperial claimant recover the Byzantine throne and, with it, control over Constantinople. But the Byzantine Empire was now reduced to little more than the city itself, leaving both Asia Minor and the Balkans open to their eventual conquest by the Ottoman Turks.

Despite the debacle of the Fourth Crusade, Western efforts to recover Jerusalem continued throughout the thirteenth century. Only in 1229, however, when the western Roman emperor Frederick II negotiated a treaty with the Egyptian sultan that returned Jerusalem to Christian control for a period of ten years, did any Western leader attempt to achieve this objective

KIEVAN STATE

Kiev

POLAND

HUNGARY

NORWAY

SWEDEN

SCOTLAND

IRELAND

ENGLAND

NORTH
SEA

DENMARK

BALTIC SEA

ATLANTIC

OCEAN

NORMANDY

MAINE

Metz

Vezelay

Regensburg

FRANCE

Clermont

HOLY
ROMAN
EMPIRE

Venice

CROATIA

Zara

SERBIA

BLACK SEA

LEON

PORTUGAL

NAVARRE

CASTILE

ARAGON

CATALUNYA

Marseilles

Genoa

Toledo

Cordoba

Rome

Constantinople

DOMINIONS OF THE
SELJUK TURKS

Edessa

EMPIRE

Granada

OF THE

ALMORAVIDS

Tunis

NORMAN

PRINCIPALITIES

BYZANTINE EMPIRE

Antioch

SULTANATE OF
DAMASCUS

RHODES

CYPRUS

Tripoli

Sidon

Tyre

Acre

Damascus

KINGDOM OF
JERUSALEM

MEDITERRANEAN   *SEA*

CRETE

Jaffa

Jerusalem

Bethlehem

Damietta

Alexandria

Cairo

CALIPHATE OF CAIRO

■ Population predominantly Christian
□ Population predominantly Muslim
→ First Crusade (1096–1099)
→ Second Crusade (1147–1149)
→ Third Crusade (1189–1192)
→ Fourth Crusade (1202–1204)
Boundaries shown are those at time of First Crusade

0   250   500 Miles
0   250   500 Kilometers

THE ROUTES OF THE CRUSADERS, 1096–1204

Compare the routes followed by the first three crusades. Why were they so similar? Why was the route of the Fourth Crusade so different? Why was Genoa so much more important than Venice as an embarkation point for crusaders?

directly. Instead, thirteenth-century crusades were aimed mainly at Egypt (1217–1219, 1248–1254) and, in 1270, Tunis. The crusaders' strategic goal was to cut the economic lifelines that supported Muslim control of the Holy Land. In explaining these later crusades, however, it becomes increasingly difficult to disentangle crusade-motivated calculations toward recapturing Jerusalem (which was, in any event, a shattered city with no walls and a tiny population) from the aspirations of Italian merchants to control the Far Eastern trade that ran through Egypt and the gold trade from sub-Saharan Africa that ran through Tunis. The great mercantile city of the thirteenth-century Latin king-

dom was Acre, not Jerusalem. Its fall in 1291 marked the end of any further Western expeditions to recover the Holy Land from Islam.

THE CONSEQUENCES OF THE CRUSADES

For Byzantium, the impact of the crusading movement was disastrous. The crusades coincided with, and to some extent caused, a decisive shift in the balance of economic and military power between western Europe and the faltering Byzantine Empire. On the Islamic

WHAT WAS THE RELATIONSHIP BETWEEN CHIVALRY AND THE CULT OF COURTLY LOVE?

SOCIAL MOBILITY AND SOCIAL INEQUALITY IN HIGH MEDIEVAL EUROPE   219

CHRONOLOGY

THE CRUSADES

First Crusade (recapture of Jerusalem)	1095–1099
Second Crusade (defeated by Seljuk Turks)	1145–1149
Third Crusade (Frederick Barbarossa and Richard the Lionheart)	1187–1192
Fourth Crusade (sack of Constantinople)	1201-1204
Fifth Crusade (capture of Damietta)	1217–1221
Peace treaty regains Jerusalem	1228–1229
Sixth Crusade (defeat of Louis IX of France)	1248–1254
Seventh Crusade (death of Louis IX of France)	1270

world, by contrast, the impact of the crusades was much more modest. Trade between Islam and the West continued despite periodic interruptions caused by crusader attacks on Syria, Egypt, and North Africa. The greatest economic gains went to Venice and Genoa; but Islamic merchants too came to depend increasingly on Western markets for their goods. Both sides also gained in military terms: Westerners learned new technques of fortification, and Muslims learned new methods of siege warfare and new respect for the uses of heavy cavalry. Finally, the crusades also helped crystallize both Christian and Islamic doctrines of holy war against the infidel. Neither Christian holy war nor Muslim *jihad* drew much doctrinally from the other. The collision between them, however, deepened the mutual hostility that already separated the Islamic world and Christian Europe.

The impact of the crusades on western Europe is more difficult to assess. From one standpoint, the crusades were an ultimately unsuccessful chapter in a generally successful story of Western expansionism during the High Middle Ages. In the Middle East, however, western Europeans could not maintain the colonies they established, and they were ultimately forced to withdraw. Nor did the crusades "open up" Europeans to a wider world of which they had previously known nothing. That wider world already existed in 1095, and Europeans were already part of it. Trade with the Islamic world did bring enormous prosperity to Italian

merchants, but these trading links had existed before the crusades and continued after they ended. Crusading may have even diminished, rather than increased, the economic and cultural exchange between western Europe and the Islamic world that might otherwise have taken place.

It would be wrong, however, to end our discussion of the crusades on such a minor note. A drive by Western merchants, backed by Western military force, to control the trade in spices, silks, and gold by "cutting out the Islamic middleman" is clearly visible in thirteenth-century crusading. This impulse would continue and would eventually lead to the creation of worldwide European mercantile and colonial empires from the sixteenth century on. Nor should we ignore or diminish the lasting influence of the crusading ideal on Europeans' image of themselves. Crusading had dramatic successes in Spain, where between 1100 and 1250 the kings of Castile and Portugal and the crown of Aragon led the reconquest of the Iberian peninsula from Islam. In Iberia particularly, crusading retained its ideological significance until the end of the sixteenth century, providing an important motivation behind the Portuguese and Spanish voyages of discovery during the fifteenth century and the conquest of the Americas during the sixteenth century. Crusading would also continue to color European relations with the Muslim world and especially with the Ottoman Turks, whose sixteenth-century conquests would lead them to the gates of Vienna and the borders of Italy. Even Napoleon, the last of the western Roman emperors, was not immune to the crusading ideal. He too would lead a successful, but short-lived, reconquest of Jerusalem.

SOCIAL MOBILITY AND SOCIAL INEQUALITY IN HIGH MEDIEVAL EUROPE

What was the relationship between chivalry and the cult of courtly love?

The increasing wealth of high medieval Europe transformed the social structure of European society. In the tenth century, it was still possible to describe European society as being divided among "those who worked, those who prayed, and those who fought." By 1300, however, new commercial and professional elites had emerged in the burgeoning cities of western Europe. By 1300, the wealthiest members of European society were merchants and bankers, not nobles. Nobles too found themselves drawn increasingly into the world of trade, despite their contempt for such "calculators." Nobles still fought, of course; but so too did knights, urban crossbowmen, peasant longbowmen, citizen militias, and peasant levies. Even work had become more complex. By 1300, half the peasants in England farmed plots of land too small to support their families. They survived, and sometimes even prospered, on a shifting combination of farming, wage labor, hunting, gathering, and charity. Such lines as existed between town and countryside were easily crossed. Schools of all sorts had emerged, and the products of those schools—lawyers, doctors, estate administrators, clerks, and government officials—made up a new and growing professional class that further complicated efforts to describe European society in terms of "three orders" of workers, prayers, and fighters.

NOBLES AND KNIGHTS

New wealth brought social mobility, but it also created a more highly stratified society, especially among the nobility. In the Carolingian period, the nobility made up a relatively small number of ancient families of approximately equal social rank who married among themselves. During the tenth and eleventh centuries, however, new families began to establish themselves as territorial lords. Some of these new families were descended from Carolingian officeholders; others were simply freebooters whose power rested on their control over castles, knights, and manors. Until the twelfth century, the old Carolingian noble families attempted to resist the claims of these new families to noble rank and status. By the end of the thirteenth century, however, a new nobility had emerged in western Europe that included these new families but that also made a series of careful distinctions in rank among dukes, counts, castellans (castle holders), and knights.

Knights were not necessarily nobles in the eleventh century. Some eleventh-century knights were the sons of great nobles, but others were little more than peasants mounted on horseback and armed with swords. As the costs of knightly equipment rose, however, the number of men who could afford the heavier horses, stronger swords, and improved armor that knights required declined dramatically. The style of domestic life expected of knights also became more elaborate and expensive. By 1300, knights throughout Europe were regarded as being part of the nobility.

CHIVALRY AND COURTLY LOVE

As the costs of knighthood rose, so too did its social prestige. From the mid-twelfth century on, the kings and nobles of Europe began to embrace and encourage the knightly code of values known as "chivalry," which stressed bravery, loyalty, generosity, skill with weapons, and proper manners as constituent elements in true nobility. *Chivalry* literally means "horsemanship," and mounted combat would for long remain the defining element in the European nobility's image of itself. First and foremost, however, chivalry was a social ideology that appealed to the knights and nobles of western Europe because it gave them a way

Images of Aristocracy. This early-fifteenth-century illustration, from the *Très Riches Heures* commissioned by Jean, Duke of Berry, depicts the leisurely elegance that became such an important feature of medieval aristocratic life.

HOW DID GOVERNMENT AND POLITICS CHANGE DURING THE HIGH MIDDLE AGES?

POLITICS AND GOVERNMENT   221

of distinguishing themselves from all those other groups in high medieval society—merchants, lawyers, artisans, and prosperous free farmers—who were their rivals in wealth and sometimes in political influence. While chivalry began as the value system of a socially diverse knightly order, by the end of the thirteenth century it had become the ideology of a social class, functioning to demarcate those who were (or aspired to be) noble from those who were (or did) not.

Closely linked to the ideology of chivalry was the so-called cult of courtly love, which made noble women into objects of veneration for their knightly admirers. Here too, there was an important element of social class. Courtly love was "refined" love, the "courteous" love appropriate to a royal or noble court. But the exponents of courtly love distinguished sharply between noble women, who alone were capable of refined love (and who should therefore be wooed and won through proper manners, poetry, and valiant deeds) and peasant women, on whom such courtliness would be wasted. Noble women were to be courted; but peasant women could be taken by force, if they would not yield willingly to the desires of a nobleman.

Courtly love literature expressed the values of a noble culture wherein upper-class women were more respected than before. Moreover, certain royal women in the twelfth and thirteenth centuries actually did rule their states on various occasions when their husbands or sons were unable to do so. From 1109 until her death in 1126, Queen Urraca ruled the combined kingdom of León-Castile in Spain. The strong-willed Blanche of Castile ruled France twice in the thirteenth century, once during the minority of her son Louis IX and again when he was off crusading. Queens are not, of course, typical women, and from a modern perspective, high medieval noblewomen were still very constrained. But from the point of view of the past, the High Middle Ages was a time of progress for the women of the upper classes. One striking symbol of this change comes from the history of the game of chess. Before the twelfth century chess was played in the Islamic world, but there the equivalent of the queen was a male figure, the king's chief minister, who could move only diagonally, one square at a time. In twelfth-century Europe, however, this piece was turned into a queen, and sometime before the end of the Middle Ages she began to move all over the board.

> Where kings or powerful feudal lords continued to rule, towns and cities often received special charters of liberty that defined their jurisdictional rights and established the basic structures of urban self-government.

POLITICS AND GOVERNMENT

How did government and politics change during the High Middle Ages?

The profound social and economic changes of the High Middle Ages also gave rise to new forms of government and political life. In the early Middle Ages, monarchy was virtually the only form of government western Europeans knew. Towns were small and usually ruled by their bishops or kings. Kingdoms too were small and were thought of as pertaining to a particular people such as the Lombards, the Visigoths, or the West Saxons. During the eighth and ninth centuries, most of these ethnic kingdoms disappeared as larger, more powerful, territorially based kingdoms emerged. In France, Catalunya, and northern Italy, however, the Carolingians' collapse came near to erasing monarchical power altogether. In the resulting power vacuum, two new structures of political authority slowly emerged in the heartland of the former Carolingian Empire: feudal principalities and self-governing cities.

URBAN GOVERNMENT

We have spoken already of the general economic factors that led to the growth of cities during the High Middle Ages: the increasing agricultural wealth of the countryside, growing population, and developing networks of local and long-distance trade. These factors brought large numbers of immigrants into the cities. They also attracted the local nobility, many of whom became involved in the burgeoning economic and political life of the city. In northern Italy especially, nobles moved to the cities, where they lived in fortified urban towers surrounded by their supporters just as they would have done in a castle in the countryside.

Considering how large the great cities of western Europe became during the twelfth and thirteenth centuries, it is astonishing to realize how informal their governmental arrangements were. Where kings or powerful feudal lords continued to rule, towns and cities often received special charters of liberty that defined

A City on Fire. Once a fire began to spread in a medieval city, women, children, and priests were swiftly evacuated, and servants of the rich would start carrying out their masters' possessions. Here the Swiss city of Bern is shown in flames: although a "bucket brigade" tried desperately to extinguish the fire with water taken from the town moat, chronicles report that the city was leveled by flames in less than half an hour.

their jurisdictional rights and established the basic structures of urban self-government. In northern Europe, these usually involved a mayor and a council elected from among the leading citizens of the town. Elsewhere, for example in Rome, powerful rulers such as the pope resisted all efforts to establish independent city governments. In northern Italy, however, only a few powerful lords—mostly bishops—remained to support or to resist demands for urban self-government. Urban dwellers in Italy therefore had to work out their governmental arrangements for themselves.

In the twelfth century, many north Italian cities entrusted their governments formally to "consuls," drawn from among the leading magnates of the city. Often, however, an informal association of citizens known as the "commune" undertook a wide variety of governmental functions side by side with the consuls. Even the communes, however, were distinctly oligarchical in character. As social stratification increased during the thirteenth century, many cities found themselves split between a ruling class of "magnates" and a popular party that felt itself excluded from the interlocking structures of power that controlled city government and the guilds. Others cities adopted the model of Venice and became more formally oligarchical, casting off even the pretence of being a popular republic. By 1300, however, even cities that remained republics in principle were becoming increasingly oligarchical in practice. Terms of office were getting longer; the jurisdictional claims of urban governments were expanding; and traditions of dynastic succession to office were beginning that would lead to the urban principalities of the later Middle Ages.

FEUDALISM AND THE EMERGENCE OF NATIONAL MONARCHIES

What was the relationship between feudalism and the rise of national monarchies?

In theory, of course, Europe remained a continent of kingdoms even during the tenth and eleventh centuries, when monarchical power in France and Italy was at its lowest ebb. In France, the Capetian dynasty

WHAT WAS THE RELATIONSHIP BETWEEN FEUDALISM AND THE RISE OF NATIONAL MONARCHIES?

FEUDALISM AND THE EMERGENCE OF NATIONAL MONARCHIES   223

succeeded the Carolingians without interruption in 987, keeping alive the memory that all France had once owed allegiance to a single king. In northern Italy, a number of local rulers vied with each other to claim the Carolingians' fallen mantle of royalty for themselves until their claims were finally trumped, after 962, by the newly crowned Ottonian emperors of Germany. In practice, however, neither the Ottonians in Italy nor the Capetians in France were able to control all the territories over which they claimed to rule. By the year 1000, effective political and military power in France lay in the hands of dukes, counts, castellans, and knights, whose power rested on their capacity to channel the increasing wealth of the countryside into their own hands. The symbol of their authority was the castle, often little more than a wooden tower set on a hill with a wooden palisade around it. From their castles, counts, castellans, and knights constructed "lordships": self-contained territories within which they exercised not only the property rights of landlords over peasants, but also the public rights to mint money, judge legal cases, raise troops, wage war, collect taxes, and impose tolls. By the year 1000, France had become a patchwork kingdom composed of essentially independent territorial principalities ruled by counts or dukes, which were in turn divided into smaller lordships ruled by castellans and knights.

THE PROBLEM OF FEUDALISM

This highly decentralized political system, in which "public" powers of minting, justice, taxation, and defense were vested in the hands of private lords, is conventionally referred to as "feudalism." Feudalism took shape first and most fully in tenth- and eleventh-century France, after the Carolingian Empire had disintegrated. From France, the language and customs of feudalism spread to other areas of Europe, changing as they were adapted to the particular social, economic, and political circumstances of different regions and countries. Finally, in the twelfth and thirteenth centuries, feudalism developed into an ideology justifying a hierarchical legal and political order that subordinated knights to counts and counts to kings. In this modified form, feudalism supported powerful monarchies and helped lay the groundwork for the emergence of European nation-states.

What then was feudalism? At its simplest level, a "fee" or "fief" (rhymes with "reef"; in Latin, *feudum*) was a kind of contract, in which someone granted something of value—often land but sometimes revenues from tolls or mills, or an annual grant of money—to some-

one else in return for service of some kind. Frequently there was a degree of inequality in such contracts, particularly if land was involved, because land was regarded as the most valuable gift one person could give to another. When a man accepted land from another in return for promises of service, a degree of subordination by the recipient toward the giver was usually implied. In some areas, the recipient of a fief might therefore become the "vassal" of the gift giver, who thereby became his "lord"; and their new relationship might be solemnized by an act of "homage," whereby the vassal became "the man" of his lord in return for his fief. It was this relationship that lay at the heart of feudalism as it emerged in the chaos of tenth-century France.

In a world in which central governmental authority had collapsed, these essentially personal relationships of service in return for land holding became an important element in ordering social and political relations among counts, castellans, and knights. At the same time, however, these relationships were entirely unsystematic. Even in northern France, where feudalism pervaded aristocratic life, many castellans and knights held their lands freely, owing no service whatsoever to the count or duke within whose territories their lands lay. Nor were feudal relationships necessarily hierarchical. Counts sometimes held lands from knights; knights frequently held lands from each other, and many landholders held fiefs from a number of different lords. Feudalism in the tenth and eleventh centuries created no "feudal pyramids," in which knights held from counts, and counts held from kings in an orderly, hierarchical system of land holding and loyalty. Feudalism of this sort emerged only in the twelfth and thirteenth centuries, when powerful kings began to insist that feudalism *should* be structured in such an orderly way, with kings at the apex of a political and social pyramid.

THE NORMAN CONQUEST OF ENGLAND

Feudalism first emerged as an ordered, hierarchical system of land holding and military service in England, in the peculiar circumstances resulting from the Norman Conquest of 1066. During the tenth and eleventh centuries, England was the wealthiest, most highly centralized, and administratively sophisticated kingdom in western Europe. In 1066, however, Duke William of Normandy laid claim to the English Crown and crossed the Channel to conquer what he had claimed. Fortunately for him the newly installed English king, Harold, had just warded off a Viking attack in the north and thus could not offer resistance at full strength. At the battle of Hastings, Harold and his English troops fought bravely but ultimately could not withstand the onslaught of the fresher Norman troops. As the day waned Harold fell, mortally wounded by a random arrow; his forces fled, and the Normans took the field—and with it, the kingdom of England. Duke William now became King William the Conqueror and set about to exploit his new prize.

William rewarded his Norman followers with extensive grants of English land. As the kingdom's conqueror, however, William could claim with some justice that all the land of England belonged ultimately to him, and therefore that all the land in England must be held from him in return for feudal service of some sort. The Norman lords were already accustomed to holding land in return for service in Normandy. In England, however, feudalism after 1066 was much more highly centralized than it had ever been in Normandy, because in England William could draw on the administrative authority of the English state to enforce his claims to be the feudal lord of the entire country.

As king of England, William also exercised a variety of public rights that did not derive from feudalism at all. In England, only the king could coin money and only the king's money was allowed to circulate. William and his sons also collected a national land tax, supervised justice in public courts, and had the sole authority to summon the population of England to arms. William was also able to insist that all the landholders in England owed loyalty to the king—even if they did not hold a scrap of land directly from him. William's kingship thus represented a powerful fusion of Carolingian-style traditions of public power with the new feudal structures of power and land holding that had grown up in northern France in the tenth and eleventh centuries.

> William's kingship thus represented a powerful fusion of Carolingian-style traditions of public power with the new feudal structures of power and land holding that had grown up in northern France in the tenth and eleventh centuries.

FEUDAL MONARCHY IN ENGLAND

The history of English government in the two centuries after William is primarily a story of kings tightening up the feudal system to their advantage until they superseded it altogether by creating a strong national monarchy. The first king to take steps in this direction was the Conqueror's energetic son Henry I (1100–1135). To supervise financial accounting at his court, Henry created a specialized administrative office known as the Exchequer, so called because it used an abacuslike checkered cloth to calculate receipts and expenditures. He strengthened the Anglo-Saxon sys-

The Bayeux Tapestry. Embroidered shortly after the Battle of Hastings, the Bayeux Tapestry is a 231-foot document of the battle and the events leading up to it. Here the Saxon Earl Harold, on a journey to Normandy, takes an oath of loyalty to Duke William of Normandy. By accepting the throne of England a few years later, Harold broke his oath, thus justifying, in Norman eyes, the Norman conquest of England.

WHAT WAS THE RELATIONSHIP BETWEEN FEUDALISM AND THE RISE OF NATIONAL MONARCHIES?

FEUDALISM AND THE EMERGENCE OF NATIONAL MONARCHIES   225

tem of local administration by appointing powerful sheriffs to supervise the counties. He also instituted a system of traveling circuit judges to administer royal justice in the countryside and to act as a check on the sheriffs. Henry's overbearing style of rule was unpopular, and after his death it helped provoke a civil war. But it also brought England many years of domestic peace and prosperity.

THE REIGN OF HENRY II

After the civil wars that marked the reign of King Stephen (1135–1154), the people of England longed for a king who would bring back the "good old days" of Henry I. They found such a king in Henry's grandson Henry II (1154–1189) who established the Angevin dynasty. Henry II was already the ruler of Normandy, Anjou, Maine, and Aquitaine when he became king of England. As a result, England quickly found itself integrated into the political and cultural world of western France. England, however, was Henry II's richest territory and his only kingdom; for both reasons, it was imperative that he repair the damage done to the country under Stephen.

Henry II restored his grandfather's administrative system with remarkable speed. In addition to reestablishing the Exchequer and the itinerant royal justices, Henry II also expanded the use of juries to determine the facts in civil cases. These innovations are the origin of our modern system of grand and trial juries. To make it easier for plaintiffs to bring civil suits into the royal courts, Henry also developed a system of "writs," which provided a regularized, inexpensive way for common people to seek justice. These legal innovations were immensely popular because they brought many more people into the royal courts. They also strengthened people's sense of attachment to the king's government.

To improve the administration of justice, Henry II also tried to reform the operations of the church courts. In Henry I's time, criminal cases involving clerics had been tried in the county courts, where sheriffs and church officials presided jointly over them. By Henry II's day, however, a new, independent system of church courts had developed in England and elsewhere in Europe, which claimed the exclusive right to try and sentence clergy accused of committing crimes. Punishment in church courts was generally much milder than in the king's courts. This struck Henry II as unjust. In 1164, Henry tried to force the bishops of England to accept his claim that by ancient custom, clerics convicted in church courts of serious crimes should first lose their clerical status and then be handed over to the royal court for sentencing as laymen. Archbishop Thomas Becket objected to this procedure, declaring that it amounted to "double jeopardy": punishing someone twice for the same crime. Becket and Henry had once been close friends, but Becket's stubborn insistence that Henry's real goal was to undermine the rights of the church shattered the relationship between them. Becket fled to the pope, who was then living in France under the protection of Henry II's enemy, King Louis VII of France. When Becket finally returned to England in 1170, he was murdered almost immediately in Canterbury Cathedral by four of Henry's knights after the king, in an outburst of anger, had rebuked them for doing nothing to rid him of "this meddlesome priest." Becket was immediately proclaimed a martyr and a saint; Henry was compelled to appear as a penitent, barefoot and dressed only in a shirt, before Becket's

Martyrdom of Thomas Becket. From a thirteenth-century English psalter. One of the knights has struck Becket so mightily that he has broken his sword.

Legend

- Angevin Empire under Henry II, c. 1180
- French royal domain, 1180
- Boundary of France, 1180
- ✕ Battle sites

France at the Death of Philip Augustus 1223

ATLANTIC OCEAN

- Royal domain
- Under English rule

ENGLAND

Paris
FRANCE
AQUITAINE
LÉON

Bay of Biscay
Compostela

0   100   200   300 Miles
0   300 Kilometers

Map labels:

Bannockburn · Edinburgh
SCOTLAND
Carlisle · Durham
IRELAND
Dublin
Stamford Bridge
York
WALES
Bosworth Field
ENGLAND
Hereford
Ely
Gloucester · Cambridge
Oxford
London
Runnymede · Canterbury
Southampton · Winchester
Hastings

ATLANTIC OCEAN

English Channel

Calais · Bruges · Antwerp
Ypres · Lille · Brussels
FLANDERS · Scheldt R. · Meuse R.
Agincourt · Bouvines
Arras
Amiens
HOLY
Rouen
Bayeux · Beauvais · VERMANDOIS
Caen · Rheims · Verdun
NORMANDY · St. Denis · ROMAN
Mont-St. Michel · Paris · LORRAINE
BRITTANY · Chartres · ISLE DE FRANCE · CHAMPAGNE
MAINE · Brétigny · Marne R. · EMPIRE
Nantes · ANJOU · Troyes
Loire R.
TOURAINE · BURGUNDY
Poitiers
POITOU · Bourges · Dijon
Autun
Seine R.
Bay of Biscay
Geneva
AQUITAINE · Saône R. · Lyon
Angoulême · Rhône R.
Bordeaux · PROVENCE
Périgueux
Garonne R.
GASCONY · Albi · Avignon
Montpellier · Marseilles
NAVARRE · TOULOUSE · Aigues-Mortes
LANGUEDOC · Narbonne
ARAGON · MEDITERRANEAN SEA
CATALUNYA · CORSICA

EUROPE
Area of detail
AFRICA

0   100   200 Miles
0   100   200 Kilometers

FRANCE AND ENGLAND, 1180–1223

Consider the vast geographical expanse of the Angevin Empire in 1180. What were the primary requirements for holding this empire together? What advantages did the kings of France enjoy in their struggles with the Angevins? What did it mean to be "French" in such a world? Would the wars between the Angevins and the Capetians have encouraged the emergence of national identities within their kingdoms? Why or why not?

WHAT WAS THE RELATIONSHIP BETWEEN FEUDALISM AND THE RISE OF NATIONAL MONARCHIES?

FEUDALISM AND THE EMERGENCE OF NATIONAL MONARCHIES   227

tomb to ask the saint's forgiveness for the rash words that had provoked his murder.

In the long run, however, these dramatic events did not seriously undermine Henry II's relationship either with the papacy or with the English church. Henry was forced to surrender several of his claims, including the right to sentence criminal clerics in royal courts and to restrict appeals from England to the papal court. But he retained the right to nominate clerics to high church offices and to have such elections held in his presence. As a result, the king's candidates were almost always confirmed to the offices for which he nominated them.

The most concrete proof of Henry II's success is that his government worked so well after his death. Henry's son, the swashbuckling Richard I, the "Lionheart," ruled his father's empire for ten years, from 1189 to 1199, but spent only about six months in England because he was otherwise engaged in crusading or defending his possessions on the Continent. Nonetheless, the legal system continued to develop, and the country raised two huge sums for Richard by taxation: one to pay for his crusade to the Holy Land, and the other to pay his ransom when he was captured by an enemy on his return. It also steadily supported his wars to defend his French lands against King Philip Augustus of France.

THE REIGN OF JOHN AND MAGNA CARTA

Had Richard lived, the map of Europe might look very different today: had he defeated King Philip, France itself might not exist with anything like its current borders. But Richard was killed in 1199 while besieging a small castle in southern France. His successor, his brother John (1199–1216), was a much less capable military leader, who quickly lost nearly all of his lands in France to King Philip.

John devoted the rest of his reign to raising the money he would need to recover his lost French territories. To do so, he pressed his feudal rights to their limits, demanding massive fines from his nobility and imposing heavy taxes on the country. When John's 1214 military expedition to France failed, the exasperated magnates of England rebelled. In 1215 they forced John to renounce his extortionate fiscal practices in a great charter of liberties known to posterity as Magna Carta. Because John had relied so heavily on his feudal powers, most of Magna Carta's provisions dealt directly with such matters, insisting that the king must in future respect the traditional rights of his vassals. But it did also establish some important general principles: that taxation could not be raised by the Crown without the consent of the kingdom and that no free man could be punished except by the judgment of his equals and by the law of the land. Above all, however, Magna Carta was important as an expression of the principle that the king is bound by the law.

In the century after Magna Carta, the progress of centralized government continued apace. In the reign of John's son, Henry III (1216–1272), the nobility vied with the king for control of the government but did so on the assumption that centralized government itself was a good thing. Throughout Henry's reign, administrators continued to perfect more efficient legal and administrative institutions, including a system of central and local courts, and a taxation system that assessed both nobles and commoners in proportion to their wealth.

The last and most famous branch of the medieval English governmental system was Parliament. This gradually emerged as a separate institution around 1300, above all owing to the wishes of Henry III's son, Edward I (1272–1307). Although Parliament later became a check against unlimited royal power, in its origins Parliament was very much a royal creation, summoned because kings found it useful to consult with their nobles, knights, and townsmen in a single assembly. Magna Carta had demanded that no taxation be imposed without the common consent of the realm. Parliament provided an efficient way to secure such consent as well as to inform those present why such taxation was necessary. Edward also used parliaments to take advice about pressing concerns, to hear judicial cases involving great men, to review local

CHRONOLOGY

NOTEWORTHY NORMAN AND ANGEVIN KINGS, 1066–1327

William I (the Conqueror)	1066–1087
Henry I	1100–1135
Stephen	1135–1154
Henry II	1154–1189
Richard I (the Lionheart)	1189–1199
John	1199–1216
Henry III	1216–1272
Edward I	1272–1307
Edward II	1307–1327

administration, to hear complaints from the countryside, and to promulgate new laws in response to those complaints. Parliaments were thus political institutions no less than financial and judicial ones. They played an essential role in English government from the fourteenth century on.

FEUDAL MONARCHY IN FRANCE

Administrative kingship developed more slowly in France than in England, but by 1300 it had reached a comparable stage in both countries. During the tenth century, most of the Carolingian institutions of local government in France had collapsed; as a result, the new Capetian dynasty of French kings (987–1328) had to rebuild such institutions from scratch. For nearly 200 years, it seemed unlikely they would ever be able to do so. As kings of France, the early Capetians ruled directly only a small area around Paris roughly the size of Vermont. Outside their home territory, the Capetian kings could claim only a vague supremacy over the independent counts and dukes who ruled the rest of France. An idea of France survived as a legacy from the Carolingian period; but in all other respects, the Capetians had to reinvent their kingdom.

In many ways the Capetians were fortunate. Quite against the biological odds, they managed to produce sons for 300 years without interruption. They also proved surprisingly long lived: on average, each Capetian king ruled for 30 years. As a result, they avoided both succession disputes and destructive minority governments. They ruled a remarkably rich agricultural territory, which provided them with a steadily rising income. They also acquired significant prestige as protectors of popes fleeing from the German emperors, and as the patrons of the University of Paris, which became the leading European center of learning during the twelfth and thirteenth centuries. Beyond all this, however, the Capetians proved to be a shrewd and wily line of kings, who carefully husbanded their strength while their more powerful enemies overreached themselves.

THE GROWTH OF ROYAL POWER IN FRANCE

The steady growth of royal power in France began under Louis VI "the Fat" (1108–1137). It was Louis who consolidated royal control over the area around Paris. Once this was accomplished, agriculture and trade could prosper and the intellectual life of Paris began to flourish. Louis's son Louis VII (1137–1180)

was thoroughly overshadowed by his rival, King Henry II of England. But he managed nonetheless to increase the resources and the prestige of the French monarchy. By inciting rebellions by Henry II's sons against their father, he also kept the Angevin Empire in a constant state of discord.

It was Louis VII's son Philip II (1179–1223) who finally turned the tide against the Angevins and who marks the true beginning of administrative kingship in France. Like his father, Philip understood that he could not win a direct military confrontation with Henry II or Richard I. King John, however—known to his detractors as "soft sword"—was another matter. To facilitate his succession to his brother's throne, John had agreed to do homage to Philip for all his lands in France. Philip then took advantage of his position as John's feudal overlord to undermine John's control over these territories. When John resisted, Philip declared all John's lands in France to be forfeit to the French crown. A war of conquest quickly followed. By 1204, the richest part of the Angevin territories in France were in Philip's hands.

Philip now had the resources to begin building an effective system of local administration. He chose to maintain most of the administrative institutions the Angevins had created there. To supervise these territories, however, he appointed new royal officials with full judicial, administrative, and military authority. Philip also adopted strict systems of financial accounting and record keeping. The administrative pattern Philip established, of combining local diversity with centralized royal control, would continue to characterize French government for the next 500 years. Philip's son, Louis VIII (1223–1226), would extend it to the newly conquered territories of southern France. His son, Louis IX (1226–1270), would deepen and extend it fur-

CHRONOLOGY

NOTEWORTHY CAPETIAN KINGS, 987–1328

Hugh Capet	987–996
Louis VI	1108–1137
Louis VII	1137–1180
Philip Augustus	1179–1223
Louis VIII	1223–1226
Louis IX	1226–1270
Philip IV	1285–1314

WHAT WAS THE RELATIONSHIP BETWEEN FEUDALISM AND THE RISE OF NATIONAL MONARCHIES?

FEUDALISM AND THE EMERGENCE OF NATIONAL MONARCHIES   229

ther. Even more important, however, Louis IX would legitimize it by his own extraordinary devotion to justice at home and crusading abroad. Louis IX became the epitome of thirteenth-century kingship; after his death, he would be canonized by the church as Saint Louis. His successors would draw on the prestige of "good King Louis" for centuries to come.

That prestige came close to being squandered, however, by Saint Louis's ruthless grandson Philip IV, "the Fair" (1285–1314). Philip waged aggressive wars against Flanders in the northeast and the remaining English territories in the southwest. To finance these campaigns, his administration became a voracious money-raising machine. But despite his enormous resources, Philip could not match the capacity of his enemy, England's Edward I, to raise cash from his subjects through voluntary taxation. Although Philip experimented with representative assemblies similar to the English Parliament, the Estates General (as they came to be called) never played a role in French government comparable to Parliament in England. There were many reasons for this, but perhaps the most fundamental one was the fact that the French nobility successfully claimed to be exempt from paying direct taxation to the crown. Ever since the Anglo-Saxon period, English monarchs had been powerful enough to ensure that their nobility must pay the taxes to which they consented. The weakness of the early Capetian kings had prevented a similar custom from taking root in France, and even Philip IV found it easier to accept this state of affairs rather than to challenge it. Noble exemptions from taxation would therefore remain a political problem for the French monarchy right on up until the French Revolution of 1789.

GERMANY

Germany in the High Middle Ages followed a very different pattern. In the year 1050, Germany appeared to be the strongest monarchy in western Europe. To rule their wide territories—which included Switzerland, eastern France, and most of the Low Countries as well as claims to northern Italy—the emperors relied heavily on cooperation with the church. The leading royal administrators were archbishops and bishops whom the German emperors appointed and installed in their sacred offices. Even the pope was frequently an imperial appointee. Often, these leading churchmen were members of the imperial family itself, who could counterbalance the strength of the regional dukes. Germany was not so administratively sophisticated as was eleventh-century England, but there was no question about the effectiveness of monarchical authority. It simply rested on other foundations.

THE CONFLICT WITH THE PAPACY

In 1056, however, the emperor Henry III died, leaving as his heir a small boy, the future Henry IV. From this point on, the strength of the monarchy began to unravel. Henry III had installed a new group of reforming clergy at the papal court, whose policies will be discussed more fully in the next chapter. Conflicts between the regents for the boy king Henry IV and the papal reformers began almost immediately. Conflicts also erupted between the regents (who came from central and southern Germany) and the nobility of Saxony. When Henry IV began to rule on his own, the Saxon conflicts escalated. In 1073, these hostilities erupted into a disastrous and destructive civil war.

Just as the Saxon war ended, however, a new conflict broke out with the papal reformers at Rome. The newly elected pope Gregory VII (1073–1085) became convinced that to reform the spiritual life of the church, it was necessary first to free the church from the control of laymen, including the emperor. Henry refused to accept Gregory's attempts to prohibit him from selecting and installing bishops and abbots in their offices, and began to plot to remove Gregory from the papacy. Gregory, in turn, allied himself with the Saxon nobility, reigniting the civil war from which Germany had not yet recovered.

The struggle between pope and emperor continued until 1122, when Henry's son Henry V finally reached a compromise with the papacy. By then, however, the German nobility had won far more practical independence from the crown than they had had before. After fifty years of nearly constant war, they had also become more militarized and dangerous. In 1125, when Henry V died childless, they gained further authority by making good on their claims to elect a new ruler regardless of hereditary succession—a principle that would thereafter often lead them to choose the weakest successors or to embroil the country in civil war. The pope's right to crown any new Roman emperor gave him a stake in the selection process also. Although the popes valued the German emperors as protectors against the Normans in southern Italy, they feared them in equal measure. Should the German emperors succeed in ruling northern and central Italy directly, the papacy—on whose spiritual independence

THE HOLY ROMAN EMPIRE, C. 1200

Are the borders of the Holy Roman Empire defined by rivers, oceans, or mountain ranges? How would you explain this fact? Does the Kingdom of Germany have any such natural borders? Note the position of the Papal States in central Italy. Why would the prospect of a single heir to the Holy Roman Empire and to the Kingdom of Sicily have frightened the popes? Were their fears well founded? Why or why not?

WHAT WAS THE RELATIONSHIP BETWEEN FEUDALISM AND THE RISE OF NATIONAL MONARCHIES?

FEUDALISM AND THE EMERGENCE OF NATIONAL MONARCHIES   231

the salvation of all Christians depended—risked becoming their puppet. This fear propelled the next century of papal-imperial conflict.

FREDERICK BARBAROSSA AND HENRY VI

A major attempt to stem the tide running against the German monarchy was made by Frederick I (1152–1190). Frederick, called "Barbarossa" ("red beard"), reasserted the independent dignity of the empire by calling his realm the "Holy Roman Empire," on the theory that it was a universal empire descending from Rome and blessed by God. At the same time, however, he also tried to rule in cooperation with the German princes, supporting their efforts to bring their own territorial nobles to heel and trusting that the princes would in turn support his attempts to reassert imperial control over the wealthy but increasingly independent cities of northern Italy.

By and large, Frederick made this system work, but at the cost of a lengthy war in Italy and destructive conflict with the papacy. Led by Milan and supported by the papacy, the north Italian cities formed an alliance, the Lombard League, to resist Frederick's claims to rule in Italy. Ultimately, Frederick achieved a compromise with both the Lombard League and the papacy, which guaranteed the political independence of the towns in return for large cash payments to the emperor. He also secured the princes' approval for his son Henry to succeed him as king and emperor, and he arranged a marriage between Henry and the sister of the Norman king of Sicily.

Barbarossa's careful planning bore fruit in the reign of his son Henry VI. Henry succeeded to his father's throne without difficulty. He enjoyed a huge income from the north Italian towns; and when his wife's brother died suddenly without heirs, he became the king of Sicily also. This was the nightmare the papacy had always feared, for now a single, enormously powerful ruler controlled both northern and southern Italy, leaving the papal lands in central Italy surrounded on all sides. Fortunately for the papacy, however, Henry VI died in 1197 at the age of thirty-two, leaving as his heir a three-year-old son, the future Frederick II. The new pope, Innocent III (1198–1216), threw all his energy into an attempt to break the links between Germany, northern Italy, and the kingdom of Sicily. When a civil war erupted in Germany over the succession to the throne, Innocent switched his support back and forth between the two main claimants, hoping to secure a promise from the successful claimant that would return Sicily to the papacy. When Otto IV, Frederick II's rival, finally appeared to have won a decisive victory, Innocent played his last card. He sent the sixteen-year-old Frederick II north with a small army, never imagining that so small a force, led by so young a man, could ever triumph. However, Otto's forces were routed at the battle of Bouvines by King Philip Augustus of France, and Frederick II wound up as the new, and undisputed, king of Germany.

FREDERICK II

Frederick II (1216–1250) was one of the most fascinating of all medieval rulers. Having grown up in Sicily, Frederick spoke Arabic as well as Latin, German, French, and Italian. He maintained a menagerie of exotic animals, a troop of Muslim archers, and a harem of veiled and secluded women, all of which traveled with him on his journeys. But despite this appearance of exoticism, he was also a very conventional medieval ruler who sought to pursue his grandfather's policies of supporting the territorial princes in Germany while enforcing imperial rights in Italy. Much had changed, however, since the death of the emperor Henry VI. In Germany, the princes had already become so entirely autonomous that there was little Frederick could do except to recognize their privileges. This he proceeded to do; in exchange, he got them to elect his sons to succeed him as kings of Germany. Frederick's bigger problems lay in Italy. In northern Italy, the cities of the Lombard League had shaken off their obligations to pay taxes to the empire; while in Sicily, the enormously powerful and administratively sophisticated kingdom created by the Normans had fallen into chaos.

Frederick spent the next twenty-five years solidifying his relationship with the German nobility and recovering as much land as he could after twenty years of war, reestablishing his authority in Sicily and northern Italy, and recovering Jerusalem through negotiations with

> Frederick spent the next twenty-five years solidifying his relationship with the German nobility and recovering as much land as he could after twenty years of war, reestablishing his authority in Sicily and northern Italy, and recovering Jerusalem through negotiations with the Muslim ruler of Egypt.

the Muslim ruler of Egypt. In 1237, however, he over-reached himself by asserting his rights as emperor to rule the north Italian cities directly, bypassing their own governmental structures. The result was another

Lombard League and another lengthy war, which continued until Frederick's death in 1250. With him went the last prospect for the continuation of effective monarchical rule in Germany. Emperors would con-

THE RECONQUEST OF IBERIA, 900–1250

Note the position of the Christian kingdoms circa 900 and the progress of the Christian reconquest over the subsequent few centuries. What factors helped shelter and sustain the small Christian kingdoms that survived Islam's initial push? Why did Castile become the largest of the Christian kingdoms as the reconquest progressed? Why did the smaller Aragon and Catalunya maintain important positions as wealthy and significant powers? How did the struggles and successes of Christians in Iberia influence the crusader movement?

tinue to be elected, but in practice, monarchical authority in Germany was now gravely weakened. Effective political power in Germany would henceforth be divided among several hundred territorial princes whose rivalries would embroil German politics until the end of the nineteenth century.

IBERIA

The Iberian peninsula was even more regionalized than was Germany. In contrast to Germany, however, Spain would emerge from the Middle Ages with the most powerful monarchy in early modern Europe. The key to the strength of the Spanish monarchies of the High Middle Ages lay in their successful reconquest of the peninsula from the Muslims and in the lands, booty, and plunder these conquests provided. During the High Middle Ages Iberia contained four major Christian kingdoms: the northern mountain state of Navarre, Portugal in the west, the combined kingdom of Aragon and Catalunya in the southeast, and Castile in the center. Throughout the twelfth century, Christian armies steadily advanced, culminating in the year 1212 in a major victory by a combined Aragonese-Castilian army over the Muslims at Las Navas de Tolosa. By the end of the thirteenth century all that remained of earlier Muslim domination was the small state of Granada, and Granada survived mostly because it was willing to pay tribute to the Christians. Castile became by far the largest Spanish kingdom in area, but it was balanced in wealth by the more urban and trade-oriented kingdom of Aragon and Catalunya. Wars between Castile and Aragon weakened both kingdoms during the later Middle Ages; but when the marriage of Ferdinand of Aragon and Isabella of Castile joined these two ancient enemies, a united Spanish monarchy was born. In 1492, the Catholic monarchs captured Granada, the last remaining Muslim territory in Spain. A few months later, Isabella commissioned an Italian adventurer named Christopher Columbus to sail to India by heading west across the Atlantic Ocean. Columbus failed. But his accidental encounter with the American continents would make sixteenth-century Spain the most powerful kingdom in Europe.

> City-states were more capable of mobilizing the loyalty of their citizens, but city-states were frequently divided by internal economic and social rivalries; and in the long run, they were not militarily strong enough to defend themselves against foreign conquerors.

CONCLUSION

In the year 1000, Europe was the least powerful, the least prosperous, and the least intellectually sophisticated of the three Western civilizations that had emerged out of the Roman world. By 1300, its position vis-à-vis both the Byzantine and the Islamic worlds had been transformed. This transformation rested on economic foundations: an increasingly efficient agriculture, a growing population, and expanding trade. These changes produced a society in which individuals cast off old roles and took on new ones with bewildering speed. No less important, however, were the political and military changes western Europe underwent during these centuries. By 1100, the heavily armored, mounted knight had emerged as the most formidable military weapon of the day. It was only during the twelfth and thirteenth centuries, however, that European governments developed the administrative and political capacity to control these knights and to direct them toward purposes larger than mere brigandage and extortion.

Until the High Middle Ages, the Western world had known two basic patterns of human government: city-states and empires. City-states were more capable of mobilizing the loyalty of their citizens, but city-states were frequently divided by internal economic and social rivalries; and in the long run, they were not militarily strong enough to defend themselves against foreign conquerors. Empires, by contrast, could win battles and maintain powerful administrative bureaucracies, but they were generally too far flung and rapacious to inspire deep loyalties among their subjects.

The national monarchies of the High Middle Ages would prove to be the "golden mean" between these extremes. They were large enough to defend themselves, and wealthy enough to develop sophisticated administrative techniques. But they also commanded sufficient citizen participation and loyalty to support them in times of stress when empires would have foundered. By 1300, the kings of England, France, and the Iberian peninsula had largely succeeded in claiming the primary loyalty of their subjects, superseding the claims of locality, region, or even the church. Their victory was not yet complete, and in the later Middle Ages, France in particular would come near to collapse. But in the end, the national monarchies of the High Middle Ages would endure to become the foundations on which the nation-states of modern Europe would be constructed. So important would this historical pedigree become that modern nation-states that did not have a medieval origin would often feel compelled to invent one.

KEY TERMS

lord	crusades	courtly love	Magna Carta
manorialism	First Crusade	Visigoths	Holy Roman Empire
serfdom	*jihad*	feudalism	
guilds	chivalry	William the Conqueror	

SELECTED READINGS

Abulafia, David. *Frederick II: A Medieval Emperor.* London and New York, 1988. The only reliable biography of Frederick II; it strips away much of the legend that has hitherto surrounded this monarch.

Abulafia, David, ed. *The New Cambridge Medieval History.* Vol. 5: *c. 1198–c. 1300.* Cambridge, 1999. An up-to-date survey, with contributions by more than thirty specialists. Excellent bibliographies.

Amt, Emily, ed. *Women's Lives in Medieval Europe: A Sourcebook.* New York, 1993. An excellent source collection.

Arnold, Benjamin. *Princes and Territories in Medieval Germany.* Cambridge and New York, 1991. The best English-language survey; it correctly avoids portraying the political history of medieval Germany as a story of failure.

Baldwin, John W. *The Government of Philip Augustus.* Berkeley and Los Angeles, Calif., 1986. A landmark scholarly account, detailed but readable.

Bartlett, Robert. *The Making of Europe: Conquest, Colonization and Cultural Change, 950–1350.* Princeton, N.J., 1993. A wide-ranging examination of the economic, social, and religious expansion of Europe, full of stimulating ideas and insights.

Clanchy, Michael. *England and Its Rulers, 1066–1307.* 3d ed. Oxford and Malden, Mass., 2006. A lively survey, highly recommended.

Dunbabin, Jean. *France in the Making, 843–1180.* 2d ed. Oxford and New York, 2000. An authoritative survey of the disparate territories that came to make up the medieval French kingdom.

Dyer, Christopher. *Making a Living in the Middle Ages: The People of Britain 850–1520.* New Haven, Conn., 2002. A splendid new synthesis that combines social, economic, and archaeological evidence.

Fuhrmann, Horst. *Germany in the High Middle Ages, c. 1050–1200.* Cambridge, 1986. A useful, short account in English of the history of twelfth-century Germany.

Gillingham, John. *The Angevin Empire,* 2d ed. Oxford and New York, 2001. The best treatment by far of its subject, brief but full of ideas.

Herlihy, David, ed. *The History of Feudalism.* New York, 1970. Collects the texts on which scholarly discussion continues to focus.

Hyde, J. Kenneth. *Society and Politics in Medieval Italy.* New York, 1973. A survey that sets the political history of the Italian city-states in its social context.

Jones, P. J. *The Italian City-State: From Commune to Signoria.* Oxford and New York, 1997. A fundamental reinterpretation, with important revisions to the standard accounts of Hyde and Waley.

Jordan, William C. *The Penguin History of Europe.* Vol. III: *Europe in the High Middle Ages.* New York and London, 2003. An outstanding new survey, the best since Southern.

Keen, Maurice. *Chivalry.* New Haven, Conn., 1984. Masterful treatment of chivalry from its origins to the sixteenth century, engagingly written.

Moore, Robert I. *The First European Revolution, c. 970–1215.* Oxford and Cambridge, Mass., 2000. A remarkable description of the ways in which European society was fundamentally reshaped during the eleventh and twelfth centuries.

Otto, Bishop of Freising. *The Deeds of Frederick Barbarossa.* Trans. C. C. Mierow. New York, 1953. A contemporary chronicle interesting enough to read from start to finish.

Reilly, Bernard F. *The Medieval Spains.* New York, 1993. A succinct account that covers the entire Iberian peninsula from 500 to 1500.

Southern, Richard W. *The Making of the Middle Ages.* New Haven, Conn., 1992. A classic work, first published in 1951 but still fresh and exciting.

Stow, Kenneth R. *Alienated Minority: The Jews of Medieval Latin Europe.* Cambridge, Mass., 1992. An excellent survey of a neglected topic.

Suger, Abbot of Saint Denis. *The Deeds of Louis the Fat.* Trans. R. Cusimano and J. Moorhead. Washington, D.C., 1992. A revealing picture of the challenges that faced the early twelfth-century kings of France as they fought to subdue the local nobility of the Île-de-France.

Waley, Daniel. *The Italian City-Republics.* New York, 1969. A classic introduction to the subject.

THE HIGH MIDDLE AGES: RELIGIOUS AND INTELLECTUAL DEVELOPMENTS, 1000–1300

THE RELIGIOUS AND INTELLECTUAL CHANGES of the High Middle Ages altered European life profoundly. Indeed, it is not too much to say that the fundamental character of European civilization was permanently transformed by the developments that occurred during these crucial centuries. With respect to religious life, the period witnessed both the emergence of the papacy as the dominant organizational force in Western Christianity and a remarkable effort on the part of the church to extend and deepen the influence of Christianity among the laity. Parish churches mushroomed across the landscape, and new monastic and religious orders developed, many of which took as their primary mission the task of ministering to the world outside the monastic walls. For the first time since the late Roman period, preaching, confession, pilgrimages, and private prayer became central elements in the religious life of European Christians. At the same time, however, these new patterns of Christian piety emphasized the religious and social distinctions between Christians and their non-Christian neighbors. The result was a marked increase in the persecution of minority groups within European society and the creation of what some historians have called a "persecuting society," in which the identification and oppression of heretics, Jews, gay people, lepers, and Muslims became an essential element in the growing power of both church and state.

The High Middle Ages also witnessed a remarkable revival of intellectual and cultural life. From the mid-twelfth century on, hundreds of new works of classical literature and philosophy, including the entirety of the surviving works of Aristotle, poured into western Europe from the Islamic world and, to a lesser degree, from Byzantium. Even before the stimulus of these new texts, however, European intellectuals had begun to think in new ways about fundamental problems in theology, philosophy, and law. Fueling this intellectual revolution was the emergence and rapid growth of universities, accompanied by an even more widespread expansion of primary schooling. New literary forms also began to emerge: vernacular lyric poetry, extended allegories, and above all romances. For the first time in centuries it began to be possible to speak of a European reading public.

FOCUS QUESTIONS

- How was the Latin Church reformed?
- How did the Latin Church control popular heresy?

- How did the recovery of classical learning affect medieval intellectual life?
- What common themes unite the literature, art, and architecture of the High Middle Ages?

In education, thought, and the arts, early medieval Europe had been a backwater, especially in comparison with Byzantium and Islam. By 1300, however, Europe had become the intellectual and artistic leader among these three Western civilizations. Europeans now boasted that learning and the arts had come to them from Egypt, Greece, and Rome; and that although they were pygmies who sat on the shoulders of giants, they nonetheless saw farther and more clearly than had the intellectual giants of antiquity on whose shoulders they sat. Such boasts were largely justified. In the High Middle Ages, Europeans built their intellectual and artistic accomplishments on ancient foundations, but they also began to make major contributions of their own.

THE REFORM OF THE CHURCH

How was the Latin Church reformed?

The combined effects of Carolingian collapse; Viking, Muslim, and Hungarian attacks; and the growing power of local noble families were disastrous for the religious life of ninth- and tenth-century Europe. For several centuries, church reformers had sought to improve the religious lives of the laity by strengthening the control that powerful bishops exercised over the local clergy within their dioceses. By the middle of the tenth century, however, that strategy lay in ruins. Many parish churches had been abandoned or destroyed, while those that survived were often regarded as the personal property of some powerful local family, whose responsibility for protecting these churches easily became a license to oppress them. Monasteries underwent a similar process of "privatization." Some became dumping grounds for aristocratic younger sons who might live in the monastery without ever taking monastic vows. Other monasteries had troops of knights thrust on them. Some even had lay abbots. It was all very distant from what Saint Benedict had outlined in his *Rule for Monasteries.*

In the absence of effective kingship, bishops were helpless against such entrenched local power. Nor could the papacy correct the situation. Indeed, as the bishops of Rome, the popes themselves were among the worst examples of the negative impact too much local influence could have on the spiritual standards of the clergy. Most of the tenth-century popes were incompetent or corrupt, the sons or tools of powerful Roman families who sought to control the papacy to rule the city of Rome itself. As the guardian of the tombs of Saints Peter and Paul and the spiritual head of Western Christendom, the papacy remained a respected institution, even in its tenth-century nadir. But the popes who occupied Saint Peter's chair left a great deal to be desired as moral and spiritual leaders of Western society.

MONASTIC REFORM, 900–1050

The first stirrings of reform emerged in the monasteries of tenth-century Europe, beginning with that of Cluny in Burgundy. Founded in 910 by a pious nobleman, Cluny was a Benedictine house, but with two important constitutional innovations. One was that to keep it free from domination by local noble families or the local bishop, Cluny was placed directly under the protection of the papacy. The second was that it undertook the reform or foundation of a large number of "daughter" monasteries. Cluny established a network of dependent Cluniac houses across Europe, all of which remained subordinate to the mother house at Cluny. By 1049, there were sixty-seven such Cluniac priories (as the daughter monasteries were called), each one performing the same elaborate round of prayer and worship for which Cluny became famous, and each entirely free from the control of local secular or ecclesiastical powers. In the eyes of the Cluniacs, their success depended on their absolute freedom from outside interference in their religious life. When Cluny reformed a monastery, therefore, it insisted on two things: first, that the Benedictine vows be strictly enforced on all monks; and second, that the selection of new abbots and priors be accomplished by a free election of the monks, without any buying or selling of the office (a sin known as "simony.")

Cluniac influence was strongest in France and Italy, where the virtual absence of effective kingship made royally sponsored monastic reforms impossible. In Germany and England, by contrast, monastic reform emerged during the tenth and eleventh centuries as an essential responsibility of a Christian king. Following Cluniac example, these kings insisted on the strict observance of poverty, chastity, and obedience within the monastery, and instituted elaborate rounds of group liturgical prayer. In contrast to Cluny, however, it was the kings themselves who guaranteed the reformed monasteries' freedom from outside interference, and it was they who appointed the abbots, just as they also appointed the bishops of their kingdoms.

As a result of these parallel movements for monastic reform, monasticism became the dominant spiritual model for tenth- and eleventh-century Latin Christianity. Monasteries also had an important influence on patterns of piety outside the cloister. For centuries, monasteries had been the repositories and guardians of the relics of departed saints, whose powers were believed to protect the monasteries that housed their earthly bodies. From the tenth century on, however, monasteries increasingly attracted the attentions of pious laypeople, who came seeking miraculous cures from the saint (or saints) whose relics were housed there. The vast majority of such pilgrimages were to local shrines. But regular long-distance pilgrimage routes also began to develop, to such places as Santiago de Compostela in Spain and the Church of Saint Faith in southern France. Traffic also increased to such traditional pilgrimage sites as Rome and Jerusalem. Pilgrimage was one of the important ways in which the new patterns of Christian piety developed in monasteries began to spread to the laity outside the monastic walls.

> Pilgrimage was one of the important ways in which the new patterns of Christian piety developed in monasteries began to spread to the laity outside the monastic walls.

THE PAPAL REFORM MOVEMENT

From the monasteries, the reform movement began to affect the bishops also. In England, kings appointed a number of reformed monks to bishoprics. In Germany, kings retained nonmonastic bishops but enforced strict requirements of personal holiness on the bishops and abbots whom they appointed to office. With royal encouragement, bishops also began to rebuild and expand their cathedral churches to make them more suitable reflections of divine majesty. The Cluniacs, however, went further and began to lobby for the reform of the entire church, including bishops, unreformed monasteries, and even the parish clergy. They centered their attacks on simony, but they also demanded that personal poverty and celibacy be enforced on all priests. This last demand was in some ways the most radical. Although a series of fourth- and fifth-century church councils had declared that priests should be celibate, this requirement had been largely ignored thereafter. In the year 1000, the vast majority of the parish priests across Europe were married.

In Rome, the papacy remained unreformed until 1046, when the German emperor Henry III came to Rome, deposed all three of the local Roman nobles who claimed to be pope, and appointed in their place his own relative, a German monastic reformer who took the name Pope Leo IX (1049–1054). Leo and his supporters quickly took control of the papal court and began to promulgate decrees against simony, clerical marriage, and immorality of all sorts throughout the church. To enforce these decrees, Leo and his entourage traveled throughout Europe, disciplining and deposing clerics who had purchased their positions or who refused to give up their wives. Implicit in Leo's reforming efforts was thus a new vision of the church

The Reliquary of Saint Faith, Early Tenth Century.

itself as a hierarchical organization in which priests obeyed bishops and bishops obeyed the pope not only as the spiritual and doctrinal leader of Western Christendom but also as the legal and jurisdictional ruler of the entire Christian church.

Leo and the reform popes were able to enforce their decrees only in those areas of Europe where they could count on the support of secular rulers. Among these secular supporters, the most important was of course the emperor Henry III, whose protection insulated the papal reformers from the Roman noble families who would otherwise have deposed them. In 1056, however, Henry III died, leaving a young child as his heir. Without their imperial protector, the reformers were now at the mercy of the Roman political factions. When the reigning reform pope died in 1058, the Roman nobles seized their opportunity to install as pope one of their own lackeys. Briefly, it looked as if the entire reform program might be lost. But the reformers rallied outside Rome and elected their own pope (who took the name Nicholas II). Allying themselves militarily with the Norman rulers of central and southern Italy, they drove the nonreformed pope out of Rome.

In 1059, Pope Nicholas II issued a new decree on papal elections, vesting the right to elect a pope solely with the cardinals, but "saving the rights of the Emperor." The decree is significant for two quite different reasons. First, it represents a milestone in the evolution of the College of Cardinals as a special body within the church. This decree was the first time that the cardinals' powers had been clearly recognized. Thereafter the College of Cardinals took on an increasingly well-defined identity, becoming an important force in creating continuity of papal policy, especially when there was a quick succession of pontiffs. The cardinals still elect the pope today.

The decree was also significant, however, because it opened up a breach between the reform party in Rome and the German imperial court. In the circumstances of 1059, the Electoral Decree was intended to justify the reformers' actions of the previous year and to protect future papal elections from the influence of the Roman aristocracy. But although the decree obviously drew on Cluniac ideals about free elections as an essential element in a reformed church, it was not intended to deprive the German emperor of his traditional role as papal protector. Nonetheless, the Electoral Decree

> Superficially, the issue that divided Gregory and Henry was whether Henry or any other layman could appoint a bishop or abbot and then dress him with the symbols of his spiritual office, a practice known as "lay investiture."

angered the advisers of the young king Henry IV, who saw it as a challenge to the emperor's right to nominate new popes and who also bitterly resented the reformers' alliance with the Normans, whose designs on imperial territories in central Italy were well known. The resulting hostility between the young king's regents and the papal court poisoned the atmosphere in which King Henry IV grew to maturity.

THE INVESTITURE CONFLICT

A new and momentous phase in the history of the reform movement began in 1073 with the election of Pope Gregory VII (1073–1085). Gregory was a Roman whose election was violently supported by a mob of Roman citizens. Gregory was already a well-known reformer with long experience at the papal court. It is likely that he would have been elected by the cardinals anyway, even without the interference of the Roman mob. But the circumstances of his election clearly violated the terms of the 1059 Electoral Decree, and this fact weakened Gregory in his first few years as pope. Henry IV was also anxious for a reconciliation with Rome, not least because between 1073 and 1075 he was involved in a major civil war with his own nobility in Saxony. Both Gregory and Henry began, therefore, by treating one another with great deference. Henry blamed the advisers of his youth for the troubles that had arisen between his own court and Rome and promised to make amends. Gregory, in turn, spoke of pope and emperor as the two eyes of a single, Christian body and promised to leave the church in Henry's care if he, Gregory, should lead a military expedition eastward against Islam. On the surface, it appeared that the harmonious relations between papacy and empire that had existed under Henry's father had been fully restored.

By the end of 1075, however, relations between the two men were at a breaking point. For the next half century, western Europe would be riven by conflict between the papacy and the empire—a conflict that would permanently alter the relationship between spiritual and temporal authority in Western Christendom. Superficially, the issue that divided Gregory and Henry was whether Henry or any other layman could appoint a bishop or abbot and then dress him with the symbols of his spiritual office, a practice known as

Henry IV and Gregory VII. In the top panel, King Henry appoints Wibert, Archbishop of Milan, to be the new pope and drives Pope Gregory from Rome. In the lower panel, Pope Gregory is received by the bishops of the Norman kingdom of southern Italy and then dies in exile. From a twelfth-century German manuscript.

to prohibit all clerics from accepting any church office from a layman. Henry IV flatly refused to accept this decree, not only because it infringed on his own traditional rights as emperor but also because the bishops and abbots of Germany and northern Italy were critically important to his own ability to rule his kingdoms. Henry proceeded, therefore, to appoint a new archbishop in Milan in defiance of Gregory's prohibition. Gregory responded by reminding Henry that he, Gregory, occupied Saint Peter's chair, and that Henry therefore owed to Gregory the same obedience he owed to Saint Peter. To drive the point home, Gregory excommunicated a number of Henry's advisers. Henry thereupon renounced his obedience to Gregory, reminding the pope that his election had violated the terms of the 1059 Electoral Decree and calling on him to resign. Gregory responded by excommunicating Henry.

In itself, the excommunication of a king was not terribly unusual. Gregory, however, went much further by declaring that since Henry was no longer a faithful son of the church, he was therefore no longer the king of Germany. Gregory now called on Henry's subjects to rebel, prompting the Saxon nobility to renew the civil war that had ended only a few months before. In January 1077, Henry was forced to make a humiliating public submission to Pope Gregory at Canossa in the Italian Alps; but when the pope absolved him of his excommunication, Henry used the opportunity to rally his forces, crush his Saxon opponents, and drive Gregory himself from Rome.

"lay investiture." In fact, however, the "Investiture Conflict" raised fundamental issues about the nature of Christian kingship, the relationship between political and religious authority, and the control that popes and kings should exercise over the clergy. Not all these issues were fully resolved by 1122, when a compromise known as the Concordat of Worms finally ended the Investiture Conflict. But the conflict was a turning point nonetheless, because it brought to a permanent end the old Carolingian traditions of sacred kingship and established once and for all the independent jurisdictional authority of the church versus all lay rulers.

Gregory was a devoted church reformer whose goals were the traditional ones of ending simony and clerical marriage. However, Gregory became convinced that these goals could not be achieved until the Cluniac goal of ensuring free elections to all church offices had first been fully realized. Gregory therefore proceeded

Although the ultimate solution to the Investiture Conflict was to distinguish between "church" and "state" by reserving the symbols of spiritual office to the clergy while permitting laymen to award the symbols of temporal rule, such a distinction was no part of Gregory's own worldview. Indeed, it was precisely because neither Henry nor Gregory could conceive of Christendom as anything other than a thoroughly unified religious and political society that the conflict between them was so intractable. Both Henry and

KINGSHIP AS A RELIGIOUS OFFICE: TWO VIEWS

The Investiture Conflict raised fundamental issues concerning the nature of royal authority and the proper relationship between kingship and the church. In a remarkable outpouring of tracts and pamphlets, Europeans continued to debate these questions from a wide variety of perspectives, even after the conflict itself had come to an end. Writing in the early twelfth century, the Anglo-Norman Anonymous presented kings as religious figures who should rule the church as partners with Christ and the bishops. Writing in the 1130s, after the Concordat of Worms, Hugh of Saint Victor sought to distinguish earthly from heavenly power by assigning kings to rule over bodies and the clergy to rule over souls.

THE ANGLO-NORMAN ANONYMOUS

By divine authority and by institution of the holy fathers, kings are ordained in the church of God and are consecrated at the altar with sacred unction and benediction, that they may have the power of ruling the people of the Lord, the Christian people, which is the holy church of God. . . . Therefore kings receive in their consecration the power to rule this church, that they may rule it and strengthen it in judgment and justice and administer it in accordance with the discipline of Christian law; for they reign in the church, which is the kingdom of God, and reign together with Christ, in order that they may rule, protect and defend it. . . . The episcopal order too is instituted and consecrated with sacred unction and benediction, that it also may rule the holy church according to the form of doctrine given to it by God. . . . In this world, then, the priestly authority and the royal power hold the power of sacred government.

Some seek to divide the power in this fashion, saying that the priesthood has the power of ruling souls, the king that of ruling bodies, as if souls could be ruled without bodies and bodies without souls, which cannot be done by any means. For if bodies are well ruled it is necessary that souls are well ruled too and vice versa, since both are ruled for this purpose, that at the resurrection they may both be saved together. . . . Therefore the king is not to be called a layman, for he is the anointed of the Lord, a God through grace, the supreme ruler, supreme shepherd, master, defender and instructor of holy church, lord over his brothers, worthy to be adored by all men, chief and highest prelate. It is not to be said that he is inferior to the bishop because the bishop consecrates him, for it often happens that lesser men consecrate a greater, inferiors their superior, as when the cardinals consecrate a pope.

HUGH OF SAINT VICTOR

There are two lives, one earthly, the other heavenly, one corporeal, the other spiritual. By one the body lives from the soul, by the other the soul lives from God. Each has its own good by which it is invigorated and nourished. . . . Therefore, in each people distributed according to each life, powers were established. Among laymen, to whose zeal and forethought the things that are necessary for earthly life pertain, the power is earthly. Among the clergy, to whose office the goods of the spiritual life belong, the power is divine. The one power is therefore called secular, the other spiritual. . . . The earthly power has as its head the king. The spiritual power has as its head the supreme pontiff. All things that are earthly and made for the earthly life belong to the power of the king. All things that are spiritual and attributed to the spiritual life belong to the power of the supreme pontiff. The spiritual power excels the earthly or secular power in honor and dignity in proportion as the spiritual life is more worthy than the earthly, and the spirit more worthy than the body. For the spiritual power has to institute the earthly power that it may exist, and to judge it if it has not been good. The spiritual power itself was instituted by God in the first place and, when it errs, can be judged by God alone.

Brian Tierney, ed., *The Crisis of Church and State, 1050–1300* (Toronto, 1988), pp. 76–77, 94–95; slightly revised by R. C. Stacey.

QUESTIONS FOR ANALYSIS

1. How might the comments of the Anglo-Norman Anonymous be used to bolster later medieval arguments of kings who claimed to rule by divine right?
2. Why did Hugh of Saint Victor seek to differentiate religious and secular power?

Gregory shared the standard Carolingian presumption that it was the responsibility of earthly rulers to lead their subjects to heaven. They disagreed only about whether the supreme ruler within this unified Christian society should be the emperor or the pope. Neither could imagine a world in which a bishop's spiritual office could be separated from the lands and military forces he controlled or in which there could be two entirely separate systems of courts, one dealing with religious matters and controlled by the papacy, the other dealing with secular matters and controlled by kings. Without such a division between the spiritual and the temporal, however, the Investiture Conflict was irresolvable. Neither pope nor emperor was powerful enough to defeat the other; and on some level, all Europe was agreed that both spiritual and temporal authorities were necessary.

The consequences of the Investiture Conflict were thus quite different from what Pope Gregory or King Henry had imagined. On the immediate issue of lay investiture, the Concordat of Worms was a compromise. The German emperor was forbidden to dress prelates with the religious symbols of their office but was allowed to invest them with the symbols of their rights as political rulers because the emperor was recognized as their overlord. In practice, the German emperors, like the other kings of western Europe, thus managed to retain a great deal of influence over appointments to bishoprics and abbeys despite allowing the appearance of free elections.

The ultimate consequence of the Investiture Conflict was to create a lasting conceptual distinction between religion and politics in western Europe, and to identify the church with religious authority and the state with political authority. Both ideas had been largely absent from western Europe since the fourth century. The boundaries between temporal and spiritual authority would continue to be subject to controversy in medieval Europe. Should kings or clerics judge clergy who committed secular crimes? Who should rule on the validity of marriages when rights to inherit property were at issue? But these were jurisdictional conflicts that sought to define the boundaries between religion and politics. These conflicts did not challenge the fundamental presumption that such a distinction existed. Therefore, these conflicts were resolvable through law—one reason that the elaboration of legal systems, both ecclesiastical and secular, became such a preoccupation for twelfth- and thirteenth-century western Europe. In this respect also, the Investiture Conflict marks a watershed in European history.

THE CONSOLIDATION OF THE PAPAL MONARCHY

The Concordat of Worms was a compromise, but the Investiture Conflict as a whole was a victory for the papacy. The conflict helped rally the Western clergy behind the pope, strengthening the papacy's claim to supremacy over the entire clergy. The dramatic struggle also galvanized the European populace. Pope Gregory and his successors had urged the common people of Europe to reject the authority of simoniac bishops and married priests. Thousands had responded, sometimes with violence. The result was a vastly greater popular interest in religious matters, which the church thereafter would struggle to contain within the bounds of orthodoxy.

Like Gregory VII, the popes of the twelfth and thirteenth centuries were committed to establishing the monarchical authority of the papacy over the church.

Specially commissioned papal officials ("legates") were sent out from Rome to convey and enforce papal commands. Many of these commands arose from the hundreds of legal cases that poured into Rome from litigants seeking justice from the pope. In turn, this growing mass of litigation encouraged the development of an authoritative body of church law, or "canon law," by which such cases could be resolved.

As the power of the papacy and the prestige of the church grew, cases in canon law courts and appeals to Rome rapidly increased. By the mid-twelfth century legal expertise had become so important that almost all popes thereafter were trained canon lawyers, whereas previously they had usually been monks. Purists decried this development, but it was an inevitable consequence of the growing power and sophistication of the papal monarchy itself.

THE REIGN OF INNOCENT III

By common consent the most capable and successful of all the high medieval popes was Innocent III (1198–1216). Innocent, who was elected at the age of thirty-seven, was one of the youngest and most vigorous individuals ever to be raised to the papacy. His major goal was to unify all Christendom under papal hegemony and thereby to recover Jerusalem. Unlike Gregory VII, Innocent never questioned the right of kings and princes to rule directly in the secular sphere.

But Innocent believed nonetheless that as pope he was obliged to discipline kings whenever they sinned.

To place papal independence on a solid foundation, Innocent consolidated and expanded the papacy's territories in central Italy. For this reason Innocent is often regarded as the founder of the Papal States, of which Vatican City is the last surviving modern remnant. In Germany, he engineered the triumph of his own candidate for the imperial office, the emperor Frederick II—a triumph his papal successors would live to regret. He also levied taxes on the clergy to support crusades to the Holy Land and authorized a crusade against heretics in southern France. The crowning achievement of Innocent's pontificate, however, was the summoning of the Fourth Lateran Council to Rome in 1215. This representative assembly of the entire Western church defined central dogmas of the faith and made the leadership of the papacy within Christendom more apparent than ever.

POPES OF THE THIRTEENTH CENTURY

Innocent's reign was the high point of the papal monarchy, but it also sowed some of the seeds of future ruin. Innocent himself could administer the Papal States and impose taxes on the clergy without seeming to compromise the spiritual dignity of his office. But future popes who followed his policies had less of his stature and thus began to appear more like ordinary,

Pope Innocent III. A thirteenth-century fresco from the lower church of Sacro Speco, Subiaco, in Italy.

CHRONOLOGY

Reform of the Church, 900–1215

Monastic reform	900–1050
Cluniac priories	910–1050
Papal reform movement	1049–1122
Pope Leo IX	1049–1054
Pope Gregory VII	1073–1085
Investiture Conflict	1075–1122
Concordat of Worms	1122
Consolidation of the Papal monarchy	1100–1216
Canon law compiled	1140
Innocent III	1198–1216
Fourth Lateran Council	1215

gence to anyone who made a pilgrimage to Rome, was a tacit recognition that Rome, not Jerusalem, would henceforth be the central goal of Christian pilgrimage.

DECLINE OF THE PAPAL MONARCHY

The temporal might of the papal monarchy finally collapsed in the reign of Boniface VIII (1294–1303). Not all Boniface's troubles were of his own making. His greatest obstacle was that the national monarchies had gained more of their subjects' loyalties than the papacy could draw on because of the steady growth of royal power and the erosion of papal prestige. Boniface also had the misfortune to succeed a particularly pious, although inept, pope who resigned his office within a year. Since Boniface was entirely lacking in conventional piety or humility, the contrast turned many Christian observers against him.

Two disputes with the kings of England and France proved to be Boniface's undoing. The first concerned the clerical taxation that had been initiated by Innocent III. Although Innocent had levied this tax to support a crusade and had collected it himself, during the course of the thirteenth century the kings of England and France had begun to levy and collect clerical taxes on the pretext that they would use the funds to help the popes on future crusades to the Holy Land or aid in papal crusades against the Hohenstaufens, Germanic kings who also ruled Sicily. Then, at the end of the century, the kings started to levy their own war taxes on the clergy without any pretexts at all. Boniface tried to prohibit this step but found that he had already lost the support of the English and French clergy. Thus when the kings offered resistance, he had to back down.

Boniface's second dispute was with King Philip IV of France, who deliberately challenged the pope by proposing to try a French bishop for treason, in violation of canon law protections for the clergy. As in the earlier struggle between Gregory VII and Henry IV of Germany, a bitter propaganda war ensued, but now hardly anyone listened to the pope. Instead, Philip pressed absurd charges of heresy against Boniface and sent soldiers to arrest the pope and bring him to France to stand trial. At the papal residence of Anagni in 1303 Boniface, who was in his seventies, was captured and mistreated by Philip's forces. Although the pope was finally rescued by the local citizens, the shock of these events was too much for the old man's strength, and he died a month later. But still Philip pressed his advantage. He forced the new pope, Clement V, not only to justify this attack on Boniface but to thank Philip

acquisitive rulers. Innocent's successors also came into conflict with Innocent's protégé Frederick II. Innocent had raised up Frederick, but he could not imagine that Frederick would later become an inveterate opponent of papal power in Italy.

At first these and other problems were not fully apparent. The popes of the thirteenth century continued to enhance their powers and centralize the government of the church. They gradually acquired the right to appoint candidates to church offices, both high and low, and they exercised control over curriculum and doctrine at the University of Paris. But they also became involved in a protracted political struggle that led to their own demise as temporal powers. This struggle began with the attempt of the popes to destroy Frederick II. To some degree they were acting in self-defense because Frederick threatened their own rule in central Italy. But in combating him they overemployed their spiritual weapons. Instead of merely excommunicating and deposing Frederick, they also called a crusade against him—the first time a crusade was called on a large scale for blatantly political purposes.

After Frederick's death in 1250 a succession of popes made a still worse mistake by renewing and maintaining their crusade against the emperor's heirs. By misusing the institution of the crusade and trying to raise increasingly large sums of money to support it, the popes lost much of their spiritual prestige. In 1291 the last crusader outpost in the Holy Land fell without any papal help being offered. Pope Boniface VIII's papal jubilee of 1300, which offered a full crusader's indulpublicly for his zealous defence of the Catholic faith. Thereafter, any shred of papal independence with respect to the French monarchy was gone. For the next seventy years, the popes would reside not in Rome, but in Avignon (*ah-veh-NYON*), on the borders of the kingdom of France; and the papacy would come to be regarded as subservient to French diplomatic interests.

The humiliating defeat of Pope Boniface VIII at the hands of King Philip of France illustrates the enormous gap that had opened up by 1300 between the rhetoric and the reality of papal power. Although Boniface continued to claim universal spiritual and temporal authority over Christendom, declaring that kings ruled only through the "will and sufferance" of the church, in fact the papal monarchy now exercised its authority only through the will and sufferance of kings. After 150 years during which the religious nature of royal authority had been steadily undermined, the kings of the later thirteenth century were beginning to restore their sacred luster. This trend would continue throughout the later Middle Ages. Only in the seventeenth century, at the end of a century of religious wars brought on by the Protestant Reformation, would the distinctions between religion and politics established by the Investiture Conflict be fully and firmly established as fundamental principles of European life.

THE OUTBURST OF RELIGIOUS VITALITY

How did the Latin Church control popular heresy?

The papal reform movement spearheaded by Pope Gregory stimulated a European religious revival for two reasons. One was that the campaign to cleanse the church actually achieved a large measure of success: the laity could now respect the clergy more, and many were inspired to join the clergy themselves. According to a reliable estimate, the number of people who joined monastic orders in England increased tenfold between 1066 and 1200, a statistic that does not include the increase in priests. The other reason that the work of Gregory VII in particular helped inspire a revival was that Gregory explicitly called on the laity to help discipline their priests. In letters of great propagandistic power he denounced the sins of "fornicating

priests" and urged the laity to drive them from their pulpits or boycott their services. It is not surprising that he touched off something close to a vigilante movement in many parts of Europe. This excitement, taken together with the fact that the papal struggle with Henry IV was one of the first European events of universal interest, increased religious commitment immensely. Until about 1050, most western Europeans were Christians in name, but after the Gregorian period Christianity was becoming an ideal and a practice that began to direct their lives.

CISTERCIANS AND CARTHUSIANS

One of the most visible manifestations of the new piety was the growth of the Cistercian order of monks. By around 1100 no form of Benedictine monasticism seemed fully satisfactory to aspirants to holiness who sought great asceticism and, above all, intense "interiority"—unrelenting self-examination and meditative striving toward knowledge of God. The result was the founding of new orders to provide for the fullest expression of monastic idealism. One was the Carthusian order, whose monks were required to live in separate cells, abstain from meat, and fast three days each week on bread, water, and salt. The Carthusians never sought to attract great numbers and therefore remained a small group. But the same was by no means true of the Cistercians. The latter were monks who were first organized around 1100 and who sought to follow the Benedictine rule in the purest and most austere way possible. To avoid worldly temptations, they founded new monasteries in forests and wastelands as far away from civilization as possible. They shunned all unnecessary church decoration and ostentatious utensils, abandoned the Cluniac stress on an elaborate liturgy in favor of more contemplation and private prayer, and committed themselves to hard manual labor. Under the charismatic leadership of Saint Bernard of Clairvaux (1090–1153), a spellbinding preacher, brilliant writer, and the most influential European religious personality of his age, the Cistercian order grew exponentially. There were only 5 houses in 1115 but no less than 343 by 1153.

At the same time more people were entering or patronizing new monasteries, the nature of religious belief and devotion was also changing. One of many examples was a shift away from the cult of saints to emphasis on the worship of Jesus and veneration of the Virgin Mary. In the new Cistercian order, the veneration of saints' relics was replaced by a concentration on the Eucharist, or sacrament of the Lord's Supper. Of course celebration of the Eucharist had always been an important part of the Christian faith, but only in the twelfth century was it made really central, for only then did theologians fully work out the doctrine of transubstantiation. According to this doctrine, the priest during mass cooperates with God in the performance of a miracle whereby the bread and wine on the altar are changed or "transubstantiated" into the body and blood of Christ. The new theology of the Eucharist greatly enhanced the dignity of the priest and encouraged the faithful to meditate on the sufferings of Christ. As a result many developed an intense sense of identification with Christ and tried to imitate his life in different ways.

THE CULT OF THE VIRGIN MARY

Coming a close second to the renewed worship of Christ in the twelfth century was veneration of the Virgin Mary. Exactly why veneration of Mary became so pronounced in the twelfth century is not fully clear, but whatever the explanation, in the twelfth century the cult of Mary blossomed throughout all of western Europe. The Cistercians made her their patron saint, Saint Bernard preached about her life and virtues, and many of the magnificent new cathedrals of the age were dedicated to her: there was Notre Dame ("Our Lady") of Paris, and also a Notre Dame in Chartres, Rheims, Amiens, Rouen, Laon, and many other places. Mary's theological role was that of intercessor with her son for the salvation of human souls. Numerous stories circulated about seeming reprobates who were saved because they venerated Mary, who then spoke for them at the hour of death. For the first time a woman was thus given a central and honored place in Western Christianity. Theologians still taught that sin had entered the world through Eve, the first woman; but they now counterbalanced this by explaining how the triumph over sin had come through Mary, who gave birth to Christ, the second Adam.

HILDEGARD OF BINGEN

Mary's spiritual prestige also contributed to the increasing visibility of living religious women within the twelfth-century church. One of the most famous of these figures was the German nun and visionary Hildegard of Bingen (1098–1179). Hildegard's descriptions of her religious visions, dictated in freshly original Latin prose, were so compelling that contem-

Mary and Eve. The "correct" medieval theological view of women. On the left (Latin: *sinister*) side of the naked Adam, the naked Eve takes the apple of sin from the serpent and feeds it to erring mortals while a skeleton waits to carry them to hell. On Adam's right, Mary counteracts Eve by feeding a different "fruit"—the Eucharistic wafer—to the devout.

poraries had no difficulty in believing that she was directly inspired by God. Consequently when the pope visited Germany he gave her his blessing, and religious and secular leaders sought her advice. She also composed religious songs whose beauty has been rediscovered in recent times. Visionary though she was, she probably would be surprised to see people today looking for her works in racks of compact discs, where she is often alphabetized as "Bingen" between Beethoven and Brahms.

THE CHALLENGE OF POPULAR HERESY

This new focus on Mary's role in salvation reflected a more general optimism during the High Middle Ages that even ordinary lay believers could lead lives worthy of salvation. Saint Bernard of Clairvaux (d. 1153) was one of the last religious teachers in western Europe to believe that it would be best if all Christian men and women were to become monks or nuns. From the mid-twelfth century on, most Christian preachers concentrated instead on encouraging ordinary Christians to devote themselves more completely to their faith without abandoning their lives in the world. These preachers were responding to an enormous surge of religious interest among the laity themselves. As time went on, however, it became increasingly difficult to control and direct such lay enthusiasm. The result was the emergence of a wide variety of popular religious movements, some of which veered off in heretical directions.

The two most important such movements were Catharism and Waldensianism. Of the two, Catharism was more obviously at variance with Christian teachings. Cathars believed that all matter was evil and that holiness therefore required extreme ascetic practices. Some Cathars even argued that there were two gods, one good, the other evil; that the created world was entirely in the power of the evil god; and that spiritual people must therefore seek to escape it. Noblewomen in southern France played an important role in the spread of Catharism, sheltering the sect's wandering preachers and converting their households to the new faith. But the sect also attracted followers in northern Italy and the Rhineland, particularly among urban craftworkers.

> By the early fourteenth century, Catharism had been effectively destroyed, but small groups of Waldensians would survive in some regions until the seventeenth century.

More typical of these twelfth-century popular religious movements was Waldensianism. The movement took its name from its founder, a layman named Peter Waldo (or Valdes), a native of the French city of Lyon, but it quickly spread through southern France, northern Italy, Switzerland, and parts of Germany. Like their founder, Waldensians were lay people who sought to imitate the life of Christ's apostles by dedicating their lives to poverty and preaching. Because the Waldensians did not initially criticize Catholic doctrine, church officials did not at first interfere with them. But when the papacy forbade them to preach without permission from church officials, Waldo's followers refused to obey and were therefore condemned as heretics.

Pope Innocent III's response to these challenges was characteristically decisive. To suppress Catharism, Innocent authorized the nobles of northern France to launch a crusade against the southern French nobles who had permitted the heresy to flourish within their territories. The crusade destroyed much of the organizational infrastructure that had supported Catharism. At the same time, however, it also dispossessed many southern lords of their lands, which fell to the northern French invaders.

To root out the heretics that remained, Innocent's successors sent papal officials throughout southern France with full powers to convict, imprison, and even execute Cathars and their supporters. Similar inquisitorial procedures were adopted against the Waldensians, but with less success. Some groups of Waldensians rejoined the church, but most did not. By the early fourteenth century, Catharism had been effectively destroyed, but small groups of Waldensians would survive in some regions until the seventeenth century.

In response to the challenge of popular heretical movements, Pope Innocent III also took steps to clarify the church's own teachings and to enhance the special status of its priests. In 1215, at the Fourth Lateran Council, he reaffirmed that the sacraments administered by the church were essential to salvation. In particular, he stressed the importance of baptism, the Eucharist, and penance, requiring for the first time that all baptized Catholics confess their sins to a priest at least once a year, and then receive the Eucharist.

FRANCISCANS AND DOMINICANS

Pope Innocent also sought to counter the appeal of heretical movements by supporting idealistic new religious orders within the church. The most important of these were the new orders of friars—the Dominicans and the Franciscans. Friars were similar to monks in vowing to follow a rule, but they differed greatly from monks in their actual conduct. Instead of withdrawing into monasteries, they imitated the life of Jesus and his apostles, wandering through town and countryside in small groups, preaching and offering spiritual guidance. They also accepted voluntary poverty and begged for their subsistence. In these respects they resembled the Waldensian heretics, but they professed unquestioning obedience to the pope and sought to fight heresy themselves.

The Dominican order, founded by the Spaniard Saint Dominic (1170–1221) and approved by Innocent III in 1216, was particularly dedicated to the fight against heresy and to the conversion of Jews and Muslims. At first the Dominicans hoped to achieve these ends by preaching and public debate. To this end, many members of the order gained teaching positions in the infant European universities, where they contributed much to the development of philosophy and theology. The Dominicans always retained their reputation for learning, but they also came to believe that stubborn heretics were best controlled by legal procedures. Accordingly, they became the leading medieval administrators of inquisitorial trials.

In its origins the Franciscan order was quite different from the Dominican, being characterized less by a commitment to doctrine and discipline and more by a sense of emotional fervor. The founder of the Franciscans, the Italian Saint Francis of Assisi (1182–1226), was a layman who behaved at first remarkably like a social rebel and a heretic. The son of a rich merchant, he became dissatisfied with the materialistic values of his father and resolved to become a servant of the poor. Giving away all his property, he threw off his clothes in public, put on the tattered garb of a beggar, and began without official approval to preach salvation in town squares and to minister to outcasts in the darkest corners of Italian cities. He rigorously imitated the life of Christ and displayed indifference to doctrine, form, and ceremony, except for revering the sacrament of the Eucharist. But he did wish to gain the support of the pope. Another pope might have rejected the layman Francis as a hopelessly unworldly religious anarchist. But Francis was thoroughly willing to profess obedience, and Innocent had the genius to approve Francis's rule and grant him permission to preach. With papal support, the Franciscan order spread, and though it gradually became more "civilized," conceding the importance of administrative stability and doctrinal training for all its members, it continued to engage in revivalistic outdoor preaching and to offer a model for "apostolic living" within an orthodox framework. Thus Innocent managed to harness a vital new force that would help maintain a sense of religious enthusiasm within the church.

The success of the Franciscans and the Dominicans in combating the appeal of heretical movements was a great victory for the church, but this success was not sufficient to make the church feel secure in its hold on the people of Europe. Quite the opposite: despite its victories over the Cathars and the Waldensians, the church's inquisitorial processes ground on, discovering heretics even where none in fact existed.

The Earliest Known Portrait of Saint Francis. Dating from the year 1228, this fresco shows the saint without the "stigmata," the wounds of Christ's crucifixion he was believed to have miraculously received toward the end of his life.

JEWS AND CHRISTIANS

The church also became more and more concerned by the threat it believed that Jews posed to the faith of Christians, despite the fact that persecution and exploitative taxation had made most Jewish communities both smaller and weaker by 1300 than they had been in 1150. Although the church did not officially endorse the wilder flights of popular anti-Semitism, it did little to combat such attitudes either. As a result, by 1300 many ordinary Christians had come to believe that the Jews who lived among them were nothing less than agents of Satan, who routinely crucified Christian children, consumed Christian blood, and profaned the body of Christ in the Eucharist. The failures of organized campaigns to convert Jews to Christianity added to the sense among Christians that there was something demonic about the continuing Jewish presence in Christian society. Fanciful stories of Jewish wealth added an economic element to the developing anti-Semitism of European society, as did the fact that across much of thirteenth-century Europe, many Jews made their living as moneylenders.

Throughout the thirteenth century, the church had cooperated with kings in imposing more and more severe restrictions on Jewish life. Starting in the late 1280s, however, kings began to expel their Jewish subjects from their kingdoms altogether: in 1288 from southern Italy, in 1290 from England, and in 1306 from France. Further expulsions followed during the fourteenth century in the Rhineland, and in 1492 from Spain. By 1500, only Italy and Poland still retained any substantial Jewish populations, where they would survive until the Nazi Holocaust during World War II.

THE MEDIEVAL INTELLECTUAL REVIVAL

How did the recovery of classical learning affect medieval intellectual life?

The major intellectual accomplishments of the High Middle Ages were the expansion of primary education and lay literacy, the origin and spread of universities, the acquisition of classical and Muslim knowledge, and the development of new philosophical and theological ideas. Any one of these accomplishments would have earned the High Middle Ages an important place in the history of Western learning. Taken together, they mark the beginning of a new era in the intellectual history of Europe that would last until the scientific revolution of the seventeenth century.

THE GROWTH OF SCHOOLS

Around 800 Charlemagne ordered that primary schools be established in every bishopric and monastery in his realm. Although it is doubtful that this command was carried out to the letter, many schools were founded during the Carolingian period, only to be destroyed in the Viking invasions. Primary education in some monasteries and cathedral towns managed to survive,

but until around 1050 the extent and quality of basic education in the European west were meager. Thereafter, however, even contemporaries were struck by the rapidity with which schools sprang up all over Europe. The economic revival, the growth of towns, and the emergence of strong government allowed Europeans to dedicate themselves to basic education as never before.

The high medieval educational boom was more than merely a growth of schools, for the nature of the schools changed, and as time went on so did the curriculum and the clientele. The first basic mutation was that cathedral schools replaced monasteries as the main centers of European education. The papal monarchy energetically supported this development by ordering in 1179 that all cathedrals should set aside income for one schoolteacher, who could then instruct all who wished, rich or poor, without fee. The papacy believed correctly that this measure would enlarge the number of well-trained clerics and potential administrators.

At first the cathedral schools existed almost exclusively to train priests, with a curriculum designed to teach only such literacy as was necessary for perform-

Medieval Conception of Elementary Education. An illumination from a fourteenth-century manuscript depicts a master of grammar who simultaneously points to the day's lesson and keeps order with a cudgel.

How did the recovery of classical learning affect medieval intellectual life?

The Medieval Intellectual Revival   251

ing the basic services of the church. But soon after 1100 the curriculum was broadened as the growth of both ecclesiastical and secular governments created a growing demand for trained officials. A thorough knowledge of Latin grammar and composition began to be inculcated, based on the study of classical Roman authors such as Cicero and Virgil. Some schools also began to focus on the study of philosophy, particularly logic, once again relying on classical authors such as Aristotle and Porphyry. This new interest in classical literary and philosophical texts has led scholars to refer to this movement as the "Renaissance of the Twelfth Century."

Until about 1200 students in urban schools remained predominantly clerical. Even those who hoped to become lawyers or administrators rather than priests usually found it advantageous to take church orders. But afterward many pupils who entered schools were not in the clergy and never intended to be. Customarily, these students would not go to cathedral schools but to ones that were more practically oriented. Such schools grew rapidly in the course of the thirteenth century and became completely independent of ecclesiastical control. Not only were their students recruited from the laity, their teachers were usually laymen as well. As time went on instruction ceased to be in Latin and was offered in the European vernacular languages instead. But schools continued to be restricted to males. Some laywomen did become highly educated, but they were taught at home by private tutors.

> By 1340 roughly 40 percent of the Florentine population could read; by the later fifteenth century about 40 percent of the total population of England was literate as well.

The rise of lay education was an enormously important development in western European history. By 1340 roughly 40 percent of the Florentine population could read; by the later fifteenth century about 40 percent of the total population of England was literate as well. When we consider that literacy around 1050 was almost entirely limited to the clergy, we can appreciate that an astonishing revolution had taken place. Without it, many of Europe's other accomplishments would have been inconceivable.

THE RISE OF UNIVERSITIES

Universities developed during the twelfth century to offer instruction in subjects that could not be pursued in cathedral schools: advanced study of the liberal arts (grammar, logic, rhetoric, arithmetic, music, astronomy, and geometry) and professional studies in law, medicine, and theology. Bologna, the first university in Italy, specialized in the study of law. Paris, the earliest university north of the Alps, was particularly known for the liberal arts and theology. At Bologna, and subsequently at other universities in Italy, Spain, and southern France, students themselves hired the teachers, paid their salaries, and fined or discharged them for poor instruction. At Paris, however, as in northern Europe generally, teachers controlled the university, licensing teachers, setting examinations, and establishing fees.

In the thirteenth century, a fairly standardized curriculum and course of study took shape at most European universities. Young men would usually begin their studies in their early teens. For at least four years, a student would study Latin grammar, rhetoric, and the rules of logic. If he passed his examinations, he would be awarded the degree of bachelor of arts. To ensure himself a place in professional life, however, he might then devote at least three additional years of study to earn an advanced degree, such as master of arts or doctor of laws, medicine, or theology. The M.A. degree involved reading and commenting on the works of ancient authorities such as Aristotle and Euclid and on modern authorities such as Peter Lombard. Strictly speaking, doctoral degrees conferred only the right to teach medicine or law, not to practice them professionally. In practice, however, university degrees of all types were pathways to a variety of professional careers, especially in law, government, and the church.

Universities markedly increased the pace of European intellectual development. Many remarkable scholars studied and taught at the monasteries and cathedral schools of eleventh-century Europe. But by and large, they had regular access only to the books in their own monastic or cathedral libraries, and their ideas did not travel much beyond the walls of their own institutions. As a result, other scholars, working in similar isolation, might never learn about them. At a university like Paris, however, the greatest minds of the age came together in a single place to argue, debate, and refine their ideas in conversation with each other and with the greatest minds of classical antiquity. Students too came from all over Europe to absorb the new learning. As a result, new ideas developed more rapidly and circulated more widely across Europe than ever before.

NORWAY   SWEDEN   ◼ Uppsala

SCOTLAND   ◼ Aberdeen

◼ St. Andrews

◼ Glasgow

DENMARK

◻ Copenhagen

NORTH
SEA

◻ Greifswald

◼ Rostock

Elbe R.

ENGLAND

◻ Cambridge

◻ Oxford

◼ Frankfurt

◼ Wittenburg

◼ Leipzig

◼ Warsaw

POLAND

Vistula R.

Oder R.

HOLY ROMAN EMPIRE

◻ Erfurt

◻ Prague

◻ Cracow

ATLANTIC
OCEAN

◼ Louvain

◻ Cologne

◼ Trier   ◼ Mainz   ◼ Würzburg

Seine R.

◻ Paris

◼ Caen

◻ Heidelberg

Danube R.

◻ Vienna

◻ Pressburg

◼ Ingolstadt

◻ Angers   ◻ Orléans

Loire R.

◻ Freiburg   ◻ Tübingen

◼ Buda

HUNGARY

◻ Bourges

◻ Basel

◼ Nantes

◼ Besançon

SWITZERLAND

◼ Fünfkirchen

Rhine R.

◻ Poitiers

◻ Dôle

AUSTRIA

◼ Bordeaux

FRANCE

◻ Lyons

◻ Vercelli

◻ Treviso

◼ Cahors

◻ Grenoble

◻ Turin

◻ Pavia   ◻ Padua

◻ Valence

Rhône R.

◻ Piacenza

◻ Ferrara

VENETIAN EMPIRE

◻ Orange

◻ Reggio

◻ Bologna

Avignon

◻ Toulouse   ◼ Montpellier   ◼ Aix

◻ Florence

PAPAL STATES

ADRIATIC SEA

◻ Siena

◻ Arezzo

◻ Perugia

PORTUGAL

◻ Palencia

◻ Valladolid

◻ Huesca

◻ Perpignan

CORSICA

◻ Rome

◻ Coimbra

◻ Salamanca

◻ Lérida

◻ Saragossa

◼ Barcelona

SPAIN

◻ Siguenza

◻ Avila

◼ Toledo

Tagus R.

◼ Naples

◼ Salerno

◻ Valencia

◼ Palma

SARDINIA

KINGDOM
OF TWO
SICILIES

◼ Lisbon

BALEARIC ISLANDS

◻ Seville

MEDITERRANEAN
SEA

◻ Palermo

◼ Catania

**CENTURY UNIVERSITY
WAS FOUNDED**

◼ Twelfth century

◼ Thirteenth century

◻ Fourteenth century

◼ Fifteenth century

— Boundaries c. 1500

0   100   200   300 Miles

0   100   200   300 Kilometers

THE RISE OF THE MEDIEVAL UNIVERSITY

This map shows the distribution and dates of origin of the major universities of medieval Europe. Why were the twelfth- and thirteenth-century universities founded primarily in France, England, and northern Italy? Notice the number and geographical distribution of universities founded in the fourteenth and fifteenth centuries. How would you explain the pattern of these later foundations?

HOW DID THE RECOVERY OF CLASSICAL LEARNING AFFECT MEDIEVAL INTELLECTUAL LIFE?

THE MEDIEVAL INTELLECTUAL REVIVAL   253

THE RECOVERY OF CLASSICAL LEARNING

Universities spurred the intellectual reawakening of Europe. So too, however, did an influx of previously unknown works by ancient Greek and contemporary Muslim authorities that reached western Europe between roughly 1150 and 1250. Because very few early medieval Europeans knew Greek or Arabic, Christian intellectuals before around 1150 had to rely on the sixth-century Latin translations made by Boethius for their knowledge of Plato and Aristotle. Boethius, however, translated only about a third of Aristotle's works and only a portion of one of Plato's dialogues. As a result, Christian intellectuals had access to only a small part of the classical tradition known by Byzantium and the Islamic world.

Starting around 1150, however, a wave of new Latin translations of Aristotelian and other Greek scientific works began to pour into western Europe, the fruits of a remarkable collaboration between Muslim, Jewish, and Christian scholars working in Sicily and especially in Spain. Plato's works would remain unknown in Europe until the fifteenth century, as would the works of the classical Greek poets and dramatists. By the mid-thirteenth century, however, all of the works of Aristotle, and most of the surviving works of Euclid, Galen, and Ptolemy were widely available in western Europe in Latin translations, as were the important commentaries on these works by Muslim scholars such as Avicenna and Averroës. For the first time, therefore, it became possible for Christians scholars working in Europe to understand fully the challenge that the Greeks in general, and Aristotle in particular, represented to Christian beliefs.

SCHOLASTICISM

Scholasticism means literally "the doctrines taught in the schools"—that is, the universities of high and late medieval Europe. More precisely, scholasticism was a method of reconciling the claims of competing authorities by applying Aristotelian principles of logic to them, a method some early scholastic thinkers called "dialectic." But scholasticism was not only a logical method; it was also a worldview that presumed a fundamental compatibility between the knowledge humans can obtain through reason and sense experience and the truths imparted to them by divine revelation. Because medieval scholars believed that the Greeks were the masters of natural knowledge and that all revelation was in the Bible, scholasticism may be best defined as an intellectual system that sought to reconcile classical Greek philosophy with Christian faith through reason.

PETER ABELARD

One of the most important thinkers who paved the way for scholasticism without yet being fully a scholastic himself was the stormy Peter Abelard, who was active in and around Paris in the first half of the twelfth century. Probably the first western European who consciously sought to forge a career as an intellectual, Abelard was so adept at logic that even as a student he easily outshone the experts of his day who had the misfortune to be his teachers. Others might have been tactful about such superiority, but Abelard gloried in openly humiliating his elders in public debate, thereby making himself many enemies. To complicate matters, in 1118 he seduced a brilliant young woman, Heloise, who had been taking private lessons with him. When Heloise became pregnant, Abelard married her (against Heloise's own wishes), but the two decided to keep the marriage secret for the sake of his career. This, however, enraged Heloise's uncle because he thought that Abelard was planning to abandon Heloise; therefore,

Abelard and Heloise. Famous for his colorful personality, Abelard was popular with students but also made many enemies. After getting Heloise, one of his students, pregnant, he was castrated by her uncle and fled to a monastery. Subsequently, he wrote his most famous work, *The Story of My Calamities.*

he took revenge for his family's honor by having Abelard castrated. Abelard sought refuge as a monk, but his enemies soon engineered his first conviction for heresy. Still restless and cantankerous, he found no spiritual solace in monasticism and after quarreling and breaking with the monks of two different communities he returned to life in the world as a teacher in Paris. This was the peak of his career. But in 1141 he again was charged with heresy, now by the highly influential Saint Bernard, and condemned by a church council. Not long afterward the persecuted thinker abjured, and in 1142 he died in retirement.

Abelard told of these trials in a letter called *The Story of My Calamities*, one of the first autobiographical accounts written in western Europe since Saint Augustine's *Confessions*. His greatest contributions to the development of scholasticism, however, were made in his *Sic et Non* (Yes and no) and in his original theological works. In the *Sic et Non* Abelard gathered a collection of contradictory statements from the church fathers that spoke for both sides of 150 theological questions. It was once thought that the brash Abelard did this to embarrass authority, but the contrary is true. Abelard was confident that the apparently conflicting opinions

of these authorities were in fact compatible with each other. The *Sic et Non* was intended as a call to arms to Christian intellectuals to use their new logical methods to demonstrate this compatibility and so to reinforce Christian truths.

PETER LOMBARD

Abelard pioneered the application of Aristotelian logical methods to Christian theology. This would become the essence of the scholastic method. In Abelard's hands, however, it remained highly controversial. It was Abelard's student Peter Lombard who brought the scholastic method to maturity by demonstrating how it could resolve theological problems while remaining firmly within the boundaries of religious orthodoxy. Taking his inspiration from Abelard's *Sic et Non*, Peter Lombard organized his *Book of Sentences* (1155–1157) around a series of rigorously ordered theological questions. But after presenting conflicting answers from the Bible and Christian authorities to each question, he then proposed logically argued resolutions to the disagreements between them. The *Sentences* quickly became a standard text, studied and commented on in medieval universities and widely imitated in its organization and approach by future scholastic thinkers, including Saint Thomas Aquinas.

SAINT THOMAS AQUINAS

Peter Lombard wrote before the full importance of the newly recovered Aristotelian texts had become apparent to Christian intellectuals. By the mid-thirteenth century, however, the potential contradictions between Aristotelian philosophy and Christian theology could not be avoided. So great had Aristotle's prestige become that he was known simply as "The Philosopher," as if there were no others. The trouble, however, was that many of Aristotle's fundamental beliefs and presumptions clashed with the claims of Christian theology. The challenge that confronted thirteenth-century scholastics, therefore, was to reconcile "reason," epitomized by Aristotle, with the doctrines of the Christian faith as stated in the Bible and developed by the Fathers of the church.

This was the challenge to which Saint Thomas Aquinas (1225–1274) responded in his two great "summaries" of theology, the *Summa Contra Gentiles* (Summary against non-Christians) and his vast *Summa Theologica* (Summary of theology). As a member of the Dominican order and the most prominent scholastic theolo-

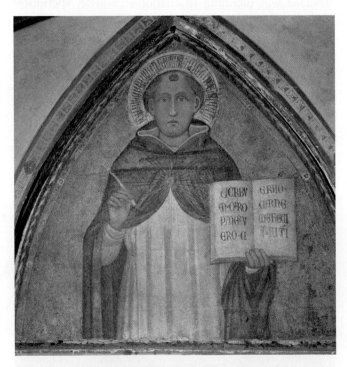

Saint Thomas Aquinas. Portrayed in this fourteenth century Florentine wall painting, Saint Thomas Aquinas defended studying the natural world through reason as a legitimate way of approaching Christian theology. He outlined his ideas about human reason in the *Summa Contra Gentiles* and the *Summa Theologica*.

WHAT COMMON THEMES UNITE THE LITERATURE, ART, AND ARCHITECTURE OF THE HIGH MIDDLE AGES?

THE BLOSSOMING OF LITERATURE, ART, AND MUSIC   255

gian at the University of Paris, Thomas was confident human reason, if properly employed, would confirm and reinforce the teachings of Christianity. He was also confident that because God had created the world, rational study of the natural world could lead human beings to knowledge of God. Reason alone was not sufficient for salvation; the Bible contained revealed truths necessary for salvation to which reason alone could not attain. But the conclusions of reason and faith were nonetheless entirely compatible. Reason supported faith and could thus take human beings a long way in their journey to God. It could also provide powerful arguments to persuade non-Christians to convert to Christianity.

SCHOLASTICISM: AN ASSESSMENT

It is often thought that medieval thinkers were constrained and timid in their willingness to embrace new ideas, but in fact scholastic thinkers were extraordinarily receptive to the new ideas that flowed out of the Islamic world during the High Middle Ages. As committed Christians, scholastics could not allow doubts to be cast on the principles of their faith, but otherwise they were glad to incorporate whatever they could from Greek and Arab philosophy. Considering that Aristotelian thought differed radically from anything accepted earlier in its emphasis on rationalism and the fundamental goodness and purposefulness of nature, its rapid acceptance by the scholastics was a philosophical revolution. Another false impression is that scholastic thinkers were greatly constrained by authority. Certainly they revered authority more than we do today, but such scholastics as Saint Thomas did not regard the mere citation of texts—except biblical revelation concerning the mysteries of the faith—as being sufficient to clinch an argument. Rather, the authorities were brought forth to outline the possibilities, but reason and experience then demonstrated the truth. Finally, it is often believed that scholastic thinkers were "antihumanistic," but modern scholars are coming to the opposite conclusion. Scholastics unquestionably gave primacy to the soul over the body and to otherworldly salvation over life in the here and now. But they also exalted the dignity of human nature because they viewed it as a glorious

> It is often thought that medieval thinkers were constrained and timid in their willingness to embrace new ideas, but in fact scholastic thinkers were extraordinarily receptive to the new ideas that flowed out of the Islamic world during the High Middle Ages.

divine creation, and they believed in the possibility of a working alliance between themselves and God. Moreover, they had extraordinary faith in the powers of human reason—probably more than we do today.

THE BLOSSOMING OF LITERATURE, ART, AND MUSIC

What common themes unite the literature, art, and architecture of the High Middle Ages?

The literature of the High Middle Ages was varied, lively, and impressive. The revival of grammatical studies in the cathedral schools and universities led to the production of some excellent Latin poetry. The best examples were secular lyrics, especially those written in the twelfth century by a group of poets known as the Goliards. Their lyrics celebrated the beauties of the changing seasons, the carefree life of the open road, the pleasures of drinking and sport, and especially the joys of love. The authors of these rollicking and satirical songs were mainly wandering students, although some were men of more advanced years. The names of most are unknown. Their poetry is notable both for its robust vitality and for its clear rejection of Christian asceticism.

VERNACULAR LITERATURE

In addition to Latin, the vernacular languages of French, German, Spanish, and Italian became increasingly popular as media of literary expression. At first, most of the literature in the vernacular languages was written in the form of the heroic epic. Among the leading examples were the French *Song of Roland*, the Norse eddas and sagas, the German *Song of the Nibelungs*, and the Spanish *Poem of the Cid*. These epics portrayed a virile but unpolished warrior society. Blood flowed freely, skulls were cleaved by battle axes, and heroic warfare, honor, and loyalty were the major themes. If women were mentioned at all, they were subordinate to men. Brides were expected to die for their beloveds, but husbands were free to beat their wives. In one French epic a queen who tried to influence her husband met with a blow to the nose; even though blood flowed she replied, "Many thanks, when it pleases you, you may do it again." Although we find such passages repugnant, the best of the vernacular epics have great literary power despite their unrelentingly masculine focus.

TROUBADOUR POETRY AND COURTLY ROMANCES

In comparison to the epics, an enormous change in both subject matter and style was introduced in twelfth-century France by the troubadour poets and the writers of courtly romances. Their style was far more finely wrought and sophisticated than that of the epic poets; and the most eloquent of their lyrics, which were meant to be sung to music, originated the theme of courtly love. The troubadours idealized women as marvelous beings who could grant intense spiritual and sensual gratification. But because the women they chose to love were usually the wives of powerful lords, they wrote more often of longing than of romantic fulfillment. The literary tradition originated by the southern French troubadours was continued by the trouvères in northern France and by the minnesingers in Germany. Thereafter many of their innovations were developed by later lyric poets in all Western languages.

An equally important twelfth-century French innovation was the composition of longer narrative poems known as romances, so called because there were written in vernacular, Romance (that is, deriving from Latin) languages. Romances told engaging stories; they often excelled in portraying character, and their subject matter was usually love and adventure. Some romances elaborated on classical Greek themes, but the most popular took their material from the legendary exploits of the British hero King Arthur and his chivalrous knights.

Not all high medieval narratives were so elevated as the romances in either form or substance. A very different new narrative form was the *fabliau*, or verse fable. Although fabliaux derived from the moral animal tales of Aesop, they quickly evolved into short stories that were written less to edify or instruct than to amuse. Often they were very coarse, treating sexual relations in a broadly humorous and thoroughly unromantic manner. Many were also strongly anticlerical, making monks and priests the butts of their jokes. They are significant as expressions of growing worldliness and as the first manifestations of the robust realism that was later to be perfected by Boccaccio and Chaucer.

THE DIVINE COMEDY

In a class by itself as the greatest work of medieval literature is Dante Alighieri's (*DAHN-tay ahl-ehg-YEE-ree*) *Divine Comedy*. Dante (1265–1321) was active dur-

The Poet Dante Driven into Exile. On the left Dante is expelled from Florence; on the right he begins work on his great poem, the *Divine Comedy*. From a mid-fifteenth-century Florentine manuscript.

A GOLIARDIC PARODY OF THE GOSPEL OF MARK, SATIRIZING THE PAPAL COURT

This selection is typical of the parodies of the liturgy and the Bible written by the freewheeling Latin poets of the twelfth century. This particular poem is written in mock biblical verse and puns on the Christian Gospel of Mark—a mark being a sum of money equal to two thirds of a pound of silver. Like all parodies, it was meant to be humorous, but its accusations—that bribery around the papal court perverted justice—were widespread in twelfth- and thirteenth-century Europe.

Here beginneth the Holy Gospel according to the marks of silver. In those days the Holy Father said unto the Romans: "When the Son of Man shall come unto the seat of our Majesty, first say unto Him: 'Friend, why art Thou come?' but if he continue knocking and give you nothing, then cast Him forth into outer darkness."

And it came to pass that a certain poor priest came to the court of the Lord Pope and cried out, saying, "Do ye at least have pity on me, servants of the Pope, for the hand of poverty hath afflicted me. Verily I am poor and have nothing. I beseech you, therefore, have mercy upon me and pity me." They, however, hearing this were sorely wroth and said unto him, "Friend, may thy poverty go with thee to hell. Get thee behind us, Satan; thou savorest not of money. Amen, Amen we say to thee: thou shalt not enter into the blessings of thy Lord until thou hast given thy last penny."

The poor man went therefore and sold his cloak and his coat and all that he had, and gave unto the cardinals and the treasurers and the papal flunkies. But they said unto him, "And this, what is this among so many?" And they cast him out utterly, and going forth he wept bitterly and would not be comforted.

After this there came to the court a rich priest, exceedingly wealthy, anointed with grease and great with wealth, who had committed murder for the sake of gain. He first gave unto the treasurer, then he gave unto the flunky, and then he gave unto the cardinals. But they reasoned among themselves, thinking they would receive more. Therefore when the Lord Pope heard that the cardinals and his servants had received many gifts from a priest he was sick, even unto death. But the rich man sent unto him a pallet of gold and silver, and immediately he was made whole.

The Lord Pope called unto him the cardinals and ministers and spake unto them saying: "Beware, brethren, lest any deceive you with vain words. For I have given you an example, so that as I have grasped, so should you grasp also."

Carmina Burana, 21, trans. Helen Waddell, in *The Wandering Scholars*, 7th ed. (London, 1934), pp. 150–151, rev. John E. Boswell.

QUESTIONS FOR ANALYSIS

1. How seriously do you think medieval men and women considered the parodies of the Goliards? For what purpose did the Goliards choose parody over other forms of literature?
2. Do you think that the Goliards were a disruptive force in medieval society? Do they have any modern parallels?

ing the early part of his career in the political affairs of his native city of Florence. In 1301 he was expelled from Florence after a political upheaval and was forced to live the rest of his life in exile. The *Divine Comedy*, his major work, was written during this final period. Dante's *Divine Comedy* is a monumental narrative in powerful rhyming Italian verse, which describes the poet's journey through hell, purgatory, and paradise. At the start Dante tells of finding himself in a "dark wood," his metaphor for a deep personal midlife crisis in which he had wandered away from his Christian faith. He is led out of this forest of despair by the Roman poet Virgil, who represents the heights of classical reason and philosophy. Virgil guides Dante on a trip through hell and purgatory; then Dante's deceased beloved, Beatrice, who symbolizes Christian wisdom and blessedness, takes over and guides him through paradise. In the course of this progress from hell to heaven Dante meets both historical personages and his own contemporaries, who explain why they met their several fates. As the poem progresses Dante grows in wisdom and understanding, until finally he returns with new confidence and certainty to his own lost Christian faith. Dante stressed the priority of salvation, but he viewed earth as existing for human benefit. He allowed humans free will to choose good and avoid evil, and he accepted Greek philosophy as authoritative in its own sphere. Above all, his sense of hope and his ultimate faith in humanity—remarkable for a defeated exile—powerfully express the dominant mood of the High Middle Ages, making Dante one of the two or three most stirringly affirmative writers who ever lived.

> The essential features of the Romanesque style were the rounded arch, massive stone walls, enormous piers (support columns), small windows, and the predominance of horizontal lines.

ART AND ARCHITECTURE

The closest architectural equivalents of the *Divine Comedy* are the great high medieval Gothic cathedrals, for they too have qualities of vast scope, balance intricate detail with careful symmetry, soaring height, and affirmative religious grandeur. But before we approach the Gothic style, it is best to introduce it by means of its high medieval predecessor, the style of architecture known as the Romanesque. This style aimed to manifest the majesty of God in stone by rigorously subordinating all architectural details to a uniform system. The essential features of the Romanesque style were the rounded arch, massive stone walls, enormous piers (support columns), small windows, and the predominance of horizontal lines. Together, these features gave Romanesque architecture a sense of stability and permanence. Interiors were plain, but sometimes relieved by mosaics or frescoes in bright colors and—a very important innovation for Christian art—the introduction of sculptural decoration, both within and without. For the first time, full-length human figures appeared on facades. These are usually grave and elongated far beyond natural dimensions, but they have much evocative power and represent the first manifestations of a revived interest in sculpting the human form.

In the course of the twelfth and thirteenth centuries the Romanesque style was supplanted throughout most of Europe by the Gothic. Although trained art historians can see how certain traits of the one style led to the development of the other, the appearance of the two styles is distinctively different. In fact, the two seem as different as the epic is different from the romance, an appropriate analogy because the Gothic style emerged in France in the mid-twelfth century exactly when the romance did and because it was far more sophisticated, graceful, and elegant than its predecessor, in the same way that the romance compared with the epic.

Gothic architecture was one of the most intricate of building styles. Its basic elements were the pointed arch, groined and ribbed vaulting, and the flying buttress. These devices made possible a much lighter and loftier construction than could ever have been achieved with the round arch and the engaged pier of the Romanesque. In fact, the Gothic cathedral could be described as a skeletal framework of stone enclosed by enormous windows. Other features included lofty spires, rose windows, delicate tracery in stone, elaborately sculpted facades, multiple columns, and the more frequent use of gargoyles, or representations of mythical monsters, as decorative devices. Ornamentation was generally concentrated on the exterior. But the inside of the Gothic cathedral was never somber or gloomy. The stained-glass windows served not to exclude the light but to glorify it, to catch the rays of sunlight and suffuse them with a richness and warmth of color that nature itself could hardly duplicate even in its happiest moods.

WHAT COMMON THEMES UNITE THE LITERATURE, ART, AND ARCHITECTURE OF THE HIGH MIDDLE AGES?

THE BLOSSOMING OF LITERATURE, ART, AND MUSIC   259

Many people still think of the Gothic cathedral as the expression of purely ascetic otherworldliness, but this estimation is highly inaccurate. Certainly all churches are dedicated to the glory of God and hope for life everlasting, but Gothic ones sometimes included stained-glass scenes of daily life that had no overt religious significance at all. Gothic sculptures of religious figures such as Jesus, the Virgin Mary, and the saints were becoming far more naturalistic than anything hitherto created in the medieval West. Each cathedral, with its many symbolic figures, was a kind of encyclopedia of medieval knowledge carved in stone. Finally, Gothic cathedrals were manifestations of urban pride. Always located in the growing medieval cities, they were meant to be both centers of community life and expressions of a town's greatness. When a new cathedral went up the people of the entire community participated in erecting it, and rightfully regarded it as almost their own property.

DRAMA AND MUSIC

Surveys of high medieval accomplishments should not omit drama and music. Our own modern drama descends at least as much from the medieval form as from the classical one. Throughout the medieval period some Latin classical plays were known in manuscript but were never performed. Instead drama was born all over again within the church. In the early Middle Ages certain passages in the liturgy began to be acted out.

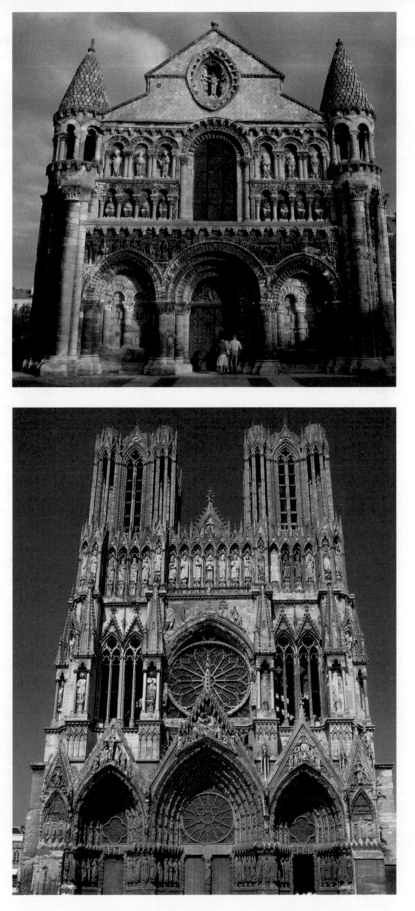

Romanesque and Gothic. Top: West front of the Church of Notre Dame la Grande, Poitiers. Constructed between 1135 and 1145, this typical example of Romanesque architecture emphasizes the repetition of rounded arches and horizontal lines. Bottom: Rheims Cathedral. Built between 1220 and 1299, this High Gothic cathedral places great stress on vertical elements. The gabled portals, pointed arches, and multitude of pinnacles all accentuate the height of this structure.

Then, in the twelfth century, short religious plays in Latin began to be composed for performance inside churches. Rapidly thereafter, these Latin plays were supplemented or supplanted by ones in the vernacular so that the whole congregation could understand them. Around 1200, these started to be performed outside, in front of the church, so that they would not take time away from the services. As soon as that happened, drama entered the everyday world: nonreligious stories were introduced, character portrayal was expanded, and the way was prepared for the Elizabethans and Shakespeare.

Just as drama developed within the liturgy and then moved beyond it, so too did music. Until the High Middle Ages Western music was homophonic—that is, it developed only one melody at a time without any harmonic background. The great high medieval invention was polyphony, the playing or singing of two or more harmonious melodies together. Some experiments along these lines may have begun as early as the tenth century, but the most fundamental breakthrough was achieved at the cathedral of Paris around 1170, when the mass was first sung by two voices weaving together two different melodies in "counterpoint." Roughly concurrently, systems of musical notation were also invented. Because performers no longer had to rely on memory, music could become more complex. All the greatness of European music followed from these first steps.

CONCLUSION

For almost 100 years, scholars have spoken of the sweeping intellectual, religious, and cultural changes of the High Middle Ages as constituting the "Renaissance of the Twelfth Century." This categorization still seems apt. Like those of the more famous Italian Renaissance of the fourteenth and fifteenth centuries, the intellectual changes of the High Middle Ages were profoundly influenced by the recovery and intensive study of classical texts. But in both periods, the use made of these classical texts was distinctive and unique. Neither of these movements were mere revivals; rather, both were creative adaptations of classical ideas to a new and distinctively Christian culture.

Even more so than the Italian Renaissance, however, the twelfth-century renaissance marks the origin of a set of distinctive attitudes and ideas that have characterized western European civilization ever since. Our modern conceptions of love and friendship, our fascination with human motivation and intention, indeed our very interest in psychology itself, all derive from twelfth-century developments. So too does our emphasis on the essential interiority of Christian piety, our vision that "true religion" ought to be expressed in practical works of charity in the world, and our presumption that religion and politics are separable spheres of human endeavor and concern. Even our modern impulse to define and persecute minority groups has roots in twelfth- and thirteenth-century efforts to suppress Jews, heretics, and sexual minorities.

Many of the people who made such important contributions to learning, thought, literature, architecture, drama, and music must have intermingled with each other in the Paris of the High Middle Ages. Some of them no doubt prayed together in the cathedral of Notre Dame. The names of the leading scholars are remembered, but the names of most of the others are unknown. Yet taken together they did as much for the civilization of Europe, and created as many enduring monuments, as did their counterparts in ancient Athens. Their names may be forgotten, but their achievements live on still.

KEY TERMS

Cluny

Investiture Conflict

cult of the Virgin Mary

Franciscan order

Dominican order

Peter Abelard

Saint Thomas Aquinas

courtly romances

Divine Comedy

Gothic style

SELECTED READINGS

Baldwin, John W. *The Scholastic Culture of the Middle Ages: 1000–1300.* Lexington, Mass., 1971. A fine introduction.

Blumenthal, Uta-Renate. *The Investiture Controversy.* Philadelphia, 1988. A clear review of a complicated subject.

Boswell, John E. *Christianity, Social Tolerance, and Homosexuality: Gay People in Western Europe from the Beginning of the Christian Era to the Fourteenth Century.* Chicago, 1980. A pioneering account, particularly good on twelfth-century poetry.

Chrétien de Troyes. *Arthurian Romances.* Trans. W. W. Kibler. New York, 1991.

Clanchy, Michael T. *Abelard: A Medieval Life.* Oxford and Cambridge, Mass., 1997. A great biography.

Cobban, Alan B. *The Medieval Universities.* London, 1975. The best short treatment in English.

Colish, Marcia. *Medieval Foundations of the Western Intellectual Tradition, 400–1400.* New Haven, Conn., 1997. An encyclopedic and exhaustive work, best used as a reference.

Dante Alighieri. *The Divine Comedy.* Trans. Mark Musa. 3 vols. Baltimore, Md., 1984–1986.

Dronke, Peter. *Women Writers of the Middle Ages.* New York, 1984. A rich literary study.

Gottfried von Strassburg. *Tristan.* Trans. A. T. Hatto. Baltimore, Md., 1960.

Knowles, David. *The Evolution of Medieval Thought.* 2d ed. London, 1988. An authoritative survey, thoroughly revised in the second edition.

Lambert, Malcolm. *Medieval Heresy.* 3d ed. Oxford and Cambridge, Mass., 2002. The standard synthesis; deeply learned and fully annotated.

Lawrence, Clifford Hugh. *The Friars: The Impact of the Early Mendicant Movement on Western Society.* London and New York, 1994. The best short introduction to the early history of the Franciscans and the Dominicans.

Lawrence, Clifford Hugh. *Medieval Monasticism: Forms of Religious Life in Western Europe in the Middle Ages.* 3d ed. London and New York, 2000. This new edition includes material on the friars drawn from his 1994 book.

Leclerq, Jean. *Bernard of Clairvaux and the Cistercian Spirit.* Kalamazoo, Mich., 1976. An empathetic account by the greatest twentieth-century scholar of Cistercianism.

Leclerq, Jean. *The Love of Learning and the Desire for God.* 3d ed. New York, 1982. A beautiful account of twelfth-century monastic culture, seen from the perspective of Saint Bernard of Clairvaux.

The Letters of Abelard and Heloise. Trans. Betty Radice. London and New York, 1974. Includes Abelard's autobiographical *Story of My Calamities.*

Miller, Maureen C. *Power and the Holy in the Age of the Investiture Conflict: A Brief History with Documents.* Boston, 2005. A stimulating approach to this eleventh-century conflict, with many newly translated sources.

Morris, Colin. *The Papal Monarchy: The Western Church from 1050 to 1250.* Oxford, 1989. An excellent scholarly survey; part of the Oxford History of the Christian Church series.

Newman, Barbara, ed. *Voice of the Living Light: Hildegard of Bingen and Her World.* Berkeley and Los Angeles, Calif., 1998. The best introduction to Hildegard's life and work; discusses her roles as abbess, religious thinker, prophet, correspondent, artist, medical writer, composer, dramatist, and poet.

Southern, Richard W. *Scholastic Humanism and the Unification of Europe.* Vol. 1: *Foundations.* Oxford and Cambridge, Mass., 1995. A major reinterpretation of scholasticism and humanism by the foremost historian of both traditions.

Southern, Richard W. *Western Society and the Church in the Middle Ages.* Baltimore, Md., 1970. An extremely insightful interpretation of the interplay between society and religion, engagingly written by one of the greatest historians of the twentieth century.

Swanson, R. N. *The Twelfth-Century Renaissance.* Manchester, UK, 1999. The most accessible and up-to-date survey of the intellectual developments of the twelfth century.

Tierney, Brian. *The Crisis of Church and State, 1050–1300.* Toronto, 1988. An indispensable collection for both teachers and students.

Wakefield, Walter, and Austin P. Evans, eds. and trans. *Heresies of the High Middle Ages.* New York, 1969, 1991. A comprehensive collection of sources, best used in conjunction with Lambert.

Wilhelm, James J., ed. and trans. *Medieval Song: An Anthology of Hymns and Lyrics.* New York, 1971. An excellent collection of sacred and secular poetry that illustrates the connections between them.

Wolfram von Eschenbach. *Parzival.* Trans. H. M. Mustard and C. E. Passage. New York, 1961.

PART IV

FROM MEDIEVAL TO MODERN

FOR MOST OF THE TWENTIETH CENTURY, historians portrayed the Italian Renaissance and the Protestant Reformation as marking a dramatic break in European history, which brought the Middle Ages to an end and ushered in the modern world. To be sure, the sixteenth and seventeenth centuries saw decisive transformations in European life. For the first time, European sailors, soldiers, and merchants forged worldwide trading networks that brought the mineral and agricultural riches of the Western Hemisphere into their Atlantic ports. The Protestant Reformation shattered the religious unity of medieval Europe, and a century of religious wars served only to cement those divisions. Meanwhile, new trends in cultural and intellectual life, many of which had begun in fourteenth- and fifteenth-century Italy, began to spread widely throughout the rest of Europe.

It is increasingly clear, however, that most of the new developments of the sixteenth and seventeenth centuries had deep roots in the later Middle Ages. The voyages that took sixteenth-century Europeans around the globe began in the thirteenth century with the conquest of the "Atlantic Mediterranean." The intensive study of classical Roman and Greek literature that characterized the Italian Renaissance developed out of the classical revival in the twelfth and thirteenth centuries. Even the theological doctrines of the Protestant reformers had roots in the theological controversies of the later Middle Ages. And all these developments took place in the context of continuing cultural and economic exchange among Europe, the Islamic world, and Byzantium.

	POLITICS	SOCIETY AND CULTURE	ECONOMY	INTERNATIONAL RELATIONS
1200	Chingiz (Genghis) Khan rules over Mongol clans (1206–1227)		"Silk Road" connects Europe with India, China, and Indonesia (1200s) Polo brothers travel to China (1200s)	Mongols conquer southern Russia (1237–1240) Mongols annihilate Hungarian army at River Sajo (1241) Mongol forces withdraw from Europe (1241)
1300	Yuan dynasty in China (1279–1368) Rise of Ottoman dynasty (1300) Babylonian Captivity of the church (1305–1378) Jacquerie rebellion in France (1358) Ming dynasty in China (1368–1644)	Civic humanism begins in Italy (1300s) Francesco Petrarch (1304–1374) Giovanni Boccaccio (1313–1375) Over a tenth of Europe dies during the Great Famine (1316–1322) John Wyclif, Oxford theologian (1330–1384) Geoffrey Chaucer (1340–1400) Onset of the Black Death, from which half of Europe dies (1347) Leonardo Bruni (1370–1444)	Development of mechanical clocks and compasses (1300) Explorers reach Azores and Cape Verde Islands (1300s) Severe flooding ruins crops, breeds pestilence (1315) Heavy cannons first employed (1330) Silver shortage begins in Europe (1340s)	 Hundred Years' War (1337–1453)
	The Great Schism, ended by Council of Constance (1378–1417) Florentine Ciompi uprising (1378) English Peasants' Revolt (1381)	Jan van Eyck (1380–1441) University of Heidelberg founded (1385)	Medici family, originators of modern banking, flourishes (1397–1494)	Poland and Lithuania united (1386) Ottomans defeat Serbian Empire at battle of Kosovo (1389)
1400	Italian territorial papacy (1417–1517) Edward, duke of York dethrones Henry VI after Wars of the Roses (1461) Reign of Ivan III, the Great, tsar of all Russias (1462–1505) Ferdinand of Aragon marries Isabella of Castile, forming modern Spain (1469)	Giovanni Aurispa returns with classical manuscripts (1423) Sandro Botticelli (1445–1510) Neoplatonism in Italy (1450–1600) Leonardo da Vinci (1452–1519) Desiderius Erasmus (1469–1536) Niccolò Machiavelli, author of *The Prince* (1469–1527) Albrecht Dürer (1471–1528) Sir Thomas More (1478–1535) Raphael (1483–1520) The High Renaissance begins (1490) The Catholic Reformation begins (1490)	Portugal establishes Atlantic colonies (1400–1460) Invention of movable type; the Gutenberg Bible (1454) Explorers round the Cape of Good Hope (1487) Dias rounds southern tip of Africa (1488) Portugal founds slave-based plantation in St. Thomas (1490) Columbus lands in West Indies (1492) Disease kills much of Native American population (1492–1538) Vasco da Gama reaches India (1498)	Rise of Grand Duchy of Moscow (1400s) Turks conquer Constantinople (1453) England loses Bordeaux (1453) French monarchy absorbs Burgundy (1477) Catholic monarchs expel Jews (1492) and Muslims (1502) from Spain
1500	Reign of Charles V, Holy Roman emperor (1519–1556)	Saint Peter's Basilica erected in Rome (1500–1520) Papacy of Julius II (1503–1513) Saint Francis Xavier, missionary in Asia (1506–1552) Andrea Palladio (1508–1580) John Calvin (1509–1564) Papacy of Leo X, son of Lorenzo de Medici (1513–1521)	Grain prices in Europe increase fivefold (1500–1650)	

POLITICS	SOCIETY AND CULTURE	ECONOMY	INTERNATIONAL RELATIONS	
				1515
		Portuguese ships reach Spice Islands and China (1515)		
	Luther posts Ninety-five Theses (1517)		Cortés conquers Aztec Empire (1519–1522)	
	Emergence of Zwinglianism, Anabaptism, and Calvinism (1520–1550)		Ottomans conquer Syria, Egypt, and the Balkans (1520–1540)	
	Edict of Worms (1521)			
	Peter Brueghel, painter of *Harvesters* and *Massacre of the Innocents* (1525–1569)		Charles V, Holy Roman emperor, sacks Rome (1527)	
	Baldassare Castiglione's *Book of the Courtier* (1528)			
	Michel de Montaigne (1533–1592)		Francisco Pizarro topples Inkas (1533)	
	Henry VIII becomes head of the Church of England (1533–1534)			
	Calvin's *Institutes of the Christian Religion* (1536)			
	Saint Ignatius Loyola publishes *Spiritual Exercises* (1541)	Rapid inflation marks the Price Revolution (1540s)		
	El Greco, painter of *View of Toledo* (1541–1614)	Silver found in Mexico and Bolivia (1543–1548)		
	Roman Inquisition begins (1542)			
	Council of Trent (1545–1563)			
Reign of Philip II of Spain (1556–1598)	Edmund Spenser, author of *The Faerie Queen* (1552–1599)		Peace of Augsburg (1555)	
Reign of Elizabeth I of England (1558–1603)				
	First *Roman Index of Prohibited Books* established (1564)			
	William Shakespeare (1564–1616)		Ottomans defeated by Habsburgs and Venetians at Lepanto (1571)	
	Papacy of Pius V (1566–1572)		Philip II of Spain annexes Portugal (1580)	
	Saint Bartholomew's Day massacre (1572)			
English navy defeats the Spanish Armada (1588)		New World silver production peaks at 10 million ounces (1590s)		
Reign of Henry IV, first of the Bourbon dynasty in France (1589–1610)				1600
Edict of Nantes (1598)				
Reign of James I, first of the Stuart dynasty in England (1603–1625)			Thirty Years' War (1618–1648)	
	John Milton (1608–1674)			
		Spanish economy collapses when silver imports drop (1620–1640)		
Cardinal Richelieu, first minister of France (1624–1642)	Blaise Pascal (1623–1662)			
Reign of Charles I of England (1625–1649)			Gustavus Adolphus of Sweden enters Thirty Years' War (1630)	
English Civil War (1642–1649)				
The Fronde, a series of French aristocratic revolts (1648–1653)			Peace of Westphalia (1648)	
Oliver Cromwell rules England (1649–1658)				
Louis XIV of France comes of age (1651)	Thomas Hobbes's *Leviathan* (1651)			
Charles II and the Restoration (1660–1685)				

THE LATER
MIDDLE AGES,
1300–1500

TEXTBOOK ACCOUNTS OF THE LATER MIDDLE AGES generally make for grim reading. The period is traditionally seen as one of disintegration and crisis, in which the high medieval world collapsed in chaos and violence, producing social and political upheaval, religious disillusionment, and widespread psychological anxiety. During these disastrous centuries, epidemic disease cut the European population in half, crops failed, and the economy shrank. The shortcomings of the church brought a storm of criticism, but few reforms in religious life resulted. Even the weather got worse. It is all enough to make the sensitive reader shudder, turn the page, and pass on to the sunnier atmosphere of the Italian Renaissance, the chapter that usually follows this late medieval litany of disaster, death, and decay.

There can be no doubt that the fourteenth and fifteenth centuries were indeed an age of adversity for Europeans. Famine and plague cut fearful swaths through the populace; war was a recurrent fact of life across most of the continent; the economy shrank; and the papacy spent 70 years in continuous exile from Italy, only to see its prestige decline even further after it returned to Rome. But to characterize these centuries as simply ones of doom and gloom would profoundly misrepresent the courage and resilience that the people of Europe displayed in the face of famine, war, and plague. It would also cause us to miss many of the fundamental transformations that shaped European society for the next 400 years. Despite the challenges it faced, European civilization did not collapse during the later Middle Ages. Instead, this was a period of creativity and innovation that preserved and extended the most enduring features of high medieval European life into the early modern era.

FOCUS QUESTIONS

- How did climate change affect early-fourteenth-century Europe?

- What were the economic consequences of the Black Death on Europe?

- To what extent were the social changes of the later Middle Ages a consequence of the plague?

- Why was warfare such a constant feature of late medieval life?

- Why did Russia develop differently from other late medieval European states?

- Why did late medieval efforts to reform the institutions of the Catholic Church fail?

- Were late medieval people disillusioned with their church?

- What accounts for the remarkable creativity of late medieval cultural life?

- How did technological advances affect everyday life?

CHANGES IN THE LAND

How did climate change affect early-fourteenth-century Europe?

By 1300, the high medieval expansion of the European economy was reaching its limits. Between 1000 and 1300, the European population tripled in size. To feed its growing numbers of people, Europe transformed itself into a continent of grain fields. The pressures to produce more grain brought dramatic changes to the landscape that undermined the long-term sustainability of European agriculture. Forests were cleared, marshes drained, and pastureland reduced, all in order to grow more grain. But still Europe was barely able to feed itself. By 1300, the continent was reaching the ecological and technological limits of its capacity to support its population.

Until the early fourteenth century, agricultural conditions generally favored the intensive cultivation of cereal crops. During the twelfth and thirteenth centuries, a gradually warming climate lengthened the growing season in northern Europe, making it possible to grow grain even on thin or boggy soils better suited to pasturing animals or planting fruit trees. Starting in the Arctic at the end of the thirteenth century, however, this warming trend reversed itself, and from the middle of the fourteenth century, the mainland of Europe became progressively colder. This change was not cataclysmic, but it was sufficient to cause substantial changes in rainfall patterns, to shorten growing seasons, and to lessen the productivity of cereal agriculture in northern Europe, especially in marginal areas such as Greenland, where European settlements disappeared entirely during the fifteenth century.

The vulnerability of the European economy to such long-term climate change was dramatically revealed in 1315, when a great famine struck northern Europe that would last for seven years. The winters in northern Europe between 1310 and 1330 were exceptionally harsh, and the summers unseasonably cold and wet. Then, starting in 1315, torrential spring and summer rains washed away sown fields, while the cold summer weather prevented the remaining crops from ripening. The result was starvation on a very large scale. Weakened by malnutrition, people and domestic animals also fell victim to epidemic diseases. By 1322, when conditions at last began to improve, 10 to 15 percent of the population of northern Europe had perished. Even after 1322, however, growing conditions did not return entirely to normal. Cold winters continued until 1330. In Italy, floods swept away the bridges of Florence in 1333, and in 1343 a tsunami destroyed the port of Amalfi. Earthquakes and comets added to the sense of alarm and uncertainty.

And then a disaster struck that was so horrifying it seemed to many to portend the end of the world.

Peasants Harvesting Grain. Harvesting with sickles was backbreaking work, as this illustration of English serfs working under the direction of a reeve indicates. By the early fourteenth century, Europe had become a continent of grain fields.

WHAT WERE THE ECONOMIC CONSEQUENCES OF THE BLACK DEATH ON EUROPE?

THE BLACK DEATH AND ITS CONSEQUENCES   269

THE BLACK DEATH AND ITS CONSEQUENCES

What were the economic consequences of the Black Death on Europe?

 The "Black Death" is the name given since the sixteenth century to a deadly illness that spread from Mongolia to China, northern India, the Middle East, and the Crimea during the 1330s and 1340s. By 1346, the disease had reached the Black Sea. From there, in 1347, Genoese galleys brought it, inadvertently, to Sicily and northern Italy. From Italy the plague (as contemporaries called it, from the Latin word *plaga*, "a blow") spread throughout western Europe along the trade routes, first striking the seaports, then moving inland. It moved with astonishing rapidity, advancing about two miles per day during 1348 and 1349 in both summer and winter. By 1350, the plague had reached Scandinavia and northern Russia, from which it then spread southward until it linked up with the earlier waves of infection that had brought it from Central Asia to the Black Sea.

After this initial pandemic outbreak, the Black Death continued to erupt in local epidemics for the next 300 years. Across most of fifteenth-century Europe, localities could expect a renewed outbreak of plague every decade. Gradually, however, the attacks of plague became less frequent and less deadly. Mortality from the Black Death was on an almost unimaginable scale. At least a third, and probably half, the population of Europe died in the initial outbreak of 1347–1350. Thereafter, the population continued to decline. By 1450, the combined effects of plague, famine, and war had reduced the total population of Europe by at least half, and perhaps by as much as two thirds, from its high point around 1300. The European population did not fully recover to its preplague levels until the end of the seventeenth century.

Initial reactions to the Black Death ran the gamut from frenzied panic to supine resignation. Observers quickly realized that the plague was contagious, but how precisely it spread remained a mystery. At the time, most medical experts believed that the plague was spread through bad air and so urged people to flee from stricken areas (thus spreading the disease even faster) or to cover their noses with sweet-smelling flowers to counteract the miasma (as the "bad air" was known). Some people locked themselves in their houses, refusing to admit anyone until the threat had passed. Others did nothing, surrendering themselves to their fate; while still others (or so at least it was alleged by moralists) abandoned themselves to their desires, declaring, "Let us eat, drink, and be merry, for tomorrow we may die."

Others looked for scapegoats. When rumors began to circulate that Jews had caused the plague by poisoning the wells, scores of Jewish communities were attacked and thousands of their inhabitants massacred in the Rhineland, southern France, and Christian Spain. Pope Clement VI (1342–1352) tried to halt these attacks, sending letters throughout Europe pointing out that Jews were dying from the plague in the same numbers as were Christians and ordering Christians to protect their Jewish neighbors from violence. But the letters did little good, and by the time they were received much of the damage had already been done.

Perhaps the most famous response to the plague was the "Flagellant Movement," so called from the whips (*flagella*) with which these traveling bands of penitents beat themselves bloody in hopes of appeasing the wrath of God, which had brought the plague down on a sinful world. But the unruly and sometimes hysterical mobs that gathered around the flagellants aroused the concern of both ecclesiastical and secular authorities, and the movement was suppressed by papal order at the end of 1349.

In focusing on the flagellants, however, we should not overlook the vastly larger number of ordinary churchmen who stayed at their posts, ministering to the dead and dying until the plague claimed them too. A few priests may have fled, but where we can count them, the huge numbers of priests who died in the plague suggest that those who fled were a small and unrepresentative minority. On the whole, the clergy of Christian Europe acquitted themselves with courage in the face of this fearsome disease. There is no evidence to suggest that their response to the plague was contemptible or that it led to religious disillusionment on the part of their parishoners.

WHAT CAUSED THE BLACK DEATH?

Until very recently, most historians were confident that the Black Death was the result of a pandemic outbreak of *Yersinia pestis*, the microbe responsible for bubonic plague and for its even deadlier cousins, pneumonic and septicemic plagues. In its bubonic

THE PROGRESS OF THE BLACK DEATH, FOURTEENTH CENTURY

Where did the Black Death come from, and where did it enter Europe, generally speaking? Why was the onslaught of the disease so devastating, and what agricultural, economic, and demographic factors helped make Europeans around 1350 so vulnerable to the disease? Note the rapid spread of the Black Death. Would such a rapid advance have been likely during the early Middle Ages or even in the ancient world? How did the growth of towns, trade, and travel contribute to the spread of the Black Death?

WHAT WERE THE ECONOMIC CONSEQUENCES OF THE BLACK DEATH ON EUROPE?

THE BLACK DEATH AND ITS CONSEQUENCES   271

form, *Y. pestis* is carried by fleas that travel on the backs of rats; humans catch it only if they are bitten by an infected flea or rat. Bubonic plague attacks the lymphatic system, producing enormous swellings (*buboes*) of the lymph nodes in the groin, neck, and/or armpit and causing boils and carbuncles to erupt on the skin. Pneumonic plague results when *Y. pestis* infects the lungs, allowing the contagion to spread in the same ways as the common cold. Septicemic plague occurs when an infected flea introduces *Y. pestis* directly into the human bloodstream, causing death within hours, often before any symptoms of the disease can manifest themselves.

Doubts about this explanation have arisen in recent years from an entirely unexpected direction. Studies of HIV/AIDS have shown that among European populations only, a genetic mutation (known as the CCR5-delta 32 mutation) occurred 2000 to 3000 years ago. This mutation renders people who carry it either entirely or substantially immune to HIV infection. Some researchers are suggesting that approximately 700 years ago, and lasting for the next 300 years, some epidemic event took place that "selected" for this particular mutation, driving up its frequency in the overall European populations.

This epidemic event can only have been the Black Death; and if the CCR5-delta 32 mutation did impart a substantial or complete immunity to the Black Death, then this would also explain why the disease gradually disappeared from Europe, whereas it has continued periodically to ravage other parts of the world into the twentieth century. Research is continuing on this possible new explanation for the Black Death, providing a striking example of the contributions to historical understanding that are emerging from modern microbiology and the genetic sciences.

THE IMPACT ON THE COUNTRYSIDE

The economic and social consequences of the plague were profound. During the plague years of 1348–1350, harvests rotted in the fields, manufacturing ceased, and trade was disrupted. Basic commodities became scarcer and prices rose, prompting efforts by governments to enforce, through legislation, a return to preplague prices and wages. By 1375, however, the new demographic realities were beginning to alter the underlying patterns of the European economy. By 1400, Europe had entered a new economic world.

With so many fewer mouths to feed and grain relatively more abundant, the price of grain fell; but with many fewer workers competing for employment, wages rose and work became more easily obtainable. With wages high and bread prices low, ordinary people could now afford not only to buy more bread but also to purchase dairy products, meat, fish, fruits, and wine on a more regular basis. As a result, the people of Europe in the later Middle Ages ate a more balanced diet and were, consequently, better nourished, than they had been for centuries.

A healthier ecological balance between arable land, pasture, and woodland was also reestablished in the wake of the plague. Faced with declining prices for cereal crops, many small farmers reduced their grain fields and expanded their sheep and cattle herds. By turning arable land into pastureland, they reduced their labor costs, increased the overall profitability of their farms, and improved the fertility of the soil

Plague Claims a Victim. An English priest gives the last rites to a bedridden plague victim, as a smiling devil pierces the victim with his spear and Christ looks on from heaven. In some English dioceses, two thirds of the priests died of the plague.

through better manuring. With land so readily available, small farmers were also able to increase the size of their landholdings, which allowed them to farm more efficiently. And with the lessened demand for fuel, forests too began to recover and expand.

Great lords were slower to adjust to the changed economic circumstances created by the plague. Some lords responded to rising wage costs by demanding additional unpaid labor from their peasant tenants. In eastern Europe, many peasants were actually forced into serfdom for the first time during the fifteenth century, as lords expanded their grain fields to supply the growing Baltic grain trade. In Castile, Poland, and Germany also, late medieval lords succeeded in imposing new forms of serfdom on the peasantry that would last until the sixteenth and seventeenth centuries. In Iberia and Italy, even outright slavery became more common after the plague, after nearly disappearing during the twelfth and thirteenth centuries (on the growing late medieval slave trade, see Chapter Eleven).

A Cured-Meat Merchant's Shop. Prepared foods, including smoked and cured meats, became increasingly popular and affordable in the later Middle Ages.

In France, by contrast, where the peasantry was already relatively freer than in most other European countries by 1300, the later Middle Ages brought few changes in peasant freedom. Rents declined, but lords made up these losses by imposing other fees on them. In England, however, where serfs in 1300 were much more burdened than they were in France, serfdom declined and ultimately disappeared altogether during the later Middle Ages. In the new world of social mobility and economic opportunity created by the plague, English serfs found it relatively easy to "vote with their feet," either by moving to the lands of a less demanding lord or by becoming town dwellers. To retain serfs on their estates, English lords were forced to offer them more favorable terms: lower rents, more animals, fewer work requirements, and greater personal freedoms. As a result of such accomodations, serfdom had effectively disappeared from England by the early sixteenth century.

For the unfree peasant farmers of late medieval Europe, the improved economic circumstances of their lives thus did not necessarily lead to greater personal freedom with respect to their lords. Except in England (and to a lesser extent in Catalunya), most serfs were not substantially freer of lordly control in 1500 than they had been before the plague. For free peasants and town dwellers, however, the economic conditions produced by the plague brought significantly increased social mobility and a wealth of new opportunities. The result was a widening gap between the rich and the poor at all levels of rural society, from peasants to the greatest lords.

THE IMPACT ON TOWNS

Towns were especially sensitive barometers of the changing economic climate of the later Middle Ages. Overcrowding, combined with the generally unsanitary conditions of medieval urban life, made Europe's cities particularly vulnerable to the plague. Warfare and local economic crises also contributed significantly to the population declines that afflicted so many late medieval cities.

After 1450, however, Europe's towns and cities were once again growing; and by 1500, approximately 20 percent of the European population lived in urban areas, a larger percentage than had been the case two centuries before. Fueling this late-fifteenth-century urban growth was the increasing specialization of the late medieval European economy, made possible by the combined effects of plague and trade. With farmers

TO WHAT EXTENT WERE THE SOCIAL CHANGES OF THE LATER MIDDLE AGES A CONSEQUENCE OF THE PLAGUE?

SOCIAL CHANGE IN THE LATER MIDDLE AGES   273

The Banker and His Wife, by Quentin Massys.

now under less pressure to produce grain, they could turn their lands to producing the agricultural products to which their lands were best suited. As a result, more specialized and efficient regional economies began to emerge. Sweden produced butter, which it traded for German and Baltic grain; England produced wool, which it traded for French wine and Italian cloth; Castile produced leather, which it traded for silks, fruits, grain, and spices; and so on in almost endless variety. Towns with links to these networks of regional exchange benefited particularly from the new economic circumstances of the later Middle Ages.

The economic world of the late Middle Ages also stimulated the development of new business, accounting, and banking techniques. New forms of business partnerships, together with the development of insurance contracts, helped minimize the risks associated with long-distance trading voyages. Double-entry bookkeeping, widely used in Italy from the mid-fourteenth century on, gave merchants a much clearer picture of their profits and losses than had been possible before. Banks too altered many of their earlier methods of doing business. The Medici family of Florence established branches of their bank in each of the major cities of Europe but were careful to organize these branches so that if one branch failed, it would no longer drag down the rest of the firm with it, as previous branch-banking arrangements had done. Banks also experimented with advanced credit techniques. Some even allowed their clients to transfer

funds between bank branches without any real money changing hands. Such "book transfers" were at first executed only by oral command, but after 1400 they started to be carried out by written orders. These were the earliest ancestors of the modern check.

SOCIAL CHANGE IN THE LATER MIDDLE AGES

To what extent were the social changes of the later Middle Ages a consequence of the plague?

Famine, plague, and war put extraordinary pressures on social order in later medieval Europe. It is perhaps surprising that revolutionary changes were avoided. Nonetheless, by 1500 European society was different in important and lasting ways from what it had been 200 years before. Not all of these changes were directly a result of the plague; but the plague's influence can be discerned behind most of them.

REVOLTS AND REBELLIONS

The economic consequences of the plague were ultimately beneficial for those who survived it. But European society did not adjust easily to the new world created by the plague. Between 1350 and 1425, hundreds of popular revolts shook later medieval Europe. In 1358, for example, French peasants in the countryside around Paris rose up against their lords in an orgy of arson, murder, and rape, in a rebellion known as the "Jacquerie" (by their social superiors, all French peasants were caricatured as being named "Jacques"). In England too, a massive rising of peasants, artisans, and town dwellers (known misleadingly as "The Peasants' Revolt") marched on London in 1381, demanding an end to serfdom, fixed rents for landholdings, and the more effective prosecution of the on-going war with France. In Florence, workers in the wool cloth industry (known as the "Ciompi"; *chee-OM-pi*), beset by high unemployment and frequently cheated by their masters who controlled both the wool industry and the Florentine government, seized control of the city, demanding tax relief, full employment, and political representation in city government.

The local circumstances that lay behind each of these revolts were unique, but certain general features

The Suppression of the Jacquerie, 1358. Although their initial attacks caught the lords off guard, the peasant rebels were no match for well-armed soldiers, who suppressed the rebellion with savage brutality.

do stand out about these and the hundreds of other similar revolts that occurred during these years. Most important, these revolts were not bread riots. Those who took part in them were not destitute, and their demands were almost never for the necessities of life. Some, like the English Peasants' Revolt and the 1408 rebellion at Lübeck in Germany, were touched off by resistance to new and higher taxes. Others, like the Jacquerie and the revolt of the Ciompi, took place at moments when unpopular governments were weakened by factionalism and military defeat. It was the nobles' political failures that led to the Jacquerie: their failure to protect their villagers from assaults by the English or by the regent of France and their collusion with the enemy in warlike pillaging of peasant property. Similarly, it was the failures of English armies in France and the rebels' belief that corruption on the part of those ruling in the name of the fourteen-year-old King Richard II caused the defeats that lay behind the Peasants' Revolt. The same point has been made about the urban rebellions of the period. Behind the social and political unrest of the period lay, therefore, not poverty and hunger but the growing prosperity and self-confidence that village communities and urban workers felt in the changed economic circumstances that arose from the plague.

ARISTOCRATIC LIFE IN THE LATER MIDDLE AGES

Some late medieval lords failed to adapt to the new world created by the plague. As grain prices fell, rents stagnated, and wages for laborers and servants rose, the fortunes of these lords declined significantly. For the most part, however, the later Middle Ages were not a period of aristocratic crisis. Quite the contrary— the great noble families of fifteenth-century Europe were almost certainly wealthier, on average, than their counterparts had been 200 years before. Nor did the plague undermine the dominant position the nobility had established in European society during the High Middle Ages. It did, however, make their world substantially more complex and uncertain, at a time when the costs of leading an appropriately noble style of life were continuing to escalate rapidly. As a result, the nobility of later medieval Europe felt themselves to be less secure in their wealth and social standing than they had been before the plague. These insecurities color almost all aspects of late medieval aristocratic life.

Across Europe, most noble families continued to derive the bulk of their revenues from their vast landholdings, just as they had done in the High Middle Ages. But many late medieval lords also tried to increase their nonagricultural sources of income. In Catalunya, Italy, Germany, and England, it was relatively common for nobles to invest in trading ventures. In France and Castile, however, direct involvement in retail commerce was regarded as socially demeaning and was, therefore, avoided by established noble families. Success in commerce could still be a route into the nobility, even in France and Castile. But when successful merchants were "ennobled" by kings or princes, they were expected to abandon their old employments and to adopt an appropriately noble way of life: living in rural castles or urban palaces surrounded by lavish households, embracing the values and conventions of chivalry (including a family coat of arms), and serving their prince at court and in war. Service to a king or great lord was an increasingly important expectation for the late medieval nobility, whose fortunes came to depend heavily on the gifts and favors that only rulers could bestow.

Nobility remained, however, an uncertain and difficult status to maintain. What made a man or woman noble? In countries where nobility entailed clearly defined legal privileges (such as exemption from taxation or the right to be tried only in special courts), proven

To what extent were the social changes of the later Middle Ages a consequence of the plague?

Social Change in the Later Middle Ages   275

descent from noble ancestors, together with a recognized coat of arms, might be sufficient to qualify a family as noble in the eyes of the law.

Fundamentally, however, nobility was a matter of social rank that was reflected by an individual's "noble" style of life. Chivalry, courtliness, political influence, deference from social inferiors, and the ostentatious display of wealth—all combined to constitute a family's "honor" and hence to mark it off as noble. In practice, however, the lines of social distinction between noble and non-noble families were often fuzzy. The newly wealthy might live like nobles, even though they had no noble ancestors. Men from obscure families might rise through royal service into the ranks of the nobility, while long-established noble families might disappear through failure of heirs or simply their own political miscalculations. Even on the battlefield, the supremacy of the mounted noble knight was being threatened by the growing importance of lower-class soldiers, archers, and artillery experts in late medieval armies.

Precisely because nobility was so contestable during the later Middle Ages, those who claimed the status took elaborate measures to assert its exclusivity and social distinctiveness. Late medieval aristocrats hosted lavish banquets, with table decorations forty-six feet high and hundreds of courses served over several days. They dressed in rich and extravagant clothing, maintained enormous households, and took part in elaborate tournaments and pageants in which the noble participants pretended to be the chivalric heroes of thirteenth-century romances. Aristocrats also emphasized their cultural taste and refinement by supporting authors and artists, and sometimes by becoming accomplished poets themselves. Nobility existed only if it was recognized; and to be recognized, noble status had to be constantly reasserted.

Rulers contributed to this process of noble self-assertion; indeed, they were among its principal supporters and patrons. Kings and princes across Europe competed with each other in founding chivalric orders, such as the Knights of the Garter in England and the Order of the Star in France. These orders honored knights who had demonstrated in an extraordinary way the idealized chivalric virtues of knightly prowess, loyalty, bravery, generosity, and courtesy on the battlefield. But although membership in these orders was strictly limited, the virtues they celebrated were seen as characterizing the nobility as a whole. By exalting the nobility as a class, chivalric orders helped cement the links that bound the nobility to their kings and princes. So too did the fees, pensions, offices, and marriages that kings and princes could provide to their noble followers. In a world in which the agricultural revenues of noble estates were declining, such rewards of princely service were critically important to maintaining noble fortunes.

It is easy to dismiss the performative aspects of late medieval aristocratic life as mere play acting. To do so, however, would be a mistake. Late medieval rulers

A Noble Hunting Party. This fifteenth-century illlustration shows an elaborately dressed group of noble men and women setting out to hunt with falcons, accompanied by their servants and their dogs. The castle at Étampes, on the Loire, can be seen in the background.

depended on the service—military, diplomatic, and political—that the nobility alone could provide, just as the nobility depended on the offices, revenues, prestige, and social affirmation that could be acquired only through service to a royal or princely court. The alliance that was forged in the fifteenth century between kings and their nobility was a response to these mutual needs and would become one of the most characteristic and enduring features of "old regime" (*ancien régime*) Europe.

WAR AND THE DEVELOPMENT OF THE LATE MEDIEVAL STATE

Why was warfare such a constant feature of late medieval life?

The ancien régime alliance between crown and nobility was in part a response to the new social and economic world created by the plague. But it was also a product of war and of the impact of war on the development of the late medieval state. The fourteenth and fifteenth centuries saw almost constant warfare at all levels of European society. To fight these wars, governments claimed new powers to tax their subjects and to control their subjects' lives. Armies became larger and military technology deadlier. Wars became more destructive and society more militarized. As a result of these developments, the largest and most successful European states (in particular, the national monarchies of Portugal, Spain, and France) were stronger and more aggressively expansionist by 1500 than they had been two centuries before. In 1500, the impact of these newly powerful states was still felt mainly in Europe. By 1600, however, their impact would be felt around the globe.

ENGLAND, FRANCE, AND THE HUNDRED YEARS' WAR

The Hundred Years' War was the largest, longest, and most wide-ranging military conflict of the later Middle Ages. England and France were its principal protagonists, but at one stage or another almost all of the major European powers became involved in it. Active hostilities between England and France lasted from 1337 until 1453, interrupted by truces of varying lengths. The roots of the conflict, however, reach back into the 1290s, when King Edward I of England attempted to conquer the neighboring kingdom of Scotland, thereby provoking the Scottish kingdom to ally itself with France.

The war had several causes. The most fundamental source of conflict, and the most difficult issue to resolve, was that the kings of England held the duchy of Gascony in southern France as vassals of the French king. In the twelfth and thirteenth centuries, this fact had seemed less of an anomaly. But as the conviction grew in the later Middle Ages that kingdoms were territorial entities, within whose borders only a single king should rule, the English presence in Gascony became more and more intolerable to the French crown. That England also had close commercial links, through the wool trade, with the French king's rebellious subjects in Flanders added further fuel to the fires of Anglo-French hostility. So too did the continuing French alliance with the Scots, who had been resolutely resisting English attempts to conquer their kingdom since the 1290s.

Greatly complicating all this, however, was a succession dispute over the French crown itself. In 1328, the last of King Philip IV's three sons died without leaving a son to succeed him. A new dynasty, the Valois, thereupon replaced the Capetians on the throne of France. Only by prohibiting inheritance through women, however, could the Valois kings claim to be the closest heirs to the Capetians. Otherwise, the rightful heir to the throne of France was King Edward III of England, whose mother, Isabella, was the only daughter of King Philip IV of France. In 1328, Edward was only fifteen years old, and he did not protest the succession of his Valois cousins. In 1337, however, when war erupted between France and England over Scotland and Gascony, Edward III responded by claiming to be the rightful king of France—a claim all subsequent English kings would uphold until the eighteenth century.

Although France was richer and more populous than England, the English political system was more effective in mobilizing the entire population behind the war effort. As a result, until the 1430s the English won most of the pitched battles. Time and again, smaller, better-organized English armies, combining archers, infantry, and cavalry, defeated vastly larger but badly led French armies on the battlefield. As English armies plundered the French countryside, the French king-

WHY WAS WARFARE SUCH A CONSTANT FEATURE OF LATE MEDIEVAL LIFE?

WAR AND THE DEVELOPMENT OF THE LATE MEDIEVAL STATE   277

Joan of Arc. A contemporary sketch, drawn in the margin of the register of the English-controlled Parlement of Paris in 1429.

dom itself began to dissolve into its constituent parts. The most dramatic and fateful instance was the breaking away of Burgundy, whose dukes from 1419 to 1435 allied with the English against the Valois monarchy, thus calling into question the very existence of an independent French crown.

It was in this dark period that the heroic figure of Joan of Arc emerged to rally the demoralized French forces. In 1429, Joan, an illiterate peasant girl, made her way to the French court to announce that an angel had told her that she, Joan, should drive the English out of France. It is a mark of the hopelessness of the French king's position that she even got a hearing—much less that he then gave her a contingent of troops, with which she promptly defeated an English army at Orleans. A series of further victories followed. But despite her victories, Joan remained an embarrassment: a peasant leading nobles, a woman leading men, and a commoner who claimed to have been commissioned by God. When the Burgundians captured her in battle and handed her over to the English, the king of France did nothing to try to save her. Accused of witchcraft and tried for heresy, Joan was burned to death in the market square at Rouen in 1431.

The French forces whom she inspired, however, continued on the offensive. In 1435, the duke of Burgundy withdrew from his alliance with England; and when the

English king Henry VI proved first to be incompetent and then to be insane, a series of French military victories during the 1440s finally brought the war to an end with the capture of Bordeaux in 1453. English kings would threaten to renew the war for another century, and Anglo-French hostility would last until the final defeat of Napoleon in 1815. But after 1453, English control over French territory would be limited to the port of Calais, which would finally fall in 1558.

The Hundred Years' War was the most dangerous challenge to its existence that the French kingdom ever faced. The disintegration of the kingdom under the pressure of war glaringly revealed the fragility of the bonds that tied the crown to its nobility and Paris to the outlying regions of Burgundy, Brittany, and Gascony. Nonetheless, the monarchy demonstrated remarkable resilience, and in the end the war strengthened the crown's capacity to rule France. To fight the war successfully, the Valois kings imposed new national taxes that would be the mainstays of French royal finance until 1789. With these new revenues, the Valois were able to create and maintain a standing national army, whose size, sophistication, and artillery ultimately overwhelmed not only the English but also the forces that dissident French nobles and regions might bring against it.

The Hundred Years' War also had dramatic effects on the English monarchy. When English armies in France were successful, the Crown rode a wave of popularity and the country prospered from the profits of booty and ransoms. When the war turned against the English, defeats abroad undermined support for the monarch at home. Of the nine English kings who ruled England between 1307 and 1485, no fewer than five were deposed and murdered by their subjects.

The particular propensity of the English for murdering their kings (a subject of comment across Europe) was a consequence of England's peculiar political system. England was the most tightly governed kingdom in Europe, but the strength of its political system depended on the king's ability to mobilize popular support for his policies through Parliament, while maintaining the support of his nobility through successful wars. As a result, incompetent or tyrannical kingship was even more destabilizing in England than it was elsewhere in Europe. In France, the nobility could endure the insanity of Charles VI (1380–1422) because his government was not powerful enough to threaten them. In England, however, the inanity and ultimate insanity of King Henry VI (1422–1461) provoked an aristocratic rebellion against him known as the Wars of

King Richard III of England, 1483–1485. Richard deposed his nephews and seized the throne for himself. He was defeated and killed by Henry Tudor (King Henry VII) at Bosworth Field in 1485.

When he died in 1509 the new Tudor dynasty was securely established on the throne, and English royal power was fully restored.

Despite the turmoil caused by war and rebellion, late medieval English political life had an essential stability. Local institutions continued to function; Parliament became increasingly important as a point of contact joining Crown, nobility, and local communities; and the political nation itself became steadily larger as prosperity brought new social groups into prominence. Most important, there was never any fundamental challenge to the power of the English state itself. When rebellions broke out, whether led by nobles or peasants, the rebels always sought to control the central government rather than to destroy or break away from it. Despite England's ultimate defeat, the Hundred Years' War strengthened this characteristically English equation between national identity and the power of the state. During the fourteenth and fifteenth centuries, mounting anti-French sentiment contributed to the triumph of English as the national language and to a patriotic vision of England itself as a country uniquely chosen by God. Having lost its continental possessions, England after 1485 became an island nation that looked to the sea as its first line of

the Roses, so called (by the nineteenth-century novelist Sir Walter Scott) from the emblems of the two competing factions: the red rose of Henry's family of Lancaster, and the white rose of Henry's cousin, the rival duke of York.

In 1461, after a six-year struggle, Edward, Duke of York finally succeeded in ousting King Henry VI. He then ruled successfully until his death in 1483. But when Edward's brother Richard seized the throne from Edward's own young sons, political stability in England collapsed once again. In 1485, Richard III was in turn defeated and killed in the battle of Bosworth Field by the Lancastrian claimant, Henry Tudor, who then resolved the dynastic feud between Lancaster and York by marrying Elizabeth of York, the only surviving child of King Edward IV. As King Henry VII, Henry Tudor systematically eliminated potential rivals for the throne. He avoided expensive foreign wars, asked for little by way of taxation, built up a financial surplus by carefully managing Crown lands, and exercised a tight (but largely welcome) control over the aristocracy.

Henry VII. A 1505 portrait by M. Sittow.

WHY WAS WARFARE SUCH A CONSTANT FEATURE OF LATE MEDIEVAL LIFE?

WAR AND THE DEVELOPMENT OF THE LATE MEDIEVAL STATE 279

defense. This too would prove to be an advantage. England in the sixteenth and seventeenth centuries would be well positioned to take advantage of the new world of overseas commerce and colonialism opened up by Columbus's discoveries in the Americas.

GERMANY AND ITALY

Elsewhere, the consequences of late medieval warfare were more uniformly destructive. In Germany, armed conflict among the territorial princes who dominated the country, and between these princes and the German emperors, weakened all the principal combatants significantly. Periodically a powerful emperor would emerge to play a major role on the European scene. But the trend was toward the continuing dissolution of central power in Germany, as princes divided their territories among their heirs and as free cities and local knights strove to shake off the rule of the princes. Between 1350 and 1450, near anarchy prevailed across much of Germany. In the east, however, the rulers of Bavaria, Austria, and Brandenburg were able to strengthen their authority by supporting the efforts of local nobles to subject their peasantry to serfdom and by conquering and colonizing new territories, particularly on the frontier between Prussia and Lithuania. The gains these rulers made during the later Middle Ages would make the Habsburg rulers of Austria and the Hohenzollern rulers of Brandenburg-Prussia the dominant powers in early modern Germany.

In northern and central Italy also, the last half of the fourteenth century was marked by incessant conflict. With the popes living at Avignon from 1309 until 1377, their control over the Papal States collapsed. Warfare between city states erupted throughout the northern half of the peninsula, further complicated by a rash of urban rebellions in the wake of the plague. By around 1400, however, Venice, Milan, and Florence had succeeded in stabilizing their own differing forms of government. Venice was now ruled by an oligarchy of merchants; Milan was ruled by a family of despots; and Florence was ruled as a republic, albeit one dominated by the influence of a few wealthy families—especially, after 1434, the Medici banking family. Having settled their internal problems, these three cities then began to expand their territories. By 1454, Venice, Milan, and Florence had subordinated almost all the other northern Italian cities and towns except Genoa, which remained prosperous and independent but gained no new lands. The papacy reasserted its control over central Italy; while in the south, the Kingdom of Naples continued to rule unchallenged by the other Italian powers, despite endemic local warfare and persistent maladministration.

A treaty in 1454 brought forty years of peace between these "five great powers." This peace was maintained by a form of "balance of power diplomacy," in which frequently shifting alliances among the five states checked the ambitions of each for further expansion. In 1494, however, a large-scale French invasion of Italy destroyed the diplomatic and military balance among the Italian powers, revealing in the process that the Italian city-states were no match for the powerful national monarchies that had developed during the fifteenth century north of the Alps. French control of the Italian peninsula would be short lived, however. The ultimate beneficiary of the French invasion of Italy would be the newly united Spanish kingdoms of Aragon and Castile.

THE EMERGENCE OF SPAIN

Spain too had seen incessant strife during the later Middle Ages. Wars between the two principal Spanish kingdoms, Castile and Aragon, had weakened both combatants, while in Castile, a disastrous civil war during the late fourteenth century was followed by a period of incompetent kingship and economic hardship during the mid-fifteenth century. In Castile, noble families took advantage of royal weakness to secure greater control over the peasantry on their estates and greater independence from the crown. After 1450, noble factions struggled for control over the Castilian court as feuds between noble families tore the kingdom apart.

The Aragonese crown preserved its authority rather better, benefiting from its alliance with the merchants of Catalunya, who were busily extending their commercial influence throughout the Mediterranean world. After 1458, however, Aragon too fell prey to civil war arising from a succession dispute, in which both France and Castile became involved. By 1469, however, King John had established his son Ferdinand as the unquestioned heir to the throne of Aragon. When, in that year, Ferdinand married Isabella, the heiress to Castile, their union became the basis on which a united Spanish kingdom would eventually be built.

In 1474, Isabella ascended to the throne of Castile; in 1479, Ferdinand became King of Aragon when his father died. Aragon and Castile continued to be ruled as separate kingdoms until 1714; even in contemporary Spain, tensions between the two former kingdoms continue. But the marriage of Ferdinand and Isabella ended the warfare between the kingdoms, and after 1479 the Catholic Monarchs (as Ferdinand and Isabella came to be known) were able to embark on united policies. Vast increases in royal revenues quickly followed. Much of this new revenue was devoted to building up Spanish military forces, which by 1500 were the most powerful in Europe. These forces were first employed to conquer Granada, the last remaining Muslim principality in Spain, which fell in 1492. A decade later, Spanish armies intervened in Italy, eventually turning all of Italy into a Spanish protectorate. But this new army also played an important role within Spain, providing honorable employment and royal service to the fractious nobles of Castile and Aragon, while overawing any nobles who might be tempted to rebel against the growing power of the Catholic Monarchs.

The conquest of Granada was a turning point for the emerging Spanish monarchy. Both Castile and Aragon had been shaped for centuries by their involvement in the reconquest of Muslim Spain. But the victory of 1492 sealed a vision of Castile in particular as a country uniquely devoted to crusading. That vision of Castile's world mission might not have been so consequential, however, had it not been for the fact that only a few months after the conquest of Granada, Queen Isabella granted three ships to a Genoese adventurer named Christopher Columbus who promised to reach India by sailing westward across the Atlantic Ocean. He failed, of course; but by landing on two new continents, which he claimed for Spain, Columbus extended the Castilian crusading tradition to the New World, with consequences that have lasted to the present day.

The year 1492 also saw the expulsion of the entire Jewish community from Spain, the culmination of a process of Jewish exclusion from Christian Europe that began in the late thirteenth century with the expulsion of the Jewish communities of southern Italy and England, continued with the expulsion of the Jews from France in 1306, and continued during the fourteenth and fifteenth centuries with a series of Jewish expulsions from the towns and cities of the Rhineland.

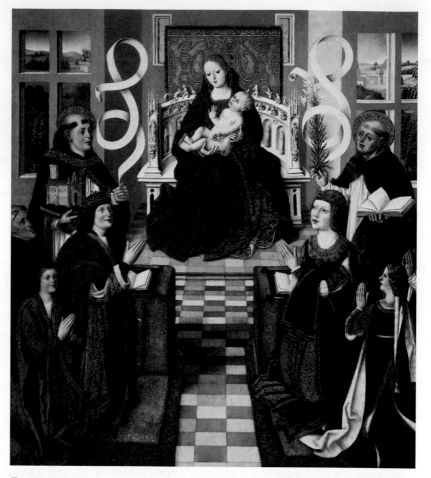

Ferdinand and Isabella Honoring the Virgin. A contemporary Spanish painting in which the royal pair are shown with two of their children in the company of saints from the Dominican order.

The Spanish expulsion stands out, however, both for the total number of Jews involved (at least 100,000, and possibly as many as 200,000) and also because of the rich cultural legacy the Jews of Spain had developed in the 1,000 years during which they had resided on the Iberian peninsula.

Historians continue to debate why Ferdinand and Isabella ordered this expulsion. Between 1391 and 1420, tens of thousands of Spanish Jews had converted to Catholicism, many as a result of coercion but some from sincere religious conviction. Until around 1450, it seemed possible that these converts (*conversos*) might successfully assimilate into Spanish Christian society. Thereafter, however, the *conversos* became the targets of discriminatory legislation and popular suspicion that they remained secretly Jews. To make "proper Christians" out of the *conversos*, the Catholic Monarchs may have concluded that they needed to remove the "bad influence" posed by the continuing presence of a practicing Jewish community in Spain.

WHY DID RUSSIA DEVELOP DIFFERENTLY FROM OTHER LATE MEDIEVAL EUROPEAN STATES?

KIEVAN RUS AND THE RISE OF MUSCOVY   281

Beyond such "practical" considerations, however, there may also have been a desire to create a new and explicitly Christian identity for the newly united country over which Ferdinand and Isabella ruled. "Spain," per se, did not exist in 1492. Its creation would be the work of centuries, work that continues today. But the need for some common identity that would transcend the rival regional identities of Castilians, Aragonese, and Catalans (not to mention Galicians, Navarrese, Valencians, Basques, and Murcians) may already have been apparent. Certainly it is implied in the title Ferdinand and Isabella took to themselves as the Catholic Monarchs. Like other monarchs in late medieval Europe, Ferdinand and Isabella may have sought to strengthen their emerging nation-state by constructing a newly explicit and exclusively Christian identity for its people and by attaching that new identity to the crown. In such a Christian nation, however, there could be no place for Jews or Muslims.

THE GROWTH OF NATIONAL MONARCHIES

In France, England, Scotland, Portugal, and Spain, the later Middle Ages saw the emergence of markedly more powerful European states than had existed in 1300. But despite the impact of war and plague in reshaping European political life, many of the basic political patterns established during the High Middle Ages endured. Germany and Italy were politically divided by 1300 and remained divided in 1500. England and France, the two most powerful monarchies of the High Middle Ages, remained powerful states in 1500, although the combined kingdoms of Aragon and Castile, together with the Kingdom of Portugal, had now emerged as powerful rivals to both. Only the position of Sicily had been fundamentally transformed. Economically exhausted by the demands of its high medieval rulers, Sicily became in the later Middle Ages the impoverished land it has remained until the present day.

Behind these continuities, however, lies one of the most notable developments in later medieval politics: the growing strength of national monarchies. By 1500, the kings of Iberia, England, France, and Scotland were all actively engaged in constructing a sense of national identity among their people and in focusing that identity on themselves. This fusion of nationalism and kingship was a product of the later Middle Ages. By 1500 it had produced a new type of political organization, the national monarchy, which was stronger and more powerful than anything Europe had seen since the heyday of the Carolingian Empire.

The superiority of the new national monarchies to older forms of political organization such as the empire and the city-state is most clearly visible in Italy. Until 1494, the Italian city-states had appeared to be well governed and powerful. But when the armies of France and Spain invaded the peninsula, the Italian political order collapsed like a house of cards. Germany would suffer the same fate only a few generations later; it would remain a battleground for the competing armies of France and Spain until the end of the seventeenth century.

The new national monarchies were not an unmitigated blessing. They were not only more powerful, they were also more intolerant and exclusionary than their high medieval predecessors, as the expulsion of Jews (and Muslims) from later medieval Europe reveals. But for better or worse, these newly powerful national monarchies would dominate Europe and the wider world for the next 500 years.

KIEVAN RUS AND THE RISE OF MUSCOVY

Why did Russia develop differently from other late medieval European states?

The fourteenth and fifteenth centuries also witnessed the consolidation of the state that would become the dominant power in eastern Europe. Russia, however, developed very differently from the national monarchies of western Europe. Unlike Spain or France or even Germany, Russia by 1500 had taken decisive steps toward becoming the largest multiethnic empire in the Eurasian world.

This development was not inevitable. Had it not been for a combination of late medieval circumstances, one or several east Slavic states might well have developed along the same lines as did the national monarchies of western Europe. But after 1200, several epoch-making developments combined to separate Russia from western Europe.

The first was the conquest of most of the eastern Slavic states by the Mongols, who cut such swaths of devastation through Russia as they advanced westward that, according to one contemporary, "no eye remained open to weep for the dead." In 1240, the Mongols overran Kiev. Two years later they created their own state on the lower Volga River—the khanate of the Golden Horde—which exercised superiority over most of Russia for the following 150 years. During the thirteenth century, the Mongols ruled Russia directly; thereafter, they tolerated the existence of several native Slavic states from which they demanded obedience and regular tribute payments. One of the most important of

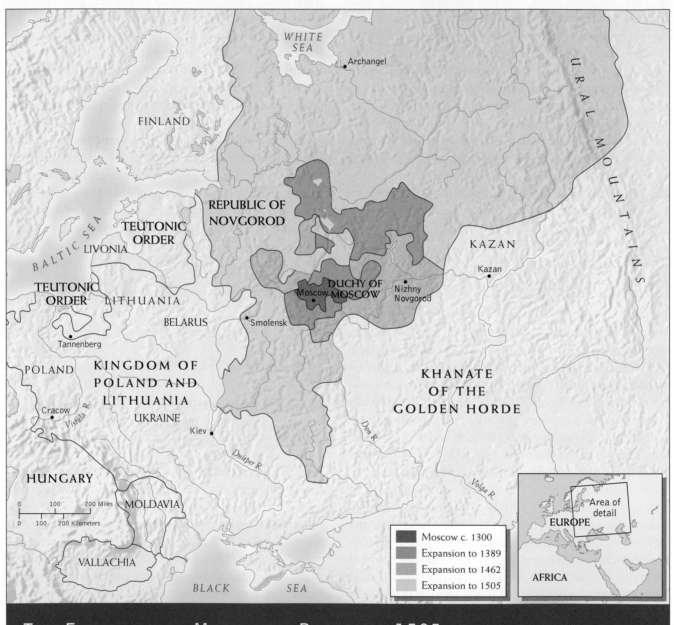

THE EXPANSION OF MUSCOVITE RUSSIA TO 1505

This map shows the expansion of the grand duchy of Moscow, the heart of what would soon become the Russian Empire. How did the relative isolation of Moscow compared with Kiev allow for the growth of Muscovite power on the one hand and Moscow's distinctively non-Western culture on the other? Why did the Muscovite Russians identify so closely with the Byzantines, and why did they reserve such pronounced hostility for the West and Latin Christianity? What role did the Kingdom of Poland-Lithuania play in the development of this Russian attitude? How did the natural direction of the expansion of Muscovite power until 1505 help encourage attitudes often at odds with those of western European civilization?

WHY DID RUSSIA DEVELOP DIFFERENTLY FROM OTHER LATE MEDIEVAL EUROPEAN STATES?

KIEVAN RUS AND THE RISE OF MUSCOVY 283

these tributary states was the grand duchy of Muscovy, with its capital at Moscow.

THE RISE OF MUSCOVY

Moscow rose to power in the early fourteenth century as a tribute-collecting center for the Mongol khanate. Its remote location made Moscow a valuable ally for the Mongols, while allowing the grand dukes of Moscow to consolidate their strength without attracting too much attention from the khans. Despite Moscow's remote location, however, the grand duchy continued to maintain commercial contacts with both the Baltic and the Black Sea regions throughout the Mongol period. What really distanced Muscovy from western Europe was not, therefore, the fact that it was under the thumb of the Mongols. Rather, it was the enormous religious hostility that existed after 1204 between the Orthodox Christian world (to which Moscow adhered) and the Latin Christian world of Europe. Hostility between these two great branches of Christianity had deep historical roots but became more pronounced after 1204, when the Latins captured Constantinople, the capital of the Orthodox world, in the Fourth Crusade. During the fourteenth and fifteenth centuries, however, what particularly excited the religious animosity of Moscow toward western European Christianity was the growing strength of the Catholic Kingdom of Poland, together with the fall of Constantinople to the Ottoman Turks in 1453.

The growing alienation of Moscow from Latin Christian Europe was further increased by events leading up to the fall of Constantinople to the Turks in 1453.

THE RIVALRY WITH POLAND

During the High Middle Ages, Poland had been a second-rate power, usually on the defensive against German encroachments. During the fourteenth century, however, Poland's situation changed dramatically, partly because German strength was declining, but above all because the marriage in 1386 of Poland's reigning queen, Jadwiga, to Jagiello, Grand Duke of Lithuania, more than doubled Poland's size, enabling the newly combined kingdom to become a major expanionist state. In 1410, combined Polish and Lithuanian forces inflicted a stunning defeat on the German military order that ruled neighboring Prussia. Poland-Lithuania then began to push its borders eastward toward Russia. Although many Lithuanian nobles were Orthodox Christians, the established church in Lithuania was Roman Catholic. So too, of course, was the Kingdom of Poland. Thus when Moscow took the offensive against Poland-Lithuania in the late fifteenth century, its campaigns appealed to religious as well as national loyalties. Prolonged warfare ensued, greatly increasing Russian antagonism not only toward Poland-Lithuania, but also toward the Latin Christian tradition it represented in the eyes of Muscovites.

MOSCOW AND BYZANTIUM

The growing alienation of Moscow from Latin Christian Europe was further increased by events leading up to the fall of Constantinople to the Turks in 1453. Connections between Byzantium and the Rus went back to the tenth century, when Byzantine missionaries had converted the Kievan Slavs to Orthodox Christianity. Thereafter, the Russian church gradually came to see itself as a special ally of Constantinople in defending and maintaining Orthodoxy. In 1438, however, Orthodox Church authorities in Constantinople agreed to submit to papal authority and unite with the Latin Christian church, in the hope that this might bring them Western military support to withstand the Turks, who were by now knocking at the gates of the besieged city. The Russian church refused to follow Byzantium in this religious submission to Rome, regarding it as a betrayal of Orthodoxy; and when Constantinople fell to the Turks without any help from the West having arrived, Muscovite churchmen regarded the Turkish victory as divine punishment for Constantinople's religious perfidy. After 1453, the Muscovite state declared itself to be the divinely appointed successor to Byzantium, adopting in the process a particularly zealous anti-Catholic ideology, which was reinforced by the military threat from Poland-Lithuania. The Muscovite ruler took the title of *tsar*—which means "caesar"—and Russians declared Moscow both "a second Jerusalem" and "the third Rome." "Two Romes have fallen," said a Russian spokesman, "the third is still standing, and a fourth there shall not be."

THE REIGN OF IVAN THE GREAT (1462–1505)

This Byzantine-derived ideology of divine election underlay both the later growth of Russian imperialism and the sacred position ascribed to the rulers of the Muscovite (and later Russian) state. Behind these developments, however, lay also the steadily growing power of the grand dukes of Moscow. Moscow itself achieved effective independence from the Mongols at the end of the fourteenth century. But it was the grand duke Ivan III, known as Ivan the Great, who transformed Moscow into a true imperial power. Under Ivan III, Muscovy evolved rapidly in the direction of political autocracy and imperialism. Between 1468 and 1485 Ivan conquered all the independent Russian principalities that lay between Moscow and the border with Poland-Lithuania. After invading Lithuania in 1492 and 1501, Ivan also succeeded in bringing parts of Belarus and Ukraine under his control. Battles between Russia and Poland-Lithuania would continue for several centuries, but by 1505, when Ivan died, he had established Muscovy as a power to be reckoned with on the European scene.

Ivan the Great.

TRIALS FOR THE CHURCH

Why did late medieval efforts to reform the institutions of the Catholic Church fail?

The later Middle Ages were a challenging and difficult period for the institutions of the Catholic Church. Like other large landowners, monasteries and bishops struggled to adapt to the economic changes brought about by the Black Death. No ecclesiastical institution suffered more severe trials, however, than did the late medieval papacy, which endured almost seventy years of continuous exile from Rome—an exile that was followed first by a thirty-year schism and then by a protracted battle with reformers who sought to reduce the popes' authority to govern the church.

THE LATE MEDIEVAL PAPACY AND CONCILIARISM

Following the humiliation and death of Pope Boniface VIII (1294–1303) at the hands of King Philip IV of France (see pp. 245–246), the late medieval papacy entered into a long period of institutional crisis. After four years of wandering in exile from Rome, the papacy resided continuously from 1309 until 1378 at Avignon, a small papal territory on the southwestern border of France. Here they built up a large and efficient bureaucracy, principally devoted to raising money to fund the reconquest of the Papal States in Italy.

When the popes first settled in Avignon, they had not intended to remain there. But Avignon soon proved to have a number of advantages over Rome. It was closer to the major centers of power in fourteenth-century Europe; it was far removed from the tumultuous local politics of Rome and the papal states; and it was safe from the aggressive attentions of the German emperors. All the popes elected during the Avignon period were natives of southern France, as were nearly all the cardinals whom they appointed; for them, Avignon felt like home. As the papal bureaucracy grew in size, it too became more difficult to move. Nor could the wishes of the king of France be ignored. The French king was the principal secular supporter of the Avignon popes, and he liked having them on the borders of his kingdom, where he could browbeat them as necessary.

But despite Avignon's advantages, the papacy never abandoned the hope of returning to Rome. To do so,

WHY DID LATE MEDIEVAL EFFORTS TO REFORM THE INSTITUTIONS OF THE CATHOLIC CHURCH FAIL?

TRIALS FOR THE CHURCH   285

however, the popes first had to win back military control over the Papal States in central Italy. This effort took decades. To finance these wars, the Avignon popes imposed new taxes and obligations on the churches of France, England, Germany, and Spain. Judicial cases from the church courts also brought large revenues into the papal coffers. More controversially, the Avignon popes also claimed the right to appoint bishops and priests directly to vacant church offices. Such appointments (known as "papal provisions") were not necessarily abusive. Although they bypassed the rights of the local clergy to elect their own officials, the men appointed were often of outstanding ability. But all such appointees had to pay large fees to the papacy in return for their appointments, fees that critics declared to be simony (the purchase of church offices for cash).

By these and other measures, the Avignon popes strengthened their administrative control over the church. But this did not make them loved. Clergy and laity alike were alienated by the papacy's insatiable demands for money, and stories quickly spread about the unbridled luxury of the papal court. In fact, most of the Avignon popes were morally upright and personally abstemious; the cash they collected went overwhelmingly to pay the costs of war in central Italy.

In 1367, Pope Urban V tried to return to Rome, but found his way blocked by the troops of King Charles V of France. In 1377, however, Pope Gregory XI succeeded in returning the papacy from Avignon to Rome. But when he died only a year later, disaster struck. Fearful that if the new pope were a Frenchman he might return to Avignon, the Romans rioted, demanding that the cardinals (who were mainly southern French) elect a Roman as the new pope. Fearing for their lives, the cardinals quickly obliged, electing an Italian who took the name Urban VI. Urban, however, immediately began quarreling with the cardinals, revealing what were probably paranoid tendencies. Fearing for their lives once again, the cardinals fled Rome, declared Urban VI's election invalid, and elected as the new pope a French cardinal who took the name Clement VII. Clement and the cardinals then marched on Rome with an army, but they could

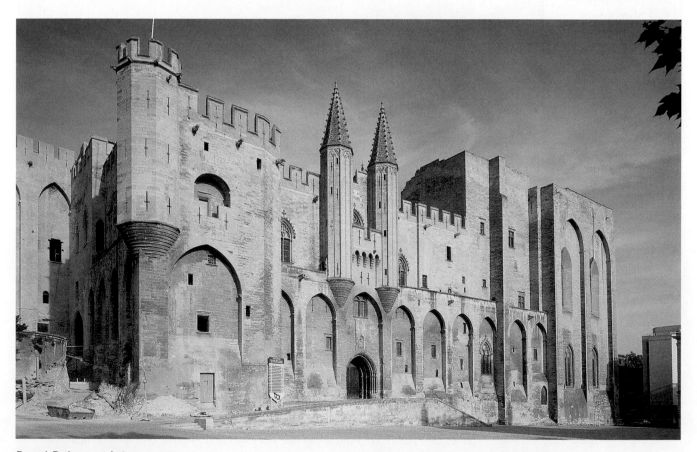

Papal Palace at Avignon. This great palace was begun in 1339 and symbolizes the apparent permanence of the papal residence in Avignon.

not dislodge Pope Urban from the city. Urban VI thereupon named a new, entirely Italian college of cardinals, while Clement VII and his cardinals withdrew to Avignon.

The result was the Great Schism, a nearly thirty-year period during which the church was ruled first by two and ultimately by three competing popes, each claiming to be the legitimate successor to Saint Peter. Europe's religious allegiances fractured along the lines of political division established by the Hundred Years' War. Nor was there any obvious way to end this embarrassing state of affairs. Both popes had been elected

THE GREAT SCHISM, 1378–1417

This map illustrates the religious divisions of Europe during the Great Schism. What common interests united the supporters of the Avignon pope? The Roman pope? Why did areas like Portugal and Austria find it so difficult to choose which side to support?

Why did late medieval efforts to reform the institutions of the Catholic Church fail?

Trials for the Church   287

by the same group of cardinals, and thereafter, whenever one of the popes died, his supporters quickly elected a successor, thus prolonging the schism. Finally, in 1409, some cardinals from both camps met at Pisa, where they deposed both popes and named a new one. But neither the Roman nor the Avignon pope accepted the council's decisions. As a result, after 1409 there were three rival popes excommunicating each other, instead of only two.

The Great Schism finally ended in 1417 at the Council of Constance, the largest ecclesiastical gathering of the Middle Ages. The council had strong support from several European princes and took care to depose all the other papal claimants before naming its own new pope, an Italian who took the name Martin V. This, however, took three years of effort, and so the council was unable to proceed with its larger goal of reforming the religious life of the church. That task was left for future councils.

The election of Pope Martin V restored the ecclesiastical unity of Europe. It did not, however, end the struggle over how the church should be governed in future. To end the schism, the Council of Constance had declared that supreme authority within the church rested not with the pope, but with itself and all future such general councils. It also ordered that general councils should meet regularly thereafter to oversee the governance and reform of the church.

These "conciliar" decrees were a revolutionary challenge to the traditions of papal monarchy. It is not surprising that Pope Martin V and his successors did

all they could to undermine them. In 1423, when the next required general council met at Siena, Pope Martin sent its representatives back home almost immediately. Constance had specified that a council must meet, but it had not specified for how long that meeting must last! In 1431, however, when the next general council met at Basel, its members immediately took steps to ensure that the pope could not dismiss it. A lengthy struggle for power then ensued, in which the popes and the conciliarists competed for the support of Europe's kings and princes.   Finally, in 1449, the Council of Basel dissolved itself in abject failure, bringing to an end this radical experiment in conciliar government over the church and dashing the hopes of those who thought it would lead to a thoroughgoing reform of religious life "in head and members."

The Growth of National Churches

The papacy's victory over the conciliarists was a costly one. To win the support of Europe's kings and princes against the conciliarists, the popes negotiated a series of treaties, known as "concordats," which granted these rulers extensive authority over the churches within their territories. The popes thus secured their own theoretical supremacy over the church at the cost of surrendering their real power to rule it. Under the terms of these concordats, kings now received many of the revenues from local churches that previously

Joan of Arc Drives Prostitutes from Her Army. This illustration, from a 1484 manuscript, tells one of the many legends that grew up around Joan after her death. It also shows the efforts that many late-fifteenth-century rulers made to present themselves as champions of moral reform within their lands.

THE CONCILIARIST CONTROVERSY

The Great Schism produced a fundamental and far-reaching debate about the nature of authority within the church. Arguments for papal supremacy rested on the traditional claims that the popes were the successors of Saint Peter, to whom Jesus Christ had delegated his own authority over the church. Arguments for the supremacy of a general council had been advanced around the University of Paris throughout much of the fourteenth century; but it was only in the circumstances of the schism that these arguments found a wide audience. The documents here trace the history of the controversy, from the declaration of conciliar supremacy at the Council of Constance (Haec Sancta), to the council's efforts to guarantee regular meetings of general councils thereafter (Frequens), to the papal condemnation of appeals to future general councils issued in 1460 (Execrabilis). Note, however, the limitations on Execrabilis. Even this condemnation does not go so far as to actually contradict Haec Sancta. It merely condemns appeals from papal judgment to future general councils that have no specified meeting date. The conciliar ideal was still powerful at the end of the fifteenth century; and in the sixteenth and seventeenth centuries, it would have a profound impact on European political thought about kings.

HAEC SANCTA SYNODUS (1415)

This holy synod of Constance . . . declares that being lawfully assembled in the Holy Spirit, constituting a general council and representing the Catholic Church Militant, it has its power directly from Christ, and that all persons of whatever rank or dignity, even a Pope, are bound to obey it in matters relating to faith and the end of the Schism and the general reformation of the church of God in head and members.

Further, it declares that any person of whatever position, rank, or dignity, even a Pope, who contumaciously refuses to obey the mandates, statutes, ordinances, or regulations enacted or to be enacted by this holy synod, or by any other general council lawfully assembled, relating to the matters aforesaid or to other matters involved with them, shall, unless he repents, be . . . duly punished. . . .

FREQUENS (1417)

The frequent holding of general councils is the best method of cultivating the field of the Lord, for they root out the briars, thorns, and thistles of heresies, errors, and schisms, correct abuses, make crooked things straight, and prepare the Lord's vineyard for fruitfulness and rich fertility. Neglect of general councils sows the seeds of these evils and encourages their growth. This truth is borne in upon us as we recall times past and survey the present.

Therefore by perpetual edict we . . . ordain that henceforth general councils shall be held as follows: the first within the five years immediately following the end of the present council, the second within seven years from the end of the council next after this, and subsequently every ten years forever. . . . Thus there will always be a certain continuity. Either a council will be in session or one will be expected at the end of a fixed period. . . .

R. L. Loomis, ed. and trans., *"Haec Sancta Synodus"* and *"Frequens"* in *The Council of Constance* (New York, 1961), pp. 229, 246–247.

EXECRABILIS (1460)

An execrable abuse, unheard of in earlier times, has sprung up in our period. Some men, imbued with a spirit of rebellion and moved not by a desire for sound decisions but rather by a desire to escape the punishment for sin, suppose that they can appeal from the Pope, Vicar of Jesus Christ; from the Pope, to whom in the person of blessed Peter it was said, "Feed my sheep" and "whatever you bind on earth will be bound in heaven"—from this Pope to a future council. How harmful this is to the Christian republic, as well as how contrary to canon law, anyone who is not ignorant of the law can understand. For . . . who would not consider it ridiculous to appeal to something which does not now exist anywhere nor does anyone know when it will exist? The poor are heavily oppressed by the powerful, offenses remain unpunished, rebellion against the Holy See is encouraged, license for sin is granted, and all ecclesiastical discipline and hierarchical ranking of the Church are turned upside down.

Wishing therefore to expel this deadly poison from the Church of Christ, and concerned with the salvation of the sheep committed to us . . . with the counsel and assent of our venerable brothers, the Cardinals of the Holy Roman Church, together with the counsel and assent of all those prelates who have been trained in canon and civil law who follow our Court, and with our own certain knowledge, we condemn appeals of this kind, reject them as erroneous and abominable, and declare them to be completely null and void. And we lay down that from now on, no one should dare . . . to make such an appeal from our decisions, be they legal or theological, or from any commands at all from us or our successors. . . .

Heiko A. Oberman, Daniel E. Zerfoss, and William J. Courtenay, eds. and trans., *Execrabilis: Defensorum Obedientiae Apostolicae et alia Documenta* (Cambridge, Mass., 1968), pp. 224–227, with modifications by R. C. Stacey.

QUESTIONS FOR ANALYSIS

1. How might the conciliar movement be seen as a subtle challenge to the authority of the medieval papacy?
2. Why would a pope fear the decisions of a general council?
3. Why was it important to guarantee regular meetings of general church councils?

had gone to the papacy. They also acquired new powers to appoint candidates to church offices within their kingdoms.

As papal authority over local churches diminished, and the spiritual prestige of the papacy declined, kings and princes became the primary figures toward whom even churchmen looked to reform the religious and moral lives of their people. Many secular rulers responded aggressively to such expectations by closing scandal-ridden monasteries, suppressing heretics, punishing women accused of witchcraft, regulating prostitution, and prohibiting the lower classes from dressing as if they were nobles. By these and other such measures, rulers could present themselves as champions of moral and religious reform while also strengthening their capacity to rule their territories. The result was an increasingly close link between national rulers and the national churches over which they ruled.

Having given away so many of their other revenues, the popes of the late fifteenth century became even more dependent on their own territories in central Italy than their predecessors had been. To build up the Papal States, however, the popes had to rule like other Italian princes: leading armies, jockeying for alliances with other princes, and undermining their opponents by every possible means. Judged in secular terms, their efforts were by no means a failure. By 1520, the Papal States was one of the better-governed and wealthier principalities in Italy. But such methods did nothing to increase the popes' reputation for piety or to respond to the calls from both clergy and laity for a thoroughgoing reform of religious life. By 1500, disillusionment with the late medieval papacy as a force for spiritual and religious reform within the church was widespread. In the Protestant Reformation, that smoldering tinder would erupt into a Europeanwide conflagration.

THE PURSUIT OF HOLINESS IN LATE MEDIEVAL PIETY

Were late medieval people disillusioned with their church?

Despite the troubles of the institutional church, religious devotion among the laity was more widespread and intense during the later Middle Ages than it had ever been before. The fundamental theme of high medieval preaching—that salvation lay open to any Christian who strove for it—bore fruit during the later Middle Ages in a rapidly multiplying variety of paths that promised to lead the individual believer to God. Some of these paths led their adherents in directions the church declared heretical. For the vast majority of late medieval Christians, however, heresy held no appeal. The church, and especially the sacraments performed by their local parish priests, stood at the center of their religious lives. To understand late medieval Christianity, we need therefore to start in the parishes.

SACRAMENT, RITUAL, AND SERMON

By 1300, nearly all of Europe was covered by a network of local parish churches, within which priests administered the sacraments of the church to the laity. Sacraments were rituals that conveyed the grace and power of God to individual Christian believers. Baptism initiated the Christian into the life of the church; without baptism, salvation was generally thought to be impossible. Confirmation "confirmed" the promises made on a child's behalf at baptism. In the Mass (which was celebrated every Sunday and on feast days as well), bread and wine became the actual body and blood of Christ, which the Christian faithful honored and consumed. Confession of sins to a priest guaranteed their forgiveness by God; but if satisfactory penance for sins were not completed on earth, then it would have to be done after death in purgatory, a nether world between heaven and hell. Marriage was a relatively new sacrament; in the later Middle Ages, only a minority of Christians would have had their unions solemnized by the church. Ordination conveyed to a priest his special power to bring God's grace to earth through the sacraments. Extreme unction (or "last rites") assured the dying that all their sins were forgiven, with the promise of salvation to come. Like baptism, extreme unction could, in an emergency, be administered by any Christian believer. The other sacraments, however, could be administered only by a properly ordained priest—or, in the case of confirmation and ordination, by a bishop.

This sacramental system was the foundation on which the other practices of late medieval popular piety rested. Pilgrimages were a form of penance that could lessen one's time in purgatory. Crusading was a kind of "extreme pilgrimage," promising the complete fulfillment of all penances the crusader might owe for all the sins of his (or her) life. Many other pious acts—saying the prayers of the rosary, for example, or giving alms to the poor—could also serve as penance for one's sins as well as constituting "good works" that would help the believer in his or her journey toward salvation.

But there was more to late medieval piety than penance. The saints generally, and the Virgin Mary in particular, were regarded as powerful intercessors with God, whose help could be solicited through prayer. In danger or ill health, believers would pray to such holy figures. Devotion to the saints might be increased by contact with the relics of a saint, typically pieces of bone or clothing that had belonged to the saint. No relic was more powerful, however, or more central to late medieval piety, than the bread and wine of the Mass, which became, through priestly consecration, the true body and blood of Christ. Believers sometimes attributed magical properties to the consecrated bread, feeding it to sick animals or rushing from church to church to see it elevated over and over again. Church reformers criticized such beliefs and practices as superstitious. But by and large, these were not practices foisted on an ignorant and credulous laity by a group of clerical con men. They arose and continued because of the deep devotion of lay people to them, frequently in opposition to the efforts of church reformers to shut them down.

RELIGION AND THE SOCIAL ORDER

Not everyone found the conventional practices of late medieval piety spiritually satisfying. Although honored in death, many late medieval saints were distinctly controversial in life. As a child, Saint Catherine of Siena refused altogether to help with the housework and then took over one of the two rooms in her working-class family's house for her prayers, forcing her parents and her dozen siblings into the one remaining room. Julianna of Norwich withdrew from the world into a small cell built next to her local church, where she spent the rest of her life in prayer and contemplation. Margery Kempe was so moved by the suffering of Jesus on the cross that she would cry hysterically for hours, disrupting the Mass and alienating her fellow parishioners.

The extraordinary piety of such individuals could be awe inspiring, but it could also threaten the church's control over religious life. Some believers who sought to achieve a mystical union with God were condemned as heretics for declaring that, having succeeded in their mystical quest, they were no longer obliged to obey God's church on earth. Even less radical figures sometimes trod on dangerous ground. Master Eckhart (c. 1260–1327), for example, a German Dominican, taught and wrote in both Latin and German that there was a power or "spark" deep within every human soul wherein God dwelt. By renouncing all sense of self one could retreat into one's innermost recesses and there find divinity. Eckhart did not discourage attendance at the sacraments, but he made clear that for those seeking God, they were of lesser importance than the inward journey he described. Church authorities charged him with inciting "ignorant and un-disciplined people to wild and dangerous excesses." Although Eckhart pleaded his own doctrinal orthodoxy, some of his teachings were ultimately condemned as heretical.

> The extraordinary piety of such individuals could be awe inspiring, but it could also threaten the church's control over religious life.

More safely orthodox was the "practical mysticism" preached to both monastic and lay audiences during the fifteenth century by such figures as Thomas à Kempis, whose *Imitation of Christ* (c. 1427) did not aim for full mystical union with God but rather for an on-going sense of divine presence during the conduct of daily life. The *Imitation* taught its readers to be pious Christians while still living actively in the world, emphasizing the importance of the Mass but otherwise stressing inward rather than outward piety and urging believers to meditate on the Bible and to live a simple, moral life. Although written in Latin, the *Imitation* was quickly translated into the leading European vernacular languages. For almost six centuries, it has been more widely read than any other Christian religious work except the Bible.

LOLLARDS AND HUSSITES

For the most part, popular heretical movements were less widespread and less dangerous to the church during the later Middle Ages than they had been in the twelfth and thirteenth centuries. In England and Bohemia, however, heretical movements did pose serious challenges to the established authorities of both church and state. In England, the Lollard heresy began with John Wyclif (c. 1330–1384), an Oxford theologian whose extreme predestinarianism (see p. 164) led him to conclude that the sacraments of a corrupt church could not save anyone. He urged the English Crown, therefore, to appropriate ecclesiastical wealth and to replace corrupt priests and bishops with men who would live according to apostolic standards of poverty and piety. Wyclif's followers, known as Lollards, went further, dismissing the sacraments altogether and declaring themselves the only true church. Instead, Lollard preachers traveled the countryside, bringing with them an English translation of the Bible and other vernacular religious literature, which they put directly into the hands of the laity.

Lollardy gained numerous adherents in the last two decades of the fourteenth century, including some nobles and knights. But after the failure of a Lollard uprising in 1414, the movement lost its noble support and went underground. Lollards survived into the sixteenth century, in numbers sufficient to cause occasional alarm to church authorities. But Lollards were never more than a tiny minority, who stood in flat opposition to almost everything (including pilgrimages, the sacraments, and religious images) that their neighbors found most satisfying in late medieval religious life.

Wyclif's ideas struck much deeper roots in Bohemia, where they were adopted by Jan Hus (c. 1373–1415), a charismatic preacher at Charles University in Prague who had already been inveighing in well-attended sermons against "the world, the flesh, and the devil." In contrast to the Lollards, however, whose dismissal of the Eucharist cost them much support, Hus emphasized the centrality of the Eucharist to Christian piety by demanding that the laity should receive not only the consecrated bread of the Mass but also the consecrated wine, which the late medieval church reserved solely for priests. This demand, known as Utraquism, gained broad popular support among the Bohemian laity and became a rallying symbol for the Hussite movement. In 1415, however, Hus agreed to travel to the Council of Constance to defend his views and try to convince the assembled prelates to undertake sweeping reforms of church life. The council had guaranteed Hus's safety, but this assurance was revoked as soon as he arrived there. Rather than being given a fair hearing, Hus was declared a heretic and burned at the stake.

Hus's supporters in Bohemia quickly raised the banner of open revolt. Nobles took advantage of the situation to seize church lands, while priests, artisans, and peasants rallied together to pursue Hus's goals of religious reform and social justice. Between 1420 and 1424 armies of radical Hussites resoundingly defeated several invading forces of crusading knights sent against them by the papacy. In 1434, however, more conservative, aristocratically dominated Hussites overcame the radicals and negotiated a settlement with the papacy that permitted Utraquism in the Bohemian church alongside Catholic orthodoxy. But Bohemia did not return fully to the Catholic fold until the seventeenth century.

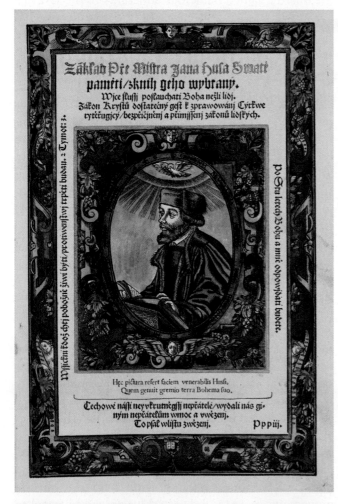

Title Page from the Teachings of Jan Hus. An eloquent religious reformer, Jan Hus was burned at the stake in 1415 for heresy. He accused the Catholic Church of being corrupt and demanded that the church reform the Eucharist.

THOUGHT, LITERATURE, AND ART

What accounts for the remarkable creativity of late medieval cultural life?

The hardships of the later Middle Ages might have led intellectual and artistic life to stagnate, but in fact the period was an extremely creative one in thought, literature, and art. In this section we postpone treatment of certain developments closely related to the early history of the Italian Renaissance but discuss some of the other important intellectual and artistic accomplishments of the fourteenth and fifteenth centuries.

THEOLOGY AND PHILOSOPHY

During the twelfth and thirteenth centuries, scholastic thinkers like Saint Thomas Aquinas had constructed a picture of a rational, organized, and comprehensible natural world that was structured to lead the inquiring human mind to a knowledge of God and hence to salvation. After 1300, however, confidence in this picture began to ebb. Nominalist thinkers such as the English Franciscan William of Ockham (d. 1349) denied that human reason could prove fundamental theological truths such as the existence of God. Instead, they argued, human knowledge of God, and hence salvation, depended entirely on what God himself had chosen to reveal through scripture. Humans could investigate the natural world but any regularities that were observable in nature existed solely because an all-powerful God actively willed them to continue in this regular way. To suggest that God had to act in accordance with certain natural laws (such as gravity), and that these laws could therefore tell us something about God himself, was an affront to the absolute power and majesty of God.

Nominalism became enormously influential in late medieval universities and had an immense impact on European thought. Ockham's concern about what God might do led his followers to raise some of the seemingly absurd questions for which medieval theology has been mocked: for example, asking whether God can undo the past or whether an infinite number of pure spirits can simultaneously inhabit the same place (the nearest medieval thinkers actually came to asking how many angels can dance on the head of a pin). Nonetheless, the nominalists' insistence on God's om-

WHAT ACCOUNTS FOR THE REMARKABLE CREATIVITY OF LATE MEDIEVAL CULTURAL LIFE?

THOUGHT, LITERATURE, AND ART   293

nipotence became one of the basic presuppositions of sixteenth-century Protestantism. At the same time, the distinction they drew between the rational comprehensibility of the natural world and the incomprehensibility of God also encouraged intellectuals to investigate the natural world without reference to supernatural explanations—one of the fundamental building blocks in the emergence of a modern scientific worldview.

VERNACULAR LITERATURE

The literature of the later Middle Ages was characterized by an intense concern to describe the world as it is. Such naturalism was not new. High medieval authors such as Wolfram von Eschenbach and Dante had already established the precedents on which their late medieval successors would build. But late medieval authors went much further, especially in describing the foibles and failings of everyday human life. They also pioneered the development of new literary forms for vernacular writing, sometimes in poetry, but especially in prose. Most late medieval authors also continued to compose in Latin; but increasingly, the most innovative and ambitious literary work was being written in the vernacular languages of Europe. Behind this development lay three fundamental changes of the later Middle Ages: a growing identification between vernacular languages and nationalism; the continuing spread of lay education; and the emergence of a substantial reading public for vernacular literature. We can see these influences at work in three of the major vernacular authors of the later Middle Ages: Giovanni Boccaccio (1313–1375), Geoffrey Chaucer (c. 1340–1400), and Christine de Pisan (c. 1365–c. 1435).

BOCCACCIO

Boccaccio (*bohk-KAHT-chee-oh*) would deserve an honored place in literary history even for his lesser works, which included courtly romances, pastoral lyrics, and learned treatises. His masterpiece, however, is the *Decameron*, a collection of 100 prose tales, mostly about love, sex, adventure, and trickery, told by a sophisticated party of seven young women and three men temporarily residing in a country villa outside Florence to escape the Black Death. Boccaccio borrowed the outlines of many of these tales from earlier sources, but he transformed them with his own characteristic exuberance and wit.

Boccaccio deliberately wrote in an unaffected, colloquial style, eschewing literary "elegance" to portray men and women exactly as they are. His women are not pallid playthings, distant goddesses, or steadfast virgins but flesh-and-blood creatures with minds and bodies, who interact with men more comfortably and naturally than any women in Western literature had ever done before. His clerics are all too human, much more like other men than they are like angels on earth. His treatment of sexual relations is often graphic, but never demeaning. For all these reasons the *Decameron* is a robust and delightful appreciation of what it means to be human.

CHAUCER

Similar in many ways to Boccaccio as a creator of naturalistic vernacular literature was the Englishman Geoffrey Chaucer (c. 1340–1400). Chaucer wrote several highly impressive works, but his masterpiece is unquestionably the *Canterbury Tales*. Like the *Decameron*, this is a collection of stories held together by a frame, in Chaucer's case the device of having a group of people tell stories while on a pilgrimage from London to Canterbury. But there are also differences between the *Decameron* and the *Canterbury Tales*. Chaucer's stories are told in sparkling verse instead of prose, and they are recounted by people of all different classes—from a chivalric knight to a dedicated university student to a thieving miller with a wart on his nose. Lively women also appear, most memorably the gap-toothed, oft-married "Wife of Bath," who knows all "the remedies of love." Each character tells a story that is particularly illustrative of his or her own occupation and outlook on the world. By this device Chaucer was able to create a highly diverse "human comedy." His range is greater than Boccaccio's, and although he is no less witty, frank, and lusty than the Italian, he is sometimes more profound.

CHRISTINE DE PISAN

The later Middle Ages also saw the emergence of professional authors who made their living with their pens. Significantly, one of the first of these professional *litterati* was a woman, Christine de Pisan (1364–1431). Although born in Italy, de Pisan spent her adult life in France, where her husband was a member of the king's household. When he died, the widowed de Pisan turned to writing to support herself and her children. She wrote in a wide variety of literary genres, including treatises on chivalry and warfare that she dedicated to her patron, King Charles VI of France. But she also wrote for a larger and more popular audience. Her

Christine de Pisan. A leading writer of late medieval vernacular prose literature, Christine de Pisan (1364–1431) was intent on upholding the dignity of women. She is shown here writing about a gigantic Amazon warrior who could defeat men effortlessly in armed combat.

imaginative tract *The City of Ladies* is an extended defense of the character, nature, and capacities of women against their male detractors, written in the form of an allegory. She also took part in a vigorous pamphlet campaign that debated the misogynistic claims commonly made against women in the literature of the period. This debate continued for several hundred years and became so famous that it was given a name: the *querelle des femmes*, "the debate over women." De Pisan was by no means the first female writer of the Middle Ages, but she was the first lay woman to earn a living by her writing.

SCULPTURE AND PAINTING

As naturalism was a dominant trait of late medieval literature, so it was of late medieval art. Whereas early medieval art had emphasized abstract design, the stress was now increasingly on realism: thirteenth-century carvings of leaves and flowers must have been made from direct observation and are clearly recognizable to modern botanists as distinct species. Statues of humans also gradually became more

> Whereas early medieval art had emphasized abstract design, the stress was now increasingly on realism: thirteenth-century carvings of leaves and flowers must have been made from direct observation and are clearly recognizable to modern botanists as distinct species.

natural and realistic in their portrayals of facial expressions and bodily proportions. By around 1290 the concern for realism had become so great that a sculptor working on a tomb portrait of the German emperor Rudolf of Habsburg allegedly made a hurried return trip to view Rudolf in person, because he had heard that a new wrinkle had appeared on the emperor's face.

In the next two centuries the trend toward naturalism continued in sculpture and was extended to manuscript illumination and painting. The latter was in certain respects a new art. Wall paintings were common in the Middle Ages and long afterward, especially in the form of *frescoes*, paintings done on wet plaster. But in addition to frescoes, Italian artists in the thirteenth century also began painting pictures on pieces of wood or canvas. These were first done in tempera (pigments mixed with water and natural gums or egg whites), but around 1400 painting in oils was introduced in the European north. These new technical developments created new artistic opportunities. Artists were now able to paint religious scenes on portable

WHAT ACCOUNTS FOR THE REMARKABLE CREATIVITY OF LATE MEDIEVAL CULTURAL LIFE?

THOUGHT, LITERATURE, AND ART   295

The Meeting of Joachim and Anna, by Giotto. Notice how the haloes merge. This aged and infertile couple will soon miraculously have their only child: Mary, the mother of Jesus.

altarpieces. They also began painting strikingly sensitive and realistic portraits.

The most innovative painter of the later Middle Ages was the Florentine Giotto (c. 1267–1337), who brought deep humanity to the religious images he painted on both walls and movable panels. Giotto was preeminently an imitator of nature. Not only do his human beings and animals look more lifelike than those of his predecessors but they seem to do more natural things. When Christ enters Jerusalem on Palm Sunday, boys climb trees to get a better view; when Saint Francis is laid out in death, one onlooker takes the opportunity to see whether the saint had really received Christ's wounds; and when the Virgin's parents, Joachim and Anna, meet after a long separation, they actually embrace and kiss—perhaps the first deeply tender kiss in Western art. After Giotto's death a reaction in Italian painting set in. Mid-fourteenth-century artists briefly moved away from naturalism and painted stern, forbidding religious figures who seemed to float in space. But by around 1400 artists came back down to earth and started to build on Giotto's

influence in ways that led to the great Italian renaissance in painting.

In the north of Europe painting did not advance impressively beyond manuscript illumination until the early fifteenth century, but then it suddenly came very much into its own. The leading northern European painters were Flemish, first and foremost Jan van Eyck (c. 1380–1441), Roger van der Weyden (c. 1400–1464), and Hans Memling (c. 1430–1494). These three were the greatest early practitioners of painting in oil, a medium that allowed them to engage in brilliant coloring and sharp-focused realism. Van Eyck and van der Weyden excelled at communicating a sense of deep religious piety and portraying minute details of familiar everyday experience. These may at first seem incompatible, but it should be remembered that contemporary manuals of practical mysticism such as the *Imitation of Christ* also sought to link deep piety with everyday existence. Thus it was by no means blasphemous when a Flemish painter portrayed behind a tender Virgin and Child a vista of contemporary life with people going about their usual business and a man even urinating against a wall. This union of the sacred and the profane tended to fall apart in the work of Memling, who excelled in either straightforward religious pictures or secular portraits, but it would return in the work of the greatest painters of the Low Countries, Brueghel and Rembrandt.

ADVANCES IN TECHNOLOGY

How did technological advances affect everyday life?

No account of enduring late medieval accomplishments would be complete without mention of certain epoch-making technological advances. Treatment of this subject has to begin with reference to the invention of artillery and firearms. The prevalence of warfare stimulated the development of new weaponry. Gunpowder itself was a Chinese invention, but it was first put to devastating military uses in the late medieval West. Heavy cannons were first employed around 1330. The earliest cannons were primitive, but by the middle of

the fifteenth century they began to revolutionize warfare. In 1453, heavy artillery played a leading role in determining the outcome of two crucial conflicts: the Ottoman Turks used German and Hungarian cannons to breach the defenses of Constantinople—hitherto the most impregnable in Europe—and the French used heavy artillery to take the city of Bordeaux, thereby ending the Hundred Years' War. Cannons thereafter made it difficult for rebellious aristocrats to hole up in their stone castles, and thus they aided in the consolidation of the national monarchies. Placed aboard ships, cannons also enabled European vessels to dominate foreign waters in the subsequent age of overseas expansion. Handheld firearms, also invented in the fourteenth century, were also gradually perfected. Shortly after 1500 the most effective new variety of gun, the musket, allowed foot soldiers to end once and for all the military dominance of heavily armored mounted knights. Once lance-bearing cavalries became outmoded and fighting could more easily be carried on by all, the monarchical states that could turn out the largest armies completely subdued internal resistance and dominated the battlefields of Europe.

Other late medieval technological developments were more life enhancing. Eyeglasses, first invented in

A Fifteenth-Century Siege with Cannon. By the mid-fifteenth century, cannons were an essential element in siege warfare.

the 1280s, were perfected in the fourteenth century. Around 1300 the use of the magnetic compass helped ships sail farther away from land and venture out into the Atlantic. Subsequent improvements in shipbuilding, map making, and navigational devices enabled Europe to start expanding overseas. In the fourteenth century the Azores and Cape Verde Islands were reached; then, after a long pause caused by Europe's plagues and wars, the African Cape of Good Hope was rounded in 1488, the West Indies reached in 1492, India reached by the sea route in 1498, and Brazil sighted in 1500. Partly as a result of technology, the world was thus suddenly made much smaller.

Among the most familiar implements of our modern life that were invented by Europeans in the later Middle Ages were clocks and printed books. Mechanical clocks were invented shortly before 1300 and proliferated in the years immediately thereafter. The earliest clocks were too expensive for private purchase, but towns vied with each other to install the most elaborate clocks in their prominent public buildings. The new invention ultimately had two profound effects. One was the further stimulation of European interest in complex machinery of all sorts. Equally if not more significant was the fact that clocks began to rationalize the course of European daily affairs. Until the advent of clocks in the later Middle Ages time was flexible. Men and women had only a rough idea of how late in the day it was and rose and retired more or less with the sun. In the fourteenth century, however, clocks first started relentlessly striking equal hours through the day and night. Thus they began to regulate work with new precision. People were expected to start and end work "on time" and many came to believe that "time is money." This emphasis on timekeeping brought new efficiencies but also new tensions: Lewis Carroll's white rabbit, who is always looking at his pocket watch and muttering "how late it's getting," is a telling caricature of time-obsessed Western humanity.

The invention of printing with movable type was equally momentous. The major stimulus for this invention was the replacement of parchment by paper as Europe's primary writing material between 1200 and 1400. Parchment, made from the skins of sheep or calves, was extremely expensive: since it was possible to get about only four good parchment leaves from one animal, it was necessary to slaughter between 200 and 300 sheep or calves to gain enough parchment for a Bible! Paper, made from rags turned into pulp by mills, brought prices down dramatically. Late medieval records show that paper sold at one sixth the price of parchment. Accordingly, it became cheaper to learn how to read and write. With literacy becoming ever more widespread, there was a growing market for still cheaper books, and the invention of printing with movable type around 1450, associated most famously with the Bible produced by Johann Gutenberg in 1454, fully met this demand. By greatly saving labor, the invention made printed books about one fifth as expensive as handwritten ones within about two decades.

As books became easily accessible, literacy increased and book culture became a basic part of European life. After about 1500, Europeans could afford to read and buy books of all sorts—not just religious tracts but instructional manuals, light entertainment, and, by the eighteenth century, newspapers. Printing ensured that ideas would spread quickly and reliably; moreover, revolutionary ideas could no longer be easily extinguished once they were set down in hundreds of copies of books. Thus the greatest religious reformer of the sixteenth century, Martin Luther, gained an immediate following throughout Germany by employing the printing press to run off pamphlets: had printing not been available to him, Luther might have died as Hus did. The spread of books also helped stimulate the growth of cultural nationalism. Before printing, regional dialects in most European countries were often so diverse that people who supposedly spoke the same language often could barely understand each other. After the invention of printing, however, each European country began to develop its own linguistic standards, which were disseminated uniformly by books. Thus communications were enhanced and governments were able to operate ever more efficiently.

CONCLUSION

Despite economic dislocation and demographic collapse, the later Middle Ages was one of the most creative and inventive periods in the history of western Europe. What lay behind the artistic, philosophical, literary, and technological developments of the period was a drive to understand, control, and replicate the workings of the natural world. This fact may help explain the sources of these developments.

Perhaps most fundamental, in the later Middle Ages intellectuals broke with the traditional, Neoplatonic vision of nature as a book in which one could read the mind of God. Instead, they came to see the natural world as operating according to its own laws, which were empirically verifiable but which could tell human beings nothing about the God who lay behind them. The resulting sense of the contingency and independence of the natural world was an essential step toward the emergence of a scientific worldview. It also encouraged Europeans to believe that nature itself could be manipulated and directed toward human ends.

Powerful economic and political factors also encouraged the technological inventiveness of the period. Despite the disruptive impact of plague and war, the market for goods was not destroyed. Instead, labor shortages encouraged European entrepreneurs to experiment with labor-saving technologies and new crops. Incessant warfare encouraged a remarkable burst of military inventiveness. It also enabled more powerful governments to extract a larger percentage of their subjects' wealth through taxation, which they proceeded to invest in ships, cannons, muskets, and the standing armies that the new weaponry made possible. Increasing per capita wealth produced the capital necessary to invest in mills, factories, clocks, books, and compasses. It also made possible a remarkable increase in the educational level of the European population.

Between 1300 and 1500 hundreds and perhaps thousands of new grammar schools were established, and scores of new universities emerged, because parents saw such schools as a reliable route to social advancement for their sons. Women were still excluded from the schools, but increasing numbers of girls were being taught at home, making women an extremely important (perhaps even the dominant) part of the "reading public" that was emerging in later medieval Europe.

Finally, it may be that dislocation itself promotes innovation, so long as it does not destroy people's confidence in the ultimate improvability of their lives. Europeans suffered enormously from war, plague, and economic crises during the later Middle Ages. But those who survived seized the opportunities their new world presented to them. The confidence they had developed in the High Middle Ages was not destroyed by the travails of the later Middle Ages. By 1500, most Europeans lived more secure lives than their ancestors had 200 years before; and they stood on the verge of an extraordinary new period of expansion and conquest that would take European armies, merchants, and settlers around the globe.

KEY TERMS

Black Death	Richard II	Joan of Arc	Ivan the Great
flagellants	Avignon	Wars of the Roses	Giovanni Boccaccio
bubonic plague	Master Eckhart	khanate	*Canterbury Tales*
Jacquerie	Hundred Years' War	tsar	William of Ockham

SELECTED READINGS

Allmand, Christopher T. *The Hundred Years' War: England and France at War, c. 1300–c. 1450*. Cambridge and New York, 1988. Still the best analytic account of the war; after a short narrative, the book is organized topically.

Allmand, Christopher T., ed. *Society at War: The Experience of England and France during the Hundred Years' War*. Edinburgh, 1973. An outstanding collection of documents.

Boccaccio, Giovanni. *The Decameron*. Trans. Mark Musa and P. E. Bondanella. New York, 1977.

Chaucer, Geoffrey. *The Canterbury Tales*. Trans. Nevill Coghill. New York, 1951. A modern English verse translation, lightly annotated.

Cohn, Samuel K., Jr. *Lust for Liberty: The Politics of Social Revolt in Medieval Europe, 1200–1425*. Cambridge, Mass., 2006. A provocative new account of popular rebellions.

Cole, Bruce. *Giotto and Florentine Painting, 1280–1375*. New York, 1976. A clear and stimulating introduction.

Crummey, Robert O. *The Formation of Muscovy, 1304–1613*. New York, 1987. The standard account.

Dobson, R. Barrie. *The Peasants' Revolt of 1381*. 2d ed. London, 1983. A comprehensive source collection, with excellent introductions to the documents and an illuminating discussion of the revolt.

Duffy, Eamon. *The Stripping of the Altars: Traditional Religion in England, 1400–1580*. New Haven, Conn., 1992. The fullest study anywhere of the patterns of fifteenth-century piety at the parish level.

Froissart, Jean. *Chronicles*. Trans. Geoffrey Brereton. Baltimore, Md., 1968. A selection from the most famous contemporary account of the Hundred Years' War to roughly 1400.

Horrox, Rosemary, ed. *The Black Death.* New York, 1994. A fine collection of documents reflecting the impact of the Black Death, especially in England.

Huizinga, Johan. *The Waning of the Middle Ages: A Study of the Forms of Life, Thought, and Art in France and the Netherlands in the Dawn of the Renaissance.* New York, 1924. A classic picture of the "expiring" Middle Ages; a book from whose influence historians are still struggling to escape. Frequently republished, the most recent translation of this work is titled *The Autumn of the Middle Ages.* Trans. Rodney J. Payton and Ulrich Mammitzsch. Chicago, 1996.

John Hus at the Council of Constance. Trans. M. Spinka. New York, 1965. The translation of a Czech chronicle with an expert introduction and appended documents.

Jordan, William Chester. *The Great Famine: Northern Europe in the Early Fourteenth Century.* Princeton, N.J., 1996. An outstanding social and economic study of the disastrous famines that swept northern Europe between 1315 and 1322.

Keen, Maurice, ed. *Medieval Warfare: A History.* Oxford and New York, 1999. The most attractive introduction to this crucially important subject. Lively and well illustrated.

Kempe, Margery. *The Book of Margery Kempe.* Trans. Barry Windeatt. New York, 1985. A fascinating autobiography by an early fifteenth-century Englishwoman who hoped she might be a saint.

Lewis, Peter S. *Later Medieval France: The Polity.* London, 1968. Still fresh and suggestive after thirty-five years. A masterwork.

Memoirs of a Renaissance Pope: The Commentaries of Pius II. Abridged ed. Trans. F. A. Gragg. New York, 1959. Remarkable insights into the mind of a particularly well-educated mid-fifteenth-century pope.

Oakley, Francis C. *The Western Church in the Later Middle Ages.* Ithaca, N.Y., 1979. The best book by far on the history of conciliarism, the late medieval papacy, Hussitism, and the efforts at institutional reform during this period. On popular piety, see Swanson.

Pernoud, Régine, ed. *Joan of Arc, by Herself and Her Witnesses.* New York, 1966. A collection of contemporary writings about Joan, including the transcripts of her trial.

Swanson, R. N. *Religion and Devotion in Europe, c. 1215–c. 1515.* Cambridge and New York, 1995. An excellent study of late medieval popular piety; an excellent complement to Oakley.

Sumption, Jonathan. *The Hundred Years' War.* Vol. 1: *Trial by Battle;* Vol. 2: *Trial by Fire.* Philadelphia, 1999. The first two volumes of a massive narrative history of the war take the story up to 1369.

Vaughan, Richard. *Valois Burgundy.* London, 1975. A summation of the author's four-volume study of the Burgundian dukes.

Ziegler, Philip. *The Black Death.* New York, 1969. A popular account, but reliable and engrossing.

CHAPTER ELEVEN

COMMERCE, CONQUEST, AND COLONIZATION, 1300–1600

B
Y 1300, THE EXPANSION of the High Middle Ages was coming to an end. In Iberia, there would be no further conquests of Muslim territory until 1492, when Granada fell to King Ferdinand and Queen Isabella. In the East, the crusader kingdoms of Constantinople and Acre collapsed in 1261 and 1291, respectively. Only the German drive into eastern Europe continued; but by the mid-fourteenth century, it too had been slowed by the rise of a new Baltic state in Lithuania. Internal expansion was also ending, as Europe reached the ecological limits of its resources. Thereafter, the pressure on resources was eased only by the dramatic population losses that resulted during the fourteenth century from the combined effects of famine, plague, and war.

But despite these checks, Europeans in the late Middle Ages did not turn inward. Although land-based conquests slowed, new sea-based empires emerged in the Mediterranean world during the fourteenth and fifteenth centuries, with colonies that extended from the Black Sea to the Canary Islands. New maritime trade routes were opened up through the Strait of Gibraltar. By the late fifteenth century, Mediterranean mariners and colonists had extended their domination out into the Atlantic, from the Azores in the north to the Canary Islands in the south. Portuguese navigators were also pushing down the west coast of Africa. In 1498 one such expedition would sail all the way around the Cape of Good Hope to India.

The fifteenth-century conquest of the "Atlantic Mediterranean" was the essential preliminary to the dramatic events that began in 1492 with Columbus's attempt to reach China by sailing westward across the Atlantic Ocean and that led, by 1600, to the Spanish and Portuguese conquests of the Americas. Because these events are so familiar, we can easily underestimate their importance. For the native peoples and empires of the Americas, the results of European contact were cataclysmic. By 1600, somewhere between 50 and 90 percent of the indigenous peoples of the Americas had perished from disease, massacre, and enslavement. For Europeans,

FOCUS QUESTIONS

• What impact did the Mongol conquests have on Europe?

• Why were slaves so important to Ottoman society?

• How were the Portuguese able to control Indian Ocean trade?

• What was the impact of New World silver on the European economy?

the results of their conquests were less lethal but no less far reaching. By 1300, Europe had eclipsed both Byzantium and the lands of Islam as a Mediterranean power, but outside the Mediterranean and the north Atlantic European power was negligible. By 1600, however, Europe had emerged as the first truly global power in world history, capable of pursuing its imperial ambitions and commercial interests wherever its ships could sail and its guns could reach. Europeans would not achieve full control over the interiors of the African, Asian, and American land masses until the end of the nineteenth century, and their control would last thereafter for less than a century. By 1600, however, European navies ruled the seas, and the world's resources were increasingly being channeled through European hands—patterns that have continued until the present day.

THE MONGOLS

What impact did the Mongol conquests have on Europe?

Trade between the Mediterranean world and the Far East dated back to antiquity, but it was not until the late thirteenth century that Europeans began to establish direct trading connections with India, China, and the "Spice Islands" of the Indonesian archipelago. For Europeans, these connections would prove profoundly important, although less for their economic significance than for their impact on the European imagination. For the peoples of Asia, however, the appearance of European traders on the "Silk Road" between Central Asia and China was merely a curiosity. The really consequential event was the rise of the Mongol Empire that made such connections possible.

THE RISE OF THE MONGOL EMPIRE

The Mongols were a nomadic people whose homeland lay to the north of the Gobi Desert in present-day Mongolia. Like many nomadic peoples throughout history, the Mongols were highly accomplished cavalry soldiers who supplemented their own pastoralism and craft production by raiding the sedentary peoples to

In 1279, Chingiz's grandson Qubilai (Kublai) Khan completed the conquest of southern (Sung) China, thus reuniting China for the first time in centuries.

their south. (It was in part to control such raiding from Mongolia that, many centuries before, the Chinese had built the famous Great Wall.) Primarily, however, China defended itself by attempting to ensure that the Mongols remained internally divided, and so turned their energies most often against each other.

In the late twelfth century, however, a Mongol chief named Temüjin began to unite the various Mongol tribes under his rule. By incorporating the army of each defeated tribe into his own army, Temüjin quickly built up a large military force. In 1206, his supremacy was formally acknowledged by all the Mongols, and he took the title Chingiz (Genghis) Khan—"the oceanic [possibly meaning universal] ruler." Chingiz now turned his enormous army against his non-Mongol neighbors.

China at this time was divided into three hostile states. In 1209, Chingiz launched an attack on northwestern China; in 1211 he invaded the Chin Empire in north China. At first these attacks were probably looting expeditions rather than deliberate attempts at conquest, but by the 1230s a full-scale Mongol conquest of northern and western China was under way, culminating in 1234 with the fall of the Chin. In 1279, Chingiz's grandson Qubilai (Kublai) Khan completed the conquest of southern (Sung) China, thus reuniting China for the first time in centuries.

Meanwhile, Chingiz turned his forces westward, conquering much of Central Asia and incorporating the important commercial cities of Tashkent, Samarkand, and Bukhara into his expanding empire. When Chingiz died in 1227, he was succeeded by his third son, Ögedei (*EHRG-uh-day*), who completed the conquest of the Chin and then laid plans for a massive invasion toward the west. Between 1237 and 1240, the Mongol horde

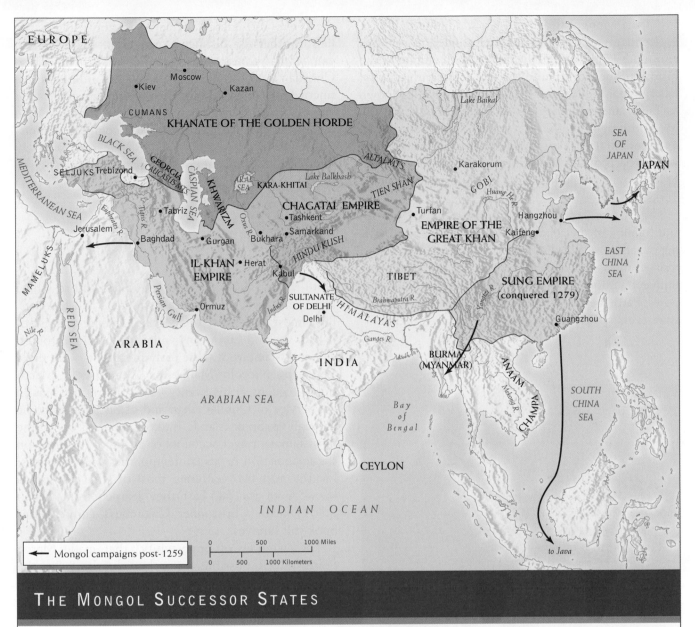

THE MONGOL SUCCESSOR STATES

Consider the breakup of Chingiz Khan's empire after 1259 and the passing similarities its fracture might possess to the disintegration of Alexander's empire, also conquered swiftly and encompassing vast swaths of Europe and Asia. Why did Chingiz Khan's empire splinter? How did the Mongol onslaught against and occupation of major sections of the Arab Muslim world possibly aid the expansion of European civilization and trade into the Mediterranean? At the same time, how did it complicate the situation for the crusader efforts in the Holy Land?

(so called from the Turkish word *ordu*, meaning "tent" or "encampment") conquered southern Russia and then launched a two-pronged assault farther west. In April 1241 the smaller Mongol force met a hastily assembled army of Germans and Poles at the battle of Liegnitz, where the two sides fought to a bloody standstill. Two days later, the larger Mongol army annihilated the Hungarian army at the River Sajo.

How much farther west the Mongol armies might have pushed will forever remain in doubt, for in December 1241 the Great Khan Ögedei died, and the Mongol forces withdrew from eastern Europe. Mongol conquests continued in Persia, the Middle East, and China; but after 1241 the Mongols never resumed their attacks on Europe. By 1300, the period of Mongol expansion had come to an end.

But the Mongol threat did not suddenly disappear. Descendants of Chingiz Khan continued to rule this enormous land empire (the largest such empire in the history of the world) until the mid-fourteenth century. Later, under the leadership of Timur the Lame (known as Tamerlane to Europeans) it looked briefly as if the Mongol Empire might be reunited. But Timur died in 1405 on his way to invade China; thereafter the various parts of the Mongol Empire fell into the hands of local rulers, including (in Asia Minor) the Ottoman Turks.

The Mongols owed their success to the size, speed, and training of their mounted armies; to the intimidating savagery with which they butchered those who resisted them; and to their ability to adapt the administrative traditions of their subjects to their own purposes. Partly because the Mongols themselves put little store even in their own shamanistic religious traditions, they were also unusually tolerant of the religious beliefs of others—a distinct advantage in controlling an empire that comprised a dizzying array of Buddhist, Christian, and Muslim sects. However, little was distinctively "Mongol" about the way they governed their empire. Except in China, where the Mongol Yuan dynasty inherited and maintained a complex administrative bureaucracy, the Mongols' rule was relatively unsophisticated, being chiefly directed at securing the steady payment of tribute from their subjects.

EUROPE, THE MONGOLS, AND THE FAR EAST

Until the Mongol conquests, the Silk Road to China had been closed to Western merchants and travelers. But almost as soon as the Mongol Empire was established, we find Europeans venturing on these routes. The most famous of these early merchants were three Venetians: Niccolo, Maffeo, and Marco Polo. Marco Polo's account of his twenty-year sojourn in China in the service of Qubilai Khan and of his journey home through the Spice Islands, India, and Iran, is one of the most famous travel accounts of all time. Its effect on the imagination of his contemporaries was enormous. For the next two centuries, most of what Europeans knew about the Far East they learned from Marco Polo's *Travels*. Christopher Columbus's copy of this book still survives.

The "window of opportunity" that made Marco Polo's travels possible was relatively short. By the middle of the fourteenth century, hostilities between the various parts of the Mongol Empire were already making travel along the Silk Road perilous. After 1368, when the Mongol (Yuan) dynasty was overthrown, Westerners were excluded from China altogether, and Mongols were restricted to cavalry service in the Ming imperial armies. The overland trade routes from China to the Black Sea continued to operate; Europeans, however, were no longer able to travel along them. But the new, more integrated commercial world the Mongols created had a lasting impact on Europe, despite the relatively short time during which Europeans themselves were able to participate directly in it. European memories of the Far East would be preserved and the dream of reestablishing direct connections between Europe and China would survive to influence a new round of European commercial and imperial expansion from the late fifteenth century onward.

The Head of Timur the Lame. A forensic reconstruction based on his exhumed skull.

MARCO POLO'S DESCRIPTION OF JAVA

The Venetian merchants Niccolo and Maffeo Polo traveled overland from Constantinople to the court of Qubilai Khan between 1260 and 1269. When they returned a few years later, they brought with them Niccolo's son Marco. A gifted linguist, Marco would remain at the Mongol court until the early 1290s, when he returned to Europe after a journey through Southeast Asia, the Spice Islands, and the Indian Ocean. Marco's account of his travels would shape European images of the Far East for centuries.

Departing from Ziamba, and steering between south and south-east, fifteen hundred miles, you reach an island of very great size, named Java. According to the reports of some well-informed navigators, it is the greatest in the world, and has a compass above three thousand miles. It is under the dominion of one king only, nor do the inhabitants pay tribute to any other power. They are worshipers of idols.

The country abounds with rich commodities. Pepper, nutmegs, spikenard, galangal, cubebs, cloves and all the other valuable spices and drugs, are the produce of the island; which occasion it to be visited by many ships laden with merchandise, that yields to the owners considerable profit.

The quantity of gold collected there exceeds all calculation and belief. From thence it is that . . . merchants . . . have imported, and to this day import, that metal to a great amount, and from thence also is obtained the greatest part of the spices that are distributed throughout the world. That the Great Khan [Qubilai] has not brought the island under subjection to him, must be attributed to the length of the voyage and the dangers of the navigation.

The Travels of Marco Polo, rev. and ed. Manuel Komroff (New York, 1926), pp. 267–268.

QUESTIONS FOR ANALYSIS

1. What effect did Marco Polo's *Travels* have on European images of the Far East?
2. Why did Marco Polo refer to various spices as "rich commodities"? Why were spices so highly valued by Europeans?

THE RISE OF THE OTTOMAN EMPIRE

Why were slaves so important to Ottoman society?

Like the Mongols, the Ottoman Turks were initially a nomadic people whose economy continued to depend on raiding even after they had conquered an extensive empire. The peoples who would become the Ottomans were already established in northwestern Anatolia when the Mongols arrived and were already at least nominally Muslims. But unlike the established Muslim powers in the region, whom the Mongols destroyed, the Ottoman Turks benefited from the Mongol conquest. By toppling the Seljuk sultanate and the Abbasid caliphate of Baghdad, the Mongols eliminated the two traditional authorities that had previously kept Turkish border chieftains like the Ottomans in check. Now the Ottomans were free to raid along their frontiers with Byzantium unhindered. At the same time, however, they remained far enough away from the centers of Mongol authority to avoid being destroyed themselves.

THE CONQUEST OF CONSTANTINOPLE

By the end of the thirteenth century, the Ottoman dynasty had established itself as the leading family among the Anatolian border lords. By the mid-fourteenth century, it had solidified its preeminence by capturing a number of important cities. These successes brought the Ottomans to the attention of the Byzantine emperor, who in 1345 hired a contingent of Ottomans as mercenaries. Thus introduced into Europe, the

Sultan Mehmet II, "The Conqueror" (1451–1481), by the Ottoman artist Siblizade Ahmed. The sultan's pose and handkerchief are central Asian conventions in portraiture, but the subdued color and three-quarter profile show the influence of Italian Renaissance portraits. The sultan wears the white turban of a scholar but also wears the thumb ring of an archer, neatly reflecting his combination of scholarly and military attainments.

Ottomans quickly made themselves at home. By 1370, they had extended their control all the way to the Danube. In 1389 Ottoman forces defeated the powerful Serbian Empire at the battle of Kosovo, enabling them to consolidate their control over Greece, Bulgaria, and the Balkans.

In 1396 the Ottomans attacked Constantinople, but withdrew to repel a Western crusading force that had been sent against them. In 1402, they attacked Constantinople again, but once more were forced to withdraw, this time to confront a Mongolian invasion of Anatolia. Led by Timur the Lame, the Mongol army captured the Ottoman sultan and destroyed his army; for the next decade it appeared that Ottoman hegemony over Anatolia might be gone forever. By 1413, however, Timur was dead, a new sultan had emerged, and the Ottomans were able to resume their conquests. Ottoman pressure on Constantinople continued during the 1420s and 1430s, producing a steady stream of Byzantine refugees who brought with them to Italy the surviving masterworks of classical Greek literature. But it was not until 1451 that a new sultan, Mehmet II, turned his full attention to the conquest of the imperial city. In 1453, after a brilliantly executed siege, Mehmet succeeded in breaching the city's walls. The Byzantine emperor was killed in the assault, the city itself was thoroughly plundered, and its population was sold into slavery. The Ottomans then settled down to rule their new capital in a style reminiscent of their Byzantine predecessors.

The effects of the Ottoman conquest of Constantinople on western Europe were modest. On the Ottomans themselves, however, their conquest was transformative. Vast new wealth poured into Ottoman society, which the Ottomans increased by carefully tending to the industrial and commercial interests of their new capital city. Trade routes were redirected to feed the capital, and the Ottomans became a naval power in the eastern Mediterranean and the Black Sea. As a result, Constantinople's population grew from less than 100,000 in 1453 to more than 500,000 in 1600, making it the largest city in the world outside China.

WAR, SLAVERY, AND SOCIAL ADVANCEMENT

Despite the Ottomans' careful attention to commerce, their empire rested on raiding and conquest. Until the end of the sixteenth century, the Ottoman Empire was therefore on an almost constant war footing. To continue its conquests, the size of the Ottoman army and administration grew exponentially. But this growth drew more and more manpower from the empire. Because the Ottoman army and administration were largely composed of slaves, the demand for more soldiers and administrators could best be met through further conquests that would capture yet more slaves. Further conquests, however, required a still larger army and an even more extensive bureaucracy; and so the cycle continued.

Slaves were the backbone of the Ottoman army and administration. But slaves were also critical to the lives of the Ottoman upper class. After 1453, new wealth permitted some Ottoman notables to maintain households in which thousands of slaves attended to their masters' whims. In the sixteenth century, the sultan's household alone numbered more than 20,000 slave attendants, not including his bodyguard and his elite infantry units, both of which were also composed of slaves.

Many of these slaves were captured in war or raids. But slaves were also recruited (some willingly, some by coercion) from rural areas of the Ottoman Empire itself. Because the vast majority of Ottoman slaves were household servants and administrators rather than laborers, some people willingly accepted enslavement, believing that they would be better off as slaves in Constantinople than as impoverished peasants in the countryside. In the Balkans especially, many people were enslaved as children, handed over by their families to pay the infamous "child tax" the Ottomans imposed on rural areas too poor to pay a monetary tribute. Special academies were created at Constantinople to train the most able of these enslaved children to act as administrators and soldiers, and some rose to become powerful figures in the Ottoman Empire. Slavery therefore carried relatively little social stigma. Even the sultan himself was most often the son of an enslaved woman.

Because Muslims were not permitted to enslave other Muslims, the vast majority of Ottoman slaves were from Christian families (although many converted to Islam later in life). But because so many of the elite positions within Ottoman government were held by slaves, the paradoxical result of this reliance on slave administrators was that Muslims, including Turks, were effectively excluded from the main avenues of social and political advancement in Ottoman society. Nor was Ottoman society characterized by a powerful, hereditary nobility of the sort that dominated contemporary European society. As a result, power in the fifteenth- and sixteenth-century Ottoman Empire was remarkably, perhaps even uniquely, open to men of ability and talent, provided that such men were slaves and therefore not Muslims by birth. Nor was this pattern of Muslim exclusion limited to government and the army. Commerce and business also remained largely in the hands of non-Muslims, most frequently Greeks, Syrians, and Jews. Jews in particular found in the Ottoman Empire a welcome refuge from the persecutions and expulsions that had characterized Jewish life in late medieval Europe. After their 1492 expulsion from Spain, more than 100,000 Spanish (Sephardic) Jews ultimately immigrated into the Ottoman Empire.

> Because the vast majority of Ottoman slaves were household servants and administrators rather than laborers, some people willingly accepted enslavement, believing that they would be better off as slaves in Constantinople than as impoverished peasants in the countryside.

RELIGIOUS CONFLICTS

The Ottoman sultans were relentlessly orthodox Sunni Muslims, who lent staunch support to the religious and legal pronouncements of the Islamic scholarly schools. In 1516, the Ottomans captured the cities of Medina and Mecca, thus becoming the defenders of the holy sites. Soon after, they captured Jerusalem and Cairo,

CHRONOLOGY

RISE OF THE OTTOMAN EMPIRE, 1300–1571

Ottomans become leading Anatolian family	1300
Byzantine emperor hires Ottoman mercenaries	1345
Ottomans enter Europe	1350s
Ottomans defeat Serbian Empire	1389
Ottomans conquer Constantinople	1453
Ottomans conquer Syria, Egypt, and the Balkans	1520s
Battle of Lepanto	1571

THE GROWTH OF THE OTTOMAN EMPIRE

Consider the patterns of Ottoman expansion revealed in this map. Did the 1453 capture of Constantinople lead to immediate further conquests? Why do you suppose this was? Compare the extent of the Ottoman Empire in 1566 with that of the Byzantine Empire under Justinian (see the map on p. 168). How would you account for these similarities? Why didn't the Ottoman Empire continue its rapid expansion after 1566?

putting an end to the Mamluk sultanate of Egypt. In 1538 the Ottoman ruler formally adopted the title of caliph, thereby declaring himself to be the legitimate successor of the Prophet Muhammad.

In keeping with Sunni traditions, the Ottomans were also religiously tolerant toward non-Muslims, especially during the fifteenth and sixteenth centuries. They organized the major religious groups of their empire into legally recognized units known as *millets*, permitting them considerable rights of religious self-government. After 1453, however, the Ottomans were particularly careful to protect and promote the author-

ity of the Greek Orthodox patriarch of Constantinople over the Orthodox Christians of their empire. As a result, the Ottomans enjoyed staunch support from their Orthodox Christian subjects during their sixteenth-century wars with the Latin Christians of western Europe. Despite the religious diversity of their empire, the Ottomans' principal religious conflicts were therefore not with their own subjects, but with the Shiite Muslim dynasty that ruled neighboring Persia. Time and again during the sixteenth century, Ottoman expeditions against western Europe had to be abandoned when hostilities erupted with the Persians.

THE OTTOMANS AND EUROPE

The contest between the Ottoman Empire and the Western powers never really lived up to the rhetoric of "holy war" that both sides employed in their propaganda. In 1396, a Western crusader army was annihilated by the Ottomans at the battle of Nicopolis. In the sixteenth and seventeenth centuries, Ottoman armies several times besieged Vienna. But despite these dramatic moments, conflicts between the Ottomans and the rulers of western Europe were fought out mainly through pirate raids and naval battles in the Mediterranean. The main result of this contest was thus a steady escalation in the scale and cost of navies. In 1571, when a combined Habsburg and Venetian force defeated the Ottoman fleet at Lepanto, both sides deployed naval forces ten times larger than they had possessed half a century before.

After 1571 both Ottoman and Habsburg interests shifted away from their conflict with each other. The Ottomans embarked on a long and costly war with Persia, while the Spanish Habsburgs turned their attention toward their new empire in the Atlantic. By the mid-seventeenth century, when a new round of Ottoman-European conflicts began, the strength of the Ottoman Empire had been sapped by a series of indolent, pleasure-loving sultans and by the tensions that arose within the Ottoman Empire itself as it ceased to expand.

MEDITERRANEAN COLONIALISM

How were the Portuguese able to control Indian Ocean trade?

During the fifteenth century, Europeans focused their colonial and commercial ambitions more and more on the western Mediterranean and the Atlantic world. Although historians have sometimes argued the contrary, this reorientation was not a result of the rising power of the Ottoman Empire. Instead, this westward orientation was the product of two related developments: the growing importance to late medieval Europe of the African gold trade and the growth of European colonial empires in the western Mediterranean Sea.

SILVER SHORTAGES AND THE SEARCH FOR AFRICAN GOLD

Europeans had been trading for African gold for centuries, mainly through Muslim middlemen who transported this precious metal in caravans from the Niger River area where it was produced to the North African ports of Algiers and Tunis. From the thirteenth century on, Catalan and Genoese merchants maintained colonies in Tunis, where they traded woolen cloth for North African grain and sub-Saharan gold.

What accelerated the late medieval demand for gold, however, was a serious silver shortage that affected the entire European economy during the fourteenth and fifteenth centuries. Silver production in Europe fell markedly during the 1340s and remained at a low level thereafter, as Europeans reached the limits of their technological capacity to extract silver ore from deep mines. This shortfall in silver production was compounded during the fifteenth century by a serious balance-of-payments problem: more European silver was flowing east in the spice trade than could be replaced using existing mining techniques on known silver deposits. Gold currencies represented an obvious alternative for large transactions, and from the thirteenth century on European rulers with access to gold were minting gold coins. But Europe itself had few natural gold reserves. To maintain and expand these gold coinages, new and larger supplies of gold were needed. The most obvious source for this gold was Africa.

> Silver production in Europe fell markedly during the 1340s and remained at a low level thereafter, as Europeans reached the limits of their technological capacity to extract silver ore from deep mines.

FROM THE MEDITERRANEAN TO THE ATLANTIC

Until the late thirteenth century, European maritime commerce had been divided between a Mediterranean and a north Atlantic world. Starting around 1270, however, Italian merchants began to sail through the Strait of Gibraltar and on to the wool-producing regions of England and the Netherlands. This was the essential first step in the extension of Mediterranean patterns of commerce and colonization into the

Atlantic Ocean. The second step was the discovery (or possibly rediscovery), during the fourteenth century, of the Atlantic island chains known as the Canaries and the Azores by Genoese sailors. Efforts to colonize the Canary Islands and to convert and enslave their inhabitants began almost immediately. But an effective conquest of the Canary Islands did not really begin until the fifteenth century, when it was undertaken by Portugal and completed by Castile. The Canaries, in turn, became the base from which further Portuguese voyages down the west coast of Africa proceeded. They were also the jumping-off point from which Christopher Columbus would sail westward across the Atlantic Ocean in hopes of reaching Asia.

THE TECHNOLOGY OF SHIPS AND NAVIGATION

The European empires of the fifteenth and sixteenth centuries rested on a mastery of the oceans. The Portuguese caravel—the workhorse ship of the fifteenth-century voyages to Africa—was based on ship and sail designs that had been in use among Portuguese fishermen since the thirteenth century. Starting in the 1440s, however, Portuguese shipwrights began building larger caravels with two masts, each carrying a triangular (lateen) sail. Such ships were capable of sailing against the wind much more effectively than were the older, square-rigged vessels. By the end of the fifteenth century, even larger caravels were being constructed, with a third mast and a combination of square and lateen sails. Columbus's *Niña* was of this design, having been refitted with two square sails in the Canary Islands to enable it to sail more efficiently before the wind during the Atlantic crossing.

Europeans were also making significant advances in navigation during the fifteenth and sixteenth centuries. Quadrants, which calculated latitude in the Northern Hemisphere by the height of the North Star above the horizon, were in widespread use by the 1450s. As sailors approached the equator, however, the quadrant became less and less useful, and they were forced instead to make use of astrolabes, which reckoned latitude by the height of the sun. Like quadrants, astrolabes had been known in western Europe for centuries. But it was not until the 1480s that the astrolabe became a really useful instrument for seaborne navigation, with the preparation of standard tables sponsored by the Portuguese crown. Compasses too were also coming into more widespread use during the fifteenth century. Longitude, however, remained impossible to

calculate accurately until the eighteenth century, when the invention of the marine chronometer finally made it possible to keep accurate time at sea. In the sixteenth century, Europeans sailing east or west across the oceans generally had to rely on their skill at dead reckoning to determine where they were on the globe.

European sailors also benefited from a new interest in maps and navigational charts. Especially important to Atlantic sailors were books known as *rutters* or *routiers*. These contained detailed sailing instructions and descriptions of the coastal landmarks a pilot could expect to encounter on route to a variety of destinations. Mediterranean sailors had had similar books, known as *portolani*, since at least the fourteenth century. In the fifteenth century, however, this tradition was extended to the Atlantic Ocean; by the end of the sixteenth century, rutters spanned the globe.

PORTUGAL, AFRICA, AND THE SEA ROUTE TO INDIA

It was among the Portuguese that these dual interests—the African gold trade and Atlantic colonization—first came together. In 1415, a Portuguese expedition captured the north African port of Ceuta. During the 1420s the Portuguese colonized both the island of Madeira and the Canary Islands. During the 1430s, they extended these colonization efforts to the Azores. In 1444 Portuguese explorers first landed in the area between the Senegal and the Gambia river mouths on the African mainland, where they began to collect cargoes of gold and slaves for export back to Portugal. By the 1470s, Portuguese sailors had rounded the African "bulge" and were exploring the Gulf of Guinea. In 1483 they reached the mouth of the Congo

CHRONOLOGY	
PORTUGUESE MARITIME EXPANSION, 1420s–1515	
Colonization of Madeira and Canary Islands	1420s
Colonization of the Azores	1430s
Dias rounds the Cape of Good Hope	1488
Da Gama reaches India	1497–1498
Portuguese reach Malacca in Southeast Asia	1511
Portuguese reach Spice Islands	1515

River. In 1488 the Portuguese captain Bartholomeu Dias rounded the southern tip of Africa. Blown around it accidentally by a gale, Dias named the point "Cape of Storms," but the king of Portugal took a more optimistic view of Dias's achievement. He renamed it the Cape of Good Hope and began planning a naval expedition to India. Finally in 1497–1498, Vasco da Gama rounded the Cape, and then, with the help of a Muslim navigator named Ibn Majid, crossed the Indian Ocean to Calicutt on the southwestern coast of India, opening up for the first time a direct sea route between Europe and the Far Eastern spice trade.

The voyages were financed heavily by the royal house of Portugal, the most famous of which was Prince Henry "the Navigator." For centuries, Henry was thought to have been a central figure in Portuguese exploration. But, in fact, he directed only eight of the thirty-five Portuguese voyages to Africa between 1419 and his death in 1460; and the stories about his gathering a school of navigators and cartographers on the Atlantic coast of Portugal, about his role in designing improved ships and navigational instruments, and about his encouragement of scientific learning generally have all been shown to be false. Henry did, however, play an important role in organizing Portuguese colonization of Madeira, the Canary Islands and the Azores; and he also pioneered the Portuguese slave trade, first on the Canaries (whose Stone Age population was almost entirely enslaved) and then along the Sene-Gambian coast of Africa. His main goal, however, was to outflank the cross-Saharan African gold trade by intercepting this trade at its source. To this end, he built a series of forts along the African coastline, most famously at Arguim, to which he hoped to divert the cross-Saharan gold caravans. This was also his reason for colonizing the Canary Islands, which he saw as a staging ground for expeditions into the African interior.

Now master of the quickest route to riches in the world, the king of Portugal swiftly capitalized on da Gama's accomplishment. After 1500, Portuguese trading fleets sailed regularly to India. In 1509, the Portuguese defeated an Ottoman fleet and then blockaded the mouth of the Red Sea, attempting to cut off one of the traditional routes by which spices had traveled to Alexandria and Beirut. By 1510 Portuguese military forces had established a series of forts along the western Indian coastline, including their headquarters at Goa. In 1511 Portuguese ships seized Malacca, a center of the spice trade on the Malay peninsula. By 1515 they had reached the Spice Islands and the coast of China. So completely

Prince Henry the Navigator, by a fifteenth-century Portuguese painter. This portrait is taken from a group portrait of the Portuguese royal family. Although thought to depict Henry, the identification is not certain.

did the Portuguese now dominate the spice trade that by the 1520s even the Venetians were forced to buy their pepper in the Portuguese capital of Lisbon.

ARTILLERY AND EMPIRE

Larger, more maneuverable ships and improved navigational aids made it possible for European mariners to reach Africa, Asia, and the Americas by sea. But fundamentally, these sixteenth-century European commercial empires were a military achievement. As such, they reflected what Europeans had learned in their wars against each other during the fourteenth and fifteenth centuries. Perhaps the most critical military advance of the late Middle Ages was the increasing sophistication of artillery, a development made possible not only by gunpowder but also by improved metallurgical techniques for casting cannon barrels.

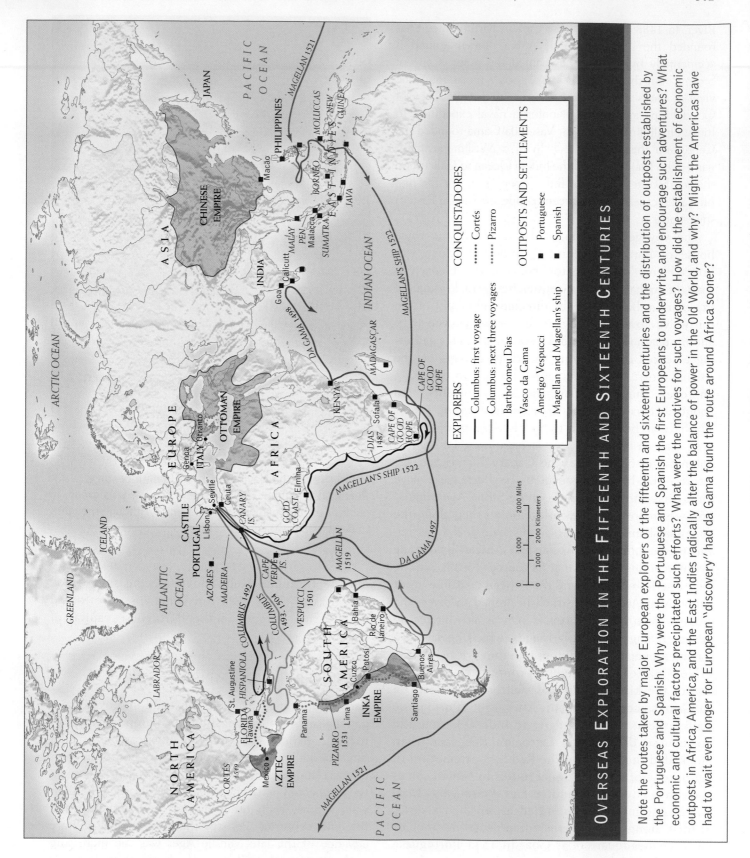

OVERSEAS EXPLORATION IN THE FIFTEENTH AND SIXTEENTH CENTURIES

Note the routes taken by major European explorers of the fifteenth and sixteenth centuries and the distribution of outposts established by the Portuguese and Spanish. Why were the Portuguese and Spanish the first Europeans to underwrite and encourage such adventures? What economic and cultural factors precipitated such efforts? What were the motives for such voyages? How did the establishment of economic outposts in Africa, America, and the East Indies radically alter the balance of power in the Old World, and why? Might the Americas have had to wait even longer for European "discovery" had da Gama found the route around Africa sooner?

A Turkish Brass Cannon of the Fifteenth Century. This eighteen-ton gun fired balls twenty-five inches in diameter.

By the middle of the fifteenth century, the use of artillery pieces had rendered the stone walls of medieval castles and towns obsolete, a fact brought home in 1453 by the successful French siege of Bordeaux (which brought to an end the Hundred Years' War), and by the Ottoman siege of Constantinople (which brought to an end the Byzantine Empire).

One of the reasons the new ship designs (first caravels, and later the even larger galleons) were so important was that their larger size made it possible to mount more effective artillery pieces on them. Increasingly during the sixteenth century, European naval vessels were conceived as floating artillery platforms, with scores of guns mounted in fixed positions along their sides and swivel guns mounted fore and aft. These guns were vastly expensive, as were the ships that carried them; but for those rulers who could afford to possess them, such ships made it possible to project military power around the world. Without this essential military component, the European maritime empires of the sixteenth century would not have existed.

> Increasingly during the sixteenth century, European naval vessels were conceived as floating artillery platforms, with scores of guns mounted in fixed positions along their sides and swivel guns mounted fore and aft.

ATLANTIC COLONIZATION AND THE GROWTH OF SLAVERY

The profits the Portuguese had hoped would come from the African gold trade did not initially materialize. They therefore had to make these expeditions pay by other means. One of those means was the slave trade. Although slavery in most of western Europe had effectively disappeared by the early twelfth century, slavery continued in Iberia (and to a lesser extent in Italy) throughout the high and late Middle Ages. Until the mid-fifteenth century, however, slavery on the Iberian mainland and in Italy remained very small in scale. The major Mediterranean slave markets of the fourteenth and early fifteenth centuries lay in Muslim lands, and especially in the Ottoman Empire. Relatively few of the slaves who passed through these markets were Africans. Most were European Christians, predominantly Poles, Ukrainians, Greeks, and Bulgarians. Thus the patterns of slavery were not racialized in the late medieval Mediterranean world, except insofar as "primitive" peoples such as the natives of the Canary Islands or of Sardinia were more likely to be regarded as targets for enslavement.

From the mid-fifteenth century on, however, Lisbon began to emerge as a significant market for enslaved Africans. Something on the order of 15,000 to 20,000 Africans were sold in Lisbon between 1440 and 1460. In the half century thereafter, the numbers grew, amounting to perhaps 150,000 African slaves imported into Europe by 1505. For the most part, these slaves were regarded as status symbols—one reason they were so frequently depicted in paintings of the period. Even in the Atlantic colonies—Madeira, the Canaries, and the Azores—the land was worked mainly by European settlers and sharecroppers. Slave labor, if it was employed at all, was generally used only in sugar mills. But even sugar production did not lead to the widespread introduction of slavery on these islands.

A new style of slave-based sugar plantations began to emerge in Portugal's Atlantic colonies only in the 1460s, starting on the Cape Verde Islands and then extending southward into the Gulf of Guinea. These islands were not populated when the Portuguese began to settle them. They were ideally located, however, to purchase laborers from the slave traders along the nearby West African coast. No comparable system of large-scale, slave-based plantation production had been seen in Europe or Africa since the Roman period.

But it was this model of sugar plantations staffed by enslaved Africans that would be exported to the Caribbean islands of the Americas by their Spanish conquerors, with incalculable consequences for Africa, the Americas, and Europe.

EUROPE ENCOUNTERS A NEW WORLD

What was the impact of New World silver on the European economy?

The decision by Spain's rulers to underwrite Columbus's famous voyage was an outgrowth of the progress of these Portuguese ventures. After 1488, when Dias successfully rounded the Cape of Good Hope, it was clear that Portugal would soon dominate the sea lanes leading eastward to Asia. The only alternative for Portugal's Spanish rivals was to finance someone bold enough to try to reach Asia by sailing west. The popular image of Christopher Columbus (1451–1506) as a visionary who struggled to convince hardened ignoramuses that the world was round does not bear up under scrutiny. In fact, the sphericity of the earth had been widely known throughout European society since at least the twelfth century. What made Columbus's scheme seem plausible to King Ferdinand and Queen Isabella was, first, the discovery and colonization of the Canary Islands and the Azores, which had reinforced a view of the Atlantic as being dotted with islands all the way to Japan; and second, the Genoese mariner's own astonishing miscalculation of the actual size of the earth, which convinced him that he could reach Japan and China in about a month's clear sailing westward from the Canary Islands. America was actually rediscovered by Europeans at the end of the fifteenth century as the result of a colossal error in reckoning. Columbus himself never realized his mistake. When he reached the Bahamas and the island of Hispaniola in 1492 after only a month's sailing, he returned to Spain to report that he had indeed reached the outer islands of Asia.

THE DISCOVERY OF A NEW WORLD

Columbus was not the first European to set foot on the American continents. Viking sailors had reached and briefly settled present-day Newfoundland, Labrador, and perhaps New England around the year 1000. But knowledge of these Viking landings had been forgotten or ignored throughout Europe for hundreds of years. In the fifteenth century, even the Scandinavian settlements in Greenland had been abandoned. It would be perverse, therefore, to deny Columbus credit for his accomplishments. Although Columbus himself never accepted the reality of what he had discovered, those who followed him soon did, and busily set out to exploit this new world.

Understandably, Columbus brought back no Asian spices from his voyages. He did, however, return with some small samples of gold and a few indigenous people, whose existence gave promise of entire tribes that might be "saved" (by conversion to Christianity) and enslaved by Europeans. This provided sufficient incentive for the Spanish monarchs to finance three more expeditions by Columbus and many more by others. Soon the mainland was discovered as well as further islands, and the conclusion quickly became inescapable that a new world had indeed been found. Awareness of this new world was most widely publicized by the Italian geographer Amerigo Vespucci. Though he may not have deserved this honor, the continents of the Western Hemisphere became known thereafter as "America" after Vespucci's first name.

The realization that this was indeed a new world was at first a disappointment to the Spanish, for with a major land mass lying between Europe and Asia, Spain could not hope to beat Portugal in the race for Asian spices. Any remaining doubt that not one, but two vast oceans separated Europe from Asia was completely removed in 1513, when Vasco Núñez de Balboa first viewed the Pacific Ocean from the Isthmus of Panama. Not entirely admitting defeat, Ferdinand and Isabella's grandson, the Holy Roman emperor Charles V, accepted Ferdinand Magellan's offer in 1519 to see whether a route to Asia could be found by sailing around South America. But Magellan's voyage demonstrated beyond question that the globe was simply too large for any such plan to be feasible. Of the five ships that left Spain under Magellan's command, only one returned three years later, having been forced to circumnavigate the globe. Out of a crew of 265 sailors, only 18 survived. Most had died from scurvy or starvation; Magellan himself had been killed in a skirmish with native peoples in the Philippines. This fiasco brought to an end all hope of discovering an easy "southwest passage" to Asia. The dream of a "northwest passage" survived, however, and continued to motivate European explorers of North America until the nineteenth century.

WHAT WAS THE IMPACT OF NEW WORLD SILVER ON THE EUROPEAN ECONOMY?

EUROPE ENCOUNTERS A NEW WORLD   315

THE SPANISH CONQUEST OF AMERICA

Although the discovery of this new continent was initially a disappointment to the Spanish, it quickly became clear that the New World had great wealth of its own. From the start, Columbus's gold samples, in themselves rather paltry, had nurtured hopes that somewhere in America gold might lie piled in ingots, ready to enrich whatever European adventurer discovered them. Rumor fed rumor, until a few freelance Spanish soldiers really did strike it rich beyond their most avaricious imaginings. Between 1519 and 1521, the *conquistador* (Spanish for "conqueror") Hernando Cortés, with a force of 600 Europeans but with the assistance of thousands of the Aztecs' unhappy subjects, overthrew the Aztec Empire of Mexico and carried off its rulers' fabulous wealth. Then in 1533 another conquistador, Francisco Pizarro, this time with only 180 men, toppled the highly centralized South American empire of the Inkas and carried off its great stores of gold and silver. Cortés and Pizarro had the advantage of some cannons and a few horses (both unknown to the native peoples of the Americas), but they achieved their victories primarily by sheer audacity, courage, and treachery. They were aided also by the unwillingness of the indigenous peoples whom the Aztecs and the Inkas had subjected to fight on behalf of their oppressors. Little did the Spaniards' erstwhile allies know how much worse their new conquerors would soon prove to be.

THE PROFITS OF EMPIRE IN THE NEW WORLD

Cortés and Pizarro were plunderers who captured in one fell swoop hoards of gold and silver that had been accumulated for centuries by the native civilizations of

Spanish Conquistadors Massacring Aztecs. Between 1519 and 1521, Cortés and a small army of conquistadors destroyed the Aztec Empire in search of gold and silver.

ENSLAVED NATIVE LABORERS AT POTOSÍ

Since the Spanish crown received one fifth of all the revenues from mines (as well as maintaining a monopoly over the mercury used to refine the silver ore into silver), it had an important stake in ensuring the productivity of the mines. To this end, the crown granted colonial mine owners the right to conscript native peoples to work in the mines. This account from about 1620 describes the conditions under which these forced native laborers worked. It is not surprising that mortality rates among such laborers were horrendous.

According to His Majesty's warrant, the mine owners on this massive range [at Potosí] have a right to the conscripted labor of 13,300 Indians in the working and exploitation of the mines, both those which have been discovered, those now discovered, and those which shall be discovered. It is the duty of the *Corregidor* (municipal governor) of Potosí to have them rounded up and to see that they come in from all the provinces between Cuzco . . . and as far as the frontiers of Tarija and Tomina. . . .

The conscripted Indians go up every Monday morning to the . . . foot of the range; the *Corregidor* arrives with all the provincial captains or chiefs who have charge of the Indians assigned him for his miner or smelter; that keeps him busy till 1 P.M., by which time the Indians are already turned over to these mine and smelter owners.

After each has eaten his ration, they climb up the hill, each to his mine, and go in, staying there from that hour until Saturday evening without coming out of the mine; their wives bring them food, but they stay constantly underground, excavating and carrying out the ore from which they get the silver. They all have tallow candles, lighted day and night; that is the light they work with, for as they are underground, they have need for it all the time. . . .

These Indians have different functions in the handling of the silver ore; some break it up with bar or pick, and dig down in, following the vein in the mine; others bring it up; others up above keep separating the good and the poor in piles; others are occupied in taking it down from the range to the mills on herds of llamas; every day they bring up more than 8,000 of these native beasts of burden for this task. These teamsters who carry the metal are not conscripted, but are hired.

Antonio Vázquez de Espinosa, *Compendium and Description of the West Indies*, trans. Charles Upson Clark (Washington, D.C.,1968), p. 62.

QUESTION FOR ANALYSIS

1. What was the human cost of the Potosí silver mine?

Mexico and Peru. Already, however, a search had begun for the sources of these precious metals. The first gold deposits were discovered in Hispaniola, where surface mines were speedily established using native laborers who died in appalling numbers from disease, brutality, and overwork. Of the approximately 1 million native people who lived on Hispaniola in 1492, only 100,000 survived by 1510. By 1538, their numbers were down to 500.

With the loss of so many workers, the Hispaniola mines became uneconomical to operate, and the European colonists turned instead to cattle raising and sugar production. Modeling their sugarcane plantations on those of the Cape Verde Islands and St. Thomas in the Gulf of Guinea, colonists imported African slaves to labor in the new industry. Sugar production was by its nature a highly capital-intensive undertaking. The need to import slave labor added further to its costs, guaranteeing that control over the sugar industry would fall into the hands of a few extremely wealthy planters and financiers.

Despite the importance of sugar production on the Caribbean islands and of cattle ranching on the Mexican mainland, mining shaped the Spanish colonies of Central and South America most fundamentally. Gold was the lure that had initially drawn the Spanish conquerors to the New World, but silver became their most lucrative export. Between 1543 and 1548, vast silver deposits were discovered north of Mexico City and at Potosí in Bolivia. Even before the discovery of these deposits, the Spanish crown had taken steps to assume direct governmental control over its Central and South American colonies. It was therefore to the Spanish crown that the profits from these astonishingly productive mines accrued. Potosí quickly became the most important mining town in the world. By 1570, it numbered 120,000 inhabitants, despite being located at an altitude of 15,000 feet where the temperature never climbs above 59°F. As in Hispaniola, enslaved native laborers died by the tens of thousands in these mines and in the disease-infested boom towns that surrounded them.

New mining techniques (in particular, the mercury-amalgamation process, introduced into Mexico in 1555 and Potosí in 1571) made it possible to produce even greater quantities of silver, at the cost of even greater mortality among the native laborers. Between 1571 and 1586, silver production at Potosí quadrupled, reaching a peak in the 1590s, when 10 million ounces of silver per year were arriving in Spain from the Americas.

This massive infusion of silver into the European economy accelerated an inflation that had begun already in the later fifteenth century. The result was what historians have termed "the Price Revolution." Although the effects of this inflation were felt throughout the European continent, Spain was affected with particular severity. Between 1500 and 1560, Spanish prices doubled; between 1560 and 1600, they doubled again. Such exceptionally high prices in turn undermined the competitiveness of Spanish industries. When the flow of New World silver to Spain slowed dramatically during the 1620s and 1630s, the Spanish economy collapsed.

CHRONOLOGY

ENCOUNTERING THE NEW WORLD, c. 1000–1545

Vikings settle Newfoundland	c. 1000
Columbus reaches Hispaniola	1492
Balboa reaches the Pacific Ocean	1513
Magellan's fleet sails around the world	1519–1522
Cortés conquers the Aztecs	1521
Pizarro conquers the Inkas	1533
Potosí silver deposits discovered	1545

After 1600, lessening quantities of New World silver entered the European economy, but prices continued to rise albeit more slowly than before. By 1650, the price of grain within Europe had risen to five or six times its level in 1500, producing social dislocation and widespread misery for many of Europe's poorest inhabitants. In England, the period between about 1590 and 1610 was probably the most desperate the country had experienced for 300 years. Standards of living were lower in England in 1600 than they had been even in the terrible years of the early fourteenth century. It is no wonder, then, that so many Europeans found emigration to the Americas a tempting prospect. We may wonder, indeed, what might have happened in seventeenth-century Europe had the new world of the Americas not existed as an outlet for Europe's growing population.

CONCLUSION

By 1600, colonization and overseas conquest had profoundly changed both Europe and the wider world. The emergence during the sixteenth century of Portugal and Spain as Europe's leading long-distance traders permanently moved the center of gravity of European economic power away from Italy and the Mediterranean toward the Atlantic. Deprived of its role as the principal conduit for the spice trade, Venice gradually declined. The Genoese moved increasingly into the world of finance, backing the commercial ventures of others, particularly of Spain. By contrast, the Atlantic ports of Spain and Portugal bustled with vessels and shone with wealth. By the mid-seventeenth century, however, economic predominance was passing to the north Atlantic states of England, Holland, and France. Spain and Portugal would retain their American colonies until the nineteenth century. But from the seventeenth century on, it would be the Dutch, the French, and especially the English who would establish new European empires in North America, Asia, Africa, and Australia. By and large, these new empires would last until World War II.

KEY TERMS

Chingiz Khan	Timur the Lame	astrolabe	Aztecs
Marco Polo	Canary Islands	Christopher Columbus	Inkas
sultan	Prince Henry the Navigator	conquistador	
Ottoman slavery	caravels	New World silver	

SELECTED READINGS

Abu-Lughod, Janet L. *Before European Hegemony: The World System A.D. 1250–1350.* Oxford and New York, 1989. A study of the trading links among Europe, the Middle East, India, and China, with special attention to the role of the Mongol Empire; extensive bibliography.

Allsen, Thomas T. *Culture and Conquest in Mongol Eurasia.* Cambridge and New York, 2001. A synthesis of the author's earlier studies, emphasizing Mongol involvement in the cultural and commercial exchanges that linked China, Central Asia, and Europe.

The Book of Prophecies, Edited by Christopher Columbus. Trans. Blair Sullivan. Ed. Roberto Rusconi. Berkeley and Los Angeles, Calif., 1996. After his third voyage, from which Columbus was returned to Spain in chains, he compiled a book of quotations from various sources, selected to emphasize the millenarian implications of his discoveries; a fascinating insight into the mind of the explorer.

Christian, David. *A History of Russia, Central Asia and Mongolia.* Vol. 1: *Inner Eurasia from Prehistory to the Mongol Empire.* Oxford, 1998. The authoritative English-language work on the subject.

Coles, Paul. *The Ottoman Impact on Europe.* London, 1968. An excellent introductory text, still valuable despite its age.

Fernández-Armesto, Felipe. *Before Columbus: Exploration and Colonisation from the Mediterranean to the Atlantic, 1229–1492.* London, 1987. An indispensible study of the medieval background to the sixteenth-century European colonial empires.

Fernández-Armesto, Felipe. *Columbus.* Oxford and New York, 1991. An excellent biography that stresses the millenarian ideas that underlay Columbus's thinking. A good book to read after Phillips and Phillips.

Flint, Valerie I. J. *The Imaginative Landscape of Christopher Columbus.* Princeton, N.J., 1992. A short, suggestive analysis of the intellectual influences that shaped Columbus's geographical ideas.

The Four Voyages: Christopher Columbus. Trans. J. M. Cohen. New York, 1992. Columbus's own self-serving account of his four voyages to the "Indies."

Goffman, Daniel. *The Ottoman Empire and Early Modern Europe.* Cambridge and New York, 2002. A revisionist account that presents the Ottoman Empire as a European state.

The History and the Life of Chinggis Khan: The Secret History of the Mongols. Trans. Urgunge Onon. Leiden, 1997. Now the standard English version of this important Mongol source.

Jackson, Peter. *The Mongols and the West, 1221–1410.* Harlow, UK, 2005. A well-written survey that emphasizes the interactions among the Mongol, Latin Christian, and Muslim worlds.

Kafadar, Cemal. *Between Two Worlds: The Construction of the Ottoman State.* Berkeley and Los Angeles, Calif., 1995. An important study of Ottoman origins in the border regions among Byzantium, the Seljuk Turks, and the Mongols.

Larner, John. *Marco Polo and the Discovery of the World.* New Haven, Conn., 1999. A study of the influence of Marco Polo's *Travels* on Europeans.

Morgan, David. *The Mongols.* 2d ed. Oxford, 2007. An accessible introduction to Mongol history and its sources, written by a noted expert on medieval Persia.

Parker, Geoffrey. *The Military Revolution: Military Innovation and the Rise of the West (1500–1800).* 2d ed. Cambridge and New York, 1996. A work of fundamental importance for understanding the global dominance achieved by early modern Europeans.

Phillips, J. R. S. *The Medieval Expansion of Europe.* 2d ed. Oxford, 1998. An outstanding study of the thirteenth- and fourteenth-century background to the fifteenth-century expansion of

Europe. Important synthetic treatment of European relations with the Mongols, China, Africa, and North America. The second edition includes a new introduction and a bibliographical essay; the text is the same as in the first edition (1988).

Phillips, William D., Jr., and Carla R. Phillips. *The Worlds of Christopher Columbus.* Cambridge and New York, 1991. The first book to read on Columbus: accessible, engaging, and scholarly. Then read Fernández-Armesto's biography.

Russell, Peter. *Prince Henry "The Navigator": A Life.* New Haven, Conn., 2000. A masterly biography by a great historian who has spent a lifetime on the subject. The only book one now needs to read on Prince Henry.

Saunders, J. J. *The History of the Mongol Conquests.* London, 1971. Still the standard English-language introduction; somewhat more positive about the Mongols' accomplishments than is Morgan.

Scammell, Geoffrey V. *The First Imperial Age: European Overseas Expansion, 1400–1715.* London, 1989. A useful introductory survey, with a particular focus on English and French colonization.

The Travels of Marco Polo. Trans. R. E. Latham. Baltimore, Md., 1958. The most accessible edition of this remarkably interesting work.

CHAPTER TWELVE

THE CIVILIZATION
OF THE RENAISSANCE,
C. 1350–1550

THE PREVALENT MODERN NOTION that a "Renaissance period" followed western Europe's Middle Ages was first expressed by numerous Italian writers who lived between 1350 and 1550. According to them, 1,000 years of unrelieved darkness had intervened between the Roman era and their own times. During these "dark ages" the muses of art and literature had fled Europe before the onslaught of barbarism and ignorance. Almost miraculously, however, in the fourteenth century the muses suddenly returned, and Italians happily collaborated with them to bring forth a glorious "renaissance of the arts."

Ever since this periodization was advanced, historians have taken for granted the existence of some sort of "renaissance" intervening between medieval and modern times. Indeed, from the late eighteenth to the early twentieth centuries many scholars went so far as to argue that the Renaissance was not just an epoch in the history of learning and culture but that a unique "Renaissance spirit" transformed all aspects of European life—political, economic, and religious, as well as intellectual and artistic. Today, however, most experts no longer accept this characterization because they find it impossible to locate any truly distinctive "Renaissance" politics, economics, or religion. Instead, most scholars reserve the term "Renaissance" to describe certain trends in thought, literature, and the arts that emerged in Italy from roughly 1350 to 1550 and then spread to northern Europe during the sixteenth century. That is the approach that we follow here: accordingly, when we refer to a "Renaissance" period in this chapter, we mean to limit ourselves to an epoch in intellectual and cultural history.

FOCUS QUESTIONS

• How did Italian Renaissance culture differ from the culture of the High Middle Ages?

• Why did the Renaissance occur in Italy?

• What were the principal characteristics of Italian Renaissance art?

• Why did the Renaissance decline around 1550?

• How did the northern and Italian Renaissances differ from one another?

THE RENAISSANCE AND THE MIDDLE AGES

How did Italian Renaissance culture differ from the culture of the High Middle Ages?

Since the word *renaissance* means literally "rebirth," it is sometimes thought that after about 1350 Italians initiated a rebirth of classical culture following a long period during which that culture had been essentially dead. In fact, however, the High Middle Ages witnessed no "death" of classical learning. It would be equally false to contrast an imaginary "Renaissance paganism" with a medieval "age of faith" because however much most Renaissance personalities loved the classics, none saw his/her classicism as superseding his/her Christianity. And finally, all discussions of the Renaissance must be qualified by the fact that there was no single Renaissance position on anything. Renaissance thinkers and artists were enormously diverse in their attitudes, achievements, and approaches. As we assess their accomplishments, we need to beware not to force them into too narrow a mold.

> In the twelfth and thirteenth centuries none of the great Greek literary masterpieces and practically none of the major works of Plato were yet known. Nor could more than a handful of medieval western Europeans read the Greek language.

RENAISSANCE CLASSICISM

Nonetheless, in the realms of thought, literature, and the arts, we can certainly find distinguishing traits that make the concept of a "Renaissance" meaningful for intellectual and cultural history. First, regarding knowledge of the classics, there was a significant quantitative difference between the learning of the Middle Ages and that of the Renaissance. Medieval scholars knew many Roman authors, such as Virgil, Ovid, and Cicero, but during the Renaissance the works of others such as Livy, Tacitus, and Lucretius were rediscovered and made familiar. Equally if not more important was the Renaissance recovery of the literature of classical Greece from Byzantium. In the twelfth and thirteenth centuries none of the great Greek literary masterpieces and practically none of the major works of Plato were yet known. Nor could more than a handful of medieval western Europeans read the Greek language. During the Renaissance, on

the other hand, large numbers of Western scholars learned Greek and mastered almost the entire Greek literary heritage that is known today.

Second, Renaissance thinkers not only knew many more classical texts than their medieval counterparts but they used them in new ways. Whereas medieval writers presumed that their ancient sources would complement and confirm their own Christian assumptions, Renaissance writers were more aware of the conceptual and chronological gap that separated their own world from that of their classical sources. At the same time, however, similarities between the ancient city-states and those of Renaissance Italy encouraged Italian thinkers to find in these ancient sources models of thought and action directly applicable to their own day. This desire to imitate classical antiquity was even more pronounced in the realms of architecture and art, areas in which classical models contributed most strikingly to the creation of Renaissance styles.

Third, although Renaissance culture was by no means pagan, it was more worldly and overtly materialistic than was the culture of the twelfth and thirteenth centuries. Italian city-states stressed the importance of the urban political arena and of living well in this world. Such ideals helped create a culture that was increasingly non-ecclesiastical. The relative weakness of the church in Italy also contributed to the more secular culture that emerged there. Italian bishoprics were small and for the most part poorly endowed. Italian universities were also largely independent of ecclesiastical supervision and control. Even the papacy was severely limited in its ability to intervene in the cultural life of the Italian city-states. All these factors helped create a space within which the worldly, materialistic culture of the Renaissance could emerge effectively untrammeled by ecclesiastical opposition.

RENAISSANCE HUMANISM

One word above all comes closest to summing up Renaissance intellectual ideals—namely *humanism*. Renaissance humanism was a program of studies that aimed to replace the thirteenth- and fourteenth-century scholastic emphasis on logic and metaphysics with the study of language, literature, rhetoric, history, and ethics. Most humanists regarded vernacular literature as at best a diversion for the uneducated.

Serious scholarship and literature could be written only in Latin or Greek. That Latin, moreover, had to be the Latin of Cicero and Virgil. Renaissance humanists were self-conscious elitists who condemned the living Latin of their scholastic contemporaries as a barbarous departure from ancient (and therefore correct) standards of Latin style. Despite their belief that they were thereby reviving the study of the classics, the humanists' position was thus inherently ironic. By insisting on ancient standards of Latin grammar, syntax, and word choice, the humanists of the Renaissance succeeded ultimately in turning Latin into a fossilized language that thereafter ceased to evolve. They thus contributed, quite unwittingly, to the ultimate triumph of the European vernaculars as the primary languages of intellectual and cultural life.

Humanists were convinced that their own educational program—which placed the study of Latin language and literature at the core of the curriculum and then encouraged students to go on to Greek—was the best way to produce virtuous citizens and able public officials. Their elitism was to this extent intensely practical, and directly connected to the political life of the city-states in which they lived. Because women were excluded from Italian political life, the education of women was therefore of little concern to most humanists, although some aristocratic women did acquire humanist training. As more and more fifteenth-century city-states fell into the hands of princes, the humanist educational curriculum lost its immediate connection to the republican ideals of Italian political life. Nevertheless, humanists never lost their conviction that the study of the "humanities" (as the humanist curriculum came to be known) was the best way to produce leaders for European society.

By insisting on ancient standards of Latin grammar, syntax, and word choice, the humanists of the Renaissance succeeded ultimately in turning Latin into a fossilized language that thereafter ceased to evolve.

THE RENAISSANCE IN ITALY

Why did the Renaissance occur in Italy?

Although the Renaissance eventually became a Europe-wide intellectual and artistic movement, it developed first and most distinctively in fourteenth- and fifteenth-century Italy. Understanding why this was so is impor-

tant not only to explaining the origins of this movement but also to understanding its fundamental characteristics.

THE ORIGINS OF THE ITALIAN RENAISSANCE

The Renaissance originated in Italy for several reasons. The most fundamental reason was that Italy in the later Middle Ages was the most advanced urban society in all of Europe. Unlike aristocrats north of the Alps, Italian aristocrats customarily lived in urban centers rather than in rural castles and consequently became fully involved in urban public affairs. The Italian aristocracy was also less sharply set off from the class of rich merchants than in the north. In Italy so many town-dwelling aristocrats engaged in banking or mercantile enterprises and so many rich mercantile families imitated the manners of the aristocracy that by the fourteenth and fifteenth centuries the aristocracy and upper bourgeoisie were becoming virtually indistinguishable. The noted Florentine family of the Medici (*MEH-dih-chee*), for example, emerged as a family of physicians (as the name suggests), made its fortune in banking and commerce, and rose into the aristocracy in the fifteenth century. The results of these developments for the history of education are obvious: not only was there a great demand for education in the skills of reading and counting necessary to become a successful merchant but the richest and most prominent families sought above all to find teachers who would impart to their sons the knowledge and skills necessary to argue well in the public arena. Consequently, Italy produced a large number of lay educators, many of whom not only taught students but also demonstrated their learning by producing political and ethical treatises and works of literature. Italian schools created the best-educated upper-class public in all of Europe, along with wealthy patrons ready to invest in new ideas and new forms of literary and artistic expression.

The Italian Renaissance could not have occurred without the underpinning of Italian wealth. The Italian economy as a whole was probably more prosperous in the thirteenth century than it was in the fourteenth and fifteenth. But late medieval Italy was wealthier in comparison with the rest of Europe than it had been before, a fact that meant that Italian writers and artists

THE HUMANISTS' EDUCATIONAL PROGRAM

These three selections illustrate the confidence of civic humanists such as Vergerius, Bruni, and Alberti that their elite educational program would be of supreme value to the state as well as to the individual students who pursued it. Not everyone agreed with the humanists' claims, however, and a good deal of self-promotion lies behind them.

VERGERIUS ON LIBERAL STUDIES

We call those studies *liberal* which are worthy of a free man; those studies by which we attain and practice virtue and wisdom; that education which calls forth, trains, and develops those highest gifts of body and of mind which ennoble men, and which are rightly judged to rank next in dignity to virtue only. . . . It is, then, of the highest importance that even from infancy this aim, this effort, should constantly be kept alive in growing minds. For . . . we shall not have attained wisdom in our later years unless in our earliest we have sincerely entered on its search. [P. P. Vergerius (1370–1444), *"Concerning Excellent Traits"*]

ALBERTI ON THE IMPORTANCE OF LITERATURE

Letters are indeed so important that without them one would be considered nothing but a rustic, no matter how much a gentlemen [he may be by birth]. I'd much rather see a young nobleman with a book than with a falcon in his hand. . . .

Be diligent, then, you young people, in your studies. Do all you can to learn about the events of the past that are worthy of memory. Try to understand all the useful things that have been passed on to you. Feed your minds on good maxims. Learn the delights of embellishing your souls with good morals. Strive to be kind and considerate [of others] when conducting civil business. Get to know those things human and divine that have been put at your disposal in books for good reason. Nowhere [else] will you find . . . the elegance of a verse of Homer, or Virgil, or of some other excellent poet. You will find no field so delightful or flowering as in one of the orations of Demosthenes, Cicero, Livy, Xenophon, and other such pleasant and perfect orators. No effort is more fully compensated . . . as the constant reading and rereading of good things. From such reading you will rise rich in good maxims and good arguments, strong in your ability to persuade others and get them to listen to you; among the citizens you will willingly be heard, admired, praised, and loved. [Leon Battista Alberti (1404–1472), *"On the Family"*]

BRUNI ON THE HUMANIST CURRICULUM

The foundations of all true learning must be laid in the sound and thorough knowledge of Latin: which implies study marked by a broad spirit, accurate scholarship, and careful attention to details. Unless this solid basis be secured it is useless to attempt to rear an enduring edifice. Without it the great monuments of literature are unintelligible, and the art of composition impossible. To attain this essential knowledge we must never relax our careful attention to the grammar of the language, but perpetually confirm and extend our acquaintance with it until it is thoroughly our own. . . .

But the wider question now confronts us, that of the subject matter of our studies, that which I have already called the realities of fact and principle, as distinct from literary form. . . . First among such studies I place History: a subject which must not on any account be neglected by one who aspires to true cultivation. . . . For the careful study of the past enlarges our foresight in contemporary affairs and affords to citizens and to monarchs lessons . . . in the ordering of public policy. From History, also, we draw our store of examples of moral precepts. . . .

The great Orators of antiquity must by all means be included. Nowhere do we find the virtues more warmly extolled, the vices so fiercely decried. From them we may learn, also, how to express consolation, encouragement, dissuasion or advice. . . .

Familiarity with the great poets of antiquity is essential to any claim to true education. For in their writings we find deep speculations upon Nature, and upon the Causes and Origins of things, which must carry weight with us both from their antiquity and from their authorship. . . .

Proficiency in literary form, not accompanied by broad acquaintance with facts and truths, is a barren attainment; whilst information, however vast, which lacks all grace of expression would seem to be put under a bushel or partly thrown away. . . . Where, however, this double capacity exists—breadth of learning and grace of style—we allow the highest title to distinction and to abiding fame. . . . [Leonardo Bruni (1369–1444), *"Concerning the Study of Literature"*]

Vergerius and Bruni: William Harrison Woodward, ed., *Vittorino da Feltre and Other Humanist Educators* (London, 1897), pp. 96–110, 124–129, 132–133. Alberti: Eric Cochrane and Julius Kirshner, eds., *University of Chicago Readings in Western Civilization*, Vol. 5: *The Renaissance* (Chicago, 1986), pp. 81–82.

QUESTIONS FOR ANALYSIS

1. Why did the Italian Renaissance produce such a strong spirit of civic humanism?
2. Do you think that Socrates' and Cicero's perceptions of virtue were identical to those of Vergerius and Bruni? Were Renaissance virtues and classical virtues one and the same thing?
3. Why did humanists such as Leonardo Bruni consider the study of history essential to a full education?

were more likely to stay at home than to seek employment abroad. During the fourteenth century, cities themselves were the primary patrons of art and learning. During the fifteenth century, however, when most Italian city-states succumbed to the hereditary rule of noble families, patronage was monopolized by the princely aristocracy. Among these great princes were the popes in Rome, who employed the greatest artists of the day and for a few decades made Rome the artistic capital of western Europe.

THE ITALIAN RENAISSANCE: LITERATURE AND THOUGHT

In surveying the accomplishments of Italian Renaissance scholars and writers it is natural to begin with the work of Petrarch (Francesco Petrarca, 1304–1374), the "father of Renaissance humanism." Petrarch was a deeply committed Catholic who believed that scholasticism was entirely misguided because it concentrated on abstract speculation rather than on teaching people how to live virtuously and attain salvation. Petrarch thought that the Christian writer should cultivate literary eloquence so that he could inspire people to do good. For him the best models of eloquence were to be found in the classical texts of Latin literature, which were doubly valuable because they were also filled with ethical wisdom. Petrarch dedicated himself, therefore, to rediscovering such texts and to writing his own poems and moral treatises in a Latin style modeled on classical authors. But Petrarch was also a remarkable vernacular poet. The Italian sonnets—later called Petrarchan sonnets—that he wrote for his beloved Laura in the chivalrous style of the troubadours were widely imitated and admired throughout the Renaissance period, and continue to be read today.

Because he was a very traditional Christian, Petrarch's ultimate ideal for human conduct was the solitary life of contemplation and asceticism. But from about 1400 to

1450, Italian thinkers and scholars, located mainly in Florence, developed a different vision customarily called civic humanism. Civic humanists such as the Florentines Leonardo Bruni (c. 1370–1444) and Leon Battista Alberti (1404–1472) agreed with Petrarch on the need for eloquence and the value of classical literature, but they also taught that man's nature equipped him for action, for usefulness to his family and society, and for serving the state—ideally a republican city-state after the classical or contemporary Florentine model. In their view ambition and the quest for glory were noble impulses that ought to be encouraged. They refused to condemn the striving for material possessions, for they argued that the history of human progress is inseparable from our success in mastering the earth and its resources.

Perhaps the most famous of the civic humanists' writings is Alberti's *On the Family* (1443), in which he argued that the nuclear family was instituted by nature for the well-being of humanity. Within this framework, however, Alberti consigned women to purely domestic roles, asserting that "man [is] by nature more energetic and industrious," and that woman was created "to increase and continue generations, and to nourish and preserve those already born." Although such dismissals of women's intellectual abilities were fiercely resisted by a few notable women humanists, for the most part Italian Renaissance humanism was characterized by a pervasive denigration of women—a denigration expressed also in the works of classical literature that the humanists so much admired.

RENAISSANCE NEOPLATONISM

The civic humanists also went far beyond Petrarch in their knowledge of classical (and especially Greek) literature and philosophy. In this they were aided by Byzantine scholars who migrated to Italy in the first half of the fifteenth century and gave instruction in the Greek language. Italian scholars also traveled to Constantinople and other Eastern cities in search of Greek texts hitherto unknown in the West. By 1500, most of the Greek classics, including the writings of Plato, the dramatists, and the historians, were available to western Europe.

From about 1450 until about 1600 Italian thought was dominated by a school of Neoplatonists who sought to blend the ideas of Plato, Plotinus, and various strands of ancient mysticism with Christianity. Foremost among these were Marsilio Ficino (1433–1499) and Giovanni Pico della Mirandola (1463–1494), both of whom were members of the Platonic Academy founded by Cosimo de' Medici in Florence. From the standpoint of posterity, Ficino's greatest achievement was his translation of Plato's works into Latin, which made them widely available to western Europeans for the first time. Ficino himself, however, regarded his *Hermetic Corpus*, a collection of passages drawn from a number of ancient mystical writings including the Hebrew Kabbalah, as his greatest contribution to learning.

It is debatable whether Ficino's own philosophy should be called humanist because he moved away from ethics to metaphysics and taught that the individual should look primarily to the hereafter. The same issue arises with respect to Ficino's disciple Giovanni Pico della Mirandola. Pico was certainly not a civic humanist because he saw little worth in mundane public affairs. He believed—and so argued in his famous *Oration on the Dignity of Man*—that there is "nothing more wonderful than man" because he believed that man is endowed with the capacity to achieve union with God if he so wills.

Pico della Mirandola. When the young nobleman Pico arrived in Florence at age nineteen he was said to have been "of beauteous feature and shape." This contemporary portrait may have been done by the great Florentine painter Botticelli.

SOME RENAISSANCE ATTITUDES TOWARD WOMEN

Italian society in the fourteenth and fifteenth centuries was characterized by marriage patterns in which men in their late twenties or thirties customarily married women in their middle to late teens. This demographic fact probably contributed to the widely shared belief in this period that wives were essentially children, who could not be trusted with important matters and who were best trained by being beaten. Renaissance humanism did little to change such attitudes. In some cases, it even reinforced them.

After my wife had been settled in my house a few days, and after her first pangs of longing for her mother and family had begun to fade, I took her by the hand and showed her around the whole house. I explained that the loft was the place for grain and that the stores of wine and wood were kept in the cellar. I showed her where things needed for the table were kept, and so on, through the whole house. At the end there were no household goods of which my wife had not learned both the place and the purpose. . . .

Only my books and records and those of my ancestors did I determine to keep well sealed. . . . These my wife not only could not read, she could not even lay hands on them. I kept my records at all times . . . locked up and arranged in order in my study, almost like sacred and religious objects. I never gave my wife permission to enter that place, with me or alone. . . .

[Husbands] who take counsel with their wives . . . are madmen if they think true prudence or good counsel lies in the female brain. . . . For this very reason I have always tried carefully not to let any secret of mine be known to a woman. I did not doubt that my wife was most loving, and more discreet and modest in her ways than any, but I still considered it safer to have her unable, and not merely unwilling, to harm me. . . . Furthermore, I made it a rule never to speak with her of anything but household matters or questions of conduct, or of the children.

Leon Batista Alberti, "On the Family," in *The Family in Renaissance Florence*, trans. and ed. Renée N. Watkins (Columbia, S.C., 1969), pp. 208–213, as abridged in *Not in God's Image: Women in History from the Greeks to the Victorians*, ed. Julia O'Faolain and Lauro Martines (New York, 1973), pp. 187–188.

QUESTIONS FOR ANALYSIS

1. For what reasons did Leon Battista Alberti argue that his wife should have no access to his books or records?
2. Would you expect Renaissance attitudes toward women to have been more liberal and more modern? Did Alberti's comments refer to Italian society as a whole or merely to a small segment of it?

MACHIAVELLI

Renaissance Italy's greatest political philosopher was the Florentine Niccolò Machiavelli (*mah-kee-uh-VEHL-ee;* 1469–1527). Machiavelli's writings reflect the unstable condition of Italy in his time. Both France and Spain had invaded the peninsula and were competing for the allegiance of the Italian city-states, which were torn by internal dissension. In 1498 Machiavelli became a prominent official in the government of the Florentine republic, set up four years earlier when the French invasion had led to the expulsion of the Medici. His duties largely involved diplomatic missions to other Italian city-states. While in Rome he became fascinated with the attempt of Cesare Borgia, son of Pope Alexander VI, to create his own principality in central Italy. He noted with approval Cesare's ruthlessness and shrewdness and his complete subordination of personal morality to political ends. In 1512 the Medici returned to overthrow the republic of Florence, and Machiavelli was deprived of his position. Disappointed and embittered, he spent the remainder of his life at his country estate, devoting his time to writing.

Machiavelli remains a controversial figure even today. Some modern scholars see him as an amoral theorist of Realpolitik, disdainful of morality and Christian piety, caring nothing about the proper purposes of political life but interested solely in the acquisition and exercise of power as an end in itself. Others see him as an Italian patriot, who viewed princely tyranny as the only way to liberate Italy from its foreign conquerors. Still others see him as a follower of Saint Augustine of Hippo, who understood that in a fallen world populated by sinful people, a ruler's good intentions do not guarantee that his policies will have good results. Instead, Machiavelli insisted that a prince's actions must be judged by their consequences and not by their intrinsic moral quality. Human beings, Machiavelli argued, "are ungrateful, fickle, and deceitful, eager to avoid dangers, and avid for gain." This being so, "the necessity of preserving the state will often compel a prince to take actions which are opposed to loyalty, charity, humanity, and religion. . . . So far as he is able, a prince should stick to the path of good but, if the necessity arises, he should know how to follow evil."

The puzzle is heightened by the fact that, on the surface, Machiavelli's two great works of political analysis appear to contradict each other. In his *Discourses on Livy* he praised the ancient Roman republic as a model for his own contemporaries, lauding constitutional government, equality among the citizens of a republic, political independence for city-states, and the subordination of religion to the service of the state. There is little doubt, therefore, that Machiavelli was a committed republican, who believed in the free city-state as the ideal form of human government. But Machiavelli also wrote *The*

Prince, "a handbook for tyrants" in the eyes of his critics, and he dedicated this work to Lorenzo, son of Piero de' Medici, whose family had overthrown the Florentine republic that Machiavelli himself had served.

Because *The Prince* has been so much more widely read than the *Discourses,* interpretations of Machiavelli's political thought have often mistaken the admiration he expressed in *The Prince* for Cesare Borgia as an endorsement of princely tyranny for its own sake. Machiavelli's real position was quite different. In the political chaos of early sixteenth-century Italy, Machiavelli saw a ruthless prince such as Borgia as the only hope for revitalizing the spirit of independence among his contemporaries, and so making them fit, once again, for republican self-rule. However dark his vision of human nature, Machiavelli never ceased to hope that his Italian contemporaries would rise up, expel their French and Spanish conquerors, and restore their ancient traditions of republican liberty and equality. Princes such as Borgia were necessary steps toward that end, but for Machiavelli, their rule was not the ideal form of government for humankind. In Italy's sunken political situation, however, a princely state such as Borgia's was the best form of government toward which Machiavelli's downtrodden contemporaries could aspire.

> In the political chaos of early sixteenth-century Italy, Machiavelli saw a ruthless prince such as Borgia as the only hope for revitalizing the spirit of independence among his contemporaries, and so making them fit, once again, for republican self-rule.

THE IDEAL OF THE COURTIER

Far more congenial to contemporary tastes than the shocking political theories of Machiavelli were the guidelines for proper aristocratic conduct offered in *The Book of the Courtier* (1528) by the diplomat and count Baldassare Castiglione. This cleverly written forerunner of modern handbooks of etiquette stands in sharp contrast to the earlier civic humanist treatises of Bruni and Alberti. Whereas they taught the sober "republican" virtues of strenuous service in behalf of city-state and family, Castiglione, writing in an Italy dominated by magnificent princely courts, taught how to attain the elegant and seemingly effortless qualities necessary for acting like a "true gentleman." More than anyone else, Castiglione popularized the ideal of the "Renaissance man": one who is accomplished in many different pursuits and is also brave, witty, and "courteous," meaning civilized and learned. Widely read throughout Europe for over a century after its publication, Castiglione's *Courtier* spread Italian ideals of civility to princely courts north of the Alps, resulting in the ever-greater patronage of art and literature by the European aristocracy.

THE ITALIAN RENAISSANCE: PAINTING, SCULPTURE, AND ARCHITECTURE

What were the principal characteristics of Italian Renaissance art?

Despite numerous intellectual and literary advances, the longest-lived achievements of the Italian Renaissance were made in the realm of art. Of all the arts, painting was undoubtedly supreme. We have already seen the artistic genius of Giotto around 1300, but it was not until the fifteenth century that Italian painting began to come fully of age. One reason for this was that in the early fifteenth century the laws of linear perspective were discovered and first employed to give the fullest sense of three dimensions. Fifteenth-century artists also experimented with effects of light and shade (*chiaroscuro*) and for the first time carefully studied the anatomy and proportions of the human body. By the fifteenth century, too, increasing private wealth and the growth of lay patronage had opened the domain of art to a variety of nonreligious themes and subjects. Artists sought to paint portraits that revealed the hidden mysteries of the soul. Paintings intended to appeal primarily to the intellect were paralleled by others whose main purpose was to delight the eye with gorgeous color and beauty of form. The introduction of painting in oil, probably from Flanders, also had much to do with the artistic advance of this period. Because oil does not dry so quickly as fresco pigment, the painter could now work more slowly, taking time with the more difficult parts of the picture and making corrections as he or she went along.

RENAISSANCE PAINTING IN FLORENCE

The majority of the great painters of the fifteenth century were Florentines. First among them was the precocious Masaccio (1401–1428). Masaccio's greatness as a painter is based on his success in "imitating nature," which became a primary value in Renaissance painting. To achieve this effect he employed perspective, perhaps most dramatically in his fresco of the Trinity; he also used chiaroscuro with strikingly dramatic effects.

Masaccio's best-known successor was the Florentine Sandro Botticelli (1445–1510), who depicted both classical and Christian subjects. Botticelli's work excels in linear rhythms and sensuous depiction of natural detail. He is most famous for paintings that portray figures from classical mythology without any overtly Christian frame of reference. His *Allegory of Spring* and *Birth of Venus* were once understood as the expression of

The Impact of Perspective. Masaccio's painting *The Trinity with the Virgin* illustrates the startling sense of depth made possible by the rules of perspective.

Birth of Venus, by Botticelli. Botticelli was a mystic as well as a lover of beauty, and this painting is most often interpreted as a Neoplatonic allegory.

"Renaissance paganism" at its fullest, a celebration of earthly delights breaking sharply with Christian asceticism. More recently, however, scholars have preferred to view them as allegories fully compatible with Christian teachings. Although Botticelli's works remain cryptic, two points remain certain: any viewer is free to enjoy them on their naturalistic sensuous level, and Botticelli had surely not broken with Christianity, since he painted frescoes for the pope in Rome at just the same time.

LEONARDO DA VINCI

Perhaps the greatest of the Florentine artists was Leonardo da Vinci (1452–1519), one of the most versatile geniuses who ever lived. Leonardo personified the Renaissance man: he was a painter, architect, musician, mathematician, engineer, and inventor. The illegitimate son of a notary and a peasant woman, Leonardo set up an artist's shop in Florence by the time he was twenty-five and gained the patronage of the Medici ruler of the city, Lorenzo the Magnificent. But

if Leonardo had any weakness, it was his slowness in working and difficulty in finishing anything. This naturally displeased Lorenzo and other Florentine patrons, who thought an artist was little more than an artisan, commissioned to produce a certain piece of work of a certain size for a certain price on a certain date. Leonardo, however, strongly objected to this view because he considered himself to be no menial craftsman but an inspired creator. Therefore in 1482 he left Florence for the Sforza court of Milan where he was given freer rein in structuring his time and work. He remained there until the French invaded Milan in 1499; after that he wandered about Italy, finally accepting the patronage of the French king, Francis I, under whose auspices Leonardo lived and worked in France until his death.

The paintings of Leonardo da Vinci began what is known as the High Renaissance in Italy. Leonardo painted like a naturalist, basing his work on his own detailed observations of a blade of grass, the wing of a bird, a waterfall. Leonardo worshiped nature and was convinced of the essential divinity in all living things.

Virgin of the Rocks, by Leonardo da Vinci. This painting reveals Leonardo's interest in the human face and in the atmosphere of natural settings.

It is not surprising, therefore, that he was a vegetarian and that he went to the marketplace to buy caged birds, which he released to their native habitat.

It is generally agreed that Leonardo's masterpieces are the *Virgin of the Rocks* (which exists in two versions), the *Last Supper,* and his portraits of the Mona Lisa and Ginevra da Benci. The *Virgin of the Rocks* typifies not only his marvelous technical skill but also his passion for science and his belief in the universe as a well-ordered place. The *Last Supper,* is a study of psychological reactions. A serene Christ, resigned to his terrible fate, has just announced to his disciples that one of them will betray him. The artist succeeds in portraying the mingled emotions of surprise, horror, and guilt in the faces of the disciples as they gradually perceive the meaning of their master's statement. The third and fourth of Leonardo's major triumphs, the *Mona Lisa* and *Ginevra da Benci,* reflect a similar interest in the varied moods of the human soul.

Last Supper, by Leonardo da Vinci.

THE VENETIAN SCHOOL

The beginning of the High Renaissance around 1490 also witnessed the rise of the so-called Venetian school, the major members of which were Giovanni Bellini (c. 1430–1516), Giorgione (1478–1510), and Titian (c. 1490–1576). The work of all these men reflected the luxurious, pleasure-loving life of the thriving commercial city of Venice. Most Venetian painters showed little of the Florentine school's concerns with philosophical and psychological issues. Their aim was to appeal to the senses by painting idyllic landscapes and sumptuous portraits of the rich and powerful. In the subordination of form and meaning to color and elegance their paintings mirrored the grandiose tastes of the wealthy merchants for whom they were created.

PAINTING IN ROME

High Renaissance painting reached its peak in the first half of the sixteenth century. During this period, Rome became the major artistic center of the Italian peninsula, although the traditions of the Florentine school still exerted a potent influence.

RAPHAEL

Among the eminent painters of this period was Raphael (1483–1520), a native of Urbino and perhaps the most beloved artist of the entire Renaissance. The lasting appeal of his style is due primarily to his ennobling portrayals of human beings as temperate, wise, and dignified creatures. Although Raphael was influenced by Leonardo, he cultivated a much more allegorical approach to his painting. His *Disputà* illustrated the relationship between the church in heaven and the church on earth. In a worldly setting against a brilliant sky, theologians debate the meaning of the Eucharist, while in the clouds above, saints and the Trinity repose in the possession of a holy mystery. Raphael's *School of Athens* depicts the harmony between Platonism and Aristotelianism. Plato (painted as a portrait of Leonardo) is shown pointing upward to empha-

School of Athens, by Raphael.

size the spiritual basis of his world of Ideas, while Aristotle stretches a hand forward to exemplify his claim that the created world embodies these same principles in physical form. Raphael is noted also for his portraits and Madonnas. To the latter, especially, he gave a softness and warmth that seemed to endow them with a sweetness and piety quite different from Leonardo's enigmatic and somewhat distant Madonnas.

MICHELANGELO

The last towering figure of the High Renaissance was Michelangelo (1475–1564), a native of Florence. If Leonardo was a naturalist, Michelangelo was an ideal-

ist; where the former sought to recapture and interpret fleeting natural phenomena, Michelangelo was more concerned with expressing enduring, abstract truths. Michelangelo was a painter, sculptor, architect, and poet—and he expressed himself in all these forms with a similar power and in a similar manner. At the center of all of his paintings is the male figure, which is always powerful, colossal, and magnificent. If humanity, embodied in the male body, lay at the center of Italian Renaissance culture, then Michelangelo, who depicted the male figure without cease, is the supreme Renaissance artist.

Michelangelo's greatest achievements in painting appear in a single location—the Sistine Chapel in Rome—

The Creation of Adam, by Michelangelo (1475–1564). One of a series of frescoes on the ceiling of the Sistine Chapel in Rome. Inquiring into the nature of humanity, it represents Renaissance affirmativeness at its height.

yet they are products of two different periods in the artist's life and consequently exemplify two different artistic styles and outlooks on the human condition. More famous are the sublime frescoes Michelangelo painted on the ceiling of the Sistine Chapel from 1508 to 1512, depicting scenes from the book of Genesis. All the panels in this series, including *God Dividing the Light from Darkness*, *The Creation of Adam*, and *The Flood*, exemplify the young artist's commitment to classical Greek aesthetic principles of harmony, solidity, and dignified restraint. But a quarter of a century later, when Michelangelo returned to work in the Sistine

Chapel, both his style and mood had changed dramatically. In the enormous *Last Judgment*, a fresco done for the Sistine Chapel's altar wall in 1536, Michelangelo repudiated classical restraint and substituted a style that emphasized tension and distortion to communicate the older man's pessimistic conception of a humanity wracked by fear and bowed by guilt.

SCULPTURE

The Italian Renaissance took a great step forward by creating statues that were no longer carved as parts of columns or doorways on church buildings or as effigies on tombs. Instead, Italian sculptors for the first time since antiquity carved free-standing statues "in the round." By freeing sculpture from its bondage to architecture the High Renaissance reestablished sculpture as a separate and potentially secular art form.

DONATELLO

The first great master of Renaissance sculpture was Donatello (c. 1386–1466). His bronze statue of David triumphant over the head of the slain Goliath imitated classical sculpture not just in the depiction of a nude body, but also in the subject's posture of resting his weight on one leg. Yet this David is clearly a lithe adolescent rather than a muscular Greek athlete. Later in his career, Donatello more consciously imitated ancient statuary in his commanding portrayal of the proud warrior Gattamelata—the first monumental equestrian statue in bronze executed in the West since the time of the Romans.

MICHELANGELO

Michelangelo regarded sculpture as the most exalted of the arts because it allowed the artist to imitate God most fully in re-creating human forms. But Michelangelo disdained slavish naturalism. Instead, he subordinated naturalism to the force of his imagination and sought restlessly to express his ideals in ever more arresting forms.

Like his painting, Michelangelo's sculpture followed a course from classicism to mannerism—that is, from harmonious modeling to dramatic distortion. The sculptor's most distinguished early work, his *David*, executed in 1501, is surely his most perfect classical statue. By sculpting a serenely confident young man at the peak of physical fitness, Michelangelo celebrated the Florentine republic's own "fortitude" in resisting

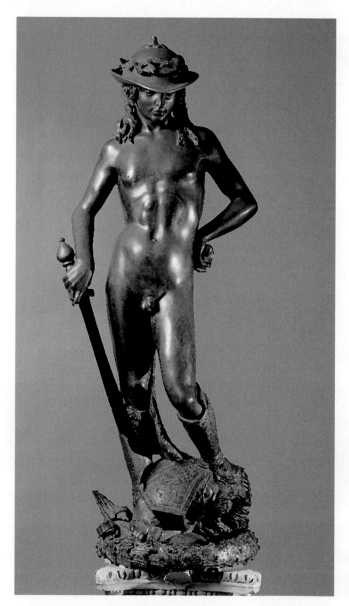

David, **by Donatello** The first free-standing nude statue executed in the West since antiquity.

tyrants and upholding ideals of civic justice. The serenity seen in *David* is no longer prominent in the works of Michelangelo's middle period; rather, in a work such as his *Moses* of about 1515, the sculptor had begun to explore the use of anatomical distortion to create effects of emotional intensity—in this case, the biblical prophet's righteous rage. As Michelangelo's life drew to a close he experimented more and more with exaggerated stylistic mannerisms for the purpose of communicating moods of brooding pensiveness or outright pathos. The culmination of this trend in Michelangelo's statuary is his unfinished but intensely moving *Descent from the Cross*, a depiction of an old man resembling the sculptor himself grieving over the distorted, slumping body of the dead Christ.

ARCHITECTURE

To a much greater extent than either sculpture or painting, Renaissance architecture had its roots in the past. The new building style was a compound of elements derived from the Middle Ages and from antiquity. The great architects of the Renaissance generally adopted their building plans from Romanesque churches, some of which they believed, mistakenly, to be Roman rather than medieval. They also copied their decorative devices from the ruins of ancient Rome. The result was an architecture based on the cruciform floor plan of transept and nave, but embodying the decorative features of the column and arch, the colonnade, and frequently the dome. Renaissance architecture also emphasized geometrical proportion because Italian builders, under the influence of Neoplatonism, concluded that certain mathematical ratios reflect the harmony of the universe. A fine example of Renaissance architecture is St. Peter's Basilica in Rome, built under the patronage of popes Julius II and Leo X and designed by some of the most celebrated architects of the time, including Donato Bramante (c. 1444–1514) and Michelangelo.

David, by Michelangelo. Over thirteen feet high, this serenely self-confident affirmation of the beauty of the human form was placed prominently by the Florentine government in front of Florence's city hall to proclaim the city's humanistic values.

CHRONOLOGY

LIVES OF ITALIAN RENAISSANCE SCHOLARS AND ARTISTS

Petrarch	1304–1374
Leon Battista Alberti	1404–1472
Giovanni Pico della Mirandola	1463–1494
Niccolò Machiavelli	1469–1527
Leonardo da Vinci	1452–1519
Titian	c. 1490–1576
Raphael	1483–1520
Michelangelo	1475–1564

THE WANING OF THE ITALIAN RENAISSANCE

Why did the Renaissance decline around 1550?

Around 1550 the Renaissance in Italy began to decline. The causes of this decline were varied. The French invasion of 1494 and the incessant warfare that ensued was one of the major factors. The French king Charles VIII viewed Italy as an attractive target for his expansive dynastic ambitions. In 1494 he led an army of 30,000 well-trained troops across the Alps to press his claims to the Duchy of Milan and the Kingdom of Naples. An alliance among Spain, the Papal States, the Holy Roman Empire, Milan, and Venice finally forced Charles to withdraw from Italy. But the respite was brief. From 1499 until 1529 warfare in Italy was virtually uninterrupted. The worst disaster came in 1527 when rampaging troops under the command of the Spanish ruler and Holy Roman emperor Charles V sacked the city of Rome, causing enormous destruction. Only in 1529 did Charles V finally manage to gain control over most of the Italian peninsula, putting an end to the fighting for a time.

To political disasters was added a waning of Italian prosperity. Italy's virtual monopoly of trade with Asia in the fifteenth century had been one of the chief economic supports for Italian Renaissance culture, but the gradual shifting of trade routes from the Mediterranean to the Atlantic region, following the overseas discoveries of around 1500, slowly but surely cost Italy its supremacy as the center of European trade. As Italian wealth diminished, there was less and less of a surplus to support artistic endeavors.

A final cause of the decline of the Italian Renaissance was the Counter-Reformation. During the sixteenth century the Roman church sought increasingly to exercise firm control over thought and art as part of a campaign to combat worldliness and the spread of Protestantism. In 1542 the Roman Inquisition was established; in 1564 the first Roman Index of Prohibited Books was published. The determination of ecclesiastical censors to enforce doctrinal uniformity could even lead to death.

Cultural and artistic achievement was by no means extinguished in Italy after the middle of the sixteenth century. On the contrary, impressive new artistic styles were cultivated between about 1540 and 1600 by painters who drew on traits found in the later work of Raphael and Michelangelo. In the seventeenth century came the dazzling Baroque style, which was born in Rome under ecclesiastical auspices. Similarly, Italian music registered enormous accomplishments virtually without interruption from the sixteenth to the twentieth century. But as Renaissance culture spread from Italy to the rest of Europe, the cultural dominance of the Italians began to wane, and the focus of European high culture shifted toward the princely courts of Spain, France, England, Germany, and Poland.

THE RENAISSANCE IN THE NORTH

How did the northern and Italian Renaissances differ from one another?

Contacts between Italy and northern Europe continued throughout the fourteenth and fifteenth centuries. Only at the end of the fifteenth century, however, did the new currents of Italian Renaissance learning begin to take firm hold in Spain and northern Europe.

A variety of explanations have been offered for this delay. Northern European intellectual life in the late Middle Ages was dominated by universities whose curricula focused on the study of philosophical logic and Christian theology. This approach left little room for the study of classical literature. In Italy, by contrast, a more secular, urban-oriented educational tradition took shape within which Renaissance humanism was able to develop. Even in the sixteenth century, northern scholars influenced by Italian Renaissance ideals usually worked outside the university system. Northern rulers were also less interested in patronizing artists and intellectuals than were the city-states and princes of Italy. Only in the sixteenth century, as northern nobles began to spend more time in residence at the royal court, did kings begin to assume a really important role as cultural leaders and patrons.

CHRISTIAN HUMANISM AND THE NORTHERN RENAISSANCE

The northern Renaissance was the product of the grafting of certain Italian Renaissance ideals onto pre-

How did the northern and Italian Renaissances differ from one another?

The Renaissance in the North   337

The States of Italy during the Renaissance, c. 1494

Note the political divisions of Italy on the eve of the French invasion in 1494. Contemporary observers often described Italy as being divided among five great powers: Milan, Venice, Florence, the Papal States, and the Kingdom of Naples. Which of these powers were most interested in expanding their territory? Which neighboring territories would be most threatened by such attempts at expansion? Why did Florence and the Papal States so often find themselves in conflict with each other?

existing northern traditions. This can be seen very clearly in the case of the most prominent northern Renaissance intellectual movement, Christian humanism. Although they shared the Italian humanists' contempt for scholasticism, northern Christian humanists

more often looked for ethical guidance from biblical and religious precepts rather than from Cicero or Virgil. Like their Italian counterparts, they sought wisdom from antiquity, but the antiquity they had in mind was Christian rather than classical—the antiquity, that is, of the New Testament and the early church fathers. Northern Renaissance artists were inspired by the accomplishments of Italian masters, but they depicted classical subject matter far less frequently than did the Italians and almost never portrayed completely nude human figures.

DESIDERIUS ERASMUS

Any discussion of northern Renaissance accomplishments in the realm of thought and literary expression must begin with the career of Desiderius Erasmus (c. 1469–1536), the "prince of the Christian humanists." The illegitimate son of a priest, Erasmus was born near Rotterdam in Holland, but later, as a result of his wide travels, became in effect a citizen of all northern Europe. Forced into a monastery against his will when he was a teenager, the young Erasmus found there little religion or formal instruction but plenty of freedom to

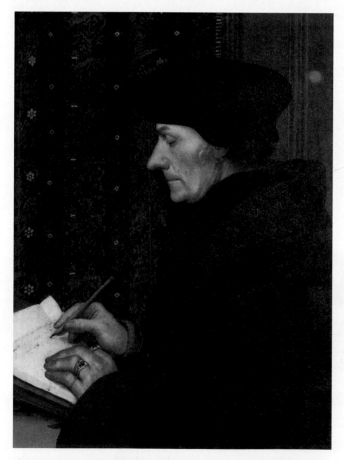

Erasmus, by Hans Holbein the Younger (1497–1543). This portrait is generally regarded as the most telling visual characterization of "the prince of the Christian humanists."

read what he liked. He devoured all the classics he could get his hands on and the writings of many of the church fathers. When he was about thirty years of age, he obtained permission to leave the monastery and enroll in the University of Paris, where he completed the requirements for the degree of bachelor of divinity. But Erasmus subsequently rebelled against what he considered the useless learning of Parisian scholasticism. Nor did he ever serve actively as a priest. Instead he made his living from teaching, writing, and the proceeds of various ecclesiastical offices that required no spiritual duties of him. By means of a voluminous correspondence that he kept up with learned friends he made wherever he went, Erasmus became the leader of a northern European humanist movement. And through the popularity of his numerous publications, he became the arbiter of northern European cultural tastes during his lifetime.

As a Latin prose stylist, Erasmus was unequaled since the days of Cicero. Above all, Erasmus excelled in the deft use of irony, poking fun at all and sundry, including himself. But although Erasmus's urbane Latin style and wit earned him a wide audience for purely literary reasons, he intended everything he wrote to promote what he called the "philosophy of Christ." Erasmus believed that the entire society of his day was caught up in corruption and immorality because people had lost sight of the simple teachings of the Gospels. Accordingly, he offered to his contemporaries three different categories of publication: clever satires meant to show people the error of their ways, serious moral treatises meant to offer guidance toward proper Christian behavior, and scholarly editions of basic Christian texts.

In the first category belong the works of Erasmus that are still most widely read today—*The Praise of Folly* (1509), in which he pilloried scholastic pedantry and dogmatism as well as the ignorance and superstitious credulity of the masses; and the *Colloquies* (1518), in which he held up contemporary religious practices for examination in a more serious but still pervasively ironic tone. The most prominent treatises in his second genre are the quietly eloquent *Handbook of the Christian Knight* (1503), which urged the laity to pursue lives of inward piety, and the *Complaint of Peace* (1517), which pleaded movingly for Christian pacifism. Erasmus's pacifism was one of his most deeply held values, and he returned to it again and again in his published works.

Despite the success of his literary works, Erasmus considered his textual scholarship his greatest achieve-

How did the Northern and Italian Renaissances differ from one another?

The Renaissance in the North   339

ment. Revering the authority of the early Latin fathers Augustine, Jerome, and Ambrose, he brought out reliable editions of all their works. He also used his extraordinary command of Latin and Greek to produce a more accurate edition of the New Testament. After reading Lorenzo Valla's *Notes on the New Testament* in 1504, Erasmus became convinced that nothing was more imperative than divesting the New Testament of the myriad errors in transcription and translation that had piled up during the Middle Ages, for no one could be a good Christian without being certain of exactly what Christ's message really was. Hence he spent ten years studying and comparing all the best early Greek biblical manuscripts he could find in order to establish an authoritative text. When it finally appeared in 1516, Erasmus's Greek New Testament, published together with explanatory notes and his own new Latin translation, was one of the most important landmarks of biblical scholarship of all time. In the hands of Martin Luther, it would play a critical role in the early stages of the Protestant Reformation.

Sir Thomas More

One of Erasmus's closest friends, and a close second to him in distinction among the ranks of the Christian humanists, was the Englishman Sir Thomas More (1478–1535). Following a successful career as a lawyer and as speaker of the House of Commons, in 1529 More was appointed lord chancellor of England. He was not long in this position, however, before he incurred the wrath of King Henry VIII. More, who was loyal to Catholic universalism, opposed the king's design to establish a national church under royal control. Finally, in 1534, when More refused to take an oath acknowledging Henry as head of the Church of England, he was thrown into the Tower of London, and a year later met his death on the scaffold as a Catholic martyr. Much earlier, however, in 1516, long before More had any inkling of how his life was to end, he published the one work for which he will ever be best remembered, *Utopia*. Purporting to describe an ideal community on an imaginary island, the book is really an Erasmian critique of the glaring abuses of the time— poverty undeserved and wealth unearned, drastic punishments, religious persecution, and the senseless slaughter of war. The inhabitants of Utopia hold all their goods in common, work only six hours a day so that all may have leisure for intellectual pursuits, and practice the natural virtues of wisdom,

Sir Thomas More, by Hans Holbein the Younger.

moderation, fortitude, and justice. Iron is the precious metal "because it is useful," war and monasticism do not exist, and toleration is granted to all who recognize the existence of God and the immortality of the soul. Although More advanced no explicit arguments in his *Utopia* in favor of Christianity, he clearly meant to imply that if the "Utopians" could manage their society so well without the benefit of Christian revelation, Europeans who knew the Gospels ought to be able to do even better.

The Decline of Christian Humanism

Despite a host of achievements, the Christian humanist movement, which possessed such an extraordinary degree of international solidarity and vigor from about 1500 to 1525, was thrown into disarray by the rise of Protestantism and subsequently lost its momentum. The irony here is obvious, for the Christian humanists' emphasis on the literal truth of the Gospels and their devastating criticisms of clerical corruption and religious ceremonialism certainly helped pave the way for the Protestant Reformation initiated by Martin Luther in 1517. But, as we will see in Chapter Thirteen, very few of the older generation of Christian humanists were willing to join Luther in rejecting the fundamental principles on which Catholicism was based, and the few who did became such ardent Protestants that they lost the sense of quiet irony that had been a hallmark of Christian humanist expression. Most Christian humanists tried to remain within the Catholic fold while still espousing their ideal of nonritualistic inward piety. But as time went on, the leaders of Catholicism grew less and less tolerant because lines were hardening in the war with Protestantism. Hence any internal criticism of Catholic religious practices seemed like giving covert aid to the "enemy." Erasmus himself, who remained a Catholic, died early enough to escape opprobrium, but several of his less fortunate followers lived on to suffer as victims of the Inquisition.

LITERATURE, ART, AND MUSIC IN THE NORTHERN RENAISSANCE

Yet if Christian humanism faded rapidly after about 1525, the northern Renaissance continued to flourish throughout the sixteenth century in literature and art. In France, Pierre de Ronsard (c. 1524–1585) and Joachim du Bellay (c. 1522–1560) wrote elegant sonnets in the style of Petrarch, and in England the poets Sir Philip Sidney (1554–1586) and Edmund Spenser (c. 1552–1599) drew impressively on Italian literary innovations. Indeed, Spenser's *Faerie Queene*, a long chivalric romance written in the manner of Ariosto's *Orlando Furioso*, communicates as well as any Italian work the gorgeous sensuousness typical of Italian Renaissance culture.

CHRONOLOGY

LIVES OF NORTHERN RENAISSANCE SCHOLARS AND ARTISTS

Erasmus	c. 1469–1536
Thomas More	1478–1535
Edmund Spenser	c. 1552–1599
François Rabelais	c. 1494–1553
Albrecht Dürer	1471–1528
Hans Holbein the Younger	1497–1543

More original than any of the aforementioned poets was the French prose satirist François Rabelais (c. 1494–1553), probably the best loved of all the great European creative writers of the sixteenth century. Like Erasmus, whom he greatly admired, Rabelais satirized religious ceremonialism, ridiculed scholasticism, scoffed at superstitions, and pilloried every form of bigotry. But unlike Erasmus, who wrote in a highly cultivated classical Latin style comprehensible to only the most learned readers, Rabelais chose to address a far wider audience by writing in an extremely down-to-earth French loaded with the crudest vulgarities. Yet there runs through all his work a common theme of glorifying the human and the natural. For Rabelais, every instinct of humanity was healthy, provided it was not directed toward tyranny over others. Thus in his ideal community, the utopian "abbey of Thélème," there was no repressiveness whatsoever, but only a congenial environment for the pursuit of life-affirming, natural human attainments, guided by the single rule of "love and do what thou wouldst."

PAINTING

The most moving visual embodiments of the ideals of Christian humanism were conceived by the foremost of northern Renaissance artists, the German Albrecht Dürer (*DOOR-er*; 1471–1528). Dürer was the first northerner to master Italian Renaissance techniques of proportion, perspective, and modeling. Dürer also shared the contemporary Italian fascination with reproducing the manifold works of nature down to the minutest details and a penchant for displaying the human nude in various postures. But whereas Michelangelo portrayed his *David* or *Adam* entirely without covering, Dürer's nudes are seldom lacking their fig leaves, in deference to more restrained northern traditions. Dürer was inspired particularly by the Christian ideals of Erasmus. Thus Dürer's serenely radiant engraving of Saint Jerome expresses the sense of accomplishment that Erasmus or any other contemporary Christian humanist may have had while working quietly in his study; and his *Four Apostles* intones a solemn hymn to the dignity and penetrating insight of Dürer's favorite New Testament authors, Saints Paul, John, Peter, and Mark.

MUSIC

Music in western Europe in the fifteenth and sixteenth centuries constitutes one of the most brilliant aspects of

Renaissance endeavor. The musical theory of the Renaissance was driven largely by the humanist-inspired effort to recover and imitate classical musical forms and modes. Musical practice, however, showed much more continuity with medieval musical tradition. At the same time, however, a new expressiveness emerges in Renaissance music, along with a new emphasis on coloration and emotional quality. New musical instruments were also developed, including the lute, the viol, the violin, and the harpsichord. New musical forms also emerged: madrigals, motets, and, at the end of the sixteenth century, a new Italian form, the opera. As earlier, musical leadership came from men trained in the service of the church. But the distinction between sacred and profane music was becoming less sharp, and most composers did not restrict their activities to a single field. Music was no longer regarded merely as a diversion or an adjunct to worship but came into its own as a serious independent art.

During the fourteenth century an early Renaissance musical movement called *ars nova* ("new art") flourished in Italy and France. Its outstanding composers were Francesco Landini (c. 1325–1397) and Guillaume de Machaut (c. 1300–1377). The fifteenth century ushered in a synthesis of French, Flemish, and Italian elements in the ducal court of Burgundy. As the sixteenth century opened, Franco-Flemish composers appeared in every important court and cathedral all over Europe, gradually establishing regional-national schools, usually in attractive combinations of Flemish with German, Spanish, and Italian musical cultures. Music also flourished in sixteenth-century England, where the Tudor monarchs Henry VIII and Elizabeth I were active patrons of the arts.

Saint Jerome in His Study, by Dürer. Saint Jerome, a hero to both Dürer and Erasmus, represents inspired Christian scholarship. Note how the scene exudes contentment, even down to the sleeping lion, which seems rather like an overgrown tabby cat.

CONCLUSION

The contrasts between the Italian and the northern Renaissance are real, but they must not be exaggerated. The intellectuals of Renaissance Italy were formed in a more secular, more urban educational environment than were the northerners, but they were no less fervent in their Christianity. Petrarch's criticism of scholasticism was not that it was too Christian but rather that it was not Christian enough. The Platonic Academy might honor Plato as if he were a saint of the church, but these men approached Plato's works in the same spirit with which thirteenth-century scholastic theologians had approached the works of Aristotle. As committed Christians, both groups were convinced that the conclusions reached by the greatest philosophical minds of classical antiquity must be compatible with Christian truth. It was the task of Christian intellectuals to reveal this compatibility and, by so doing, to strengthen the one true faith.

Nor should we overdraw the contrasts between the Renaissance and the High Middle Ages. Both Italian and northern humanists shared an optimistic view of human nature as improvable despite the consequences of Adam and Eve's disobedience; but none was more optimistic on this score than was Saint Thomas Aquinas. Both groups emphasized the importance of personal introspection and self-examination; but none took this injunction more seriously than did the Cistercian thinkers of the twelfth century. And finally, both groups shared a belief that the exhortations of intellectuals would lift everyone's morals and conduct them to new heights of virtue. In this regard, High Renaissance intellectual life has a kind of naive optimism that contrasts sharply with the darker, more psychologically complex world of the Middle Ages and with the Reformation era that was about to begin.

KEY TERMS

humanism	Baldassare Castiglione	Desiderius Erasmus
Medici	Leonardo da Vinci	*The Praise of Folly*
Petrarch	Raphael	*Utopia*
The Prince	Michelangelo	François Rabelais

SELECTED READINGS

Alberti, Leon Battista. *The Family in Renaissance Florence (Della Famiglia)*. Trans. Renée Neu Watkins. Columbia, S.C., 1969.

Baxandall, Michael. *Painting and Experience in Fifteenth Century Italy.* Oxford, 1972. A classic study of the perceptual world of the Renaissance.

Brucker, Gene. *Florence, the Golden Age, 1138–1737.* Berkeley and Los Angeles, Calif., 1998. The standard account by a master historian.

Bruni, Leonardo. *The Humanism of Leonardo Bruni: Selected Texts.* Trans. Gordon Griffiths, James Hankins, and David Thompson. Binghamton, N.Y., 1987. Excellent translations, with introductions, to the Latin works of a key Renaissance humanist.

Burke, Peter. *The Renaissance.* New York, 1997. A brief introduction by an influential modern historian.

Castiglione, Baldassare. *The Book of the Courtier.* Many editions. The translations by C. S. Singleton (New York, 1959) and by George Bull (New York, 1967) are both excellent.

Cellini, Benvenuto. *Autobiography.* Trans. George Bull. Baltimore, Md., 1956. This Florentine goldsmith (1500–1571) is the source for many of the most famous stories about the artists of the Florentine Renaissance.

Cochrane, Eric, and Julius Kirshner, eds. *The Renaissance.* Chicago, 1986. An outstanding collection, from the University of Chicago Readings in Western Civilization series.

Erasmus, Desiderius. *The Praise of Folly.* Trans. J. Wilson. Ann Arbor, Mich., 1958.

Fox, Alistair. *Thomas More: History and Providence.* Oxford, 1982. A balanced account of a man too easily idealized.

Grendler, Paul, ed. *Encyclopedia of the Renaissance.* New York, 1999. A valuable reference work.

Hale, John R. *The Civilization of Europe in the Renaissance.* New York, 1993. A synthetic volume summarizing the life's work of a major Renaissance historian.

Jardine, Lisa. *Worldly Goods.* London, 1996. A revisionist account that emphasizes the acquisitive materialism of Italian Renaissance society and culture.

Kanter, Laurence, Hilliard T. Goldfarb, and James Hankins. *Botticelli's Witness: Changing Style in a Changing Florence.* Boston, 1997. This catalog, for an exhibit of Botticelli's works at the Gardner Museum in Boston, offers an excellent introduction to the painter and his world.

King, Margaret L. *Women of the Renaissance.* Chicago, 1991. Deals with women in all walks of life and in a variety of roles.

Martines, Lauro. *Power and Imagination: City-States in Renaissance Italy.* New York, 1979. Insightful account of the connections among politics, society, culture, and art.

Murray, Linda. *High Renaissance and Mannerism.* London, 1985. The place to start for fifteenth- and sixteenth-century Italian art.

Olson, Roberta. *Italian Renaissance Sculpture*. New York, 1992. The most accessible introduction to the subject.

Perkins, Leeman L. *Music in the Age of the Renaissance*. New York, 1999. A massive new study that nonetheless needs to be read in conjunction with Reese.

Rabelais, François. *Gargantua and Pantagruel*. Trans. J. M. Cohen. Baltimore, Md., 1955. A robust modern translation.

Reese, Gustave. *Music in the Renaissance*. Rev. ed. New York, 1959. A great book; still authoritative, despite the more recent work by Perkins, which supplements but does not replace it.

Rice, Eugene F., Jr., and Anthony Grafton. *The Foundations of Early Modern Europe, 1460–1559*. 2d ed. New York, 1994. The best textbook account of its period.

Rowland, Ingrid D. *The Culture of the High Renaissance: Ancients and Moderns in Sixteenth-Century Rome*. Cambridge and New York, 2000. Beautifully written examination of the social, intellectual, and economic foundations of the Renaissance in Rome.

Chapter Thirteen

Chapter Contents

FVIT·CONSILIO·D·IOANNIS·IACOBI·PASTORIS·HVIVS·ECCLES

Reformations of Religion

AFTER TWO CENTURIES of economic, social, and political turmoil, Europe in the year 1500 was well on the road to recovery. Population was increasing, the economy was expanding, and the national monarchs of France, England, Spain, Scotland, and Poland were all securely established on their thrones. Throughout Europe, governments at every level were extending their control over their subjects' lives. Europe had also resumed its commercial and colonial expansion. Even Catholic Christianity appeared to be going from strength to strength as the sixteenth century dawned. Although the papacy remained mired in territorial wars in Italy, the church had weathered the storms that beset it during the fifteenth century. The Lollards had been suppressed and the Hussites reincorporated into the church. In the struggle over conciliarism, the papacy had won the support of all the major European rulers, reducing the conciliarists to academic isolation at the University of Paris. Meanwhile, at the parish level, the devotion of ordinary Christians to their faith had probably never been higher. To be sure, there were also problems. Although the educational standards of the parish clergy were higher than they had ever been, reformers were quick to note that too many priests were still absent, ignorant, or neglectful of their spiritual duties. Monasticism, by and large, seemed to have lost its spiritual fire; among the populace, religious enthusiasm sometimes led the faithful into gross superstition and doctrinal error. But these were manageable problems. On the whole, the "prospect of Europe" had not looked brighter for several centuries.

No one in 1500 could have predicted that within fifty years Europe's religious unity would be irreparably shattered by a new and powerful Protestant reform movement—or that in the century thereafter an appallingly destructive series of religious wars would shake to their core the foundations of European political life. Yet remarkably, these extraordinary events began with a single German monk named

FOCUS QUESTIONS

• What were the theological premises of Lutheranism?

• Why did Switzerland emerge as such an important center for sixteenth-century Protestantism?

• How did notions of family and marriage change during the Reformation?

• Why did England become a Protestant country?

• How did the Catholic Reformation differ from the Counter-Reformation?

Martin Luther (1483–1546), whose personal quest for a more certain understanding of sin, grace, and Christian salvation set off a chain reaction throughout Europe, resulting in the secession of millions of Europeans from the Roman Catholic Church and affecting the religious practices of nearly every Christian in Europe, whether Catholic or Protestant. The religious movement that Luther touched off was much larger than Luther himself; nor should Martin Luther's own spiritual journey be seen as an epitome for all of Protestantism. But that said, there is no doubt that the Reformation movement began with Martin Luther—and so must we if we are to understand the extraordinary upheaval this new religious movement brought about.

THE LUTHERAN UPHEAVAL

What were the theological premises of Lutheranism?

To explain the success of the Lutheran revolt in Germany, we must answer three central questions: (1) Why did Luther's theological ideas lead him to break with Rome? (2) Why did large numbers of Germans rally to his cause? (3) Why did so many German princes and towns impose the new religion within their territories? As we shall see, those who followed Luther found his message appealing for different reasons. Many peasants hoped the new religion would free them from the exactions of their lords; towns and princes thought it would allow them to consolidate their political independence; nationalists thought it would liberate Germany from the demands of foreign popes bent on feathering their own nest in central Italy.

What Luther's followers shared, however, was a conviction that their new, Lutheran understanding of Christianity would lead them to heaven, whereas contemporary Catholicism would not. To this degree, *reformation* is a misleading label for the movement Luther initiated. Although Luther himself did begin as a reformer seeking to cleanse contemporary Christianity from its abuses, he quickly developed into an uncompromising opponent of the basic principles of Catholic belief and practice. Many of his followers became even more radical. The religious movement that began with Martin Luther was thus no mere "reformation." It was a frontal assault on the foundations of late medieval religious life.

LUTHER'S QUEST FOR RELIGIOUS CERTAINTY

Although Martin Luther became an inspiration to millions, he was at first a terrible disappointment to his father. The elder Luther was a Thuringian peasant who had prospered by leasing some mines. Eager to see his clever son rise still further, he sent young Martin to the University of Erfurt to study law. In 1505, however, Martin shattered his father's hopes by becoming a monk of the Augustinian order. In some sense, however, Luther always remained faithful to his father's humble roots. Throughout his life, Martin Luther lived simply and expressed himself in the vigorous, earthy vernacular of the German peasantry.

Like many great figures in the history of religion, Luther arrived at his new understanding of religious truth by a dramatic conversion experience. As a monk, young Luther zealously pursued all the traditional means for achieving his own salvation. Yet, try as he might, Luther could find no spiritual peace because he

Martin Luther. A portrait by Lucas Cranach.

feared that he could never perform enough good deeds to deserve so great a gift as salvation. But in 1513 he hit on an insight that granted him relief and changed the course of his life.

Luther's guiding insight pertained to the problem of the justice of God. For years he had worried that it seemed unjust for God to issue commandments that he knew human beings could not observe and then punish them with eternal damnation for not observing them. But after becoming a professor of biblical theology at the University of Wittenberg, it suddenly struck him that God's justice had nothing to do with his power to punish but rather with his mercy in saving sinful mortals through faith. As Luther later wrote, ". . . I felt as though I had been born again, and had gone through open gates into paradise."

After that, everything seemed to fall into place. Lecturing at Wittenberg in the years immediately after 1513, Luther pondered a passage in Saint Paul's Letter to the Romans (1:17): "[T]he just shall live by faith" until he reached his central doctrine of "justification by faith alone." Luther concluded that God's justice does not demand endless good works and religious rituals for salvation, because humans can never be saved by their own efforts. Rather, humans are saved by God's grace alone, which God offers as an utterly undeserved gift to those whom he has predestined for salvation. Because this grace comes to humans through the gift of faith, from the human perspective men and women are "justified" (that is, made worthy of salvation) by faith alone. Those whom God has justified through faith will manifest that fact by performing works of piety and charity, but such works are not what saves them. Piety and charity are merely visible signs of each believer's invisible spiritual state, which is known to God alone.

The essence of this doctrine was not original to Luther. It harked back to around the year 400 with the predestinarianism of Saint Augustine (see Chapter Six), the patron saint of Luther's own monastic order. During the twelfth and thirteenth centuries, however, theologians developed a very different understanding of salvation, emphasizing the role that both the church itself (through its sacraments) and the individual believer (through acts of piety and charity) could play in the process of salvation. None of these theologians claimed that a human being could earn his or her way

> By the end of the fifteenth century, however, indulgences were often being granted in return for monetary payments to favored papal causes. To many reformers, this looked like simony: the sin of selling grace in return for cash.

to heaven by good works alone. But the late medieval church unwittingly encouraged such misunderstandings by presenting the process of salvation in increasingly quantitative terms, declaring, for example, that by performing a specific meritorious act (such as a pilgrimage or a pious donation), a believer could reduce the penance she or he owed to God by a specific number of days. From the fourteenth century on, popes claimed to dispense such special grace to the living from the "Treasury of Merits," a storehouse of surplus good works piled up by Christ and the saints in heaven. Most commonly, grace was withdrawn from this Treasury and reassigned to needy sinners through indulgences: special remissions of the penitential obligations imposed on Christians by their priests as part of the sacrament of penance. By the end of the fifteenth century, however, indulgences were often being granted in return for monetary payments to favored papal causes. To many reformers, this looked like simony: the sin of selling grace in return for cash.

Abuses of this sort were widely criticized by early sixteenth-century church reformers such as Erasmus. But Luther's objections to indulgences and prayers for the dead had much more radical consequences, because they rested on a set of Augustinian theological presuppositions that, if taken to their logical conclusion, could result only in dismantling much of contemporary Catholic religious practice. Luther himself may not have realized this when he took the first steps that would lead to his breach with Rome. But as the implications of his ideas became clear, Luther did not withdraw from them. Instead, he pressed on, declaring to his opponents, "Here I stand; God help me, I can do no other."

THE REFORMATION BEGINS

Luther first developed his theological ideas as an academic lecturer, but in 1517 he was goaded into attacking some of the actual practices of the church by a provocation that was too much for him to bear.

A Dominican friar named Tetzel was hawking indulgences throughout much of northern Germany, deliberately giving people the impression that an indulgence was an automatic ticket to heaven for oneself or one's loved ones in purgatory. For Luther, this was doubly offensive: not only was Tetzel violating Luther's conviction that people are saved by faith, not works, he was also misleading people into thinking that if they purchased an indulgence, then they no longer needed to confess their sins to a priest. Tetzel was thus putting their very salvation at risk. So on October 31, 1517, Luther offered to his university colleagues a list of ninety-five theses objecting to Catholic indulgence doctrine, an act conventionally seen as the beginning of the Protestant Reformation.

Luther wrote his theses in Latin, not German, and meant them only for academic discussion within the University of Wittenberg. But when some unknown person translated and published Luther's theses, the hitherto obscure monk suddenly gained widespread notoriety. Tetzel and his allies demanded that Luther withdraw his theses. Rather than backing down, however, Luther became even bolder in his attacks on the church hierarchy. In 1519, in a public disputation held before throngs in Leipzig, Luther defiantly maintained that the pope and all clerics were merely fallible men and that the highest authority for an individual's conscience was the truth of the Bible. Pope Leo X responded by charging Luther with heresy; after that Luther had no alternative but to break with the Catholic Church entirely.

Luther's year of greatest creative activity came in 1520 when, in the midst of the crisis caused by his defiance, he composed a series of pamphlets setting forth his three primary theological premises: justification by faith, the primacy of scripture, and "the priesthood of all believers." We have already examined the meaning of the first premise. By the second he simply meant that the literal meaning of scripture took precedence over church traditions and that beliefs (such as purgatory) or practices (such as prayers to the saints) not explicitly grounded in scripture could be rejected as human inventions. Luther also declared all Christian believers to be spiritually equal before God. Denying that priests, monks, and nuns had any special spiritual qualities by virtue of their vocations, Luther argued instead for "the priesthood of all believers."

From these premises a host of practical consequences followed. Because works could not lead to salvation, Luther declared fasts, pilgrimages, and the veneration of relics to be spiritually valueless. He also called for the dissolution of all monasteries and convents. He also took steps to "demystify" the rites of the church, proposing the substitution of German for Latin in church services and reducing the number of sacraments

Denying that priests, monks, and nuns had any special spiritual qualities by virtue of their vocations, Luther argued instead for "the priesthood of all believers."

from seven to two (baptism and the Eucharist). To further emphasize that those who presided in churches had no supernatural authority, he insisted on calling them ministers or pastors rather than priests. He also proposed to abolish the entire ecclesiastical hierarchy of popes, bishops, and archdeacons. Finally, firm in the belief that no spiritual distinction existed between clergy and laity, Luther argued that ministers could marry, and in 1525 he took a wife himself.

THE BREAK WITH ROME

Luther's brilliant polemical pamphlets of 1520 electrified much of Germany, gaining him passionate popular support and touching off a national religious revolt against the papacy. As word of Luther's defiance spread, his pamphlets became a publishing sensation. Whereas the average press run of a printed book before 1520 had been 1,000 copies, the first run of *To the Christian Nobility* (1520) was 4,000, which sold out in a few days. Many more thousands of copies quickly followed. Even more popular were woodcut illustrations mocking the papacy and exalting Luther. These sold in the tens of thousands and could be readily understood even by the illiterate.

Luther's denunciations of the papacy reflected widespread public dissatisfaction with recent popes. Pope Alexander VI (1492–1503) had bribed the cardinals to gain the papacy, used the money raised from the jubilee of 1500 to support the military campaigns of his son Cesare, and was so morally corrupt that he was suspected of incest with his own daughter. Julius II (1503–1513) devoted his reign to enlarging the Papal States through war; a contemporary remarked of him that he would have gained the greatest glory if only he had been a secular prince. Leo X (1513–1521), Luther's opponent, was a member of the Medici family of Florence. Although not spectacularly corrupt or immoral, he was a self-indulgent aesthete who, in the words of a modern Catholic historian, "would not have been deemed fit to be a doorkeeper in the house of the Lord had he lived in the days of the apostles."

In Germany, however, resentment of the papacy ran especially high. Because fifteenth-century Germany was so politically fractured, there were no agreements (known as concordats) between pope and emperor limiting papal authority in Germany, as there were

Pope Leo X. Raphael's highly realistic portrait shows the pope with two of his nephews.

with the rulers of Spain, France, and England. As a result, by 1500 the German princes were complaining that papal taxes were so high they were draining the country of its coin. But despite paying such large sums of money to Rome, Germans had almost no influence over papal policy. Frenchmen, Spaniards, and Italians dominated the college of cardinals and the papal bureaucracy, and the popes themselves were invariably Italian (as they would continue to be until 1978). As a result, graduates from the rapidly growing German universities almost never found employment in Rome. Instead, many joined the throngs of Luther's supporters to become leaders of the new religious movement.

THE DIET OF WORMS

Luther's personal drama was now moving swiftly toward a crisis. Late in 1520, Luther responded to Pope Leo X's bull ordering him to recant by casting not only the bull but all of church law onto a roaring bonfire in front of a huge crowd. Because in the eyes of the church Luther was now a stubborn heretic, he was formally "released" for punishment to his lay overlord, the

elector Frederick the Wise of Saxony. Frederick, however, was loath to silence the pope's antagonist. Rather than burning Luther at the stake for heresy, Frederick declared that Luther had not yet received a fair hearing. Early in 1521, he therefore brought him to the city of Worms to be examined by a formal assembly (a "diet") of the princes of the Holy Roman Empire.

At Worms the initiative lay with the presiding officer, the newly elected Holy Roman emperor, Charles V. Charles was not a German; indeed, it is doubtful if he had any national identity at all. As a member of the Habsburg family, he had been born and bred in his ancestral holding of the Netherlands. By 1521, however, through the unpredictable workings of dynastic inheritance, marriage, election, and luck, he had become not only the ruler of the Netherlands but also king of Germany and Holy Roman emperor, duke of Austria, duke of Milan, and ruler of Franche-Comté. As the grandson of Ferdinand and Isabella on his mother's side, he was also king of Spain; king of Naples, Sicily, and Sardinia; and ruler of all the Spanish possessions in the New World.

Governing such an extraordinary combination of territories posed enormous challenges. Charles's empire had no capital and no centralized administrative institutions; it shared no common language, no common culture, and no geographically contiguous borders. It thus stood completely apart from the growing nationalism of late medieval political life. Charles recognized the diversity of his empire and tried wherever possible to rule it through local officials and institutions. But he could not tolerate threats to the two fundamental forces that held his empire together: the emperor himself and Catholicism. Beyond such political calculations, however, Charles was also a faithful and committed Catholic, who was deeply disturbed by the prospect of heresy within his empire. There was therefore little doubt that the Diet of Worms would condemn Martin Luther for heresy. But when Luther refused to back down, even before the emperor himself, Frederick the Wise once more intervened, this time by arranging a "kidnapping" whereby Luther was spirited off to the elector's castle of the Wartburg and kept out of harm's way for a year.

Thereafter Luther was never again to be in danger of his life. Although the Diet of Worms proclaimed him an outlaw, this edict was never enforced. Instead, Luther went into hiding, and Charles V left Germany to conduct a war with France. In 1522 Luther returned in triumph from the Wartburg to Wittenberg to find that the changes he had called for in ecclesiastical government and worship had already been put into practice by his university supporters. Then, in rapid succession, several German princes formally converted to Lutheranism, bringing their territories with them. By 1530, a considerable part of Germany had thus been brought over to the new faith.

THE EMPIRE OF CHARLES V, C. 1550

Note the dispersed lands Charles V ruled directly through inheritance and marriage; as Holy Roman emperor, he was also the titular ruler of Germany. Which countries and rulers were most threatened by Charles's extraordinary combination of territories? Where might these threatened rulers and countries look for allies against Charles V? How did the threat posed by the Ottoman Empire complicate the political and religious struggles within Christian Europe?

THE GERMAN PRINCES AND THE LUTHERAN REFORMATION

At this point, then, the last of the three major questions regarding the early history of Lutheranism arises: Why did some German princes, secure in their own powers, nonetheless heed Luther's call by establishing Lutheran religious practices within their territories? This is a crucial question, because despite Luther's popular support, his cause surely would have failed had it not been embraced by a number of powerful German princes and free cities. In 1520, Luther was more or less equally popular throughout Germany, but it was only in those territories where rulers formally established Lutheranism (mostly in the north) that the new religion prevailed. Elsewhere, Luther's sympathizers were forced to flee, face death, or conform to Catholicism.

Luther recognized that he could never hope to institute new religious practices without the strong arm of the princes behind him. At first the princes bided their time, but when they realized that Luther had enormous public support and that Charles V would not act swiftly to defend the Catholic faith, several moved to introduce Lutheranism into their territories. Personal piety surely played a role in individual cases, but political and economic considerations were more generally decisive. By instituting Lutheranism within their territories, Protestant princes could consolidate their authority by naming pastors, cutting off fees to Rome, and curtailing the jurisdiction of church courts. They could also guarantee that the political and religious boundaries of their territories would now coincide. No longer, therefore, would a rival ecclesiastical prince (such as a bishop or archbishop) be able to use his spiritual position to undermine a neighboring secular prince's sovereignty over his territory.

Similar considerations also moved a number of free cities (so called because they were not ruled by territorial princes) to adopt Lutheranism. By adopting the

The Seven-Headed Papal Beast. Around 1530 a Lutheran cartoon was circulated in Germany that turned the papacy into the "seven-headed beast" of the Book of Revelation. The papacy's seven heads consist of pope, cardinals, bishops, and priests; the sign on the cross reads "for money, a sack full of indulgences"; and a devil is seen emerging from an indulgence treasure chest below.

The Seven-Headed Martin Luther. In response, a German Catholic propagandist showed Luther as Revelation's "beast." In the Catholic conception Luther's seven heads show him by turn to be a hypocrite, a fanatic, and "Barabbas"—the thief who should have been crucified instead of Jesus.

new religion, town councils and guild masters could establish themselves (rather than local aristocrats or bishops) as the supreme governing authority within their towns. Given the added fact that under Lutheranism monasteries and convents could be shut down and their lands appropriated by the newly sovereign secular authorities, the practical advantages of the new faith were overwhelming, quite apart from any considerations of religious zeal.

Once safely ensconced in Wittenberg under princely protection, Luther began to express ever more vehemently his own profound conservatism in political and social matters. In a treatise of 1523, *On Temporal Authority*, he insisted that "godly" rulers must be obeyed in all things and that even ungodly ones should never be actively resisted since tyranny "is not to be resisted but endured." Then, in 1525, when peasants throughout Germany rebelled against their landlords, Luther responded with intense hostility. In his vituperative pamphlet of 1525, *Against the Thievish, Murderous Hordes of Peasants*, he urged all who could to hunt the rebels down like mad dogs, to "strike, strangle, stab secretly or in public, and remember that nothing can be more poisonous than a man in rebellion." After the ruthless suppression of the Peasants' Revolt (which may have cost as many as 100,000 lives), the firm alliance of Lutheranism with state power helped preserve and sanction the existing social order. Never again would there be a mass lower-class uprising in Germany.

As for Luther himself, he concentrated in his last years on debating with younger, more radical religious reformers and on offering spiritual counsel to all who sought it. Never tiring in his amazingly prolific literary

activity, he wrote an average of one treatise every two weeks for twenty-five years. To the end Luther was unswerving in his new faith: on his deathbed in 1546 he responded to the question "Will you stand firm in Christ and the doctrine which you have preached?" with a resolute yes.

THE SPREAD OF PROTESTANTISM

Why did Switzerland emerge as such an important center for sixteenth-century Protestantism?

Originating as a term applied to Lutherans who "protested" an action of the German Imperial Diet of 1529, the word *Protestant* was soon applied to a much wider range of European Christians in rebellion against Rome. Lutheranism itself struck lasting roots only in northern Germany and Scandinavia. Elsewhere in Europe, competing forms of Protestantism soon emerged from the seeds that Luther had sown. By the 1550s, Protestantism had become an international movement; in so doing, however, it also split into a number of competing traditions.

THE REFORMATION IN SWITZERLAND

In the early sixteenth century Switzerland was neither ruled by kings nor dominated by all-powerful territorial princes; instead, prosperous Swiss cities were either independent or on the verge of becoming so. Hence when the leading citizens of a Swiss municipality decided to adopt Protestant reforms no one could stop them, and Protestantism in Switzerland could usually take its own course. Although religious arrangements varied from city to city, three main forms of Protestantism emerged in Switzerland between 1520 and 1550: Zwinglianism, Anabaptism, and Calvinism.

ULRICH ZWINGLI

Zwinglianism, founded by Ulrich Zwingli (*ZWIHNG-lee*; 1484–1531) in Zürich, was the most theologically moderate form of the three. Although Zwingli began his career as a somewhat indifferent Catholic priest, around 1516 his humanist-inspired study of the Bible

---

CHRONOLOGY	
ORIGINS OF THE REFORMATION, 1450–1529	
Christian humanists call for reforms	1400s–1500s
Growth of German universities	1450–1517
Luther posts the Ninety-five Theses	1517
Luther charged with heresy	1519
Publication of Lutheran theological premises	1520
Diet of Worms declares Luther an outlaw	1521
Peasant Revolt defeated	1525
Luther's break with Zwingli	1529

WHY DID SWITZERLAND EMERGE AS SUCH AN IMPORTANT CENTER FOR SIXTEENTH-CENTURY PROTESTANTISM?

THE SPREAD OF PROTESTANTISM   353

convinced him that Catholic theology and practice conflicted with the Gospels. But he did not speak out publicly until Luther set the precedent. In 1522, however, Zwingli began attacking the authority of the Catholic Church in Zürich. Soon all Zürich and much of northern Switzerland had accepted his religious leadership. Zwingli's reforms closely resembled those of the Lutherans in Germany. Zwingli differed from Luther, however, concerning the theology of the Eucharist: whereas Luther believed in the real presence of Christ's body in the sacrament, for Zwingli the Eucharist conferred no grace at all; it was simply a reminder and communal celebration of Christ's historical sacrifice on the cross. This fundamental disagreement prevented Lutherans and Zwinglians from uniting in a common Protestant front. Zwingli fell in battle against Catholic forces in 1531. Soon thereafter, his movement was absorbed by the more systematic Protestantism of John Calvin.

ANABAPTISM

Before Calvinism prevailed, however, an even more radical form of Protestantism arose in Switzerland and Germany. The first Anabaptists were members of Zwingli's circle in Zürich, but they broke with him around 1525 on the issue of infant baptism. Because Anabaptists were convinced that the sacrament of baptism was only effective if administered to willing adults who understood its significance, they rejected infant baptism altogether and required followers who had been baptized as infants to be baptized again as adults (the term *Anabaptism* means "rebaptism"). This doctrine reflected the Anabaptists' fundamental belief that the true church was a small community of believers gathered out of the world whose members had to make a deliberate, inspired decision to join it. No other Protestant groups were prepared to go so far in rejecting the medieval Christian view of the church as a single body to which all members of society belonged from birth. Yet in its first few years the movement did gain numerous adherents in Switzerland and Germany, above all because it appealed to sincere religious piety in calling for extreme simplicity of worship, pacifism, and strict personal morality.

Disastrously, however, an unrepresentative group of Anabaptist extremists managed to gain control of the German city of Münster in 1534. These zealots believed that God wished to institute a completely new order throughout the world, beginning with Münster, which they declared the new Jerusalem. Anabaptist religious practices were made obligatory; private property was abolished; and even polygamy was permitted on the grounds of Old Testament precedents. Such practices

The Anabaptists' Cages, Then and Now. After the three Anabaptist leaders who had reigned in Münster for a year were executed in 1535, their corpses were prominently displayed in cages hung from a tower of the marketplace church. As can be seen from the photo on the right, the bones are now gone but the iron cages remain to this very day as a grisly reminder of the horrors of sixteenth-century religious strife.

were deeply shocking to both Protestants and Catholics alike. Münster was besieged and captured by Catholic forces little more than a year after the Anabaptist takeover, and the Anabaptist leaders were put to death by excruciating tortures. Thereafter, Anabaptists throughout Europe were ruthlessly persecuted from all sides. Among the few who survived were some who banded together in the Mennonite sect, named for its founder, the Dutchman Menno Simons (c. 1496–1561). This sect, dedicated to pacifism and the simple "religion of the heart" of original Anabaptism, has continued to exist to the present day.

RELIGIOUS SITUATION IN EUROPE, C. 1560

The religious boundaries of Europe around 1560, roughly forty years after Martin Luther's movement began, were quite complicated. To what extent did the religious divisions of Europe follow its political boundaries? How would you account for the dispersed areas in which Calvinists predominated? Why did Lutheranism spread north into Scandinavia but not south into Bavaria or west across the Rhine?

WHY DID SWITZERLAND EMERGE AS SUCH AN IMPORTANT CENTER FOR SIXTEENTH-CENTURY PROTESTANTISM?

THE SPREAD OF PROTESTANTISM   355

JOHN CALVIN'S REFORMED THEOLOGY

A year after events in Münster sealed the fate of Anabaptism, a twenty-six-year-old French Protestant named John Calvin (1509–1564), who had fled to the Swiss city of Basel to escape religious persecution, published the first version of his *Institutes of the Christian Religion*, the most influential systematic formulation of Protestant theology ever written. Born in northern France, Calvin originally had been trained for the law. But then, as he later wrote, while he was "obstinately devoted to the superstitions of Popery," a stroke of light made him feel that God was extricating him from "an abyss of filth." He thereupon became a Protestant theologian and propagandist.

Although some of these details resemble the early career of Luther, the two men were very different figures. Luther was an emotionally volatile personality and a controversialist. He responded to theological problems as they arose or as the impulse struck him, but he never attempted to write systematic theology. Calvin, however, was a coolly analytical legalist, who resolved in his *Institutes* to set forth all the principles of Protestantism comprehensively, logically, and systematically. As a result, after several revisions and enlargements (the definitive edition appeared in 1559), Calvin's *Institutes* became the most theologically authoritative statement of Protestant beliefs and the nearest Protestant equivalent to Saint Thomas Aquinas's *Summa Theologica*.

Calvin's austere theology started with the omnipotence of God and worked downward. For Calvin the entire universe depends utterly on the will of the Almighty, who created all things for his greater glory. Because of the original fall from grace, all human beings are sinners by nature, heirs to an evil inheritance they cannot escape. Nevertheless, the Lord for reasons of his own has predestined some for eternal salvation and damned all the rest to the torments of hell. Nothing that human beings may do can alter their fate; their souls are stamped with God's blessing or curse before they are born. Nevertheless, Christians cannot be indifferent to their conduct on earth. If they are among the elect, God will implant in them the desire to live according to his laws. Upright conduct is thus a sign, though not an infallible one, that an individual has been chosen for salvation. Membership in the reformed church (as Calvinist churches are often known) is another presumptive sign

> Calvin also insisted on the utmost simplicity in worship, prohibiting (among much else) vestments, processions, instrumental music, and religious images of any sort—including stained-glass windows.

of election to salvation. But most of all, Calvin urged Christians to conceive of themselves as chosen instruments of God, charged to work actively to fulfill God's purposes on earth. Because sin offends God, Christians should do all they can to prevent it, not because their actions will lead to anyone's salvation (they will not) but simply because God's glory is diminished if sin is allowed to flourish unchecked by the efforts of those whom he has chosen for glory.

Calvin always acknowledged a great theological debt to Luther, but his religious teachings differed from those of the Wittenberg reformer in several essentials. First of all, Luther's attitude toward proper Christian conduct in the world was much more passive than Calvin's. For Luther, a Christian should endure the trials of this life in suffering, whereas for Calvin the world was to be mastered in unceasing labor for God's sake. Calvin's religion was also more legalistic than Luther's. Luther, for example, insisted that his followers attend church on Sunday, but he did not demand that during the remainder of the day they refrain from all pleasure or work. Calvin, on the other hand, issued stern strictures against worldliness of any sort on the Sabbath day of rest and forbade all sorts of minor self-indulgences even on non-Sabbath days.

The two men also differed on fundamental matters of church government and worship. Although Luther broke with the Catholic system of hierarchical church governance, Lutheran district superintendents continued to exercise some of the powers of bishops, including supervision of the parish clergy. Luther also retained many features of traditional worship, including altars, music, ritual, and vestments (special clothing for the clergy). Calvin, however, rejected everything that smacked to him of "popery." Each congregation should elect its own ministers, and assemblies of ministers and "elders" (laymen responsible for maintaining proper religious conduct among the faithful) were to govern the reformed church as a whole. Calvin also insisted on the utmost simplicity in worship, prohibiting (among much else) vestments, processions, instrumental music, and religious images of any sort—including stained-glass windows. He also dispensed with all remaining vestiges of Catholic sacramental theology by making the sermon, rather than the Eucharist, the centerpiece of reformed worship. When these teachings were put into practice, Calvinist services became little more than "four bare walls and a sermon."

CALVINISM IN GENEVA

Calvin was intent on putting his religious teachings into practice. Sensing an opportunity in the French-speaking Swiss city of Geneva, he moved there late in 1536 and began preaching and organizing. In 1538 his activities caused him to be expelled, but in 1541 he returned and the city soon came completely under his sway. Under Calvin's guidance Geneva's government became a theocracy. Supreme authority was vested in a "Consistory" composed of twelve lay elders and between ten and twenty pastors, whose weekly meetings Calvin dominated. Aside from passing legislation proposed to it by a congregation of ministers, the Consistory's main function was to supervise morality, both public and private. To this end, Geneva was divided into districts, and a committee of the Consistory visited every household without warning to check on the behavior of its members. Dancing, card playing, attending the theater, and working or playing on the Sabbath—all were outlawed as works of the devil. Innkeepers were forbidden to allow anyone to consume food or drink without first saying grace or to permit any patron to stay up after nine o'clock. Murder, treason, adultery, "witchcraft," blasphemy, and heresy were all capital crimes. Even penalties for lesser crimes were severe. During the first four years after Calvin gained control in Geneva, there were no fewer than fifty-eight executions out of a total population of only 16,000.

As objectionable as such interference in the private sphere may seem today, in the mid-sixteenth century Calvin's Geneva was a beacon of light to thousands of Protestants throughout Europe. Calvin's disciple John Knox, who brought reformed religion to Scotland, declared Geneva under Calvin "the most perfect school of Christ that ever was on earth since the days of the Apostles." Converts such as Knox flocked to Geneva for refuge or instruction and then returned home to become ardent proselytizers for the new religion. Geneva thus became the center of an international movement dedicated to spreading reformed religion to France and the rest of Europe through organized missionary activity and propaganda.

These missionary efforts were remarkably successful. By the end of the sixteenth century, Calvinists were a majority in Scotland (where they were known as Presbyterians), Holland (where they founded the Dutch Reformed Church), and England (where the Church of England adopted reformed theology but not reformed worship; Calvinists who sought further reforms in worship were known as Puritans). There were also substantial Calvinist minorities in France (where they were called Huguenots), Germany, Hungary, Lithuania, and Poland. God's kingdom on earth had not yet been fully realized; on his deathbed in 1564, Calvin pronounced the Genevans to be still "a perverse and unhappy nation." But an extraordinary revolution had taken place nonetheless in the religious life and practice of Europe.

THE DOMESTICATION OF THE REFORMATION, 1525–1560

How did notions of family and marriage change during the Reformation?

Protestantism had begun as a revolutionary doctrine whose radical claims for the spiritual equality of all true Christian believers had the potential to undermine the social, religious, political, and even gender hierarchies on which European society rested. Luther himself seems not to have anticipated that his ideas might have such implications, and he was genuinely shocked when the rebellious German peasants and the religious millenarianists at Münster interpreted his teachings in this way. In response to the social and political radicals, the social ideology of the Reformation movement became increasingly conservative after 1525. The Protestant reformers began to emphasize the patriarchal family as the central institution of reformed life.

REFORM AND DISCIPLINE

Protestant rulers took the need to enforce godly discipline on their people with particular seriousness, because the depravity of human nature was a fundamental tenet of their Protestant beliefs. Like Saint Augustine at the end of the fourth century, Protestants believed that people would inevitably turn out badly unless they were compelled to be good. It was, therefore, the responsibility of pastors and magistrates to discipline and control the behavior of their people—not because their good deeds would lead them to heaven but because

HOW DID NOTIONS OF FAMILY AND MARRIAGE CHANGE DURING THE REFORMATION?

THE DOMESTICATION OF THE REFORMATION, 1525–1560   357

their evil deeds would anger God and destroy human society.

Protestant godly discipline began with the education of children. Luther himself wrote two catechisms (statements of belief) to teach children the tenets of their faith and the obligations—toward parents, masters, and rulers—that God imposed on them. Luther also insisted that all children, boys and girls alike, should be taught to read the Bible in their own vernacular language. Schooling thus became a characteristically Protestant preoccupation. Even the Protestant family was conceived of as a "school of godliness," in which fathers were expected to instruct and discipline their wives, their children, and their household servants.

But family life in the early sixteenth century still left much to be desired in the eyes of Protestant reformers. Drunkenness, domestic violence, illicit sexual relations, lascivious dancing, and the blasphemous swearing of oaths were commonplace, even among the religiously reformed. Various methods were tried by Protestant congregations to discipline their unruly members, including private counseling, public confessions of wrongdoing, public penances and shamings, exclusion from church services, and even imprisonment. All these efforts met with varying, but generally modest, success. To create godly Protestant families, and to enforce godly discipline on entire communities, was going to require the active cooperation of godly authorities in both church and state.

> Because marriage involved rights of inheritance to property, most families regarded it as far too important a matter to be left to the free choice of their children.

PROTESTANTISM AND THE FAMILY

Protestantism brought a new emphasis on the family as a "school of godliness," in which an all-powerful father figure was expected to assume responsibility for instructing and disciplining his household according to the precepts of reformed religion. At the same time, Protestantism also introduced a new religious ideal for women. No longer was the celibate nun the exemplar of female holiness; in her place now stood the married and obedient Protestant "goodwife." As one Lutheran prince wrote in 1527: "Those who bear children please God better than all the monks and nuns singing and praying." To this extent, Protestantism resolved the tensions between piety and sexuality that had characterized late medieval Catholicism by declaring firmly in favor of the holiness of marital sexuality.

This did not reflect a newly elevated view of women's spiritual potential, however—quite the contrary. Luther, like his medieval predecessors, continued to regard women as more sexually driven than men and less capable of controlling their sexual desires (although, to be fair, Luther had only a slightly higher view of men's capacity for celibacy). His opposition to convents rested on his belief that, except in extraordinary circumstances, it was impossible for women to remain celibate, so convents simply made illicit sexual behavior inevitable. To control women and prevent sin, it was therefore necessary that all women should be married, preferably at a young age, and so placed under the governance of a godly husband.

PROTESTANTISM AND CONTROL OVER MARRIAGE

Protestantism also increased parents' control over their children's choice of marital partners. The medieval Catholic Church defined marriage as a sacrament that did not require the involvement of a priest. The mutual free consent of the two parties, even if given without witnesses or parental approval, was enough to constitute a legally valid marriage in the eyes of the church; at the same time, however, the church would annul a marriage if either of the parties could prove that they had not freely consented to it. Opposition to this doctrine came from many quarters, but especially from parents and other relatives. Because marriage involved rights of inheritance to property, most families regarded it as far too important a matter to be left to the free choice of their children. Instead, parents wanted the power to prevent unsuitable matches and, ideally, to force their children to accept the marriage arrangements their families might negotiate on their behalf. Protestantism offered an opportunity to achieve such control. Luther had declared marriage to be a purely secular matter, not a sacrament at all, that could be regulated however the governing authorities thought best. Calvin largely followed suit, although Calvinist theocracy drew less of a distinction than did Lutheranism between the powers of church and state. Even Catholicism was eventually forced to give way. Although it never entirely abandoned its insistence that

MARRIAGE AND CELIBACY: TWO VIEWS

These two selections illustrate the strongly contrasting views on the spiritual value of marriage versus celibacy that came to be embraced by Protestant and Catholic religious authorities. The first selection is part of Martin Luther's more general attack on monasticism but emphasizes his view that marriage is the natural and divinely intended state for all human beings. The second selection, from the decrees of the Council of Trent (1545–1563), restates traditional Catholic teaching on the holiness of marriage but also emphasizes the spiritual superiority of virginity to marriage and the necessity of clerical celibacy.

LUTHER ON CELIBACY AND WOMEN

Listen! In all my days I have not heard the confession of a nun, but in the light of Scripture I shall hit upon how matters fare with her and know I shall not be lying. If a girl is not sustained by great and exceptional grace, she can live without a man as little as she can without eating, drinking, sleeping, and other natural necessities. Nor, on the other hand, can a man dispense with a wife. The reason for this is that procreating children is an urge planted as deeply in human nature as eating and drinking. That is why God has given and put into the body the organs, arteries, fluxes, and everything that serves it. Therefore what is he doing who would check this process and keep nature from running its desired and intended course? He is attempting to keep nature from being nature, fire from burning, water from wetting, and a man from eating, drinking, and sleeping.

E. M. Plass, ed., *What Luther Says* (St. Louis, 1959), pp. 2:888–889.

CANNONS ON THE SACRAMENT OF MATRIMONY (1563)

Canon 1. If anyone says that matrimony is not truly and properly one of the seven sacraments . . . instituted by Christ the Lord, but has been devised by men in the Church and does not confer grace, let him be anathema [cursed].

Canon 9. If anyone says that clerics constituted in sacred orders or regulars who have made solemn profession of chastity can contract marriage . . . and that all who feel that they have not the gift of chastity, even though they have made such a vow, can contract marriage, let him be anathema, since God does not refuse that gift to those who ask for it rightly, neither does *he suffer us to be tempted above that which we are able* [I Cor. 10:13].

Canon 10: If anyone says that the married state excels the state of virginity or celibacy, and that it is better and happier to be united in matrimony than to remain in virginity or celibacy, let him be anathema.

H. J. Schroeder, *Canons and Decrees of the Council of Trent* (St. Louis and London, 1941), pp. 181–182.

QUESTION FOR ANALYSIS

1. Why did Luther believe that the monastic demands for celibacy were impossible to meet? How important an issue was celibacy in the context of sixteenth-century religious conflicts?

both members of the couple must freely consent to their marriage, by the end of the sixteenth century the Catholic Church required formal public notice of intent to marry and insisted on the presence of a priest at the actual wedding ceremony. Both were efforts to prevent elopements, allowing families time to intervene before an unsuitable marriage was concluded. Individual Catholic countries sometimes went even further in trying to reassert parental control over their children's choice of marital partners. In France, for example, although couples might still marry without parental consent, those who did so now forfeited all of their rights to inherit their families' property. In somewhat different ways, both Protestantism and Catholicism thus moved to strengthen the control that parents could exercise over their children—and, in the case of Protestantism, that husbands could exercise over their wives.

THE ENGLISH REFORMATION

Why did England become a Protestant country?

In England, the Reformation took a rather different course than it did in continental Europe. By 1527 the imperious King Henry VIII had been married for eighteen years to Ferdinand and Isabella's daughter Catherine of Aragon, yet all the offspring of this union had died in infancy, save only Princess Mary. Because Henry needed a male heir to preserve the succession of his Tudor dynasty and because Catherine was now past childbearing age, Henry had good reasons of state to break his marriage bonds. He also had more personal motives, having become infatuated with a dark-eyed lady-in-waiting named Anne Boleyn. To marry Anne, Henry appealed to Rome to annul his marriage to Catherine, arguing that because Queen Catherine had previously been married to Henry's older brother Arthur (who had died shortly after the ceremony was performed), Henry's marriage to Catherine had been invalid from the beginning. As Henry's representatives pointed out, the Bible pronounced it "an unclean thing" for a man to take his brother's wife and cursed such a marriage with childlessness (Leviticus 20:31). Even a papal dispensation (which Henry and Catherine had obtained for their marriage) could not dispose of such a clear prohibition, as the marriage's childlessness proved.

HENRY VIII AND THE BREAK WITH ROME

Henry's suit put Pope Clement VII (1523–1534) in a quandary. Both Henry and Clement knew that popes in the past had granted annulments to reigning monarchs on far weaker grounds than the ones Henry was alleging. If, however, the pope granted Henry's annulment he would cast doubt on the validity of all papal dispensations. More seriously, however, he would also provoke the wrath of the emperor Charles V, Catherine of Aragon's nephew, whose armies were in firm command of Rome and who at that moment held the pope himself in captivity. Clement was trapped; all he could do was procrastinate and hope for better days. For two years, he allowed the suit to proceed in England without ever reaching a verdict. Then, suddenly, he transferred the case to Rome, where the legal process began all over again.

Exasperated by these delays, Henry began to increase the pressure on the pope. In 1531 he compelled an assembly of English clergy to declare him "protector and only supreme head" of the church in England. In January 1533, Henry married Anne Boleyn (already

Henry VIII, by Hans Holbein the Younger.

pregnant) even though his marriage to Queen Catherine had still not been annulled. (The new archbishop of Canterbury, Thomas Cranmer, provided the required annulment in May.) In September, Princess Elizabeth was born; her father, disappointed again in his hopes for a son, refused to attend her christening. Nevertheless, Parliament settled the succession to the throne on the children of Henry and Anne, redirected all papal revenues from England into the king's hands, prohibited appeals to the papal court, and formally declared "the King's highness to be Supreme Head of the Church of England [having] the authority to redress all errors, heresies, and abuses." In 1536, Henry executed Sir Thomas More for his refusal to endorse this declaration of supremacy and took the first steps toward dissolving England's monasteries. By the end of 1539, the monasteries and convents were gone and their lands and wealth confiscated by the king, who distributed them to his supporters.

These measures broke the bonds that linked the English church to Rome, but they did not make England a Protestant country. Although certain traditional practices (such as pilgrimages and relics) were prohibited, the English church remained overwhelmingly Catholic in organization, doctrine, ritual, and language. The Six Articles promulgated by Parliament in 1539 at Henry VIII's behest left no room for doubt as to official orthodoxy: oral confession to priests, masses for the dead, and clerical celibacy were all confirmed; the Latin Mass continued; and Catholic eucharistic doctrine was not only confirmed but its denial made punishable by death. To most English people, only the disappearance of the monasteries and the king's own continuing matrimonial adventures (he married six wives in all) gave certain evidence that their church was no longer part of the Roman obedience.

EDWARD VI

For truly committed Protestants, and especially those who had visited Calvin's Geneva, the changes Henry VIII enforced on the English church did not go nearly far enough. In 1547, the accession of the nine-year-old king Edward VI (Henry's son with his third wife, Jane Seymour) gave them their opportunity to finish the task of reformation. Encouraged by the clear Protestant sympathies of the young king himself, Edward's government moved quickly to reform the creeds and ceremonies of the English church. Priests were permitted to marry; English services replaced Latin ones; the veneration of images was abolished,

and the images themselves defaced or destroyed; prayers for the dead were abolished and endowments for such prayers were confiscated; and new articles of belief were drawn up, repudiating all sacraments except baptism and communion and affirming the Protestant doctrine of justification by faith alone. Most important, a new prayer book was published to define precisely how the new, English-language services of the church were to be conducted. Much remained unsettled with respect to both doctrine and worship; but by 1553, when the youthful Edward died, the English church appeared to have become a distinctly Protestant institution.

MARY TUDOR AND THE RESTORATION OF CATHOLICISM

Edward's successor, however, was his pious and deeply Catholic sister Mary (1553–1558), Henry VIII's daughter with Catherine of Aragon. Mary speedily reversed her brother's religious policies, restoring the Latin Mass and requiring married priests to give up their wives. She even prevailed on Parliament to vote a return to papal allegiance. Hundreds of Protestant leaders fled abroad, many to Geneva; others, including Archbishop Thomas Cranmer, were burned at the stake for refusing to abjure their Protestantism. News of the martyrdoms spread like wildfire through Protestant Europe. In England, however, Mary's policies sparked relatively little outright resistance at the local level. After two decades of religious upheaval, most English men and women were probably hoping that Mary's reign would bring some stability to their religious lives.

This, however, Mary could not do. The executions she ordered were insufficient to wipe out religious resistance—instead, Protestant propaganda about "Bloody Mary" and the "fires of Smithfield" caused widespread disaffection, even among those who welcomed the return of traditional religious forms. Nor could she do anything to restore monasticism: too many leading families had profited from Henry VIII's dissolution of the monasteries for this to be reversed. Mary's marriage to her cousin Philip, Charles V's son and heir to the Spanish throne, was another miscalculation. Although the marriage treaty stipulated that in the event of Mary's death Philip could not succeed her, her English subjects never trusted him. When the queen allowed herself to be drawn by Philip into a war with France on Spain's behalf in which England lost

Calais, its last foothold on the European continent, many English people became highly disaffected. Ultimately, however, what doomed Mary's religious counterrevoution were simply the accidents of biology. Mary was unable to conceive an heir, and when she died after only six years of rule, her throne passed to her Protestant sister, Elizabeth.

THE ELIZABETHAN RELIGIOUS SETTLEMENT

The daughter of Henry VIII and Anne Boleyn, and one of the most capable and popular monarchs ever to sit on the English throne, Queen Elizabeth I (1558–1603) was predisposed in favor of Protestantism by the circumstances of her parents' marriage as well as by her upbringing. But Elizabeth was no zealot and wisely recognized that supporting radical Protestantism in England might provoke bitter sectarian strife. Accordingly, she presided over what is customarily known as "the Elizabethan settlement." By a new Act of Supremacy (1559), Elizabeth repealed Mary's Catholic legislation, prohibiting foreign religious powers (that is, the pope) from exercising any authority within England and declaring herself "supreme governor" of the English church—a more Protestant title than Henry VIII's "supreme head" insofar as most Protestants believed that Christ alone was the head of the church. She also adopted many of the Protestant liturgical reforms instituted by her brother, Edward, including a revised version of the Edwardian prayer book. But she also retained vestiges of Catholic practice, including bishops, church courts, and vestments for the clergy. On most doctrinal matters, including predestination and free will, Elizabeth's Thirty-Nine Articles of Faith (approved in 1562) struck a decidedly Protestant, even Calvinist, tone. But the prayer book was more moderate, and on the critical issue of the Eucharist was deliberately ambiguous. By combining Catholic and Protestant interpretations ("this is my body. . . . Do this in remembrance of me") into a single declaration, the prayer book permitted an enormous latitude for competing interpretations of the service by priests and parishioners alike.

Despite such "latitudinarianism," religious tensions persisted in Elizabethan England, not only between Protestants and Catholics but also between moderate and more extreme Protestants. The queen's artful "fudging" of these differences was by no means a recipe guaranteed to succeed. Rather, what preserved the Elizabethan religious settlement, and ultimately made England a Protestant country, was the extraordinary length of Queen Elizabeth's reign combined with the fact that for much of that time Protestant England was at war with Catholic Spain. Under Elizabeth, Protestantism and English nationalism gradually fused together into a potent conviction that God himself had

Queen Elizabeth. Elizabeth managed to mediate between the Catholic and the Protestant faiths and became one of England's most popular monarchs.

CHRONOLOGY	
SPREAD OF PROTESTANTISM, 1520–1560	
Lutheranism becomes state religion in Denmark, Norway, and Sweden	1520s
England breaks with Rome	1534
Geneva adopts theocratic government based on Calvinism	1541
Calvinism spreads to Scotland, England, Netherlands, and France	1540–1560s
Elizabethan settlement	1559

chosen England for greatness. After 1588, when English naval forces won an improbable victory over the "invincible" Spanish Armada, Protestantism and Englishness became nearly indistinguishable to most of Queen Elizabeth's subjects. Laws against Catholic "recusants" became increasingly severe; and although an English Catholic tradition did survive, its adherents were a persecuted minority. Much more alarming was the situation in Ireland, where the vast majority of the population remained Catholic despite the government's efforts to impose Protestantism on them. By 1603, "Irishness" was as firmly identified with Catholicism as was "Englishness" with "Protestantism"; but it was the Protestants who were in the ascendant in both countries.

CATHOLICISM TRANSFORMED

How did the Catholic Reformation differ from the Counter-Reformation?

The historical novelty of Protestantism inevitably casts the spotlight on such religious reformers as Luther and Calvin, but there was also a powerful internal reform movement within the Catholic Church during the sixteenth century. Historians differ about whether to call this movement the "Catholic Reformation" or the "Counter-Reformation." Some prefer the former term because it emphasizes that significant efforts to reform the Catholic Church began before Luther posted his theses and continued long after. Others, however, insist that from the mid-sixteenth century on, most Catholic reformers were inspired primarily by the urgent need to resist the Protestant schism. We will use both terms to refer to two complementary phases of Catholic reform: a Catholic Reformation that came before Luther, and a Counter-Reformation that came after him.

> In northern Europe, Christian humanists such as Erasmus and Thomas More also played a role in this Catholic reform movement, not only by criticizing abuses and editing sacred texts but also by encouraging the laity to lead lives of simple but sincere religious piety.

THE CATHOLIC REFORMATION

The Catholic Reformation began around 1490, and was primarily a movement for moral and institutional reform within the religious orders. Although these efforts received strong support from several secular rulers, the papacy showed little interest in them. As a result, the Catholic Reformation never became a truly international movement. In Spain, reform activities directed by Cardinal Francisco Ximenes de Cisneros (1436–1517) and supported by the monarchy led to the imposition of strict rules of behavior on Franciscan friars and the elimination of abuses prevalent among the diocesan clergy. In Italy, reformers established several new religious orders dedicated to high ideals of piety and social service. In northern Europe, Christian humanists such as Erasmus and Thomas More also played a role in this Catholic reform movement, not only by criticizing abuses and editing sacred texts but also by encouraging the laity to lead lives of simple but sincere religious piety.

As a response to the challenges posed by Protestantism, however, the Catholic Reformation proved entirely inadequate. Starting in the 1530s, therefore, a second, more aggressive phase of reform under a new style of vigorous papal leadership began to gather momentum. The leading Counter-Reformation popes—Paul III (1534–1549), Paul IV (1555–1559), Saint Pius V (1566–1572), and Sixtus V (1585–1590)—were collectively the most zealous reforming popes since the High Middle Ages. All led upright personal lives. Some, indeed, were so grimly ascetic that contemporaries wondered whether they were not too holy. But these Counter-Reformation popes were not merely holy men. They were also accomplished administrators who reorganized papal finances and filled ecclesiastical offices with bishops and abbots no less renowned for austerity and holiness than were the popes themselves.

These papal reform efforts intensified at the Council of Trent, a general council of the entire church convoked by Paul III in 1545 and which met at intervals thereafter until 1563. The decisions taken at Trent provided the foundations on which a new, Counter-Reformation Catholic Church would be erected. Although the council began by debating some form of compromise with Protestantism, Trent ended by reaffirming all of the Catholic doctrinal tenets challenged by Protestant critics. Good works were declared necessary for salvation, and all seven sacraments were declared indispensable means of grace, without which salvation was impossible. Transubstantiation, purgatory, the invocation of saints, and the rule of

How did the Catholic Reformation differ from the Counter-Reformation?

Catholicism Transformed   363

celibacy for the clergy were all confirmed as essential elements in the Catholic system. The Bible and the traditions of apostolic teaching were held to be of equal authority as sources of Christian truth. The Council of Trent even reaffirmed the doctrine of indulgences that had touched off the Lutheran revolt, although it did condemn the worst abuses connected with their sale.

The legislation of Trent was not confined to matters of doctrine. To improve pastoral care of the laity, bishops and priests were forbidden to hold more than one spiritual office. A theological seminary was to be established in every diocese. The council also decided to censor or suppress dangerous books. In 1564, a specially appointed commission published the first Index

The Council of Trent. This fresco depicts the general council of the entire Catholic Church that met from 1545 to 1563 and produced the foundation for the new Counter-Reformation church.

of Prohibited Books, an official list of writings that ought not to be read by faithful Catholics. All of Erasmus's works were immediately placed on the Index, even though he had been a chosen Catholic champion against Martin Luther only forty years before: a chilling sign of the doctrinal intolerance that characterized sixteenth-century Christianity, both in its Catholic and Protestant varieties.

SAINT IGNATIUS LOYOLA AND THE SOCIETY OF JESUS

In addition to the independent activities of popes and the legislation of the Council of Trent, a third main force propelling the Counter-Reformation was the foundation of the Society of Jesus, commonly known as the Jesuit order, by Saint Ignatius Loyola (1491–1556). In the midst of a youthful career as a worldly soldier, the Spanish nobleman Loyola was wounded in battle in 1521 (the same year in which Luther defied Charles V at Worms). While recuperating, he decided to change his ways and become a spiritual soldier of Christ. For ten months he lived as a hermit, during which time he experienced ecstatic visions and worked out the principles of his subsequent meditational guide, the *Spiritual Exercises*. This manual, completed in 1535 and first published in 1541, offered practical advice on how to master one's will and serve God through a systematic program of meditations on sin and the life of Christ. Soon made a basic handbook for all Jesuits and widely studied by numerous Catholic laypeople as well, Loyola's *Spiritual Exercises* has had an influence second only to Calvin's *Institutes* among all the religious writings of the sixteenth century.

Originating as a small group of six disciples who gathered around Loyola in Paris in 1534, the Society of Jesus was formally constituted as an order of the church by Pope Paul III in 1540; by the time of Loyola's death it already numbered 1,500 members. The Society of Jesus was by far the most militant of the religious orders fostered by the Catholic reform movements of the sixteenth century. Its organization was patterned after that of a military company, with a general as commander in chief and iron discipline enforced on all members. The Jesuit general, sometimes known as the "black pope" (from the color of the order's habit), was elected for life and was not bound to take advice offered by any other member. His sole superior was the pope, to whom all senior Jesuits took a special vow of strict obedience. As a result of this

OBEDIENCE AS A JESUIT HALLMARK

The necessity of obedience in the spiritual formation of monks and nuns had been a central theme in Catholic religious thought since the Rule of Saint Benedict. By focusing its demands for obedience specifically on the papacy, however, the Society of Jesus brought a new militancy to this old ideal.

RULES FOR THINKING WITH THE CHURCH

1. Always to be ready to obey with mind and heart, setting aside all judgment of one's own, the true spouse of Jesus Christ, our holy mother, our infallible and orthodox mistress, the Catholic Church, whose authority is exercised over us by the hierarchy.

2. To commend the confession of sins to a priest as it is practised in the Church; the reception of the Holy Eucharist once a year, or better still every week, or at least every month, with the necessary preparation. . . .

4. To have a great esteem for the religious orders, and to give the preference to celibacy or virginity over the married state. . . .

6. To praise relics, the veneration and invocation of Saints: also the stations, and pious pilgrimages, indulgences, jubilees, the custom of lighting candles in the churches, and other such aids to piety and devotion. . . .

9. To uphold especially all the precepts of the Church, and not censure them in any manner; but, on the contrary, to defend them promptly, with reasons drawn from all sources, against those who criticize them.

10. To be eager to commend the decrees, mandates, traditions, rites and customs of the Fathers in the Faith or our superiors. . . .

13. That we may be altogether of the same mind and in conformity with the Church herself, if she shall have defined anything to be black which to our eyes appears to be white, we ought in like manner to pronounce it to be black. For we must undoubt-ingly believe, that the Spirit of our Lord Jesus Christ, and the Spirit of the Orthodox church His Spouse, by which Spirit we are governed and directed to salvation, is the same. . . .

FROM THE CONSTITUTIONS OF THE JESUIT ORDER

Let us with the utmost pains strain every nerve of our strength to exhibit this virtue of obedience, firstly to the Highest Pontiff, then to the Superiors of the Society; so that in all things . . . we may be most ready to obey his voice, just as if it issued from Christ our Lord . . . leaving any work, even a letter, that we have begun and have not yet finished; by directing to this goal all our strength and intention in the Lord, that holy obedience may be made perfect in us in every respect, in performance, in will, in intellect; by submitting to whatever may be enjoined on us with great readiness, with spiritual joy and perseverance; by persuading ourselves that all things [commanded] are just; by rejecting with a kind of blind obedience all opposing opinion or judgment of our own. . . .

Henry Bettenson, ed., *Documents of the Christian Church*, 2d ed. (Oxford, 1967), pp. 259–261.

QUESTIONS FOR ANALYSIS

1. Did total obedience to the church contradict the aspirations of Renaissance humanism?

2. What role did the Jesuits play in the Catholic Reformation? Did the establishment of the Jesuit order somehow serve as a general indictment of the church itself?

vow, all Jesuits were held to be at the pope's disposal at all times.

The activities of the Jesuits consisted primarily of missionary work and establishing schools. Early Jesuits preached to non-Christians in India, China, and Spanish America. Yet, although Loyola had not at first conceived of his society as making up shock troops against Protestantism, that is what it primarily became as the Counter-Reformation mounted in intensity. Through preaching and diplomacy—sometimes at the risk of their lives—Jesuits in the second half of the sixteenth century fanned out across Europe in direct confrontation with Calvinists. In many places the Jesuits succeeded in keeping rulers and their subjects loyal to Catholicism, in others they met martyrdom, and in some others—notably Poland and parts of Germany and France—they succeeded in regaining territory previously lost to Protestantism. Wherever they were allowed to settle, the Jesuits set up schools and colleges, for they firmly believed that a vigorous Catholicism depended on widespread literacy and education. Their schools were so well regarded that, after the fires of religious hatred began to subside, upper-class Protestants sometimes sent their children to receive a Jesuit education.

Early Jesuits preached to non-Christians in India, China, and Spanish America.

COUNTER-REFORMATION CHRISTIANITY

The greatest achievement of these sixteenth-century Catholic reform movements was to defend and revitalize the faith. Had it not been for the determined efforts of these reformers, Catholicism would not have swept over the globe during the seventeenth and eighteenth centuries or reemerged in Europe as the vigorous spiritual force it remains today. But other results stemmed from the Counter-Reformation as well. One was the spread of literacy in Catholic countries due to the edu-

cational activities of the Jesuits. Another was the enormous importance of charitable activities to Counter-Reformation Catholicism. Spiritual leaders such as Saint Francis de Sales (1567–1622) and Saint Vincent de Paul (1581–1660) urged almsgiving in their sermons and writings, and a wave of founding of orphanages and houses for the poor swept over Catholic Europe.

The Counter-Reformation also brought a new emphasis on the importance of religious women. Counter-Reformation Catholicism did not exalt marriage as a route to holiness for women to the same degree as did Protestantism, but it did foster a distinctive role for a female religious elite—countenancing the mysticism of Saint Teresa of Avila (1515–1582) and establishing new orders of nuns such as the Ursulines and the Sisters of Charity. Both Protestants and Catholics continued to exclude women from the priesthood or ministry, but Catholic celibate women could pursue religious lives with at least some degree of independence.

The Counter-Reformation did not, however, perpetuate the tolerant Christianity of Erasmus. Instead, Christian humanists lost favor with Counter-Reformation popes. But sixteenth-century Protestantism was just as theologically intolerant as sixteenth-century Catholicism, and even more hostile to the cause of rationalism. Indeed, because Counter-Reformation theologians returned for guidance to the scholasticism of Saint Thomas Aquinas, they tended to be much more committed to the dignity of human reason than were their Protestant counterparts, who emphasized pure scriptural authority and unquestioning faith. It is not entirely coincidental, therefore, that René Descartes, one of the pioneers of seventeenth-century rationalism (and who coined the famous phrase "I think, therefore I am"), was trained as a youth by the Jesuits.

CONCLUSION

Protestantism emerged after the height of the Italian Renaissance and before the scientific revolution and the Enlightenment. It may be tempting, therefore, to think of historical events advancing in an inevitably cumulative way, from the Renaissance to the Reformation to the Enlightenment to the "Triumph of the Modern World." But history is seldom as neat as that. Although scholars continue to disagree on points of detail, most agree that the Protestant Reformation

CHRONOLOGY

THE COUNTER-REFORMATION, 1534–1590

Counter-Reformation popes	1534–1590
Saint Ignatius Loyola founds the Jesuits	1534
Council of Trent convenes	1545–1563
Index of Prohibited Books	1564

drew relatively little from the civilization of the Renaissance. Indeed, in certain basic respects Protestant principles were completely at odds with the major assumptions of most Renaissance humanists.

Certainly the Renaissance contributed something to the origins of the Protestant Reformation. Criticisms of religious abuses by Christian humanists helped prepare Germany for the Lutheran revolt. Close textual study of the Bible led to the publication of new, more reliable biblical editions used by the Protestant reformers. In this regard a direct line ran from the Italian humanist Lorenzo Valla to Erasmus to Luther. For these and related reasons, Luther addressed Erasmus in 1519 as "our ornament and our hope."

But in fact Erasmus quickly showed that he had no sympathy whatsoever with Lutheran principles. Most other Christian humanists followed suit, shunning Protestantism as soon as it became clear to them what Luther and other Protestant reformers were actually teaching. The reasons for this split are clear enough. Most humanists believed in free will, whereas Protestants believed in predestination; humanists tended to think of human nature as basically good, whereas Protestants found it unspeakably corrupt; and most humanists favored urbanity and tolerance, whereas the followers of Luther and Calvin emphasized obedience and conformity.

The Protestant Reformation did, however, contribute to certain traits characteristic of modern European historical development. Foremost among these was the increasing power of Europe's sovereign states. But we must not make any simple equation between state power and Protestantism. The power of the state was growing already by 1500, especially in such countries as France and Spain, where Catholic kings already exercised most of the same rights over the church that were forcibly seized by Lutheran German princes and Henry VIII in the course of their own reformations.

Nationalism too was already a part of this world, as we can see from the way Luther played on it in his appeals during the 1520s. But Luther also did much to foster German cultural nationalism, not least by translating the Bible into vigorous, colloquial German. Until the sixteenth century, Germans from different regions spoke such different dialects of German that they often could not understand each other. Luther's Bible, however, gained such currency that it eventually became the linguistic standard for the entire nation. Protestantism did not unite the German nation politically; instead, Germany soon divided into Protestant and Catholic camps. But elsewhere, as in Holland or parts of central Europe, where Protestants fought successfully against a foreign, Catholic overlord, Protestantism enhanced a sense of national identity. Perhaps the most familiar case of all is that of England, where a sense of nationhood existed long before the advent of Protestantism, but where the new faith lent to that nationalism a new confidence that England was indeed a nation peculiarly favored by God.

Finally, we come to the subject of Protestantism's effects on relationships between the sexes. No consensus among historians exists on this subject. What does seem clear, however, is that Protestant men as individuals could be just as ambivalent about women as their medieval Catholic predecessors had been. But if one asks how Protestantism as a belief system affected women's social roles, the answer appears to be that it enabled women to become just a shade more equal to men within a framework of continuing subjection. Because Protestantism called on women as well as men to undertake serious study of the Bible, it encouraged primary schooling for both sexes. But Protestant male leaders still insisted that women were naturally inferior to men and should defer to men both within the family and in the larger society. As Calvin himself said, "[L]et the woman be satisfied with her state of subjection and not take it ill that she is made inferior to the more distinguished sex." Both Luther and Calvin appear to have been happily married, but that clearly meant being happily married on their own terms.

KEY TERMS

Martin Luther	Desiderius Erasmus	John Calvin	Counter-Reformation
Reformation	Diet of Worms	Henry VIII	Council of Trent
Catholicism	Protestantism	Church of England	Jesuits
indulgences	Ulrich Zwingli	Mary Tudor	Society of Jesus
Lutheranism	Anabaptists	Elizabeth I	

SELECTED READINGS

Bainton, Roland. *Erasmus of Christendom*. New York, 1969. Still the best biography in English of the Dutch reformer and intellectual.

Bainton, Roland. *Here I Stand: A Life of Martin Luther*. Nashville, 1950. Although old and obviously biased in Luther's favor, this remains an absorbing and dramatic introduction to Luther's life and thought.

Benedict, Philip. *Christ's Churches Purely Reformed: A Social History of Calvinism*. New Haven, Conn., 2002. A wide-ranging recent survey of Calvinism in both western and eastern Europe.

Bossy, John. *Christianity in the West, 1400–1700*. Oxford and New York, 1985. A brilliant, challenging picture of the changes that took place in Christian piety and practice as a result of the sixteenth-century reformations.

Bouwsma, William J. *John Calvin: A Sixteenth-Century Portrait*. Oxford and New York, 1988. The best biography of the magisterial reformer.

Collinson, Patrick. *The Religion of Protestants: The Church in English Society, 1559–1625*. Oxford, 1982. A great book by the best contemporary historian of early English Protestantism.

Dillenberger, John, ed. *John Calvin: Selections from His Writings*. Garden City, N.Y., 1971. A judicious selection, drawn mainly from Calvin's *Institutes*.

Dillenberger, John, ed. *Martin Luther: Selections from His Writings*. Garden City, N.Y., 1961. The standard selection, especially good on Luther's theological ideas.

Dixon, C. Scott, ed. *The German Reformation: The Essential Readings*. Oxford, 1999. A collection of important recent articles.

Duffy, Eamon. *The Stripping of the Altars: Traditional Religion in England, c. 1400–c. 1550*. New Haven, Conn., 1992. The best study of the hesitant way in which England eventually became a Protestant country.

Hillerbrand, Hans J., ed. *The Protestant Reformation*. New York, 1967. Source selections are particularly good for illuminating the political consequences of Reformation theological ideas.

Loyola, Ignatius. *Personal Writings*. Trans. Joseph A. Munitiz and Philip Endean. London and New York, 1996. An excellent collection that includes Loyola's autobiography, his spiritual diary, some of his letters, and his *Spiritual Exercises*.

Luebke, David, ed. *The Counter-Reformation: The Essential Readings*. Oxford, 1999. A collection of nine important essays.

MacCulloch, Diarmaid. *Reformation: Europe's House Divided, 1490–1700*. London and New York, 2003. A definitive new survey; the best single-volume history of its subject in a generation.

McGrath, Alister E. *Reformation Thought: An Introduction*. Oxford, 1993. A useful explanation, accessible to non-Christians, of the theological ideas of the major Protestant reformers.

Mullett, Michael A. *The Catholic Reformation*. London, 2000. A sympathetic survey of Catholicism from the mid-sixteenth to the eighteenth century that presents the mid-sixteenth-century Council of Trent not as a response to Protestantism but as a continuation of reform efforts dating from the fifteenth century.

Oberman, Heiko A. *Luther: Man between God and the Devil*. Trans. Eileen Walliser-Schwarzbart. New Haven, Conn., 1989. The best recent biography of Luther, stressing his preoccupations with sin, death, and the devil.

O'Malley, John W. *The First Jesuits*. Cambridge, Mass., 1993. A scholarly account of the origins and early years of the Society of Jesus.

O'Malley, John W. *Trent and All That: Renaming Catholicism in the Early Modern Era*. Cambridge, Mass., 2000. Short, lively, up to date, and with a full bibliography.

Pelikan, Jaroslav. *Reformation of Church and Dogma, 1300–1700*. Vol. 4: *A History of Christian Dogma*. Chicago, 1984. A masterful synthesis of Reformation theology in its late medieval context.

Pettegree, Andrew, ed. *The Reformation World*. New York, 2000. An exhaustive multiauthor work representing the most recent thinking about the Reformation.

Roper, Lyndal. *The Holy Household: Women and Morals in Reformation Augsburg*. Oxford, 1989. A pathbreaking study of how Protestantism was adopted and adapted by the town councilors of Augsburg, with special attention to its impact on attitudes toward women, the family, and marriage.

Shagan, Ethan H. *Popular Politics and the English Reformation*. Cambridge, 2002. Argues that the English Reformation reflects an ongoing process of negotiation, resistance, and response between government and people.

Tracy, James D. *Europe's Reformations, 1450–1650*. 2d ed. Lanham, Md., 2006. An outstanding survey, especially strong on Dutch and Swiss developments, but excellent throughout.

Williams, George H. *The Radical Reformation*. 3d ed. Kirksville, Mo., 1992. Originally published in 1962, this is still the best book on Anabaptism and its offshoots.

Chapter FOURTEEN

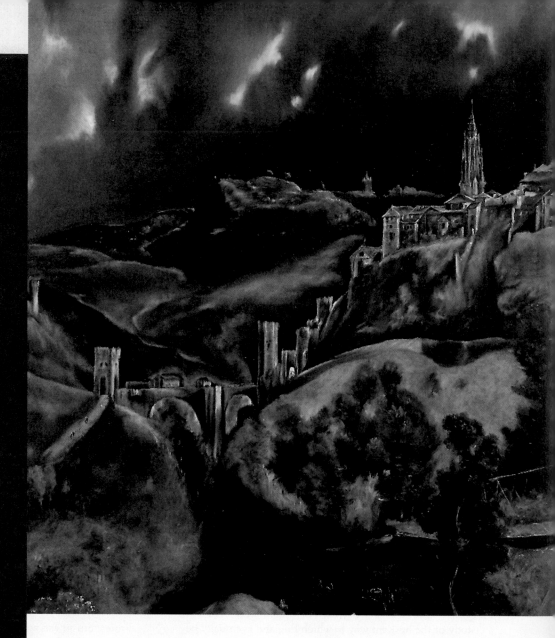

RELIGIOUS WARS AND STATE BUILDING, 1540–1660

STRANGE AS IT MAY SEEM in retrospect, Martin Luther never intended to fracture the religious unity of Europe. He sincerely believed that once the Bible was available to everyone in an accurate, vernacular translation, then everyone who read the Bible would interpret it in exactly the same way as did he himself. The result, of course, was quite different, as Luther quickly discovered in his bitter disputes with Zwingli and Calvin. Nor did Catholicism crumble in the face of reformed teachings as Luther had believed that it would. Instead, Europe's religious divisions multiplied, speedily crystallizing along political lines. By Luther's death in 1546, a clear pattern had already emerged. With only rare exceptions, Protestantism triumphed in those areas where political authorities supported the reformers. Where rulers remained Catholic, so too did their territories.

This was not the result Martin Luther had intended, but it did faithfully reflect the most basic presumptions of sixteenth-century European life. Anabaptists apart, neither Protestant nor Catholic reformers set out to challenge the standard medieval beliefs about the mutual interdependence of religion and politics—quite the contrary. Sixteenth-century Europeans continued to believe that the proper role of the state was to enforce true religion on its subjects, and sixteenth-century rulers remained convinced that religious pluralism would bring disunion and disloyalty to any state that embraced it. Ultimately, both Catholics and Protestants believed that western Europe had to return to a single religious faith enforced by properly constituted political authorities. What they could not agree on was, "Which faith?" and "Which authorities?"

The result was a brutal series of religious wars between 1540 and 1660 whose reverberations would continue to be felt until the eighteenth century. Vastly expensive and enormously destructive, these wars affected everyone in Europe, from peasants to princes. They did not arise solely from conflicts over religion. Regionalism, dynasticism, and nationalism were also potent contributors to the chaos into which Europe now plunged. Together, however, these forces of division

FOCUS QUESTIONS

- Why was the period 1540–1660 one of the most turbulent in European history?
- Why did religious conflicts become so deeply entwined with political conflicts during this period?
- What caused the decline of Spain in the seventeenth century?

- Why was this period such a fertile one for political philosophy?
- What was the relationship between the Baroque school and the Counter-Reformation?

and disorder brought into question the very survival of the European political order that had emerged since the thirteenth century. Faced with the prospect of political collapse, Europeans by 1660 were forced to embrace, gradually and grudgingly, a notion that in 1540 had seemed impossible to conceive: that religious toleration, however limited in scope, might be the only way to preserve the political, social, and economic order of the European world.

ECONOMIC, RELIGIOUS, AND POLITICAL TESTS

Why was the period 1540–1660 one of the most turbulent in European history?

The troubles that engulfed Europe between 1540 and 1660 caught contemporaries unaware. From the mid-fifteenth century on, most of Europe had enjoyed steady economic growth, and the discovery of the New World seemed the basis of greater prosperity to come. Political trends too seemed auspicious, because most western European governments were becoming ever more efficient and providing more internal peace for their subjects. By the middle of the sixteenth century, however, thunderclouds were gathering that would soon burst into terrible storms.

THE PRICE REVOLUTION

Although the causes of these storms were interrelated, we can examine each separately, starting with the great price inflation. Nothing like the upward price trend that affected western Europe in the second half of the sixteenth century had ever happened before. In Flanders the cost of wheat tripled between 1550 and 1600, grain prices in Paris quadrupled, and the overall cost of living in England more than doubled. The twentieth century would see much more dizzying inflations than this, but since the skyrocketing of prices in the later sixteenth century was a novelty, most historians agree on calling it a "price revolution."

Two developments in particular underlay the soaring prices. The first was demographic. Starting in the later fifteenth century, Europe's population began to grow again after the plague-induced falloff: roughly estimated, Europe had about 50 million people around 1450 and

90 million around 1600. Because Europe's food supply remained more or less constant, food prices were driven sharply higher by greater demand. At the same time, wages stagnated or even declined. As a result, workers around 1600 were paying a higher percentage of their wages to buy food than ever before, even though their basic nutritional levels were declining.

Population trends explain much, but since Europe's population did not increase nearly so rapidly in the second half of the sixteenth century as did prices, other explanations for the great inflation are necessary. Foremost among these is the enormous influx of bullion from Spanish America. From 1556 to 1560 roughly 10 million ducats worth of silver passed through the Spanish entry port of Seville. Between 1576 and 1580 that figure doubled, and between 1591 and 1595 it more than quadrupled. Most of this silver was used by the Spanish crown to pay its foreign creditors and its armies abroad; as a result, this bullion quickly circulated throughout Europe, where much of it was minted into coins. This dramatic increase in the volume of money

Peasants Harvesting Wheat, Sixteenth Century. The inflation that swept through Europe in the late 1500s affected workers the most as the abundant labor supply dampened wages while the cost of food rose from poor harvests.

WHY DID RELIGIOUS CONFLICTS BECOME SO DEEPLY ENTWINED WITH POLITICAL CONFLICTS DURING THIS PERIOD?

A CENTURY OF RELIGIOUS WARS   371

in circulation fueled the spiral of rising prices. "I learned a proverb here," said a French traveler in Spain in 1603, "everything costs much here except silver."

The price revolution also placed new pressures on the sovereign states of Europe. Since the inflation depressed the real value of money, fixed incomes from taxes and tolls yielded less and less. Thus merely to keep their incomes constant governments would have been forced to raise taxes. But to compound this problem, most states needed much more real income than previously because they were undertaking more wars; and warfare, as always, was becoming increasingly expensive. The only recourse, then, was to raise taxes precipitously, but such draconian measures aroused great resentment. Hence governments faced continuous threats of defiance and potential armed resistance.

After 1600 prices rose less rapidly, as population growth slowed and the flood of silver from America began to abate. On the whole, however, the period from 1600 to 1660 was one of economic stagnation rather than growth. The Black Death also returned, wreaking havoc in London and elsewhere during the 1660s.

RELIGIOUS CONFLICTS

It goes without saying that most people would have been far better off had there been fewer wars during this difficult century, but given prevalent attitudes, newly arisen religious rivalries made wars inevitable. Simply stated, until religious passions began to cool toward the end of the period, most Catholics and Protestants viewed each other as minions of Satan who could not be allowed to live. Worse, sovereign states attempted to enforce religious uniformity on the grounds that "crown and altar" offered each other mutual support and in the belief that governments would totter where diversity of faith prevailed. Rulers on both sides felt certain that religious minorities, if allowed to survive in their realms, would inevitably engage in sedition; nor were they far wrong because militant Calvinists and Jesuits were indeed dedicated to subverting constituted powers in areas where their parties had not yet triumphed. Thus states tried to extirpate all potential religious resistance but, in the process, sometimes provoked civil wars in which each side tended to assume there could be no victory until the other was exterminated. And of course civil wars might become international in scope if foreign powers chose to aid their embattled religious allies elsewhere.

POLITICAL INSTABILITY

Compounding the foregoing problems were the inherent weaknesses of the major European kingdoms. Most of the major states of early modern Europe had grown during the later Middle Ages by absorbing smaller, traditionally autonomous territories, sometimes by conquest but more often through marriage alliances or inheritance arrangements between their respective ruling families (a policy known as "dynasticism"). At first some degree of provincial autonomy was usually preserved in these newly absorbed territories. But between 1540 and 1660, when governments were making ever greater financial claims on all their subjects or trying to enforce religious uniformity, rulers often rode roughshod over the rights of these traditionally autonomous provinces. The result, once again, was civil war, in which regionalism, economic grievances, and religious animosities were compounded into a volatile and destructive mixture. Nor was that all, since most governments seeking money and/or religious uniformity tried to rule with a firmer hand than before and thus sometimes provoked armed resistance from subjects seeking to preserve their traditional constitutional liberties. Given this bewildering variety of motives for revolt, it is not surprising that the long century between 1540 and 1660 was one of the most turbulent in all of European history.

A CENTURY OF RELIGIOUS WARS

Why did religious conflicts become so deeply entwined with political conflicts during this period?

The greatest single cause of warfare during this period was religious conflict. The wars themselves divide into four phases: a series of German wars from the 1540s to 1555; the French wars of religion from 1562 until 1598; the Dutch wars with Spain between 1566 and 1609; and the Thirty Years' War in Germany between 1618 and 1648.

> On the whole, however, the period from 1600 to 1660 was one of economic stagnation rather than growth.

THE GERMAN WARS OF RELIGION TO 1555

Wars between Catholics and Protestants in Germany began in the 1540s when the Holy Roman emperor Charles V, a devout Catholic, tried to reestablish Catholic unity in Germany by launching a military campaign against several German princes who had instituted Lutheran worship in their territories. Despite some notable victories, Charles's efforts to defeat the Protestant princes failed. Partly this was because he was simultaneously involved in wars against France, and so could not devote his entire attention to German affairs. Primarily, however, Charles failed because the Catholic princes of Germany feared that if Charles succeeded in defeating the Protestant princes, he might then suppress their own independence also. As a result, the Catholic princes' support for the foreign-born Charles was only lukewarm; at times, they even joined with the Protestant princes in battle against the emperor. Accordingly, religious warfare sputtered on and off

***The Emperor Charles V at Muehlberg*, by Titian.** Charles V's attempts to re-create a united Catholic Germany by military means failed, and he ultimately settled with the Peace of Augsburg in 1555.

until a compromise settlement was reached in the Peace of Augsburg (1555). This rested on the principle of *cuius regio, eius religio* ("as the ruler, so the religion"), which meant that in those principalities where Lutheran princes ruled, Lutheranism would be the sole state religion; where Catholic princes ruled, their territories would be Catholic also. Although the Peace of Augsburg was a historical milestone inasmuch as Catholic rulers for the first time acknowledged the legality of Protestantism, it boded ill for the future in assuming that no sovereign state larger than a free city (for which it made exceptions) could tolerate religious diversity. Moreover, in excluding Calvinism entirely, it ensured that the German Calvinists would become aggressive opponents of the status quo.

THE FRENCH WARS OF RELIGION

From the 1560s on, Europe's religious wars became far more brutal, partly because the combatants had become more intransigent (Calvinists and Jesuits customarily took the lead on their respective sides) and partly because the later religious wars were aggravated by regional, political, and dynastic hostilities. Calvinist missionaries made considerable headway in France between 1541 (when Calvin took power in Geneva) and the outbreak of religious warfare in 1562. By 1562, Calvinists made up between 10 and 20 percent of France's population, with their numbers swelling daily. Greatly assisting the Calvinist (Huguenot; *HYOO-guh-noh*) cause in France was the conversion of many aristocratic Frenchwomen to Calvinism. Such women often won over their husbands, who in turn maintained large private armies. But Calvinism in France was also nourished by long-standing regional hosilities within the French kingdom, especially in southern France, where the animosities aroused by the thirteenth-century Albigensian crusade continued to fester.

Until 1562, an uneasy peace continued between Catholic and Calvinist forces in France. In 1562, however, the French king died unexpectedly, leaving a young child as his heir. A struggle immediately broke out between Huguenot and Catholic courtiers for control of the regency government. And since both Catholics and Protestants assumed that France could have only a single *roi, foi,* and *loi* (king, faith, and law), this political struggle immediately took on a religious aspect. Soon all France was aflame. Rampaging mobs ransacked churches and settled local scores. Although the Huguenots were not strong or numerous enough to gain victory, they were too strong to be defeated, espe-

WHY DID RELIGIOUS CONFLICTS BECOME SO DEEPLY ENTWINED WITH POLITICAL CONFLICTS DURING THIS PERIOD?

A CENTURY OF RELIGIOUS WARS   373

cially in their southern French stronghold. Hence, despite intermittent truces, warfare dragged on at great cost of life until 1572, when a truce was arranged by which the Protestant leader, Henry of Navarre, was to marry the Catholic sister of the reigning French king. At this point, however, the cultivated queen mother Catherine de Medici, normally a woman who favored compromise, panicked. Instead of honoring the truce, she plotted to kill the Huguenot leaders while they were assembled in Paris for her daughter's wedding to Henry of Navarre. In the early morning of St. Bartholomew's Day (August 24) most of the Huguenot chiefs were murdered in their beds and 2,000 to 3,000 other Protestants were slaughtered in the streets or drowned in the Seine by Catholic mobs. When word of the Parisian massacre spread to the provinces, some 10,000 more Huguenots were killed in a frenzy of blood lust that swept through France. Henry of Navarre escaped, along with his new bride; but after 1572, the conflict entered a new and even more bitter phase.

Only when the politically astute Henry of Navarre succeeded to the French throne as Henry IV (1589–1610) did the civil war finally come to an end. In 1593 Henry abjured his Protestantism in order to placate France's Catholic majority, declaring as he did so that "Paris is worth a mass." In 1598, however, he offered limited religious freedom to the Huguenots by the Edict of Nantes. Although the Edict recognized Catholicism as the official religion of the kingdom, Huguenot nobles were now allowed to hold Protestant services privately in their castles; other Huguenots were allowed to worship at specified places and to fortify some towns, especially in the south and west, for their own military defense. Huguenots were also guaranteed the right to serve in all public offices, and to enter the universities and hospitals without hindrance.

Although the Edict of Nantes did not countenance absolute freedom of worship, it nevertheless took a major stride in the direction of toleration. But despite its efforts to create one kingdom with two faiths, the effect of the Edict was to divide the French kingdom into separate religious enclaves. In southern and western France, Huguenots came to have their own law courts, staffed by their own judges. They also received substantial powers of self-government, because it was presumed on all sides that the members of one reli-

gious group could not be ruled equitably by the adherents of a competing religion. In some ways, indeed, the Huguenot areas became "a state within a state," thus raising again the perpetual fear in Paris that the kingdom of which it was the capital might once again fly apart into its constituent parts, as had happened during the Hundred Years' War. On its own terms, however, the Edict of Nantes was a success. With religious peace established, France quickly began to recover from decades of devastation, even though Henry IV himself was cut down by the dagger of a Catholic fanatic in 1610.

THE REVOLT OF THE NETHERLANDS

Bitter warfare also broke out between Catholics and Protestants in the Netherlands, where national resentments exacerbated the predictable religious hatreds. For almost a century the Netherlands had been ruled by the Habsburg family of Holy Roman emperors. But when Charles V retired to a monastery in 1556 (dying two years later) he ceded all his vast territories outside of the Holy Roman Empire and Hungary—not only the Netherlands but also Spain, Spanish America, and half of Italy—to his son Philip II (1556–1598). Unlike Charles, Philip viewed the Netherlands primarily as a source of income necessary for pursuing Spanish affairs. Philip also tried to tighten his control over the government of the Netherlands. This aroused the resentment of the local magnates who had dominated the government under Charles V. A religious storm was also brewing. After 1559, when a long war between France and Spain ended, French Calvinists began to stream over the border into the southern Netherlands, making converts wherever they went. Soon there were more Calvinists in Antwerp than in Geneva. To Philip, an ardent supporter of Counter-Reformation Catholicism, this was intolerable. As he declared to the pope on the eve of conflict, "rather than suffer the slightest harm to the true religion and service of God, I would lose all my states and even my life a hundred times over because I am not and will not be the ruler of heretics."

Worried by the growing tensions, a group of local Catholic noblemen led by William of Orange appealed to Philip to allow toleration for Calvinists. But

> In some ways, indeed, the Huguenot areas became "a state within a state," thus raising again the perpetual fear in Paris that the kingdom of which it was the capital might once again fly apart into its constituent parts, as had happened during the Hundred Years' War.

before Philip could respond, radical Protestant mobs began ransacking Catholic churches throughout the country. Local troops soon brought the situation under control, but Philip II nonetheless decided to dispatch an army of 10,000 Spanish troops, led by the duke of Alva, to wipe out Protestantism in the Netherlands. Alva's rule quickly became a reign of terror. Operating under martial law, his "Council of Blood" examined some 12,000 people on charges of heresy or sedition, of whom 9,000 were convicted and 2,000 to 3,000 executed. William fled the country, and all hope for a free Netherlands seemed lost.

But the tide turned quickly. Instead of giving up, William of Orange converted to Protestantism; sought help from Protestants in France, Germany, and England; and organized bands of sea rovers to harass Spanish shipping on the Netherlandish coast. Alva's tyranny also helped William's cause. With internal disaffection growing, in 1572 William was able to seize the northern Netherlands even though the north until then had been predominantly Catholic. Thereafter geography played a major role in determining the outcome of the conflict. Spanish armies repeatedly attempted to win back the north, but they were stopped by a combination of impassable rivers and dikes that could be opened to flood out the invaders. Although William of Orange was assassinated by a Catholic in 1584, his son continued to lead the resistance until 1609, when the Spanish crown finally recognized the independence of the northern Dutch Republic. Meanwhile, the pressures of war and persecution had made the whole north Calvinistic, whereas the south—which remained under Spanish control—returned to uniform Catholicism.

ENGLAND AND THE DEFEAT OF THE SPANISH ARMADA

Religious strife could spark civil war, as in France, or political rebellions, as in the Netherlands. It also provoked warfare between sovereign states, as it did between England and Spain. A seafaring and trading people, the English in the later sixteenth century were steadily making inroads into Spanish naval and commercial domination and were determined to resist any Spanish attempt to block England's lucrative trade with the Low Countries. But the greatest source of antagonism lay in the Atlantic, where English privateers, with the tacit consent of Queen Elizabeth, regularly attacked Spanish treasure ships.

Because Philip II had his hands full in the Netherlands, he resolved to invade England only after the English openly allied with the Dutch rebels in 1585. Even then, Philip moved slowly and made careful plans. Finally, in 1588 he dispatched an enormous fleet, confidently called the "Invincible Armada," to invade insolent Britannia. After an initial standoff in the English Channel, however, the smaller, longer-gunned English warships outmaneuvered the Spanish fleet, while English fireships set Spanish galleons ablaze. "Protestant gales" did the rest. After a disastrous circumnavigation of the British Isles and Ireland, the shattered armada limped home with almost half its ships lost.

The defeat of the Spanish Armada was one of the decisive battles of Western history. Had Spain conquered England, the Spanish might have gone on to crush Holland and perhaps even to destroy Protestantism elsewhere in Europe. But as it was, the Protestant day was saved, and not long afterward Spanish power began to decline, as English and Dutch ships seized command of the seas. In England, patriotic Protestant fervor intensified. Popular even before then, "Good Queen Bess" was virtually revered by her subjects until her death in 1603, and England embarked on its golden "Elizabethan Age" of literary endeavor. War with Spain dragged on inconclusively until 1604, but the fighting never brought England any serious harm and was just lively enough to keep the English people deeply committed to their queen, their country, and the Protestant religion.

THE THIRTY YEARS' WAR

With the promulgation of the Edict of Nantes in 1598, the peace between England and Spain of 1604, and the truce between Spain and Holland of 1609, religious warfare in northwestern Europe came briefly to an end. But in 1618 a major new war broke out, this time in Germany. Because this struggle raged more or less unceasingly until 1648 it is known as the Thirty Years' War. Spain and France quickly became engaged in the conflict in Germany and eventually in war with one another. Meanwhile, domestic resentments in Spain, France, and England flared up during the 1640s into concurrent outbreaks of civil war. As an English preacher said in 1643, "these are days of shaking, and this shaking is universal."

The Thirty Years' War began as a war between Catholics and Protestants but ended as an international struggle in which the initial religious dimension was almost entirely forgotten. Between the Peace of Augsburg in

THE DESTRUCTIVENESS OF THE THIRTY YEARS' WAR

Hans Jakob Christoph von Grimmelshausen (1621–1676) lived through the horrors of the Thirty Years' War. His parents were killed, probably when he was thirteen years of age, and he himself was kidnapped the following year. By age fifteen, he was a soldier. His comic masterpiece, Simplicissimus, *from which this extract is taken, drew heavily on these wartime experiences. Although technically "fiction," it portrays with brutal accuracy the cruelty and destructiveness of this war, especially for its peasant victims.*

Although it was not my intention to take the peaceloving reader with these troopers to my dad's house and farm, seeing that matters will go ill therein, yet the course of my history demands that I should leave to kind posterity an account of what manner of cruelties were now and again practised in this our German war: yes, and moreover testify by my own example that such evils must often have been sent to us by the goodness of Almighty God for our profit. For, gentle reader, who would ever have taught me that there was a God in Heaven if these soldiers had not destroyed my dad's house, and by such a deed driven me out among folk who gave me all fitting instruction thereupon? . . .

The first thing these troopers did was, that they stabled their horses: thereafter each fell to his appointed task: which task was neither more nor less than ruin and destruction. For though some began to slaughter and to boil and to roast so that it looked as if there should be a merry banquet forward, yet others there were who did but storm through the house above and below stairs. Others stowed together great parcels of cloth and apparel and all manner of household stuff, as if they would set up a frippery market. All that they had no mind to take with them they cut in pieces. Some thrust their swords through the hay and straw as if they had not enough sheep and swine to slaughter: and some shook the feathers out of the beds and in their stead stuffed in bacon and other dried meat and provisions as if such were better and softer to sleep upon. Others broke the stove and the windows as if they had a never-ending summer to promise. House-ware of copper and tin they beat flat, and packed such vessels, all bent and spoiled, in with the rest. Bedsteads, tables, chairs, and benches they burned, though there lay many cords of dry wood in the yard. Pots and pipkins must all go to pieces, either because they would eat none but roast flesh, or because their purpose was to make there but a single meal.

Our maid was so handled in the stable that she could not come out; which is a shame to tell of. Our man they laid bound upon the ground, thrust a gag into his mouth, and poured a pailful of filthy water into his body: and by this, which they called a Swedish draught, they forced him to lead a party of them to another place where they captured men and beasts, and brought them back to our farm, in which company were my dad, my mother, and our Ursula.

And now they began: first to take the flints out of their pistols and in place of them to jam the peasants' thumbs in and so to torture the poor rogues as if they had been about the burning of witches: for one of them they had taken they thrust into the baking oven and there lit a fire under him, although he had as yet confessed no crime: as for another, they put a cord round his head and so twisted it tight with a piece of wood that the blood gushed from his mouth and nose and ears. In a word each had his own device to torture the peasants, and each peasant his several tortures.

Hans Jakob Christoph von Grimmelshausen, *Simplicissimus*, trans. S. Goodrich (New York, 1995), pp. 1–3, 8–10, 32–35.

QUESTION FOR ANALYSIS

1. Defend the statement that the Thirty Years' War was the first modern war and the Peace of Westphalia was the first modern peace.

1555 and the outbreak of war in 1618, Calvinists had replaced Lutherans in a few German territories, but the overall balance between Protestants and Catholics within the Holy Roman Empire had remained undisturbed. In 1618, however, war broke out after Ferdinand, the Catholic Habsburg prince of Poland, Austria, and Hungary, was elected king of the Protestant territory of Bohemia. The staunchly Protestant Bohemian nobility had opposed Ferdinand's election, and when Ferdinand began to suppress Protestantism in Bohemia, they rebelled. German Catholic forces ruthlessly counterattacked, first in Bohemia and then in Germany proper, led by Ferdinand, who in 1619 also became Holy Roman emperor. Within a decade, a German Catholic league seemed close to extirpating Protestantism throughout Germany.

Ferdinand's success raised once again the prospect that an overly powerful Holy Roman emperor might threaten the political autonomy of the German princes, Catholic and Protestant alike. Thus when the Lutheran king of Sweden, Gustavus Adolphus, the "Lion of the North," marched into Germany in 1630 to champion the Protestant cause, he was welcomed by several German Catholic princes who preferred to see the former religious balance restored rather than risk surrendering their sovereignty to Ferdinand II. To make matters still more ironic, Gustavus's Protestant army was secretly subsidized by Catholic France, whose policy was then dictated by a cardinal of the church, Cardinal Richelieu (RIH-shub-loo). This was because Habsburg Spain had been fighting in Germany on the side of Habsburg Austria, and Richelieu was determined to prevent France from being surrounded by a strong Habsburg alliance on the north, east, and south. In any event, the military genius Gustavus Adolphus started routing the Habsburgs, but after he fell in battle in 1632, French armies entered the war directly on Sweden's side. From then until 1648 the struggle was really one of France and Sweden against Austria and Spain, with Germany a helpless battleground.

Nor did the Peace of Westphalia, which finally ended the Thirty Years' War in 1648, do much to vindicate anyone's death, even though it did establish some abiding landmarks in European history. Above all, from the international perspective, the Peace of Westphalia marked the emergence of France as the predominant power on the continental European

> Above all, from the international perspective, the Peace of Westphalia marked the emergence of France as the predominant power on the continental European scene, replacing Spain.

scene, replacing Spain. France would hold this position for the next two centuries. The greatest losers in the conflict (aside, of course, from the German people themselves) were the Austrian Habsburgs, who were forced to surrender all the territory they had gained in Germany and to abandon their hopes of using the office of Holy Roman emperor to dominate central Europe. Otherwise, something very close to the German status quo of 1618 was reestablished, with Protestant principalities in the north balancing Catholic ones in the south, and Germany so divided that it could play no united role in European history until the nineteenth century.

DIVERGENT PATHS: SPAIN, FRANCE, AND ENGLAND, 1600–1660

What caused the decline of Spain in the seventeenth century?

The long century of war between 1540 and 1660 decisively altered the balance of power among the major kingdoms of western Europe. Germany emerged from the Thirty Years' War a devastated and exhausted land. But after 1600, Spain too was crippled by its unremitting military commitments and exertions. The French monarchy, by contrast, steadily increased its authority over France. By 1660 France had become the most powerful country on the European mainland, decisively eclipsing Spain. In England, meanwhile, a bloody civil war broke out between the king and his critics in Parliament; but after a short-lived experiment in republican rule, England in 1660 returned to its constitutional status as a "mixed" monarchy in which power was shared between king and Parliament.

THE DECLINE OF SPAIN

Spain's greatest underlying weakness was economic. Lacking either rich agricultural or mineral resources, Spain desperately needed to develop industries and a

WHAT CAUSED THE DECLINE OF SPAIN IN THE SEVENTEENTH CENTURY?

DIVERGENT PATHS: SPAIN, FRANCE, AND ENGLAND, 1600–1660   377

balanced trading pattern as its Atlantic rivals were doing. But the Spanish nobility preferred to use American silver to buy manufactured goods from other parts of Europe while living in splendor and dedicating itself to military exploits. As a result, few new industries were established; and when the influx of silver began to decline, the Spanish economy was left with nothing except increasing debts.

Nonetheless, the crown, dedicated to supporting the Counter-Reformation and maintaining Spain's international dominance, could not cease fighting abroad. Even in the relatively peaceful year of 1608, more than half the total revenues of the Spanish crown went to military expenditures. Thus when Spain became engaged in the Thirty Years' War it overextended itself. In 1643 French troops inflicted a stunning defeat on the famed Spanish infantry at Rocroi, the first time that a Spanish army had been overcome in battle since the reign of Ferdinand and Isabella. Worse still was the fact that by then two territories belonging to Spain's European empire were in open revolt.

To understand the causes of these revolts, we must recognize that in the seventeenth century the governing power of Spain lay entirely in Castile. After the marriage of Isabella of Castile and Ferdinand of Aragon in 1469, Castile had emerged as the dominant partner in the Spanish union, becoming even more dominant when it took over Portugal in 1580. In the absence of any great financial hardships, semi-autonomous Catalunya (the most fiercely independent part of Aragon) endured Castilian hegemony. But in 1640, when the strains of warfare induced Castile to limit Catalan liberties in order to raise more money and men for combat, Catalunya revolted and drove out its Castilian governors. When the Portuguese learned of the Catalan uprising, they revolted as well, followed by southern Italians who rose up against Castilian viceroys in Naples and Sicily in 1647. Only the momentary inability of Spain's greatest external enemies, France and England, to take advantage of its plight saved the Spanish Empire from utter collapse. This gave the Castilian government time to put down the Italian revolts; by 1652 it had also brought Catalunya to heel. But Portugal retained its independence; and by the Peace of the Pyrenees, signed with France in 1659, Spain in effect abandoned its ambition of dominating Europe.

THE GROWING POWER OF FRANCE

The Thirty Years' War imposed enormous strains on both Spain and France. France, however, weathered the storm, to emerge by 1660 as the most powerful country in Europe. The rich and varied agricultural resources of France, combined with the wise stewardship of King Henry IV, gave the French economy a resilience that the Spanish economy could not match. These were the foundations on which the power of seventeenth-century France was built. The architect of French greatness, however, was Cardinal Richelieu who as the first minister to the ineffectual King Louis XIII ruled France from 1624 until his death in 1642.

CARDINAL RICHELIEU (1585–1642)

As de facto ruler of France, Richelieu had two main objectives: to strengthen and centralize royal power and to undermine the Habsburg powers that surrounded France on all sides. Richelieu deprived the Huguenots of their political and military rights and instituted a new system of local government through royal officials, known as "intendants," who were expressly commissioned to ride roughshod over any provincial resistance. He also revoked the semi-autonomous status of several French regions. By these and other measures Richelieu doubled the crown's income during his rule. He turned these new revenues against the Habsburgs, first subsidizing their enemies and then committing French troops against them in the Thirty Years' War. Richelieu succeeded in destroying Habsburg power, but the costs of his ambitious foreign policy would create problems for his successors as rulers of France.

THE FRONDE

A reaction against French governmental centralization manifested itself in a series of revolts between 1648 and 1653, collectively known as "the slingshot tumults" or, in French, the *Fronde.* By this time Louis XIII had been succeeded by his son Louis XIV; but because the latter was still a boy, France was governed by a regency consisting of Louis's mother, Anne of Austria, and her paramour, Cardinal Mazarin. Both were foreigners (Anne was a Habsburg, and Mazarin originally an Italian adventurer named Giulio Mazarini), and many of their subjects, including some extremely powerful nobles, hated them. Popular resentments were greater still because the costs of war, combined with several consecutive years of bad harvests, had brought widespread misery to France. Thus when cliques of nobles expressed their disgust with Mazarin for primarily self-interested reasons, they found much support throughout the country, and uncoordinated revolts against the regency government flared on and off for several years.

EUROPE AT THE END OF THE THIRTY YEARS' WAR

What was at issue in the Thirty Years' War? Why did Catholic France ally with Lutheran Sweden against German and Austrian Catholics? Why did this war, which began as a religious conflict within the Holy Roman Empire, turn into an international struggle? Which European powers stayed out of the war? Why did they do so?

Map labels

RUSSIA

SWEDEN

NORWAY

Christiana

Stockholm

TEUTONIC ORDER

BALTIC SEA

POLAND

Kiev

Warsaw

Vistula R.

Danzig

EAST PRUSSIA

DENMARK

Copenhagen

Christiana

SCOTLAND

Edinburgh

NORTH SEA

Hamburg

MECKLEN-BURG

BRANDENBURG

Berlin

HANOVER

SAXONY

Elbe R.

HOLY ROMAN EMPIRE

HUNGARY

Budapest

AUSTRIA

Vienna

Danube R.

BLACK SEA

OTTOMAN EMPIRE

Constantinople

CYPRUS (to Ottoman Empire)

AEGEAN SEA

CRETE (to Spain)

NETHERLANDS

Amsterdam

HESSE

Rhine R.

WÜRTTEM-BERG

BAVARIA

SWITZ.

SPANISH NETH.

LORRAINE

FRANCHE-COMTÉ

Liverpool

ENGLAND

London

English Channel

IRELAND

Dublin

Seine R.

Paris

FRANCE

Loire R.

Bordeaux

Garonne R.

Rhône R.

SAVOY

MILAN

VENICE

GENOA

PIEDMONT

AVIGNON

FLORENCE

Marseilles

CORSICA (to Genoa)

SARDINIA (to Spain)

PAPAL STATES

Rome

ITALY

ADRIATIC SEA

Zara (to Venice)

(to Venice)

Ragussa

Cattaro

KINGDOM OF THE TWO SICILIES

Naples

MEDITERRANEAN SEA

ATLANTIC OCEAN

BALEARIC ISLANDS

ARAGON

CASTILE

Madrid

Tagus R.

SPAIN

PORTUGAL

Lisbon

Strait of Gibraltar

Legend

The church
Spain
Austria
Brandenburg–Prussia
Boundary of the Holy Roman Empire

Inset

EUROPE

Area of detail

AFRICA

Scale

500 Miles

500 Kilometers

250

250

0

WHAT CAUSED THE DECLINE OF SPAIN IN THE SEVENTEENTH CENTURY?

DIVERGENT PATHS: SPAIN, FRANCE, AND ENGLAND, 1600–1660   379

France, however, did not come close to falling apart. The French crown retained great reservoirs of prestige. Neither the aristocratic leaders of the Fronde nor the commoners who joined them in revolt claimed to be resisting the young king but only the alleged corruption and mismanagement of Mazarin. Thus when Louis XIV began to rule in his own name in 1651 and pretexts for revolt against "corrupt ministers" no longer existed, the opposition was soon silenced. Remembering the turbulence of the Fronde for the rest of his life, Louis XIV resolved never to let his aristocracy or his provinces get out of hand again and ruled as the most effective royal absolutist in all of French history.

THE ENGLISH CIVIL WAR

Of all the revolts that shook mid-seventeenth-century Europe, the most radical in its consequences was the English civil war. The causes of this conflict were similar to those that sparked rebellions in Spain and France. Only in England, however, did these conflicts lead to the deposition and execution of the king (1649), an eleven-year "interregnum" during which England was officially a republic (1649–1660), and ultimately to the restoration of the monarchy under conditions designed to safeguard Parliament's place in government and to guarantee a limited degree of religious toleration for all Protestants.

THE ORIGINS OF THE ENGLISH CIVIL WAR

The chain of events that led to war between king and Parliament in 1642 began in the last decades of Queen Elizabeth's reign (1559–1603). During the 1590s, the expenses of war with Spain, together with a rebellion in Ireland, widespread crop failures, and the inadequacies of the antiquated English taxation system drove the queen's government deeply into debt. Factional disputes around the court also became more bitter as courtiers, anticipating the aging queen's death, jockeyed for position under her presumed successor, the Scottish king James Stuart. Only on her deathbed, however, did the queen finally confirm that her throne should go to her Scottish cousin. As a result, neither James nor his new English subjects knew very much about one another when he took the throne at the end of 1603.

The relationship did not begin well. James's English subjects looked down on the Scots whom he brought with him to London, whom they blamed, quite unreasonably, for the Crown's indebtedness. James, meanwhile, saw clearly that to resolve his debts he had to have more revenue. But rather than bargain with

parliamentary representatives for increased taxation he chose to lecture them on the prerogatives of kingship. When this approach failed to produce the taxation he needed, James made peace with Spain and then took steps to raise revenues without parliamentary approval, imposing new tolls on trade and selling trading monopolies to favored courtiers. These measures aroused further resentments against the king, and so made voluntary grants of taxation from Parliament even less likely to be approved. As a result, the king's financial situation steadily worsened.

James was more adept with respect to religious policy. Scotland had been a firmly Calvinist country since the 1560s. In England, however, the Elizabethan religious settlement had produced much less theological definition. By 1603 England was clearly a Protestant country, but a significant number of English Protestants continued to hope for a "second" or "further" reformation that would bring their church more firmly into line with Calvinist principles. Other Protestants resisted such efforts and labeled those who supported them "Puritans." As king, James was compelled to mediate

James I. "The wisest fool in Christendom."

these conflicts. By and large, he did so successfully. Only in Ireland, which remained overwhelmingly Catholic, did James stir up future trouble. By encouraging the "plantation" of more than 8,000 Scottish Calvinists in the northern province of Ulster, he undermined the property rights of Irish Catholics and created religious animosities that have lasted until the present day.

The delicate religious balance preserved by James I was shattered in 1625 by the accession of Charles I. Throwing his father's habitual caution to the winds, Charles immediately launched a new war with Spain, exacerbating his financial problems and alarming his Protestant subjects by proposing to raise Irish Catholic troops for military service in Germany. Protestant alarm was further increased when Charles married Henrietta Maria, the Catholic daughter of King Louis XIII of France. The situation became truly dangerous, however, when Charles openly began to favor the most anti-Calvinist elements in the English church and then attempted to impose this religious policy on Scotland. The Scots rebelled, and in 1640 a Scottish army marched south into England to demand the withdrawal of Charles's "Catholicizing" religious reforms.

To meet the Scottish threat, Charles was forced to summon the English Parliament for the first time in eleven years. Relations between the king and Parliament had broken down in the late 1620s, when Charles responded to Parliament's refusal to grant him additional funds by demanding forced loans from his subjects and then punishing those who refused to comply by quartering soldiers in their homes or throwing them into prison without trial. In response, in 1628 Parliament forced the king to accept the Petition of Right, which declared all taxes not voted by Parliament illegal, condemned the quartering of soldiers in private houses, and prohibited arbitrary imprisonment and martial law in time of peace. Angered rather than chastened by the Petition of Right, Charles resolved to rule without Parliament entirely, funding his government during the 1630s with a variety of levies and fines imposed without parliamentary consent.

> Angered rather than chastened by the Petition of Right, Charles resolved to rule without Parliament entirely, funding his government during the 1630s with a variety of levies and fines imposed without parliamentary consent.

The Scottish invasion forced Charles to summon a new parliament. Once summoned, however, the parliamentarians were determined to impose a series of radical reforms on the king's government before they would even consider granting him funds to raise an army against the Scots. Charles initially cooperated with these reforms, even allowing Parliament to execute his chief minister. But it soon became clear that the parliamentary leaders had no intention of fighting the Scots. Instead, a de facto alliance emerged between them, which was reinforced by their common, Calvinist, religious outlook. By 1642, Charles had had enough. Marching his guards into the House of Commons, he tried (but failed) to arrest five of its leaders. Charles then withdrew from London to raise an army. Parliament responded by summoning its own force and voting the taxation to pay for it. By the end of 1642, open warfare had erupted between king and Parliament.

CIVIL WAR AND COMMONWEALTH

Arrayed on the king's side were most of England's aristocrats and largest landowners, who were loyal to the established Church of England despite their opposi-

Charles I. This portrait by Anthony Van Dyck vividly captures the ill-fated monarch's arrogance.

WHAT CAUSED THE DECLINE OF SPAIN IN THE SEVENTEENTH CENTURY?

DIVERGENT PATHS: SPAIN, FRANCE, AND ENGLAND, 1600–1660   381

tion to some of Charles's own religious innovations. The parliamentary forces were made up of smaller landholders, tradesmen, and artisans, most of whom were Puritans. At first the royalists, having obvious advantages of military experience, won most of the victories. In 1644, however, the parliamentary army was reorganized, and soon afterward the fortunes of battle shifted. The royalist forces were badly beaten, and in 1646 the king was compelled to surrender. Soon thereafter, the episcopate was abolished and a Calvinist-style church was established throughout England.

The struggle might now have ended had not a quarrel developed within the parliamentary party. The majority of its members were ready to restore Charles to the throne as a limited monarch under an arrangement whereby a uniformly Calvinist faith would be imposed on both Scotland and England as the state religion. But a radical minority of Puritans, commonly known as Independents, distrusted Charles and insisted on religious toleration for themselves and all other Protestants. Their leader was Oliver Cromwell (1599–1658), who had risen to command the parliamentary army.

Taking advantage of the dissension within the ranks of his opponents, Charles renewed the war in 1648 but, after a brief campaign, was forced to surrender. Cromwell now resolved to end the life of "that man of blood" and, ejecting all the moderate Protestants from Parliament by force of arms, obliged the "Rump" Parliament that remained to vote an end to the monarchy. On January 30, 1649, Charles I was beheaded; a short time later, the hereditary House of Lords was abolished, and England became a republic.

But founding a republic was far easier than maintaining one. Officially called a Commonwealth, the new form of government did not last long. Technically the Rump Parliament continued as the legislative body; but Cromwell, with the army at his command, possessed the real power and soon became exasperated by the legislators' attempts to enrich themselves by confiscating their opponents' property. Accordingly, in 1653 he marched a detachment of troops into the Rump Parliament. Declaring "Come, I will put an end to your prating," he ordered the members to disperse. The Commonwealth thus ceased to exist and was soon replaced by the "Protectorate," a thinly disguised autocracy established under a constitution drafted by officers of the army. Called the Instrument of Government, this text was the nearest approximation to a written constitution England has ever had. Extensive powers were given to Cromwell as "lord protector" for life, and his office was made hereditary. At first a new Parliament

exercised limited authority to make laws and levy taxes, but in 1655 Cromwell abruptly dismissed its members also. Thereafter the government became a virtual dictatorship, with Cromwell wielding a sovereignty more absolute than any Stuart monarch ever dreamed of claiming.

THE RESTORATION OF THE MONARCHY

Given the choice between a Puritan military dictatorship and the old royalist regime, when the occasion arose England unhesitatingly opted for the latter. Years of unpopular Calvinist austerities had discredited the Puritans, making most people long for the milder style of the Elizabethan church. Thus not long after Cromwell's death in 1658, one of his generals seized power and called for elections to a new parliament, which met in the spring of 1660 and proclaimed as king Charles I's exiled son, Charles II, after Charles first gave the traditional promises of good government and then promised a limited religious toleration for all Protestants.

Charles II (1660–1685) restored bishops to the Church of England, but he did not return to the provocative religious policies of his father. Declaring with characteristic good humor that he did not wish to "resume his travels," Charles agreed to respect Parliament and observe the Petition of Right. He also accepted all the legislation passed by Parliament immediately before the outbreak of civil war in 1642, including the requirement that Parliament be summoned at least once every three years. After one further test in the late seventeenth century, England thus emerged from its civil war as a limited monarchy, in which power was exercised by "the king in parliament."

CHRONOLOGY

THE ENGLISH CIVIL WAR, 1603–1660

Reign of the Stuarts begins	1603
Reign of Charles I	1625–1649
Rule without Parliament	1629–1640
English civil war	1642–1649
Charles I beheaded	1649
Commonwealth	1649–1653
Protectorate	1653–1658
Restoration of the monarchy	1660

DEMOCRACY AND THE ENGLISH CIVIL WAR

The English civil war raised fundamental issues about the political rights and responsibilities of Englishmen. Many of these issues were addressed in a lengthy debate held within the General Council of Cromwell's New Model Army at Putney in October 1647. It is interesting that none of the participants in these debates seems to have recognized the implications their arguments might have for the political rights of women. Only King Charles, speaking moments before his execution in 1649, saw the radical implications of the constitutional experiment on which the parliamentary forces had embarked—but ironically, it was his own radical assertions of monarchical authority that prompted the rebellion that overthrew him.

THE ARMY DEBATES, 1647

Colonel Rainsborough: Really, I think that the poorest man that is in England has a life to live as the greatest man; and therefore truly, sir, I think it's clear, that every man that is to live under a government ought first by his own consent to put himself under that government; and I do think that the poorest man in England is not at all bound in a strict sense to that government that he has not had a voice to put himself under . . . insomuch that I should doubt whether I was an Englishman or not, that should doubt of these things.

General Ireton: Give me leave to tell you, that if you make this the rule, I think you must fly for refuge to an absolute natural right, and you must deny all civil right; and I am sure it will come to that in the consequence. . . . For my part, I think it is no right at all. I think that no person has a right to an interest or share in the disposing of the affairs of the kingdom, and in determining or choosing those that shall determine what laws we shall be ruled by here, no person has a right to this that has not a permanent fixed interest in this kingdom, and those persons together are properly the represented of this kingdom who, taken together, and consequently are to make up the representers of this kingdom. . . .

We talk of birthright. Truly, birthright there is. . . . [M]en may justly have by birthright, by their very being born in England, that we should not seclude them out of England. That we should not refuse to give them air and place and ground, and the freedom of the highways and other things, to live amongst us, not any man that is born here, though he in birth or by his birth there come nothing at all that is part of the permanent interest of this kingdom to him. That I think is due to a man by birth. But that by a man's being born here he shall have a share in that power that shall dispose of the lands here, and of all things here, I do not think it is a sufficient ground.

David Wootton, ed., *Divine Right and Democracy: An Anthology of Political Writing in Stuart England* (New York, 1986), pp. 286–287, language modernized.

CHARLES I ON THE SCAFFOLD, 1649

I think it is my duty, to God first, and to my country, for to clear myself both as an honest man, a good king, and a good Christian.

I shall begin first with my innocence. In truth I think it not very needful for me to insist long upon this, for all the world knows that I never did begin a war with the two Houses of Parliament; and I call God to witness, to whom I must shortly make an account, that I never did intend to incroach upon their privileges. . . .

As for the people—truly I desire their liberty and freedom as much as anybody whatsoever. But I must tell you that their liberty and freedom consists in having of government those laws by which their lives and goods may be most their own. It is not for having share in government. That is nothing pertaining to them. A subject and a sovereign are clean different things, and therefore, until they do that—I mean that you do put the people in that liberty as I say—certainly they will never enjoy themselves.

Sirs, it was for this that now I am come here. If I would have given way to an arbitrary way, for to have all laws changed according to the power of the sword,

I needed not to have come here. And therefore I tell you (and I pray God it be not laid to your charge) that I am the martyr of the people.

Brian Tierney, Donald Kagan, and L. Pearce Williams, eds., *Great Issues in Western Civilization* (New York, 1967), pp. 46–47.

QUESTIONS FOR ANALYSIS

1. What issues did the English civil war raise regarding the rights of freeborn Englishmen? What are the natural rights of man? What are civil rights?
2. For what reasons was Charles I brought to trial and ultimately beheaded? Was Charles truly the "martyr of the people"?

THE PROBLEM OF DOUBT AND THE QUEST FOR CERTAINTY

Why was this period such a fertile one for political philosophy?

Between 1540 and 1660, Europeans were forced to confront a world in which all that they had once taken for granted was suddenly cast into doubt. An entirely new world had been discovered in the Americas, populated by millions of people whose very existence compelled Europeans to rethink some of their most basic ideas about humanity and human nature. Equally disorienting, the religious uniformity of Europe, although never absolute, had been shattered to an unprecedented extent by the Reformation and the religious wars that arose from it. In 1540, it was still possible to imagine that these religious divisions might be temporary. By 1660, it was clear they would be permanent. No longer, therefore, could Europeans regard revealed religious faith as an adequate foundation for universal philosophical conclusions, for even Christians now disagreed about the fundamental truths of the faith. Political allegiances were similarly under threat, as intellectuals and common people alike began to assert a right to resist princes with whom they disagreed on matters of religion. Even morality and custom were

beginning to seem arbitrary and detached from the natural ordering of the world.

Europeans responded to this pervasive climate of doubt in a variety of ways, ranging from radical skepticism to authoritarian assertions of religious fideism and political absolutism. What united their responses, however, was a sometimes desperate search for new foundations on which to reconstruct some measure of certainty in the face of Europe's new intellectual, religious, and political challenges.

WITCHCRAFT ACCUSATIONS AND THE POWER OF THE STATE

Adding to the fears of Europeans was their conviction that witchcraft was a mortal and increasing threat to their world. Although most people in the Middle Ages believed that certain individuals, usually women, could heal or harm through the practice of magic, it was not until the fifteenth century that learned authorities began to insist that such powers could derive only from some kind of "pact" made by the "witch" with the devil. Once this belief became accepted, judicial officers became much more active in seeking out suspected witches for prosecution. In 1484 Pope Innocent VIII ordered papal inquisitors to use all the means at their disposal to detect and eliminate witchcraft, including torture of suspected witches. Predictably, torture increased the number of accused witches who confessed to their alleged crimes; and as more accused witches confessed, more and more witches were "discovered," accused, and executed—even in areas (such as England) where torture was not employed and where the Inquisition did not operate.

In considering the rash of witchcraft persecution that swept early modern Europe, we need to keep two facts in mind. First of all, the witchcraft trials were by no means limited to Catholic countries. Protestant reformers believed in the insidious powers of Satan just as much as Catholics did. Second, it was only when the efforts of religious authorities to detect witchcraft were backed up by the coercive powers of secular governments to execute them that the fear of witches became truly murderous. Between 1580 and about 1660, however, enthusiasm for catching and killing "witches" claimed tens of thousands of victims, of whom at least three quarters were women. After 1660, accusations of witchcraft gradually diminished, but isolated incidents, such as the one at Salem, Massachusetts, continued to crop up for another half century.

This witch mania reflects the fears that early modern Europeans held about the devil. But it also reflects their growing conviction that only the state, and not the church, had the power to protect them. One of the most striking features of the mania for hunting down

Supposed Witches Worshiping the Devil in the Form of a Billy Goat. In the background other witches ride bareback on flying demons. This is one of the earliest visual conceptions of witchcraft, dating from around 1460.

witches is the extent to which these prosecutions, in both Catholic and Protestant countries, were carried out under the supervision of the state. In both Catholic and Protestant countries, the result of these witchcraft trials was thus a considerable increase in the scope of the state's powers and responsibilities to regulate the lives of its subjects.

THE SEARCH FOR AUTHORITY

The crisis of Europe's iron century (as even contemporaries sometimes called it) was fundamentally a crisis of authority. Attempts to reestablish some foundation for agreed authority took many forms. For the French nobleman Michel de Montaigne (1533–1592), who wrote during the height of the French wars of religion, the result was a searching skepticism about the possibilities of any certain knowledge whatsoever. Although the range of subjects of his *Essays* is wide, two main themes are dominant. One is a pervasive skepticism. Making his motto *Que sais-je?* ("What do I know?"), Montaigne decided that he knew very little for certain. From this Montaigne's second main principle followed—the need for moderation. Because all people think they know the perfect religion and the perfect government, yet few agree on what that perfection might be, Montaigne concluded that no religion or government is really perfect and consequently no belief is worth fighting for to the death. Instead, people should accept the teachings of religion on faith and obey the governments constituted to rule over them, without resorting to fanaticism in either sphere.

Montaigne sought refuge from the trials of his age in skepticism, distance, and resigned dignity. His contemporary, the French lawyer Jean Bodin (1530–1596), looked instead to resolve the disorders of the day by reestablishing the powers of the state on new and more secure foundations. Like Montaigne, Bodin was particularly troubled by the upheavals caused by the religious wars in France—he had even witnessed the frightful St. Bartholomew's Day Massacre of 1572 in Paris. But instead of shrugging his shoulders about the bloodshed, he resolved to offer a political plan to make sure turbulence would cease. This he did in his monumental *Six Books of the Commonwealth* (1576), the earliest fully developed statement of absolute governmental sovereignty in Western political thought. For Bodin, sovereignty was "the most high, absolute, and perpetual power over all subjects," consisting principally in the power "to give laws to subjects without their consent." Bodin insisted that monarchs could in no way be limited, either by legislative or judicial bodies or even

WHAT WAS THE RELATIONSHIP BETWEEN THE BAROQUE SCHOOL AND THE COUNTER-REFORMATION?

LITERATURE AND THE ARTS   385

by laws made by their predecessors or themselves. Even if the ruler proved a tyrant, the subject had no warrant to resist, for any resistance would open the door "to a licentious anarchy which is worse than the harshest tyranny in the world."

Like Bodin, who was moved by the events of St. Bartholomew's Day to formulate a doctrine of political absolutism, Thomas Hobbes (1588–1679) was moved by the turmoil of the English civil war to do the same in his classic of political theory, *Leviathan* (1651). Yet Hobbes differed from Bodin in several respects. For one, whereas Bodin assumed that the absolute sovereign power would be a royal monarch, Hobbes made no such assumption. Any form of government capable of protecting its subjects' lives and property might act as a sovereign (and hence all-powerful) Leviathan. Then too, whereas Bodin defined his state as "the lawful government of families" and hence did not believe that the state could abridge private property rights because families could not exist without property, Hobbes's state existed to rule over atomistic individuals and thus was licensed to trample over both liberty and property if the government's own survival was at stake.

Perhaps the most moving attempt to respond to the problem of doubt in seventeenth-century culture was offered by the French moral and religious philosopher Blaise Pascal (1623–1662). Pascal began his career as a mathematician and scientific rationalist. But at age thirty Pascal abandoned science as the result of a conversion experience and became a firm adherent of Jansenism, a puritanical faction within French Catholicism. From then until his death he worked on a highly ambitious philosophical-religious project meant to persuade doubters of the truth of Christianity by appealing simultaneously to their intellects and their emotions. Pascal's *Pensées* (Thoughts) expresses the author's own terror, anguish, and awe in the face of evil and eternity but presents that awe itself as evidence

for the existence of God. Pascal's hope was that on this foundation, some measure of hopefulness about humanity and its capacity for self-knowledge could be re-erected that would avoid both the dogmatism and the extreme skepticism that were so prominent in seventeenth-century society.

LITERATURE AND THE ARTS

What was the relationship between the Baroque school and the Counter-Reformation?

Doubt and the uncertainty of human knowledge were also primary themes in the literature and art produced during western Europe's iron century. The greatest writers and painters of the period were moved by a realization of the ambiguities and ironies of human existence not unlike that expressed in different ways by Montaigne and Pascal. They all were fully aware of the horrors of war and human suffering so rampant in their day, but they also sought some measure of redemption for human beings caught up in a world that treated them so cruelly. Out of this tragic balance came some of the greatest works in the entire history of European literature and art.

MIGUEL DE CERVANTES (1547–1616)

Cervantes's masterpiece, the satirical romance *Don Quixote*, recounts the adventures of a Spanish gentleman, Don Quixote of La Mancha, who becomes slightly unbalanced by his constant reading of chivalric epics. In his distorted fancy he mistakes inns for castles and serving girls for courtly ladies on fire with love. Set off in contrast to the "knight-errant" is the figure of his faithful squire, Sancho Panza. The latter represents the ideal of the practical man, with his feet on the ground and content with the modest but substantial pleasures of eating, drinking, and sleeping. Yet Cervantes clearly does not wish to say that the realism of a Sancho Panza is categorically preferable to the "quixotic" idealism of his master. Rather, the two men represent different facets of human nature. Without any doubt, *Don Quixote* is a devastating satire on the anachronistic chivalric mentality that was already hastening Spain's decline. But for all that, the reader's sympathies remain with the protagonist, the man from La Mancha who dares to "dream the impossible dream."

CHRONOLOGY

THE SEARCH FOR AUTHORITY, 1572–1670

Montaigne's *Essays*	1572–1580
Bodin's *Six Books of the Commonwealth*	1576
Hobbes's *Leviathan*	1651
Pascal's *Pensées*	1670

ELIZABETHAN AND JACOBEAN DRAMA

Among a bevy of great Elizabethan and Jacobean play-wrights, the most outstanding were Christopher Marlowe (1564–1593), Ben Jonson (c. 1572–1637), and William Shakespeare (1564–1616). Of the three, the fiery Marlowe, whose life was cut short in a tavern brawl before he reached the age of thirty, was the most popular in his own day. In plays such as *Tamburlaine* and *Doctor Faustus*, Marlowe created larger-than-life heroes who seek and come close to conquering everything in their path and feeling every possible sensation. But they meet unhappy ends because, for Marlowe, there are limits on human striving, and wretchedness as well as greatness lies in the human lot.

In contrast to the heroic tragedies of Marlowe, Ben Jonson wrote corrosive comedies that expose human vices and foibles. In the particularly bleak *Volpone* Jonson shows people behaving like deceitful and lustful animals, but in the later *Alchemist* he balances an attack on quackery and gullibility with admiration for resourceful lower-class characters who cleverly take advantage of their supposed betters.

The plays from Shakespeare's second period are far darker in mood, being characterized by bitterness, pathos, and a troubled searching into the mysteries and meaning of human existence.

The greatest of the Elizabethan dramatists, William Shakespeare was born into the family of a tradesman in the provincial town of Stratford-on-Avon. Little is known about his early life. He left his native village, having gained a modest education, when he was about twenty and went to London where he found employment in the theater. How he eventually became an actor and still later a writer of plays is uncertain, but by the age of twenty-eight he had definitely acquired a reputation as an author sufficient to excite the jealousy of his rivals. Before he retired to his native Stratford about 1610 to spend the rest of his days in ease, he had written or collaborated in writing nearly forty plays, over and above 150 sonnets, and two long narrative poems.

Shakespeare's dramas fall thematically into three groups. Those written during the playwright's early years are characterized by a sense of confidence that, despite human foolishness, the world is fundamentally orderly and just. These include a number of the history plays, which recount England's struggles and glories leading up to the triumph of the Tudor dynasty; the lyrical romantic tragedy *Romeo and Juliet*; and a number of comedies including the magical *Midsummer Night's Dream*, *Twelfth Night, As You Like It*, and *Much Ado about Nothing*.

The plays from Shakespeare's second period are far darker in mood, being characterized by bitterness, pathos, and a troubled searching into the mysteries and meaning of human existence. The series begins with the tragedy of indecisive idealism represented by *Hamlet*, goes on to the cynicism of *Measure for Measure* and *All's Well That Ends Well*, and culminates in the searing tragedies of *Macbeth* and *King Lear*, wherein characters assert that "life's but a walking shadow . . . a tale told by an idiot, full of sound and fury signifying nothing," and that "as flies to wanton boys are we to the gods; they kill us for their sport." Despite their gloom, however, the plays of Shakespeare's second period contain some of the dramatist's greatest flights of poetic grandeur.

Shakespeare ended his dramatic career, however, with a third period characterized by a profound spirit of reconciliation and peace. Of the three plays (all idyllic romances) written during this final period, the last, *The Tempest*, is the widest ranging in its reflections on human nature and the power of art. Ancient animosities are buried and wrongs are righted by a combination of natural and supernatural means, and a wide-eyed, youthful heroine rejoices on first seeing men with the words "O brave new world, that has such people in it!" Here, then, Shakespeare seems to be saying that despite humanity's trials, life is not so bitter after all, and the divine plan of the universe is ultimately benevolent and just.

MANNERISM

The ironies and tensions inherent in human existence were also portrayed with eloquence and profundity by several immortal masters of the visual arts who flourished during this tumultuous century. The dominant goal in Italian and Spanish painting between about 1540 and 1600, was to fascinate the viewer with special effects achieved by means of two entirely different styles. (Confusingly, both styles are sometimes referred to as "Mannerism.") The first was based on the style of the Renaissance master Raphael but moved from that painter's gracefulness to a highly self-conscious elegance bordering on the bizarre and surreal. Representatives of this approach were the Florentines Pontormo (1494–1557) and Bronzino (1503–1572). Their sharp-focused portraits are flat and cold, yet strangely riveting.

WHAT WAS THE RELATIONSHIP BETWEEN THE BAROQUE SCHOOL AND THE COUNTER-REFORMATION?

LITERATURE AND THE ARTS   387

The other extreme was theatrical in a more conventional sense—highly dramatic and emotionally compelling. Painters who followed this approach were indebted to Michelangelo but went much farther than he did in emphasizing shadowy contrasts, restlessness, and distortion. Of this second group, the two most outstanding were the Venetian Tintoretto (1518–1594) and the Spaniard El Greco (c. 1541–1614). Combining aspects of Michelangelo's style with the traditionally Venetian taste for rich color, Tintoretto produced monumental canvases that still inspire awe. More emotional still is the work of Tintoretto's disciple, El Greco. Born on the Greek island of Crete, this extraordinary artist absorbed some of the stylized elongation characteristic of Greco-Byzantine icon painting before traveling to Italy to learn color and drama from Tintoretto. Finally he settled in Spain, where he was called "El Greco"—"the Greek." His stunning portraits of gaunt, dignified Spaniards radiate a rare blend of austerity and spiritual insight that reflects the painter's own deeply mystical Catholic fervor.

BAROQUE ART AND ARCHITECTURE

The dominant artistic school of southern Europe from about 1600 until the early 1700s was that of the Baroque. Originating in Rome as an expression of the ideals of the Counter-Reformation papacy and the Jesuit order, Baroque architecture in particular aimed to promote a specifically Catholic worldview. Similarly, Baroque painting often was done in the service of the Counter-Reformation church, which at its high tide around 1620 seemed everywhere to be on the offensive. When Baroque painters were not celebrating Counter-Reformation ideals, most of them worked in the service of monarchs who sought their own glorification.

The most imaginative and influential figure of the Roman Baroque was the architect and sculptor Gianlorenzo Bernini (1598–1680), a frequent employee of the papacy who created a magnificent celebration of papal grandeur in the sweeping colonnades leading up to St. Peter's Basilica. Breaking with Renaissance classicism, Bernini's architecture retained such classical elements as columns and domes, but combined them in ways meant to express both aggressive restlessness and great power. Harking back to the restless motion of Hellenistic statuary—particularly the *Laocoön* group— and building on tendencies already present in the later sculpture of Michelangelo, Bernini's statuary emphasizes drama and incites the viewer to respond to it rather than serenely to observe.

David, by Bernini (1598–1680). Whereas the earlier conceptions of David by the Renaissance sculptors Donatello and Michelangelo were reposeful (see pp. 334 and 335), the Baroque sculptor Bernini chose to portray his young hero at the peak of physical exertion.

To view the very greatest masterpieces of southern European Baroque painting one must look to Spain and the work of Diego Velázquez (1599–1660). Velázquez was not an entirely typical exponent of the Baroque style. Certainly many of his canvases display a characteristically Baroque delight in motion, drama, and power, but Velázquez's best work is characterized by a more restrained thoughtfulness than is usually found in the Baroque. Thus his famous *Surrender of Breda* shows muscular horses and splendid Spanish grandees on the one hand but un-Baroque sympathy for defeated, disarrayed troops on the other. Velázquez's greatest painting, *The Maids of Honor,* done around 1656 after Spain's collapse, is one of the most thoughtful and probing artistic examinations of illusion and reality ever executed.

The Maids of Honor, by Diego Velázquez. The artist himself is at work on a double portrait of the king and queen of Spain (who can be seen in the rear mirror), but reality is more obvious in the foreground in the persons of the delicately impish princess, her two maids, and a misshapen dwarf. The twentieth-century Spanish artist Picasso gained great inspiration from this work.

DUTCH PAINTING IN THE GOLDEN AGE

Southern Europe's main rival for artistic laurels was the Netherlands, where three extremely dissimilar painters all explored the greatness and wretchedness of humanity to the fullest. The earliest, Peter Brueghel (c. 1525–1569), worked in a vein related to earlier Netherlandish realism. But unlike his predecessors, who favored quiet urban scenes, Brueghel exulted in portraying the life of the peasantry. Late in his career Brueghel became appalled by the intolerance and bloodshed he witnessed in the Netherlands and expressed his criticism in an understated yet searing manner. Most powerful is Brueghel's *Massacre of the Innocents,* which from a distance looks like a snug scene of a Flemish village buried in snow. In fact, however, heartless soldiers are methodically breaking into homes and slaughtering babies, the simple peasant folk are fully at their mercy, and the artist—alluding to a Gospel forgotten by warring Catholics and Protestants alike—seems to be saying "as it happened in the time of Christ, so it happens now."

Vastly different from Brueghel was the Netherlandish Baroque painter Peter Paul Rubens (1577–1640). Since the Baroque was an international movement closely linked to the spread of the Counter-Reformation, it should offer no surprise that Baroque style was extremely well represented in just that part of the Netherlands, which—after long warfare—had been retained by Spain. In fact, Rubens of Antwerp was a far more typical Baroque artist than Velázquez of Madrid, painting hundreds of robust canvases that glorified resurgent Catholicism or exalted second-rate aristocrats by portraying them as epic heroes. But unlike a host of lesser Baroque artists, Rubens was not lacking in subtlety and was a man of many moods. His gentle portrait of his son Nicholas catches unaffected childhood in a moment of repose; and his late *Horrors of War* movingly portrays what he himself called "the grief of unfortunate Europe, which, for so many years now, has suffered plunder, outrage, and misery."

In some ways a blend of Brueghel and Rubens, the greatest of all Netherlandish painters, Rembrandt van Rijn (1606–1669), defies all attempts at easy characterization. Living across the border from the Spanish Netherlands in staunchly Calvinistic Holland, Rembrandt belonged to a society that was too austere to tolerate the unbuckled realism of a Brueghel or the fleshy Baroque pomposity of a Rubens. Yet Rembrandt managed to put both realistic and Baroque traits to new uses. In his early career he gained fame and fortune as a painter of biblical scenes characterized by swirling forms and stunning experiments with light. Rembrandt was also active as a portrait painter who knew how to flatter his subjects by emphasizing their Calvinistic steadfastness, to the great advantage of his purse. As personal tragedies mounted in the painter's middle and declining years, his art became

WHAT WAS THE RELATIONSHIP BETWEEN THE BAROQUE SCHOOL AND THE COUNTER-REFORMATION?

LITERATURE AND THE ARTS   389

Massacre of the Innocents, by Brueghel. This painting shows how effectively art can be used as a means of social commentary. Many art historians believe that Brueghel was tacitly depicting the suffering of the Netherlands at the hands of the Spanish in his own day.

Horrors of War, by Rubens. The war god, Mars, here casts aside his mistress, Venus, and threatens humanity with death and destruction. In his old age Rubens took a far more critical view of war than he did for most of his earlier career.

Self-Portraits. Self-portraits became common during the sixteenth and seventeenth centuries, reflecting the intense introspection of the period. Left: Rembrandt painted more than sixty self-portraits; this one, dating from around 1660, captures the artist's creativity, theatricality (note the costume), and the honesty of his self-examination. Right: Judith Leyster (1609–1660) was a Dutch contemporary of Rembrandt who pursued a successful career as an artist during her early twenties, before she married. Respected in her own day, she was all but forgotten for centuries thereafter.

more pensive and somber, but it gained in dignity, subtle lyricism, and awesome mystery. Thus his later portraits, including several self-portraits, are imbued with introspective qualities and a suggestion that only half the story is being told. Equally moving are explicitly philosophical paintings such as *Aristotle Contemplating the Bust of Homer,* in which the philosopher seems spellbound by the radiance of the epic poet, and *The Polish Rider,* in which realistic and Baroque elements merge in a portrayal of a pensive young man setting out fearlessly into a perilous world. Like Shakespeare, Rembrandt knew that life's journey is full of perils, but his most mature paintings suggest that these can be mastered with a courageous awareness of one's human shortcomings.

CONCLUSION

Between 1540 and 1660, Europe was racked by a combination of religious wars, political rebellions, and economic crises that undermined confidence in traditional structures of social, religious, and political authority. The result was fear, skepticism, and a search for new, more certain foundations on which to rebuild the social, political, and religious order of Europe. For artists and intellectuals, the period proved to be one of the most creative epochs in the history of Europe. But for common people, the century was one of extraordinary suffering.

After a hundred years of destructive efforts to restore the religious unity of Europe through war, a de facto religious toleration between states was beginning to emerge by 1660 as the only way to preserve the European political order. Within states, toleration was still very limited when this terrible century ended. But in territories where religious rivalries ran too deep to be overcome, rulers were beginning to discover that loyalty to the state was a value that could override even the religious divisions among their subjects. The result of this century of crises was thus to strengthen Europeans' confidence in the powers of the state to heal their wounds and right their wrongs, with religion relegated more and more to the private sphere of individual conscience. In the following centuries, this new confidence in the state as an autonomous moral agent that acts in accordance with its own "reasons of state," and for its own purposes, would prove a powerful challenge to the traditions of limited consensual government that had emerged out of the Middle Ages.

KEY TERMS

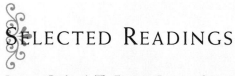

Peace of Augsburg	Spanish Armada	Oliver Cromwell	William Shakespeare
Huguenots	Thirty Years' War	Michel de Montaigne	Rembrandt van Rijn
Henry of Navarre	Cardinal Richelieu	*Leviathan*	
St. Bartholomew's Day massacre	James I	*Don Quixote*	
Edict of Nantes	Puritans	Baroque	

SELECTED READINGS

Bonney, Richard. *The European Dynastic States, 1494–1660.* Oxford and New York, 1991. An excellent survey of continental Europe during the "long" sixteenth century.

Briggs, Robin. *Early Modern France, 1560–1715.* 2d ed. Oxford and New York, 1997. Updated and authoritative, with new bibliographies.

Briggs, Robin. *Witches and Neighbors: The Social and Cultural Context of European Witchcraft.* New York, 1996. An influential recent account of continental witchcraft.

Cervantes, Miguel de. *Don Quixote.* Trans. Edith Grossman. New York, 2003. A splendid new translation, far better than its competitors.

Cochrane, Eric, Charles M. Gray, and Mark A. Kishlansky. *Early Modern Europe: Crisis of Authority.* Chicago, 1987. An outstanding source collection from the University of Chicago Readings in Western Civilization series.

Held, Julius S., and Donald Posner. *Seventeenth- and Eighteenth-Century Art: Baroque Painting, Sculpture, Architecture.* New York, 1971. The most complete and best-organized introductory review of the subject in English.

Hibbard, Howard. *Bernini.* Baltimore, Md., 1965. The basic study in English of this central figure of Baroque artistic activity.

Hirst, Derek. *England in Conflict, 1603–1660: Kingdom, Community, Commonwealth.* Oxford and New York, 1999. A complete revision of the author's *Authority and Conflict* (1986), this is an up-to-date and balanced account of a period that has been a historical battleground over the past twenty years.

Hobbes, Thomas. *Leviathan.* Ed. Richard Tuck. 2d ed. Cambridge and New York, 1996. The most recent edition, up-to-date and complete.

Holt, Mack P. *The French Wars of Religion, 1562–1629.* Cambridge and New York, 1995. A clear account of a confusing time.

Kors, Alan Charles, and Edward Peters. *Witchcraft in Europe, 400–1700: A Documentary History.* 2d ed. Philadelphia, 2000. A superb collection of documents, significantly expanded in the second edition, with up-to-date commentary.

Levack, Brian P. *The Witch-Hunt in Early Modern Europe.* 2d ed. London and New York, 1995. The best account of the persecution of suspected witches; coverage extends from Europe in 1450 to America in 1750.

Limm, Peter, ed. *The Thirty Years' War.* London, 1984. An outstanding short survey, followed by a selection of primary-source documents.

Lynch, John. *Spain, 1516–1598: From Nation-State to World Empire.* Oxford and Cambridge, Mass., 1991. The best book in English on Spain at the pinnacle of its sixteenth-century power.

MacCaffrey, Wallace. *Elizabeth I.* New York, 1993. An outstanding traditional biography by an excellent scholar.

Martin, Colin, and Geoffrey Parker. *The Spanish Armada.* London, 1988. Incorporates recent discoveries from undersea archaeology with more traditional historical sources.

Martin, John Rupert. *Baroque.* New York, 1977. A thought-provoking, thematic treatment, less a survey than an essay on the painting, sculpture, and architecture of the period.

Mattingly, Garrett. *The Armada.* Boston, 1959. A great narrative history that reads like a novel; for more recent work, however, see Martin and Parker.

Parker, Geoffrey. *The Dutch Revolt.* 2d ed. Ithaca, N.Y., 1989. The standard survey in English on the revolt of the Netherlands.

Parker, Geoffrey. *Philip II.* Boston, 1978. A fine biography by an expert in both the Spanish and the Dutch sources.

Parker, Geoffrey, ed. *The Thirty Years' War.* Rev. ed. London and New York, 1987. A wide-ranging collection of essays by scholarly experts.

Pascal, Blaise. *Pensées* (French-English edition). Ed. H. F. Stewart. London, 1950.

Quint, David. *Montaigne and the Quality of Mercy: Ethical and Political Themes in the "Essais."* Princeton, N.J., 1999. A fine treatment that presents Montaigne's thought as a response to the French wars of religion.

Roberts, Michael. *Gustavus Adolphus and the Rise of Sweden.* London, 1973. Still the authoritative English-language account.

Russell, Conrad. *The Causes of the English Civil War.* Oxford, 1990. A penetrating and provocative analysis by one of the leading "revisionist" historians of the period.

PART V
EARLY MODERN EUROPE

SEVENTEENTH- AND EIGHTEENTH-CENTURY European life was shaped by the combined effects of commerce, war, and a steadily growing population. A commercial revolution spurred the development of overseas colonies and trade while opening up new markets for European industry. Agricultural productivity increased, making it possible for Europe to feed a population that had now reached unprecedented levels. Population growth in turn enabled European governments to wage more frequent wars and to employ larger and larger armies.

Although monarchs continued to meet with opposition from the various estates within their realms, they increasingly asserted their power as absolute rulers. Warfare remained the chief instrument of European foreign policy; but slowly the notion of a diplomatic and military "balance of power" began to displace the pursuit of unrestrained aggrandizement as the primary goal of European state relations.

Profound changes were also occurring in European intellectual life during these centuries. Using new instruments and applying new mathematical techniques, astronomers proved beyond question that the earth was not the center of the universe. Biologists and physicians pioneered a more sophisticated understanding of the nature and processes by which life was created and sustained, and physicists such as Sir Isaac Newton established for the first time a true science of mechanics. During the eighteenth century, these discoveries gave rise to a new confidence in the capacity of human reason alone to understand nature and so to improve human life—a confidence those who held to it declared to be a sign of enlightenment.

	POLITICS	SOCIETY AND CULTURE	ECONOMY	INTERNATIONAL RELATIONS
1500		Copernicus's *On the Revolutions of the Heavenly Spheres* (1543)	Enclosure movement (1500–1700s)	
		Claudio Monteverdi, father of opera (1567–1643)	Demand for sugar escalates in Europe (late 1500s)	Sir Francis Drake leads attack on Spanish fleet at Cadíz (1587)
		Johannes Kepler (1571–1630)		
		William Harvey (1578–1657)	Widespread crop failure in France (1597–1694)	
1600		Literacy increases across Europe (1600–1800)	Mechanically powered saws and calico-printing from the Far East (1600s)	A total of 11 million Africans forcibl[y] shipped across the middle passage (1500–1800)
		Increased urbanization (1600–1750)	Dutch East India Company founded (1602)	
		Smoking spreads in Europe (early 1600s)		
		Over 80,000 leave England for the New World (1607–1650)		English colonists establish Jamestow[n] (1607)
		Galileo's *Starry Messenger* (1610)		
	Jean Baptiste Colbert, French finance minister (1619–1683)	Bacon's *New Instruments* (1620)		*Mayflower* lands in the New World (1620)
		Galileo charged with heresy (1633)		
		John Locke (1632–1704)		
		Descartes's *Discourse on Method* (1637)	French government introduces head tax (c. 1645)	
	Reign of Louis XIV, the Sun King (1643–1715)	Plague outbreaks (1649–1665)	Coffee consumption escalates in Europe (1650s)	
	England promulgates Navigation Acts (1651, 1660)	Edmond Halley (1656–1742)	Bank of Sweden founded (1657)	
	Restoration and return of Charles II (1660)	Founding of the Royal Society of London and the French Academy of Sciences (1660)		Dutch surrender New Amsterdam to England (1667)
		Daniel Defoe, author of *Robinson Crusoe* (1660–1731)		Austrian Habsburgs repulse Turks' assault on Vienna (1683)
		The Great Fire in London (1666)		Peace of Augsburg (1686)
	Louis XIV revokes the Edict of Nantes (1685)	Johann Sebastian Bach (1685–1750)		Portugal regains independence from Spain (1688)
		George Frideric Handel (1685–1759)		William of Orange rules England and Holland (1688)
		Newton's *Principia Mathematica* (1687)		War of the League of Augsburg (1688–1697)
	Glorious Revolution in England (1688–1689)	Locke's *Treatise of Civil Government* and *Essay Concerning Human Understanding* (1690)		Battle of the Boyne, English solidify control of Ireland (1690)
	Reign of Peter the Great of Russia (1689–1725)		Bank of England founded (1694)	
1700		Maize and the potato are introduced in Europe (1700s)	Fly shuttle for weaving loom invented (early 1700s)	
		Proliferation of salons and coffee-houses (1700s)	Physiocrats promote concept of laissez-faire (1700s)	
		First daily newspaper in England (1702)		War of Spanish Succession (1702–1713)
	Reign of Charles VI, emperor of Holy Roman Empire (1711–1740)	Rousseau's *Social Contract* (1712–1778)		England and Scotland unite to form Great Britain (1707)
	Treaty of Utrecht (1713)			
	Reign of George I, first of Hanoverian dynasty in England (1714–1727)			
	Reign of Louis XV of France (1715–1774)			
	Robert Walpole serves as England's first prime minister (1720–1742)			

POLITICS	SOCIETY AND CULTURE	ECONOMY	INTERNATIONAL RELATIONS	
		German imperial law prohibits journeyman associations (1731) France establishes the Road and Bridge Corps of Engineering (1747)		1731
eign of Frederick the Great, the enlightened despot," of Prussia 1740–1786)	Voltaire's *The Philosophical Letters* (1734) Montesquieu's *Spirit of Laws* (1748) Steady increase in population begins (1750) *Encyclopedia* published by Diderot and d'Alembert (1751–1772) Wolfgang Amadeus Mozart (1756–1791) Beccaria's *On Crimes and Punishment* (1764)	Antislavery movements emerge in Europe (1760s)	Seven Years' War/ French and Indian War (1756–1763)	
eign of George III of England 1760–1820) eign of Catherine the Great of Russia (1762–1796) aria Theresa and Joseph II of Austria rule jointly (1765–1780)		James Cook explores Pacific (1768–1779) Abbe Raynal's *Philosophical History of Europeans in the Two Indies* (1770)	Treaty of Paris: France concedes Canada and India to England (1763) French East India Company dissolves (1769) Russo-Turkish War (1769–1792) American Revolution (1775–1783)	
eign of Louis XVI of France 1774–1792) ench Revolution breaks out (1789)	Kant's "What Is Enlightenment?" (1784) Wollstonecraft's *Vindication of the Rights of Woman* (1792) Austen's *Pride and Prejudice* (1813)	Smith's *Inquiry into the Nature and Causes of the Wealth of Nations* (1776)	Russia, Austria, and Prussia fully partition Poland (1795)	1800

Chapter FIFTEEN

Absolutism and Empire, 1660–1789

THE PERIOD FROM around 1660 (when the English monarchy was restored, and Louis XIV of France began his personal rule) to 1789 (when the French Revolution erupted) is traditionally known as the age of absolutism. *Absolutism* was a political theory that encouraged rulers to claim complete sovereignty within their territories. To seventeenth- and eighteenth-century absolutists, complete sovereignty meant that a ruler could make law, dispense justice, create and direct a bureaucracy, declare war, and levy taxation without the formal approval of any other governing authorities. Frequently, such absolutist rulers claimed to govern their territories by the same divine right that established a father's absolute authority over his household. After the chaos of Europe's "iron century," many Europeans had come to believe that it was only by exalting the sovereignty of such "patriarchal" rulers that order could be restored to European life.

The age of absolutism was also an age of empire. By 1660, the French, Spanish, Portuguese, English, and Dutch had all established important colonies in the Americas and in Asia. Rivalry among these competing colonial powers was intense and fraught with consequence. In the late seventeenth century, European wars almost always had a colonial aspect. By the middle of the eighteenth century, however, Europe's wars were being driven by colonial considerations and imperial conflicts, as worldwide trade assumed a larger and larger role in the European economy.

Absolutism was not the only political theory according to which European governments sought to rule during this period. England, Scotland, the Dutch Republic, Switzerland, Venice, Sweden, and Poland-Lithuania were all either limited monarchies or republics; in Russia, an extreme autocracy was emerging that ascribed to the tsar a degree of control over his subjects' lives and property far beyond anything imagined by western European absolutists. Even in Russia, however, absolutism was never so

FOCUS QUESTIONS

- What were the aims of absolutist rulers?
- Did John Locke's political principles lie behind the Glorious Revolution in England?
- How did Louis XIV strengthen his control over France?
- What changes lay behind the growing power of Prussia?
- In what ways did Russian absolutism differ from its western European counterparts?

- What factors facilitated the commercial revolution?
- How did the patterns of European colonial settlement in the Americas differ from each other?
- In what ways did eighteenth-century European colonialism differ from seventeenth-century European colonialism?

unlimited in practice as it was in theory. Even the most absolute monarchs of seventeenth- and eighteenth-century Europe could rule effectively only so long as their subjects (and particularly their nobility) were prepared to consent, at least tacitly, to their policies. When outright opposition erupted, even absolutists were forced to back down. And when, in 1789, an outright political revolution occurred, the entire structure of absolutism came crashing to the ground.

THE APPEAL AND JUSTIFICATION OF ABSOLUTISM

What were the aims of absolutist rulers?

Absolutist monarchs sought to gather into their own hands command of the state's armed forces, control over its legal system, and the right to collect and spend the state's financial resources at will. To achieve these goals, they also needed to create an efficient, centralized bureaucracy that owed its allegiance directly to the monarch himself. The legally privileged estates of nobility and clergy, the political authority of semi-autonomous regions, and the pretensions of independent-minded representative assemblies were all obstacles, in the eyes of absolutists, to strong, centralized monarchical government. The history of abolutism is, as much as anything, a history of attempts by aspiring absolutists to bring such institutions to heel.

In most Protestant countries, the independent power of the church had already been subordinated to the interests of the state when the age of absolutism began. In France, Spain, and Austria, however, where Roman Catholicism had remained the state religion, absolutist monarchs now devoted concerted attention to "nationalizing" the church and its clergy within their territories. Even Charles III, the devout Spanish king who ruled from 1759 to 1788, pressed successfully for a papal concordat granting him control over ecclesiastical appointments and the right to nullify any papal bull affecting Spain of which he did not approve.

The most important potential opponents of royal absolutism were not churchmen, however, but nobles.

Monarchs dealt with their threat in various ways. Louis XIV deprived the French nobility of political power in the provinces while increasing their social prestige by requiring them to reside at his own lavish court at Versailles. Peter the Great of Russia (1689–1725) forced all his nobles into lifelong government service. Later in the century, Catherine II of Russia (1762–1796) struck a bargain whereby in return for vast estates and a variety of social and economic privileges (including exemption from taxation) the Russian nobility virtually surrendered the administrative and political power of the state into the empress's hands. In Prussia the army was staffed by nobles, as was generally the case in Spain, France, and England also. But in eighteenth-century Austria, the emperor Joseph II (1765–1790) adopted a policy of confrontation rather than accommodation, denying the nobility exemption from taxation and deliberately blurring the distinctions between nobles and commoners. Rarely, however, was the path of confrontation between crown and nobility successful in the long run. The most effective absolutist monarchies of the eighteenth century established a *modus vivendi* with their nobility, in which nobles came to see their own interests as tied to those of the crown. For this reason, cooperation more often characterized the relations between kings and nobles during the eighteenth-century "old regime" (ancien régime) than did conflict.

ALTERNATIVES TO ABSOLUTISM

Did John Locke's political principles lie behind the Glorious Revolution in England?

Although absolutism was the dominant model for seventeenth- and eighteenth-century European monarchs, it was by no means the only system by which Europeans governed themselves. In Venice, a republican oligarchy continued to rule the city. In the Netherlands, the territories that had won their independence from Spain during the early seventeenth century combined to form the United Provinces, the only truly new country to take shape in Europe during the early modern era. The Spanish wars created a deep distrust among the Dutch toward monarchs of any

DID JOHN LOCKE'S POLITICAL PRINCIPLES LIE BEHIND THE GLORIOUS REVOLUTION IN ENGLAND?

ALTERNATIVES TO ABSOLUTISM   399

stripe. As a result, the House of Orange never attempted to transform the new country from a republic into a monarchy.

LIMITED MONARCHY: THE CASE OF ENGLAND

At a time when representative assemblies were being undermined across much of Europe, the English Parliament was the longest-surviving and most highly developed such body in Europe. English political theorists had for centuries seen their government as a "mixed" monarchy, composed of monarchical, noble, and non-noble elements. During the seventeenth century, however, these traditions had come under threat, first through Charles I's attempts to rule without Parliament, and then during Oliver Cromwell's dictatorial Protectorate. The restoration of the monarchy in 1660 resolved the question of whether England would in future be a republic or a monarchy; but the sort of monarchy England would become remained an open question as the reign of Charles II began.

THE REIGN OF CHARLES II

Despite the fact that he was the son of the hated Charles I, Charles II (1660–1685) was initially welcomed by most English men and women. On his accession, he declared limited religious toleration for Protestant "dissenters" (Protestants who were not members of the official Church of England). He also promised to observe Magna Carta and the Petition of Right, declaring, with characteristic good humor, that he did not wish to "resume his travels." The unbuttoned moral atmosphere of his court, with its risqué plays, dancing, and sexual licentiousness, also reflected a public desire to forget the restraints of the Puritan past.

Charles was an admirer of all things French. During the 1670s he began openly to model his kingship on the absolutism of Louis XIV. As a result, the great men of England soon came to be publicly divided between Charles's supporters (called by their opponents "Tories," a popular nickname for Irish Catholic bandits) and his opponents (called by their opponents "Whigs," a nickname for Scottish Presbyterian rebels). Both sides feared absolutism, just as both sides feared a return to the "bad old days" of the 1640s, when resistance to the Crown had led to civil war and ultimately to republicanism. What they could not agree on was which possibility frightened them more.

Religion also remained a divisive issue. Charles was sympathetic to Roman Catholicism, even to the point of a deathbed conversion in 1685. During the 1670s, he briefly suspended civil penalties against Catholics and Protestant dissenters by asserting his right as king to ignore parliamentary legislation. The resulting public outcry compelled him to retreat; but this controversy, together with rising opposition to Charles's ardently Catholic brother, James, as the heir to the throne, led to a series of Whig electoral victories between 1679 and 1681. When a group of radical Whigs attempted to exclude James by law from succeeding his brother on the throne, however, Charles stared the opposition down in the so-called Exclusion Crisis. Thereafter, Charles found that his rising revenues from customs duties, combined with a secret subsidy from Louis XIV, enabled him to govern without relying on Parliament for money. Charles further alarmed Whig politicians by executing several of them on charges of treason, and by remodeling local government to make it more amenable to royal control. Charles died in 1685 with his power enhanced, but he left behind a political and religious legacy that was to be the undoing of his less able and adroit successor.

Charles II.

BOSSUET ON THE NATURE OF MONARCHICAL AUTHORITY

This selection shows how a political theorist justified royal absolutism by deriving it from the absolute authority of a father over his household. Bishop Jacques-Benigne Bossuet (1627–1704) was a famous French preacher who served as the tutor to the son of King Louis XIV of France before becoming bishop of Meaux.

There are four characteristics or qualities essential to royal authority. First, royal authority is sacred; Secondly, it is paternal; Thirdly, it is absolute; Fourthly, it is subject to reason. . . . All power comes from God. . . . Thus princes act as ministers of God, and his lieutenants on earth. It is through them that he exercises his empire. . . . In this way . . . the royal throne is not the throne of a man, but the throne of God himself. . . .

We have seen that kings hold the place of God, who is the true Father of the human race. We have also seen that the first idea of power that there was among men, is that of paternal power; and that kings were fashioned on the model of fathers. Moreover, all the world agrees that obedience, which is due to public power, is only found . . . in the precept which obliges one to honor his parents. From all this it appears that the name "king" is a father's name, and that goodness is the most natural quality in kings. . . .

Royal authority is absolute. In order to make this term odious and insupportable, many pretend to confuse absolute government and arbitrary government. But nothing is more distinct, as we shall make clear when we speak of justice. . . . The prince need account to no one for what he ordains. . . . Without this absolute authority, he can neither do good nor suppress evil: his power must be such that no one can hope to escape him. . . . [T]he sole defense of individuals against the public power must be their innocence. . . .

One must, then, obey princes as if they were justice itself, without which there is neither order nor justice in affairs. They are gods, and share in some way in divine independence. . . . It follows from this that he who does not want to obey the prince . . . is condemned irremissibly to death as an enemy of public peace and of human society. . . . The prince can correct himself when he knows that he has done badly; but against his authority there can be no remedy. . . .

Jacques-Benigne Bossuet, *Politics Drawn from the Very Words of Holy Scripture,* trans. Patrick Riley (Cambridge, 1990), pp. 46–69, 81–83.

QUESTION FOR ANALYSIS

1. Why did some political theorists argue the necessity of absolutism based on the model of the father? Was there an alternative to this model?

Did John Locke's political principles lie behind the Glorious Revolution in England?

ALTERNATIVES TO ABSOLUTISM   401

THE REIGN OF JAMES II

James II was the very opposite of his worldly brother. A zealous Catholic convert, he alienated his Tory supporters, almost all of whom were members of the established Church of England, by suspending the laws preventing Catholics and Protestant dissenters from holding political office. James also flaunted his own Roman Catholicism, openly declaring his wish that all his subjects might be converted, and publicly parading papal legates through the streets of London. When, in June 1688, he ordered all Church of England clergymen to read his decree of religious toleration from their pulpits, seven bishops refused and were promptly thrown in prison on charges of seditious libel. At their trial, however, they were declared not guilty, to the enormous satisfaction of the Protestant English populace.

The trial of the bishops was one event that brought matters to a head. The other was the unexpected birth of a son in 1688 to James and his second wife, Mary of Modena. This child, who was to be raised a Catholic, replaced James's much older Protestant daughter Mary Stuart as heir to the thrones of Scotland and England. So unexpected was this birth that there were widespread rumors that the child was not in fact James's son at all but had been smuggled into the royal bedchamber in a warming pan.

With the birth of the "warming-pan baby," events moved swiftly toward a climax. A delegation of Whigs and Tories invited Mary Stuart and her Protestant husband, William of Orange, to cross to England with an invading army to preserve Protestantism and English liberties by summoning a new parliament. As the leader of a continental coalition then at war with France, William also welcomed the opportunity to make England an ally against Louis XIV's expansionist foreign policy.

THE GLORIOUS REVOLUTION

William and Mary's invasion became a bloodless coup (although James is reputed to have suffered a nosebleed at the moment of crisis). A Bill of Rights, passed by Parliament and accepted by the new king and queen in 1689, reaffirmed English civil liberties such as trial by jury and habeas corpus (a guarantee that no one could be imprisoned unless charged with a crime), and declared the monarchy subject to the law of the land. An Act of Toleration granted Protestant dissenters the right to worship freely, though not to hold political office. And in 1701, an Act of Succession ordained that every future English monarch must be a member of the Church of England. With the childless Queen Mary now dead, this meant that the throne would pass, after King William's death, first to Mary's Protestant sister Anne (1702–1714) and then, if Anne died childless, to George, elector of the German principality of Hanover and the Protestant great-grandson of James I. In 1707, a formal Act of Union between Scotland and England ensured that the Catholic heirs of King James II would in future have no more right to the throne of Scotland than they did to the throne of England.

The English soon referred to the events of 1688 and 1689 as the "Glorious Revolution": glorious because it occurred without bloodshed and also because it firmly established England as a mixed monarchy governed by the "King in Parliament." Although William and Mary and their successors continued to exercise a large measure of executive power, after 1688 no English monarch attempted to govern without Parliament, which has met annually from that time on. Parliament, and especially the House of Commons, also strengthened its control over taxation and expenditure.

Mary Stuart. Queen Mary and her husband William of Orange became Protestant joint rulers of England in a bloodless coup, taking power from her father, the Catholic James II.

Yet 1688 was not all glory. It was a revolution that consolidated the position of large property holders, whose control over local government had been threatened by Charles II and James II. It thus restored the status quo on behalf of a wealthy class of magnates that would soon become even wealthier from government patronage and the profits of war. It also brought misery to the Catholic minority in Scotland and to the Catholic majority in Ireland. After 1690, when King William won a decisive victory over James II's forces at the battle of the Boyne, power in Ireland would lie firmly in the hands of a "Protestant Ascendancy," whose dominance over Irish society would last until modern times.

> Locke maintained that humans had originally lived in a state of nature characterized by absolute freedom and equality, in which there was no government of any kind.

JOHN LOCKE AND THE CONTRACT THEORY OF GOVERNMENT

The Glorious Revolution was the product of unique political circumstances, but it also reflected antiabsolutist theories of politics that were taking shape in the late seventeenth century. Chief among these opponents of absolutism was the Englishman John Locke (1632–1704), whose *Two Treatises of Government* were written before the revolution but published for the first time in 1690.

Locke maintained that humans had originally lived in a state of nature characterized by absolute freedom and equality, in which there was no government of any kind. The only law was the law of nature, by which individuals enforced for themselves their natural rights to life, liberty, and property. Soon, however, humans began to perceive that the inconveniences of the state of nature outweighed its advantages. Accordingly, they agreed first to establish a civil society based on absolute equality, and then to set up a government to arbitrate the disputes that might arise within this civil society. But they did not make government's powers absolute. Government was simply the combined power of all members of the society; as such, its authority could "be no more than those persons had in a state of nature before they entered into society, and gave it up to the community." All powers not expressly surrendered to the government were reserved to the people. If a government exceeded or abused the authority granted to it, society had the right to dissolve it and create another.

Locke condemned absolutism in every form. He denounced absolute monarchy, but he was no less critical of claims for the sovereignty of parliaments. Government, he argued, had been instituted to protect life, liberty, and property; no political authority could infringe an individual's natural rights to preserve these inviolate.

In the late eighteenth century, Locke's ideas would become an important element in the intellectual background to both the American and French revolutions. Between 1690 and 1720, however, they served a far less radical purpose. The landed magnates who replaced James II with William and Mary read Locke as a defense of their conservative revolution. Rather than protecting their liberty and property, James II had threatened both; hence the magnates were entitled to overthrow the tyranny he had established and replace it with a government that would defend their interests by preserving these natural rights. English government after 1689 would be dominated by Parliament; Parliament in turn was controlled by a landed aristocracy whose common interests far outweighed their incessant competition for office or their occasional disagreements over principle.

THE ABSOLUTISM OF LOUIS XIV

How did Louis XIV strengthen his control over France?

In Louis XIV's state portrait, it is all but impossible to discern the human being behind the facade of the absolute monarch, dressed in his coronation robes and surrounded by the symbols of his authority. That facade was artfully constructed by Louis, who recognized, perhaps more fully than any other early modern ruler, the importance of theater to effective kingship. Louis and his successors deliberately staged theatrical demonstrations of their sovereignty to enhance their position as rulers endowed with godlike powers far removed from common humanity.

PERFORMING ROYALTY AT VERSAILLES

Louis's most elaborate exhibitions of his sovereignty took place at his palace at Versailles (*vuhr-SY*), the town outside of Paris to which he moved his court. The palace and its grounds became a stage on which Louis mesmerized his nobles into obedience by his performance of the daily rituals and demonstrations of royalty. Noblemen vied to attend him when he arose from bed, ate his meals (usually stone cold after having traveled the distance of several city blocks from kitchen to table), strolled in his gardens (even the way the king walked was choreographed by the royal dancing master), or rode to the hunt. France's leading nobles were required to reside with him at Versailles for a portion of the year; the splendor of Louis's court was deliberately calculated to blind them to the possibility of disobedience while raising their prestige by associating them with himself.

Louis understood such theatricality as part of his duty as sovereign, a duty that he took with utmost seriousness. Though far from brilliant, he was hard working and conscientious. Whether or not he actually remarked *"L'état, c'est moi"* ("I am the state"), he clearly saw himself as serving the interests of the state. As such, he considered himself personally responsible for the well-being of his subjects. "The deference and the respect that we receive from our subjects," he wrote in a memoir he prepared for his son on the art of ruling, "are not a free gift from them but payment for the justice and the protection that they expect from us. Just as they must honor us, we must protect and defend them."

ADMINISTRATION AND CENTRALIZATION

Louis defined his responsibilities in absolutist terms: to concentrate royal power so as to produce domestic tranquillity. While coopting the nobility into his own theater of royalty, he conciliated the upper bourgeoisie by enlisting them as royal administrators. These men were not actors in the theater of Louis the Sun King; rather, they were the hard-working assistants of Louis the royal custodian of his country's welfare.

Louis's administrators devoted much of their time and energy to collecting the taxes necessary to finance the large standing army on which his aggressive and highly personal foreign policy depended. In addition to the *taille*, or land tax, which increased throughout the seventeenth century and on which a surtax was levied as well, Louis's government introduced a *capitation* (a head tax) and pressed successfully for the collection of indirect taxes on salt (the *gabelle*), wine, tobacco, and other goods. Because the nobility was exempt from the *taille*, its burden fell most heavily on the peasantry, whose local revolts Louis easily crushed.

Regional opposition was curtailed, but by no means eliminated, during Louis's reign. By removing the provincial nobility to Versailles, Louis cut them off from their local sources of power and influence. To put an end to the obstructive powers of regional parlements, Louis also decreed that members of any parlement that refused to approve and enforce his laws would be summarily exiled. He also crippled the authority of the provincial estates of Brittany, Languedoc, and Franche-Comté. The Estates-General, the national French representative assembly last summoned in 1614, did not meet at all during Louis's reign. It would not meet again until 1789.

LOUIS XIV'S RELIGIOUS POLICIES

Both for reasons of state and of personal conscience, Louis was determined to impose religious unity on France, regardless of the economic and social costs this entailed. Louis believed firmly that God would favor him in return for such fidelity.

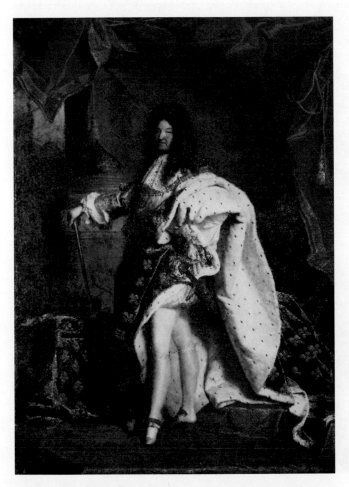

Louis XIV's State Portrait. This portrait by Hyacinthe Rigaud illustrates the degree to which absolute monarchy was defined in terms of studied performance.

Although the vast majority of the French population was Roman Catholic, French Catholics were divided among Quietists, Jansenists, Jesuits, and Gallicans. Quietists preached personal mysticism, emphasizing a direct relationship between God and the individual human heart. Jansenism held to an Augustinian doctrine of predestination that could sound and look surprisingly like a kind of Catholic Calvinism. Louis vigorously persecuted Quietists and Jansenists. Instead, he supported the Jesuits in their efforts to create a Counter-Reformation Catholic church in France. Louis's support for the Jesuits upset the traditional Gallican Catholics of France, however, who desired a French church independent of papal, Jesuit, and Spanish influence (which they tended to equate). As a result of this dissension between Catholics, the religious aura of Louis's kingship diminished during the course of his reign.

Against the Protestant Huguenots, however, Louis waged unrelenting war. Protestant churches and schools were destroyed, and Protestants were banned from many professions. In 1685, Louis revoked the Edict of Nantes, the legal foundation of the toleration Huguenots had enjoyed since 1598. Protestant clerics were exiled; laymen were sent to the galleys as slaves; and their children were forcibly baptized as Catholics. Many families converted, but 200,000 Protestant refugees fled to England, Holland, Germany, and America, bringing with them their professional and artisanal skills. This was an enormous loss to France. Among many other examples, the silk industries of Berlin and London were established by Huguenots fleeing Louis XIV's persecution.

COLBERT AND ROYAL FINANCE

Louis's drive to unify and centralize France depended on a vast increase in royal revenues engineered by Jean Baptiste Colbert, the king's finance minister from 1664 until his death in 1683. Colbert tightened the process

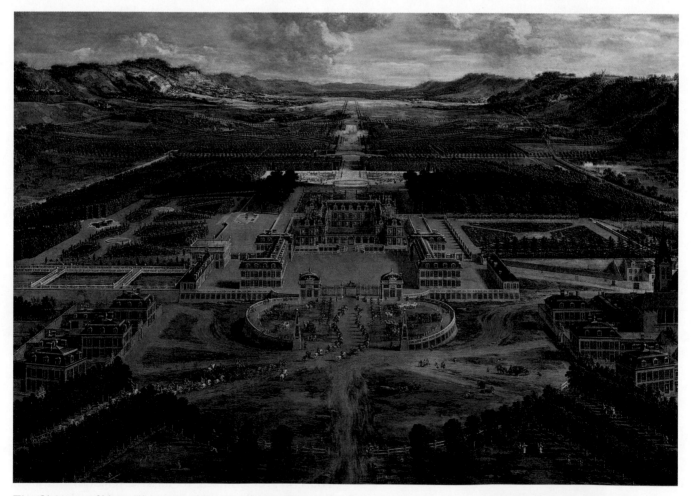

The Château of Versailles. Dramatically expanded by Louis XIV in the 1660s from a hunting lodge to the principal royal residence and the seat of government, the château became a monument to the international power and prestige of the Grand Monarch.

of tax collection and eliminated wherever possible the practice of tax farming (which permitted collection agents to retain for themselves a percentage of the taxes they gathered for the king). When Colbert assumed office, only about 25 percent of the taxes collected throughout the kingdom reached the treasury. By the time he died, that figure had risen to 80 percent. Colbert also tried to increase the nation's income by controlling and regulating its foreign trade. As a confirmed mercantilist (see "Mercantilism and War" on p. 406), Colbert believed that France's wealth would increase if its imports were reduced and its exports increased. He therefore imposed tariffs on foreign goods imported into France, promoting the domestic manufacture of such formerly imported goods as silk, lace, tapestries, and glass. He was especially anxious to create domestic industries capable of producing all the goods France would need for war. To encourage domestic trade, he also improved France's roads, bridges, and waterways.

Despite Colbert's efforts to increase crown revenues, his policies ultimately foundered on the insatiable demands of Louis XIV's wars. Colbert himself foresaw this result when he lectured the king in 1680: "Trade is the source of public finance and public finance is the vital nerve of war. . . . I beg your Majesty to permit me only to say to him that in war as in peace he has never consulted the amount of money available in determining his expenditures." Louis, however, paid him no heed. As a result, by the end of Louis's reign, his aggressive foreign policy lay in ruins and his country's finances had been shattered by the unsustainable costs of war.

THE WARS OF LOUIS XIV TO 1697

From 1661, when Louis began his personal rule, until his death in 1715, Louis kept France on an almost constant war footing. His wars had two main objectives: to lessen the threat posed to France by the Habsburg powers that surrounded it and to promote the dynastic interests of his own family. Happily for Louis, these two objectives frequently coincided. In 1667–1668 he attacked the Spanish Netherlands, which he claimed on behalf of his wife. In 1672, Louis attacked Holland and its new leader William of Orange (1672–1702). The great-grandson of the sixteenth-century Protestant champion William the Silent, William of Orange would become the leading figure in Europe resisting Louis's wars of conquest.

The Dutch war ended in 1678–1679 with the Treaty of Nijmegen. Although Louis made little headway in

the Low Countries, he did succeed in conquering and holding the eastern territory of Franche-Comté. Thus encouraged, he now turned his attentions eastward, capturing Strasbourg (1681), Luxembourg (1684), and Cologne (1688). He then pillaged and burned the middle Rhineland, which he claimed on behalf of his unhappy sister-in-law, the daughter of the territory's ruler, the Elector Palatine.

In response to these new aggressions, William of Orange organized the League of Augsburg, which eventually united Holland, England, Spain, Sweden, Bavaria, Saxony, the Rhine Palatinate, and the Austrian Habsburgs against Louis. The resulting Nine Years' War (1689–1697) was extraordinarily destructive. Most of its campaigns were fought in the Low Countries, but the conflict extended from Ireland to India to North America (where it was known as King William's War). Finally, in 1697, the Peace of Ryswick compelled Louis to return most of France's recent gains, except for Strasbourg and its surrounding territory of Alsace. This treaty also recognized William of Orange as the new king of England, thus legitimizing the Glorious Revolution of 1688 that had replaced the Catholic king James II with the Protestant monarchs William and Mary.

THE WAR OF THE SPANISH SUCCESSION

The League of Augsburg reflected the emergence of a new diplomatic goal in western and central Europe: the preservation of a "balance of power" designed to prevent any single country, such as France, from becoming so powerful as to threaten the position of the other major powers within the European state system. This goal would animate European diplomacy for the next 200 years, until the entire balance-of-power system collapsed in 1914 with the outbreak of World War I.

A balance of power was not, however, a goal to which Louis XIV subscribed. Louis made peace in 1697 with the League of Augsburg because his country was exhausted by war and famine. But he was also looking ahead to the real prize: a French claim to succeed to the throne of Spain, and so to control the Spanish Empire in the New World, Italy, the Netherlands, and the Philippines.

Louis had married, as his first wife, the elder daughter of King Philip IV of Spain (1621–1665). Philip's younger daughter had married the Holy Roman emperor, Leopold I of Austria (1658–1705). Neither daughter was expected to inherit the Spanish

MERCANTILISM AND WAR

Jean-Baptiste Colbert (1619–1683) served as Louis XIV's finance minister from 1664 until his death. He worked assiduously to promote commerce, build up French industry, and increase exports. However much Colbert himself may have seen his economic policies as ends in themselves, to Louis they were always means to the end of waging war. Ultimately, Louis's wars undermined the prosperity that Colbert tried so hard to create. This memorandum, written to Louis in 1670, illustrates clearly the mercantilist presumptions of self-sufficiency on which Colbert operated: every item needed to build up the French navy must ultimately be produced in France, even if it could be acquired elsewhere at a lower cost.

And since Your Majesty has wanted to work diligently at reestablishing his naval forces, and since afore that it has been necessary to make very great expenditures, since all merchandise, munitions and manufactured items formerly came from Holland and the countries of the North, it has been absolutely necessary to be especially concerned with finding within the realm, or with establishing in it, everything which might be necessary for this great plan.

To this end, the manufacture of tar was established in Médoc, Auvergne, Dauphiné, and Provence; iron cannons, in Burgundy, Nivernois, Saintonge and Périgord; large anchors in Dauphiné, Nivernois, Brittany, and Rochefort; sailcloth for the Levant, in Dauphiné; coarse muslin, in Auvergne; all the implements for pilots and others, at Dieppe and La Rochelle; the cutting of wood suitable for vessels, in Burgundy, Dauphiné, Brittany, Normandy, Poitou, Saintonge, Provence, Guyenne, and the Pyrenees; masts, of a sort once unknown in this realm, have been found in Provence, Languedoc, Auvergne, Dauphiné, and in the Pyrenees. Iron, which was obtained from Sweden and Biscay, is currently manufactured in the realm. Fine hemp for ropes, which came from Prussia and from Piedmont, is currently obtained in Burgundy, Mâconnais, Bresse, Dauphiné; and markets for it have since been established in Berry and in Auvergne, which always provides money in these provinces and keeps it within the realm.

In a word, everything serving for the construction of vessels is currently established in the realm, so that Your Majesty can get along without foreigners for the navy and will even, in a short time, be able to supply them and gain their money in this fashion. And it is with this same objective of having everything necessary to provide abundantly for his navy and that of his subjects that he is working at the general reform of all the forests in his realm, which, being as carefully preserved as they are at present, will abundantly produce all the wood necessary for this.

Charles W. Cole, *Colbert and a Century of French Mercantilism*, 2 vols. (New York, 1939), p. 320.

QUESTIONS FOR ANALYSIS

1. Could Colbert's economic policies have been used more wisely by Louis XIV?
2. Can mercantilist policies be implemented without resorting to warfare?
3. Is war a necessary component of mercantilism?

throne. But Philip's only son, King Charles II of Spain (1665–1700), was a mental and physical invalid throughout his life. As it became clear during the 1690s that he would not live much longer, all the major European powers began to concern themselves with the succession to the Spanish throne. The stakes were high. If one of Leopold's sons succeeded, then France would be surrounded by a united Habsburg power. If Louis XIV's son or grandson succeeded, however, then France would become the preponderant power in Europe and the Americas.

Several schemes to resolve the crisis were floated during the 1690s. Most involved dividing the Spanish Empire between the competing claimants. King Charles II's advisers, however, wanted the entire Spanish Empire to pass to a single heir. To achieve this, they arranged for King Charles, in his will, to leave all his possessions to Louis XIV's younger grandson, Philip of Anjou. As soon as Charles II died, Philip V (1700–1746) was therefore proclaimed the new king of Spain, and Louis XIV rushed French troops into the Spanish Netherlands. Louis also sent French merchants into Spanish America and withdrew recognition from William of Orange as king of England.

The resulting war pitted England, the United Provinces, Austria, and Prussia against France, Bavaria, and Spain. The allied forces fought a series of fierce battles in the Low Countries and Germany, including an extraordinary march deep into Bavaria, where they inflicted a devastating defeat on the French and their Bavarian allies at Blenheim (1704). Soon thereafter, the English navy captured Gibraltar and the island of Minorca, thus establishing a foothold in the Mediterranean and opening a new military theater in Spain itself.

By 1709, France was on the verge of defeat. But the allies overreached themselves by demanding that Louis join their war against his own grandson in Spain. The war therefore continued, at enormous cost to both sides.

Queen Anne of England (Mary's sister and William's successor) gradually grew disillusioned with the war. English and Dutch merchants were also complaining about the damage the war was doing to trade. Meanwhile, the diplomatic situation in Europe was also changing. Leopold I of Austria had died in 1705. When his elder son and successor, Joseph I, died in 1711, the Austrian monarchy fell to Leopold's younger son, the archduke Charles, who had been the allies' candidate for the throne of Spain. With Charles VI (1711–1740) now the Austrian ruler and the Holy Roman emperor, the prospect of his accession to the Spanish throne threatened to upset the balance of power in Europe all over again.

THE TREATY OF UTRECHT

In 1713 the war finally came to an end with the Treaty of Utrecht. Its terms were reasonably fair to all sides. Philip V, Louis XIV's grandson, remained on the throne of Spain and retained Spain's colonial empire intact; but in return, Louis agreed that France and Spain would never be united under the same ruler. The biggest winner by far was Great Britain (as the combined kingdoms of England and Scotland were known after 1707), which kept Gibraltar and Minorca and also acquired large chunks of French territory in the New World. Even more valuable, however, Britain also extracted from Spain the right to transport and sell African slaves in Spanish America. As a result, the British were now poised to become the principal slave merchants and the dominant colonial and commercial power of the eighteenth-century world.

The Treaty of Utrecht reshaped the balance of power in western Europe. Spain's collapse was already precipitous; by 1713 it was complete. Spain would remain the "sick man of Europe" for the next two centuries. Holland's decline was more gradual, but by 1713 its greatest days were also over. The Dutch would continue to control the Spice Islands, but in the Atlantic world Britain and France were now the dominant powers. They would continue to duel for another half century for control over North America, but at Utrecht the balance of colonial power shifted decisively in Britain's favor. Britain's navy, not France's army, would rule the new imperial and commercial world of the eighteenth century.

THE REMAKING OF CENTRAL AND EASTERN EUROPE

What changes lay behind the growing power of Prussia?

The decades between 1680 and 1720 were equally decisive in reshaping the balance of power in central and eastern Europe. As Ottoman power waned, the Austro-Hungarian Empire of the Habsburgs emerged as the dominant power in central and southeastern Europe.

EUROPE AFTER THE TREATY OF UTRECHT (1713)

To what extent did the balance of power within Europe change as a result of the Treaty of Utrecht? Would this map lead you to expect the Habsburg lands to dominate eighteenth-century Europe? Why or why not?

To the north, Brandenburg-Prussia was also a rising power. The most dramatic changes, however, were occurring in Russia, which would emerge from a long war with Sweden as the dominant power in the Baltic Sea and would soon become a mortal threat to the combined kingdom of Poland-Lithuania.

THE HABSBURG EMPIRE

In 1683, the Ottoman Turks launched their last assault on Vienna. Only the arrival of 70,000 Polish troops saved the Austrian capital from capture. Thereafter,

however, Ottoman power in southeastern Europe declined rapidly. By 1699, Austria had reconquered most of Hungary from the Ottomans; by 1718, it controlled all of Hungary and also Transylvania and Serbia. In 1722, Austria acquired the territory of Silesia from Poland. With Hungary now a "buffer state" between Austria and the Ottomans, Vienna emerged as one of the great cultural and political capitals of eighteenth-century Europe, and Austria became one of the arbiters of the European balance of power.

After 1740, the empress Maria Theresa (1740–1780) and her son Joseph II (1765–1790; from 1765 until 1780 the two were co-rulers) pioneered a new style of "enlightened absolutism" within their empire: centralizing the administration on Vienna, increasing taxation, creating a professional standing army, tightening their control over the church, creating a statewide system of primary education, relaxing censorship, and instituting a new, more liberal criminal code. But in practice, Habsburg absolutism, whether enlightened or not, was always limited by the diversity of its imperial territories and by the weakness of its local governmental institutions.

THE RISE OF BRANDENBURG-PRUSSIA

After the Ottoman collapse, the main threat to Austria came from the rising power of Brandenburg-Prussia. Like Austria, Prussia was a composite state, made up of several geographically divided territories acquired through inheritance by the Hohenzollern family. Their two main holdings, however, were Brandenburg, centered on its capital city, Berlin, and the duchy of East Prussia. Between these two territories lay Pomerania (claimed by Sweden) and an important part of the kingdom of Poland, including the port of Gdansk (Danzig). The Hohenzollerns' aim was to unite their state by acquiring these intervening territories. Over the course of more than a century of steady state building, they finally succeeded in doing so. In the process, Brandenburg-Prussia became the dominant military power of central Europe and a key player in the balance-of-power diplomacy of the mid-eighteenth century.

The foundations of Prussian greatness were laid by Frederick William, the "Great Elector" (1640–1688). By siding with Poland in a war against Sweden in the late 1650s, he obtained the Polish king's surrender of East Prussia. He also protected his western provinces from French attack by returning Pomerania, captured in a recent war, to France's Swedish ally. Behind these diplomatic triumphs, however, lay the elector's success in building an army and mobilizing the resources to pay for it. By granting to the powerful nobles of his territories (known as *Junkers*) the right to enserf their peasants, by relying on them to staff the officer corps of his army, and by guaranteeing their immunity from taxation, Frederick William gained their support for the effective and highly autocratic taxation system he imposed on the rest of the country.

By supporting Austria in the War of the Spanish Succession, the Great Elector's son, Frederick I (1688–1713), received the right to style himself king of Prussia. (As Holy Roman emperor, the Austrian monarch had the right to create kings.) And by joining the Great Northern War on the side of Russia against Sweden (discussed later in this chapter), Frederick paved the way for Prussia to recover and extend its control over Pomerania. As king, however, his main attention was devoted to developing the cultural life of his new royal capital, Berlin, along the lines laid down by Louis XIV of France.

Frederick William I (1713–1740) returned to the policies of his grandfather. During his reign, the Prussian army grew from 30,000 to 83,000 men, the fourth largest army in Europe after those of France, Russia, and Austria. To support his army, Frederick William I increased taxes and streamlined their collection, while shunning the expensive luxuries of court life. For him, the "theater" of absolutism was not the palace but the office, where he personally supervised his beloved army and the offices of state that sustained it.

> To support his army, Frederick William I increased taxes and streamlined their collection, while shunning the expensive luxuries of court life.

Frederick William I made Prussia a strong state. Frederick the Great (1740–1786) raised his country to the status of a major power. As soon as he became king in 1740, Frederick mobilized the army his father had never taken into battle and occupied the Austrian province of Silesia. Emboldened by this early success, Frederick spent the rest of his reign consolidating his gains in Silesia and extending his control over the Polish territories that lay between Prussia and Brandenburg. Through relentless diplomacy and frequent war, Frederick succeeded by 1786 in transforming Prussia into a powerful, contiguous territorial kingdom.

To ensure a united domestic front against Prussia's enemies, Frederick was careful to guarantee the support of the Junkers for his policies. His father had recruited civil servants according to merit rather than birth, but Frederick relied on the nobility to staff the army and his expanding administration. Remarkably, Frederick's strategy worked. His nobility remained loyal, while Frederick fashioned the most highly professional and efficient bureaucracy in Europe.

Frederick showed the same concern for Junker sensibilities in his domestic policies. Like his contemporary Joseph II of Austria, Frederick was an enlightened absolutist who supervised a series of social reforms, prohibited the judicial torture of accused criminals and the bribing of judges, and established a system of elementary schools. Although strongly anti-Semitic, he encouraged religious toleration toward all Christians and even declared that he would happily build a mosque in Berlin if he could find enough Muslims to fill it. On his own royal estates he abolished capital punishment, curtailed the forced labor services of his peasantry, and granted them long leases on the land they worked. But he never attempted to extend these reforms to the estates of the nobility. To have done so would have alienated the very group on whom Frederick's rule depended.

AUTOCRACY IN RUSSIA

In what ways did Russian absolutism differ from its western European counterparts?

An even more dramatic transformation took place in Russia under Tsar Peter I (b. 1672–d. 1725). Peter's accomplishments alone would have earned him his title of "Great." But his imposing height—he was six feet eight inches tall—as well as his mercurial personality—jesting one moment, raging the next—certainly added to the outsized impression he made on his contemporaries. Peter was not the first tsar to bring his country into contact with western Europe, but his policies were decisive in making Russia a great European power.

THE EARLY YEARS OF PETER'S REIGN

Like Louis XIV of France, Peter came to the throne as a young boy, and his minority was marked by political dissension and court intrigue. In 1689, however, at the age of seventeen, he overthrew the regency of his half-sister Sophia and assumed personal control of the state. Determined to make Russia a great military power, the young tsar traveled to Holland and England during the 1690s to study shipbuilding and to recruit skilled foreign workers to help him build a navy. While he was abroad, however, his palace guard rebelled, attempting to restore Sophia to the throne. Peter quickly returned home from Vienna and crushed the rebellion with striking savagery. About 1,200 suspected conspirators were summarily executed, many of them gibbeted outside the walls of the Kremlin, where their bodies rotted for months as a graphic re-

minder of the fate awaiting those who dared challenge the tsar's authority.

THE TRANSFORMATION OF THE TSARIST STATE

Peter is most famous as the tsar who attempted to westernize Russia by imposing a series of social and cultural reforms on the traditional Russian nobility: ordering noblemen to cut off their long beards and flowing sleeves; publishing a book of manners that forbade spitting on the floor and eating with one's fingers; encouraging polite conversation between the sexes; and requiring noblewomen to appear, together with men, in Western garb at weddings, banquets, and other public occasions. The children of Russian nobles were sent to western European courts for their education, and thousands of western European experts were brought to Russia to staff the new schools and academies Peter built; to design the new buildings he constructed; and to serve in the tsar's army, navy, and administration.

These measures were important, but it is misleading to see them as driven by the tsar's desire to modernize or westernize Russia. Peter's real goal was to make Russia

Peter the Great. As tsar Peter I westernized Russia with social and cultural reforms, among them the mandate that traditional nobles cut off their long beards.

IN WHAT WAYS DID RUSSIAN ABSOLUTISM DIFFER FROM ITS WESTERN EUROPEAN COUNTERPARTS?

AUTOCRACY IN RUSSIA   411

a great military power, not to remake Russian society. His new taxation system (1724), for example, which assessed taxes on individuals rather than on households, rendered many of the traditional divisions of Russian peasant society obsolete. It was created, however, to raise more money for war. His Table of Ranks, imposed in 1722, had a similar impact on the nobility. By insisting that all nobles must work their way up from the lower (landlord) class to the (higher) administrative class and to the (highest) military class, Peter reversed the traditional hierarchy of Russian noble society, which had valued landlords by birth above administrators and soldiers who had risen by merit. But he also created a powerful new incentive to lure his nobility into service to the tsar.

> By insisting that all nobles must work their way up from the lower (landlord) class to the (higher) administrative class and to the (highest) military class, Peter reversed the traditional hierarchy of Russian noble society, which had valued landlords by birth above administrators and soldiers who had risen by merit.

As autocrat of all the Russias, Peter the Great was the absolute master of his empire to a degree unmatched elsewhere in Europe. After 1649, Russian peasants were legally the property of their landlords; by 1750, half were serfs, and the other half were state peasants who lived on lands owned by the tsar himself. State peasants could be conscripted to serve as soldiers in the tsar's army, workers in his factories (whose productive capacity increased enormously during Peter's reign), or forced laborers in his building projects. But serfs too could be taxed by the tsar and summoned for military service, as could their lords. All Russians, of whatever rank, were thus expected to serve the tsar, and all Russia was considered in some sense to belong to him.

To further consolidate his power, Peter replaced the Duma—the rudimentary national assembly—with a hand-picked senate, a group of nine administrators who supervised military and civilian affairs. In religious matters, he took direct control over the Russian Orthodox Church by appointing an imperial official to manage its affairs. To cope with the demands of war, he also fashioned a new, larger, and more efficient administration, for which he recruited both nobles and nonnobles. But rank in the new bureaucracy did not depend on birth. One of his principal advisers, Alexander Menshikov, began his career as a cook and finished as a prince. This degree of social mobility would have been impossible in any contemporary western European country. Instead, noble status depended on governmental service, with all nobles expected to participate in Peter's army or administration. Peter was not entirely successful in enforcing this requirement, but the administrative machinery he devised furnished Russia with its ruling class for the next 200 years.

PETER'S FOREIGN POLICY

The goal of Peter's foreign policy was to secure warm-water ports for Russia on the Black Sea and the Baltic Sea. In the Black Sea, his enemy was the Ottomans. Here, however, he had little success; Russia would not secure its position in the Black Sea until the end of the eighteenth century. In the north, however, Peter achieved much more. In 1700, he began what would become a twenty-one-year war with Sweden, hitherto the dominant power in the Baltic Sea. By 1703, Peter had secured a foothold on the Gulf of Finland and immediately began to build a new capital city there, which he named St. Petersburg. After 1709, when Russian armies, supported by Prussia, decisively defeated the Swedes at the battle of Poltava, work on Peter's new capital city accelerated. An army of serfs was now conscripted to build

CHRONOLOGY

ABSOLUTIST RULERS

France	
Louis XIV	1643–1715
Louis XV	1715–1774
Louis XVI	1774–1792
Brandenburg-Prussia	
Frederick William, the "Great Elector"	1640–1688
Frederick I	1688–1713
Frederick William I	1713–1740
Frederick the Great	1740–1786
Austria	
Leopold I	1658–1705
Charles VI	1711–1740
Maria Theresa	1740–1780
Joseph II	1765–1790
Russia	
Peter the Great	1689–1725
Catherine the Great	1762–1796

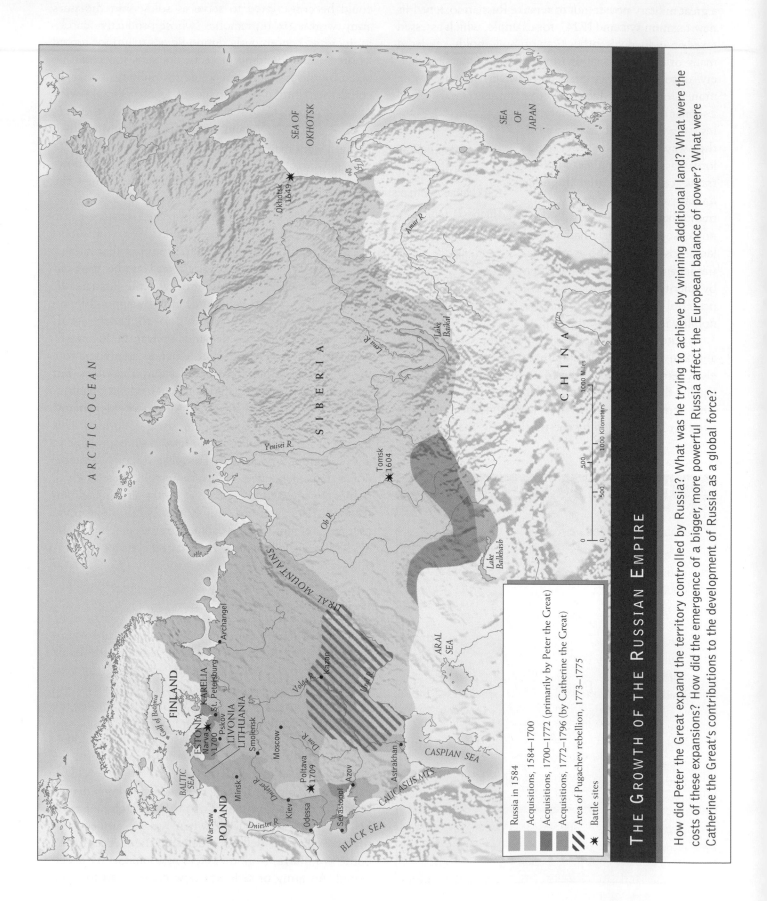

THE GROWTH OF THE RUSSIAN EMPIRE

How did Peter the Great expand the territory controlled by Russia? What was he trying to achieve by winning additional land? What were the costs of these expansions? How did the emergence of a bigger, more powerful Russia affect the European balance of power? What were Catherine the Great's contributions to the development of Russia as a global force?

IN WHAT WAYS DID RUSSIAN ABSOLUTISM DIFFER FROM ITS WESTERN EUROPEAN COUNTERPARTS?

AUTOCRACY IN RUSSIA   413

the new city, whose centerpiece was a royal palace designed to imitate and rival Louis XIV's Versailles.

The Great Northern War with Sweden ended in 1721 with the Peace of Nystad. This treaty marks a realignment of power in eastern Europe comparable to that effected by the Treaty of Utrecht in the west. Sweden lost its North Sea territories to Hanover and its Baltic German territories to Prussia. Its eastern territories, including the entire Gulf of Finland, Livonia, and Estonia, passed to Russia. Poland-Lithuania was a declining power also; by the end of the eighteenth century, the kingdom would disappear altogether, its territories swallowed up by its more powerful neighbors. The victors at Nystad were the Prussians and the Russians, both of whom secured their position along the Baltic coast and so positioned themselves to take advantage of the lucrative eastern European grain trade with western Europe.

Peter's victory had come at enormous cost. Direct taxation increased 500 percent during his reign, and his army in the 1720s numbered more than 300,000 men. Peter had made Russia a force to be reckoned with on the European scene; but in so doing, he had also aroused great resentment, especially among his nobility. Peter's only son and heir, Alexis, became the focus for conspiracies against the tsar, until finally Peter had him arrested and executed in 1718. As a result, when Peter died in 1725, he left no son to succeed him. A series of ineffective tsars followed, mostly creatures of the palace guard, under whom the resentful nobles reversed many of Peter the Great's reforms. In 1762, however, the crown passed to Catherine the Great, a ruler whose ambitions and determination were equal to those of her great predecessor.

CATHERINE THE GREAT AND THE PARTITION OF POLAND

Catherine was a German who came to the throne in 1762 on the death of her husband, the weak (and possibly mad) Tsar Peter III, who was deposed and executed in a palace coup that Catherine herself may have helped to arrange. Although she cultivated an image of herself as an enlightened ruler (she corresponded with French philosophers, wrote plays, and began to compose a history of Russia), Catherine was determined not to lose the support of the nobility who had placed her on the throne. As a result, her efforts at social reform did not extend much beyond the founding of hospitals and orphanages and the creation of an elementary school system for the children of the provincial nobility.

Catherine's greatest achievements were gained through war and diplomacy. In 1769, she renewed Peter the Great's push to secure a warm-water port on the Black Sea. In the resulting war with the Ottoman Turks (which ended in 1774), Russia won control over the northern coast of the Black Sea, secured the independence of Crimea (which Russia would annex in 1783), and obtained safe passage for Russian ships through the Bosporus and into the Mediterranean Sea. In the course of this campaign, Russia also won control over several Ottoman provinces along the Danube River.

Russia's gains in the Balkans alarmed Austria, however, which now found itself with the powerful Russian Empire on its southern doorstep. Prussia too was threatening to become involved in the war as an ally of the Ottomans. Frederick the Great's real interests, however, lay much closer to home. To preserve the peace among Russia, Prussia, and Austria, he proposed instead a partition of Poland. Russia would abandon its Danubian conquests and, in return, would acquire the grain fields of eastern Poland, along with a population of 1 to 2 million Poles. Austria would take Galicia, acquiring 2.5 million Poles. Prussia, meanwhile, would take the coastal regions of Poland,

Dividing the Royal Spoils. A contemporary cartoon showing the monarchs of Europe at work carving up a hapless Poland.

including the port of Gdansk (Danzig), that separated Brandenburg and Pomerania from East Prussia. As a result of this agreement, finalized in 1772, Poland lost about 30 percent of its territory and about half of its population.

Poland was now paying the price for its political conservatism. Alone among the major central European powers, the Polish nobility had successfully opposed any move toward monarchical centralization as a threat to its liberties, among which was the right of every individual noble to veto any measure proposed in the Polish representative assembly, the Diet. To make matters worse, Polish aristocrats were also quite prepared to accept bribes from foreign powers in return for their vote in elections for the Polish king. In 1764, Catherine the Great had intervened in this way to secure the election of one of her former lovers, Stanislaus Poniatowski, as the new king of Poland. In 1772, King Stanislaus reluctantly accepted the partition of his country because he was too weak to resist it. In 1788, however, he took advantage of a new Russo-Turkish war to try to strengthen his control over what remained of his kingdom. In May 1791 a new constitution was adopted that established a much stronger monarchy than had previously existed. But it was too late. In January 1792 the Russo-Turkish war ended, and Catherine the Great pounced. Together the Russians and Prussians took two more enormous bites out of Poland in 1793, destroying the new constitution in the process. A final swallow by Russia, Austria, and Prussia in 1795 left nothing of Poland or Lithuania at all.

> Combined with improved transportation systems, the new farming methods resulted in fewer famines and a better-nourished population.

COMMERCE AND CONSUMPTION

What factors facilitated the commercial revolution?

 Despite the increased military power of Russia, Prussia, and Austria, the balance of power within Europe was shifting steadily toward the west during the eighteenth century. The North Atlantic economies in particular were growing more rapidly than those anywhere else in Europe. As a result, France and Britain were becoming preponderant powers both in Europe and the wider world.

ECONOMIC GROWTH IN EIGHTEENTH-CENTURY EUROPE

The reasons for this rapid economic and demographic growth in northwestern Europe are complex. In Britain and Holland, new, more intensive agricultural systems were producing more food per acre than ever before. Combined with improved transportation systems, the new farming methods resulted in fewer famines and a better-nourished population. New crops, especially maize and potatoes (both introduced to Europe from the Americas), also helped increase the supply of food available to feed Europe's growing population. But although famines became less common and less widespread, infectious disease continued to kill half of all Europeans before they reached the age of twenty. Even here, however, some progress was being made. Plague in particular was ceasing to be a major killer, as a degree of immunity (perhaps the result of a genetic mutation) began to emerge within the European population. Together with a better diet, improved sanitation may also have played some role in reducing the infection rates from such killers as typhoid, cholera, smallpox, and measles.

Northwestern Europe was also becoming increasingly urbanized. Across Europe as a whole the total number of urban dwellers did not change markedly between 1600 and 1800. At both dates, approximately 200 cities in Europe had a population of over 10,000. What did change was, first, the fact that these cities were increasingly concentrated in northern and western Europe; and second, the extraordinary growth of the very largest cities. Amsterdam, the hub of early modern international commerce, increased from 30,000 in 1530 to 115,000 in 1630 and 200,000 by 1800. Naples, the busy Mediterranean port, went from a population of 300,000 in 1600 to nearly half a million by the late eighteenth century. But even more spectacular population growth occurred in the administrative capitals of Europe. London grew from 674,000 in 1700 to 860,000 a century later. Paris went from 180,000 people in 1600 to more than 500,000 in 1800. Berlin grew from a population of 6,500 in 1661 to 60,000 in 1721 to 140,000 in 1783, of whom approximately 65,000 were state employees or members of their families.

Increased food supplies were needed to feed these burgeoning cities; but to the rising prosperity of northwestern Europe as a whole, developments in trade and manufacturing contributed even more than did agriculture. Spurred by improvements in transportation—better roads and bridges, and new canals—entrepreneurs began to promote the production of textiles in the countryside by distributing ("putting out") wool and flax to rural workers who would card, spin, and weave it into cloth on a piece-rate basis. The entrepreneur would then collect and sell the finished cloth in a market that now extended from local towns to international exporters. For country dwellers, this system (sometimes called "protoindustrialization") provided welcome employment during otherwise slack seasons of the agricultural year. For the merchant-entrepreneurs who administered it, the system allowed them to avoid expensive guild restrictions in the towns and to reduce their levels of capital investment, thus reducing their overall costs of production. Urban cloth workers suffered, but the system led nonetheless to markedly increased employment and to much higher levels of industrial production, not only for textiles but also for iron, metalworking, and even toy and clock making.

Despite rural protoindustrialization, the role of cities as manufacturing centers continued to grow during the eighteenth century. Most urban manufacturing continued to be carried out in small shops employing anywhere from five to twenty journeymen working under the supervision of a master. But the scale of such enterprise was growing and also becoming more specialized, as workshops began to group together to form a single manufacturing district in which several thousand workers might be employed to produce the same product.

Techniques in some crafts remained much as they had been for centuries. In others, however, inventions changed the pattern of work as well as the nature of the product. Knitting frames, simple devices to speed the manufacture of textile goods, made their appearance in Britain and Holland. Wire-drawing machines and slitting mills, the latter enabling nail makers to convert iron bars into rods, spread from Germany into Britain. Techniques for printing colored designs directly on calico cloth were imported from Asia. New

and more efficient printing presses appeared, first in Holland and then elsewhere. The Dutch even invented a machine called a "camel," with which the hulls of ships could be raised in the water so that they could be more easily repaired.

Workers did not readily accept innovations of this kind. Labor-saving machines threw people out of work. Often, therefore, governments would intervene to block the widespread use of machines if they threatened to increase unemployment or in some other way to create unrest. States might also intervene to protect the interests of their powerful commercial and financial backers. But the pressures for economic innovation were irresistable, because behind them lay an insatiable eighteenth-century appetite for goods.

A WORLD OF GOODS

In the eighteenth century, for the first time, a mass market for consumer goods emerged in Europe, and especially in northwestern Europe. Houses became larger, particularly in towns; but even more strikingly, the houses of relatively ordinary people were starting to be crammed with hitherto uncommon luxuries such as sugar, tobacco, tea, coffee, chocolate, newspapers, books, pictures, clocks, toys, china, glassware, pewter, silver plate, soap, razors, furniture (including beds with mattresses, chairs, and chests of drawers), shoes, cotton cloth, and spare clothing. Demand for such products consistently outstripped the supply, causing prices for these items to rise faster than the price of foodstuffs throughout the century. But the demand for them continued unabated. Such goods were indulgences, of course, but they were also repositories of value in which families could invest their surplus cash, knowing that they could pawn them in hard times if cash were needed.

The exploding consumer economy of the eighteenth century spurred demand for manufactured goods of all sorts. But it also encouraged the provision of services. In eighteenth-century Britain, the service sector was the fastest-growing part of the economy, outstripping both agriculture and manufacturing. Almost everywhere in urban Europe, the eighteenth century was the golden age of the small shopkeeper. People bought more prepared foods and more ready-made (as opposed to personally tailored) clothing. Advertising became an important part of doing business, helping create

> The exploding consumer economy of the eighteenth century spurred demand for manufactured goods of all sorts. But it also encouraged the provision of services.

Topsy-Turvy World, **by Jan Steen.** This Dutch painting depicts a household in the throes of the exploding consumer economy that hit Europe in the eighteenth century. Consumer goods ranging from silver and china to clothing and furniture cluttered the houses of ordinary people as never before.

demand for new products and shaping popular taste for changing fashions. Even political allegiances could be expressed through consumption when people purchased plates and glasses commemorating favorite rulers or causes.

The result of all these developments was a European economy vastly more complex, more specialized, more integrated, more commercialized, and more productive than anything the world had seen before.

COLONIZATION AND TRADE IN THE SEVENTEENTH CENTURY

How did the patterns of European colonial settlement in the Americas differ from each other?

Many of the new consumer goods that propelled the economy of eighteenth-century Europe, including such staples as sugar, tobacco, tea, coffee, chocolate, china, and cotton cloth, were the products of Europe's

colonial empires in Asia, Africa, and the Americas. Europe's growing wealth was not simply the result of its colonial possessions, but it is impossible to imagine this prosperity without them. We need, therefore, to examine these European empires and the developing role they played in the economy of the eighteenth-century world. To do so, however, we need to begin by looking at the patterns of seventeenth-century European colonialism.

SPANISH COLONIALISM

After the exploits of the conquistadors, the Spanish established colonial governments in Peru and in Mexico, which they controlled from Madrid. In keeping with the doctrines of mercantilism, the Spanish government allowed only Spanish merchants to trade with their American colonies, requiring all colonial exports and imports to pass through a single Spanish port where they were registered at the government-operated customs house. During the sixteenth century, this system worked reasonably well. The Spanish colonial economy was dominated by mining; the lucrative market for silver in East Asia even made it profitable to establish an outpost in Manila, where Spanish merchants exchanged Asian silk for South American bullion. But Spain also took steps to promote farming and ranching in Central and South America, and established settlements in Florida and California.

The wealth of Spain's colonial trade tempted the merchants of other countries to win a share of the treasure for themselves. Probably the boldest challengers were the English, whose leading buccaneer was the "sea dog" Sir Francis Drake. Three times Drake raided the east and west coasts of Spanish America. In 1587 he attacked the Spanish fleet at its anchorage in Cadíz harbor; and in 1588 he played a key role in defeating the Spanish Armada. His career illustrates the mixture of piracy and patriotism that characterized England's early efforts to break into the colonial trade. Until the 1650s, however, the English could only dent the lucrative Spanish trade in bullion, hides, silks, and slaves.

How did the patterns of European colonial settlement in the Americas differ from each other?

Colonization and Trade in the Seventeenth Century   417

English Colonialism

England's own American colonies had no significant mineral wealth. As a result, English colonists sought profits by establishing agricultural settlements in North America and the Caribbean basin. Their first permanent, though ultimately unsuccessful, colony was founded in 1607 at Jamestown, Virginia. Over the next forty years, 80,000 English emigrants would sail to more than twenty autonomous settlements in the New World. Many of these early settlers were driven by religious motives. The Pilgrims who landed at Plymouth, Massachusetts, in 1620 were one of many dissident groups, both Protestant and Catholic, that sought to escape the English government's attempt to impose religious conformity by emigrating to North America.

Most of these early English settlements were privately organized. As they began to prosper, however, the governments of both Oliver Cromwell and Charles II began to intervene in their management. Mercantilist-inspired navigation acts, passed in 1651 and 1660 and rigorously enforced thereafter, decreed that all exports from English colonies to the mother country be carried in English ships and forbade the direct exporting of certain "enumerated" products directly from the colonies to continental ports.

The most valuable of those colonial products were sugar and tobacco. Sugar, virtually unknown in Christian Europe during the Middle Ages, became a popular luxury item in the late fifteenth century, when Europeans began to produce it in their Mediterranean and African colonies. Only in the New World, however, did sugar production reach such volumes as to create a mass market for the product. By the middle of the seventeenth century, European demand for sugar had already reached enormous proportions. In the eighteenth century, the sugar England imported from its tiny West Indian colonies of Barbados and Jamaica was worth more than all of its imports from China and India combined.

> In the eighteenth century, the sugar England imported from its tiny West Indian colonies of Barbados and Jamaica was worth more than all of its imports from China and India combined.

Sugar, however, could be grown only in a fairly limited geographical and climatic area. Tobacco was much more adaptable. Although tobacco was first imported into Europe by the Spaniards in the mid-sixteenth century, another half century passed before Europeans took up the habit of smoking. Governments at first joined the church in condemning the use of tobacco, but by the end of the seventeenth century, having realized the profits to be made from it, they were actively encouraging its production and consumption.

French Colonialism

French colonial policy matured during the administration of Louis XIV's mercantilist finance minister, Jean Baptiste Colbert, who regarded overseas expansion as an integral part of state economic policy. To compete with the English, he encouraged the development of sugar-producing colonies in the West Indies, the largest of which was St. Domingue (present-day Haiti). France also dominated the interior of the North American continent, where French traders bought furs and missionaries preached Christianity to the Indians in a vast territory that stretched from Acadia to Quebec to Louisiana. Yet the financial returns from these lands were never commensurate with their size. Furs, fish, and tobacco were exported to European markets in large quantities but never matched the profits from the Caribbean sugar colonies or from the trading outposts the French maintained in India.

Dutch Colonialism

Until the 1670s, the Dutch controlled the most prosperous commercial empire of the seventeenth century. Dutch colonialism generally followed the "fort and factory" model established by the Portuguese in Asia. In Southeast Asia, the Dutch East India Company, founded in 1602, seized control of Sumatra, Borneo, and the Moluccas (Spice Islands), driving Portuguese traders from an area they had previously dominated and establishing a Dutch monopoly within Europe over pepper, cinnamon, nutmeg, mace, and cloves. The Dutch also secured an exclusive right to trade with Japan and maintained military and trading outposts in China and India as well. In the Western Hemisphere, however, their achievements were less spectacular. After a series of trade wars with England, in 1667 they formally surrendered their colony of New Amsterdam (subsequently renamed New York), retaining only Surinam (off the northern coast of South America) and Curaçao and Tobago (in the West Indies). Although they dominated the seventeenth-century slave trade with Africa, after 1713 the Dutch would lose this position also to the British.

As the primary financiers of seventeenth-century Europe, the Dutch also pioneered new mechanisms for investing in colonial enterprises. One of the most important of these was the joint-stock company, of which the Dutch East India Company was among the first. Such companies raised cash by selling shares in their enterprise to investors. Even though the investors might not take any role in managing the company, they were joint owners of the business and therefore entitled to a share in its profits in proportion with the amount they had invested. Initially, the Dutch East India Company had intended to pay off its investors ten years after its founding, but the directors soon recognized the impossibility of this plan. The directors therefore urged investors anxious to realize their profits to sell their shares on the Amsterdam stock exchange to other investors, thereby ensuring the continued operation of their enterprise and, in the process, establishing a method of continuous business financing that would soon spread elsewhere in Europe.

> As the primary financiers of seventeenth-century Europe, the Dutch also pioneered new mechanisms for investing in colonial enterprises. One of the most important of these was the joint-stock company, of which the Dutch East India Company was among the first.

CONTRASTING PATTERNS OF COLONIAL SETTLEMENT

Differences in the commercial relationships European countries established with their New World colonies reflected important differences in settlement patterns among these colonies. In Central and South America, a relatively small number of Spaniards had conquered complex, highly populous Native American societies. To rule these new territories, the Spanish quickly replaced native elites with Spanish administrators and churchmen. But by and large they did not attempt to uproot or eliminate existing native cultures. Instead, Spain focused its efforts on controlling and exploiting native labor, so as to extract the maximum possible profit for the crown from the colonies' mineral resources. The native peoples of Spanish America already lived, for the most part, in large, well-organized villages and towns. Spanish colonial policy was to collect tribute from such communities and to convert them to Catholicism, but to do so without fundamentally disrupting their existing patterns of life.

The result was widespread cultural assimilation between the Spanish colonizers and the native populace, combined with a relatively high degree of intermarriage between them. Out of this reality emerged a complex and distinctive system of racial and social castes, with "pure-blooded" Spaniards at the top, peoples of mixed descent in the middle (native, Spanish, and African, in various combinations), and Indians at the bottom. In theory, these racial categories corresponded with class distinctions; but in practice race and class did not always coincide, and race itself was often a social fiction. Mixed-race individuals who prospered economically often found ways to establish their "pure" Spanish ancestry by adopting the social practices that characterized elite (that is, Spanish) status. Spaniards, however, always remained at the top of the social hierarchy, even when they fell into poverty.

Like the Spanish colonies, the French colonies were established and administered as direct crown enterprises. French colonial settlements were conceived mainly as military outposts and trading centers; as a result, they were overwhelmingly populated by men. The elite members of French colonial society were the military officers and administrators sent out from Paris. But fishermen, fur traders, small farmers, and common soldiers constituted the bulk of the French settlers of North America. Except in the Caribbean, French colonies depended largely on the fur trade and on fishing; both enterprises relied in turn on cooperative relationships with native peoples. A mutual economic interdependence therefore grew up between these French colonies and the peoples of the surrounding region. Intermarriage, especially between French fur traders and native women, was common. But most French colonies in North America remained dependent on the wages and supplies sent to them from the mother country. Only rarely did they become truly self-sustaining economic enterprises.

The English colonies along the Atlantic seaboard followed a different model. English colonies did not begin as Crown enterprises. Instead they were established either by joint-stock companies (as in Virginia and the Massachusetts Bay colony) or as private, proprietary colonies (such as Maryland and Pennsylvania). Building on their experience in Ireland, English colonists established planned settlements known as plantations, in which they attempted to replicate as many features of English life as possible. Geography

How did the patterns of European colonial settlement in the Americas differ from each other?

Colonization and Trade in the Seventeenth Century   419

THE ATLANTIC WORLD

Why were European governments so concerned with closely controlling the means by which certain products traveled from the colonies to European ports? How and why did the financial institutions of the late medieval period thrive on and encourage the economic policies of colonial powers? Why are the trade routes carrying slaves so prominently marked on this map? What does this suggest about the importance of unfree labor to the economic achievements of Europeans in the New World?

also contributed to the resulting concentration of English settlement patterns. The rivers and bays of eastern North America provided the first footholds for English colonists in the New World, and the Atlantic Ocean helped tie these separated settlements together. But aside from the Hudson, there were no great rivers to lead colonists very far inland. Instead, the English colonies clung to the seacoast, and so to each other.

Like the French colonies, the early English colonies relied on fishing and the fur trade for their exports. But primarily, English colonies were agricultural communities, populated by small- and medium-scale landholders for whom control over land was the key to wealth. Partly this was a reflection of the kinds of people whom these privately sponsored colonial enterprises could persuade to immigrate to the New World. But this focus on agriculture was also the result of the demographic catastrophe that had struck the native populations of the Atlantic seaboard during the last half of the sixteenth century. European diseases—brought by Spanish armies and by the French, English, and Portuguese fishermen who frequented the rich fishing banks off the New England coast—had already decimated the native peoples of eastern North America even before the first European colonists set foot there. By the early seventeenth century, a great deal of rich

agricultural land had been abandoned simply because there were no longer enough native farmers to till it—one reason that many native groups initially welcomed the new arrivals.

Unlike the Spanish, English colonists along the Atlantic seaboard therefore had neither the need nor the opportunity to control a large native labor force. What they wanted, rather, was complete and exclusive control over native lands. To this end, the English colonists soon set out to eliminate, through expulsion and massacre, the indigenous peoples of their colonies. To be sure, there were exceptions. In the Quaker colony of Pennsylvania, colonists and Native Americans maintained friendly relations for more than half a century. In the Carolinas, by contrast, there was widespread enslavement of native people, either for sale to the West Indies or, from the 1690s, to work on the rice plantations along the coast. Elsewhere, however, attempts to enslave the native peoples of North America failed. When English planters looked for bond laborers, they therefore either recruited indentured servants from England (most of whom would be freed after a specified period of service) or else they purchased African captives (who would usually be enslaved for life).

Social relations between the English colonists and native peoples also differed from the patterns we find

Illinois Indians Trading with French Settlers. This engraving from Nicholas De Fer's 1705 map of the Western Hemisphere illustrates the economic interdependence that developed between early French colonies and the native people of the surrounding region.

elsewhere in the New World. In contrast to the Spanish and French colonies, intermarriage between English colonists and natives was rare. Instead, a rigid racial division emerged that distinguished all Europeans, regardless of class, from all Native Americans and Africans. Intermarriage between natives and Africans was relatively common, but between the English and the indigenous peoples of their colonies an unbridgeable gulf soon developed.

COLONIAL RIVALRIES

The fortunes of these colonial empires changed dramatically in the course of the seventeenth and early eighteenth centuries. Spain, mired in persistent economic stagnation and embroiled in a series of expensive wars and domestic rebellions, proved unable to defend its monopoly over colonial trade. In a war with Spain in the 1650s, England captured not only the island of Jamaica but treasure ships lying off the Spanish harbor of Cadíz. Further profit was obtained by bribing Spanish customs officials on a grand scale. During the second half of the century, two thirds of the imported goods sold in Spanish colonies were smuggled in by Dutch, English, and French traders. By 1700, although Spain still possessed a colonial empire, that empire lay at the mercy of its more dynamic rivals. A brief revival of fortunes under more enlightened leadership in the mid-eighteenth century did nothing to prevent its ultimate eclipse.

Portugal, too, found it impossible to prevent foreign penetration of its colonial empire. England in particular worked diligently to win commercial advantages there. In 1703, the English signed a treaty with Portugal allowing English merchants to export woolens duty free into Portugal and allowing Portugul to ship its wines duty free into England. Increasing English trade with Portugal also led to English trade with the Portuguese colony of Brazil, an important sugar producer and the largest of all the New World markets for African slaves. In the eighteenth century, English merchants would dominate these Brazilian trade routes.

COLONIALISM AND EMPIRE

In what ways did eighteenth-century European colonialism differ from seventeenth-century European colonialism?

The 1713 Treaty of Utrecht opened a new era in these colonial rivalries. As we have seen, the biggest losers in these negotiations were the Dutch, who gained only a guarantee of security for their own borders, and the Spanish, who were forced to concede to Britain the right to market slaves in the Spanish colonies. The winners were the British (who acquired large chunks of French territory in North America) and, to a lesser extent, the French, who retained Cape Breton Island, Quebec, the interior portions of North America, and their

The Defense of Cadíz against the English, by Francisco Zurbaran. The rivalry between European powers that played out over the new colonial possessions further proved the decline of Spain, which lost the island of Jamaica and ships in the harbor of Cadíz to the English in the 1650s.

foothold in India. The eighteenth century would witness a continuing struggle between Britain and France for control over the expanding commerce that now bound the European economy to the Americas and to Asia.

THE TRIANGULAR TRADE IN SUGAR AND SLAVES

During the eighteenth century, European colonial trade came to be dominated by transatlantic routes that developed in response to the lucrative West Indian sugar industry and to the demand for slaves from Africa to work those Caribbean plantations. In this "triangular" trade, naval superiority gave Britain a decisive advantage over its French, Spanish, Portuguese, and Dutch rivals. Typically, a British ship might begin its voyage from New England with a consignment of rum and sail to Africa, where the rum would be exchanged for a cargo of slaves. From the west coast of Africa the ship would then cross the South Atlantic to the sugar colonies of Jamaica or Barbados, where slaves would be traded for molasses. It would then make the final leg of the journey back to New England, where the molasses would be made into rum. A variant triangle might see manufactured goods move from England to Africa, where they would be traded for slaves. Those slaves would then be shipped to Virginia and exchanged for tobacco, which would be shipped to England and processed there for sale throughout Europe.

The cultivation of New World sugar and tobacco depended on slave labor. As European demand for these products increased, so too did the traffic in enslaved Africans. At the height of the Atlantic slave trade in the eighteenth century, 75,000 to 90,000 Africans were shipped across the Atlantic yearly: at least 6 million in the eighteenth century, out of a total of over 11 million for the entire history of the trade. About 35 percent went to English and French Caribbean plantations; 5 percent (roughly 500,000) to North America; and the rest to the Portuguese colony of Brazil and to the Spanish colonies in Central and South America. By the 1780s, there were more than

How Slaves Were Stowed Aboard a Ship during the Middle Passage. Men were "housed" on the right; women on the left; children in the middle. The human cargo was jammed onto platforms six feet wide without sufficient headroom to permit an adult to sit up. This diagram is from evidence gathered by English abolitionists and depicts conditions on the Liverpool slave ship *Brookes.*

500,000 slaves on the largest French plantation island, St. Domingue, and at least 200,000 on its English counterpart, Jamaica.

Although run as a monopoly by various governments in the sixteenth and early seventeenth centuries, the slave trade in the eighteenth century was open to private entrepreneurs who operated ports on the West African coast. These traders exchanged Indian cloth, metal goods, rum, and firearms with African slave merchants in return for their human cargo, who would then be packed by the hundreds into the holds of slave ships for the gruesome "middle passage" across the Atlantic (so called to distinguish it from the slave ship's voyage from Europe to Africa, and then from the colonies back to Europe). Shackled below decks without sanitary facilities, the captive men, women, and children suffered horribly. The mortality rate, however, remained at about 10 percent, not much higher than the rate for a normal sea voyage of 100 days or more. Since traders had to invest as much as £10 per slave in their enterprise, they were generally anxious to ensure that their consignment would reach its destination in good enough shape to be sold for a profit.

The Commercial Rivalry between Britain and France

British dominance of the slave trade gave it decisive advantages in its colonial struggles with France. As one Englishman wrote in 1749, the slave trade had provided "an unexhastible fund of wealth to this nation." But even apart from the slave trade, the value of colonial commerce was increasing dramatically during the eighteenth century. French colonial trade, valued at 25 million livres in 1716, rose to 263 million livres in 1789. In England, during roughly the same period, foreign trade increased in value from £10 million to £40 million, the latter amount more than twice that for France.

The growing value of colonial commerce tied the interests of governments and transoceanic merchants together in an increasingly tight embrace. Merchants engaged in the colonial trade depended on their governments to protect and defend their overseas investments; but governments depended in turn on merchants and their financial backers to build the ships and sustain the trade on which national power depended. In the eighteenth century, even the ability to wage war rested largely (and increasingly) on a government's ability to borrow the necessary funds from wealthy investors, and then to pay back those debts, with interest, over time. As it did in commerce, so too in finance, Britain came to enjoy a decisive advantage in this respect over France. The Bank of England, founded in the 1690s, managed the English national debt with great success, providing the funds required for war by selling shares to investors, then repaying those investors at moderate rates of interest. In contrast, chronic governmental indebtedness forced the French crown to borrow at ruinously high rates of interest, provoking a series of fiscal crises that in 1789 finally led to the collapse of the French monarchy.

War and Empire in the Eighteenth-Century World

After 1713, western Europe remained largely at peace for a generation. In 1740, however, that peace was shattered when Frederick the Great of Prussia seized the Austrian province of Silesia (see p. 409). In the resulting War of the Austrian Succession, France and Spain fought on the side of Prussia, hoping to reverse some of the losses they had suffered in the Treaty of Utrecht. As they had done since the 1690s, Britain and the Dutch Republic sided with Austria. Like those earlier wars, this war quickly spread beyond the frontiers of Europe. In India, the English East India Company lost control over the coastal area of Madras to its French rival; but in North America, British colonists from New England captured the important French fortress of Louisbourg on Cape Breton Island, hoping to put a stop to French interference with their fishing and shipping. When the war finally ended in 1748, Britain recovered Madras and returned Louisbourg to France.

Eight years later, these colonial conflicts reignited when Prussia once again attacked Austria. This time, however, Prussia allied itself with Great Britain. Austria found support from both France and Russia. In Europe, the Seven Years' War (1756–1763) ended in stalemate. In India and North America, however, the war had decisive consequences. In India, the British East India Company joined with native allies to eliminate their French competitors. In North America (where the conflict was known as the French and Indian War), British troops captured Louisbourg and Quebec and drove French forces from the Ohio River valley and the Great Lakes. In 1763, France formally surrendered both Canada and India to the British. Six years later, the French East India Company was dissolved.

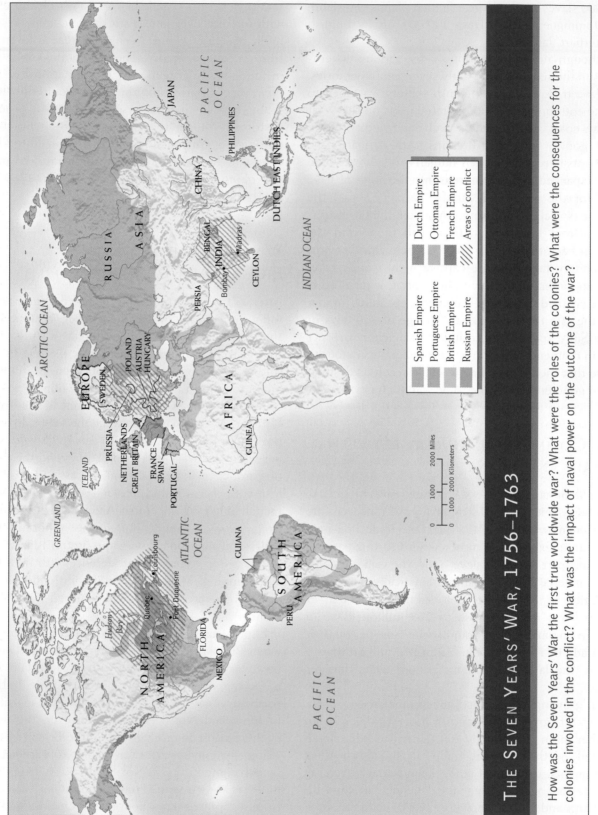

THE SEVEN YEARS' WAR, 1756–1763

How was the Seven Years' War the first true worldwide war? What were the roles of the colonies? What were the consequences for the colonies involved in the conflict? What was the impact of naval power on the outcome of the war?

Legend:
- Spanish Empire
- Portuguese Empire
- British Empire
- Russian Empire
- Dutch Empire
- Ottoman Empire
- French Empire
- Areas of conflict

Map labels: ARCTIC OCEAN, RUSSIA, ASIA, PACIFIC OCEAN, JAPAN, CHINA, PHILIPPINES, DUTCH EAST INDIES, BENGAL, Madras, INDIA, Bombay, CEYLON, PERSIA, INDIAN OCEAN, EUROPE, SWEDEN, POLAND, AUSTRIA, HUNGARY, PRUSSIA, NETHERLANDS, GREAT BRITAIN, FRANCE, SPAIN, PORTUGAL, ICELAND, AFRICA, GUINEA, GREENLAND, ATLANTIC OCEAN, GUIANA, SOUTH AMERICA, PERU, Hudson Bay, Quebec, Louisbourg, Fort Duquesne, NORTH AMERICA, FLORIDA, MEXICO, PACIFIC OCEAN

Scale: 0 1000 2000 Miles / 0 1000 2000 Kilometers

THE AMERICAN REVOLUTION

Along the Atlantic seaboard, however, the rapidly growing British colonies were beginning to chafe at rule from London. To recover some of the costs of the Seven Years' War and to pay for the continuing costs of protecting its colonial subjects, the British Parliament imposed a series of new taxes on its American colonies. These taxes were immediately unpopular. Colonists complained that because they had no representatives in Parliament, they were being taxed without their consent—a fundamental violation of their rights as British subjects. They also complained that British restrictions on colonial trade, particularly the requirement that certain goods pass first through British ports before being shipped to the Continent, were strangling American livelihoods and so making it impossible to pay even the king's legitimate taxes.

The British government, led since 1760 by the young and inexperienced King George III, responded to these complaints with a badly calculated mixture of vacillation and force. Various taxes were imposed and then withdrawn in the face of colonial resistance. In 1773, however, when East India Company tea was dumped in Boston Harbor by rebellious colonials objecting to the customs duties that had been imposed on it, the British government closed the port of Boston and curtailed the colony's representative institutions. These "Coercive Acts" galvanized the support of the other American colonies for Massachusetts. In 1774, representatives from all the American colonies met at Philadelphia to form the Continental Congress to negotiate with the Crown over their grievances. In April 1775, however, local militiamen at Lexington and Concord clashed with regular British troops sent to disarm them. Soon thereafter, the Continental Congress began raising an army, and an outright rebellion erupted against the British government.

On July 4, 1776, the thirteen colonies formally declared their independence from Great Britain. During the first two years of the war, it seemed unlikely that such independence would ever become a reality. In 1778, however, France, anxious to undermine the colonial hegemony Great Britain had established since 1713, joined the war on the side of the Americans. Spain entered the war in support of France, hoping to recover Gibraltar and Florida (the latter lost in 1763 to Britain). In 1780, Britain also declared war on the Dutch Republic for continuing to trade with the rebellious colonies. Now facing a coalition of its colonial rivals, Great Britain saw the war turn against it. In 1781, combined land and sea operations by French and American troops forced the surrender of the main British army at Yorktown in Virginia. Negotiations for peace began soon after but were not concluded until September 1783. The Treaty of Paris left Great Britain in control of Canada and Gibraltar. Spain retained its possessions west of the Mississippi River and recovered Florida. The United States gained its independence; its western border was fixed on the Mississippi River, and it secured valuable fishing rights off the eastern coast of Canada. France gained only the satisfaction of defeating its colonial rival; but even that satisfaction was short lived. Six years later, the massive debts France had incurred in supporting the American Revolution helped bring about another, very different kind of revolution in France that would permanently alter the history of Europe.

In 1781, combined land and sea operations by French and American troops forced the surrender of the main British army at Yorktown in Virginia.

CONCLUSION

Seen in this light, the American War of Independence was the final military conflict in a century-long struggle between Great Britain and France for colonial dominance. But the consequences of Britain's defeat in 1783 were far less significant than might have been expected. Even after American independence, Great Britain would remain the most important trading partner for its former American colonies, while elsewhere around the globe, the commercial dominance Britain

CHRONOLOGY

EIGHTEENTH-CENTURY WARS

War of the Spanish Succession	1702–1713
War of the Austrian Succession	1740–1748
Seven Years' War	1756–1763
American Revolution	1775–1783
The Russo-Turkish War	1787–1792

had already established would continue to grow. The profits of slavery certainly helped fuel the eighteenth-century British economy; by the end of the century, however, British trade and manufacturing had reached such high levels of productivity that even the abolition of the slave trade (in 1808) and of slavery itself (in 1833) did not impede its continuing growth.

The economic prosperity of late-eighteenth-century Britain was mirrored to some degree throughout northwestern Europe. Improved transportation systems, more reliable food supplies, and growing quantities of consumer goods brought improved standards of living to large numbers of Europeans, even as the overall population of Europe was rising faster after 1750 than it had ever done before. Population growth was especially rapid in the cities, where a new urban middle class was emerging whose tastes drove the market for goods and whose opinions were reshaping the world of ideas.

But the prosperity of late-eighteenth-century Europe remained very unevenly distributed. In the cities, rich and poor lived separate lives in separate neighborhoods. In the countryside, regions bypassed by the developing commercial economy of the period continued to suffer from hunger and famine, just as they had done in the sixteenth and seventeenth centuries. In eastern Europe the contrasts between rich and poor were even more extreme, as many peasants fell into a new style of serfdom that would last until the end of the nineteenth century. War too remained a fact of European life, bringing death and destruction to hundreds of thousands of people across the Continent and around the world—yet another consequence of the worldwide reach of these European colonial empires.

Political change was more gradual. Throughout Europe, the powers of governments steadily increased. Administrators became more numerous, more efficient, and more demanding, partly to meet the mounting costs of war but also because governments were starting to take on a much wider range of responsibilities for the welfare of their subjects. Despite the increasing scope of government, however, the structure and principles of government changed relatively little. Apart from Great Britain and the Dutch Republic, the great powers of eighteenth-century Europe were still governed by rulers who styled themselves as absolutist monarchs in the mold of Louis XIV. By 1789, however, the European world was a vastly different place than it had been a century before, when the Sun King had dominated European politics. The full extent of those differences was about to be revealed.

KEY TERMS

absolutism	Treaty of Utrecht	Catherine the Great
balance of power	Habsburg empire	English navigation acts
Louis XIV	Versailles	triangular trade
William and Mary	Frederick the Great	East India Company
Two Treatises on Government	Peter the Great	Seven Years' War

SELECTED READINGS

Blanning, T. C. W., ed. *The Eighteenth Century: Europe 1688–1815.* Oxford and New York, 2000. Chapters on political, economic, cultural, and religious developments written by leading experts.

Cameron, Euan, ed. *Early Modern Europe: An Oxford History.* Oxford and New York, 1999. A wide-ranging, stimulating, multiauthor survey, topically arranged, that spans the entire period from the Renaissance to the French Revolution.

Campbell, Peter R. *Louis XIV, 1661–1715.* London, 1993. A reliable recent biography; short, with primary source material and a good bibliography.

Collins, James B. *The State in Early Modern France.* Cambridge and New York, 1995. A challenging new account of French government and finance between 1620 and 1789.

Doyle, William. *The Old European Order, 1660–1800.* Oxford and New York, 1992. An excellent account of European society during the ancien régime, with chapters on population, trade, the social order, and public affairs.

Hufton, Olwen. *The Prospect before Her: A History of Women in Western Europe, 1500–1800.* New York, 1996. A great book by a great social historian.

Hughes, Lindsey. *Russia in the Age of Peter the Great.* New Haven, Conn., 1998. A detailed, scholarly account by the leading British authority on Peter's reign.

Ingrao, Charles. *The Habsburg Monarchy, 1618–1815.* 2d ed. Cambridge and New York, 2000. A recently revised and updated edition of this standard work.

Kishlansky, Mark A. *A Monarchy Transformed: Britain, 1603–1714.* London, 1996. An excellent survey that takes seriously its claims to be a "British" rather than merely an "English" history.

Koch, H. W. *A History of Prussia.* London, 1978. Still the best account of its subject.

Locke, John. *Two Treatises of Government.* Rev. ed. Ed. Peter Laslett. Cambridge and New York, 1963. Laslett has revolutionized our understanding of the historical and ideological context of Locke's political writings.

Miller, John, ed. *Absolutism in Seventeenth-Century Europe.* London, 1990. An excellent, multiauthor survey, organized by country.

Quataert, Donald. *The Ottoman Empire, 1700–1822.* Cambridge and New York, 2000. Well balanced, up to date, and intended to be read by students.

Saint-Simon, Louis. *Historical Memoirs.* Many editions. The classic source for life at Louis XIV's Versailles.

Thomas, Hugh. *The Slave Trade: The History of the Atlantic Slave Trade, 1440–1870.* London and New York, 1997. A survey notable for its breadth and depth of coverage, and for its attractive prose style.

RULERS OF PRINCIPAL STATES

THE CAROLINGIAN DYNASTY

Pepin of Heristal, Mayor of the Palace, 687–714
Charles Martel, Mayor of the Palace, 715–741
Pepin III, Mayor of the Palace, 741–751; King, 751–768
Charlemagne, King, 768–814; Emperor, 800–814
Louis the Pious, Emperor, 814–840

WEST FRANCIA
Charles the Bald, King, 840–877; Emperor, 875–877
Louis II, King, 877–879
Louis III, King, 879–882
Carloman, King, 879–884

MIDDLE KINGDOMS
Lothair, Emperor, 840–855
Louis (Italy), Emperor, 855–875
Charles (Provence), King, 855–863
Lothair II (Lorraine), King, 855–869

EAST FRANCIA
Ludwig, King, 840–876
Carloman, King, 876–880
Ludwig, King, 876–882
Charles the Fat, Emperor, 876–887

HOLY ROMAN EMPERORS

SAXON DYNASTY
Otto I, 962–973
Otto II, 973–983
Otto III, 983–1002
Henry II, 1002–1024

FRANCONIAN DYNASTY
Conrad II, 1024–1039
Henry III, 1039–1056
Henry IV, 1056–1106
Henry V, 1106–1125
Lothair II (Saxony), 1125–1137

HOHENSTAUFEN DYNASTY
Conrad III, 1138–1152
Frederick I (Barbarossa), 1152–1190
Henry VI, 1190–1197
Philip of Swabia, 1198–1208 } Rivals
Otto IV (Welf), 1198–1215
Frederick II, 1220–1250
Conrad IV, 1250–1254

INTERREGNUM, 1254–1273

EMPERORS FROM VARIOUS DYNASTIES
Rudolf I (Habsburg), 1273–1291
Adolf (Nassau), 1292–1298
Albert I (Habsburg), 1298–1308
Henry VII (Luxemburg), 1308–1313
Ludwig IV (Wittelsbach), 1314–1347
Charles IV (Luxemburg), 1347–1378
Wenceslas (Luxemburg), 1378–1400
Rupert (Wittelsbach), 1400–1410
Sigismund (Luxemburg), 1410–1437

HABSBURG DYNASTY
Albert II, 1438–1439
Frederick III, 1440–1493
Maximilian I, 1493–1519
Charles V, 1519–1556
Ferdinand I, 1556–1564
Maximilian II, 1564–1576
Rudolf II, 1576–1612

Matthias, 1612–1619
Ferdinand II, 1619–1637
Ferdinand III, 1637–1657
Leopold I, 1658–1705
Joseph I, 1705–1711
Charles VI, 1711–1740

Charles VII (not a Habsburg), 1742–1745
Francis I, 1745–1765
Joseph II, 1765–1790
Leopold II, 1790–1792
Francis II, 1792–1806

RULERS OF FRANCE FROM HUGH CAPET

CAPETIAN DYNASTY
Hugh Capet, 987–996
Robert II, 996–1031
Henry I, 1031–1060
Philip I, 1060–1108
Louis VI, 1108–1137
Louis VII, 1137–1180
Philip II (Augustus), 1180–1223
Louis VIII, 1223–1226
Louis IX (St. Louis), 1226–1270
Philip III, 1270–1285
Philip IV, 1285–1314
Louis X, 1314–1316
Philip V, 1316–1322
Charles IV, 1322–1328

VALOIS DYNASTY
Philip VI, 1328–1350
John, 1350–1364
Charles V, 1364–1380
Charles VI, 1380–1422
Charles VII, 1422–1461
Louis XI, 1461–1483
Charles VIII, 1483–1498
Louis XII, 1498–1515
Francis I, 1515–1547

Henry II, 1547–1559
Francis II, 1559–1560
Charles IX, 1560–1574
Henry III, 1574–1589

BOURBON DYNASTY
Henry IV, 1589–1610
Louis XIII, 1610–1643
Louis XIV, 1643–1715
Louis XV, 1715–1774
Louis XVI, 1774–1792

AFTER 1792
First Republic, 1792–1799
Napoleon Bonaparte, First Consul, 1799–1804
Napoleon I, Emperor, 1804–1814
Louis XVIII (Bourbon dynasty), 1814–1824
Charles X (Bourbon dynasty), 1824–1830
Louis Philippe, 1830–1848
Second Republic, 1848–1852
Napoleon III, Emperor, 1852–1870
Third Republic, 1870–1940
Péain regime, 1940–1944
Provisional government, 1944–1946
Fourth Republic, 1946–1958
Fifth Republic, 1958–

RULERS OF ENGLAND

ANGLO-SAXON DYNASTY
Alfred the Great, 871–899
Edward the Elder, 899–924
Ethelstan, 924–939
Edmund I, 939–946
Edred, 946–955
Edwy, 955–959
Edgar, 959–975
Edward the Martyr, 975–978
Ethelred the Unready, 978–1016

Canute, 1016–1035 (Danish Nationality)
Harold I, 1035–1040
Hardicanute, 1040–1042
Edward the Confessor, 1042–1066
Harold II, 1066

HOUSE OF NORMANDY
William I (the Conqueror), 1066–1087
William II, 1087–1100

Henry I, 1100–1135
Stephen, 1135–1154

HOUSE OF PLANTAGENET
Henry II, 1154–1189
Richard I, 1189–1199
John, 1199–1216
Henry III, 1216–1272
Edward I, 1272–1307
Edward II, 1307–1327
Edward III, 1327–1377
Richard II, 1377–1399

HOUSE OF LANCASTER
Henry IV, 1399–1413
Henry V, 1413–1422
Henry VI, 1422–1461

HOUSE OF YORK
Edward IV, 1461–1483
Edward V, 1483
Richard III, 1483–1485

HOUSE OF TUDOR
Henry VII, 1485–1509
Henry VIII, 1509–1547
Edward VI, 1547–1553
Mary, 1553–1558
Elizabeth I, 1558–1603

HOUSE OF STUART
James I, 1603–1625
Charles I, 1625–1649

COMMONWEALTH AND PROTECTORATE, 1649–1659

HOUSE OF STUART RESTORED
Charles II, 1660–1685
James II, 1685–1688
William III and Mary II, 1689–1694
William III alone, 1694–1702
Anne, 1702–1714

HOUSE OF HANOVER
George I, 1714–1727
George II, 1727–1760
George III, 1760–1820
George IV, 1820–1830
William IV, 1830–1837
Victoria, 1837–1901

HOUSE OF SAXE-COBURG-GOTHA
Edward VII, 1901–1910
George V, 1910–1917

HOUSE OF WINDSOR
George V, 1917–1936
Edward VIII, 1936
George VI, 1936–1952
Elizabeth II, 1952–

RULERS OF AUSTRIA AND AUSTRIA-HUNGARY

*Maximilian I (Archduke), 1493–1519
*Charles V, 1519–1556
*Ferdinand I, 1556–1564
*Maximilian II, 1564–1576
*Rudolf II, 1576–1612
*Matthias, 1612–1619
*Ferdinand II, 1619–1637
*Ferdinand III, 1637–1657
*Leopold I, 1658–1705
*Joseph I, 1705–1711
*Charles VI, 1711–1740
Maria Theresa, 1740–1780

*Joseph II, 1780–1790
*Leopold II, 1790–1792
*Francis II, 1792–1835 (Emperor of Austria as Francis I after 1804)
Ferdinand I, 1835–1848
Francis Joseph, 1848–1916 (after 1867 Emperor of Austria and King of Hungary)
Charles I, 1916–1918 (Emperor of Austria and King of Hungary)
Republic of Austria, 1918–1938 (dictatorship after 1934)
Republic restored, under Allied occupation, 1945–1956
Free Republic, 1956–

*also bore title of Holy Roman Emperor

RULERS OF PRUSSIA AND GERMANY

*Frederick I, 1701–1713
*Frederick William I, 1713–1740
*Frederick II (the Great), 1740–1786
*Frederick William II, 1786–1797
*Frederick William III,1797–1840
*Frederick William IV, 1840–1861
*William I, 1861–1888 (German Emperor after 1871)
Frederick III, 1888

*Kings of Prussia

*William II, 1888–1918
Weimar Republic, 1918–1933
Third Reich (Nazi Dictatorship), 1933–1945
Allied occupation, 1945–1952
Division into Federal Republic of Germany in west and
    German Democratic Republic in east, 1949–1991
Federal Republic of Germany (united), 1991–

RULERS OF RUSSIA

Ivan III, 1462–1505
Vasily III, 1505–1533
Ivan IV, 1533–1584
Theodore I, 1534–1598
Boris Godunov, 1598–1605
Theodore II,1605
Vasily IV, 1606–1610
Michael, 1613–1645
Alexius, 1645–1676
Theodore III, 1676–1682
Ivan V and Peter I, 1682–1689
Peter I (the Great), 1689–1725
Catherine I, 1725–1727
Peter II, 1727–1730

Anna, 1730–1740
Ivan VI, 1740–1741
Ellzabeth, 1741–1762
Peter III, 1762
Catherine II (the Great), 1762–1796
Paul, 1796–1801
Alexander I,1801–1825
Nicholas I, 1825–1855
Alexander II,1855–1881
Alexander III, 1881–1894
Nicholas II, 1894–1917
Soviet Republic, 1917–1991
Russian Federation, 1991–

RULERS OF SPAIN

Ferdinand
{ and Isabella, 1479–1504
{ and Philip I, 1504–1506
{ and Charles I, 1506–1516
Charles I (Holy Roman Emperor Charles V), 1516–1556
Philip II, 1556–1598
Philip III, 1598–1621
Philip IV, 1621–1665
Charles II, 1665–1700
Philip V, 1700–1746
Ferdinand VI, 1746–1759
Charles III, 1759–1788
Charles IV, 1788–1808

Ferdinand VII, 1808
Joseph Bonaparte, 1808–1813
Ferdinand VII (restored), 1814–1833
Isabella II, 1833–1868
Republic, 1868–1870
Amadeo, 1870–1873
Republic, 1873–1874
Alfonso XII, 1874–1885
Alfonso XIII, 1886–1931
Republic, 1931–1939
Fascist Dictatorship, 1939–1975
Juan Carlos I, 1975–

RULERS OF ITALY

Victor Emmanuel II, 1861–1878
Humbert I, 1878–1900
Victor Emmanuel III, 1900–1946

Fascist Dictatorship, 1922-1943 (maintained in northern
  Italy until 1945)
Humbert II, May 9–June 13, 1946
Republic, 1946–

PROMINENT POPES

Silvester I, 314–335
Leo I, 440–461
Gelasius I, 492–496
Gregory I, 590–604
Nicholas I, 858–867
Silvester II, 999–1003
Leo IX, 1049–1054
Nicholas II, 1058–1061
Gregory VII, 1073–1085
Urban II, 1088–1099
Paschal II, 1099–1118
Alexander III, 1159–1181
Innocent III, 1198–1216
Gregory IX, 1227–1241
Innocent IV, 1243–1254
Boniface VIII, 1294–1303
John XXII, 1316–1334
Nicholas V, 1447–1455
Pius II, 1458–1464

Alexander VI, 1492–1503
Julius II, 1503–1513
Leo X, 1513–1521
Paul III, 1534–1549
Paul IV, 1555–1559
Sixtus V, 1585–1590
Urban VIII, 1623–1644
Gregory XVI, 1831–1846
Pius IX, 1846–1878
Leo XIII, 1878–1903
Pius X, 1903–1914
Benedict XV, 1914–1922
Pius XI, 1922–1939
Pius XII, 1939–1958
John XXIII, 1958–1963
Paul VI, 1963–1978
John Paul I, 1978
John Paul II, 1978–2005
Benedict XVI, 2005–

GLOSSARY

Peter Abelard (1079–1142) Famed French theologian, logician, and university lecturer.

abolition of feudalism The end of the feudal system in France, which was brought about by the popular revolts of 1789. Louis XVI and other nobles established the National Assembly, which abolished all forms of privilege, such as the church tax on harvests, the labor requirement of peasants (known as the corvee), the nobility's hunting privileges, and a variety of tax exemptions and monopolies.

absolutism Form of government in which one body, usually the monarch, controls the right to make war, tax, judge, and coin money. The term was often used to refer to the state monarchies in seventeenth- and eighteenth-century Europe.

abstract expressionism The mid-twentieth-century school of art based in New York that included Jackson Pollock, Willem de Kooning, and Franz Kline. It emphasized form, color, gesture, and feeling instead of figurative subjects.

African National Congress (ANC) Multiracial organization founded in 1912 whose goal was to end racial discrimination in South Africa.

Afrikaners Descendants of the original Dutch settlers of South Africa; formerly referred to as Boers.

AIDS Acquired immune deficiency syndrome. AIDS first appeared in the 1970s and has developed into a global health catastrophe; it is spreading most quickly in developing nations in Africa and Asia.

Akhenaten The fourteenth-century B.C.E. pharaoh who developed a sun-oriented religion and ultimately damaged Egypt's position in the ancient world.

Alexander (356–323 B.C.E.) The Macedonian general who conquered northwest Asia Minor, and Persia, and built an empire that stretched as far east as the Indus River.

Algerian War The war in the 1950s and 1960s between France and Algerians seeking independence. Led by the National Liberation Front (FLN), guerrillas fought the French army in the mountains and desert of Algeria. The FLN also initiated a campaign of bombing and terrorism in Algerian cities that led French soldiers to torture Algerians and attract world attention and international scandal.

Allied Powers The World War I coalition of Great Britain, Ireland, Belgium, France, Italy, Russia, Portugal, Greece, Serbia, Montenegro, Albania, and Romania.

al Qaeda The radical Islamic organization founded in the late 1980s by former *mujahedin* who had fought against the Soviet Union in Afghanistan. Al Qaeda carried out the 9/11 terrorist attacks and is responsible as well for attacks in Africa, Southeast Asia, Europe, and the Middle East.

Americanization The fear of many Europeans from the 1920s and on that U.S. cultural products, such as film, television, and music, exerted too much influence. Many of the criticisms centered on America's emphasis on mass production and organization. The fears about Americanization were not limited to culture. They extended to corporations, business techniques, global trade, and marketing.

Amnesty International Nongovernmental organization formed in 1961 to defend "prisoners of conscience"—those detained for their beliefs, color, sex, ethnic origin, language, or religion.

Anabaptists Swiss Protestant movement that began in 1521 and insisted that only adults could be baptized Christians. The movement's first generation, who had been baptized as infants according to Catholic practice, was "re-baptized," hence the name.

anarchism The social and political movement that began in the mid-nineteenth century and advocated the destruction of the state through violence and terrorism.

Antigonus Greek general who established his own rule over Macedon in 276 B.C.E.

apartheid The racial segregation policy of the Afrikaner-dominated South African government. Legislated in 1948 by the Afrikaner National Party, it existed in South Africa for many years.

appeasement The policy pursued by Western governments in the face of German, Italian, and Japanese aggression leading up to World War II. The policy, which attempted to accommodate and negotiate peace with the aggressive nations, was based on the belief that another global war like World War I was unimaginable, a belief that Germany and its allies had been mistreated by the terms of the Treaty of Versailles, and a fear that fascist Germany and its allies protected the West from the spread of Soviet Communism.

aqueducts Engineering system that brought water from the mountains down to Roman cities.

Saint Thomas Aquinas (1225–1274) Italian Dominican monk and theologian whose intellectual style encouraged the study of ancient philosophers and science as complementary to theology.

Arians The fourth-century followers of a priest named Arius, who rejected the idea that Christ could be equal with God.

Aristotelian   The system of thought based on the ideas of the Greek philosopher Aristotle. Aristotelian ideas distinguished between the works of humans and those of nature and posited that as God's creation, nature belonged to a different, higher order.

Assyrians   A Semitic-speaking people that emerged around 2400 B.C.E. in northern Mesopotamia. Their highly militarized empire dominated Near-Eastern politics for close to two thousand years.

astrolabe   An ancient navigational instrument, thought to have been invented in 150 B.C.E., which was used to find latitude while at sea.

Saint Augustine (c. 354–397)   One of the most influential Christian theologians of all time, Saint Augustine described his conversion in his autobiographical *Confessions* and formulated new aspects of Christian theology in *On the City of God*.

Augustus (63 B.C.E.–14 C.E.)   The grandnephew and adopted son of Julius Caesar and first emperor of the Roman empire.

Auschwitz-Birkenau   The Nazi concentration camp in Poland that was designed to systematically murder Jews and gypsies. Between 1942 and 1944 over one million people were killed in Auschwitz-Birkenau.

Austrian empire   The dual monarchy of Austria-Hungary established by the Habsburg family in 1867; it collapsed at the end of World War I.

authoritarianism   A centralized and dictatorial form of government, proclaimed by its adherents to be superior to parliamentary democracy and especially effective at mobilizing the masses. Authoritarianism was prominent in the 1930s.

Avignon   City on the southeastern border of France. Between 305 and 378 it was the seat of the papacy.

Aztecs   Native American people of central Mexico; their empire was conquered by the Spanish in the sixteenth century.

Francis Bacon (1561–1626)   British philosopher and scientist who pioneered the scientific method and inductive reasoning. In other words, he argued that thinkers should amass observations and then make general observations or theories.

balance of power   Initated by the League of Augsburg in 1689, a new diplomatic goal emerged in western and central Europe to preserve a balance of power to prevent any single country from becoming so powerful as to threaten the position of the other major powers within the European state system.

Balfour Declaration   A letter dated November 2, 1917, by Lord Arthur J. Balfour, British Foreign Secretary, that promised a homeland for the Jews in Palestine.

Baroque   An ornate style of art and music associated with the Counter Reformation (from the French word for "irregularly shaped pearl").

Bay of Pigs (1961)   The unsuccessful invasion of Cuba by Cuban exiles, supported by the U.S. government. The rebels intended to incite an insurrection in Cuba and overthrow the Communist regime of Fidel Castro.

Beer Hall Putsch (1923)   The Nazi invasion of a meeting of Bavarian leaders and supporters in a Munich beer hall; Adolf Hitler was imprisoned for a year after the incident.

Saint Benedict of Nursia (c. 480–c. 547)   Considered the father of western monasticism, Saint Benedict created the Benedictine rule that became the guide for nearly all western monks. Monks were required to follow the rules laid down by Saint Benedict: poverty, sexual chastity, obedience, labor, and religious devotion.

Berlin airlift (1948)   The supply of vital necessities to West Berlin by air transport primarily under U.S. auspices. It was initiated in response to a blockade of the city that had been instituted by the Soviet Union to force the Allies to abandon West Berlin.

Berlin blockade   From June 1948 until May 1949, the Soviets cut all road, train, and river access from the Western zone of Germany to West Berlin. Unwilling to cede control of their portion of the capital, France, Britain, and the United States airlifted supplies over Soviet territory to the Western zone of Berlin.

Berlin Wall   The wall built in 1961 by East German Communists to prevent citizens of East Germany from fleeing to West Germany; it was torn down in 1989.

Otto von Bismarck (1815–1890)   The prime minister of Prussia and later the first chancellor of Germany, Bismarck helped consolidate the German people's economic and military power.

Black Death   The epidemic of bubonic plague that ravaged Europe, East Asia, and North Africa in the fourteenth century, killing one-third of the European population.

Black Shirts   The troops of Mussolini's fascist regime; the squads received money from Italian landowners to attack socialist leaders.

Black Tuesday (October 24, 1929)   The day on which the U.S. stock market crashed, plunging the U.S. and international trading systems into crisis and leading the world into the "Great Depression."

Blitzkrieg   The German "lightning war" strategy used during World War II; the Germans invaded Poland, France, Russia, and other countries with fast-moving well-coordinated attacks using aircraft, tanks and other armored vehicles, followed by infantry.

Bloody Sunday   On Sunday, January 22, 1905, the Russian tsar's guards killed 130 demonstrators who were protesting the tsar's mistreatment of workers and the middle class.

Giovanni Boccaccio (1313–1375)   Italian prose writer famed for his *Decameron*, one hundred short stories about the human condition, mostly from a comic or cynical point of view.

Boer War   Conflict between British and ethnically European Afrikaners in South Africa, 1899–1902, with terrible casualties on both sides. Resulted in bringing two Afrikaner republics under control of the British.

Simón de Bolívar (1783–1830)   Venezuelan-born general called "The Liberator" for his assistance in helping Bolivia, Panama, Colombia, Ecuador, Peru, and Venezuela win independence from Spain.

Bolsheviks   Former members of the Russian Social Democratic Party who advocated the destruction of capitalist political and economic institutions and started the Russian Revolution. In 1918 the Bolsheviks changed their name to the Russian Communist Party.

Napoleon Bonaparte (1769–1821)   Corsican-born French general who seized power and ruled as dictator 1799–1814. After successful conquest of much of Europe, he was defeated by Russian and Prussian forces and died in exile.

bourgeoisie The French term for the middle class, which emerged in Europe during the Middle Ages. The Bourgeoisie sought to be recognized not by birth or title, but by capital and property.

Boxer Rebellion (1899–1900) Chinese peasant movement that opposed foreign influence, especially that of Christian missionaries; it was finally put down after the Boxers were defeated by a foreign army comprised mostly of Japanese, Russian, British, French, and American soldiers.

bubonic plague An acute infectious disease caused by a bacterium that is transmitted to humans by fleas from infected rats. It ravaged Europe and parts of Asia in the fourteenth century. Sometimes referred to as the "black death."

Julius Caesar (100–44 B.C.E.) The Roman general who conquered the Gauls, invaded Britain, and expanded Rome's territory in Asia Minor. He became the dictator of Rome in 46 B.C.E. and was murdered by Brutus and Cassius, which led to the rise of Augustus and the end of the Roman republic.

caliphs Rulers of the Islamic community who claimed descent from Muhammad.

John Calvin (1509–1564) French-born Protestant theologian who stressed the predestination of all human beings according to God's will.

Canary Islands Islands off the western coast of Africa conquered by Portugal and Spain in the mid-1400s. Used to supply expeditions around the African coast and across the Atlantic.

Canterbury Tales Middle English verse stories by Geoffrey Chaucer (c.1340–1400) that reflect different classes and experiences in late medieval England.

caravans Companies of men who transported and traded goods along overland routes in North Africa and central Asia; large caravans consisted of 600 to 1,000 camels and as many as 400 men.

caravels Sailing vessels suited for nosing in and out of estuaries and navigating in waters with unpredictable currents and winds.

Carthage A great maritime empire that rivaled Rome; at its height, it stretched across the northern coast of Africa from modern-day Tunisia to the Strait of Gibraltar. Carthage fought against Rome in the Punic Wars that began in 264 B.C.E. The wars ended with the destruction of Carthage in 146 B.C.E.

Cassiodorus (490–583) Author of the *Institutes*, which instructed medieval readers on the essential works of literature a monk should know before moving on to more intensive study of theology and the Bible.

Baldassare Castiglione (1478–1529) Author of *The Book of the Courtier*, a popular treatise on upper-class social graces.

Catherine the Great (1729–1796) German-born empress of Russia who maintained an absolutist feudal system but encouraged Enlightenment philosophy and the arts at court.

Catholicism Branch of Christianity headed by the pope.

Camillo Benso di Cavour (1810–1861) Anti-papist Italian leader who led the initial stages of revolution against the Habsburgs.

Central Powers The World War I alliance between Germany, Austro-Hungary, Bulgaria, and Turkey.

Charlemagne (742–814) Frankish ruler 767–813 who consolidated much of western Europe by adding Lombardy and Saxony to the Frankish kingdoms. With a strong sense of divine purpose, he forced the Christian conversion of pagan peoples and sponsored arts and learning at court. In 800 he became the first Roman emperor in the west since the 5th century.

Chartist movement (1834–1848) Mass democratic movement to pass the Peoples' Charter in Britain, granting male suffrage, secret ballot, equal electoral districts, and annual Parliaments, and absolving the requirement of property ownership for members of Parliament.

chivalry From the word for "horsemanship"; an aristocratic ideology originating with the knights of eleventh-century Europe that encouraged military prowess and social graces.

Winston Churchill (1874–1965) The British prime minister who led the country during World War II. He also coined the phrase "Iron Curtain" in a speech at Westminster College in 1946.

Church of England Founded by Henry VIII in the 1530s after his excommunication from the Catholic Church by Pope Clement VII, it is the established form of Christianity in England.

Cicero (106–43 B.C.E.) The most famous Stoic philosopher and orator of Rome.

Civil War (1861–1865) Conflict between the northern and southern states of America that cost over 600,000 lives; this struggle led to the abolition of slavery in the United States.

Cluny A Benedictine monastery, founded in 910, whose reform ideology tried to separate its network of religious houses from control by lay people.

cold war (1945–1990) Ideological conflict in which the U.S.S.R. and Eastern Europe opposed the United States and Western Europe.

collectivization The process under Stalin in the 1920s and 1930s where peasants were forced to give up private farmland and join collective farms, which were supported by the state.

Christopher Columbus (1451–1506) The Italian sailor who persuaded King Ferdinand and Queen Isabella of Spain to fund his expedition across the Atlantic to discover a new trade route to Asia. He miscalculated the size of the Earth and rather than landing in China or Japan, Columbus reached the Bahamas and the island of Hispaniola in 1492.

Committee of Public Safety Political body during the French Revolution that was controlled by the Jacobins, who enforced party rule by executing thousands during the Reign of Terror, September 1793–July 1794.

Communist Manifesto (1818–1883) Radical pamphlet by Karl Marx that predicted the downfall of the capitalist system and its replacement by a system that operated in the interests of the working class (proletariat).

Congo Free State Large colonial state in Africa created by Leopold II, king of Belgium, during the 1880s, and ruled by him alone. After reports of mass slaughter and enslavement, the Belgian parliament took the land and formed a Belgian colony.

Congress of Vienna (1814–1815) International conference to reorganize Europe after the downfall of Napoleon. European monarchies agreed to respect each other's borders and to cooperate in guarding against future revolutions and war.

conquistador   Spanish term for "conqueror," applied to European leaders of campaigns against indigenous peoples in central and southern America.

conservativism   Reactionary mode of thinking that held that tradition, including hereditary monarchy, would dispel the divisive ideas of the Enlightenment.

Constantinople   Former capital of the Byzantine empire, eventually renamed Istanbul after its conquest by the Ottomans in 1453.

Nicholas Copernicus (1473–1543)   Polish astronomer who advanced the radical idea that the earth moved around the sun in *De Revolutionibus*.

Council of Trent   Intermittent meeting of Catholic leaders (1545–1563) that reaffirmed Catholic doctrine against Protestant criticisms while also reforming the church.

Counter-Reformation   To counter the spread of the Reformation, the Counter-Reformation was initiated by the Catholic Church at the Council of Trent in 1545.

coup d'état   Overthrow of established state by a group of conspirators, usually from the military.

courtly love   Codes of refined romantic behavior between men and women of high station.

courtly romances   Long narrative poems written in vernacular languages based on myths and legends but expressing ideals of medieval aristocratic conduct.

Crimean War (1854–1856)   War waged by Russia against Great Britain and France. Spurred by Russia's encroachment on Ottoman territories, the conflict revealed Russia's military weakness when Russian forces fell to British and French troops.

Oliver Cromwell (1599–1658)   Puritan leader of the Parliamentary army that defeated the royalist forces in the English Civil War. After the 1649 execution of King Charles I and dispersion of Parliament, Cromwell ruled as self-styled Lord Protector from 1653 until his death.

crusades (1096 to 1291)   Series of wars undertaken to free Jerusalem and the Holy Lands from Muslim control.

cult of domesticity   Concept associated with Victorian England that idealized women as nurturing wives and mothers.

cult of the Virgin Mary   A surge in veneration of the mother of Jesus beginning in the twelfth century that seemed to portend a change in how women were regarded as religious and moral beings.

cuneiform   One of the earliest writing systems, beginning around 3500 B.C.E., it was the Mesopotamian form of writing on clay tablets using a stylus.

Cyrus (c.585–529 B.C.E.)   The ruler of the Persians from circa 559 B.C.E. until 529 B.C.E.

Charles Darwin (1809–1882)   British naturalist who wrote *The Origin of Species* and developed the theory of natural selection to explain the evolution of organisms.

David   King of the Hebrews from around 1000 B.C.E. to 973 B.C.E. David united Israel and made Jerusalem his capital.

Leonardo da Vinci (1452–1519)   Florentine painter, architect, musician, and inventor whose breadth of interests typifies Renaissance ideals.

D-Day (June 6, 1944)   Date of the Allied invasion of Normandy under General Dwight Eisenhower to liberate Western Europe from German occupation.

Decembrists   Russian army officers who were influenced by events in France and formed secret societies that espoused liberal governance. They were put down by Nicholas I in December 1825.

Declaration of the Rights of Man and of the Citizen (1789)   French charter of liberties formulated by the National Assembly that marked the end of dynastic and aristocratic rule. The seventeen articles later became the preamble to the new constitution, which the Assembly finished in 1791.

Olympe de Gouges (1745–1793)   French political radical and feminist whose *Declaration of the Rights of Women* demanded an equal place for women in the new French republic.

Charles Dickens (1812–1870)   Hugely popular English novelist whose fiction exposed urban crime, poverty, and injustice but maintained Victorian domestic ideals.

Dien Bien Phu (1954)   Defining battle in the war between French colonialists and the Viet Minh that secured North Vietnam for Ho Chi Minh and his army and left the south to form its own government to be supported by France and the United States.

Diet of Worms   Examination of Luther by a church council in 1521. The council condemned him, and Luther was rescued by Frederick of Saxony.

Directory   Temporary military committee that took over the affairs of the state of France in 1795 from the radicals and held control until the coup of Napoleon Bonaparte.

Discourse on Method   Philosophical treatise by René Descartes (1596–1650) proposing that the path to knowledge was through logical speculation, beginning with one's own self: "I think, therefore I am."

Divine Comedy   Italian verse narrative by Dante Alighieri (1265–1321); its complex themes exemplify the concerns of medieval learning.

DNA (deoxyribonucleic acid)   Discovered by James Watson and Francis Crick in 1953, DNA contains an organism's genetic information and hereditary characteristics.

Dominican Order   Founded by the Spaniard Saint Dominic (1170–1221) and approved by Innocent III in 1216, the order was dedicated to the fight against heresy and the conversion of Jews and Muslims. Many members of the order gained teaching positions in the infant European universities and contributed much to the development of philosophy and theology. The Dominicans always retained their reputation for learning, but they also came to believe that stubborn heretics were best controlled by legal procedures. Accordingly, they became the leading medieval administrators of inquisitorial trials.

Don Quixote   Comical adventure by Spanish writer Miguel de Cervantes (1547–1616) that mocks chivalric ideas.

Dreyfus Affair   The 1894 French scandal surrounding accusations that a Jewish captain, Alfred Dreyfus, sold military secrets to the Germans. Convicted, Dreyfus was sentenced to life in prison. However, after public outcry, it was revealed that the trial documents were forgeries and Dreyfus was released.

Duma   The Russian parliament.

Dunkirk The French port on the English Channel where the British and French forces retreated after sustaining heavy losses against the German military. Between May 27 and June 4, 1940, the Royal Navy evacuated over three hundred thousand troops using commercial and pleasure boats.

Eastern Front Battlefront between Berlin and Moscow during World War I and World War II.

East India Company (1600–1858) British charter company created to outperform Portuguese and Spanish traders in the Far East; in the eighteenth century the company became, in effect, the ruler of a large part of India. There was also a Dutch East India Company.

Master Eckhart (c. 1260–1327) Dominican monk who preached an introspective and charismatic version of Christian piety.

Edict of Nantes (1598) Edict issued by Henry IV to end the French Wars of Religion. The edict declared France a Catholic country, but tolerated some Protestant worship.

Albert Einstein (1879–1955) German physicist who developed the theory of relativity, which states that space and motion are relative to each other instead of being absolute.

Elizabeth I (1533–1603) Protestant daughter of Henry VIII, Queen of England 1558–1603. During her long reign, the doctrines and services of the Church of England were defined and the Spanish Armada was defeated.

enclosure Long process of privatizing what had been public agricultural land in the eighteenth century that changed the nature of economic activity in England.

the *Encyclopedia* Joint venture of French *philosophe* writers, helmed by Denis Diderot (1713–1784), which proposed to summarize all modern knowledge.

Friedrich Engels (1820–1895) German social and political philosopher who collaborated with Karl Marx on many publications.

English navigation acts (1651 and 1660) Acts stipulating that only English ships could carry goods between the mother country and its colonies.

Enlightenment Intellectual movement stressing natural laws and classifications in nature, in eighteenth-century Europe.

Epicureanism Greek philosophy that emphasized the individual, denied the existence of spiritual forces, and proposed that the highest good is pleasure.

Desiderius Erasmus (c. 1469–1536) Dutch-born scholar and social commentator who proclaimed his humanist views in lively treatises like *In Praise of Folly* and the *Colloquies*.

Estates General French quasi-parliamentary body called in 1789 to deal with the financial problems that afflicted France at the time. It had not met since 1614.

Etruscans Non-Indo-European-speaking settlers of the Italian peninsula who dominated the region from the late Bronze Age until the rise of the Romans in the sixth century B.C.E.

Euclid Hellenistic mathematician whose book *Elements of Geometry* was the basis of modern geometry.

eugenics Term, meaning "good birth," referring to the project of "breeding" a superior human race. It was popularly championed by scientists, politicians, and social critics in the late nineteenth and early twentieth centuries.

European Union (EU) An international political body that was organized after World War II to reconcile Germany and the rest of Europe as well as to forge closer industrial cooperation. Over time, member states of the EU have relinquished some of their sovereignty, and cooperation has evolved into a community with a single currency, the euro, and a common European parliament.

existentialism The philosophy that arose out of World War II and emphasized the human condition. Led by Jean Paul Sartre and Albert Camus, existentialists encouraged humans to take responsibility for their own decisions and dilemmas.

fall of the Bastille On July 14, 1789, the sans culottes, led by the electors of Paris, stormed the Bastille, an ancient fortress, in search of weapons to protect themselves from Louis XVI's troops rumored to be heading toward the city. The fall of the Bastille was the first popular revolt in the French Revolution.

fascists Radical right-wing group of the disaffected that formed around Mussolini in 1919 and a few years later came to power in Italy.

February Revolution (1917) The first of two uprisings of the Russian Revolution, which led to the end of the Romanov dynasty.

Federal Republic of Germany (1949–1990) Country formed of the areas occupied by the Allies after World War II. Also known as West Germany, this country experienced rapid demilitarization, democratization, and integration into the world economy.

The Feminine Mystique Groundbreaking book by feminist Betty Friedan (b. 1921), which tried to define "femininity" and explored how women internalized those definitions.

Fertile Crescent An area of fertile land in what is now Syria, Israel, Turkey, eastern Iraq, and western Iran that was able to sustain settlements due to its wetter climate and abundant natural food resources. Some of the earliest known civilizations emerged there between 9000 and 4500 B.C.E.

feudalism A loose term reflecting the political and economic situation in eleventh- and twelfth-century Europe. In this system, lords were owed agricultural labor and military service by their serfs, and in turn owed allegiance to more powerful lords and kings.

First Crusade (1095–1099) Forces were sent by Pope Urban II to assist Byzantine emperor Alexius Comnenus in fighting Turkish forces in Anatolia. The struggle to recapture Jerusalem for western Christianity was eventually successful. This crusade prompted attacks against Jews throughout Europe and resulted in six subsequent military campaigns to the Holy Land.

Five-Year Plan Soviet effort launched under Stalin in 1928 to replace the market with a state-owned and state-managed economy in order to promote rapid economic development over a five-year period and thereby "catch and overtake" the leading capitalist countries. The First Five-Year Plan was followed by the Second Five-Year Plan (1933–1937), and so on, until the collapse of the Soviet Union in 1991.

flagellants European social group that came into existence during the bubonic plague in the fourteenth century; they believed that the plague was caused by the wrath of God and chose to beat and mutilate themselves as a form of religious penance.

Franciscan order Order of monks established in 1209 by Saint Francis of Assisi (1182–1226); its members strove to imitate the life and example of Jesus.

Frankfurt Assembly   An 1848 gathering of delegates from all German states that attempted to unify them into one nation. The liberal agenda and squabbling over whose plan for the nation was best led to the failure of the gathering.

Franz Ferdinand (1863–1914)   Archduke of Austria and heir to the Austro-Hungarian empire; his assassination led to the beginning of World War I.

Frederick the Great (1740–1786)   Prussian ruler who engaged the nobility in maintaining a strong military and bureaucracy, and led Prussian armies to notable military victories. He also encouraged Enlightenment rationalism and artistic endeavors.

French new wave   A group of filmmakers in the 1950s and 1960s that emphasized naturalistic and unsentimental portrayals of ordinary life. Famous new wave directors included François Truffaut (1932–1984), Jean-Luc Godard (b. 1930), and Eric Rohmer (b. 1920).

French Revolution of 1830   The French popular revolt against King Charles's July Ordinances of 1830, which dissolved the French Chamber of Deputies and restricted suffrage to exclude almost everyone except the nobility. After several days of violence, Charles abdicated the throne and was replaced by a constitutional monarch, King Louis Philippe.

French Revolution of 1848   Brief uprising caused by economic grievances; it was violently quelled by the government.

Sigmund Freud (1865–1939)   The Austrian physician who founded the discipline of psychoanalysis and suggested that human behavior was largely motivated by unconscious and irrational forces.

Galileo Galilei (1564–1642)   Italian physicist and inventor. The implications of his ideas raised the ire of the Catholic Church, and he was forced to retract most of his findings.

Mohandas K. (Mahatma) Gandhi (1869–1948)   The Indian leader who advocated nonviolent noncooperation and helped win home rule for India in 1947.

Giuseppe Garibaldi (1807–1882)   Italian revolutionary leader who led the fight to free Sicily and Naples from the Habsburg empire; the lands were then peaceably annexed by Sardinia.

garrisons   Military bases inside cities that were often used for political purposes, such as protecting the rulers and putting down domestic revolt or enforcing colonial rule.

Gaul   The region of the Roman empire that is modern Belgium, Germany west of the Rhine, and France.

Geneva Accords (1954)   Drawn up at an international conference to restore peace in Korea and Indochina and resulted in the division of North and South Vietnam. The chief participants were the United States, the Soviet Union, Great Britain, France, the People's Republic of China, North Korea, South Korea, Vietnam, the Viet Minh party, Laos, and Cambodia.

German Democratic Republic   Nation founded from the Soviet zone of occupation of Germany after World War II; also known as East Germany.

German Social Democratic Party   Founded in 1875, it was the most powerful Socialist party in Europe before 1917.

Gilgamesh   The hero of the Sumerian epic, which was recorded in written form around 2000 B.C.E. Gilgamesh was a powerful ruler who, along with his friend Enkidu, battled monsters and gods and searched for immortality.

globalization   The term used to describe political, social, and economic networks that span the globe. These global exchanges are not limited by nation states and often rely on new technologies, international laws, and economic imperatives.

Arthur de Gobineau (1816–1882)   French writer whose pseudoscientific, racist ideology provided a rationale for European imperialism.

Gothic style   Period of graceful architecture emerging after the Romanesque style in twelfth- and thirteenth-century France. The style is characterized by pointed arches, delicate decoration, and large windows.

Great Depression   Period following the U.S. stock market crash on October 29, 1929, and ending in 1941 with America's entry into World War II.

Great Terror   The systematic murder of nearly a million people and the deportation of another million and a half to labor camps by Stalin's regime during 1937 in an attempt to consolidate power and remove perceived enemies.

The Great War (1914–1918)   World War I.

Greek civil war (1821–1827)   Conflict between Greek Christians and Muslim Ottomans.

Pope Gregory I (540?–604)   Roman Catholic Pope 590–604. Used his political influence and theological teachings to separate the western Latin from the eastern Greek church. He also encouraged the Benedictine monastic movement and missionary expeditions.

guerrillas   Portuguese and Spanish peasant bands who resisted the revolutionary and expansion efforts of Napoleon; after the French word for war, *guerre*.

Guernica   The Basque town bombed by German planes in April 1937 during the Spanish Civil War. It is also the subject of Pablo Picasso's famous painting from the same year.

guilds   Professional organizations in commercial towns that regulated the business conditions and privileges of those practicing a particular craft.

gulag   The vast system of forced labor camps under the Soviet regime; it originated in 1919 in a small monastery near the Arctic Circle and spread throughout the Soviet Union and to other Soviet-style socialist countries. Penal labor was required of both ordinary criminals and those accused of political crimes (counterrevolution, anti-Soviet agitation).

Gulf War (1991)   Armed conflict between Iraq and a coalition of thirty-two nations, including the United States, Britain, Egypt, France, and Saudi Arabia. The seeds of the war were planted with Iraq's invasion of Kuwait on August 2, 1990.

Habsburg empire   Ruling house of Austria, which once ruled the Netherlands, Spain, and Central Europe but came to settle in lands along the Danube River. It played a prominent role in European affairs for many centuries. In 1867, the Habsburg empire was reorganized into the Austro-Hungarian Dual Monarchy, and in 1918 it collapsed.

Hammurabi   The ruler of Babylon from 1792 to 1750 B.C.E. Hammurabi issued a collection of laws that were greatly influential in the Near East for centuries.

harem   Secluded women's quarters in Muslim households.

heliocentric The sun-centered view of the planetary system, which displaced the Earth from the center of the universe.

Henry VIII (1491–1547) Oft-married English monarch who broke with the Roman Catholic church when the pope refused to grant him an annulment. The resulting modified version of Christianity became the Church of England, or Anglicanism.

Henry of Navarre (1553–1610) Crowned King Henry IV of France, he renounced his Protestantism but granted limited toleration to Huguenots (French Protestants) with the 1598 Edict of Nantes.

Prince Henry the Navigator (1394–1460) Portuguese noble who encouraged conquest of western Africa and trade in gold and slaves.

hero cults Important ancient Greek families would claim that an impressive Mycenean tomb was that of their own famous ancestor and would practice sacrifices and other observances to strengthen their claim. This devotion could extend to their followers, and eventually whole communities would identify with such local heroes.

Hiroshima Japanese port devastated by an atomic bomb on August 6, 1945.

Adolf Hitler (1889–1945) The author of *Mein Kampf* and leader of the Nazis. Hitler and his Nazi regime started World War II and orchestrated the systematic murder of over five million Jews.

Hittites An Indo-European-speaking people that migrated into Anatolia (now Turkey) around the beginning of the second millennium B.C.E.

Ho Chi Minh (1890–1969) The Vietnamese communist resistance leader who drove the French out of Vietnam and controlled North Vietnam after the Geneva Accords divided the region into four countries.

Holy Roman Empire The collection of lands in central and western Europe ruled over by the kings of Germany (and later Austria) from the twelfth century until 1806.

Homo sapiens Term defined by Linnaeus in 1737 and commonly used to refer to fully modern human beings.

hoplite A Greek foot soldier armed with a spear or short sword and protected by a large round shield (a hopla). In battle, hoplites stood shoulder to shoulder in a close formation called a phalanx.

Huguenots French Protestants who endured severe persecution in the sixteenth and seventeenth centuries.

humanism Medieval program of study built around the seven liberal arts: grammar, logic, rhetoric, arithmetic, music, geometry, and astronomy.

humanitarianism The dignity and worth of all individuals.

Hundred Years' War (1337–1453) Long conflict, fought mostly on French soil, between England and France, centering on English claims to the throne of France.

Saddam Hussein (1937–2006) The former dictator of Iraq who invaded Iran in 1980 and started the eight-year-long Iran-Iraq War; invaded Kuwait in 1990, which caused the Gulf War of 1991; and was overthrown when the United States invaded Iraq in 2003. Involved in Iraqi politics since the mid-1960s, Hussein became the official head of state in 1979.

Imhotep The chief adviser to the Pharaoh Djoser, who ruled in the 27th century B.C.E. Often considered to be the first architect, Imhotep designed tombs and other structures to express the power of the Egyptian pharaohs.

Indian National Congress Formed in 1885, this political party was deeply committed to constitutional methods, industrialization, and cultural nationalism.

Indian rebellion of 1857 The uprising began near Delhi when the military disciplined a regiment of Indian soldiers employed by the British for refusing to use rifle cartridges greased with pork fat—unacceptable to either Hindus or Muslims. Rebels attacked law courts and burned tax rolls, protesting debt and corruption. The mutiny spread through large areas of northwest India before being violently suppressed by British troops.

Indo-Europeans A group of people that spoke variations of the same language and moved into the Near East and Mediterranean shortly after 2000 B.C.E.

indulgences Remissions of the penances owed by Catholics as part of the process by which their sins are forgiven.

Inkas The highly centralized South American empire that was toppled by the Spanish conquistador Francisco Pizarro in 1533.

Inquisition Tribunal of the Roman Catholic Church that aimed to enforce religious orthodoxy and conformity.

International Monetary Fund Established in 1945 to promote the health of the world economy, the IMF is a specialized agency of the United Nations.

intifada Uprising in the Palestinian occupied territories from 1987 to 1993, in protest against the Israeli occupation and politics. The Oslo Agreement (1993) helped to reduce the tension between the two sides and the Intifada all but ceased by the end of 1993. In early 2000, the Intifada resumed.

Investiture Conflict A disagreement between Pope Gregory VII and Emperor Henry IV of Germany that tested the power of kings over church matters. After years of diplomatic and military hostility, it was settled by the Concordat of Worms in 1122.

invisible hand Described in Adam Smith's *The Wealth of Nations*, the idea that the operations of a free market would produce economic efficiency and economic benefits for all.

Irish home rule The late-nineteenth- and early-twentieth-century movement, led by Sinn Fein (established 1905), for Irish self-government.

Irish potato famine Period of agricultural blight from 1845 to 1849 whose devastating results prompted a mass emigration to America.

Iron Curtain Term coined by Winston Churchill in 1946 to refer to the division of Western Europe, under American influence, from Eastern Europe, under the domination of the Soviet Union.

Ivan the Great (1440–1505) Emperor of Russia who annexed neighboring territories and began Russia's career as a European power.

Jacobins Radical French political group that came into existence during the French Revolution, executed the French king, and sought to remake French culture.

Jacquerie Violent 1358 peasant uprising in northern France, incited by disease, war, and taxes.

James I (1566–1625)   Monarch of Scotland and England from 1603 to 1625. He oversaw the English vernacular translation of the Bible known by his name.

Jesuits   Religious order founded in 1540 by Ignatius Loyola to counter the inroads of the Protestant Reformation; the Jesuits were active in politics, education, and missionary work.

jihad   A struggle and, if need be, a holy war toward the advancement of the cause of Islam.

Joan of Arc (c. 1412–1431)   French teenager, supposedly divinely inspired, who led forces against the English during the Hundred Years' War. Burned at the stake for heresy by the English and later made a Catholic saint.

Justinian (527–565)   Emperor of eastern Rome. Justinian codified Roman law in the Corpus Juris Civilis and tried to reunify the eastern and western halves of the old Roman empire.

Das Kapital (Capital)   The 1867 book by Karl Marx that outlined the theory behind historical materialism and attacked the socio-economic inequities of capitalism. Mixing economic theory and revolutionary politics, the book became the preeminent socialist critique of capitalism.

Johannes Kepler (1571–1630)   Mathematician and astronomer who elaborated on and corrected Copernicus's theory and is chiefly remembered for his discovery of the three laws of planetary motion that bear his name.

Chingiz Khan (c. 1167–1227)   Title taken by Mongol chief Temujin meaning "The Oceanic Ruler." Began dynasty that conquered much of southern Asia.

khanate   Major political unit of the vast Mongol empire. There were four Khanates, including the Yuan empire in China, forged by Chingiz Khan's grandson Kubilai in the 13th century.

Nikita Khrushchev (1894–1971)   Leader of the Soviet Union during the Cuban Missile Crisis, Khrushchev had quickly reached power soon after Stalin's death in 1953. His reforms and criticisms of the excesses of the Stalin regime led to his fall from power in 1964.

Kristallnacht   The Nazi destruction of seventy-five hundred Jewish stores and two hundred synagogues on November 9, 1938.

kulaks   Originally a pejorative term used to designate better-off peasants, it was used in the late 1920s and early 1930s to refer to any peasant, rich or poor, perceived as an opponent of the Soviet regime. Russian for "fist."

Labour Party   Founded in Britain in 1900, this party represented workers and was based on socialist principles.

League of Nations   International organization founded after World War I to solve international disputes through arbitration; it was dissolved in 1946 and transferred its assets to the United Nations.

Vladimir Lenin (1870–1924)   Leader of the Bolshevik Revolution in Russia (1917) and the first leader of the Soviet Union.

Leopold II (1835–1909)   Belgian king who sponsored colonizing expeditions into Africa.

Leviathan   A book by Thomas Hobbes (1588–1679) that recommended a ruler have unrestricted power.

liberalism   Political and social theory that advocates representative government, free trade, and freedom of speech and religion.

lord   Privileged landowner who exercised authority over the people who lived on his land.

Louis XIV (1638–1715)   The "Sun King," known for his opulent court and absolutist political style.

Louis XVI (1754–1793)   Well-meaning but ineffectual king of France, finally deposed and executed with his family by revolutionaries.

Lusitania   The passenger liner that was secretly carrying war supplies and was sunk by a German U-boat (submarine) on May 7, 1915.

Martin Luther (1483–1546)   A German monk who led the Reformation movement. At the center of his ideas is the doctrine, "justification by faith alone," which challenged many of the medieval practices of the Catholic Church and led to the religious wars between Protestants and Catholics.

Lutheranism   Branch of Protestantism that followed Martin Luther's (1483–1546) rejection of the Roman Catholic "doctrine of works."

lycées   System of high schools instituted by Napoleon as part of his domestic reform campaign.

Magna Carta   "Great Charter" of 1215 signed by King John of England, which limited the king's fiscal powers and is seen as a landmark in the political evolution of the West.

Nelson Mandela (b. 1918)   The South African opponent of *apartheid* who led the African National Congress and was imprisoned from 1962 until 1990. After his release from prison, he worked with Prime Minister Frederik Willem De Klerk to establish majority rule. Mandela became the first black president of South Africa in 1994.

Manhattan Project   The secret U.S. government research project in Los Alamos, New Mexico, to develop the first nuclear bomb. The first test of a nuclear bomb was near Los Alamos on July 16, 1945.

manorialism   System common to England, northern France, and Germany in the Middle Ages of communal peasant farming under the protection of a landholding lord.

Mao Zedong (1893–1976)   The leader of the Chinese Revolution who defeated the Nationalists in 1949 and established the Communist regime in China.

Marshall Plan   Economic aid package given to Europe after World War II in hopes of a rapid period of reconstruction and economic gain and to secure the countries from a Communist takeover.

Karl Marx (1818–1883)   German philosopher and economist who believed that a revolution of the working classes would overthrow the capitalist order and create a classless society. Author of *Das Kapital* and the *Communist Manifesto*.

Maxim gun   Invented in 1885 by an American, Hiram Maxim, the Maxim gun was the first portable machine gun. Quickly adopted by the majority of European armies and capable of firing 500 rounds per minute, it played a major role in the imperial conquests of the African continent.

Giuseppe Mazzini (1805–1872)   Founder of Young Italy and an ideological leader of the Italian Nationalist movement.

Mecca   Major commercial city of the Arabian peninsula in the sixth century C.E., at which time the founder of Islam, Muhammad, was born and achieved prominence. From the earliest days of the spread of Islam, the city was the destination of the chief religious pilgrimage for Muslims, and it is now considered the holiest site in the Islamic world.

Medici Dynasty of Florentine bankers and politicians known for their patronage of the arts.

mercantilism A popular Western belief between 1600 and 1800 that a country's wealth and power was based on a favorable balance of trade (more exports and fewer imports) and the accumulation of precious metals.

Michelangelo (1475–1564) Virtuoso artist, best known for the Sistine Chapel ceiling in Rome and his sculptures *David* and *Pieta*.

John Stuart Mill (1806–1873) English radical philosopher whose writings advocated aspects of socialism and civil liberties.

Slobodan Milosevic (1941–2006) The Serbian nationalist politician who took control of the Serb government and orchestrated the genocide of thousands of Croatians, Bosnian Muslims, Albanians, and Kosovars. After ten years of war, he was ousted by a popular revolt in 2000.

Minoans A sea empire that flourished on Crete and in the Aegean Basin from 1900 B.C.E. until the middle of the second millennium B.C.E.

modernism The series of artistic movements, manifestos, innovations, and experiments that redefined art in the first half of the twentieth century. Modernism rejected history and tradition in favor of expressive and experimental freedom.

Michel de Montaigne (1533–1592) French philosopher known for his *Essays*.

mosque Place of worship for the people of Islam.

Wolfgang Amadeus Mozart (1756–1791) Austrian child prodigy and composer of instrumental music and operas.

Muhammad (570–632 C.E.) The founder of Islam, he claimed to be the prophet whom God (Allah) had chosen for his final revelation to mankind.

Muslim Brotherhood Egyptian organization founded in 1938 by Hassan al-Banna. It attacked liberal democracy as a façade for middle-class, business, and landowning interests and fought for a return to a purified form of Islam.

Muslim League National Muslim party of India.

Benito Mussolini (1883–1945) The Italian founder of the Fascist party who came to power in Italy in 1922 and allied himself with Hitler and the Nazis during World War II.

Mycenaens The ancient Greek civilization that settled in Greece during the second millennium B.C.E. and organized around powerful citadels.

Nagasaki Second Japanese city on which the United States dropped an atomic bomb. The attack took place on August 9, 1945; the Japanese surrendered shortly thereafter, ending World War II.

Napoleonic Code Legal code drafted by Napoleon in 1804; it distilled different legal traditions to create one uniform law. The code confirmed the abolition of feudal privileges of all kinds and set the conditions for exercising property rights.

National Assembly Governing body of France that succeeded the Estates General in 1789 during the French Revolution. It was composed of, and defined by, the delegates of the Third Estate.

nationalism Movement to unify a country based on a people's common history and social traditions.

National Liberation Front (FLN) An anti-colonial, nationalist party that waged an eight-year war, beginning in 1954, against French troops for Algerian independence; the war forced nearly all of the 1 million French colonists to leave.

nation building refers to the process of creating new states and reconstructing older ones, a process in which the nineteenth century marked a crucial stage.

NATO The North Atlantic Treaty Organization, which was a 1949 agreement between the United States, Canada, Great Britain, and 8 European countries that declared that an armed attack against any one of the members would be regarded as an attack against all. Other European countries have since joined.

"navvies" Slang for laborers who built railroads and canals.

Nazi Party Founded in the early 1920s, the National Socialist German Workers' Party (NDSAP) gained control over Germany under the leadership of Adolf Hitler in 1933 and continued in power until Germany was defeated in 1945.

Nefertiti The wife of Akhenaten, the fourteenth-century B.C.E. Egyptian pharaoh.

Neolithic The "New" Stone Age, which began around 11,000 B.C.E., saw new technological and social developments, including managed food production, the beginnings of semipermanent and permanent settlements, and the rapid intensification of trade.

New Deal President Franklin Delano Roosevelt's package of government reforms that were enacted during the 1930s to provide jobs for the unemployed, social welfare programs for the poor, and security to the financial markets.

new imperialism Expansion of colonial power by Western European nations, especially in Asia, in the last three decades of the nineteenth century.

Isaac Newton (1642–1727) One of the foremost scientists of all time, Newton was an English mathematician and physicist; he is noted for his development of calculus, work on the properties of light, and theory of gravitation.

New World silver The most lucrative export from the Spanish colonies in Central and South America was silver. The massive infusion of New World Silver into the sixteenth-century European economy accelerated inflation and eventually caused the collapse of the Spanish economy and widespread misery for the rest of Europe's poorest inhabitants who could not afford the rising prices of goods.

Nicholas I (1796–1855) Russian tsar who executed the leaders of the 1825 December Revolution and pursued an absolutist reign.

Nicholas II (1868–1918) The last Russian tsar, who abdicated the throne in 1917. He and his family were executed by the Bolsheviks on July 17, 1918.

Nicomachean Ethics The treatise on moral philosophy by Aristotle, which teaches that the highest good consists of the harmonious functioning of the individual human mind and body.

Friedrich Nietzsche (1844–1900) The German philosopher who denied the possibility of knowing absolute "truth" or "reality," since all knowledge comes filtered through linguistic, scientific, or artistic systems of representation. He also criticized Judeo-Christian morality for instilling a repressive conformity that drained civilization of its vitality.

Novum Organum   Work by English statesman and scientist Francis Bacon (1561–1626) that advanced a philosophy of study through observation.

OPEC (Organization of Petroleum Exporting Countries)   Organization created in 1960 by oil-producing countries in the Middle East, South America, and Africa to regulate the production and pricing of crude oil.

Operation Barbarossa   The codename for Hitler's invasion of the Soviet Union.

Opium Wars (1839–1842)   Wars fought between the British and Qing China to protect British trade in opium; resulted in the ceding of Hong Kong to the British.

Oracle at Delphi   Dating to 1400 B.C.E., the oracle was the most important shrine in ancient Greece. A priestess of Apollo who attended the shrine was believed to be able to predict the future. The shrine ceased to function in the fourth century C.E.

Ottoman slavery   Social system of using slave labor for domestic, administrative, and military work that permitted social advancement and religious diversity within the Muslim empire.

Pan-African Conference   1900 assembly in London which sought to draw attention to the sovereignty of African people and their mistreatment by colonial powers.

pan-Slavism   Cultural movement that sought to unite native Slavic peoples within the Russian and Habsburg empires.

papal   Of, relating to, or issued by a pope.

patricians   The uppermost elite class of ancient Rome.

Paul   One of the twelve apostles of Jesus, Paul spread Christianity throughout the Near East and Greece.

Peace of Augsburg   The 1555 settlement between factions within the Holy Roman Empire that stated a territory would follow the religion of its ruler, whether Catholic or Protestant.

Pearl Harbor   The American Navy base in Hawaii that was bombed by the Japanese on December 7, 1941, which brought the United States into World War II.

Peloponnesian War   The ancient Greek war between Sparta and Athens that began in 431 B.C.E. and ended with the destruction of the Athenian fleet in 404 B.C.E.

People's Charter   An action of the Chartist Movement (1839–1848); between 1839 and 1842 over 3 million British signed this document calling for universal suffrage for adult males, the secret ballot, electoral districts, and annual parliamentary elections.

perestroika   Introduced by Soviet leader Mikhail Gorbachev in June 1987, perestroika was the name given to economic and political reforms begun earlier in his tenure. It restructured the state bureaucracy, reduced the privileges of the political elite, and instituted a shift from the centrally planned economy to a mixed economy, combining planning with the operation of market forces.

Pericles   The fifth-century B.C.E. Athenian leader who served as strategos for thirty years and pushed through reforms to make Athens more democratic by giving every citizen the right to propose and amend legislation and making it easier for citizens to participate in the assembly and the great appeals court of Athens by paying an average day's wage for attendance.

Peter the Great (1672–1725)   Energetic tsar who transformed Russia into a leading European country by centralizing government, modernizing the army, creating a navy, and reforming education and the economy.

Petrarch (Francesco Petrarca, 1304–1374)   Italian scholar and writer who revived interest in classical writing styles and was famed for his love sonnets.

Pharisees   A group of Jewish teachers and preachers that emerged in the third century B.C.E. and insisted that all of Yahweh's (God's) commandments were binding on all Jews.

Philip II (382–336 B.C.E.)   The Macedonian king who consolidated the southern Balkans and the Greek city-states; he was the father of Alexander.

Phoenicians   The semitic-speaking residents of present-day Lebanon from around 1200 to 800 B.C.E. The Phoenician cities were centers for trade throughout the Mediterranean.

Plato's *Republic*   The first systematic treatment of political philosophy ever written, it argued for an elitist state in which most people would be governed by intellectually superior "philosopher-kings."

plebians   The citizen population of ancient Rome that included farmers, merchants, and the urban poor; plebians comprised the majority of the population.

Polis   One of the major political innovations of the ancient Greeks was the Polis, or city-state. They were independent social and political structures, organized around an urban center, containing markets, meeting places, and a temple; they controlled a limited amount of the surrounding territory.

Marco Polo (1254–1324)   Venetian merchant who traveled through Asia for twenty years and published his observations in a widely read memoir, *Travels*.

Prague spring   A period of political liberalization in Czechoslovakia between January and August 1968 that was initiated by Alexander Dubĉek, the Czech leader. This period of expanding freedom and openness in this Eastern bloc nation ended on August 20, when the USSR and Warsaw Pact countries invaded with 200,000 troops and 5,000 tanks.

The Praise of Folly   A 1511 satire by Erasmus that attacked the corruption of the papacy.

pre-Socratics   A group of philosophers on the Greek island of Miletus, including Thales, Anaximander, and Anaximenes, who raised questions about the relationship between the natural world, the gods, and humans, and formulated rational theories to explain the physical universe they observed.

The Prince   Influential treatise by Niccolò Machiavelli (1469–1527) that attempts to lay out methods to secure and maintain political power.

Protestantism   Division of Christianity that emerged in sixteenth-century western Europe at the time of the Reformation. It focused on individual spiritual needs and rejected the social authority of the papacy and the Catholic clergy.

Ptolemy (c. 85–165 C.E.)   One of the most influential ancient Greeks; he was a leading astronomer, mathematician, and geographer who lived his entire life in Alexandria and helped to transform that city into a center of scientific study and scholarship.

puppet state A government that has little power in the international arena and follow the dictates of their more powerful neighbors or patrons.

Puritans Seventeenth-century reform group of the Church of England; also known as dissenters or nonconformists.

Qur'an (often Koran) Islam's holy book, comprised of Allah's revelations.

Sayyid Qutb (1906–1966) The Egyptian critic who became one of the most important intellectual leaders of the Muslim Brotherhood and whose writings are often cited as philosophical inspiration for Osama bin Laden and other Islamic radicals.

François Rabelais (c. 1494–1553) French humanist satirist best known for his crudely comic *Gargantua and Pantagruel*, in which he espouses the "eat, drink, and be merry" lifestyle. Originally a novice in the Franciscan order, later a Benedictine monk who left the order to study medicine, Rabelais spent time in hiding for fear of being labeled a heretic, and some of his books were banned.

radicals Widely used term in nineteenth-century Europe that referred to those individuals and political organizations that favored the total reconfiguration of Europe's old state system.

raj Term referring to the British crown's administration of India following the end of the East India Company's rule after the Indian Mutiny of 1857.

Raphael (1483–1520) Italian painter noted for his warmly human treatment of religious subjects, particularly his Madonnas and large-figure compositions in the Vatican in Rome.

realism Artistic and literary style which sought to portray common situations as they would appear in reality.

Realpolitik Political strategy advancing power for its own sake.

reason According to thinkers like Descartes, reason is a subjective faculty, or unaided ability, to form concepts.

Reds The Bolsheviks.

Reformation Religious and political movement in sixteenth-century Europe that led to the breakaway of Protestant groups from the Catholic Church; notable figures include Martin Luther and John Calvin.

Reich A term for the German state. The first Reich corresponded to the Holy Roman Empire (9th century to 1806), the second Reich was from 1871 to 1919, and the third Reich lasted from 1933 through May 1945.

Reign of Terror Campaign at the height of the French Revolution (1793–1794) in which violence, including systematic executions of opponents of the Revolution, was used to purge France of its "enemies" and to extend the Revolution beyond its borders; radicals executed as many as 40,000 persons who were judged enemies of the state.

Rembrandt Van Rijn (1606–1669) A Dutch painter famous for his portraits, biblical scenes, and imaginative experiments with light and shading.

Renaissance Term meaning "rebirth" that historians use to refer to the expanded cultural production of European nations between 1300 and 1600.

Restoration period (1815–1848) European movement after the defeat of Napoleon to restore Europe to its pre-French revolutionary status and to prevent radical movements from arising.

Richard II (1367–1400) King of England (r. 1377–1399), chiefly remembered for his successful resolution of the Peasants' Rebellion (1381) and as a vacillating, yet tyrannical monarch. He was deposed by his cousin Henry Bolingbroke (Henry IV) and assassinated.

Cardinal Richelieu (1585–1642) First minister to French King Louis XIII, who centralized political power and deprived the Huguenots of many rights.

Romanticism Beginning in Germany and England in the late 18th century and continuing up to the end of the 19th century, a movement in art, music, and literature that countered the rationalism of the Enlightenment by stressing a highly emotional response to nature.

Jean-Jacques Rousseau (1718–1778) Philosopher and radical political theorist whose *Social Contract* attacked privilege and inequality. One of the primary principles of Rousseau's political philosophy is that politics and morality should not be separated.

Russification Programs designed to assimilate people of over 146 dialects into the Russian empire by the tsars in the late 19th century.

Rwanda A former Belgian colony in central Africa that has been torn by ethnic violence between the Hutus and the Tutsis since before the country's independence in 1962.

St. Bartholomew's Day massacre Massacre of French Protestants (Huguenots) by Catholic crowds that began in Paris on August 24, 1572, spreading to other parts of France and continuing into October of that year. More than 70,000 were killed.

St. Domingue Former French Caribbean colony and site of a slave rebellion in 1791, which embroiled English and French forces until 1804, when St. Domingue was declared the independent nation of Haiti.

salons Informal gatherings of intellectuals and aristocrats that allowed discourse about Enlightenment ideas.

Santa Sophia The Byzantine church in Constantinople, constructed by emperor Justinian I in the sixth century, and famous for its dome, which rested on the keystones of four great arches.

Sargon (r. 2334–2279 B.C.E.) The Akkadian leader who unified Mesopotamia.

Schlieffen Plan Devised by Count Alfred von Schlieffen in 1905 and put into operation on August 2, 1914, the Schlieffen Plan required France to be attacked first through Belgium and a quick victory to be secured so that the German army could fight Russia on the Eastern Front.

scientific societies Organizations that emerged in the seventeenth century to promote the improvement of scientific knowledge, experiments, and collaboration by scientists and philosophers.

scramble for Africa European rush to colonize parts of Africa at the end of the nineteenth century.

second industrial revolution The technological developments in the last third of the nineteenth century, which included new techniques for refining and producing steel; increased availability of electricity for industrial, commercial, and domestic use; advances in chemical manufacturing; and the creation of the internal combustion engine.

Seleucus (d. 280 B.C.E.)   The Macedonian general who ruled the Asian territory of Alexander the Great's empire and founded Greek colonies such as Antioch and Selsucia.

Semitic   The Semitic language family has the longest recorded history of any linguistic group and is the root language for most of the languages of the Middle and Near East. Ancient Semitic languages include the language of the ancient Babylonians and Assyrians, Phoenician, the classical form of Hebrew, early dialects of Aramaic, and the classical Arabic of the Qur'an.

sepoys   Hindu and Muslim recruits of the East India Company's military force.

serfdom   Slavery-like system of customs and laws whereby peasants were kept poor and stationary by their manor lords; it had spread throughout the West by the 10th century and its peak was the Middle Ages.

Seven Years' War (1756–1763)   Worldwide war that ended when Prussia defeated Austria, establishing itself as a European power, and when Britain gained control of India and many of France's colonies through the Treaty of Paris. It is known as the French and Indian War in the United States.

shah   Traditional title of Persian rulers.

William Shakespeare (1564–1616)   The greatest Elizabethan playwright, Shakespeare worked as actor before becoming a dramatist. The author of *Hamlet, King Lear,* and *Much Ado about Nothing* wrote nearly 40 plays and over 150 sonnets.

Shiism   One of the two main branches of Islam. Shiites recognize Ali, the fourth caliph, and his descendants as rightful rulers of the Islamic world; practiced in the Safavid empire.

Shiites   An often-persecuted minority religious party within Islam that insists only descendants of Ali can have any authority over the Muslim community. Today, Shiites rule Iran and are numerous in Iraq but make up only 10 percent of the worldwide population of Islam.

Sinn Fein   The Irish revolutionary organization that formed in 1900 to fight for Irish independence.

Adam Smith (1723–1790)   Scottish economist and philosopher who proposed that individual self-interest naturally promoted a healthy national economy. He became famous for his influential book, *The Wealth of Nations* (1776).

Social Darwinism   Belief that Charles Darwin's theory of natural selection (evolution) was applicable to human societies and justified the right of the ruling classes or countries to dominate the weak.

socialism   Political ideology that calls for a classless society with collective ownership of all property.

the social question   In the wake of the Industrial Revolution and rapid urbanization, topics such as criminality, water supply, sewers, prostitution, tuberculosis and cholera, alcoholism, wet nursing, wages, and unemployment were studied by political leaders, social scientists, and public health officials throughout Europe and collectively referred to as the social question. Reformers and politicians believed that these issues needed to be addressed to avoid popular revolts in Europe's cities.

Society of Jesus   Also called the Jesuit order, a group of priests influenced by military discipline. The society was founded by Saint Ignatius of Loyola (1491–1556) and is still very active in the field of education.

Socrates (469–399 B.C.E.)   The ancient Greek philosopher who emphasized the reexamination of all inherited assumptions and tried to base his philosophical speculations on sound definitions of words. He also wished to advance to a new system of truth by examining ethics rather than by studying the physical world.

Solidarity   The communist bloc's first independent trade union; it was established in Poland at the Gdansk shipyard in 1980.

Solon (d. 559 B.C.E.)   Elected archon in 594 B.C.E., this ancient Greek aristocrat enacted a series of political and economic reforms that made Athenian democracy possible.

Aleksandr Solzhenitsyn (1918–2008)   This Soviet novelist was a critic of the Soviet regime and wrote *The Gulag Archipelago,* which was published in 1974.

Sophists   Ancient Greek professional teachers who taught that sense perception was the source of all knowledge and that only particular truths could be valid for the individual knower.

Soviet bloc   International alliance that included the East European countries of the Warsaw Pact as well as the Soviet Union, but also came to include Cuba.

Spanish-American War (1898)   War between the United States and Spain in Cuba, Puerto Rico, and the Philippines. It ended with a treaty in which the United States took over the Philippines, Guam, and Puerto Rico; Cuba won partial independence.

Spanish Armada   Supposedly invincible fleet of warships sent against England by Philip II of Spain in 1588, but routed by the English and bad weather in the English Channel.

Spartiate   A full citizen of Sparta who was a professional soldier of the hoplite phalanx.

spinning jenny   Invention of James Hargreaves (c. 1720–1774) that revolutionized the British textile industry.

S.S. (*Schutzstaffel*)   Formed in 1925 to serve as Hitler's personal security force and to guard Nazi party (NDSAP) meetings, the SS was notorious for participation in carrying out Nazi policies.

Joseph Stalin (1879–1953)   The Bolshevik leader who succeeded Lenin as the leader of the Soviet Union in 1924 and ruled until his death.

Stoicism   The ancient Greek and Roman philosophy that held that the cosmos is an ordered whole in which all contradictions are resolved for ultimate good. Everything that happens is rigidly determined in accordance with rational purpose, and no individual is master of his or her fate. Founded in the fourth century B.C.E. and still popular well into the fifth century C.E.

Suez Canal   Built in 1869 across the Isthmus of Suez to connect the Mediterranean Sea with the Red Sea and to lower the costs of international trade.

Sufism   Emotional and mystical form of Islam that appealed to the common people.

sultan   An Islamic political leader. In the Ottoman empire, the sultan combined a warrior ethos with an unwavering devotion to Islam.

Sumerians   The civilization and people that arose in southern Mesopotamia (modern Iraq and Kuwait) around 4000 B.C.E. and developed one of the first written languages.

Sunnism   Orthodox Islam, as opposed to Shiite Islam.

survival of the fittest   A main concept of Charles Darwin's theory of natural selection (evolution), which holds that as animal populations grow and resources become scarce, a struggle for existence arises, the outcome of which is that only the "fittest" survive.

sweatshops   Textile factories with poor pay and work conditions.

tabula rasa   Term used by John Locke (1632–1704) to describe man's mind before he acquired ideas as a result of experience; Latin for "clean slate."

Testament of Youth   The memoir by Vera Brittain about the home front and the changing social norms during World War I.

tetrarchy   Diocletian's political reform, which divided the Roman empire into two halves ruled by two rulers and two lieutenants.

Third Estate   Delegates from the common class to the Estates General, the French legislature, whose refusal to capitulate to the nobility and clergy in 1789 led to the Revolution.

Third Reich   The German state from 1933 to 1945 under Adolf Hitler and the Nazi party.

Third World   Nations—mostly in Asia, Latin America, and Africa—that are not highly industrialized and developed.

Thirty Years' War (1618–1648)   Beginning as a conflict between Protestants and Catholics in Germany, it escalated into a general European war fought in Germany by Sweden, France, and the Holy Roman Empire.

the three estates   Eighteenth-century French society was divided into three estates. An individual's status determined his or her legal rights, taxes, and so on. The First Estate was the clergy; the Second was the nobility; and the Third Estate included everyone from wealthy merchants to poor peasants.

Tiananmen Square   Largest public square in the world, located in Beijing, the site of the Chinese pro-democracy movement in 1989 that resulted in the killing of as many as 1,000 protesters by the Chinese army.

Timur the Lame (1336–1405)   Mongol ruler who was the last leader of the Khans' south Asian empire. Also known as Tamerlane.

total war   All-out war involving civilian populations as well as military forces, often used in reference to World War II.

Treaty of Brest-Litovsk (1918)   Separate peace between imperial Germany and the new Bolshevik regime in Russia. The treaty acknowledged the German victory on the Eastern Front and withdrew Russia from the war.

Treaty of Nanking (1842)   Treaty between China and Britain following the Opium War; it called for indemnities, the opening of new ports, and the cession of Hong Kong to the British.

Treaty of Utrecht (1713)   Resolution to the War of Spanish Succession that redistributed territory among the warring nations of Europe and encouraged England's colonial conquests.

Treaty of Versailles   Signed on June 28, 1919, this peace settlement ended World War I and required Germany to surrender a large part of its most valuable territories and to pay huge reparations to the Allies.

trench warfare   The twenty-five thousand miles of holes and ditches that stretched across the Western Front during World War I and where most of the fighting took place.

triangular trade   The eighteenth-century commercial Atlantic shipping pattern that took rum from New England to Africa, traded it for slaves taken to the West Indies, and brought sugar back to New England to be processed into rum.

Triple Entente   Alliance developed before World War I that eventually included Britain, France, and Russia.

Truman Doctrine (1947)   Declaration promising U.S. economic and military intervention, whenever and wherever needed, for the sake of preventing further communist expansion.

tsar   Russian translation, similar to the German *kaiser*, of the Roman title "caesar" (emperor), a title claimed by the rulers of medieval Muscovy and then the Russian empire.

Mary Tudor (1516–1558)   Catholic daughter of Henry VIII who reinstituted Catholicism in England when she acceded to the throne; she was called "Bloody Mary" for her violent suppression of Protestants during her five-year reign.

Two Treatises on Government   Published in 1690, this work by John Locke (1632–1704) defended humans' right to freedom against absolutist ideas and served as one of the underpinnings of the U.S. Constitution.

Ubaid   This culture flourished in Mesopotamia between 5500 and 4000 B.C.E., characterized by large village settlements and the first temples built in that area. A precursor to the Sumerians and the development of "urban" civilizations.

Universal Declaration of Human Rights (1948)   United Nations declaration that laid out the rights to which all human beings were entitled.

Utopia   Humanist social critique by English statesman Thomas More (1478–1535).

utopian socialism   The most visionary of all Restoration-era movements, Utopian socialists, like Charles Fourier, dreamt of transforming states, workplaces, and human relations, and proposed actual plans to do so.

velvet revolutions   The peaceful political revolutions throughout Eastern Europe in 1989.

Versailles   Splendid palace outside Paris where Louis XIV and his nobles resided.

Versailles conference (1919)   Peace conference between the victors of World War I; resulted in the Treaty of Versailles, which forced Germany to pay reparations and to give up its colonies to the victors.

Viet Cong   Vietnamese communist group formed in 1954; committed to overthrowing the government of South Vietnam and reunifying North and South Vietnam.

A Vindication of the Rights of Woman   Noted work of Mary Wollstonecraft (1759–1797), English republican who applied Enlightenment political ideas to issues of gender.

Virgil (70–19 B.C.E.)   One of the most influential Roman authors, his surviving works include the Eclogues and the Roman epic poem, the *Aeneid*.

Visigoths The German "barbarians" who sacked Rome in 410.

Voltaire Pseudonym of French philosopher and satirist François Marie Arouet (1694–1797), who championed the cause of human dignity against state and church oppression. Noted Deist and author of *Candide*.

Wars of the Roses Fifteenth-century conflicts between the English dynastic houses of Lancaster and York (each symbolized in heraldry by the rose), ultimately won by Lancastrian Henry VII.

Warsaw Pact (1955–1991) Military alliance between the U.S.S.R. and other Communist states that was established as a response to the creation of the NATO alliance.

James Watt (1736–1819) Scottish inventor and scientist who developed the steam engine.

The Wealth of Nations 1776 treatise by Adam Smith, whose *laissez-faire* ideas predicted the economic boom of the Industrial Revolution.

Weimar Republic The government of Germany between 1919 and the rise of Hitler and the Nazi party.

Western Front Military front that stretched from the English Channel through Belgium and France to the Alps during World War I.

Whites Refers to the "counterrevolutionaries" of the Bolshevik Revolution (1918–1921) who fought the Bolsheviks (the "Reds"); included former supporters of the tsar, Social Democrats, and large independent peasant armies.

William and Mary (1650–1702 and 1662–1694) Dutch noble couple who supplanted the deposed Catholic king James II in 1688 as monarchs of England.

William of Ockham (d. 1349) An English Franciscan monk, Ockham denied that human reason could prove fundamental theological truths such as the existence of God. He argued that there was no necessary connection between the observable laws of nature and the unknowable essence of divinity, and no hope of reason from the laws of nature to the nature of God. Ockham's ideas encouraged intellectuals to investigate the natural world without reference to the supernatural and encouraged empiricism.

William the Conqueror (1027–1087) Duke of French Normandy who crossed the English Channel and defeated Harold for the English throne in 1066. Imposed a centralized feudal system on England and introduced French as the official language.

woman suffrage The movement to win legal and political rights, including the right to vote for all women.

World Bank International agency established in 1944 to provide economic assistance to war-torn and poor countries. Its formal title is the International Bank for Reconstruction and Development.

World War I A total war from August 1914 to November 1918, involving the armies of Britain, France, and Russia (the Allies) against Germany, Austria-Hungary, and the Ottoman empire (the Central Powers). Italy joined the Allies in 1915, and the United States joined them in 1917, helping to tip the balance in favor of the Allies, who also drew upon the populations and material of their colonial possessions. Also known as the Great War.

World War II Worldwide war that began in September 1939 in Europe, and even earlier in Asia (1930s), and that pitted Britain, the United States, and especially the Soviet Union (the Allies) against Nazi Germany, Italy, and Japan (the Axis).

yellow journalism Newspapers that sought increased circulation by featuring sensationalist reporting that appealed to the masses.

Boris Yeltsin (1931–2007) The President of Russia who led the country after the disintegration of the Soviet Union in 1991.

Young Turks The 1908 Turkish nationalist movement to depose Sultan Abdul Hamid II.

Yugoslavia The Eastern European country that broke apart after the fall of the Soviet Union. Driven by nationalism and ethnic rivalries, the former Yugoslavia divided into six countries: Bosnia-Herzegovina, Croatia, Macedonia, Montenegro, Serbia, and Slovenia.

Zionism Formally founded in 1897, a political movement holding that the Jewish people constitute a nation and are entitled to a national homeland, originally advocating the reestablishment of a Jewish homeland in Palestine.

Zoroastrians Founded by Zoroaster around 600 B.C.E., this Persian religion urged people to be truthful, to help each other, and to practice hospitality. Those who did would be rewarded in an afterlife after a "judgment day."

Ulrich Zwingli (1484–1531) A former Catholic priest from Zurich, Zwingli joined Luther and Calvin in attacking the authority of the Catholic Church. Zwingli's reforms resembled those of Luther's except that Zwingli believed that the Eucharist conferred no grace at all. At his peak, Zwingli converted much of northern Switzerland. After Zwingli's death in a battle with Catholic forces, most of his supporters began following John Calvin.

TEXT CREDITS

PHOTO CREDITS

Part I: **2–3**: *King Tutankhamen fighting the Nubians* (Giraudon/Art Resource, NY)

Chapter 1: **6**: *An Egyptian Scribe* (The Louvre, Paris. Photo: Giraudon/Art Resource, NY); **8**: Science Museum, Minnesota; **9 (top)**: Joerg Carstensen/epa/Corbis; **11**: Himer Fotoarchiv; **14**: Oriental Institute; **16**: Hirmer Fotoarchiv; **17**: From *The Origins of War*, by Arthur Ferrill, published by Thames and Hudson, Inc., New York; **18, 23**: *A Sumerian Banquet* (Bettmann/Corbis); **20 (left)**: Iraq Museum, Baghdad, Iraq. Photo: Scala/Art Resource, NY; **20 (right)**: University of Pennsylvania Museum; **21**: The Nelson-Atkins Museum of Art, Kansas City, Missouri (Purchase: Nelson Trust); **22**: Réunion des Musées Nationaux/Art Resource, NY; **27**: Copyright Jurgen Liepe, Berlin; **28**: Bettmann/Corbis; **29**: Roger Wood/Corbis; **29**: Charles & Josette Lenars/Corbis; **31**: British Museum. Photo: HIP/Art Resource, NY; **32**: Excavations of The Metropolitan Museum of Art, 1929; Rogers Fund, 1930. (30.3.31) Photograph © 1978 The Metropolitan Museum of Art

Chapter 2: **36**: *Egyptian Slaves at Work* (Egyptian expedition of The Metropolitan Museum of Art, Rogers Fund, 1930 (30.3.77) Photograph © The Metropolitan Museum of Art; **40**: British Museum, London. Photo: Erich Lessing/Art Resource, NY; **41**: Erich Lessing/Art Resource, NY; **42**: Courtesy Museum of Fine Arts, Boston; **43**: Eric Lessing/Art Resource, NY; **44, 58**: *King Tutankhamen fighting the Nubians* (Giraudon/Art Resource, NY); **48**: Gianni Dagli Orti/Corbis; **52**: Ancient Civilizations, 2/e by Scarre/Fagan, © 2003. Reprinted by permission of Pearson Education, Inc., Upper Saddle River, NJ; **56**: *Assyrian Winged Human-Headed Bull* (Courtesy of The Oriental Institute of The University of Chicago); **59**: British Museum, London. Photo: Erich Lessing/Art Resource, NY; **62**: British Museum/Bridgeman Art Library; **64**: Courtesy Zev Radovan (www.bibleandpictures.com); **92**: Staatliche Museen zu Berlin. Photo: Bildarchiv Preussischer Kulturbesitz/Art Resource, NY

Part II: **68–67**: *Battle of Issus* (Scala/Art Resource, NY)

Chapter 3: **72**: *The School of Plato* (Scala/Art Resource, NY); **75**: Art Resource, NY; **78, 94**: *A symposium—a festive meal. 4th century B.C.E.*. (Kunsthistorisches Museum, Vienna, Austria. Photo: Erich Lessing/Art Resource, NY; **76**: Hirmer Fotoarchiv; **77**: Réunion des Musées Nationaux/Art Resource, NY; **79**: Scala/Art Resource, NY; **86**: Scala/Art Resource, NY; **87**: Vanni/Art Resource, NY; **88 (left)**: Hartwig Koppermann; **88 (center)**: Réunion des Musées Nationaux/Art Resource, NY; **88 (right)**: Nimatallah/Art Resource, NY; **89**: Bildarchiv Preussicher Kulturbesitz/Art Resource, NY; **92**: Photo: Paul Lipke/Trireme Trust, Montague, MA; **93**: Erich Lessing/Art Resource, NY

Chapter 4: **98**: *The colossal statue of the Nile River* (Scala/Art Resource, NY); **101**: Scala/Art Resource; **104 (top)**: Gianni Dagli Orti/Corbis; **104 (bottom)**: Erich Lessing/Art Resource, NY; **111, 155, 156**: *Dionysus Anaploga. Floor mosaic.* 1st century C.E. Corinth, Greece (Vanni/Art Resource, NY); **112**: University Prints; **113 (top)**: The Metropolitan Museum of Art, Rogers Fund, 1909. (09.39) Photograph © 1977 The Metropolitan Museum of Art; **113 (left)**: Giraudon/Art Resource, NY; **113 (right)**: Nimatallah/Art Resource, NY

Chapter 5: **118**: *Portrait of Pasquio Proculo and his wife* (Alinari/Art Resource, NY); **121**: Musei Capitolini, Rome, Italy; Photo: Scala/Art Resource, NY; **129, 139**: Mosaic in red tesserae. 2nd C.E. Corinth, Greece. Photo: Vanni/Art Resource, NY; **124**: Scala/Art Resource, NY; **125**: British Museum, London; **130**: Erich Lessening/Art Resource, NY; **132**: Scala/Art Resource, NY; **133**: Scala/Art Resource, NY; **137**: Scala/Art Resource, NY; **138 (top)**: British Museum. Photo: HIP/Art Resource, NY; **138 (bottom)**: British Museum; **141**: Scala/Art Resource, NY

Chapter 6: **146**: *Constantine IV with his brothers Heraclius and Tiberius Conceding Privileges of the Church of Ravenna to Reparato who is protected by Archbishop Mauro* (Alinari/Art Resource, NY); **150**: Scala/Art Resource, NY; **151**: Scala/Art Resource, NY; **154**: Scala/Art Resource, NY; **155, 161**: Mausoleum of Galla Piacidia Ravenna, Italy, Scala/Art Resource, NY; **166**: Biblioteca Medicea Laurenziana, Florence; **167 (top)**: Scala/Art Resource, NY; **167 (bottom)**: Scala/Art Resource, NY

Part III: **172–173**: Anoymous, 15th century. *The Death of Charlemagne.* Vincent de Beauvais, Le Miroir Historical. Ms. 722/1196, fol. 113 v. French, 15th c. (Photo: Giraudon/Art Resource, NY)

Chapter 7: **176**: *Muslim Pilgrims on Their Way to Mecca* (Bibliothèque Nationale de France, Paris); **179**: Werner Forman/Art Resource, NY; **181**: Vanni/Art Resource, NY; **182, 186**: *Inlaid marble floor, Byzantine.* (Mosaic Museum, Istanbul, Turkey. Photo: Werner Forman/Art Resource, NY); **183**: The Art Archive/HarperCollins Publishers; **188 (left)**: encyclopedia.quickseek.com; **188 (right)**: www.destoop.com; **191**: Giraudon/Art Resource, NY; **194**: Kunsthistorisches Museum, Vienna; **196**: The Art Archive/Biblioteca del duomo Moderna/Dagli Orti (A); **198**: Vatican Library: MS Reg. Ret. 762, fol. 82r, written at Tours 800 A.D. (detail)

Chapter 8: 204: Limbourg Brothers (15th C.E.). *June. Tres Riches Heures du Duc De Berry*, (Palace and Ste. Chapelle in background). (Giraudon/Art Resource, NY); 207: Biblioteca Riccardiana, Florence, Manuscript Ricc. 492 c. 18, with the permission of the Ministero per I Beni Culturali e Ambientali; 208: British Library/Art Resource, NY; 220: Art Resource, NY; 211, 216: *View of Paris* (cliché Bibliothèque National de France, Paris); 222: Diebold Schilling, Official Bernese Chronicle, vol. 1, Burgerbibliothek, Berne, Ms. h.h.I.1, 289; 224: Musee de la Tapisserie, Bayeux, France. Photo: Erich Lessing/Art Resource, NY; 225: The Walters Art Gallery, Baltimore

Chapter 9: 236: *A Lecture Class in a Medieval University* (Bettmann/Corbis); 243, 257: 12th century sleeve of the Dalmatic (detail) (Kunsthistorisches Museum, Vienna, Austria. Photo: Erich Lessing/Art Resource, NY); 239: Treasury, Abbey Ste. Foy, Conques, France. Photo: Giraudon/Art Resource, NY; 241: Thüringer Universität-und Landesbibliothek, Jena, Ms. Bos. Q. 6, fol. 79r; 244: Bettmann/Corbis; 247: Bayerische Staatsbibliothek, München; 249: Scala/Art Resource, NY; 250: cliché Bibliothèque Nationale de France, Paris; 253: Giraudon/Art Resource, NY; 254: Alinari Archives/Corbis; 256: cliché Bibliothèque Nationale de France, Paris; 259 (both): Richard List/Corbis

Part IV: 262–263: *A Portuguese galleon* (National Maritime Museum, London)

Chapter 10: 266: *Les Grandes Chroniques de France* (Erich Lessing/Art Resource, NY); 268: British Museum. Photo: Snark/Art Resource, NY; 271: British Library. Photo: HIP/Art Resource, NY; 272: Bibliothèque Nationale, Paris. Photo: Snark/Art Resource, NY; 273: Réunion des Musées Nationaux/Art Resource, NY; 274: British Library. Photo: HIP/Art Resource, NY; 288: detail from *The Plague of a Murrain Among the Cattle, c. 1250* (The Pierpont Morgan Library, New York. Photo: The Pierpont Morgan Library/Art Resource, NY); 275: Musee Conde, Chantilly, France. Photo: Réunion des Musées Nationaux/Art Resource, NY; 277: Bibliotheque Nationale, Paris. Photo: Snark/Art Resource, NY; 278 (left): King's College, Cambridge. Photo: Bildarchiv Preussischer Kulturbesitz/Art Resource, NY; 278 (right): National Portrait Gallery, London; 280: Art Archive/ Museo del Prado, Madrid; 284: Vova Pomortzeff/Alamy; 285: Angelo Hornak/Corbis; 287: Bibliotheque Nationale, Paris. Photo: Bildarchiv Preussischer Kulturbesitz/Art Resource, NY; 288: detail from *The Plague of a Murrain Among the Cattle, c. 1250* (The Pierpont Morgan Library, New York. Photo: The Pierpont Morgan Library/Art Resource, NY); 292: The Art Archive/British Library; 293: By permission of the British Library; 295: Scrovegni Chapel, Padua, Italy. Photo: Scala/Art Resource, NY; 296: Bibliothèque Royale Albert I, Brussels

Chapter 11: 300: *Army of Suleiman the Magnificent conquering Europe* (The Art Archive/Topkapi Museum, Istanbul/Dagli Orti); 304: John Massey Stewart Picture Library; 305, 316: *Persian panel of mosaic tilework, 14th–15th century* (Victoria & Albert Museum, London. Photo: Victoria & Albert Museum/Art Resource, NY; 306: Werner Forman Archive/Topkapi Palace Library, Istanbul/Art Resource, NY; 311: José Pessoa, Arquivo Nacional de Fotografia, Instituto Português de Museus; 313: Royal Armouries Museum; 315: The Art Archive/Biblioteca Nacional de Madrid/Dagli Orti

Chapter 12: 320: *The School of Athens*, by Raphael (Scala/Art Resource, NY); 324, 327: detail from *Ceiling of Sala di Giove* (Palazzo Farnese, Caprarola, Italy. Photo: Scala/Art Resource, NY); 326: Art Resource, NY; 329: Erich Lessing/Art Resource, NY; 330: Erich Lessing/Art Resource, NY; 331 (top): Réunion des Musées Nationaux /Art Resource, NY; 331 (bottom): Scala/Art Resource, NY; 332: Scala/Art Resource, NY; 333: Scala/Art Resource, NY; 334: Nimatallah/Art Resource, NY; 335: Scala/Art Resource, NY; 338: Bildarchiv Preussischer Kulturbesitz / Art Resource, NY; 339: Réunion des Musées Nationaux /Art Resource, NY; 341: Bildarchiv Preussischer Kulturbesitz/Art Resource, NY

Chapter 13: 344: *Martin Luther preaching to faithful and communion and baptism from altarfront from Torslunde, 1561, Denmark* (The Art Archive/ Nationalmuseet Copenhagen Denmark / Dagli Orti (A); 346: Scala/Art Resource, NY; 348: Alinari/Art Resource, NY; 351 (left): Staatliche Museen zu Berlin—Preußischer Kulturbesitz Kupferstichkabinett; 351 (right): By permission of the British Library; 353: The Warder Collection, NY; 358, 364: *Reformation monument on front of Vor Frue Kirke, Copenhagen, Denmark*. Photo: Bridgeman Art Library; 359: National Trust/Art Resource, NY; 361: Scala/Art Resource, NY; 363: Scala/Art Resource, NY

Chapter 14: 368, 376, 382: *View of Toledo* by El Greco (The Metropolitan Museum of Art, H.O. Havemeyer Collection, Bequest of Mrs. H. O. Havemeyer, 1919 (29.100.6) Photograph © 1992 The Metropolitan Museum of Art; 370: Bettmann/Corbis; 372: Gianni Dagli Orti/Corbis; 379: Courtesy of the National Portrait Gallery, London; 380: Photo Bulloz Collection, Privèe; 384: Bibliotheque des Arts Decoratifs, Paris. Photo: Bridgeman Art Library; 387: Scala/Art Resource, NY; 388: Museo del Prado, Madrid; 389 (top): Erich Lessing/Art Resource, NY; 389 (bottom): Nimatallah/Art Resource, NY; 390 (left): © English Heritage Photo Library; 390 (right): Gift of Mr. and Mrs. Robert Woods Bliss, © 1997 Board of Trustees, National Gallery of Art, Washington, D.C.

Part V: 392–393: *Last Naval Battle in the Dutch-English War. August 11, 1637*, by Backhuyzen Ludolf, 1631–1708 (Erich Lessing/Art Resource, NY)

Chapter 15: 396: *Marriage a la Mode* by William Hogarth (National Gallery Collection; By kind permission of the Trustees of the National Gallery, London/Corbis); 400, 406: *A fountain at Versailles* (Giraudon/Art Resource, NY); 399: Courtesy of the National Portrait Gallery, London; 401: Scottish National Portrait Gallery, Edinburgh, Scotland/Bridgeman Art Library; 403: Erich Lessing/Art Resource, NY; 404: Giraudon/Art Resource, NY; 410: The Art Archive/Russian Historical Museum Moscow/Dagli Orti (A); 413: Giraudon/Art Resource, NY; 416: Ali Meyer/Corbis; 420: John R. Freeman & Co.; 421: Corbis; 422: The Warder Collection, NY

INDEX

Page numbers in *italics* refer to illustrations.

NORTH POLAR REGION

GLOBAL SATELLITE MOSAIC

The beauty and complexity of Earth's landscapes above and below the oceans is revealed with the Global Satellite Mosaic. The mosaic was produced for the National Geographic Society by NASA's Jet Propulsion Laboratory using more than 500 satellite images from the National Oceanic and Atmospheric Administration. The cloud-free images show Earth in its natural colors as it would be seen from space. One can easily identify the world's major glaciers, deserts, mountain ranges, and rain forests. For example, follow the green ribbon of lush vegetation along the Nile into the stark, dry Sahara. The mountain ranges seem to rise off the map thanks to digital elevation databases from the Department of Defense. The deepest areas of the ocean realm are colored dark blue in contrast to the light blue areas highlighting continental shelves, submarine ridges, and underwater mountains.

BIOSPHERE

Thousands of satellite images were combined to show a picture of biological productivity. In the oceans, red, yellow, and green indicate waters rich in phytoplankton. On land, green areas show high-potential plant productivity; tan to brown areas suffer from productivity limitations due to aridity and temperature.

THE
SATE

OCEAN

20° 40° 60° 80° 100° 120° 140° 160° 180°

80°

SOUTH POLAR REGION

30° 0° 30°

60° ANTARCTIC CIRCLE 60°

Drake Passage

Antarctic Peninsula

Weddell Sea

Queen Maud Land

75°

Alexander I. **ANTARCTICA**

Bellingshausen

Marie Byrd Land

WEST ANTARCTICA

South Pole

Transantarctic Mountains

EAST ANTARCTICA

Ross Ice Shelf

Wilkes Land

Ross Sea

150° 180° 150°

ANTARCTIC CIRCLE

90°

120°

40°

N O R T H

P A C I F I C

O C E A N

TROPIC OF CANCER

20°

Franz Josef Land

North Land

S I B E R I A

ARCTIC CIRCLE

Kamchatka Peninsula

E U R O P E

A S I A

Aral Sea

Black Sea

Caspian Sea

Lake Baikal

PHILIPPINE SEA

Plateau of Tibet

ARABIAN PENINSULA

INDIA

ARABIAN SEA

BAY OF BENGAL

SOUTH CHINA SEA

M I C R O N E S I A

A F R I C A

Congo Basin

Lake Tanganyika

Lake Malawi

I N D O N E S I A

EQUATOR 0°

M E L A N E S I A

Madagascar

New Guinea

CORAL SEA

Kalahari Desert

I N D I A N

O C E A N

A U S T R A L I A

Fiji Islands

20°

New Caledonia

TROPIC OF CAPRICORN

S O U T H

P A C I F I C

O C E A N

Cape of Good Hope

SOUTHWEST INDIAN RIDGE

NINETYEAST RIDGE

SOUTHEAST INDIAN RIDGE

TASMAN SEA

North Island

40°

KERGUELEN PLATEAU

Tasmania

NEW ZEALAND

South Island

THE NEED FOR SATELLITES

The Global Satellite Mosaic along with the biosphere image (lower left) and the temperature image (lower right) provides an integrated view of our world. The very high elevations of the Himalaya and Tibet show up as a cold area (blue, temperature imageland as a plant-poor area (tan, biosphere image). Temperature, vegetation, and landscape are interrelated. The need to understand the forces shaping environmental change has led to a space race among various countries. In 1997 alone some 85 rockets launched more than 140 satellites–mostly from China, Europe, Japan, Russia, and the United States. Some satellites provide vital communication links propelling economic development, other satellites supply data on patterns and trends associated with agricultural productivity, pollution monitoring, weather forecasting, and many other environmental concerns.

Wilkes Land

WINKEL TRIPEL PROJECTION, CENTRAL MERIDIAN 0°

SCALE 1:38,931,000

1 CENTIMETER = 389 KILOMETERS; 1 INCH = 614 MILES AT THE EQUATOR

KILOMETERS

STATUTE MILES

TICA

20° 40° 60° 80° 100° 120° 140° 160° 180°

ORLD

MAP

SURFACE TEMPERATURE

Reddish colors vividly show average high temperatures on the two largest continents, Africa and Asia, from the Sahara to Central Asia. Latitude, mountains, and oceans influence land temperatures.